ASK THE EXPERTS

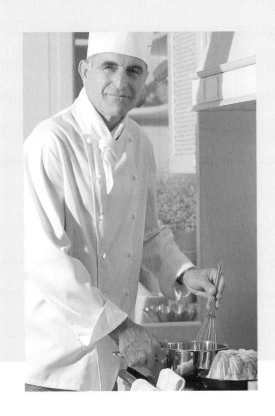

READER'S DIGEST CANADA

ASK THE EXPERTS

2500
GREAT HINTS & SMART TIPS FROM THE PROS

Reader's Digest

The Reader's Digest Association (Canada) Ltd., Montreal

Editorial

Project Editor
Andrew R. Byers

Associate Editor
Anita Winterberg

Copy Editor
Gilles Humbert

Art

Designer
Cécile Germain

Production

Production Manager
Holger Lorenzen

Production Coordinator
Susan Wong

Contributors

Researchers
Martha Plaine
Aleli Balagtas
Pamela Boyle
Dolores LaPratt
  Houseman

Indexer
Pat Buchanan

Production Artist
Yves Lachance

Photographer
Mike Haimes

Books and Home Entertainment

Vice President
Deirdre Gilbert

Managing Editor
Philomena Rutherford

Art Director
John McGuffie

U.S. Staff

Senior Editor
Nancy Shuker

Designer
Eleanor Kostyk

A Reader's Digest Book produced by Lightbulb Press, Inc.

Editorial Director
Virginia Morris

Editors
Sophie Forrester
Renée Ryerson

Contributing Editors
Sarah Lang
Lenore Person

Copy Editor
Sarah Norris

Editorial Assistants
Ann Fisher
Linda Hetzer
Miranda Pinckert

Proofreader
Elaine Durbach

Creative Director
Dean Scharf

Art Director
Dave Wilder

Designers
Dianne Athey
Jeff Badger
Kara W. Hatch
Karen Robbins

Photographer
Simon Metz

Photography Staff
Jennifer Abadi
Lisa Homa
Amy Lord
Ciaran Tully

Illustrator
Jeffrey Chandler

Production Artists
Holly Duthie
Cassandra Johnson
Katie Lyness
Sally Minker
Sarah Price
Thomas F. Trojan

The acknowledgments that appear on pages 351–352 are hereby made a part of this copyright page.

Canadian Cataloguing in Publication Data

Main entry under title:
    Ask the experts: 2500 great hints & smart tips from the pros

Includes index.

ISBN 0-88850-679-1

    1. Home economics. 2. Do-it-yourself work.

TX158.A853 2000   640'.41   C00-900227-8

Printed in Canada

00 01 02/5 4 3 2

Address any comments about ASK THE EXPERTS to Editor, Books and Home Entertainment, c/o Customer Service, Reader's Digest, 1125 Stanley Street, Montreal, Quebec H3B 5H5.

For information on this and other Reader's Digest products or to request a catalogue, please call our 24-hour Customer Service hotline at 1-800-465-0780.

You can also visit us on the World Wide Web at
http://www.readersdigest.ca

Contents

Chapter 1

Your Home Inside and Out

Chapter 4

The Green Thumb's Yard and Garden

Chapter 7

The Business of Living

CHAPTER ONE

Your Home, Inside and Out

Creating a Distinctive Style

Make your home a personal expression of the people who live there.

BUCKING THE TRENDS

The proliferation of home furnishing stores and catalogs offering fully coordinated, attractive products at affordable prices has made home decorating easier, but has also increased the chances that your living room will resemble that of your friends and relatives. How can you avoid the homogenized look? Robert Warsh, owner of the design and textile store called Department of Interiors in Toronto, suggests:

- Plan the look you want, including a base, secondary, and accent color. Collect photographs, clippings, and swatches of things you like. These will help guide you as you begin to shop.

- Use textiles, which provide color, texture, and pattern, to personalize a room. In addition to upholstery and drapes, think about using textiles, such as old tapestries, as throws, table toppers, or on fabric screens. Subtle colors and weaves can provide interest. Even a small amount of fabric can make a big statement.

- Don't be afraid to mix colors and textures. "If things match too much, it's boring," says Warsh.

- When you travel, visit flea markets, outdoor shows, antique stores, yard sales, and auctions. You never know when you will find something that calls out to you. Also, search for places that sell quality merchandise off-price.

- Follow your interests and incorporate them into your decorating, whether that's model airplanes, Turkish rugs, or antique egg cups. Chances are no one you know will have exactly those elements in his or her home.

Smart Moves

A distinctive front door helps to welcome guests and sets the tone for the rest of your home. To pique interest in what's beyond, says Bunny Meals, try this front door treatment: Paint the door a different color from the rest of the exterior surfaces, and use that color as an accent in the entryway of your home. Set up a "welcoming committee" outside the door. A group of frogs greets guests outside one of Meals' cottages that's across from a pond where frogs can often be heard, making a transition between the outdoors and indoors.

COLLECTIONS CARRY IT

Bunny Meals is an innkeeper on Whidbey Island in Puget Sound off the coast of Washington State, where guests rave about her two cottages, Dove House and Chauntecleer House. Part of what makes the cottages so special is Meals' thematic approach and incredible attention to detail.

Dove House, for instance, reflects the area's history as home to Native North Americans who were fishermen, as well as the current popularity of fishing. Antique fishing creels— or baskets—hold linen napkins, carved fish, and flower arrangements. Antique fishing poles, along with hand-painted tiles of fishermen, fish, and flies, adorn the walls of the cottage.

In Chauntecleer House, a collection of 35 roosters, and a rooster motif in everything from the sign to the light fixtures, reinforce the theme in surprising and charming ways. A cottage currently being renovated will have a garden theme, and Meals is already pre-pared with a collection of antique garden tools, framed antique seed packets, and dishes with trowels and bird houses on them. Some lamps will be made out of watering cans, others out of long-handled tools, and the bed will be fashioned from twigs.

"What I do is take an object that I receive aesthetic pleasure from and try to collect a few of them," says Meals, explaining her approach. "Before you know it, it starts you thinking about colors and fabrics and all of that." Meals enjoys being on "an eternal treasure hunt" as she gathers her collections, and points out that the collected items need not be expensive. "Collections can heighten people's senses— they'll say they've never seen so many whatever— and collections are a lot of fun to put together."

Whimsy and the unexpected are also an important part of Meals' decorating. In the corner of one of her rooms is an old basket lined with straw, home to a family of wooden baby

COMMON THEMES

What's the difference between an impersonal room and one that you couldn't imagine belonging to anyone but its owner? "Personality comes through loud and clear," says design expert Chris Casson Madden, author of *A Room of Her Own: Women's Personal Spaces* and other books. *A Room of Her Own* looks at the distinctive personal spaces of women. Although each room is unique— a true reflection of its owner—common themes can be found among them. Madden lists some of the common elements among the intimate and very personal rooms of these women:

- Favorite artwork, such as antique prints
- Topiaries or plants
- Unusual baskets
- A comfortable chair or chaise longue
- Personal collections, such as kilim boxes
- Old family photographs
- Unusual picture frames
- Candles
- Throw pillows
- Coffee table books
- Fragrant oils or incense
- Favorite postcards
- Interesting fabrics used as throws or chair covers
- A teapot, cup, and a favorite tea

pigs. Next to it sits the mother pig. At the top of a stairway, a sea otter, created by a local sculptor, sits perched on the railing waiting to greet you as you climb up. The fun continues outside, where a sculpture of a little wood elf perches on an old tree stump, and old iron bedsteads, mounded with dirt, serve as planters for wildflowers. "All these little touches say you have spent time thinking about your home and setting a tone," says Meals.

KNOW YOUR STUFF

Interior designer Elke Oppinger of Hudson, Quebec, sums up the dilemma a lot of people feel as they look around their bare living room: "People who aren't trained in the business of design know what they like, but often don't know how to put it together to achieve a coordinated look that's exciting and pleasurable."

The solution is to go to books about the period or style of interest to you, says Oppinger.

Look at what the experts have done. Study the pictures to see how the rooms came together, and as a guide for color and fabrics.

Oppinger also recommends the research approach to collecting. "What's interesting is when you go to someone's house and they're knowledgeable about their collections," she says. "As they begin to tell you about their Indian folk art or French clocks or English creamware, the house begins to take on a personality." In other words, your interest in and excitement about the things in your home make them come alive for your guests.

MOVE IT IN MINIATURE

If you want the aerobic exercise, you can move your furniture around to try out a new look. Or you can buy an interior design kit and try a dozen new arrangements without any heavy lifting.

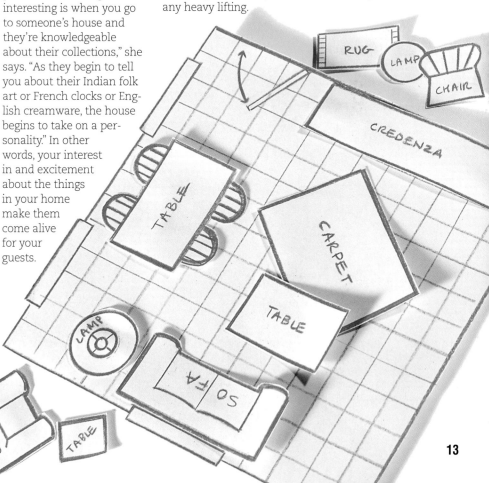

A Fresh Coat of Paint

Create a personal touch with color.

USE COLOR WITH COURAGE

White walls may make you feel safe—but what are they doing for your room? Paula Perlini, a New York City decorator, says, "Don't be a color coward. Color warms up a room, adds drama, and makes everything else pop out. Your furnishings will look better against a background color." The challenge, as many people know from experience, is getting the right color. "Often, people choose too sharp a color," says Perlini, "one that has too much of an acid feel.

"Not all pretty colors translate to good wall colors. It's essential to paint a patch of the color you're considering on a wall and live with it for a bit. See what it looks like at night and during the day." And don't try to salvage an unsuccessful color by adding white to it. "That just leaves you with an unattractive color that has white in it," says Perlini.

When Perlini starts working with clients, she uses a brief questionnaire to find out what colors they like. She has them collect examples of colors they think they might want to live with from magazine and catalog photos, material swatches, or coffee mugs. Perlini will then start to choose fabrics in the preferred colors, and from the fabrics will come the choice of paint or wall cover. It might be one of the colors in the fabrics, or one that's compatible.

Although a neutral palette of beige and cream is quite popular, Perlini is not fond of it. "You can make everything so understated that there's no statement at all," she says. In addition, it's not a practical choice for homes where children, pets, and guests abound because it shows dirt quickly.

WHAT YOU NEED

Choosing high-quality paints and hand-crafted tools will make your painting job much easier and improve the look and durability of the finished product, says Eric Oxley, owner of Eric's Paints of Hanford, California.

■ Oxley prefers latex- and water-based paints to oil- and solvent-based ones for most painting jobs, whether interior or exterior. They are better for the environment, safer for the do-it-yourselfer, easier to work with, and fade and yellow less quickly.

■ Nylon or nylon-polyester brushes work best with latex paint products. Use more-expensive boar hair brushes—usually known as Chinese bristle—only when applying solvent- or oil-based paints.

■ When using paint rollers, choose a longer nap for painting highly textured surfaces, such as stucco, and a shorter nap for flatter surfaces. The best rollers are made from lambskin, but many good, less-expensive rollers are made from synthetics, such as Orlon.

The Right Way

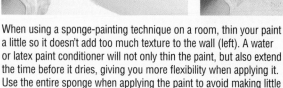

When using a sponge-painting technique on a room, thin your paint a little so it doesn't add too much texture to the wall (left). A water or latex paint conditioner will not only thin the paint, but also extend the time before it dries, giving you more flexibility when applying it. Use the entire sponge when applying the paint to avoid making little round blobs of paint (center). The goal is to cover the entire surface of the wall, and not be able to tell where you have started and finished an application. You will get a lacier look if you work with the whole sponge, or use a crinkled plastic grocery bag dipped in paint and blotted on a newspaper before applying (right).

DECORATIVE PAINTING

Most decorative painting techniques fall into the category of broken color, explains Lisa Teague, a decorative painter from New Hampshire. Color is applied in a mottled, broken way that makes it softer and easier to live with than a deep, flat, solid color. "This enables you to use a color that you might not otherwise be comfortable with in your house," says Teague.

There are two basic ways to do broken color: through an applied technique or a removal technique. In the applied technique, glaze or paint is applied in a pattern over a solid ground coat. This might be done with a sponge, rag, brush, comb, or other applicator that creates texture. In the removal technique, a glaze is applied over a base coat, then partially removed with cheesecloth or a rag. The key to successful broken color is combining the right colors. Teague suggests staying within one color tone for an entire job, and varying the strengths of the different coats. Often, she says, she will apply a base coat that is half strength, then sponge it with a coat that is full strength, followed by a coat that is one-quarter strength. "The closer your ground coat and your glaze color, the softer the overall feeling you're going to get, which is what I encourage," says Teague. "If your finishes have a lot of contrast, it's hard on your eyes and doesn't feel restful. What you're really trying to do is replicate light and shadow on your walls."

A different kind of decorative technique that can be fun but requires some artistic ability is *trompe l'oeil*, which means, literally, to deceive the eye. This can be anything from a mural to a little bird's nest painted on your windowsill. In her house, Teague has painted pots of geraniums and African violets sitting on her mantelpiece. With *trompe l'oeil*, "you can pop in little surprises and really personalize your house," says Teague.

Know Your Terms

James Martin, a Denver-based architectural colorist and color consultant, explains the three main aspects to color that can help you choose paint colors for your home:

Hue indicates the position of the color within the spectrum. Red, green, and blue are all hues.

Value is the lightness or darkness of a color. For example, the value of red might range from light pink to red-brown.

Chroma is the color's intensity or saturation. Bubble-gum pink and fuchsia may be the same value, but fuchsia has more chroma.

A SMART EXTERIOR

An effective use of color on the exterior of your home can add thousands of dollars to its value, says James Martin, who has been hired by landlords and real estate developers to increase the market value of their properties or improve occupancy rates in their buildings with eye-catching color schemes.

■ Perception of color is very relative. For instance, if you put a mid-value color, such as tan, next to pure white, it will look beige. But if you put it next to dark green, it will look off-white. Keep this in mind when choosing colors—main and trim. And when you are choosing a color from a fan deck at the paint store, you should mask off the colors next to it with a white sheet of paper.

■ Design your color scheme first according to value. That is, decide whether you want a dark, medium, or light main color.

■ Highlight detail carefully to create a balanced effect between the top and bottom of your home. For instance, if there is a lot of detail on the top of your home, you will need to create detail and interest on the bottom.

■ Put darker colors toward the bottom of the house to avoid creating an "uncomfortable, top-heavy feel," says Martin.

■ Pick colors outside in natural light on a cloudy day or in open shade. Bright light creates glare and can distort your perception of the color.

■ Make sure the paint colors you choose complement the colors of the other materials of your home, such as the roof, brick, stone, or stucco.

■ Paint window sashes and overhead surfaces, such as porch ceilings and soffits, a lighter color to reflect light and "lift the spirit of your home."

■ Use warm colors as opposed to cool. For instance, use a warm yellow-white as opposed to a cool blue-white.

■ Use light colors to make a small house look bigger, and dark colors to make a large house that is squeezed onto a small lot look smaller.

Smart Moves

Good painters use tricks like adding burnt umber to a color to warm it up, which is why it makes sense to consult with a professional even if you can't afford to hire one to do the whole job for you. Be up front as to what you can afford, and request basic advice.

Decorating with Wallpaper

Create variety and interest in your home with wallpaper.

PAPERHANGING BASICS

The biggest mistake people make when hanging wallpaper, says Walter Green III, author of *The Joy of Paperhanging*, is assuming that it's going to be easy. He recommends doing some homework before starting a wallpapering project so you have some idea of the challenges in store and how to handle them.

According to Green, the most important part of paperhanging is wall preparation. This is because wallpaper must be applied to a clean, smooth surface. If the room already has wallpaper, the first step is to strip off the old paper.

When you're stripping, the first thing you have to know is whether your walls were sized during construction. Sizing means that the walls were either primed with a waterproof sealer, or had commercial sizing applied to them. Sizing provides a base on which to glue the wallpaper. Without it, glue goes right through the sheetrock. If you try to remove wallpaper from walls that have not been sized, you will tear off the surface of the sheetrock.

On plaster walls or sheetrock walls that have been sized, stripping off old wallpaper is a fairly simple operation: Apply a solution that you can buy at the hardware or wallpaper store, and scrape off the paper. If sheetrock walls haven't been sized, stripping off the wallpaper is more complicated. There are two ways to handle this problem: Prime and then hang paper over the existing wallpaper, or strip the wallpaper and call in an experienced drywall finisher. After either type of stripping, wash all the old paste off, spackle, and prime the walls.

When hanging wallpaper, use as little paste as possible. And expect to paste even prepasted paper, using the activators specially made for that purpose. In Green's experience, most prepasted products work better with the activator than with water.

OFF THE WALL

A variety of lovely effects can be achieved with the skillful use of wallpaper borders. Here are some of the industry's favorite tricks:

- Use borders instead of a wooden chair rail in your dining room.
- Miter—or bevel—paper borders around window and door frames.
- Run them around the top of a wall like a crown molding or around the bottom as a lower border or dado.
- If you have a large picture that you'd like to highlight, you can miter border paper around the edges of the frame to create a shadow-case effect.

WHAT'S WHAT IN WALLPAPER

Adriana Galdau is co-owner of Maison de Wallpaper in Scarsdale, New York. According to Galdau, customers frequently come into her store with preconceived—and not necessarily accurate—notions of how wallpaper should and should not be used.

A common mistake people make is getting caught up in the wallpaper fad of the moment, choosing an "in" style that is almost always out of fashion the following season. And changing your wallpaper is a big deal. Instead, Galdau recommends going with a more timeless look.

Another common misconception is the idea that small

The Right Way

Wallpaper expands and contracts when it gets damp during the hanging process, says MaryAnne Fisher. Here's how to prevent your paper from pulling away from the seams as it dries:

- Cut the wallpaper and apply the paste to the wall.
- Allowing the ends of the paper to curl inwards and meet, roll the paper from its center up and down the wall.
- Let the paper sit on the wall at least three to five minutes before hanging the adjacent piece to achieve a clean, tight seam.

A CREATIVE WAY TO USE EXTRA PAPER

To add a finishing touch to your room, and put leftover wallpaper to clever use, cover a graduated set of hat boxes or rigid gift boxes and stack them on a dresser or table. You can use them to store scarves, letters, or whatever you like. Or leave the top one uncovered, filled with a fragrant potpourri. Coordinated extras like these add to the richness of your environment.

Smart Moves

Interior designer MaryAnne Fisher learned a lot about wallpapering in 14 years as owner and operator of Wallflowers Ltd. in Greensboro, North Carolina.

■ If you will be papering the ceiling as well as walls, do not use up-and-down or striped patterns, advises Fisher, since this can create a "tunnel effect." Instead, choose a trellis or plaid pattern, which will appear to open up the dimensions of the room. And always paper the ceiling first—then the walls.

■ Fisher agrees that big patterns can work well in small rooms. However, if you will be using this approach, always paper at least two of the walls. If you only paper one wall, a large pattern can close in on you visually.

■ Quality control is terrible among wallpapers, says Fisher. If you buy a roll of wallpaper with a dark background and a non-bleed edge—or white unprinted strip along the side—send it back to the store. If the strip is narrow, Fisher sometimes blends the seam with the background color using a matching eye shadow and a cotton swab.

■ When decorating your home, try to carry one "key color" into every room to give your color scheme continuity and flow. Make it the primary color in a few rooms, and secondary in the others.

bathrooms require small, light-colored prints. On the contrary, large, bold prints and strong colors attract attention to themselves and away from the size of the room, making it appear larger. Dark colors add drama to a small room and tend to downplay its perimeters. Galdau also recommends papering the ceiling of a small room, eliminating any contrast in color and adding to the sense of space.

To test out a particular wallpaper in your home, don't stop at the sample book, says Galdau. For a minimal amount of money, you can get a three-foot sample, which you can pin on your wall and live with for a little while before making a final decision.

MORE THAN JUST WALLPAPER

For Bruce Bradbury, owner and president of Bradbury and Bradbury Wallpapers (www.bradbury.com), wallpaper is a fine art. Specializing in Victorian, Arts and Crafts, and neo-Classical reproductions and original designs, all of Bradbury's papers are hand silk-screened with oil-based inks on clay-coated paper. Bradbury's 10 craftspeople and designers make by hand in one month what a machine would make in one day, says the owner.

Bradbury's designs have been hung in historic homes throughout North America and Europe, including Abraham Lincoln's home in

Springfield, Illinois. "If you can imagine it, we can do it," says Bradbury. New to his collection is a wallpaper from a historic farmhouse in Burnaby, British Columbia. "The wallpaper is so perfectly evocative of an early 1900s interior that we decided to reproduce it and the companion border."

Bradbury's offers 13 types of wall- and ceiling papers. Modular wall elements include dados, fillings, and upper friezes. Ceiling elements include perimeter enrichments, corner fans, corner blocks, panels, and rosettes. Customers can choose many coordinating elements from a period decorative program to create a full-bore, or highly elaborate, effect. Or customers can incorporate one or two elements, such as a border, frieze, or simple wall filling, into a less-structured decorative scheme.

HOW MANY ROLLS WILL YOU NEED?

You can estimate the number of single rolls of wallpaper you'll need using this chart. Just find where your room's size intersects with the height of its ceiling. For example, for a room that's 10' x 14' and has 10' ceilings, you'll need about 15 single rolls.

Room Size	Ceiling Height in Feet				
	8	9	10	11	12
8' x 10'	9	10	11	12	13
10' x 14'	12	14	15	16	18
12' x 16'	14	16	17	19	21
14' x 16'	15	17	19	20	22
16' x 20'	18	20	22	24	27

Beautiful Natural Floors

Hardwood, tile, and marble are winning floor choices.

TALKING ABOUT CERAMIC TILE

Ceramic tile is a smart floor choice for areas that frequently get wet or dirty, which explains its popularity in restaurants and kitchens. Its glasslike glaze cleans easily with just water, says Elaine Nikiforuk, who owns World Mosaic Inc., in Ottawa, Ontario. In addition, it's attractive, and lasts for a long time: Ceramic tiles have even been found intact in some ancient Roman buildings.

The body of a ceramic tile is made out of clay and other earth components, explains Nikiforuk. Tiles for residential and commercial use are typically glazed, then fired in a kiln to fuse the glaze to the tile body. The glaze forms the hard, impervious surface that homeowners value. But not all tiles or glazes are the same. There are four characteristics it's smart to be aware of when choosing tile, all of which should be indicated on the manufacturer's specification sheet:

- Breaking strength, or what it takes to crack the tile. Nikiforuk says that reputable tile dealers will all carry tile with sufficient breaking strength for residential usage.
- Wear rating, which is expressed on a scale of one to five. Grade 1, the rating of most wall tiles, wears easily. That means it doesn't take much abrasion to wear off the glaze and expose the body of the tile. Grade 2, light residential, is appropriate for bathrooms and other areas that don't get heavy traffic. Grade 3, residential, is for any home application, including entryways and kitchens. Grade 4, commercial, is for businesses with moderate traffic. Grade 5, heavy commercial, is for heavy traffic locales, such as shopping malls. You can also use commercial-grade tile in the home, if you wish.
- Glaze hardness is measured on a scale of 1 to 10, 10 being a diamond-like hardness that can't be scratched. Most tiles have a glaze hardness of 6 or above, which is usually acceptable.
- Water absorption. Look for low water absorption if you're using tiles outside or in a wet area inside, like the bathroom. The best way to make sure you are getting reliable tiles, says Nikiforuk, is to shop at a reputable tile store or supplier that guarantees its products. Another safe way to go is to buy only well-known brands.

There are hundreds of different types of tiles available in an array of material, such as ceramic, slate, marble, and granite.

Oak Cherry

CHOOSING HARDWOOD FLOORS

Today, hardwood floors are in greater demand than ever before, says Ron Knight of Stanley Knight Limited, a manufacturer of fine flooring in Meaford, Ontario. The company's Beaver Brand hardwood floors were even installed at some sites of the 1993 Barcelona Olympics. The beauty of wood and a heightened awareness of the natural environment have encouraged consumers to turn to this renewable resource. Plus, hardwood flooring is a good alternative for people allergic to carpet fibers. Beyond the ever-popular oak, there are Canadian hardwoods such as northern hard maple, hickory, and black cherry to choose from. Consider the following when choosing your floor:

Color. Visit a hardwood floor showroom where you can see the variety of colors available. More people choose their floor by color than by the type of wood. If you are installing the floor in a room where there's hardwood already—a kitchen with cabinets, for instance—bring in a sample of the wood (e.g., a cabinet drawer) to see how it will

Maple

Walnut

Ash

look in combination with different woods. Combining two dark woods is probably too dark for a kitchen, but might be fine for a library. Natural maple, oak, or hickory contrasts well with dark woods. Knight recommends against mixing different stain colors.

Hardness. For high-traffic areas, you will probably want a hardwood that won't dent. Soft woods, such as American cherry, are appropriate for a casual or historic look where some dents will fit in with the rest of the room's decor.

Finish. Prefinished floors have polyurethane baked on when they arrive at your house. Unfinished floors must be sanded and finished on site. Unfinished floors provide more flexibility, allowing you to stain a floor a particular color, as well as finish it according to your preference—with either polyurethane or oil.

Quality. Drying and milling are the most important factors to ensure you are getting quality hardwood flooring, regardless of the grade, in both on-site finished and prefinished products. The grade of hardwood flooring has more to do with the look of the floor than the measure of its quality. The pricier

grades such as Clear offer a uniform color, relatively free of knots, checks, and mineral discoloration. The less expensive grades such as Number 1 Common permit more rustic characteristics and the full range of color and mineral stains found in the species. The lower grade is a darker floor when coated with a clear finish. A stain will even out the color variation.

AN OLD APPROACH TO HARDWOOD FLOORS

The old-fashioned approach to finishing floors is alive and well, thanks to people like Leonard L. Morgan Jr., a New York real estate developer who specializes in restoring antique homes. He prefers the glowing, natural finish of wood treated with linseed oil. Plus, naturally treated floors don't have to be refinished for an extended period of time. Here are the basic finishing methods Morgan uses:

■ A heavy-duty sander will remove most finishes. Sand the floor three times—with coarse sandpaper the first time, then medium, and then fine.

■ Combine mineral spirits and pure linseed oil in a ratio of 2½ to 1. (The greater the amount of lin-

seed oil, the harder the sealer.) Brush, roll, or spray this mixture on the floor, then let it dry for two days if the humidity is low—or up to a week if the humidity is high. When the first coat is dry, apply another coat and let it dry. Caution: Mineral spirits are very toxic. Ventilate the area thoroughly while you are applying the seal and allowing it to dry.

■ Apply butcher's wax to the floor in a thin, even coat using a lamb's wool pad, vigorously pressing the wax into the floor. Let it dry at least 20 minutes—but no more than 45—before buffing.

■ Using a floor-polishing machine, buff the floor thoroughly with a medium pad and polish it to the desired level of shine with a soft pad. If the floor is slippery when you are finished, it needs more buffing.

Once you've finished, all you have to do to care for your floor is wipe it with a dust mop every week. Every few months, you can mix Murphy's Oil Soap with lukewarm water, and damp-mop the floor. This will enhance the shine. Once a year, buff the floors to achieve a glossier finish.

MAD ABOUT MARBLE

"With marble, you've got to realize that every piece is going to be different," says Linda Abbott, showroom manager at Arizona Tile in Phoenix, Arizona. The color and veining of marble tiles, even those cut from the same block, can vary quite dramatically. When you are shopping for marble, ask to see several samples from the lot you are interested in so you get an idea of how wide the variation will be.

Another important characteristic of marble is its relative softness. Scratching is especially apparent on marble that has a very high polish. Recently, honed and tumbled marbles, on which scratches are less apparent, have become available.

Marble floor care is fairly easy. Dust regularly with a dust mop, and then mop with warm water.

The Right Way

Stay away from chemicals, vinegar, and acid-based cleaners for floor tiles. They can eat away the grout, and create build-up over time that will need to be removed. Instead, use water and commercial grout and tile cleaners.

Beautiful Floor Coverings

Enjoy the luxury and comfort of carpeting and rugs.

BROADLOOM CARPET

When shopping for carpeting, you know you want a color that will look good with the rest of your decor and a price that will fit within your budget. Where things can get confusing is in the different fibers and fiber treatments available.

Almost every branded fiber you can purchase is a good, high-quality product, says Eric Scharff, broadloom marketing manager at Karastan. Nylon and wool are still pretty much the fibers of choice for high-quality indoor carpeting, and it's pretty hard to go wrong if you choose a branded fiber. Special features, such as stain resistance, are largely a matter of individual preference based on your family's day-to-day lifestyle.

Wool, the original carpet fiber, offers a "unique luster and feel that you can't get with anything else," says Scharff. Plus, "wool today is

just as easy to clean and stain-resistant as nylon."

Nylon is a more affordable option. "We're at a point now where nylon is more durable and stain-resistant than ever," says Scharff. Acrylic is a less-popular carpet fiber. At Karastan, it is sometimes blended with wool to "achieve some of the rich look of wool carpeting at a somewhat lower price."

Cotton is making slow inroads into the broadloom market. However, it hasn't quite made the move from bath mats and area rugs because it is soft and easily worn, and therefore unsuitable for heavy use.

One of the key differences between most nylon and wool carpets is how they're produced. Nylon is usually tufted, a process ("like a big sewing operation," says Scharff) where the nylon is stitched in loops into a primary backing, sealed with latex, and a secondary backing is then applied. Wool, by contrast, is woven into a backing yarn, then sealed with latex, creating "the most dimensionally stable type of carpet there is."

Because it is extremely durable, woven carpet is often used in commercial installations where it's subjected to both heavy use and minimal upkeep.

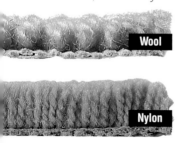

Wool

Nylon

Cotton

FLOORCLOTHS

Floorcloths are hand-painted floor coverings made out of canvas, then finished with varnish so that the final result is stiff—almost like plastic. In North America, floorcloths were popular during the late 1700s as a cheaper alternative to the linoleum that was being imported from Europe, explains Michele Hollick, owner of Stenciling by Michele, a floorcloth business located in Hollis, New Hampshire.

The floorcloth designs from this era, many of which are recreated in floorcloths today, were imitations of the geometric patterns used in the linoleum. Floorcloths made a comeback in the 1930s and '40s, and are once again popular for their decorative, retro designs that can be simple or quite elaborate.

For her unique floorcloths,

Hollick generally uses specially manufactured canvas, which is pre-primed, and water-based paints and finishes. Some purists insist on oil-based materials, but Hollick dislikes them because of their smell and the long drying time they require. The larger the floorcloth, the more expensive it will be. Nonstandard sizes also raise the price.

Because floorcloths are flat, they are great for entryways, where they won't slow down the doors the way a carpet might. As they are both durable and attractive, they are also appropriate for high-traffic, high-visibility areas, such as foyers and hallways. Since they are relatively easy to clean they are a favorite in the kitchen.

Know Your Terms

The terms "carpet" and "rug" are pretty much interchangeable, although some experts use "rug" to refer to anything four feet by six feet or less, and "carpet" for anything larger than that.

A painted canvas floorcloth is an attractive alternative for high-traffic areas.

Smart Moves

Maintain your carpets by vacuuming them at least once a week. This simple routine prevents carpet fibers from getting sticky, clumping together, and becoming matted, says Eric Scharff. Cleaning your carpets every 18 to 24 months will further ensure that you get maximum wear out of them.

ORIENTAL CARPETS

When people in the carpet business refer to Oriental carpets, they mean handwoven carpets produced in Istanbul and everywhere east of it, explains Meryl Gardner, sales manager for Elte Carpets and Home in Toronto, Ontario. The good news, says Gardner, is that "it's never been a more exciting time to buy new Oriental carpets. The golden age of carpet weaving was the late 19th century, but what's available today far exceeds what was available then. The production and creativity and variety are just unbelievable." The bad news is that the proliferation of carpets makes judging quality very complicated. In the 1940s, "the perceived quality of carpets fit into nice little categories," says Gardner. "Persian was good, Indian was bad, the more knots per square inch, the better. Today, every country is capable of making high- and low-quality carpets, and the number of knots per square inch is just one factor. You also have to look at the quality of the dyes, the quality of the wool, and a host of other factors."

Given this complexity, explains Gardner, the most important thing you can do when buying a carpet is to go to a reputable dealer who's been around a long time. Always buy from a store that will let you try out a carpet before you purchase it, or that will issue a refund if you are not happy with your choice.

Be prepared before you buy. Take some photographs of the room the carpet is going in, including artwork and furniture, if possible, and bring along a piece of fabric that is or will be used in the room so the salesperson can get a sense of the space—as well as your taste. Also have an idea of what you want to spend, though you should be prepared for "being romanced" into something more expensive. "A carpet lasts a lifetime," says Gardner. "It should not be something you compromise on. You should be able to get up every day, look at it, and say 'I'm glad I bought it.' "

THE BEAUTY OF NATURAL FIBERS

Synthetic-fiber carpets and carpets treated with stain repellent and other chemicals may represent an environmental and—for some people—a health challenge. That's why Elte stocks one of the largest selections of natural-fiber floor coverings in Canada, says Meryl Gardner.

Wall-to-wall carpets and area rugs in the collection are made from wool, coir, sisal, flax, linen, and jute. In developing the line, attention was paid not only to design and weave, but also to environmental soundness. Unspoiled yarns are used in these "green carpets," which have no backing and receive no topical treatments.

Wool is the most popular fiber in the line, followed by coir and sisal. With the price of wool coming down, many wool carpets are very affordable, says Gardner. Coir and sisal are also well-priced and versatile fibers. They work well in all settings and decors. Area rugs from these fibers look equally good in casual family rooms, traditional living rooms, and sleek contemporary settings. Since their hard fibers make coir and sisal naturally anti-static, these carpets are often used in offices and computer rooms. Another advantage to these hard fibers is that they won't support bacterial growth.

Flax, linen, and jute are all bast fibers, which means that they are harvested from the stalk of the plant. They are beautiful yarns, but because they are relatively soft, they are appropriate in areas that receive only moderate traffic, such as living rooms and bedrooms. Wool is a very durable fiber that can be used in central, high-traffic areas.

Natural-fiber carpets are best cleaned using a dry-cleaning method. Shampooing and steam cleaning can shrink them and cause damage. In addition, says Gardner, shampooing often leaves a soap residue in carpets, which attracts soil. For wool carpets, use a suction vacuum to clean away surface dirt, not one with a rotating bar that beats the fibers, advises Gardner. With proper care, natural fibers wear well and age nicely, developing an attractive patina with time.

The knotting on the back of an Oriental carpet tells a lot about its quality.

Getting Your Windows in Focus

Dress and maintain your windows in great style.

INSIDE OUT

When Roslyn, New York, interior designer Diane Alpern Kovacs goes into clients' homes, she's "always opening the curtains or window treatments. I like to be able to see out—that's my sensibility." When creating drapery treatments, Kovacs frees up windows and makes them appear larger by placing the drapes above the window and on the wall to each side, rather than on the window frame. This way, the fabric just brushes the interior of the window. The drapes themselves are stationary. Since this doesn't take care of privacy or light, Kovacs combines the drapes with a shade—a porch, woven wood, or tortoise shade, for instance. This treatment prevents what Kovacs feels is the biggest mistake most people make with drapes, which is hanging them so that they shorten the appearance of the window and block out the light.

Unlined, unstructured curtains hung on rings on wrought-iron curtain rods are also an attractive way to frame a window without enveloping it. These curtains can be pulled back easily and pinned out of the way when you want to see out of your windows.

Another look that Kovacs likes is that of thick wooden blinds or plantation shutters with thick slats—anywhere from 2½ to 4½ inches. "They are very handsome and architectural, and look great if there are pretty moldings around the window," she says.

Increasingly, Kovacs is being asked to design window treatments in media rooms requiring total darkness. Kovacs handles this with vinyl blackout shades (matching the wall color) behind a wooden blind. The blackout shades can be controlled with a switch that rolls them up or down. Automatic privacy shades also come in handy in a bathroom with a hot tub, where one side of the tub is underneath a window. A switch allows you to close the shade without having to climb into the tub.

TRENDS IN WINDOW TREATMENTS

Vice president of merchandising for Country Curtains in Stockbridge, Massachusetts, Lillian Bender says the current trend in window treatments is simplicity—casual looks that provide privacy and control light as needed without a lot of material around the window. This includes inside-window treatments, such as Roman shades, cloth roll-up shades, and wooden blinds, and light, natural-fiber curtains. Coziness and comfort are other priorities, judging by the popularity of soft, plush curtain fabrics, such as corduroys and velvets.

Bender has these suggestions for covering windows:
- In a new home with large windows, a lot of light, and little privacy, try combining a wooden blind with a sheer curtain on a decorative rod. The blind affords privacy and darkness, while the curtain softens the look.
- In a home with a lot of wood, attach a piece of cloth across the top of the window as an informal valance.
- Where privacy is not an issue, create a great style by attaching a couple of interesting swag holders and draping a few yards of beautiful material in between them to make a swag. Depending on the materials you choose and how you hang them, this approach can give the room a traditional or contemporary look.
- In an apartment, try a tailored swag, a valance with a window shade, or a decorative rod with a sheer curtain. Any of these is easy to remove.
- Crane rods—L-shaped rods that swing out from a window—are great for door panels, French doors, and in situations where there is not enough room for a curtain rod to project out from the side of the window.

Use a variety of accessories to tie your curtains back into an attractive swag. The clamp pictured here uses magnets to hold the fabric up.

RUBBER STAMP FABRIC

Add a special touch to your curtains with a stamped design. Find a rubber stamp you like or have one made from your own drawing at a stationery store. Then use it with permanent ink in any color to make a playful pattern.

The Right Way

Windows will stay cleaner during the winter if you remove the screens. Water from rain and snow coming through a metal screen will leave stains on the windows that are difficult to remove.

KEEPING YOUR WINDOWS CLEAN

It takes Andrew Hock and his two partners four months to clean the 6,500 windows of the Empire State Building in New York City—and then they start all over again. And there are a few lessons amateurs can learn from these professionals. Hock says the essential ingredients for clean windows are a good

squeegee with a new rubber, mild detergent, ammonia, water, a soft, highly absorbent cloth, a sponge, and a razor blade.

Before washing windows, remove any caked-on matter with a razor blade. To wash the windows, add a small squirt of detergent and a half-cup of ammonia to a gallon of hot water. (The detergent helps the squeegee slide.) Sponge the mixture over the glass, and then drag the squeegee once across the whole window—going over it more than once will leave marks. Use the soft cloth to clean the sides of the squeegee where liquid accumulates.

Smart Moves

Here's how you can give your windows a smart new look:
- Use curtain jewelry—a star pinned on a valance, for instance— to add interest to the top or bottom of your curtains.
- Change the appearance of your window by experimenting with the placement of curtain holdbacks and how you attach the curtains to them. The higher the top of the curtain and the higher the holdback, the longer your window will look. Leaving a lot of fabric draped in the center softens the window and makes it look more elegant.
- Attach fabric to the top of a Roman shade with buttons so you can change it for different seasons. Simply unbutton the winter fabric and button on the spring fabric.
- When you want privacy but not a complete absence of light or scenery, use a shade that pulls up from the bottom.

SOME UPS AND DOWNS OF BLINDS

Jerry Lacey, owner of Parker Window Covering in Huntsville, Alabama, offers practical advice about blinds and shutters that could save you time and money:
- One-inch wood blinds usually come with hardware designed for one-inch aluminum blinds. Since wood is much heavier than aluminum, the hardware does not work very well. Two-inch wooden blinds come with heavy-duty hardware specially designed for them. So, if you want hardware that can stand up to wood, either buy two-inch blinds or purchase the two-inch blind hardware for one-inch blinds.
- Wood blinds with slats that are wider than two inches are often difficult to operate because they are typically hard to open and close.
- Some wood blinds come

with no cord holes in the slats. Instead, they have notches cut in the edge of the blind. This is great for privacy and blocking light, but be careful during installation—the slats can fall out if you stand the blind on its end. Also, if the blinds have wide cloth tapes, these may fray and need to be replaced if they get caught in the notches.
- Buy products that have a Canadian Standards Association (CSA) label. Standards for blinds are currently voluntary, but

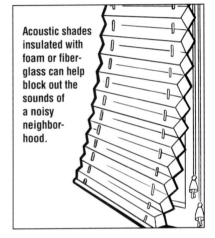

Acoustic shades insulated with foam or fiberglass can help block out the sounds of a noisy neighborhood.

new CSA standards are in the works. Take precautions to make sure that lift cords are out of reach of curious children and pets. Don't position a crib or playpen next to a window with blind lift cords. Alternatively, eliminate the cord altogether by using a shade that can be opened and closed by a remote switch.
- In areas that are likely to get wet or humid—on a window next to a hot tub, or in a garage—try a wood (sometimes called wonder wood) blind that won't warp or crack if it gets damp or wet.

Lighting up Your Life

Illuminate your home effectively, indoors and out.

Dramatic light

Ambient light

Reading light

LIGHTING YOUR INTERIOR

A well-lit room will combine three different types of light, explains New York City interior designer Benjamin Noriega-Ortiz:

- Ambient light, which is the overall light of a living space.
- Reading light, which focuses illumination in a particular place.
- Dramatic light, which highlights certain objects or areas in a room.

Too often, says Noriega-Ortiz, people have only ambient light, and it comes from only one source: the ceiling. He dislikes ceiling light because it produces shadows under the eyes and tends to be harsh. His preferred choices for ambient light are lamps and sconces, which provide light that glows in the face and lights up the furniture, creating a homier feeling. He recommends using floor lamps that are no higher than four feet six inches—these will provide comfortable light when you sit down, and don't allow you to see the naked lightbulb when you stand up.

If you use halogen lighting, says Noriega-Ortiz, combine it with incandescent lighting. Halogen shows colors well, but is too harsh for human skin. The relative warmth of incandescent lighting will help cut the harshness and is kinder to people's faces. With either type of light, dimmers allow you to create a more flattering environment by reducing brightness.

Noriega-Ortiz avoids overhead light even in the dining room, preferring to use candlelight. "Dinner is one of the only ceremonies left in our daily lives," he remarks, "and candlelight helps to make it special. It reflects on your face, and lends a sense of poetry."

PERIOD LIGHTING

The right light fixtures can make an important contribution to an authentic period look. Jim Kelly's Rejuvenation Lamp and Fixtures Company in Portland, Oregon, a producer of reproduction light fixtures, has helped restorers of old homes, libraries, capitol buildings, and county courthouses achieve the appearance of historic lighting using the safety features and wattage available today.

The first step in recreating an authentic period look, says Kelly, is to do some research on what kind of lights were used during the time period in which you are interested. In general, he says, what you will find is that rooms in older homes were lit with multiple light sources—wall and ceiling lights as well as lamps—for a combination of direct and indirect light.

LIGHTING ART

As an artist and an installer of pictures and lighting in the northeastern United States, Frank Keller is doubly sensitive to the interplay of art and lighting. "Picture lighting is designed to supply illumination to the artwork, not to draw attention to itself," he says. "If picture lights are too dressy or showy, they're a distraction. They should fade into the sidelines and not be an identity in themselves."

There are three ways of lighting artwork, Keller explains. One is a lamp that attaches onto the picture frame, most commonly the Richardson Reflector. Second is a framing projector or pin lights, which are placed in a hollow above the ceiling and project light through a lens that distributes light evenly over the surface of the picture. And third is track lighting or another form of ceiling light that floods the wall, rather than the picture, with a wash of light. Lamps such as the Richardson Reflector are most appropriate for substantial picture

frames, which help to obscure the fixture. Pictures with very thin frames call for one of the other lighting methods.

The ultimate picture lighting evenly lights just the artwork, not the frame.

LANDSCAPE LIGHTING

Landscape lighting is difficult to do successfully, says Jan Lennox Moyer, landscape lighting expert and author of *The Landscape Lighting Book*. Landscape lighting can turn the darkness outside your home into a place of magic and mystery, or it can call up images of high-security government buildings. Moyer notes some of the most important factors to consider: "First, you're starting with a big, open darkness with no walls. Any amount of brightness has to relate to the surrounding environment, and it's easy to overdo it. Second, the outdoor environment is always growing and changing. A lighting system has to be flexible so it doesn't get buried by plants or knocked over by people working or

playing in the garden. Third, the outdoor environment is extremely destructive and you have to make sure to get fixtures that can withstand the threats of corrosion and breakage."

Moyer suggests starting a landscape lighting design with the main structural feature of your garden. Moyer believes simple is more effective than cluttered: Choose to light one beautiful tree and perhaps a hedge behind it rather than four trees, which can create a "hodgepodge effect." At the same time, pay attention to lighting paths and stairs for safety, and the outer edges of your property for security. By using layers of lights on the tree you have chosen, you may be able to accomplish all your lighting objectives.

When lighting paths, consider the fact that, as vertical beings, we see vertical surfaces long before we see horizontal surfaces. This means it's more effective to send light to the plantings bordering a path than onto the path itself, though you will want some light directly on the path.

Tools of the Trade

Solar-powered fixtures are an energy-efficient way to illuminate the footpaths around your home. Use them to highlight the greenery along the edges of a footpath, which are easier to see in the dark than the flat surface of the path itself.

Smart Moves

Jan Lennox Moyer tells how to make landscape lighting effective:
- Use a combination of down lighting (from above) and up lighting (from below) to incorporate natural overall coverage and dramatic effects.
- Use low-wattage bulbs, especially on accent lights for trees.
- Use more fixtures, rather than fewer, in order to sculpt the three-dimensional qualities of what you are lighting. Three fixtures are an absolute minimum for up lighting a tree and showing its three-dimensionality. An 80-foot tree could take 10 to 15 fixtures.
- Avoid do-it-yourself landscape lighting kits available at discount stores. The fixtures tend to be poorly made, and typically have a very short lifespan. Buy quality instead.

Decorating with Flowers

Enhance your environment with fresh and dried varieties.

Silk rose

Silk cockscomb

Freeze-dried greens

Silk rose

Freeze-dried yarrow

Combine natural and silk elements to create appealing arrangements.

DESIGNING WITH DRIED AND SILK FLOWERS

Dried, silk, or fabric flower arrangements allow you to have long-lasting beauty with a minimum of work. Patricia Cull, owner of Allan's Flowers in Calgary shares her approach to creating these designs:

- The current trend in designing arrangements is to use botanically correct fabric flowers in contemporary acrylic vases. Always start with beautiful products, says Cull. She discourages combining "fresh look" fabric flowers and dried flowers. However, she points out that "dried look" fabric flowers combined with dried natural materials such as pods and branches do work well together.

- Look for a variety of textures to "enlarge the vocabulary" of your arrangement. Besides flowers, you can use things available all year-long—like curly willow branches, dried poppy pods, amaranthus, cockscomb, and pepper berry—to provide visual interest.

- When choosing colors, try to pick up tones in the room where the arrangement will be placed. This helps ensure that the arrangement enriches and enhances the room decor. If you can't match an exact tone, you can take a pointillist approach, using two colors that together create the effect of the desired tone. To create a chartreuse effect, for instance, you can combine certain shades of greens and yellows.

- When building the arrangement of dried flowers, take the same approach you would if you were making a live arrangement. Cull compares this to the structure of a house. She advises making small groupings of each variety, rather than mixing them in singly. Begin by making a foundation of greenery and branches. Next, lay in the big or focal flowers, which form the base of the arrangement. Then, build upward, adding architectural details, such as texture—the second and third stories of the house—with different kinds of flowers and materials.

FRESH FLOWER CHOICE AND CARE

To make sure your cut flowers look their best and last as long as possible, follow this advice from Claire Won Kang, instructor at the New York Botanical Gardens:

- For a beautiful arrangement, buy all one kind of flower, such as daisies or tulips, and mass them in a container.

- If you want a mixed arrangement, consider combining four different types of flowers: spike flowers (such as snap-dragons, larkspur, or gladiolas), face flowers (like carnations and roses), filler flowers (such as baby's breath or statice), and multi-flora flowers (like pompons).

- Color combinations can be challenging. If you are overwhelmed by them, use all one color. If you're mixing colors, stay within a theme, using all pastels or all jewel tones, for instance. Avoid too many colors.

- When you get home from the farmer's market or flower store, place flowers in a bucket of warm water and, using very sharp scissors, cut the stems. This opens up an air hole through which flowers can receive water. The air hole is often blocked when you buy flowers. Sharp scissors are important to prevent mashing the stems.

Buy florists' supplies to anchor your arrangement.

The Right Way

When buying roses for your home, make sure they are open just a little. If you buy them with tight buds, they are unlikely to open once you get them home.

MUSEUM-QUALITY ARRANGEMENTS

Some 5½ million people a year view the floral spectaculars arranged by Chris Giftos, manager of special events and floral master at the Metropolitan Museum of Art in New York City and author of *A Bouquet from the Met*. Every Monday, Giftos creates arrangements that appear in four large urns in the museum's Great Hall. His designs are guided by a variety of factors: a current exhibition, the season, a particular holiday, and what's available in the flower market. For instance, if there's a special display of Impressionist paintings, he might do pastel arrangements that suggest those art works. For the Fourth of July, he'll create a display reminiscent of fireworks bursting in the air, using tall, spiky plants and flowers.

Typically, Giftos uses four or five different types of flowers in a bouquet, staying within a color theme. He's careful to combine flowers with similar lifespans, and those that are equally sturdy or fragile. Giftos' rule of thumb for containers is that the flowers should generally be 1½ to 2 times the height of the container.

- Use a container that has been washed with a solution of one teaspoon of bleach to two quarts of water to remove bacteria.
- Remove all leaves on flowers and greenery that would be below the water line in the container. For best results, put only bare stems in the water.
- Fill the container with clean, cold water and flower food. Place the flowers in it loosely. Don't jam them together.
- Change the water in the container every day to prevent bacterial growth.

Tools of the Trade

Pour water into an amaryllis's hollow stem and plug it with a cotton ball to keep the bloom hydrated.

Smart Moves

Dried flowers
- Air-dry your own flowers to use in dried arrangements. After cutting, simply hang them upside down until they have dried. (If they crumble, use them for potpourri.)
- Keep dried, silk, or fabric flower arrangements out of the sun, where they can fade to unnatural shades.
- Add artificial fruits and vegetables to your dried flower centerpieces for a different, slightly off-beat look.

Fresh flowers
- If you're using flowers and greenery from your garden, be sure to spray them with water when you bring them inside to remove any insects. If you still see insects, don't use the materials, or you may find yourself with an infestation.

IKEBANA FLOWER ARRANGING

Ikebana is a Japanese approach to flower arranging that dates back to the sixth century. Originally, the flower arrangements, designed to show the connection between heaven, humans, and earth, were given as gifts or offerings to Shinto priests or deities, says Lauren Tillman, associate master, Ichiyo school of Ikebana and past president of Ikebana, Pittsburgh Chapter. Gradually, the approach spread throughout Asia, and is now practiced in many places around the world. When describing the difference between Ikebana and the typical North American approach to flower arranging, Tillman says, "The North American approach focuses on quantity. In Ikebana, a guiding principle is less is more. Line and form are more important than masses of flowers." Space, line, beauty, color, and form are all important elements.

The following are keys to Ikebana arrangements:
- They use odd numbers of flowers, and usually small numbers—one, three, or five.
- Only seasonal materials are acceptable.
- They use many elements of the environment in addition to flowers, including water, rock, moss, twigs, and pottery, and must blend with the environment they are in.
- They are based on prescribed structures that are passed along from master to student.

Focus on Photographs

Beautify your home and enhance personal memories with photographs.

FRAMING THE FAMILY

Leslie Linsley, a designer and author of *Leslie Linsley's High-Style, Low-Cost Decorating Ideas*, advocates an easy, inexpensive, but creative approach to framing family photographs. Start by purchasing unornamented discount frames. Then let the photographs guide you in how to decorate the frames. For instance, suggests Linsley, pictures of young children in colorful clothes might lead you to glue Legos on the frame, or miniature colored pencils, or little bicycles. To complement a wedding picture, you can cut out roses from greeting cards or wrapping paper and attach them to the frame. Shells on the frame of a beach vacation photograph can enhance a memory. So can pressed flowers gathered on a walk in the woods. Faux finishing, sponge painting, stenciling, and other applications can all add interest without a great deal of work. Decorat-

ing the frames can be a great family activity.

For displaying family photographs, says Linsley, narrow walls filled with photos can make a striking display and serve as an effective way of separating one space from another.

The Right Way

Without proper care and maintenance, family photographs and negatives will deteriorate, says Lionel Suntop, owner of Exhibits/Prairie Book Arts Center. He specializes in the preservation of fine art and photography.

- Photographs should be stored in a low-heat (68°F), low-humidity (30 to 50 percent). "The basement and the attic are the worst places to store photographs," says Suntop.
- Very old pictures or those of special personal value should be professionally rephotographed and the originals stored in a safe deposit box.
- Do not glue pictures in albums or use albums with pre-pasted, sticky pages. Not only are these adhesives destructive to the photograph, but you can easily damage photographs if you decide to remove them. Instead, use pre-pasted

plastic photo corners made of polypropylene or albums with pocket pages sheathed in thin strips of mylar.

- There is not much you can do to prevent color images that were poorly processed from decomposing, says Suntop. Take photos you care about to a custom processing outlet and avoid one-hour convenience-store photo developers. For especially precious color images, request *cibachrome* processing.
- Store negatives in the dark, and they won't deteriorate as quickly as photos. Negatives can be preserved and catalogued in plastic page preservers in three-ring or clip binders. Suntop recommends storing negatives of black and white photos with the contact sheet for easy identification and cataloging.

FAMILY ARCHIVES

When art photographer Bea Nettles inherited her family's extensive collection of historical photographs—some dating back to the mid-1800s—she became inspired to turn them into the subject of two books, *Memory Loss* and *Grace's Daughter*. Nettles is chair of the Photography Program at the University of Illinois in Champaign. Her work is displayed in major collections, including the Museum of Modern Art in New York City and the International Museum of Photography at

Eastman House in Rochester, New York.

Nettles' two books incorporate images, mementos, and excerpts from family members' letters, memoirs, and journal entries. While Nettles produced the books for publication, hobbyists can put together similar collections for personal pleasure and to share with family and friends.

- Take time with older relatives to identify people in your old family photographs. Nettles recommends gently penciling in names, locations, and dates directly on the back

Plastic photo corners are the best way to mount your family pictures.

Family photographs, clustered together on a single wall or shelf, make an effective display.

DISPLAYING ART PHOTOGRAPHS

David Winter owns Winter Works on Paper, a New York City art and photo gallery, where displaying photographs is an important part of the business.

For an informal look, display framed photographs on shelves 4 inches deep with a lip on the front to prevent slippage. In his home, Winter has an entire wall devoted to these shelves, which are placed 30 inches apart.

In a more formal approach, Winter also hangs photographs using a rod or wire that hangs from the picture molding in the room. The advantage of this technique is that you can easily move photos by positioning the rod without leaving nail holes in your wall. This hanging system comes with special attachments in case you do not have picture moldings in your room. Winter buys many of his frames at flea markets, and mixes old frames and clean-lined, modern ones.

Mat size is also an important consideration, says Winter. Mats provide some "breathing room" around an image. Winter prefers simple, eight-ply mats, usually in white. There's not a lot of color choice in acid-free mats, so when he does want a colored mat, he paints it with acrylic paint.

of the photograph using a 2B or 3B pencil. Never use a ball-point pen.

- Nettles scanned family photos into a computer, which she then used to help restore the images. While this process may be beyond the scope of the amateur, readable results can be obtained on a black-and-white copier using the "photo" setting, and excellent results with color.
- Nettles' father sent out copies of photographs to the extended family, who provided further background.
- Pictures and artifacts can be arranged chronologically, around branches of the family, or around specific individuals. In *Memory Loss*, Nettles organizes around the two sides of her family, beginning with her great-grandparents and ending with her parents and their 12 grandchildren at their 50th wedding anniversary.
- Include different types of artifacts in your album, such as letters, programs from events and other mementos.

FRAMING ART PHOTOGRAPHS

Art photographs need the same care and attention as paintings or other artwork to maintain their appearance and value over time, explains Greg O'Halloran, vice president of design at APF/Visions, an archival framing studio in New York City.

- Use acid-free framing materials, including the mat, backing, and hinges that hold the photo to the backing. Acidic materials

Tools of the Trade

Pocketed plastic shower curtains and room dividers are a playful way to display photographs and other mementos.

will eventually break down the paper fibers and burn the photograph.
- Photographs should not be hung in direct sunlight. Consider using a frame with ultraviolet-filtering Plexiglas in it.

O'Halloran suggests that "there should be a good marriage between the period of the photograph and the frame." A 1930s photograph of a Montreal street scene, for instance, would be complemented by an Art Deco-style frame. Another consideration is color. If your photographs are black and white, you will probably want to stay with frames that are black, white, or silver because a color frame can give them a commercial appearance.

Treat each photograph as a separate framing decision, advises O'Halloran. Using one kind of frame for a whole collection "tends to run one image into the next."

A little imagination and an inexpensive frame can make an unforgettable gift.

Imaginative Recycling

Find new and attractive uses for old or discarded items.

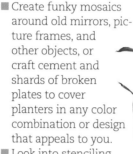

GARGOYLES AND OTHER BUILDING DETAILS

Artefacts Architectural Antiques is a store in St. Jacobs, Ontario, specializing in architectural salvage. Interesting things that come off of and out of old buildings often end up here, and go on to serve new and surprising purposes. Co-owner Chris Blott and the staff are skilled and creative and able to help clients imagine new applications for each antique piece. To help with the custom design, Artefacts maintains a forge and metal studio, a glass studio, and consults with local artisans. Here are some ideas:

- Old iron grille topped with sheet glass to make a coffee table.
- Marble or wood balusters from an altar railing or old staircase that become table legs.
- Iron or marble balusters and newel posts made into bed frames.
- Column capitals—in everything from marble to granite to cast iron—used as end tables or as bases for plants.
- Carved gargoyles turned into bathtub spigots.

A new trend is the reuse of old industrial items. Bases from knitting machines, for example, are popular with wood or glass tops. Medical cabinets are rescued and are reused as towel cabinets.

A TOUCH OF COLOR

Donna Proietti, decorating consultant and assistant editor at *Country Living* magazine, maintains that a quick coat of oil-based paint in a fresh color is a great way to add flash to shabby furniture found in the basement or at a garage sale. Here are a few of Proietti's other suggestions for bringing old, dingy items to new life:

- Consider a crackle paint kit for two-tone, aged look. The process is reasonably simple. Paint the object a solid color first. Then spray on a second coat that peels away as it dries, revealing the original color beneath it between the cracks.
- Create funky mosaics around old mirrors, picture frames, and other objects, or craft cement and shards of broken plates to cover planters in any color combination or design that appeals to you.
- Look into stenciling. Craft stores offer a wide variety of stencils, paints, and brushes that let you create a new look in just a few minutes.
- Update an old lamp by painting the base a favorite color and gluing ribbons or sea shells around the bottom edge of a simple lampshade.

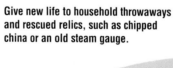

Give new life to household throwaways and rescued relics, such as chipped china or an old steam gauge.

A rag rug 27 inches wide by 4 feet long requires about 3½ pounds of medium-weight material. Very large rag rugs can be made by sewing smaller rugs together.

RUGS FROM RAGS

Pioneers used to strip up their old clothing once it was beyond repair and take it to the local weaver, who would make it into rag rugs. In a modern variation, on this theme, Lizzie and Charlie's Rag Rugs in Utah weaves rag rugs from scrap fabric purchased by the pound from sewing factories. Much of the scrap, once it's cut and stripped, is appropriate for the rugs: odds and ends left over from making jeans, dresses, shirts—even the loops that are snipped off pairs of socks as they leave the assembly line. Glenda Bushman, one of the owners of Lizzie and Charlie's, explains that they used to use old clothing, but stopped when they discovered that scrap fabric requires less time and effort to recycle.

Lizzie and Charlie's produces about 2,000 rugs a year on eight traditional looms, two of which date back to 1913 and 1914. The rugs have no backing and are completely reversible. "Once one side gets dirty, just flip it over and use the other side," recommends Bushman.

Explore the color spectrum with your kids with plastic bottles filled with water and food coloring.

Wash a rag rug by putting it on the driveway and cleaning it with a liquid soap, a broom, and a hose. If it fits, you can also put it in the washing machine—but not the dryer. Dry cleaning is best for a special rug. With care a rag rug can last a long time.

Quick Tricks

In her European Flower Shop, in Boulder, Colorado, Cindy Lennon uses beautiful ceramic and glass vases for customers' flowers. In her home, though, Lennon is a little looser. "I use anything that holds water," says Lennon, "and lots of things food and drink come in." For Lennon, "anything" might include:
- olive oil cans
- old milk bottles
- wine bottles
- fish bowls
- brandy snifters
- shells
- 1930s glass building blocks

KIDSTUFF

Parents needn't spend a bundle on toys, says Ann Fisher, former program coordinator for The Family Farm, a North Carolina educational and care facility for teen parents.

- Children love to play with old household items, such as dented pots or a set of measuring spoons. Older children will enjoy playing dress-up with old clothes and shoes. Make sure all items are safe for kids.
- Fill large plastic bottles with water and food coloring and seal them tightly with glue. Children can play with them or you can line them up on the window sill to let the light shine through.
- Make nestling containers or building blocks with old containers and boxes decorated with non-toxic paints, construction paper, tissue paper, and magazine cutouts.

Smart Moves

Old, commonplace items can often be put to new and distinctive uses. Following are a few suggestions:
- Turn old glass condiment and juice jars and bottles into storage containers for foodstuffs, such as grains, legumes, and pasta. These can be artfully and conveniently displayed on open shelves in the kitchen.
- Decorate old coffee cans with wrapping paper, magazine pictures, or color photographs, and arrange them together on open shelves. They can be used as storage containers for everything from paper clips and thumbtacks to perishable foods.
- Hang plastic—or even better, metal—milk crates on the wall in a checkerboard pattern to create lively and playful shelf space.
- Old yogurt and cottage cheese containers are terrific for freezing sauces, soups, and stews, and for storing leftovers.
- Cut the bottoms off old cardboard juice and milk cartons to use as cloches in the garden to protect tender young seedlings.
- Old newsprint and cardboard make a perfect base for mulch in the garden. The paper will decompose slowly over time.
- Instead of throwing away old and damaged CDs, hang them in the garden—they scare away birds and catch and reflect the sunlight in interesting ways.

Organizing Your Closets

Maximize space while you minimize disorder.

A well-designed closet combines different organizational elements for accessibility, visibility, and versatility.

DEALING WITH CLUTTER

Professional organizer Laura Lakin, president of ClutterBusters in New York City, specializes in "compassionate chaos abatement." Here are her tips for becoming clutter-free:

- Everything you own should have a home. If you can't accommodate all your belongings, donate them to charity, have a garage sale, or rent a small storage unit.
- Don't waste accessible or "hot" storage space on things you rarely or never use. Items such as back tax returns and holiday ornaments should be stored out of the way, such as at the top of the closet or under the bed.
- Open your mail every day. Throw out any catalogs, coupons, and other junk mailings you are never going to use.
- If you buy and subscribe to lots of magazines, consider how many you really get a chance to read. If the magazines are not being read, recycle the issues you have and cancel the subscriptions.
- Pair odd socks. If you can't find a match, throw the sock away.
- Designate one drawer as the "clutter drawer" for everything you don't have time to deal with immediately but don't want to part with. When it starts to overflow, sort through it and start again.

Tools of the Trade

Drawer dividers, which you can buy at housewares stores or have installed by a carpenter or closet designer, make it easy to keep accessories, undergarments, and jewelry organized and dust-free.

CLOSET MAKEOVER

In her 10 years working as a design consultant with California Closets—North America's best-known designers of custom closets—Ginny Snook Scott says she has "never created the same closet twice." Here are her tips for efficient use of closet space:

- If you share your master closet with other people, maintain separate areas for each person's clothing.
- Keep like clothes, such as all your shirts, pants, and skirts, together in separate sections of their own. Also keep your business and leisure clothes separate for convenience.
- Keep everything off the floor, especially footwear. Shoes and boots are best kept on shelves at eye level, or in clear plastic shoe boxes, which can be purchased at many housewares stores.
- Keep folded clothing, such as sweaters, t-shirts, and jeans, on open shelves, rather than in drawers, where you can't easily see them.

■ Wire hampers on wheels work well for dirty laundry and dry cleaning.

■ Store belts and ties on a separate hanging rack, rather than draping them over a coat hanger.

GETTING THE HANG OF IT

"Most people have a love/hate relationship with their closets," says Ronni Eisenberg, co-author with Kate Kelly of *Organize Your Home!* and *Organize Yourself!* "They love to stuff in everything they ever owned, bought, or borrowed, but hate it when they can't find what they're looking for."

■ If you have lots of separates, create space in your closet to double-hang clothes. Divide your hanging space in half (you can do it yourself or hire a carpenter to help), with one side for longer clothes and the other side with an upper and lower pole for separates.

■ Clothes need breathing space, or they wrinkle. Don't overcrowd.

■ Use sturdy, high-quality hangers that won't rust.

■ After hanging, run your hand down the garment to prevent twisted lapels and bunched sleeves.

■ Empty all pockets before hanging a suit or jacket.

■ Don't hang dresses and jackets inside out, which can damage the fabric.

■ Hang dresses on a well-padded hanger of the appropriate size.

■ Hang pants from the bottom using a pants hanger. Or fold them over a hanger with a wide rounded bottom to prevent creasing or damaging your clothes.

An uncluttered pantry not only makes mealtime easier, but looks great and creates a feeling of serenity in your home.

■ Don't hang sweaters, which can sag and become damaged.

■ Avoid hangers designed to hold more than one item, since clothes can become wrinkled.

■ Check your clothes for dropped hems, missing buttons, and stains before hanging them up.

MANAGING THE DETAILS

"The key to organization is simplification," says Christy Best, a member of the National Association of Professional Organizers in the United States and owner of Details Professional Organizing. "There seems to be a tendency to hang on to excess things, because there was an initial monetary output. But keeping these items won't make the money reappear!"

Best recommends keeping a donation box going at all times. When it's full, drop it off at a donation station. "It's impossible to get organized until items that aren't being used are cleared. Once that process is underway, life becomes much simpler."

THE LINEN CLOSET

Ronni Eisenberg tells you how to create order out of chaos in your linen closet.

■ Line shelves with easy-to-clean vinyl fabric or paper.

■ Keep only frequently used towels and sheets in the linen closet. Recycle worn towels and sheets as rags.

■ Fold sheets by set. Fold pillow cases, fitted, and flat sheets separately, then place the flat sheet and cases within the fitted sheet so they can be pulled out as a unit.

■ Stack sheets according to family member and towels according to the bathroom in which they are used.

■ When storing sheets, towels, or tablecloths, place the folded side facing the door.

■ Use the floor of the linen closet to store large, bulky items, or smaller items in storage bins.

Smart Moves

Storing out-of-season clothing can help you keep the chaos in check.

■ Try to store clothes in a well-ventilated part of the house. Overheated attics can cause clothes to discolor or hidden stains to appear, while damp basements may cause mildew.

■ Clean everything before storing it. Moths will attack food-stained and dirty clothes first. And stains will set over time.

■ Store folded items like sweaters in cedar chests or plastic bins. Use mothballs, but don't let them touch clothing. Don't store clothes directly on wood, which can discolor them.

■ Suits, dresses, and skirts can be stored on rolling clothing racks.

■ If you're short on storage space at home, find a dry cleaner who offers box storage for your winter clothes over the summer.

Creating Children's Spaces

Create children's environments that are appealing, comfortable, and safe.

ROOM WITH A VIEW

Kids who are lucky enough to have Jill Avery paint a mural in their room enter an environment where cartoon characters, jungle animals, dragons and princesses, or any number of other fantasy friends cavort on the wall. Avery, who owns Murals and Artistic Finishes in Santa Barbara, California, explains how a mural comes about: "I meet with the child and the parents to see who they are and what they like. They have the vision, and I try to make their vision come true. For the parents, I'm sensitive to everything that's already in the room—the furniture, carpets, pillows, and curtains. I try to match the existing palette so the grownups will be happy. Working within those parameters, I put in a scene and characters for the children, usually at the children's eye level."

Favorite themes for babies' rooms are nursery rhymes. Older children prefer adventure scenes, fairy-tale themes, and animals. When creating her murals, Avery tries to find a space where they won't be blocked by anything in the room. She might also incorporate architectural features, such as winding a rubber plant around a window as a perch for a toucan.

Color is an important element in Avery's work. "I tend to blend the color that's on the wall with my paint so it softens the mural. That keeps it from being too strong or distracting. And I always blend in the opposite color of the dominant one I'm using—for instance, if I'm doing a lot of green, I add pink or red to the green to temper the color."

Avery works primarily with acrylic paints because they are fast-drying and do not smell. She uses oils when a mural needs more detail or depth, or for glazes.

MAKING THE BEST OF IT

A less-than-ideal room—one that's too small, low, dark, or far away—is often a source of dissension in families. The fact is, someone has to have it. In Wendy Smolen's family, that someone is her older daughter, who lost best-room privileges after acquiring twin siblings. Smolen, lifestyles editor at *Parents Magazine*, knew how to soften the blow. "We compensate with color," she says. "Her room is always the most colorful and the most fun, and she's always involved in the decorating."

Let your child choose the color, suggests Smolen. Then pick out a few paint colors and fabric samples in that color range, and allow the child to choose those that he or she likes most. "I wouldn't show her something I hated," says Smolen, "but the point is to give the kids some say."

Smolen's twins used to share a room, a situation that can be equally challenging to family harmony. Smolen suggests giving each child in a shared space a personal area—his or her own desk, bookshelf, or toy shelf, for instance—that's private. Also, allow both children some expression of personal taste. Maybe one likes pink and one likes polka dots—work out a creative solution that incorporates both of these elements. "You can tie the two tastes together in a way that acknowledges their individuality but also unifies the room."

Speaking of sharing spaces, parents and children also share other parts of the house. "At *Parents*," says Smolen, "we believe that children's bedrooms aren't the only places in the house where they spend time. It's their house, too." Have a special seat for them in the living room. Frame a piece of art they did in first grade and hang it in the hall. Have a step stool in the kitchen so they can join in the action, and a low drawer for their toys and art supplies.

Smart Moves

Give kids a space where they can be creative without worrying about ruining the walls. Provide them with a firm primed panel, maybe pine or Masonite, approximately four feet by eight feet, where they can paint to their hearts' content.

BREAKING AWAY

The trend in children's rooms is moving away from the traditional pink or blue theme to a more gender-free treatment that is appropriate for both boys and girls, says Alex Jordan, principal, Bruce Gregga Interiors in Chicago. Some recent examples from Gregga Interiors:

■ A baby's room based on a "wonderful small rug" from the late 1940s or early 1950s that was discovered in an antique store. The rug, featuring Disney characters in red, turquoise, yellow, blue, and black, was mounted and hung above the crib. These colors were picked up in the rest of the room: yellow on the walls, white and turquoise on the tiered valances, and the rest in the bed linens and other fabrics.

■ A baby's room and adjoining playroom in hot tropi-

Use your child's interests as a springboard for painting whimsical, personalized wooden furniture.

cal colors. The bedroom walls are lime green, the armoires French blue, the changing table, "pinky-red". The playroom walls are seafoam green. Multi-colored linens on a white bed help to keep color interest high.

Experimenting with different colors is all part of "thinking outside the box" when it comes to kids' rooms, says Jordan. So is choosing furniture that's not necessarily designed for children, but works well in their rooms.

A good pad with bumpers added to the top of a chest can transform it into a changing table—and removing the pad can transform it back into a regular piece of furniture as the child grows.

"Old-fashioned rockers and beautifully scaled chests and tables can be painted with non-toxic paints and made whimsical by changing the hardware," says Jordan, opening up worlds for you to explore in designing a child's habitat.

Professional mural painters can turn children's rooms into magical fantasy lands. Painter Jill Avery turned this child's room into the main deck of a pirate ship.

SAFE SPACES

In a contest for the most dangerous area in the house for kids, the bathroom would probably head the list. The tub, faucets, toilet, hard ceramic tile, and under-sink storage all pose threats: slipping, drowning, and poisoning, for example. Next would come the kitchen, then stairs, exits to the outdoors, and swimming pools. Obviously, vigilance on the part of caregivers is the most effective preventive against accidents. But several types of safety products on the market today can add another element of protection.

Mindy Moss, a buyer for The Right Start, a chain of children's specialty stores, lists items to make homes safer:

Bathroom	Toilet lid lock, children's bath seat, faucet covers, water temperature indicator (can be in the form of a bath toy), cabinet locks.
Kitchen	Cabinet locks, stove burner shield, stove knob covers.
Stairs	Steel gates. (Gates at the top of the stairs should never be tension gates, which can give under pressure.)
Throughout the house	Electrical outlet covers, power strip safety covers (especially in the home office or wherever there is a computer), furniture corner covers, furniture safety brackets (which attach furniture to the wall to prevent it from toppling over during rough play), window blinds with CSA-approved blind cords.
Outdoors	Locks on doors, and an alarm that sounds when a child leaves the house or jumps into the pool.

Barrier-Free Design

Good design should work for everyone.

WHEELCHAIR ACCESS

Sometimes you have to modify your environment to allow you to do what you want to do, advises Nancy Mannucci, a residential and commercial interior designer who has multiple sclerosis. Now in a wheelchair, Mannucci, who has remodeled her downtown apartment and her Victorian home outside the city, attributes the success of her designs to "creative problem solving." For example, she has consolidated two small closets into one larger one to allow her greater access and independence. She keeps seasonal clothes on open shelves and on low closet rods.

Many of these modifications are also appropriate as people get older.

- Remove all door saddles—the wooden frame at the base of the door. If you live in a rental home, you can simply put them back in place at the end of your occupancy.
- Mannucci has installed grab bars all over her house, wherever she finds a need for them. She has two above her bed that she uses for physical therapy, as well as for leverage when getting in and out of bed, and some along the edge of her kitchen counters and in her bathroom. When attaching grab bars, anchor them securely into wall studs.
- Centralize control of your light switches, advises Mannucci. About half of her lights are controlled at a central wall switch.
- Use tight, flat-woven rugs, such as sisal and rag rugs, which should be secured on the floor with strong, double-sided tape.
- If you are ambulatory, install a second handrail on the staircase so you can always support yourself on your stronger side.
- If you cannot negotiate stairs, consider installing a chair lift along the wall of the staircase.
- Reorganize your kitchen pantry and cupboards so that everything you might need is accessible and at eye level.

USER-FRIENDLY KITCHENS AND BATHS

It makes good design sense to take into account safety and ease of use, says Scott Puddicomb, a designer and owner of Home Access, an Ottawa-based company that creates baths and kitchens to make life easier for everyone, especially people with limited mobility.

- Showers are now available that have a built-in bench and footrest. New tubs have a wide lip that allows you to sit comfortably on them.
- Select flooring for durability, safety, and ease of care. Some vinyl flooring is slippery and wears poorly. Puddicomb prefers large ceramic tiles that have been treated for slip resistance and have narrow grout lines.
- Bathroom vanities are now available in standard (30- to 32-inch) and tall (36-inch) sizes for people who find the standard size uncomfortably low. When designing a bathroom vanity for wheelchair users, make sure the pipes are recessed and there is sufficient clearance for a wheelchair underneath the counter.
- Puddicomb creates kitchens that allow cooks to sit down or use a wheelchair while preparing food. Counters and cupboards are lowered and there is plenty of room for knees underneath. He places appliances, such as cooktops, at counter height. A wall oven with a door that swings out and has a shelf underneath to rest pots on is a smart design for everyone.

Raised appliances

Grab bars

Lowered counters

Toe kick for wheelchair access

Lighted cabinetry with 180-degree hinges affords accessibility and ease of use.

THE HOME OF THE FUTURE

A few alterations can help make your home safer, more convenient, and more comfortable, says Tom Parker of the Canada Mortgage and Housing Corporation. If you're elderly or have difficulty getting around, these changes can help you enjoy your own home and remain independent longer:

■ Large rocker light switches are the easiest to use, whether you have an armful of groceries or limited dexterity.
■ Replace round doorknobs with lever door handles that open more easily.
■ Lever- or pedal-operated bathroom and kitchen faucets might make life a little easier.
■ If you have limited mobility, consider buying a seat or bench designed for use in the bath or shower to prevent falls. Choose a model with slip-proof caps on the legs.
■ Hand-held shower heads mounted on a vertical sliding bar can make showering safer.
■ Choose appliances for convenience: front-loading dishwashers are easier to load, stacking washer-dryers simplify the transfer of wet clothes to the dryer.
■ As you get older, poor lighting is a potential safety hazard. Two-bulb fixtures are wise. Also, add more fixtures, or use bulbs with a higher wattage where the fixtures can safely accommodate them.

BATHROOM SAFETY

Here are some ideas from Tom Parker, senior researcher at Canada Mortgage and Housing Corporation (CMHC), on making bathrooms safe for kids and grandparents alike.

■ Use ground-fault circuit interrupter (GFCI) outlets, which prevent shocks by shutting off electricity to the outlet when current leakage is detected.
■ Protect your family from burns with anti-scalding devices on showers and tubs that prevent water from getting too hot, even if someone pushes the faucet the wrong way or mistakenly turns off the cold water. Or install a central thermostatic control to limit hot-water temperature to 109°F.
■ Shower and bathroom doors can be dangerous for children, older adults, and anyone who might have difficulty opening them in an emergency. Doors that swing out when they open are the safest option.

Smart Moves

If you are doing renovations or building from scratch, consider making these changes for maximum comfort and adaptability:

■ Use three-quarter-inch plywood as floor-to-ceiling reinforcement to anchor towel and grab bars more securely.
■ Allow for a five-foot turning space in kitchen and bath.
■ Install 36-inch-wide doorways instead of the standard 32.
■ Have 48-inch-wide hallways rather than 36 inches.
■ Make sure to allow for 36 inches of clearance next to the toilet.

DESIGNING FOR PEOPLE WITH MEMORY LOSS

If someone you love suffers from Alzheimer's or some other illness that causes forgetfulness and confusion, there are some simple adjustments you can make around the house to generally enhance the occupant's memory and orientation, says Cynthia Leibrock, MA, an interior designer, lecturer, and co-author with James Evan Leery of *Beautiful Universal Design*.

Here are a few of Leibrock's suggestions for rearranging the homes of people with memory difficulties and confusion:

■ Try to keep things simple, orderly, and logical. For instance, keep socks in one drawer, underwear in another, and night clothes in another—eliminating distractions and reducing random clutter.
■ Older people who suffer from memory loss may understand traditional appliances and fixtures better than their modern counterparts. For example you might consider replacing a digital clock with an analog clock, a push-button phone with a rotary phone, or levered door handles with round doorknobs.
■ Reinforce memory with well-defined spaces and visual cues. Rooms and their functions should be distinct and well articulated: A dining room should look like a dining room. Visual cues might include a distinctive piece of furniture or painting outside the bathroom or bedroom to help residents find their way around the space.

The Right Way

Adapting modern appliances for people who are confused, forgetful, or visually impaired doesn't have to be complicated. For example, you can put a large, easily legible sticker on a remote control to make it easier for people dealing with a variety of physical and mental challenges.

Lazy-Day Furniture

Choose outdoor furnishings to fit your lifestyle and budget.

THE LONGEVITY OF TEAK

"Teak is historically considered the best wood for extended use outdoors in all seasons," says Dave Wideman, owner of Wideman and William Wallace Garden Furniture in Fordwich, Ontario, who specializes in teak and iroko furniture. Teak is used on battleship decks, yacht handrails, and anywhere else on a seagoing vessel where wood is exposed to the elements. Why? Wideman explains that because of the natural oils and silicates in the wood, teak can withstand destructive forces without warping, splintering, or rotting.

Wideman and William Wallace Garden Furniture uses teak from Indonesia, where teak plantations operate on a "sustained source" basis. This means that for every tree felled, at least one is planted. Iroko is similar to teak with the exception that it can be painted and it is somewhat less expensive. When buying teak furniture, check to see if the manufacturer has a certification showing where the wood came from, or if the manufacturer's literature identifies the source. The term to look for is "plantation-grown teak." If this is absent, the teak is likely to have been cut from natural forest, and should be avoided for environmental reasons.

The quality and price of teak furniture is based on the grade of lumber, thickness of the boards, and type of hardware used in its construction. Although the wood itself will last a long time, lower-grade lumber is likely to have wormholes and knots that, if used on high-stress areas, such as legs, joints, or seat and back slats, can cause a break. Thinner wood also increases susceptibility to breakage. At Wideman's company, the teak furniture has mortise and tenon joinery. The fewer metal fittings on the furniture, the finer the quality. Some teak furniture is made with long-lasting marine brass fittings. Avoid inexpensive brass which can stain the wood, and break easily.

Shop around to compare quality, comfort, price, and design, advises Wideman.

Teak turns silvery when it weathers, or you can preserve its golden hue with a teak sealer.

You want the design to look as good 15 years from now as it does today. Well-made teak furniture lasts a lifetime.

Maintaining teak furniture is as simple as scrubbing it with soapy water once or twice a year.

THE STYLE OF METAL

You have a little spot under a tree that's perfect for drinking coffee or an aperitif. You've spent some of your happiest moments in European parks. You want a sleek, modern look outdoors. If any or all these statements apply, you will probably want to consider metal outdoor furniture.

Metal furniture, says Patricia Kittredge, furniture buyer for Smith and Hawken stores in the United States, is a rapidly expanding category in outdoor furnishings. Strong but lightweight, it ranges in design from the classic French bistro table and chairs to cutting-edge looks from France and Italy. Metal furniture is the perfect solution if you have limited space outdoors, and some of it even folds for easy storage.

Since finishes on metal furniture vary, be sure to check the manufacturer's information on how to protect and care for it to ensure

Powdercoated aluminum outdoor furnishings are low-maintenance and durable.

Smart Moves

When buying an umbrella for your yard or terrace, be sure to choose one with a heavy, mildew- and weather-resistant fabric. Look for those that contain the same kind of canvas that's used in awnings for commercial buildings.

that you will enjoy it for as long as possible. Some finishes are designed for protected areas only, while others can withstand a little rain, but in general, no metal is going to be as weatherproof as teak. Eventually, the paint will chip away and you will need to have the furniture refinished.

THE ROMANCE OF WICKER

Fran's Wicker and Rattan Furniture store in Succasunna, New Jersey, has contributed some of its wares to the exotic Siamese stage setting of the Broadway musical *The King and I*, and has added the gracefulness of wicker and rattan to the homes of the famous and the humble for more than 30 years.

The secrets of owner Fran Gruber's success are high-quality products and service, a huge variety of pieces in stock, and the public's continued love affair with the look of wicker and rattan furniture.

While light and airy in appearance, high-quality wicker and rattan furniture is actually quite sturdy. Gruber says that when shopping for it,

you should make sure the base is solid wood or steel, and that the frame has been properly secured with screws and glue, rather than just nails.

Finishing should be consistent on the entire piece, and on top-quality items you can expect multiple stain coats and multiple-layer topcoats, as well as specialty treatments, such as antiquing. The wicker or rattan poles should have a consistent diameter, and their surfaces should contain no holes or impurities.

Care for wicker and rattan involves vacuuming it to keep out the dust, and preventing its exposure to continual moisture. The need for refinishing will vary depending on how hard you are on your furniture, and how well you care for it.

Myth: *Wicker furniture can look great, but is too delicate for regular use.* **Fact:** *Sturdy, high-quality wicker furniture with solid bases wears quite well.*

HISTORY OF A FRONT PORCH

As visitors approach the Grand Hotel at Mackinac Island in Michigan, they are met with a magnificent front porch 660 feet long, where 100 white wicker rocking chairs invite them to while away the hours reading, chatting, or just enjoying their leisure.

Bob Tagatz, Grand Hotel's concierge and resident historian, says that the chairs and the 280 Chippendale-style white planters filled with 1,400 geraniums have been at the heart of the resort's signature look for over 100 years. For Grand Hotel guests of a more reclining nature, a sprinkling of chaise longues with yellow-and-white-striped cushions dot the porch among the rocking chairs.

The Right Way

To get rid of rust on wrought-iron furniture, rub it with steel wool dampened with paint thinner, a wire brush, or 600-grit sandpaper. In tough cases, naval jelly can help to dissolve the rust.

The Grand Hotel's rockers are purchased en masse from a source in North Carolina. Each summer, five or so disappear on any given day for their annual painting. About every five years, half of the rockers are replaced with new ones.

Given the old-fashioned charm of this porch, it's not hard to imagine back to the 1890s, when it was called Flirtation Walk. Elegant 19th-century ladies on summer holidays would enjoy the fine view from the rocking chairs—and each day soldiers from the nearby fort would appear in full military regalia and stroll along the front porch, hoping to meet them.

A porch lined with wicker chairs is a classic North American look. The front porch of the Grand Hotel in Michigan has played a central role in the hotel's ambience since the late 19th century.

The Roof over Your Head

Let it rain, let it shine.

CHOOSING YOUR ROOF

There are many considerations when choosing a roofing material, including budget and climate, says Peter Kalinger, technical director for the Canadian Roofing Contractors' Association in Ottawa. Here are descriptions of some roofing materials.

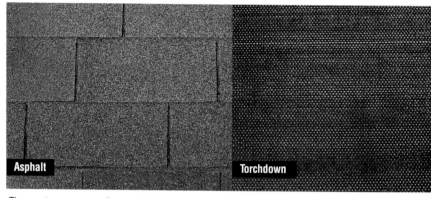

Asphalt

Torchdown

The most common roofing material, asphalt composition shingles are moderately priced. They are made from fiberglass and asphalt granules, are highly durable, and available in many colors. They last 15 to 30 years.

Torchdown, a rubberized asphalt rolled material, is suitable for wet climates and flat or low-pitch roofs. As the name implies, it is torched onto a suitable non-combustible base.

HARNESS THE SUN

Solar—or photovoltaic (PV)—roofing makes sense across the country, says Peter Kalinger. Consult a solar designer or a builder who has experience with solar roofing about the elements you will need to add a system to your home.

- Depending on the solar availability in your area and the energy efficiency of your home, solar energy can supply some of your power needs.
- Solar roofing can be a cost-effective option in areas of the country where utility rates are high, or where there is plenty of sunlight.
- It is also economical to consider solar roofing if you need to supply power to a home that is at least a mile off the power grid. In that case, solar roofing is usually cheaper than installing power lines.
- PV shingles require no more expertise than installing conventional roofing shingles; however, the cost of the internal power grid needed to store the power is very high. PV shingles are available in the US.

WATER SPOTS

Before you can fix a leak, you have to identify where it's coming from, says Al Carrell, host of the weekly radio show "The Super Handyman" and author of seven books, including *Super Handyman Al Carrell's 1000 Questions about Home Repair and Maintenance*.

- Check your attic. Water will usually run down a rafter before soaking through the plaster on your ceiling.
- Many leaks occur in a roof's valley, where two surfaces meet, and the seam is covered with a metal flashing. The seam where the chimney meets the roof is another vulnerable spot. If you can locate the source, cover it temporarily with black asphalt roofing compound and call a roofer.
- If the leak originates from a torn shingle, insert a metal strip underneath the shingle and nail it in place. Cover the heads of the nails with asphalt roofing compound to seal.

The Right Way

If your composition asphalt shingle roof has started to turn black, it's probably a fungal growth, says Al Carrell. Fortunately, there are several simple ways to treat it:

Don't scrub the roof to remove the fungus since you risk loosening the surface granules and damaging the roof tiles. Instead, spray the roof thoroughly with a solution of half chlorine bleach and half water to kill the fungus.

Fungus thrives in shady, humid places. To prevent its growth on the roof, trim back overhanging trees to improve sunlight and air flow to the roof. This will also preserve your roof by keeping tree branches from beating against shingles during high winds.

Purchase zinc strips from the hardware store and insert them under roof shingles. The zinc will leech out during rainstorms and kill the fungus. Alternatively, roofing shingles are now available with copper and zinc embedded in the surface granules.

Cedar

Slate

Standing seam metal

Cedar shakes give a rustic look to your home. They are a natural product and have a natural resistance to decay. However, they are expensive. Shakes are thicker, rougher, and longer than cedar shingles.

One of the most durable roofing materials is natural slate. Each tile is unique. Slate tiles are heavy, and extra roof support may be necessary. Good slate roofs can last 50 to 200 years or more and are fireproof.

Once reserved for commercial use, metal is an increasingly popular, modern-looking roofing choice. It is durable and fireproof. Have a roof snow guard installed to prevent injuries from sliding snow and ice.

GOOD PITCH

The pitch—or angle—of your roof is described as a ratio of height to depth at 12 feet. If your roof has a pitch of 7:12, your roof is 7 feet high at a depth of 12 feet. A roof less than 4:12 is generally considered to be a low-pitch one.

Asphalt shingles, cedar shakes, and slates are not recommended on roofs with a pitch less than 4:12.

SAFETY FIRST

Safety should come first when using a ladder:

■ Check your ladder for damage and wear before each use. Make sure all parts are in working order. You should never use a warped, cracked, or corroded ladder. If your fiberglass ladder starts blistering or cracking, or the coating starts to wear off, it is time to buy a new one.

■ Be aware of your surroundings when working on a ladder. Be conscious of electrical equipment and power lines.
■ Always place the ladder on firm, level ground. Never use a ladder on a slippery or loose surface.
■ Make sure the top section of the extension ladder is fully supported on both sides. The support area should extend at least 12 inches beyond the ladder on both sides.
■ Always be sure the locks are fully engaged and the fly section is in front of the base before climbing.
■ Never stand above the fourth rung from the top of an extension ladder.
■ Try to keep your body centered over the ladder. Hold on to the ladder with one hand while working with the other hand.
■ Haul materials and tools up on a line rather than carrying them up an extension ladder.
■ Never allow more than one person to work on a single-sided ladder at the same time.

CLIMBING HIGH

Choosing the right ladder for a roofing job is imperative, says Pino Commisso, who has worked in rental sales at Dickie Moore for more than 20 years. Dickie Moore rents construction equipment for home, industry, and construction. They have stores in Montreal, Ottawa, and Toronto.

■ Ladders can be made from three materials: wood, fiberglass, and aluminum. Wooden ladders are economical and electrically nonconductive, provided they are clean and dry. Aluminum ladders are sturdy, lightweight, and corrosion-resistant, but must not be used when working with or near electrical equipment. Fiberglass ladders are strong, nonconductive, weather-resistant, and will last about three times longer than wooden ladders.
■ When doing roof work, the ladder should extend at least three feet above the roof line, says Commisso. Also, an extension ladder should be placed at about a 75° angle to the building—or a one-foot set-back for every four feet of height.
■ All ladders are rated by the Canadian Standards Association (CSA). Make sure you are using a ladder with the correct rating for the task you are performing and your body weight, warns Commisso.

Rating	Load Capacity	Typical Uses
IA	300 pounds	Extra-heavy-duty/professional use: industrial construction, building, roofing
I	250 pounds	Heavy-duty/industrial use: general contracting, building, maintenance
II	225 pounds	Medium-duty/commercial use: light commercial, painting, cleaning, light repair
III	200 pounds	Light-duty/household use: painting, yardwork, chores
IV and V	300-350 pounds	Industrial use

Pampering Wood Furniture

Take a kid-glove approach to caring for wood furniture.

THE BASICS

Caring for wood furniture that has a good finish, whether oil, lacquer, or varnish, doesn't require a lot of time or effort. Here are some easy do's and a don't from Chris Erickson, supervisor of finishing and sanding operations at Thomas Moser, Cabinetmakers:

- Keep your furniture clean by dusting it frequently. As necessary (after each meal for a dining table, every two weeks or so for an end table that doesn't get much use), wipe it with a damp cloth that's been dipped in a solution of water and Murphy's Oil Soap, then wrung out. Immediately dry furniture with another soft cloth. Basic cleaning may seem obvious, but Erickson says failure to do it is at the top of the list of furniture mistreatment.
- If there is a spill on the furniture, wipe it up immediately with a damp cloth, then dry the area. If you don't, that spill will attract dust, and you'll have a bigger cleaning challenge down the road.
- Keep furniture out of direct sunlight. The sun's ultraviolet rays can discolor and prematurely age wood and break down a finish. If furniture does get direct sun and you have stable objects, such as lamps

or vases, on top of it, rings will eventually form under the objects as discoloration occurs.
- When placing hot objects on a wood table, always use a heatproof pad or trivet. Otherwise, you might scorch the wood or create a white moisture ring on the surface of the table.
- Don't place wood furniture over a forced hot air vent, which will dry it out. A humidity level of 40 to 50 percent is ideal for wood furniture.

Erickson says that most finishing professionals prefer lemon oil over the popular silicone-based waxes. These waxes produce a good shine, but can build up in the cracks of the wood over time.

CARING FOR OIL-FINISHED WOOD FURNITURE

George Nakashima, a woodworker in New Hope, Pennsylvania, makes and sells handmade solid wood furniture, none of it stained, all of it finished with a rubbed oil finish, says his daughter and studio designer Mira Nakashima-Yarnau. She has these guidelines for caring for such furniture:
- Understand that a certain amount of scratching and denting, known in the trade as distress-

ing, adds character to a piece. Don't coddle your wood furniture. Live with it comfortably.
- If spots occur, remove them by rubbing them hard with 3/0 steel wool with the grain of the wood, blending off the edges. If steel wool isn't effective, use a 280-grit garnet paper and rub the same way. Afterwards, apply a light oil, such as lemon oil, rubbing oil, or mineral oil, and allow it to sit on the surface several hours before rubbing it off. If light oil isn't sufficient, use tung oil, letting it sit on the surface for about 20 minutes. Rub off thoroughly so that no film remains and allow to dry for 24 hours.
- For small dents and scratches, place a piece of wet paper towel over the damaged area and leave it overnight. The water will cause the wood fibers to swell to their original size. Treat the spot remaining as described above.

CONSERVING WOOD FURNITURE

How do museums and other historical institutions treat the wood furniture that comes into their possession? Donald Webster, curator emeritus, Western Art and Culture and Canadiana, Royal Ontario

Museum, and author of several books, including *Canfake, An Expert's Guide to the Tricks of the Canadian Antiques Trade*, explains that the conservator's code of ethics requires them to "maintain the integrity of the material as it's presented and preserve it in the least intrusive way possible. There is a tremendous amount of information contained in any fine or decorative art object—who made it, what materials it was made with, how it was used—and so we're careful not to disturb what came before. Full-blown strip-and-finish work is not something you see much of in a museum setting or with valuable furniture because there's a sense today that furniture of value is not to be abused."

Conservators operate like forensic scientists. Taking a tiny piece of finish from a wooden chair or table, they will examine it under a microscope. They're able to analyze the history of finishes used on the piece, layer by layer. Information like this about an object can be used by historians to further their understanding of an historical period. After analysis, conservators use special cleaning systems that allow them to "unpack" the layers of finish, one by one. This is similar to what painting conservators do to clean old paintings. The goal is to "maximize the harmonious appearance of the object, while restoring it as unintrusively as possible."

Webster advises consult-

True Stories

One of the beauties of old wood furniture is that it contains clues about family history. Bruce Hamilton once had a customer, an elderly woman who was downsizing in preparation for moving into senior housing. She asked him to restore a slant-front secretary desk with a drop-down lid that she'd received when she was married 50 years before. She wanted to give it to her grandson. Somewhere along the line, she had lost the key that opened the front of the desk. For many years the woman had opened it by putting two fingers between the lid and the desk case. Gradually, two little depressions were worn into the wood from this action. When Hamilton restored the desk, he left in these notches so the grandson would have that bit of history from his grandmother.

ing with a professional if you have or acquire a piece of wood furniture that has value, whether financial, religious, or personal, and you think it needs some kind of restoration. Most conservators will be happy to tell you what you have and to recommend the best way to treat it.

The Canadian Conservators Institute, a branch of the Department of Canadian Heritage, in Ottawa, will answer your questions about furniture and may be able to refer you to a conservator. Or you can contact a local museum. Gerald Fitzgerald, president of the Canadian Association of Professional Conservators (CAPC), says that his organization can give you referrals to accredited conservators in Canada. Write to CAPC, c/o Canadian Museum Association, 280 Metcalfe Street, Suite 400, Ottawa, ON K2P 1R7 or call (613) 567-0099.

TO REFINISH OR NOT REFINISH

Before deciding whether to strip and refinish a piece of furniture, first ask yourself several questions, says Bruce Hamilton, who runs an antique restoration firm in West Newbury, Massachusetts. Does the piece have financial, historical, or personal value? Will refinishing decrease its value? How severe is the damage? Can the piece be restored in some less drastic way? Will refinishing it make it look better? Should you pay a professional to do the restoration, or will you tackle the job yourself?

A piece of furniture that you purchased for a song at a flea market may have value that is not immediately apparent, says Hamilton. But you may need a professional's assistance. For example, some 1920s furniture was finished in very sophisticated ways. The time and effort put into coloring and finishing were equal to that spent actually constructing the furniture. Hamilton has developed a solvent that enables him to restore furniture like this to its original state.

If furniture has been subjected to extreme moisture, and the finish is crumbling off, stripping and refinishing is usually the only solution. Hamilton cautions that stripping is a messy, caustic, and potentially dangerous job that must be undertaken with extreme care.

Tools of the Trade

Before you start preserving or refinishing a wood furniture surface, you need to decide what type of finish to apply. Here are some guidelines:

- Lacquer enhances wood grains, darkens less than oil-based finishes, and provides medium protection, but can be difficult to apply evenly.
- Linseed oil is a wood preservative as opposed to a finish. Typically you mix it with solvent and rub it into the wood with a rag. The wood's color will probably deepen over time.
- A polyurethane coating is extremely durable, so it is useful for ordinary pieces that will get heavy use. It is not suitable for fine furniture, as it can make wood look plastic-coated.
- Shellac finishes may enhance wood grain, but pieces are vulnerable to damage from liquids.
- Varnish is available in many shades, and protects pieces that get average use. Tung-oil varnish is the most natural looking, but also the least durable.

43

Making Metals Shine

Protect your household metals, from pots and pans to family heirlooms.

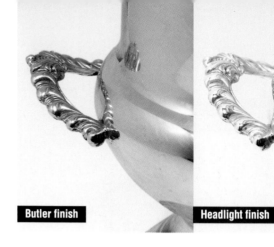

Butler finish

Headlight finish

PRESERVING YOUR FINE METALS

Doris Couture-Rigert's main concern as conservator of Sculpture and Decorative Arts at the National Gallery of Canada in Ottawa is providing the right environment to display and preserve precious objects. Temperature, humidity, and air quality are just some of the factors that can affect your metals.

- Avoid storing objects on newly painted surfaces, which can emit formaldehyde, sulfur, ammonia, acids, and other volatile compounds that can damage the metal. Avoid the use of drying oils and alkyd paints.
- Never wrap rubber bands around metal objects, such as silver spoons.
- Don't display or store fine metal on or in unsealed wood, which can corrode and discolor metals.
- Before using fabric for display or storage, verify the type of fibers. Wrap items in silver cloth (from fabric stores) or acid-free, unbuffered tissue paper (from art suppliers).

Ultrasonic jewelry cleaners use sound vibrations to gently polish your metal jewelry.

THE HARD WAY

Nothing beats hot breath and elbow grease to keep silver and other fine metals bright, according to silversmith William Manfredi, who decorated the Kentucky Derby cup in 1976. He is a professor of silversmithing and restoration at New York's Fashion Institute of Technology. There are basically two finishes to polished silver: a "headlight," or bright glossy, shine, or a softer "butler" finish. To achieve the latter, polish highlights only, allowing recesses and details to oxidize naturally. Here are some other tips:

- Use a high-quality silver polish and clean, soft cotton or a soft sponge on brass, copper, and silver. Never use terry cloth, which is too abrasive. Wear latex gloves and a dust mask to protect your hands and lungs from dirt and chemicals.
- Sea air, salt, and citrus are all corrosive to fine metals. If you live on the coast, protect your pieces in a display case and don't use them as vases.
- Keep silver pieces away from lead pewter, which will destroy it.

LACQUERING

Lacquering decorative metal pieces, such as wall sconces, keeps them from tarnishing and collecting dust. However, never lacquer antiques, advises Michael Dotzel, since it can diminish their value.

The Right Way

You should never put silverware in the dishwasher, warns antique metal restorer Michael Dotzel, owner of Michael Dotzel and Sons in New York City. Keep silverware away from heat and stainless steel, which interact with silver and corrode it. Instead, soak silverware in lukewarm water and dry it thoroughly. Also avoid abrasive cleansers and ammonia.

CARING FOR YOUR HARDWARE

If you oil and polish your locks regularly, they should last as long as you live in your home, says Robert Campbell, senior manager of the US firm Champion Locksmiths. When buying exterior hardware, be sure it is treated with duronodic or some other finish to help it withstand harsh outdoor conditions such as the cold of Canada's winters. Buff brass hardware with an antioxidant polish, available in different strengths from hardware stores.

HEAVY METAL

"Metal objects aren't always what they appear to be," says Gene Olson, a metal sculptor who is also a participant in the ArtMetal Project (www.artmetal.com), a cooperative educational website. He describes how different finishes and compositions require different care:

Plated metals. Many objects sold as brass or bronze are actually plated steel or zinc alloy—the same material from which your cooking pots are made. Some are even plated plastic. You can often tell if a piece is plated by looking at its recesses, which may be poorly finished. Plated surfaces should be cleaned very gently with a metal polish so that you don't rub right through the finish.

Faux finishes. Some nonmetal objects are painted to look like metal. Treat them as you would any other painted surface.

Lacquered finishes. Copper, bronze, and brass are often sealed with lacquer or a powder coating to protect their shine. Make sure the piece is not lacquered before you polish it. You can tell if your piece has

been lacquered if it doesn't tarnish after long periods of time. If the piece has dark spots or tarnishes unevenly, then the lacquer is wearing off. Clean lacquered items with a clean, dry, soft cloth.

Copper, brass, and bronze. Mirror glaze—an automotive finish—seals the surface and protects the shine on these metals.

Wrought iron. Remove surface rust with steel wool. Recoat with a high-quality carnauba floor wax, which is made from the leaves of Brazilian palm trees.

Pewter and aluminum. These can be polished with most silver polishes. Avoid using lye- or sodium-based cleaners on aluminum. They can harm the metal.

ANTIQUE HUNTING

Don't go out there cold, warns Shelley Sturman of the National Gallery in Washington, DC. She has also contributed to *Caring For Your Collections*, a publication of the National Committee to Save America's Cultural Heritage. Metal objects have specific characteristics that indicate the manufacturing process and any alloys that might have been widely used during the period when it was made, says Sturman. For example, if you

are looking at 18th-century silver pieces, make sure you understand what qualities and telltale signs of the period to look for. Before you invest in an antique, call a curator or do some research to make sure you understand what you are spending your money on. Here are a few of Sturman's helpful guidelines:

- Is the piece solid or plated? Check the underside to see whether a base metal shows through.
- Does it feel solid and heavy, or light and thinly made?
- Are there maker's marks or stamps? These can tell you about the age and origin of a piece.
- Does the piece have mold lines and seams, or does it appear to be handmade?
- How carefully finished are the details? Do they look realistic? If the piece appears to be mold-made, has any additional handwork been done on it?
- Has the appearance or finish of the metal been artificially altered? For instance, patinas—or alterations of the surface of the metal from corrosion—are sometimes artificially induced on copper alloys, turning them green. Artificially induced patinas can corrode metals, reducing their value.

Smart Moves

Use your household metals wisely:
- Copper is poisonous. If the tin lining of your copper cookware wears out, have the pot or pan relined before using it again.
- Some pewter objects contain lead, which is very toxic, warns Gene Olson. Unless you are certain that your pewter pieces are intended for everyday use, you should not use them for serving food or drink.
- Some kitchen items, such as ice cream molds, pots, and ice trays, used to be cast out of lead. If you have dull, gray, heavy kitchenware that has been passed down to you, it might be made of lead and should be thrown out.

A solid, hallmarked piece will almost always have more value than one that has been screwed or soldered together.

Quick Tricks

Shelley Sturman avoids commercial polishes when cleaning precious objects.
- Make a "slurry," or polishing paste, out of water, calcium carbonate (available at art supply stores), and a drop of mild detergent or rubbing alcohol.
- Roll it on gently with a cotton swab, changing swabs frequently. Rinse the object thoroughly and dry briefly with a blow dryer.
- Polish as infrequently as possible: "Every time you polish, you are removing a fine layer of metal."

Keeping Bathrooms Clean and Fresh

You can make an onerous job easy.

DOING THE DIRTY WORK

Water deposits, soap film, rust stains, mildew, and germs are some of the challenges you face when cleaning the bathroom, says Jane Meyer, education director of the Soap and Detergent Association, a US trade association of cleaning products manufacturers.

- Rinse the tub after each use to prevent soap film and hard water deposits from forming.
- Use a sponge, towel, or squeegee to wipe down tub or shower walls. Dry faucets and handles to prevent water spots.
- Leave shower curtains open after use to prevent mildew. If mildew does appear, use diluted household bleach to remove it.
- Avoid using products containing bleach to remove rust stains—they may intensify the color.

ON THE SURFACE OF THINGS

Jane Meyer provides these pointers for cleaning and sanitizing different types of bathroom surfaces:

Porcelain bathtubs and sinks. Scour gently with a non-abrasive all-purpose cleaner or mild abrasive cleanser.

Fiberglass shower stalls, bathtubs, and sinks. These surfaces are easily scratched. Use an all-purpose or disinfectant cleaner, or a solution of baking soda and water, and soft cloths.

Vitreous china toilet bowls. Hard water deposits can collect on the inside of the bowl. Use a toilet bowl cleaner and a long-handled toilet brush to clean under the rim and as far into the trap as possible. Don't mix different types of toilet bowl cleaners together. For instance, if you use an in-tank cleaner, remove it and flush the toilet before using another type of cleaner. Do not use toilet bowl cleaners to clean anything else.

Plastic toilet seats. These seats scratch easily. Use a non-abrasive all-purpose or disinfectant cleaner.

Ceramic tile. Use a non-abrasive all-purpose or disinfectant cleaner, or mild abrasive cleanser. Use a mildew remover or solution of three-quarters of a cup of bleach to one gallon of water to remove mildew on grout between tiles.

USING CLEANSERS WISELY

"Chemicals are not our enemies," says Joe Schwarcz, PhD, director of McGill University's Office for Chemistry and Society (MOCS) in Montreal. Insecticides, germicides, and disinfectants used cautiously can protect your health, the quality of your living environment, and your food supply. They can also make household cleaning chores considerably easier. When using commercial cleaners and strong chemicals around the house, it is always advisable to follow these guidelines:

- Always ventilate the area well as you work. After you have finished, leave the bathroom vent on and the door open until the room airs out.
- Never mix cleansers. If you use two different types of cleanser on nearby surfaces, such as in the toilet bowl and in the bathtub, the air vapors from the two cleansers can become toxic when combined. This is especially true of bleach- and ammonia-based cleansers, which create very toxic gases when mixed. As a precaution, let the room ventilate between tasks with different products.
- Never use more of a product than label directions indicate. "More does not mean cleaner or easier." Using too much can make the product less effective and may leave

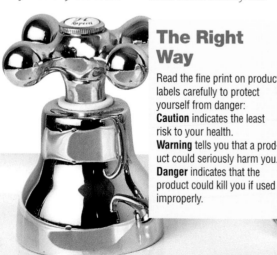

The Right Way

Read the fine print on product labels carefully to protect yourself from danger:
Caution indicates the least risk to your health.
Warning tells you that a product could seriously harm you.
Danger indicates that the product could kill you if used improperly.

harmful residues that can trigger headaches, allergic reactions, and other health problems.

Be aware that clean does not have a color or scent. Perfumes and dyes are added to cleaning supplies to make them more appealing to consumers.

HEAVY-DUTY CLEANING

Better known as the "Clean Guy," George F. Gaebler Jr. is chief information officer at Pride Services, a US firm specializing in extra-tough corporate and industrial cleaning jobs. Here are some of the industrial-strength methods Pride's cleaning crews use:

■ When cleaning bath and shower stalls, remove all soaps, shampoos, razors, and anything else in the bathing area.

■ Spray the entire area with a phosphoric acid de-scaler. Avoid contact with

CLEAN UP YOUR ACT

Many communities in Canada have recycling programs, such as the blue-box program. Call your municipality to find out what items they collect for recycling. Dr. Len Shaw, president of the Canadian Association of Recycling Industries, says most companies collect glass, metal, plastic, and paper. Some communities have return-to-retailer programs and depots for hazardous products and containers. Inform yourself about the recycling facilities in your area. A local environmental organization may be able to help. Learn how to identify hazardous products in your home and how to dispose of them.

Pour down the drain:

Contact your municipality to learn if you can safely pour the following products down the drain and flush with plenty of water: alcohol-based lotions, bleach, ammonia-based disinfectants, toilet-bowl cleaners, tub and tile cleaners, and window cleaners.

Check with your municipality about the following:

Full aerosol cans	Solvent-based metal polish
Alkaline batteries	Paint thinner
Button batteries	Turpentine
Battery acid	Lacquer thinner
Solvent-based cleaners	Oil-based paints, spot remover
Dry-cleaning solvent	Solidified latex paint

Cosmetics: some companies, such as M.A.C., take back empty lipstick tubes.
Medicines and needles: return unused medicines and needles to your pharmacist.

skin and eyes. Let it sit for a minute or two to penetrate mineral deposits and soap scum.

■ Scrub the entire area vigorously with a nylon or plastic scouring pad. Use a nylon bristle brush to scrub the floor of the shower or tub.

■ Now flush the entire area thoroughly with very hot water until the surface rinses clean. Your bath or shower stall should be sparkling and sanitary.

DO IT THE OLD-FASHIONED WAY

"When in doubt, get the baking soda out," say Joan Wilen and Lydia Wilen, authors of *Shoes in the Freezer, Beer in the Flower Bed and Other Down-Home Tips for House and Garden*. These ideas will help you save money and cut down on corrosive chemicals:

■ Leave a small bowl of vinegar or lemon juice, or an open box of baking

soda, in the bathroom to absorb odors.

■ White vinegar will remove hard water spots and soap scum from chrome fixtures. Dry them with a soft cloth. To really make them shine, buff them with a fabric softener sheet.

■ Leave a few charcoal briquettes in the bathroom to help absorb moisture and prevent mildew.

■ White vinegar and baking soda will clean your toilet bowl. So will orange drink powder, a can of cola, vitamin C capsules, or effervescing denture-cleaning tablets, if they are allowed to stand in the bowl for a few hours or overnight.

■ To keep your bathroom mirror steam-free, clean it with shaving cream before showering.

■ Add two tablespoons of baking soda to your bath water to eliminate ring-around-the-tub problems.

■ Spritz glass shower doors with white vinegar. Wait five minutes to see if the soap residue and mineral deposits will wipe off easily with a washcloth or sponge. If not, scour the glass with baking soda and a soft rag.

■ To whiten grout between ceramic bathroom tiles, trace over it with a wet nail whitener pencil.

Smart Moves

Here are some useful guidelines to keep in mind when purchasing household cleaning products:

■ Think twice before you buy any strong, new product. Switch to a safer substitute whenever possible.

■ Purchase only the amount you need and use up what you buy. Give leftovers to someone who will use them for their intended purpose.

■ Avoid aerosols. Use pump sprays or other alternatives.

■ Use water-based, rather than solvent-based, products when they are available.

The Laundry Basket

There are ways to take the drudgery out of laundry day.

THE LINEN CLOSET

Gentle handling and common sense are the rule when washing fine linens, says Elizabeth Barbitelli, president of the Laundry at Linens Ltd., a fine linen laundry and restoration service in Milwaukee. She also owns Liz's Linens, a fine linens shop in Aspen, Colorado. Here are more of her commonsense tips:

■ Never dry-clean linens, warns Barbitelli. "Cotton and linen were meant to be laundered."

■ Most stains in linen and cotton will respond to soaking, which loosens fibers and allows the stain to float away from the fabric.

■ Use gentle, pure detergents without additives. Avoid harsh cleaning agents and bleach.

■ Never include fabric-softening dryer sheets. They coat fabrics and prevent towels from absorbing water.

■ Air-dry linens (except for towels) on a line until they are damp. Iron them while still damp on a low to medium setting.

■ Do not wash fine linens in a washing machine with an agitator.

■ Avoid washing fine linens in very hot water, which can damage fabrics.

■ Make repairs to hems, tears, or moth holes before you launder.

■ Store fine linens in acid-free tissue paper, which can be purchased at art or photo supply stores.

Myth: *Club soda or seltzer helps remove stains.* **Fact:** *Club soda is no more effective at removing stains from fabrics than plain water.*

THE CLOTHES ON YOUR BACK

Fine garment care begins at home, says Wayne Edelman, president of Meurice Garment Care, one of New York's most reputable laundry and dry-cleaning services.

■ Directions for care on garment labels are mass produced and are not always accurate, warns Edelman. Many natural fabrics, such as cotton and linen, are better wet-laundered than dry-cleaned, regardless of what the manufacturer's label says. If you are not sure how to care for a garment, take it to a good dry cleaner or laundry that can advise you.

■ Take dry-cleaned clothes out of plastic bags to allow them to breathe. It is generally a bad idea to store textiles in plastic, says Edelman, since the acids in the plastic can discolor them.

■ Don't clean leather and suede routinely, but only when necessary. Leather and suede are professionally cleaned using a water-based process. If your leather or suede jacket or skirt gets soaked in a downpour, dry it away from a direct source of heat. Then brush the nap back with a foam rubber block or pad. Edelman recommends wearing a scarf with suede and leather jackets to prevent discoloration around the collar.

■ Edelman is a fan of sodium-based bleaches for home cleaning since they are gentler on fabrics than chemical products and better for the environment.

Smart Moves

Some dry cleaners are better than others, warns Wayne Edelman. Take your business to another establishment if you notice any of these telltale signs that your dry cleaner is cutting corners with your fine garments:

■ Your clothes smell like dry-cleaning solvent when you bring them home. That smelly residue indicates that your dry cleaner is not cleaning the equipment and changing the solvent often enough.

■ There is a sign hanging in the establishment reading "Not responsible for belts, buckles, buttons, and zippers." A good dry cleaner should take pains to protect the accessories on your clothes, says Edelman. At Meurice, for example, employees cover all buttons with aluminum foil before processing.

■ Your cleaned clothes have the impressions of seams showing through the cloth where the garment has been pressed.

Tools of the Trade

Always keep the following on hand to attack fresh spills and stains, advises Don Aslett, author of 26 books on cleaning and household management, including *The Stainbuster's Bible*. He is also founder and chairman of the board of Varsity Contractors, Inc., a commercial cleaning company with many locations.

- A spotting brush, available at professional janitorial supply stores.
- A butter knife to use as a scraper.
- Clean white terry cloth (so you can check for colorfastness and if the stain is coming out).
- Liquid dishwashing detergent (diluted 20:1 for stains).
- Clear household ammonia (not for use on silk or wool).
- White vinegar.
- Hydrogen peroxide (3% solution).
- Isopropyl alcohol.
- Enzyme digestant cleaner for extra-tough stains. (Soak washables in a solution of digestant for up to an hour. For dry cleanables, mix into a paste with water and apply for 15 to 30 minutes.)

CLEANING UP YOUR ACT

Consumers, employees in the dry-cleaning industry, and environmental activists are becoming increasingly concerned about the health and environmental impact of perchloroethylene—or perc—the solvent used in most dry-cleaning establishments. This highly toxic chemical has been linked to central nervous system damage, reproductive disorders, vital organ damage, and some types of cancer.

Marcia Todd, editor of *Fabric Care* magazine (www.fabricarecanada.com) in Oakville, Ontario, says that about 20 percent of the Canadian dry-cleaning industry have switched to alternatives to perc. Other dry-cleaning methods use hydrocarbons and petroleum-based solvents, silicon-based products, carbon dioxide under pressure, and chlorinated solvents.

Interesting new solvents are on the horizon, but the cost of switching technologies is prohibitive for many businesses.

There are many dry-cleaning businesses that use perc in a responsible way and handle the solvent with extreme care. Nat Kurtzman, owner of Bellingham Cleaners in Montreal, says that perc is 99.9 percent recoverable when used in totally enclosed machines, such as the updated equipment he uses. The solvent evaporates during the drying cycle, condenses, is filtered to remove impurities, and transferred to a sealed drum.

If you are concerned about the health and environmental effects of perc, ask dry cleaners in your area how they handle the solvent or if they are using safer alternatives.

Quick Tricks

Don Aslett recommends these tips for removing extra-tough stains:

Alcohol (liquor, beer, and wine): Blot up all you can and sponge with water. Next, sponge with a detergent solution, then vinegar, blotting after each application. Rinse. Bleach with hydrogen peroxide if necessary.

Blood: Blot or scrape up all you can. Soak old blood stains in salt water or enzyme digestant. Blot with cool water, then with ammonia, and rinse. Bleach with hydrogen peroxide if necessary. If stain remains, try commercial rust remover from a janitorial supply store, observing all safety precautions.

Candle wax: Scrape up all you can. Put a clean, absorbent cloth over and under the spot, and iron with a warm iron to melt and absorb the wax into the blotting cloth. Remove residue with a spot remover.

Grass: Sponge with water, then alcohol (except wool, silk, or acetate). If the stain remains, use enzyme digestant, sponge with detergent solution, and rinse. If necessary bleach with hydrogen peroxide.

Ballpoint pen ink: Sponge with detergent solution, and rinse. If the stain remains, saturate with inexpensive hair spray, and blot. If that doesn't work, try alcohol, acetone, non-oily nail polish remover, or a bleach safe for the fabric—in that order. If a yellow stain remains, try rust remover.

Oil: Absorb fresh oil with cornmeal, then blot with paint thinner. If the stain remains, sponge with detergent solution, and blot again.

The Right Way

- If possible, treat a stain while it's fresh. Don't iron or hot-air dry until the stain is gone—heat will set most stains.
- Test any chemical you plan to use on a hidden area of the garment to make sure it won't discolor or damage the fabric.
- Blot, don't scrub. Strike with the flat face of a spotting brush if necessary to break up the stain.

Keeping Clothes Shipshape

Here are some home appliances to get excited about.

NOT A WRINKLE

Donna Wallace, product manager for Rowenta Irons, a leading manufacturer of premium irons, offers these tips to achieve perfectly pressed clothes and linens:

- Sort clothes according to temperature, working from coolest to hottest. Iron silks and synthetics on low to medium heat (approximately 350°F), wool on medium to high, and cotton and linens at high temperatures (400°F to 425°F). Since the right temperature is critical, let the iron sit for a few minutes after you have adjusted the controls.
- Hang up or fold your garments immediately after ironing them.
- Never use circular strokes—you can stretch the fabric. Iron lengthwise and eliminate wrinkles by blasting the area with steam.

- When ironing large items, such as a tablecloth or curtains, set up two chairs next to the ironing board and fold the piece carefully onto the chairs as you work on it. You could also iron large items on a tabletop padded with a towel, provided that the table won't be harmed by the steam or hot temperatures.
- Iron sensitive fabrics with a pressing cloth—a clean cotton cloth, handkerchief, or napkin. Iron fabrics inside out to protect them from becoming singed or shiny.
- If you must use an extension cord with your iron, use a 12-ampere cord. Lighter-weight cords could overheat, causing fires. Make sure that you arrange the cord so you won't trip over it.
- Press pleats starting from the bottom, working from the inside of the pleat to the outside. Set pleats with a shot of steam.
- Let clothes sit for a few hours after you've finished ironing to allow the creases to set.

THE RIGHT STUFF

For professional sewers and textile artists, ironing is a serious business. The use of high-quality ironing appliances will make the job easier and you will be less likely to damage fabrics, says Annette McLeroy of The Versatile Needle in Greenville, South Carolina. She specializes in textile restoration, costuming, and private commissions, and has pieces in private and church collections. Here's what to look for when you buy ironing equipment:

- A wide temperature range, with an accurate thermostat.
- A thick soleplate for good heat retention.
- Good steam capability, with lots of steam vents on the soleplate. The best irons have a "burst of steam" or "shot of steam" option that will blast out wrinkles and blast in permanent creases when you want them.

Multiple steam vents

Thick soleplate

Smart Moves

- To reduce the shine caused by wear or over-pressing, dampen a pressing cloth and wring it out. Place the cloth over the shiny area and press repeatedly until the area is almost dry. Using a soft brush, brush back the nap of the fabric.
- To avoid build-up on your iron's soleplate from materials such as synthetics and bonded fabrics, make sure your iron is set to the correct temperature, and use a pressing cloth. Fresh build-up on your soleplate can be removed by rubbing it with all-cotton terry cloth while the iron is still hot. Buy a soleplate cleaning kit to remove burnt-on stains.
- Use a Teflon-covered soleplate or a protective soleplate cover to keep debris from sticking to your iron.

- Substantial weight. Your iron should be heavy enough so you don't need to use your weight to get the pressure you want.
- Comfort and ease of use.
- Automatic cut-off in case the iron is left unattended for a certain amount of time.

Steam options

ALL ON BOARD

All ironing boards were not created equal, says Ira Blank, owner and president of Blanks Fabric Center in Maryland. The store caters to homemakers, hobbyists, and professionals. Top-of-the-line ironing boards will offer certain features.

Stability is essential for ease and safety. Some good boards feature a leveling system on the legs so you can stabilize your board on an uneven surface.

Adjustable height lets you iron comfortably without stooping or slouching, whether you are standing up or sitting down.

A wide ironing surface—approximately 48 by 16 inches—means you don't have to reposition your clothes as often.

Wide mesh ventilation allows steam to travel through the fabric and prevents mildew and rot in the board's padding.

An iron rest and cord minder will help to keep the cord out of your way while you are working.

Blank does not recommend adding attachments, such as sleeve boards, to your ironing board because

they can make the board unstable. Depending on your needs, you should also consider fold-out boards, travel-size boards, and tabletop boards.

TAKING A TUMBLE

There are many options to consider when buying laundry appliances, says Maureen Chittenden, a salesperson specializing in washers and dryers. Consider some of these now-available appliances and features:

- Look for one of the new "front-loading" washers—also known as "tumble-action" or "high-efficiency" machines. Because they gently tumble clothes, rather than spinning them around an agitator—as in the traditional machines—they are much kinder to delicate fabrics. They also use one-third to two-thirds the water of agitator machines, which saves you on both your water and energy bills because there is much less water to be heated.
- Consider a machine with automatic temperature control, which heats up water as the machine fills, preventing blotchy laundry. This is especially

The Right Way

If you are using one of the new high-efficiency front-load washers, look for a detergent specifically formulated for it. The tumble action in these machines, which is gentler on clothes and uses less water than traditional agitator machines, creates more suds, advises Maureen Chittenden. If front-load detergent is not yet available in your area, pretreat the stains on all your laundry items and use less than the recommended amount of your regular detergent. If your clothes don't come out clean, call the washing machine manufacturer for suggestions on where to get the proper detergent.

Tools of the Trade

You can quickly remove wrinkles from hanging draperies, tablecloths, or wool blazers with a small upright steamer.

useful where winters are cold or if your water is supplied from a well, which can make the water exceptionally cold.

- Some washing machines offer a "hand-wash intermittent" cycle, which allows you to machine-wash silks and other delicate fabrics.
- If you live in a small space, consider the new portable machines that can be stacked and take up about half the space of large machines. These machines often come with a low-noise feature, called a "quiet pack," in case your laundry room is near the main living or sleeping quarters of the house.
- Gas dryers are usually more energy efficient than electric dryers, suggests Chittenden.
- Choose a dryer with a "soft-heat" system that cools off during the last few minutes of the cycle, preventing wrinkles and too-hot-to-touch laundry.
- If you own a lot of delicates and knits, choose a dryer with removable racks that allow you to dry clothes flat inside the drum of the machine.

Simple Plumbing Repairs

A little common sense goes a long way.

Phillips-head screwdriver

Pipe wrench

WATER HEATER PROBLEMS

Hot-water heaters are a very hot topic with visitors to www.theplumber.com, says Hill Daughtry, creator of the website, who also owns Hill's Plumbing in the Seattle area. Daughtry's site has one of the most extensive lists of frequently asked questions on the Internet, and provides links to more than 500 other websites.

Always make sure the power is off before servicing an electric water heater, warns Daughtry. If your tank is more than 10 years old, you should consider replacing it with a new one. Old tanks can grow rusty and leak, and newer tanks are typically much more energy efficient.

Here are some of the most common electric water heater problems Daughtry can help solve:

Very hot water at first and then none. Most likely, the upper thermostat on your water heater is jammed, causing the water to overheat. When the water tank gets too hot, the safety switch automatically shuts the tank down. Pressing the red reset button on the side of the tank will turn the power back on, but if your tank continues to overheat and shut itself off, you will probably have to replace your upper thermostat.

■ First turn off the power to the water heater (p.54). Then test to be sure the power is off, using a voltage tester.

■ Most thermostats can be removed with a Phillips-head screwdriver and replaced inexpensively. Take the old one with you to the hardware store.

Not enough hot water. First ask yourself, says Daughtry, whether hot water use in your household has changed. If not, the lower element or heating coil has probably burned out and needs to be replaced.

■ Turn off the power supplying your tank.

■ Turn off the cold water intake valve to the water heater and open a hot-water tap somewhere in the house to drain the water out of the tank. You can also connect a garden hose running to a sump pump, or out to the street, to the drain spigot at the bottom of the tank and open the valve to let the tank drain.

■ Unscrew the lower panel on the side of the tank.

■ Take out the mounting bolts and remove the heating element. Replacement elements are inexpensive and can be purchased at the hardware store. Make sure that your new element has the same wattage rating as the element you are replacing.

■ Gaskets wear out, too. Always replace the gasket when attaching the new heating element.

■ Screw the panel back into place and turn off the drain spigot, if open.

■ Fill the tank before you turn the water heater on or it will burn out.

■ Now turn the power to the heater back on.

Smart Moves

■ Before installing that extra-deep tub or whirlpool, find out how long it will take to fill it. One of the most common mistakes people make when designing bathrooms is forgetting to check what the fill time is for the new bath, says Doris LaCroix, a certified kitchen and bathroom designer in Ottawa. In many areas, water pressure is too low to accommodate whirlpools or oversized tubs. Plus, you may need a larger supply line. Call your water company and ask what the fill time is in your neighborhood. Also, ask a plumber if your water heater's capacity is sufficient.

■ If you are remodeling a bathroom or kitchen in an older house, check to see what the pipes are made of, advises LaCroix. Many houses built more than 50 years ago have lead pipes that should be replaced. Lead that leeches into the water and then gets absorbed into the body can cause brain and nervous system damage and other serious health problems.

■ Always have an emergency shut-off wrench handy to shut off water at the main valve in the event of a flood. The main valve is usually in the basement, garage, or on the side of the house.

Estimate the fill time for your tub by timing how long it takes to fill a gallon jug from the bathtub faucet and multiplying that figure by the number of gallons the tub will hold.

before replacing it on the stem of the faucet. This type of lubricant is used by plumbers and is available at most hardware stores.

■ Re-assemble the faucet. If the leak persists, replace the assembly and O-ring. Take the parts to the hardware store to ensure that you get exact replacements.

DOWN THE DRAIN

"Whatever you pour down your drain eventually becomes someone else's drinking water," warns plumber Terre Packham. She became interested in plumbing after "bugging and begging" her landlord to take care of recurring plumbing problems.

■ To help keep your drains clear, an easy solution is simply to pour a tea kettle of boiling water down the kitchen, laundry, and bathroom sinks, as well as the bathtub or shower drains. The boiling water is much more effective if you add baking soda to dissolve the oils—and just as safe ecologically.

■ Do not, however, pour boiling water down the toilet or any other fixture that has an integrated trap (such as a bidet or a urinal) since the sudden change in temperature could damage the porcelain surface. "This is the best kind of preventive maintenance homeowners can do."

■ Use chemicals in clogged drains only as a last resort, after plunging, pouring boiling water down the drains, and using an auger or

Assorted washers and seals

Standard pliers

LEAKY HANDLES

If there is a leak around the handle of your faucet, you need to tighten or replace faucet hardware, advises Michael Okiishi, assistant manager at San Francisco's Cole Hardware.

■ Turn off the water supply first. Plug the drain and cover the basin with a towel in case you drop one of the pieces. Remove the faucet handle with an Allen wrench or screwdriver, depending on the faucet model.

■ Tighten the ring and any washers underneath the handle. If they are slightly corroded, clean them with fine steel wool. If the stem uses an O-ring, coat it lightly with a silicon lubricant

plumber's snake. "The gases that are formed by the chemicals in the drain cleaner seep into the air in your home," warns Packham. After using chemicals, flush them completely with water. Never plunge drains after using chemicals, since they could splash up in your face.

■ Water-saving appliances, such as 6-liter-per-flush toilets and lower-flow shower heads are worth considering if you want to conserve water. These appliances now provide much better performance than when they were first introduced, says Packham. Also, look for water-saving toilets with a pressure assist feature.

HOME WATER TREATMENT

"Municipal water in Canada is healthy, but some homeowners have to deal with water that is "hard" or poor tasting," says Jon Eakes, host of HGTV Canada's *Just Ask Jon Eakes*, who is always present at his website: www.joneakes.com. To deal with these problems, Eakes offers this advice:

■ Install an "ion-

exchange" water softener, which exchanges calcium and magnesium in the water for sodium. Softening water makes soaps lather better and reduces

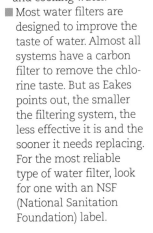

mineral residues in appliances and pipes, but it also elevates the sodium level. To solve this problem, install your water softener only on the hot-water pipes, or put in a separate tap for drinking and cooking water.

■ Most water filters are designed to improve the taste of water. Almost all systems have a carbon filter to remove the chlorine taste. But as Eakes points out, the smaller the filtering system, the less effective it is and the sooner it needs replacing. For the most reliable type of water filter, look for one with an NSF (National Sanitation Foundation) label.

Electrical Know-how

Turn on the power, and keep it running safely.

BLOWING YOUR FUSE

Suddenly the electricity goes out in one part of the house. You have probably blown a fuse or tripped a breaker, says Bob Nelson, a Hamilton-based commercial and industrial electrician. Here is his advice on dealing with a blown fuse:

The first thing to do is find your service panel. In most Canadian houses, the service panel is located in the basement. If you're living in an older house, you may have round fuses. The blown fuse will look sooty or the circuit connection within it will have blown apart. Simply unscrew or unplug it and replace it with a good fuse of the same amperage. You'll find that the amperage is clearly marked on the fuse. Never replace a blown fuse with one of the wrong amperage, warns Nelson. That creates a fire hazard.

If you live in a more recent home, you will probably have a breaker box. Scan the box to see which switch is in a different position from the others. The blown—or tripped—circuit will be set between the *Off* and *On* positions and may display a red bar next to the circuit switch. To restart your electricity, first push the breaker all the way to the *Off* position and then back to the *On* position. The electricity should be restored immediately.

LIVE WIRES

No matter what the electrical repair job, double-check normally energized circuits with a voltage tester, warns Joseph Da Mour, a retired electrical power station worker who's used to working on live power circuits of 345,000 volts. (Most homes carry 240 volts.) Here's how:

- Switch off the breaker, or pull out or unscrew the fuse for the circuit you will be working on.
- Check that your voltage tester or neon light tester is working by using it on a circuit that you know is energized. You should get a reaction. Make sure it is rated for your home's voltage—120 or 240 volts.
- Recheck the circuit you're going to be working on to be sure it's dead by plugging the tester into an outlet on that circuit. You should get no reaction.

Tools of the Trade

Surge protectors help keep your appliances safe if there is a spike or surge in the power grid.

BLACKOUTS (AND BROWNOUTS)

The first stop for Internet-savvy do-it-yourselfers is www.doityourself.com, created by David Goldscholle. This website provides thousands of helpful hints for homeowners, and hosts 20 live forums concerning home-maintenance issues. Here are Goldscholle's tips for surviving household electrical emergencies:

Blackouts. Total power failures are often caused by weather conditions, such as lightning striking the power lines or lines that are blown down during storms. Sometimes power is temporarily shut off by the power company during an emergency.

- Keep a flashlight and extra batteries available at all times. Battery-operated night lights that light up in the dark are also helpful. Always be careful with candles and live flames, which can be fire hazards.
- Turn off all unnecessary appliances. Leave the water pump, furnace, refrigerator, and freezer turned on, but turn off all air conditioning units.
- Keep the freezer and refrigerator doors closed to prevent the food inside from spoiling.
- Avoid flushing toilets or using too much water if your home has its own pump. With a municipal water system, water will probably still be available in a limited quantity.

Brownouts. These occur when power suppliers reduce electrical voltage during emergencies. They are usually announced on the radio and television. If everyone cooperates and limits their electric consumption, the duration of the brownout is reduced. During brownouts, power suppliers try to maintain voltage levels so they do not go below 10 percent of their

normal level, which for limited periods of time should not damage consumers' equipment. If the brownout is not planned, however, shut down all equipment running on motors since the low power could cause them to burn out.

- Use only those lights and appliances that are absolutely necessary.
- Delay chores, such as dish washing and laundry, until after the brownout is officially over.
- Turn off your air conditioning unless it is necessary for health reasons.
- Continue to limit energy consumption right after a brownout, or the voltage may have to be reduced again.
  - Keep cooking to a minimum if your house has an electric stove.

Labeling the wires will make your repairs easier— and safer.

SAFETY FIRST

Loose connections and overloaded circuits can cause electrical fires, warns Bob Nelson. Here's how to prevent them:

- Check all outlets, or receptacles, with a plug-in circuit tester, which can tell you if a circuit is functioning properly or identify potential fire hazards, such as improper grounding or reverse connections.
- Observe voltage and amperage ratings when using extension cords, which can overheat and possibly catch fire if they are overloaded.
- Always use lightbulbs of the correct wattage, which will be marked on the socket. Otherwise bulbs can overheat or even explode.

SIMPLE REPAIRS

Allegra Bennett, author of *Renovating Woman: A Guide to Home Repair, Maintenance and Real Men*, gives the following tips for basic repairs:
Replacing an outlet. Replace outlets when they come loose from the wall or when anything plugged into them starts flickering.

Smart Moves

- Always turn off power at the service panel before starting work.
- Unplug any appliances you will be working on.
- Post a sign on the service panel indicating that you are working on the circuits so nobody tries to restore power.
- Avoid making yourself an electrical conductor in the event of an emergency: Make sure you are not standing on a wet floor. Use a wooden, rather than a metal, stepladder. Don't touch bare metal, such as pipe or ducts, in the work area.
- Use shoes with rubber soles and tools with rubber grips.
- Have a friend or family member assist you.
- Have all tools on hand before you start.
- When in doubt, call an electrician.

- Turn off the power to the circuit at the service box.
- Test both sockets of the outlet with a voltage tester to be sure they are dead.
- Remove the screw from the cover plate and the screws that are holding the receptacle in the box.
- Gently pull the receptacle from the box.
- Before loosening wires, label them with masking tape—top silver (ts), lower silver (ls), top brass (tb), lower brass (lb), and the green ground screw (g).
- Loosen the terminal screws and free the wires.
- Install the new receptacle, matching the wires with the corresponding terminal screw.
- Gently push the wires back into the box. Reposition the receptacle and screw it in place.
- Restore power, and test both sockets to make sure your new outlet is properly installed.
  Installing a dimmer switch. Dimmer switches are easy to install and will save you money on your electric bill, says

Safety should be your first concern when you are making electrical repairs.

Bennett. Here are instructions for replacing a single-pole switch—one that controls a light from one location—with a dimmer. Make sure the wattage rating for the dimmer switch does not exceed that of the switch you are replacing. The wattage is marked on the side of the switch.

- Turn off the power at the service panel.
- Push the switch to the *Off* position and unscrew the cover plate.
- Double-check that the power in the circuit is off using a voltage tester.
- Gently pull the switch forward. Label all wires.
- Remove the switch.
- Match the wires on the new dimmer.
- Now gently push the wires back into the box and screw it into place.

Home Security

Prevention is the best protection.

CRIME BUSTING

"Most burglaries are opportunistic," says staff sargeant Michael Rice of Ottawa-Carleton regional police. In more than half of all house burglaries, thieves enter through an open door or window. If you make it difficult for burglars to enter, they'll probably head elsewhere. Here are some of Rice's tips:

- Some local police departments will do a free security inspection of your home on request and offer advice on how to make your home safer and more crimeproof.
- You don't have to spend a fortune on high-tech equipment to protect your family and home. You can discourage criminals with locking devices from the local hardware store. All reasonably accessible doors and windows should be secured, as well as any skylights.
- Make sure louvered or awning windows are completely closed, or they can be dislodged from their frames easily. As an extra precaution-

Motion sensor

Centralized alarm system

Five- to six-pin, pick-resistant locks

ary measure, you can reinforce them with epoxy or rubber cement. To secure sliding windows, screw the bottom rail of the upper sash and the top rail of the lower sash together.
- Practice security landscaping: Trim back trees and shrubbery so thieves can't hide or lie in wait on your property. Plant low-growing, thorny

plants "that hurt," advises Rice, such as yew and Explorer roses.
- If you go away, have a trusted neighbor pick up your newspaper and mail and put a trash bag outside your home on trash day. Or have your mail held at the post office. As a precaution, do not cancel your paper while you are away. Ask your neighbor to park their car in your driveway at night. Hire a teenager to cut the grass or clear the snow if you'll be away for an extended period.
- Never hide keys under the doormat, on a window ledge, or in any other conspicuous place. "Those are the first places a thief will look,"

says Rice. Instead, leave a key with a trusted neighbor. Buy light timers and set them so that the lights go on at different times each night.
- Organizations such as Neighborhood Watch are good deterrents provided they stay active. Contact your local police about crime prevention in your neighborhood.

SAFE HAVEN

There are many different devices to protect yourself, your family, and your home, says Professor Robert D. McCrie, PhD, of the John Jay College of Criminal Justice in New York City. A certified protection professional, McCrie has worked

Tools of the Trade

Carbon monoxide detectors will alert you to dangerously high and potentially fatal levels of this invisible, odorless gas in your home before it's too late.

Carbon Monoxide DETECTOR

0.0.0.

PARTS PER MILLION OF CO
(Lb = Low or No Battery)

TEST-RESET   PEAK LEVEL

Sturdy dead bolt

as a security consultant for almost 30 years.

- Centralized alarm systems can protect residents in two ways, says McCrie. They decrease the incidence of burglary, and cause burglars to flee the site during a break-in.
- Passive infrared detectors that you can install yourself are available at many hardware stores and are reasonably priced.
- Motion-sensitive outdoor lighting is an inexpensive, effective way of deterring potential burglars.
- Houses that have a "territorial" appearance can discourage criminals. A fence around your property, exterior lighting, and signs alerting trespassers to alarm and surveillance systems all increase the territoriality of your home. Even if you don't have an alarm system, you can purchase warning signs from hardware stores that may deter potential criminals.
- Doors that give access to the outside should be equipped with five- to six-pin, pick-resistant locks and a dead bolt with a good throw, or cylinder. You can tell how many pins your lock has by the number of grooves or notches on the key.
- Closed-circuit cameras, which show who is entering your property, are a good value for the amount of security they provide, says McCrie.

IT'S ALARMING

Designing a security system requires analyzing a client's needs, lifestyle, and budget, says Ivan Spector, president of Sentinel Alarm Company in Montreal. A security system will not only detect and deter burglars, but can also incorporate features such as fire, smoke, and carbon monoxide detectors. Spector recommends you consider the following:

Burglar alarms: The most cost-effective system is a combination of perimeter detection with contacts on doors and windows, and with backup motion detectors.

Hardwire versus wireless: Hardwire systems are more effective in the long run. But wireless technology has improved dramatically. One advantage of a wireless system is that it does not depend on the telephone line to transmit an alarm to the receiving station. Most of today's control panels will support a combination of both technologies.

Monitored or not: Monitored security systems alert a monitoring center that will contact the appropriate authorities. Spector warns that local-only systems will simply sound at the protected location. This is not usually sufficient. Your system should be monitored by an Underwriters Laboratories of Canada-listed monitoring station.

The alarm company: Ask friends for referrals to reliable alarm companies, which should belong to the Canadian Alarm and Security Association. Sign a contract. You should feel comfortable about your choice since this is the beginning of a long-term relationship.

FIRE SAFETY

Fire detection devices and extinguishers that are maintained properly can save lives, says Emile Therien, president, Canada Safety Council in Ottawa.

- Smoke detectors use two technologies: ionization and photoelectricity. Install one of each type on each level of your house, close to the bedrooms. For extra security, install a detector in each bedroom.
- Use a combination of battery- and electricity-operated detectors.
- Install smoke detectors on an open ceiling area, away from corners, where smoke would take longer to reach the sensor.
- Change batteries on smoke detectors every six months. Change batteries at the same time you set the clock forward or back in spring and fall. Keep smoke detectors clean and dust-free, and replace them every five years.
- Sprinkler systems are recommended for use in private homes. Some systems automatically alert the fire department if they are activated.
- Keep a fire extinguisher on each floor of the house. An ABC, or dry chemical, fire extinguisher is best since it can be used on grease and electrical fires as well as on wood and paper fires. Install one near, but not inside, the kitchen. Have extinguishers checked every six months and recharged if necessary.
- Never go up to the roof during a fire. Heat and smoke rise.

The Right Way

The initials **P.A.S.S.** may help you remember the four key steps required when using an ABC fire extinguisher during an emergency.

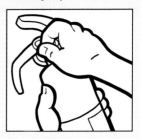

Pull out the pin.

Aim at the base of the fire. Chemical extinguishers shoot from about 15 feet, water extinguishers from about 20 feet.

Squeeze the handles together.

Sweep the hose back and forth across the base of the fire.

Long-distance Housekeeping

Make the most of your home away from home.

CLOSING UP FOR THE WINTER

For Jody and Bates Littlehales, paradise is an isolated log cabin on top of a small mountain in West Virginia. The couple bought the 159 acres of forest to photograph, study, and protect the indigenous wildlife and plant life in the area. Although they presently use the property as a weekend retreat from their hectic city lives, the Littlehales eventually plan to live there for six months of the year.

Closing the cabin for the winter months is a serious business, since it is too isolated for neighbors to routinely check in, and is too inaccessible because of icy roads and heavy snow. Here's what they suggest:

■ Put curtains, quilts, blankets, pillows, linens, and other items that might be tempting to mice and moths in a chest or cedar closet for the winter.

■ Turn off the water pump and water heater at the fuse box. Consider draining the pipes and toilets.

■ Empty the ash trap on the wood stove/heat pump.

■ Make sure the fireplace is cold. Close the damper.

■ Take valuable equipment, such as computers, cameras, and musical instruments, away with you.

■ Leave the electricity on so that you can keep non-perishables, such as preserves, and some frozen foods in the refrigerator over the winter.

Snow can bury the Littlehales' cabin roof-deep in wintertime, so to protect the timber, they put a fresh coat of finish on it every year or two. They also installed a heavy-duty steel fence at the entrance to their property, which they lock to deter trespassers.

The Right Way

If you are coming in as an outsider to an area, learn to understand and respect your neighbors—especially the local people—advises Jody Littlehales. And demand respect in return. Cultivating good relations with your neighbors will not only make your second home more enjoyable, but will also help ensure your own security and the security of your property.

THE GUEST BOOK

Whether you have family, friends, or tenants staying at your home, it's a good idea to leave behind a guest book, telling your visitors everything they might need to know about the home and the area, says Cathy Ruizgoubert, general manager at Sandbridge Realty in Virginia. The company manages some 200 privately owned vacation properties. Here's what Ruizgoubert suggests you include in your guest book:

■ Instructions on how to open and close the property, including tasks such as disposing of garbage, turning down the thermostat, and returning recyclable items.

■ Instructions for operating appliances your guests may not know how to use, including dishwashers, hot tubs, ice makers, and garbage disposals.

■ Telephone numbers for local doctors and dentists, as well as hospital and other emergency numbers.

■ Warnings about any local health concerns, such as sunstroke and poison ivy, and how to prevent and treat them if necessary.

■ Information about hiking trails, beaches, and other natural attractions in the surrounding area.

■ Recommendations for local restaurants, shops, and activities.

■ Reminders about what's expected of guests. For instance, would you like them to strip the beds or restock the refrigerator before leaving?

RENTING IT OUT

If the house is in good condition when tenants arrive, they will leave it good condition, says Cathy Ruizgoubert. Her firm recommends these tips to their clients who are going to rent their homes:

■ Make sure everything is clean, lubricated, freshly painted, and in good working order.

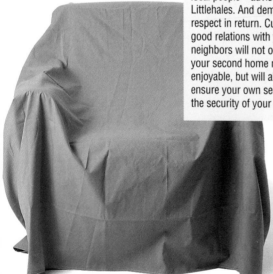

Cover furniture and wood to protect them from fading.

Important Numbers:

Fire Department   555-7000
Police   555-1221
Snow Removal   555-3435
Fire wood   555-1668
Towing and Repair   555-2324

A guest book describing your home and neighborhood will make visitors feel welcome and provide necessary information.

- Keep cleaning supplies, such as a broom, bleach, and pine cleaner, on hand so guests can clean up after themselves.
- Stock a few basic necessities, such as toilet paper, garbage bags, and lightbulbs, for when your guests arrive.
- Leave a written reminder to leave the property in the same condition in which it was found.

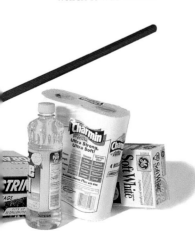

SAFE AND SOUND

A few years ago Cathy Asher and her husband learned the hard way about the vulnerability of vacation homes when their Connecticut getaway dwelling was broken into. As a result, they now take extra precautions to ensure the security of their 40-acre vacation property.

- The Ashers have installed such devices as motion-sensitive exterior lights, timers on their indoor lights, and an alarm system to deter thieves.
- The Ashers use two codes on their alarm system— one for themselves and one for their guests. The alarm company can read the code being used.
- Neighbors down the road keep an eye on the house when it's empty and stop

by to mow the lawn and check things out from time to time.

- The Ashers hire local caretakers to oversee the property and manage emergencies when they are not there. They also clean the house once a month and tend to the Ashers' garden.

NO VACANCY

If you hire people to look after your second home while it is vacant, make sure they care about it as much as you do, says Bill Mogg of Mountain Property Management in Crested Butte, Colorado. Bill and his wife Tammy oversee about 30 homes, many of which are vacant most of the year. Here are their tips:

- Draw the shades to keep furniture and wood from fading in the sun.
- Cover the furniture with sheets and blankets.
- Keep easy-to-maintain plants, such as philodendrons and cacti.
- Natural surfaces, such as oiled wood, are much easier to maintain than paint, which flakes off. Oil wood decks and other wooden surfaces once a year to keep them in tip-top shape.

Once a week, the Moggs do a complete inventory of the houses, checking for vermin, leaks under sinks, and other problems. If there is a car in the garage, the Moggs start it up once a month to prevent the batteries from dying. If requested, they will take it in for service. Before the owners arrive, the Moggs wash windows, do a thorough cleaning, and bring out deck furniture.

Smart Moves

How to prevent burst pipes:

Consider having your pipes professionally winterized by a plumber, who will drain them to prevent freezing.

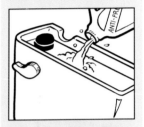

If you are handling the job yourself, turn off the pump and water heater. Drain the pipes by opening all faucets and letting them run dry. Flush the toilet until the tank stops refilling, and add antifreeze.

If you plan to leave the heat on, maintain the temperature at 55°F to 60°F, and have a system installed to alert your caretaker or a neighbor if the heat goes off unexpectedly.

During the winter, four to six feet of snow is routine in Crested Butte. To prevent decks and roofs from being damaged, the Moggs recommend having snow cleared from the property regularly.

CHAPTER TWO

In the Kitchen

The Basic Kitchen

The right equipment can make cooking easier.

KNIVES

Balance and sensitivity are the two most important qualities to look for when purchasing a knife, says Matthias Merges, chef de cuisine at Charlie Trotter's in Chicago. Balance refers to the equilibrium between the weight of the handle and that of the blade. If this weight is evenly distributed and you have good cutting techniques, "the knife should do the work for you," says Merges. Sensitivity has to do with how well you can feel what the tip of the knife is doing when you're holding the handle. For example, you should be able to tell where the tip is inside a fish when filleting it. A good way to test for sensitivity is to place the tip of the knife sideways on a counter surface and push down. You should feel some flexibility. Test a range of knives, from low- to high-end, to experience the dif-ferences in their sensitivity.

The four essential knives to own are a chef's (or French) knife for chopping and julienning, a paring knife, a slicer, and a boning knife. Additional nice-to-have knives include a serrated knife, a cleaver, a fish filleting knife, and a pair of scissors.

You will also need a steel for maintaining the knife edges. Using the steel between all your cutting jobs helps keep the edge on your knives and means you don't have to sharpen them as often. Sharpening, which is ideally done with a triple stone, reapplies the edge to the knife. Merges uses the steel on his knives constantly, and sharpens them every two to three weeks. How often you need to sharpen your knives will depend on how much you use them. Wash knives with mild hand soap, and avoid harsh detergents.

The four essential knives

Chef's knife Paring knife Slicer Boning knife

Nice-to-have knives

Serrated knife Cleaver Filleting knife Scissors

THE A LIST

The following list includes just about everything you need to cook, says Chef Stefan Czapalay, owner of Seasons in Thyme restaurant in Summerside, P.E.I., who is also vice-president of the Atlantic Chapter of the Canadian Federation of Chefs and Cooks.

Cooking Basics

1½- and 3-quart saucepans
Large surface sauté pan
Medium sauté pan
Omelet pan
Steamer insert

Medium covered casserole
Large covered casserole
Pasta pot with colander
Nonstick fry pan
Stainless steel double boiler

Stainless steel roasting pan
Instant meat thermometer
Stainless steel bulb baster
Pepper grinder
Heat diffuser

Griddle
Top-of-the-stove grill
Kitchen timer
Basting brush

Preparation Utensils

Food processor
Stainless steel mixing bowls
Rubber scrapers
Wire whisk
Wooden spoons
Stainless steel ladle
Cutting board(s)
Stainless steel strainer
Pancake turner

Colander
Stainless steel grater
Long-handled pot fork
Stainless steel tongs
Vegetable peeler
Stainless steel funnel
Slotted spoon and solid spoon
Vegetable brush
Kitchen shears

Can opener
Stainless steel potato ricer
Stainless steel food mill
Stainless steel garlic press
Stainless steel tea kettle
Vegetable slicer
Juicer
Melon baller
Coffee maker

Measuring and Baking

Dry measuring cup set
Dry measuring spoon set
Liquid measuring cup(s)
Mercury oven thermometer
Heavy-duty mixer
8- or 9-inch square baking pans
8- or 9-inch round baking pans
Removable-bottom tart pan
Two cookie sheets

Cooling racks
9-inch pie plate
Muffin pan
Loaf pan (9 x 5 x 3 inches)
Sheet pan (9 x 13 x 2 inches)
Jelly roll pan
Flour sifter
Tube cake pan
Parchment paper

Springform cheesecake pan
Gram/ounce scale
Cake-icing spatulas
Rolling pin and cover
Pastry blender
Pastry cloth
Pastry brush
Pastry weights
Pastry bag and tips

POTS AND PANS—MADE IN PRINCE EDWARD ISLAND

Paderno and Chaudier Cookware, based in Prince Edward Island, has developed a reputation as a top-notch North American manufacturer of high-quality kitchenware, whose products are found in the residence of Canada's Prime Minister and on board Air Force One, the US President's jet.

Scott Chandler, in charge of marketing and development for Paderno, advises cooks to consider these recommendations when they go shopping for kitchenware:

■ Pick pots and pans that are made with stainless steel, which is far more durable than any other metal used for cookware and much easier to clean. Chandler explains that stainless steel is a poor conductor of heat. As a result, kitchenware manufacturers must bond a more effective conductor to the bottom of the pot. Paderno Cookware uses an aluminum bond on the bottom of its pots and pans. Apart from durability, an aluminum bottom provides fast and even heat control.

■ Always choose a pot with a thick, heavy bottom. In the very best kind of cookware, the bottom may be as much as two millimeters thick.

■ Avoid pots and pans with plastic and wooden handles, which can fall off. The best choice is a stainless steel handle, which, as Scott Chandler points out, does not get hot even when the pot is boiling. Check to see whether the handles are welded to the pot. If the handle is attached by bolts or screws to the pot, there is a risk that it may become loose and fall off.

Choosing and Using

Look for the best equipment for your kitchen.

CONSIDERING COOKTOPS

Chances are good that much of the cooking that gets done in a basic kitchen takes place on a cooktop. The range of cooktop choices is growing, though public awareness of them seems to be lagging behind. Rick Wiseman, a buyer at Sears Canada Inc., points out that the newer cooktops are worth exploring because they can be easier to clean, easier to control, and easier on the eye than the more conventional options. For example:

Sealed gas burner. This operates like a conventional gas burner, but because the burners are sealed to the cooktop, spills can't flow into hard-to-clean spots. And simmering on this cooktop is easier because the flame is more evenly spread out.

Gas or electric downdraft modular cooktop. Related to the basic gas or electric cooktops, but with interchangeable modules, this one usually has a grill and options for additional burners or accessories, such as a griddle or wok. It's highly flexible, but expensive.

Ceramic glass with a radiant element. Radiant elements beneath the smoothtop surface transfer heat to cookware via conduction and radiation. These flat tops look elegant, give good heat control, and stand up to high temperatures and hard knocks, but require flat-bottom pans that do not extend more than one inch over the element edge.

Ceramic glass with a halogen element. Quartz halogen lamp tubes encircled by electric resistance coils underneath the smoothtop surface transfer heat to cookware. These cooktops are tough, like their radiant cousins, but heat up faster. They are, however, expensive and less available.

Your cooktop should suit your family's cooking and eating habits, existing energy sources, available space, and budget.

A food processor for basic chopping, slicing, and shredding is also helpful when mixing dough and puréeing.

APPLIANCES TO GET STARTED WITH

There are very few small appliances that are absolute necessities in the kitchen. A lot depends on an individual's cooking style, expertise, and food preferences. But Barbara Pool Fenzl, owner of Les Gourmettes Cooking School in Phoenix and past president, International Association of Culinary Professionals, thinks the following are pretty basic:

A mini-chop or coffee grinder can be used for grinding spices.

A toaster or toaster oven is essential for breakfast.

A hand-held or stand mixer is important if you bake frequently.

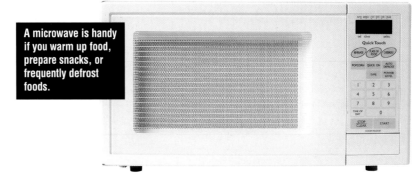

A microwave is handy if you warm up food, prepare snacks, or frequently defrost foods.

MICROWAVE OVENS

Microwave ovens are the most commonly used kitchen appliance in North America, says Jim Griffin, associate dean, Johnson and Wales University, College of Culinary Arts in Providence, Rhode Island. Whether you're a new buyer or you're replacing an outdated machine, consider these shopping tips:

Your needs. Microwaves come with a whole variety of "bells and whistles," including alarms to remind you to walk your dog! But if you're only going to be heating spaghetti sauce and coffee, a basic, inexpensive model should do. The more features, the more you'll pay.

Construction. Look at a model of the oven you're interested in on the display floor to see how well it is put together. Do the door hinges line up properly? Does the door align with the oven cavity, and does it close properly? A flimsy or poorly assembled oven will probably have to be replaced in a short time.

Wattage. Wattage will determine the output of the oven—how effective it will be in heating foods. Generally speaking, the higher the wattage, the more powerful the oven, and the greater the range of cooking you can do in it.

Smart Moves

- When purchasing a small appliance, choose one sold by a major manufacturer. It is likely to be of higher quality than a lesser-known brand.
- Before using a small appliance for the first time, wash it in warm, soapy water and rinse well.
- Put appliances out of reach when you're not using them. Otherwise, it's easy to knock over hard-to-replace parts like blender containers or mixing bowls. And never place appliances close to the edge of a counter.
- Always store appliance accessories, such as mixer beaters or processor blades, in the same place as the appliance so you can find them when you need them.
- When considering whether to buy an appliance that's new to the market, you might want to wait a year or so to see how it performs. Like a new model car, it can take a while for the manufacturer to work out the kinks.
- Once you've bought a new appliance, start using it right away and keep at it. That way you'll get comfortable with it, figure out how to use all the features, and become efficient in creating dishes with it.

SMALL APPLIANCES

Small appliances are as varied as tasks in the kitchen. Rose Mary Schaefer, selling manager for the department store division of the Minneapolis-based Dayton Hudson Corporation, gives some tips on what to think about when choosing and using some of today's more-popular small appliances:

Mixer. If you cook or bake in large batches for many people, you'll want to consider a stand mixer rather than a hand mixer. For the average cook, a 200-watt stand mixer is sufficient. Someone who cooks a lot and prepares stiff batters and doughs should consider a machine with 300 watts or more.

Food processor. At a minimum, look for the capacity to slice and shred, mix with a steel blade, and mix dough with a plastic blade. Wattage is not an issue here—size is. If you usually cook for two to four people, a seven-cup capacity should be sufficient. If you cook for larger groups, a machine with a larger capacity is better. (Some processors come with more than one size work bowl.) When you get your processor home, store it in an easily accessible place so you won't have to haul it out every time that you want to use it.

Hand or immersion blender. This device does the work of a blender, but allows you to do it right in the pan. For example, you can purée a soup without taking it off the stove. For maximum versatility, purchase one with more speeds and multi-functions. If you buy a brand that has its own plastic beaker, you can whip up salad dressings.

Rice cooker. The choice here is single- (just rice) versus multi-function (rice plus steaming, so you can do vegetables and fish), and size. Choose a size that fits the amount of rice you ordinarily cook. The steamers will have a larger capacity.

Bread maker. Two important features to look for here are the size of the loaf produced and the number of programmable cycles, which determines how many different kinds of bread you can make. Stay away from a machine with windows because they allow heat to escape.

THE SOUL OF A KITCHEN

The right tools and machines can make a kitchen efficient. But it takes something more to make it sing. Joyce Goldstein, author of *Kitchen Conversations* and many other cookbooks, and former chef/owner of Square One Restaurant in San Francisco, reflects, "A kitchen is wonderful if it looks like people use it—if there are cut marks on the butcher block, if the pots have a few dents, if there are personal containers that hold spatulas and wooden spoons. I don't like kitchens where everything is stored away, there's nothing on the counter, and it looks like it came out of a fancy magazine. I like kitchens where things aren't too manufactured, where there's a mixture of pots and pans, and there's memorabilia around.

"A good kitchen is a personal kitchen," Goldstein continues. "It emits imperfections."

True Stories

When Barbara Pool Fenzl got her first food processor, she used it to prepare a large batch of peanut soup for a fundraiser. She poured the hot soup into the processor, turned it on, and jumped back, horrified, as the soup exploded all over the kitchen—and all over her. As a result, she always warns her students to remove the food tube or pusher from the processor when puréeing hot food, and to read all the instructions that come with new machines.

Organizing Kitchen Space

Today's cooks need workable kitchens.

A NEW ANGLE ON KITCHENS

The work triangle consisting of sink-stovetop-refrigerator has dominated home kitchen design for many years. So, too, has the notion that kitchen means same-height countertops, matching cabinets, and a seamless look.

"The problem if you have a triangle is that only one person can be in the middle of it," says Deborah Krasner, a kitchen designer based in Putney, Vermont, and author of *Kitchens for Cooks*. Today, it's more common to find multiple cooks in one home. So, she designs kitchens with her clients based on the way they live and cook. "I ask a lot of questions about who cooks, what foods are prepared, and whether people cook together. And I measure all the people who are going to be cooking."

The result of Krasner's approach is a kitchen designed around different zones for different functions. She has dubbed the

zones hot (cooking), cold (refrigerating), wet (rinsing, washing), and dry (chopping, pastry-making). Major appliances anchor each zone, and each zone has its own storage system. For instance, colanders are stored in the wet zone, saucepans in hot, refrigerator storage con-

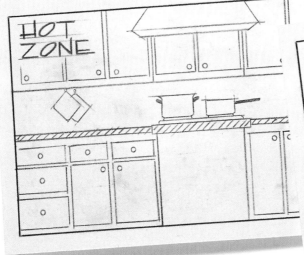

tainers in cold. Individual zones may also have different surfaces—for example, butcher block in the dry zone, and ceramic or heat-resistant stone in the hot zone. A key design element in Krasner's kitchens is an 18- to 36-inch space on both sides of each zone for putting pots and pans beside a stovetop, or drying dishes next to the sink.

Krasner doesn't shy away from diversity. She creates counters of varying heights, and uses different woods and a variety of styles. Her clients end up with kitchens that are "magazine-beautiful" as well as very functional, while accommodating the needs of everyone in the home.

KITCHEN ENHANCEMENTS

What makes a kitchen the heart of the family? For Charles Morris Mount of Charles Morris Mount Interior Design in New York City, it's when the kitchen is a place where everybody meets and can enjoy talking, cooking, and eating together. That's why his kitchens usually include an eating area that's an extension of the island, or a peninsula.

"Nobody has to go into the dining room or into a nook—it's all happening here," says Mount. The eating area is often in the

same material as the island top—stone or marble—and several inches lower—27 or 28 inches, versus 36 inches for the island work space. But you need careful design to make sure that the transition in heights looks natural, not awkward.

Lighting is another important element in creating a kitchen that's both

functional and warm. Mount says task lighting (needed for food preparation) should be mounted under upper cabinets and shine down against the wall. The important thing is never to work in shadow or dim light, so your risk of accidents is lower.

Lighting for ambience is also critical. But how you create it is largely a matter of taste. Mount has clients who have used such unique items as old-fashioned wooden chandeliers to light their kitchens. However you do it, the goal is a warm, welcoming feeling.

The Right Way

Don't have unlimited funds for a kitchen renovation? Put your money into the equipment that really matters to you and make do with everything else. If you're a real cook, invest in a great stove. Granite countertops and top-of-the-line cabinets can wait.

SUPER STORAGE

There's no excuse for clattering pot lids, crammed counters, or bulging drawers. Today, you can find solutions for every kitchen item. Marty Marston, public relations manager at Ikea, North America, provides some examples:

■ Cupboards with space for a microwave oven.

You can create a lot more storage space if you remove the soffits in your kitchen and fill the space with to-the-ceiling cabinets. Frameless (versus full-frame) cabinets also provide more storage. How to tell the difference? If you can see the hinges on the cabinets, they

galleys. The key to small-kitchen survival is simplicity. "If you measure how much space you need in the kitchen, you'll find how concentrated it is." Three feet is enough distance between facing counters, and the counters themselves don't have to be more than two feet in depth.

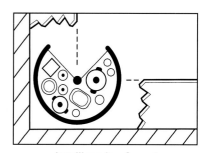

Installing a lazy Susan in a corner cabinet gives you easy access to the items you store inside.

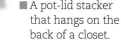
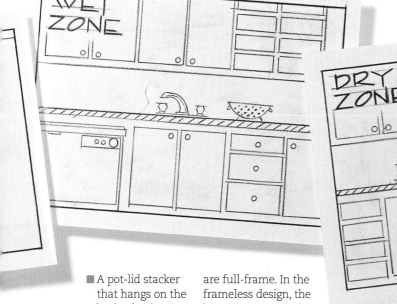

■ A pot-lid stacker that hangs on the back of a closet.
■ An under-the-counter recycling unit that fits in a corner space. Three trash bins whirl on a pole and can be removed when recycling day comes.
■ A chrome-plated steel railing that attaches to the bottom of hanging cabinets. Various gadgets can slide along the railing, such as spice holders, cookbook holders, a drying rack, or coffee filters.
■ A half-moon lazy Susan that fits in that empty space in the back of a cabinet for odds and ends.
■ A pull-out holder for flat cookware, such as roasting or baking trays.

are full-frame. In the frameless design, the hinges are recessed inside the cabinets.

Marston, who recently renovated her own kitchen, recommends storage drawers as an alternative to cabinets. Because they pull out, everything is within easy reach.

DESIGNING FOR SMALL SPACES

Jay Benford, a yacht designer in the Benford Design Group, St. Michaels, Maryland, understands small kitchens. Having spent more than half his adult life on boats, he has become adept at both designing and cooking in

Benford points out that there's a lot of wasted space in most kitchen cabinets. (Check out the area above your dishes.) In a galley kitchen, he'll save space by making shelf heights of 7 or 8 inches rather than the standard 12 or 16. What goes in cabinets is also important. Nesting pots and pans and equipment that serves multiple purposes cut down on the space you need.

The best way to plan your small kitchen, recommends Benford, is to make a miniature cardboard mock-up of the space beforehand.

True Stories

Sometimes "less is more" says Doris Lacroix, Ottawa-based kitchen designer. She finds European appliances are often the solution when designing a small kitchen. Stylish and energy efficient, they are also wonderfully compact. A 24-inch oven with convection features, a 24-inch cooktop, and an 18-inch dishwasher will suffice for the most elaborate cooking style. Lacroix should know because she cooks daily, and entertains often, with these appliances in her own 150-square-foot kitchen.

Kitchen Clean-up

You can form habits that help keep you safe.

USE THE DISHWASHER DAILY

You always knew your dishwasher was convenient. But did you also know that it's one of your best allies in keeping your kitchen safe from contaminants? The dishwasher sanitizes everything that goes in it, says Bonnie Richmond, senior lecturer in food safety and sanitation at the Hotel School at Cornell University, if you use the dry cycle. During that cycle, the internal temperature of the dishwasher reaches 170°F, which is required for sanitizing. (Sanitizing is the process of reducing harmful microbes to an acceptable level. Sterilizing is the process of removing all living organisms—something we can't aspire to in our own homes.)

Here's Richmond's first rule of thumb: Run anything through the dishwasher that can go into it, including plateware, glassware, flatware, plastic cutting boards, and sponges. Anything that touches raw meat and fish, or their juices or blood, should be placed in the dishwasher immediately. That means if you use a sponge to wipe up the counter where meat juices have spilled, you should toss it right in the dishwasher and get out a clean one. At the very least, your sponges should go into the dishwasher every time you run it. Be sure to keep a backup supply on hand so you are not tempted to use a dirty one.

One thing you can't put through the dishwasher is your hands. Always keep a bar of soap or soap dispenser next to the kitchen sink. To ensure that you are not spreading contaminants, wash your hands thoroughly whenever you enter the kitchen, between each kitchen task, and before you leave the kitchen.

Your dishwasher is the first line of defense against germs in the kitchen. You can sanitize almost anything in it.

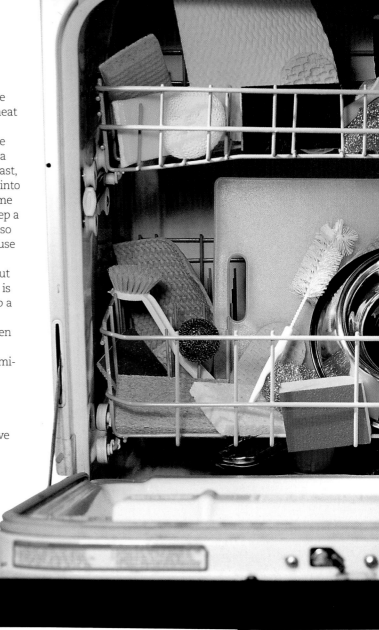

HOW THE PROS DO IT

If you're serving food to millions of people around the world, your kitchen sanitation had better be rigorous. At McDonald's it is, thanks to strict procedures, intensive training, on-site management, and peer supervision, says McDonald's Corporation spokesperson Julie Cleary. Kitchen cleanliness at McDonald's focuses on three major areas that you can use in the home kitchen as well:

- Hand washing. Crew and management teams alike are required to wash their hands on a schedule, including when they change shifts. They use antimicrobial hand-washing soap.
- Proper and consistent cleaning and sanitizing of all utensils, equipment, and surfaces with hot water and sanitizer.
- The use of disposable dishware and cleaning rags, which are more sanitary than reusable sponges or cloths.

Myth: *Antibacterial sponges, soaps, and sprays protect you from dangerous microbes in the kitchen.*

Fact: *The jury is still out on the effectiveness of these products. Consistent cleaning and sanitizing is the best insurance against illnesses caused by kitchen germs.*

ing a safe cleaning routine," says Sandy Sullivan, spokesperson for the Clorox Company. A prime example is the drain in your sink. If you throw some raw meat scraps into your garbage disposal, then drop a spoon down there, retrieve it with your hand, and go on to prepare a salad, chances are good that you have just contaminated your lettuce. To get rid of bacteria, mix three-quarters of a cup of bleach in a gallon of water. Pour it into your sink, let it sit for two to five minutes, and drain it out.

The three-quarter-cup to one gallon water bleach solution applied for two to five minutes can also take care of other kitchen hot spots: dishcloths, faucet handles, refrigerator door handles, countertops, and moldy areas in the refrigerator. For wooden cutting boards, first wash with hot, soapy water, then use a solution of three tablespoons bleach to a gallon of water to scrub the boards and eliminate dangerous germs.

BLEACH IT

"Understanding where germs hang out is an important part of develop-

Smart Moves

You've finished preparing a meal and have washed your hands, but cooking odors still cling to them. What to do?
- For general cooking odors, rub your hands with toothpaste or mouthwash and rinse them with water.
- For garlic odors, wet your hands with cold water and rub against a stainless steel sink or faucet.

KNOW YOUR CLEANING AGENTS

Use detergents made for the job you are doing, says Rich Vergili, professor of food safety at the Culinary Institute of America in Hyde Park, New York.

Having the right product for each job can make cleaning a lot easier.

- Make sure that your detergent contains a degreaser if you're washing a greasy pot.
- Use an abrasive cleaner that contains bleach if you want to clean and sanitize a smooth metal surface (e.g., sinks, soiled flatware). Be aware that before an item can be sanitized, it must first be cleaned, that is, have all the visible particles removed.
- Read the labels on your cleaning products to become better informed about their uses and any precautions you should take. For instance, you should not use household ammonia on food contact surfaces. Nor should you mix chemicals. In particular, never use bleach and household ammonia together because the resulting fumes can be dangerous.
- Expect some new iodine-based sanitizing products coming on the market to be more widely available. Right now, they are primarily used in home brewing, where sanitizing is critical. The iodine-based sanitizers are milder on the hands and nose than bleach is, but are very effective.
- Choose your detergents to match the quality of your water, since water influences their effectiveness. If your water is very hard, it can interfere with the cleaning process by preventing detergents from sudsing up. But if your water is very soft, you may get lots of suds that you can't rinse properly. If either of these problems sounds familiar, you can have your water analyzed and treated.
- Buy the smallest-sized container of any new cleaning product you've decided to try. While you may have found the perfect answer to a tough job, you may discover that you don't like the aroma or that the product is too harsh on your hands.
- If you prefer to use small containers, save money by buying the economy size and refilling.

Keeping a Safe Kitchen

You need to know the why's and how's of food safety.

SAFETY ISSUES TODAY

Why are food-related illnesses on the rise? According to Nicols Fox, author of *Spoiled: Why Our Food is Making Us Sick and What We Can Do About It*, the basic problem is that "we've changed our relationship with food. We've changed what we eat, where we get it, how we grow it, how we produce it, and our expectations from it. We want convenience foods, novelty, year-round availability, and cheap food. All of these things are driving the producers who are interested in efficiency and profit. When you apply these pressures to food production, you're setting up situations in which food can become contaminated or in which contamination can be spread in new and different ways."

The old model for food-borne disease was the church picnic. Everybody who went and ate the potato salad got sick. It was a contained, localized outbreak. Now outbreaks are widespread as a result of a variety of preparation and distribution practices:

Smart Moves

When in doubt about some aspect of food safety, contact the Canadian Food Inspection Agency. You can visit the website at www.cfia-acia.agr.ca.

- Processed foods that are widely distributed. For example, an ice cream mix may be spoiled because it was transported in tanker trucks that had hauled contaminated raw eggs, or some spoiled beef may contaminate a huge batch of ground meat.
- Food animals that are raised for specific qualities or functions, reducing their diversity and making large flocks more susceptible to disease. The conditions in which the animals are raised, shipped, and processed, which may be stressful or dirty, can also contribute to the development and spread of disease.
- The popularity of pre-prepared foods, such as those at salad bars. One food preparer with unwashed hands can potentially infect all who purchase the food.
- Fruits and vegetables imported from other countries where sanitation standards or practices may be less rigorous than in North America.

HOLIDAY SAFETY

Follow appropriate safety precautions, and don't let food-borne illness contaminate your holidays. The Canadian Food Inspection Agency issues *Food Safety Facts for the Holidays* and *Turkey Facts for Food Safety*, with this advice about holiday food safety:

- Turkey, the centerpiece of many a holiday meal, needs special treatment. When buying it, place it in its own plastic bag to avoid contaminating other foods, and put it in the refrigerator immediately when you get home. Place it on a plate big enough to catch any leaking juices. Buy fresh turkey just a day or two before cooking it. Defrost a frozen turkey in the refrigerator—*not* on the counter—allowing 24 hours for every five pounds of turkey. You can also defrost a turkey wrapped in leak-proof plastic in cold water, but you need to change the water every half-hour. Allow 30 minutes of defrosting per pound.
- Clean everything that touches the turkey and its juice thoroughly with hot, soapy water.
- The safest way to cook stuffing is on the stove or in the oven, not inside the turkey. If you do stuff the turkey, do it loosely and just before you put the bird in the oven. The center of the stuffing should reach 160°F on a meat thermometer.
- A meat thermometer is also the most reliable way to tell when the turkey is done. It should reach

For safety's sake, buy only a commercial, pasteurized eggnog.

185°F in the inner thigh and the juices should run clear.
- If you buy a hot, pre-cooked turkey, keep it at 140°F or above if you'll eat it within two hours. Otherwise, remove the stuffing, cut the turkey

off the bone, and refrigerate everything separately, including any side dishes.

- When serving, don't leave the turkey unrefrigerated for more than two hours.
- Store stuffing in shallow containers so it gets cold quickly and completely. Stuffing in deep containers may not get cold in the center and, thus, bacteria may grow there.
- Use all leftovers, except for stuffing and gravy, within four days. Reheat leftovers at 160°F. Use stuffing and gravy within two days. Boil the gravy.

The Right Way

Test molluscan shellfish for freshness by holding the shell between your thumb and forefinger and pressing as though sliding the two parts of the shell across one another. If the shells move, the shellfish is not fresh. Throw away any that do not close tightly.

Discard any clams, mussels, or oysters that do not open during cooking.

SHELLFISH SAFETY

Health Canada advises that eating raw or partially cooked molluscan shellfish, such as oysters, clams, and mussels, carries a higher potential for causing illness than eating them thoroughly cooked. In healthy individuals, the illnesses that can result from consuming raw or partially cooked shellfish aren't life threatening, and commonly range from mild intestinal disorders to acute gastroenteritis. They are caused by bacteria and viruses present in water due to human pollution or natural causes, such as warm waters.

Some experts say individuals with compromised immune systems shouldn't eat raw or partially cooked molluscan shellfish at all. These people are susceptible to far more serious illnesses caused by naturally occurring marine bacteria or human pollution.

Here are some guidelines on how to avoid molluscan shellfish-related illnesses:

Shopping. Buy from a store or market where shellfish is properly chilled. Mollusks in the shell should always be alive when you buy them. When a clam, oyster, mussel, or scallop is alive, the shell will be tightly closed or will close when it is tapped lightly or iced.

Storing. Store live mollusks in the refrigerator in containers covered loosely with a clean, damp cloth. Do not store live shellfish in airtight containers or in water.

Cooking. Use one or more pots to boil or steam shellfish. If you crowd them, the ones in the middle won't get thoroughly cooked. Discard any clams, mussels, or oysters that don't open during cooking. Closed shells may mean the shellfish haven't received adequate heat. When boiling molluscan shellfish, wait until shells open, then continue to boil three to five more minutes. When steaming, cook four to nine minutes from the start of steaming.

SAFE FREEZER STORAGE

You regularly check the temperature of your oven. How about your freezer? According to Lawrie Hall, director of external affairs at the Tupperware Corporation, her firm recommends a freezer temperature of 0°F for optimal long-term storage. The following list sets out Tupperware's recommended maximum storage times for a variety of home-frozen foods:

Food in freezer	Maximum storage
Breads, rolls	6-8 months
Butter and margarine	9 months
Citrus fruits	4-6 months
Cut-up chicken (uncooked)	9 months
Frozen juice concentrate	12 months
Frozen vegetables	8-12 months
Fruits except citrus	8-12 months
Ice cream and sherbet	1 month
Lamb and beef roast (uncooked)	12 months
Pork and veal roast (uncooked)	8 months
Whole chickens and turkeys (uncooked)	12 months

Hall cautions that if your freezer temperature is above 0°F, or if you have a frost-free freezer where the temperature fluctuates, you may have to shorten these suggested maximum times to maintain high quality.

There are a few simple keys to ensuring that your food survives its time in the freezer. Only freeze fresh foods of good quality and prepare them following the procedure recommended for that food type. Cool in the refrigerator before freezing to prevent raising the temperature in the freezer. Store in airtight freezer containers that are sized to allow for some expansion during the freezing process while minimizing air exposure. Label with the date when you put them in.

Creating Tasty, Healthy Meals

You can make meals that taste good and are good for you.

TIPS FOR EASIER MEALS

Most people want to serve delicious, easy, inexpensive, low-calorie, and kid-friendly meals every time. But they often have to compromise, and do what's possible. Michele Urvater, author of the *Monday to Friday Cookbook* series, offers these suggestions for staying sane in the kitchen:

- Cook one dish—chicken breasts, for example— and fill in the rest of the meal with store-bought frozen or prepared items.
- Let taste, not rules, determine what you cook. There is no point preparing something nobody likes, even if it's healthful.
- Cook once for two meals, but vary the dish the second time. Say it's a stew. Next time, add beans or serve it over pasta.
- Simplify getting a salad ready by making a quart of vinaigrette salad dressing at a time. To vary it, add Parmesan or blue cheese, extra mustard, or fresh or dried herbs.
- Plan ahead. Choose your recipes, check which of the necessary ingredients you have on hand, and make a shopping list.
- Make menu planning easier by serving at least one favorite meal every week, chosen either by popular demand or by rotating the decision among family members.

RECOMMENDED DAILY SERVINGS

Canada's Food Guide to Healthy Eating recommends the following daily servings from the four basic food groups. Amounts vary depending on age, body size, activity level, gender, and if you are pregnant or breast-feeding.

Daily servings for each food group	What counts as a serving?
Vegetables and Fruits 5-10 servings	1 medium size vegetable or fruit 1 cup salad ½ cup juice ½ cup frozen or fresh fruit or vegetable
Grain Products 5-12 servings	1 slice of bread 30 grams cold cereal ¾ cup hot cereal 1 bagel, pita, or bun 1 cup cooked pasta or rice
Milk Products *Children 4-9 years:* 2-3 servings *Youth 10-16 years:* 3-4 servings *Adults:* 2-4 servings *Pregnant and breast-feeding women:* 3-4 servings	1 cup milk 50 grams cheese ¾ cup yogurt
Meat and Alternatives 2-3 servings	50-100 grams meat, poultry, or fish 1-2 eggs 125-250 ml beans ⅓ cup tofu 2 tablespoons peanut butter

ONCE-A-MONTH COOKING

If you dread being asked "What's for dinner?" every day, one way to cope is by having a freezer full of tasty, homemade main dishes. This is the approach devised by Mary Beth Lagerborg and Mimi Wilson, co-authors of *Once a Month Cooking*. Lagerborg explains, "You do one big shopping trip and have one intense cooking day, but the rest of the month all you have to do is heat up your entree and throw together a salad or cook some vegetables."

Planning is the key to this system. Another essential: efficient cooking methods. The authors advise, for instance, doing all similar processes—such as browning all the ground beef, grating all the cheeses, or chopping all the vegetables —at one time.

One way to make the most of this system is to collaborate with a friend. Not only does the time in the kitchen go faster, but by splitting the dishes you create, you can add more variety to your menus.

Another hint: Label each dish and make a master list to keep track of what you've served. That way you won't have several similar meals left at the end of the month.

Myth: *You should take vitamins to supplement your diet.* **Fact:** *Most people can get all the nutrients they need by eating a variety of foods in the proportions shown in* **Canada's Food Guide to Healthy Eating.**

For a meal in a bowl, try black bean soup topped with yogurt and garnished with corn chips and a crunchy celery stalk. Grapes add the perfect finishing touch.

TASTY, HEALTHY, INEXPENSIVE

Ingredients	Amount	Cost
Black beans	1 pound	$1.45
Chopped onions	1 cup	$.30
Whole tomatoes	1 standard can	$.90-1.30
Chopped red pepper (imported)	1 cup	$1.00-2.00
Yogurt	1 cup	$.80

VEGETABLE APPEAL

If it is a challenge to get your family to eat vegetables, here are some helpful hints on how to enhance vegetable appeal from Rosie Schwartz, a Toronto-based consulting dietitian, who is also the author of *The Enlightened Eater*:
■ Enlist your children's aid when buying vegetables. At the store, let them make the choices. At home, let them select a recipe for the vegetable dish and prepare it. And always be appreciative of the end result.
■ Some kids find vegetables more appealing raw than cooked. Add nutritional value by serving raw vegetables with healthy dips. In time, the kids may be willing to try vegetables slightly steamed.
■ Find ways of putting vegetables into soups.

The Right Way

What's the best way to save money on meat and kitchen staples? Buy in bulk, which saves both money and time. Buying in large quantities is almost always cheaper, and you shop less often, which means you'll probably make fewer impulse buys. You can always shop with a friend or relative, splitting large quantities. That way you get the advantage of lower prices, but you won't have more perishables on hand than you can use within a reasonable period of time.

Make a broth with potatoes and onions, add cut-up zucchini, broccoli, or cauliflower, and purée the mixture. This soup has a mild flavor likely to appeal to young children.
■ When local fresh produce is available, prepare and freeze batches of soup such as minestrone. For a tasty dish, defrost one batch, and use the soup to create layers between thick crusty bread and parmesan cheese in a casserole. Heat the dish in a hot oven until it is thoroughly cooked and bubbling.

STAR ATTRACTIONS

What's harder than preparing meals that please everyone in your immediate family? Try planning healthy meals that please a crowd, such as a family reunion or a volunteer work party. Linda LaViolette knows—she's president of LaViolette Fancy Foods, a full-service caterer specializing in feeding film crews on location.

Many film people are vegetarian, and others want a low-fat or no-fat diet. The crew, on the other hand, "want it all." To satisfy a variety of tastes, LaViolette builds her menus around a formula:
■ Two protein items, such as a red meat and a white meat, or a white meat and a fish.
■ A vegetarian pasta.
■ Plenty of vegetables and fruits.
■ Simple desserts.

The most popular menu is barbecue—chicken and ribs, grilled vegetables, pasta salad, spicy coleslaw, and watermelon. Most people perceive barbecue as greasy and high-calorie, but LaViolette keeps the fat down at barbecue time by blanching the meats in advance.

She recommends a number of other tricks to provide tasty low-fat food. She blanches or steams vegetables, eliminates butter and oil in rice dishes, marinates foods in oil-free sauces, and uses spices and herbs to add interest. LaViolette also recommends cooking in a convection oven, which she finds requires less oil and cooks a bit faster than a regular oven.

One of the challenges of cooking on a large scale is having pots and pans big enough to handle the job if you cook for a crowd only occasionally. One solution may be to borrow the equipment from a local club, church, or other organization—or even arrange to use their kitchen.

Satisfying Soups

Soup is the ultimate feel-good food.

Chilled fruit soups, like this honeydew and canteloupe combination, make for creative summer desserts.

RIB-STICKING SOUPS

For main-dish soups, think stew, recommends James Peterson, author of *Splendid Soups*. Turn your favorite stew (maybe boeuf bourguignon) into a soup by thinning it with liquid and cutting up the meat and vegetables into smaller pieces. Peterson's other tips for adding oomph to an ordinary dish:

- Finish a vegetable soup by whisking in a flavorful paste or sauce, such as pistou—a purée of Parmesan cheese, garlic, tomato paste, basil, olive oil, and salt. Or chop fresh herbs and add them toward the end of the cooking time.
- Use an old European trick: Take a chunk of stale bread from a hearty country loaf (not the packaged variety), rub it with garlic, put it in the bowl, and pour the soup over it. For a variation, sprinkle croutons on top of the soup.
- Add any kind of cooked beans, cooked pasta, rice, or hominy to turn a soup into a meal.
- Enrich a thin soup by adding cream or plain yogurt. Whisk together until blended.
- Use a turkey carcass to make turkey broth, and let it be the basis for your favorite French onion soup. After it's ready, pour the soup into individual crocks, add croutons or pieces of stale bread, sprinkle with grated Gruyère cheese, and bake until the soup is heated through and the cheese is brown and bubbly.

Make a hearty winter soup by adding more liquid to your favorite meat stew. This version of boeuf bourguignon tastes as wonderful as it looks.

CHILL OUT WITH SOUP

"People tend to have strong reactions to cold soups," says Crescent Dragonwagon, co-owner of the Dairy Hollow House Country Inn in Eureka Springs, Arkansas, and author of *Dairy Hollow House Soup and Bread*: "They either love them or hate them."

She recommends chilled fruit soup—particularly the following delicious and beautiful approach—as the way to win the hearts of all. She purées five cups of ripe cantaloupe with three cups of white wine, adds a little honey and cinnamon, and sometimes buttermilk or a dollop of yogurt. When she uses honeydew melon instead of cantaloupe, she also adds a little Midori liqueur for flavor.

For an eye-catching presentation featuring both soups, Dragonwagon puts each purée in its own Pyrex measuring cup with a spout and then pours them simultaneously into two sides of a glass bowl. Topped with a mint leaf, the result is a showy mixture, half peach color and half green, that looks like it's right off the pages of a gourmet cooking magazine.

AN ASIAN TOUCH

Asian cooks prepare clear soup stocks with lots of flavor. To get it right, they use only fresh, meaty bones, water, and perhaps a piece of ginger or scallion, according to Bruce Cost, partner in the Big Bowl restaurants in Chicago. As the stock simmers, they skim

Aromatic flavorings such as lemon grass or basil can transform Asian shrimp soup into an exotic first course.

Smart Moves

- Freeze soup stock in ice cube trays, then pop the cubes into plastic bags. Use as needed.
- Let meat and chicken stocks sit, covered, in the refrigerator overnight. Then remove the fat that has congealed at the top.
- To thicken soups, purée some of the soup vegetables, then return them to the pot. Or add flour, beaten with a little of the soup liquid. Other thickening methods include adding oatmeal, rice, or barley, adding arrowroot or cornstarch mixed with a little water, and adding cream or yogurt.
- For a beautiful finish, garnish soups with vegetable cutouts, strips, or shreds, sprinkles of fresh herbs, puréed vegetables of contrasting colors, or tortilla strips or bread squares sautéed in oil.

it frequently to remove impurities. Here are some suggestions from Cost:

- Make a chicken stock and turn it into a Thai treat. Cook aromatics, such as chopped fresh lemon grass, chilies, and fresh ginger slices, in the stock for 20 minutes. Discard aromatics, then add Asian fish sauce (which you can find bottled in Asian markets), lemon juice, coconut milk, black pepper, and maybe some basil or cilantro leaves. Cook fresh shrimp or thinly sliced chicken breast in the stock just until it's done.
- For beef stock, cook well-rinsed beef bones in water to which you have added a few drops of dark soy sauce, light soy sauce, star anise, and maybe a cube or two of yellow rock sugar (a crystallized sugar you can buy at Asian markets). Again, skim often as the stock simmers. Strain the stock, then pour it over rice noodles and very thin slices of beef for a Vietnamese-style soup. The ingredients will cook in the hot broth.

CLAM CHOWDER: A NEW TAKE ON AN OLD FAVORITE

Chowder and heavy cream are almost synonymous. At the restaurant Kitchen Little in Mystic, Connecticut, though, owner Flo Klewin serves a clear broth clam chowder that makes a light beginning to a lunch or dinner. Klewin says it's even better if it sits overnight.

1 quart quahog or other hard shell clams with their own juice
1 medium-sized onion, chopped
2 tablespoons bacon drippings
4 medium-sized red potatoes
Water
Freshly ground black pepper
Fresh basil

1. Ask the fish vendor to open the **quahogs** for you and to give you the juice.
2. At home, place the clams over a strainer and collect

Individual crocks of French onion soup topped with bubbly cheese set the mood for a festive meal.

all the juice from them.
3. Bring the clam juice briefly to a boil. Strain all the foam and grit off the top of the juice, leaving behind the clean broth.
4. Chop the clams coarsely.
5. Sauté the **onion** in the **bacon drippings**.
6. Dice, but don't peel, the **potatoes** and add to the sautéed onion.
7. Add **water** to cover, the clam juice, freshly ground **pepper** to taste, and some fresh **basil**.
8. Add the chopped clams. Stir and bring to a boil for a few minutes.

Myth: *Using up old, wilted vegetables in your soup stock will give it better flavor.* **Fact:** *The fresher your ingredients, the better your stock will taste.*

9. Shut off heat and let the chowder sit a few minutes. If you are not serving it right away, refrigerate or ice immediately.

Clam chowder doesn't have to be rich and buttery to be delicious and satisfying. It just needs lots of clams.

True Stories

Stevie Cameron, editor of *Elm Street* magazine, cooks once a week with a Toronto organization called Out of the Cold. Through churches, synagogues, and professional groups, the organization's volunteers offer meals and services to the city's homeless. At St. Andrew's Church, Cameron and other volunteers prepare a full-course dinner, which begins with a nourishing soup course. The ingredients for Out of the Cold's corn chowder include five pounds of bacon, plus celery, potatoes, onions, chicken stock, 8 to 10 two-pound bags of frozen corn, and, as Cameron adds, "any amount of creamed corn that's in the pantry." Quantities are sufficient to feed as many as 200 people.

Star Salads

You can create salads with crowd appeal.

GREAT GREENS

Introduce new greens into your diet gradually. That's the advice from Tina Vandenheuvel and Antony John, owners of Soiled Reputations, an organic vegetable farm at Seabringville, Ontario. Their summer gourmet salad mix, served in Toronto restaurants, contains about 35 different

Beyond iceberg

You can add unusual texture and a refreshing crunch.

You can add unusual flavors that pique your taste buds and your curiosity.

You can add appealing color in a range of shades and shapes.

ingredients. About a third of the mix is green, pink, and red lettuces, while the remainder consists of herbs, cresses, and sprouts. Some other salad suggestions:

■ Mix roughly three-quarters of the sweet lettuces you already know and about one-quarter of the more unfamiliar greens. Experiment with textures, flavors, and colors. Try something curly, something bitter, something purple. Work up to a combination that's half familiar and half new. And always use a light vinaigrette to enhance, rather than mask, the flavors.

■ Add lots of herbs to your salads. Delicate herbs like chervil can be chopped coarsely and added generously. Strong herbs like rosemary or sage should be chopped finely and added sparsely.

■ Enhance your salads with different kinds of easy-to-grow basils, say Vandenheuvel and John. Also, consider adding chives, sorrel, hot and spicy Asian mustards, salad burnet, and beet greens. Be lavish with parsley, but always use the flat-leaved variety.

BUILDING A SALAD

In the fashionable resort town of Easthampton, New York, a salad from The Barefoot Contessa is a summer must. That's because the salads look as wonderful as they taste. Ina Garten, sometime salad-composer and author of *The Barefoot Contessa Cookbook*, says her salads often start with a

single, fresh ingredient around which she builds flavors. Here are some other salad approaches from this pro:

■ Take something traditional—think tuna salad, for instance—and make it more interesting. How about salmon? Grilling brings out its flavor, so use grilled salmon, chilled and broken into big flakes. Add celery (traditional) or fresh dill (new), and dress with raspberry vinaigrette to bring out the sweetness of the salmon. You have a whole new salad. Turn it into a main course by adding asparagus spears or another vegetable that won't overwhelm the subtle flavors.

■ Salad garnishes should relate to salad ingredients so your eye gets clued in to what your mouth is about to experience. Sprinkle mustard seeds on mustard chicken salad, sesame seeds on Asian vegetables with sesame oil, or dill seeds on shrimp salad with dill.

■ Dress your basic salad ingredient—chicken, pasta, or fish—when it's hot because it absorbs the dressing better, and then chill it. Just before serving the salad, add chilled vegetables and additional dressing. This will help prevent soggy, wilted vegetables.

Rosemary ——————
Dill ——————
Cilantro ——————

ALL ABOUT DRESSING

All dressings are not equal from a lettuce's point of view. Hearty greens, such as escarole, like a strong vinaigrette, perhaps one where you've added a shallot to the acid in the dressing, says Hallie Harron, executive chef at Quiessence Culinary Center in Phoenix, Arizona. Delicate greens, such as those contained in mesclun, prefer a more refined treatment.

In either case, start by putting your acid—lemon juice or vinegar—into a glass bowl or cup and adding salt. (Never sprinkle salt directly on the lettuce because it won't dissolve and will wilt the lettuce.) For a classic dressing, add oil in a ratio of three parts oil to one part acid, stirring briskly to combine.

When dressing tender greens, Harron recommends that you pour the

If you want to dress the salad ahead of time, add only the acid and place it in the refrigerator covered with a damp kitchen towel. Toss with the oil at the last minute. Oil, not vinegar, wilts the salad.

dressing around the sides of the bowl—not directly on the greens—and toss gently. The greens should look "almost as if they're jumping off the plate," says Harron, not like a saturated and soggy pile.

Harron also recommends trying something new now and then. Vary your dressings. Experiment with hazelnut and walnut oils, which go well with blue cheese. Add an Asian flavor by using half a teaspoon of sesame oil and garnishing the salad with toasted sesame seeds, or go for a Southwestern taste by using lime juice and seasoning with cumin and cilantro. Harron's favorite creamy dressing is the simplest to make: a bit of heavy cream thinned with lemon juice and seasoned with chives, then served on a buttery-flavored lettuce.

The Right Way

To keep a molded gelatin salad from sticking, spray the mold lightly with oil before adding the gelatin mix. Or try using less liquid when you prepare the gelatin. If the instructions say to use two cups, use a quarter-cup less.

Classic dressings use:

3
parts oil to

1
part acid (lemon juice or vinegar)

Smart Moves

■ Always taste salad dressing before you add it to the salad, and taste it again before serving it. You may want to add salt or pepper, or make other adjustments, once the dressing has mixed with the salad ingredients.

■ Adjust the proportions of vinegar and oil in a salad dressing according to their quality and character. If using a very heavy oil and a very light vinegar, for instance, add more vinegar. Conversely, if you're using a light oil and strong vinegar, you will need less vinegar.

■ If a dressing tastes too acidic, try adding more salt.

■ When entertaining, present your salad first, then dress it, so guests can enjoy the beauty of your arrangement.

SALAD COMBINATIONS

A salad will be more interesting and appealing if you combine ingredients with different colors, textures, and flavors, says Anne Willan, author of *Cook It Right* and many other cookbooks, and founder and president of LaVarenne Cooking School in France and at the Greenbrier in West Virginia. Examples? Consider, says Willan, the classic watercress (a dark green, peppery, tender leaf) and Belgian endive (a white, bland, crispy leaf), or beets with walnuts and lamb's lettuce, or red tomatoes with mozzarella cheese and basil.

Keep in mind that salad ingredients should complement—not clash with—one another. So, for instance, if you're adding meat to tender greens, it would make sense to julienne the meat very finely in order to maintain the delicate feeling of the salad. If you're working with chunks of meat—leftover pork, say—you might consider combining them with blanched root vegetables, which are similar in shape but provide variety in texture and taste.

Croutons are a good way to add last-minute crispi-

ness to a salad, says Willan. Choose from baked or fried, or use little cheese crackers cut in squares. Cheese itself—goat, feta, grated Cheddar, or Parmesan—can be the extra element that makes your salad special.

When adding leftover meat to salad, do as the French do: Marinate sliced meat first in a vinaigrette highly flavored with garlic, shallots, herbs, and chilies. Then combine the meat and the greens, and serve.

Tools of the Trade

When choosing a salad spinner, keep in mind that heavier-weight spinners are more stable than lightweight ones. And check to see if the model you're considering must be used in the sink rather than on the countertop.

The Bread Basket

Whether you're buying or baking, fresh bread is a treat.

BREAD BOUNTY

The choice of breads available now is exciting, but a bit overwhelming. Which kind of loaf do you want? Here are some suggestions from James MacGuire, the chef and owner of Le Passe-Partout Restaurant and Bakery in Montreal, where you can choose from nine different varieties of bread:

- When you're in sandwich-making mood, try a French baguette, a sourdough loaf, or a genuine rye bread.
- Genuine rye bread is a delicacy that is all too often overlooked by both bakers and consumers, says MacGuire. With your breakfast coffee, try thinly sliced rye with unsalted butter and bitter orange marmalade.
- For a tasty combination, there's walnut bread with French goat's cheese. Raisin bread, or raisin or walnut bread, also marry well with a blue cheese, such as Roquefort. It is delicious for breakfast, lunch, or a light meal.
- Use sourdough or country-style loaves in bread pudding to improve its texture. Adding different breads to the pudding is another way of enhancing its flavor.
- Another MacGuire tip: Use sourdough bread to make tasty croutons that do not turn to mush in onion soup.

BAKING BASICS

The secret to great home-baked bread? It's kneading, says Denis Weadon, director of technology for Five Roses Flour, Canada. According to Weadon, most people don't realize this, and they under-mix and underknead bread. For homemade breads, he recommends all-purpose and bread flours, beached or unbleached, according to personal taste. For storage, James MacGuire prefers the old-fashioned bread boxes. Avoid storing bread in the refrigerator because it will go stale quickly there.

Flour + Yeast + Salt + Water =

Flour. Canadian flour is great for breadmaking, says Denis Weadon. Because the flour is milled from red spring wheat, it has a high level of gluten (protein), an essential for breadmaking success. (Breadmakers compare gluten to rubber bands that keep carbon dioxide in the loaf as it's rising.) Be aware that, with a high gluten level, Canadian flour absorbs more liquid than U.S. or European flours. You may have to adjust your recipe depending on its source.

Yeast. Weadon recommends using bulk yeast instead of yeast in packets because the bulk variety will be fresher and perform better. A good source of bulk yeast is a health food store. Instant yeast gets going quickly, but it frequently stays on the shelf too long. It is advisable to check the date on the package before you buy the packaged variety. A long, slow rise is what your bread dough needs to produce the best results.

Smart Moves

- The more fat you add to bread, the more tender it will be. For sandwich bread, be sure to add milk, butter, or eggs. The fat from these ingredients will produce a soft bread that doesn't go stale quickly.
- Bread will have a finer crumb if you let it rise twice in the bowl before shaping it into a loaf.
- If you have a choice, make bread dough in a bread machine rather than a food processor. In order to get the dough out of the food processor, you have to add too much flour.

- Yeast needs sugar to feed on, but too much slows the action of the yeast. When making sweet breads, don't add more than half a cup of sugar per three cups of flour or your dough will take forever to rise. Instead, increase the amount of sweetening you put on the outside of the bread.
- Don't throw away leftover bread. Transform it. Stale bread is great for making French toast, croutons, bread crumbs, and a tasty and satisfying bread pudding.

The Right Way

The biggest mistake you can make with home-baked bread is adding too much flour while kneading. This produces a loaf that's dry, heavy, and crumbly. Resist the impulse to keep adding flour to the mix. Instead, lightly oil your kneading surface with a spray oil to keep the dough from sticking.

WHY BAKE?

Fabulous fresh bread is more widely available than ever before, yet people continue to bake their own. Not only that, they are interested in sharing recipes, experiences, and advice, judging by the rapid growth of Reggie Dwork's two Internet mailing lists about bread.

Dwork, a passionate home baker from San Jose, California, explains the appeal of bread baking: "It's therapeutic. If you've had a rough day, you can take it out on the bread. You can get your hands in it and feel like you're connected to something. It's something you produce totally from scratch, and you can put anything in it you want. You can learn from it, adjust it, and it will eventually work. And you don't get any additives and preservatives." Another plus: a home full of the inviting aroma of baking bread.

MUFFINS ARE THE PLACE TO START

Muffin baking is the amateur baker's best friend, according to Helene Siegel, author of the *Totally Muffins Cookbook*. That's because it's easy, doesn't require special equipment, and the results are always better than what you buy in the store. Hard to believe? Siegel suggests you try this classic buttermilk muffin recipe.

6 tablespoons butter, softened
$^2/_3$ cup sugar
2 eggs
1 cup buttermilk
2 teaspoons vanilla
2$^1/_2$ cups flour
$^1/_2$ teaspoon salt
1 teaspoon baking soda
2 teaspoons baking powder

1. Preheat oven to 400°F. Grease muffin tins or line with paper muffin cups.
2. Cream together **butter** and **sugar** until light and fluffy.
3. Add **eggs**, **buttermilk**, and **vanilla**. Beat lightly until blended.
4. In another bowl, stir together **flour**, **salt**, **baking soda**, and **baking powder.**
5. Add dry mixture to liquid and stir. Fill muffin cups to top. Bake 20 minutes, and cool 5 minutes.

If you want to experiment, try one of the following variations: (Add the additional ingredients as part of step 5.)
- Add 1$^1/_2$ cups fresh or frozen berries and $^1/_8$ teaspoon nutmeg.
- Add 1$^1/_2$ cups peeled and chopped apple and $^1/_2$ teaspoon cinnamon.
- Substitute brown sugar for white and add 1 cup chopped pecans and $^1/_2$ teaspoon each of cinnamon and nutmeg.

AS GOOD AS IT GETS

Bread machines have put wonderful home-baked bread within the reach of every home cook. Lora Brody, co-author of *Bread Machine Baking: Perfect Every Time* and creator of a line of products designed to give great machine-made results, says breaking some of the manufacturer's rules can actually help you get a better loaf. Here's how:
- Open the lid of the bread machine during the first knead cycle and correct the proportions of flour and water as necessary. Just like making bread by hand, you have to adjust the amounts according to

the condition of the ingredients. If the dough is dry and crumbling, add water by the tablespoon. If it is too wet, add flour the same way. Your goal is a soft, supple ball of dough.
- Use the machine as a kneader and let the dough rise once in the machine. Then remove it, shape it, give it a final rise, and bake it in the oven. You can tell it's done when the center of the bread registers 190°F to 200°F on an instant-read thermometer inserted into it.

Brody often takes the dough out of the machine after the first rise, puts it in

You can open the machine in the first knead cycle to adjust the proportions of flour and water.

a plastic bag, and stores it in the refrigerator overnight. This provides the long, slow, cool rise that allows the yeast to develop the flavor of the bread. Then she shapes the bread and bakes it in the oven.

Great Vegetables

It's time to get enthusiastic about veggies.

BROCCOLI AND FRIENDS

Many people tend to avoid Brussels sprouts, cauliflower, cabbage, and other cruciferous vegetables with very robust flavors. But these vegetables are good for you—they may even help prevent cancer. Deborah Madison, author of *Vegetarian Cooking for Everyone*, offers these ideas for renewing your acquaintance with crucifers:

■ Cook the vegetables quickly by blanching them in lots of boiling salted water in an uncovered pot. This will help get rid of the sulfurous compounds that give these vegetables a strong odor and a bitter taste.

■ Serve the crucifers with mustard vinaigrette or mustard butter. Other additions that work well are lemon zest, capers, and garlic.

■ Broccoli stems are an undiscovered treat. Peel the tough outside, thinly slice what's left, blanch for 30 seconds, and enjoy the delicate flavor.

■ Slice raw cauliflower very thinly and toss with diced green peppers and cucumbers, watercress, capers, and Spanish olives. The perfect dressing is a sherry vinaigrette.

■ For an Asian-style salad, mix raw bok choy with other cabbages and add a dressing of sesame oil, rice wine, orange peel, and ginger.

TURNIPS AND RUTABAGAS

Turnips and rutabagas are a favorite of chefs. Clifford Harrison, co-owner and chef of Bacchanalia Restaurant in Atlanta, cooks them in the French way, which caramelizes them and enhances their sweetness. His method:

Pare away the tough outer skin, then cut the vegetables into a medium-sized dice. Heat a small amount of olive oil in a large pan until hot but not smoking. Add the vegetables. Cook until they are brown, shaking the pan occasionally. Add a bit of sugar to encourage browning, if necessary. When brown, add salt and pepper to taste. Add chicken or beef stock to barely cover the vegetables, turn off the heat, cover the pan, let sit for 5 to 10 minutes until the vegetables puff up.

MAIN COURSE VEGGIES

Stuffed vegetables make great main courses that even pass muster with meat-lovers. At the Moosewood Restaurant in Ithaca, New York, eggplant, zucchini, and peppers stuffed with grains are favorite menu items. David Hirsch, Moosewood co-owner and author of *The Moosewood Restaurant Kitchen Garden*, suggests a few ways to go with these popular dishes:

■ If stuffing eggplant, slice it in half lengthwise, and braise it in some tomato juice or wine until it is almost soft. Then make a well in the center for the stuffing. If stuffing zucchini or peppers, cut them open and remove the seeds. Blanch peppers in boiling water for three to four minutes before stuffing. Zucchini does not have to be precooked before stuffing.

Add flavor to green vegetables with a creamy mustard vinaigrette, and contrasting color with several shakes of crushed rose peppercorns.

Three Ways to Make Zucchini a Main Dish

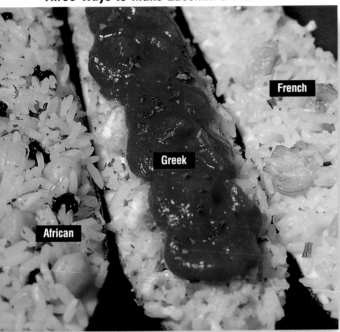

African

Greek

French

- Try an African-inspired stuffing. Make saffron rice, then add cooked chickpeas, currants, cumin, sautéed onions, and parsley.
- For a Greek version, combine cooked rice pilaf with feta cheese, eggs, cottage cheese, lots of fresh herbs, scallions, and bread crumbs. Top the stuffed vegetable with a light tomato sauce.
- For stuffing with a French flavor, mix rice with mushrooms that have been sautéed in wine and mixed with tarragon and Gruyère cheese.

To cook any of the stuffed vegetables, place them in a baking pan, add a little liquid, cover tightly, and bake at 350°F until heated all the way through, from 10 to 30 minutes, depending on the size of the vegetable. Or, for a real feast, stuff some peppers, eggplant, and zucchini with different fillings and sample all of them.

FORMING A CO-OP

If you want the freshest produce—organic, if possible—you should consider getting together with like-minded people to set up your own co-op. So says Jacynthe Godard, who runs the Montreal organic food supplier, Distribue-Vie.

Godard's company provides year-round food supplies to some 20 co-ops. In season, Distribue-Vie guarantees customers fresh Quebec and Ontario produce. Throughout the year, the company goes to Canadian suppliers first. Only when necessary does the company buy from suppliers in the United States. All Distribue-Vie produce, domestic or American, is organic, which means it is grown without pesticides on farms that practice crop rotation and other sound agricultural methods.

Godard offers this advice to those who are thinking about forming their own co-op. Organize a group of 6 to 10 families. The bigger, the better. As part of a big group, you can always insist on better service.

Dividing up produce is easier with a large group. Most suppliers require a minimum purchase of one case. A case of lettuce has 24 heads, far too generous for a small group to consume. A large group can order fresh produce more often, every week instead of every two weeks. As a result, you'll enjoy fresher food, and you won't have to throw away any excess that might go bad.

Always make sure that your co-op group can satisfy credit requirements, recommends Godard. Bear in mind that a typical organic food order for 6 to 10 families might cost more than $1,000 every two weeks.

Godard also points out that co-ops may also purchase other certified products such as soya and dairy products.

Myth: *Raw vegetables are healthier for you than those that are cooked.* **Fact:** *The nutrients in some vegetables, like carrots, become more available to the body after cooking. And if fresh vegetables are stored for a long time or overcooked, they may have fewer nutrients than frozen vegetables.*

The Right Way

Many experts offer advice on how to dice an onion. Here's one of the easiest:

- Peel the onion and stand it upright on the root end. Make parallel deep cuts into the onion, being careful not to cut completely through the base.

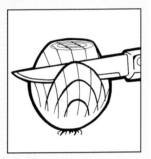

- Hold the onion firmly and turn it a quarter turn. Make another set of parallel deep cuts, close together if you want tiny dice and further apart if you want larger pieces or chunks.

- Still holding the onion firmly, turn it on its side and slice it. You'll end up with perfect squares of onion.

Beans and Grains

Beans and grains are perfect partners or super solo.

THE BEAN/GRAIN CONNECTION

Beans and grains are a potent source of good nutrition, and they encourage creative cooking because you can experiment with so many delicious combinations of tastes and textures.

According to Dr. James Anderson, professor of medicine and clinical nutrition at the University of Kentucky, "Mixing and matching foods is important to our diets because we get a variety of nutrients from a range of different foods. They can have benefits we don't even recognize."

One bean benefit: oligosaccharides, the sugars from beans that cause flatulence, also generate health-promoting bacteria in the colon, says Anderson. These bacteria help to preserve colon function and may protect against cancer.

The Right Way

Soaking beans softens them so that they cook more evenly. Here are two soaking methods:
Quick hot soak: Cover beans with water and boil them for two minutes. Put a lid on the pot and soak for one to four hours before cooking.
Overnight cold soak: Cover the beans with room-temperature water and allow to sit overnight (12 hours or more).

After soaking with either method, be sure to discard the soaking water and cover the beans with fresh water for cooking.

Black bean
Red kidney bean
Pinto bean
Black-eyed pea
Adzuki bean
Green split pea
Lentil
Fava bean
Chickpea
Lima bean

BEAN BONANZA

Beans give new meaning to the old saying that variety is the spice of life. There are dozens of beans currently available in the markets, including some old-fashioned varieties that have been reintroduced and dubbed "heirloom" beans. The chart below describes some of your choices.

Type of Bean	Appearance	Flavor	Common Use
Pinto	Medium size, brown with pink streaks. Loses streaks when cooked.	Full-bodied, earthy	Refried beans and other Mexican and South American dishes. Stews and soups.
Lentil	Small, flat. Green, brown, pink varieties.	Mild	Soups, casseroles, salads.
Black-eyed pea	Smallish oval, with distinctive black spot.	Mild, sweet	Rice and beans, casseroles, salads.
Great Northern	Flat, oval, white.	Mild	Soups, stews, baked dishes, and mixed with other varieties.
Adzuki	Small, dark red.	Sweet, delicate	Asian cuisine. Good with rice, or in sweet dessert sauce.
Red kidney	Kidney-shaped, large, red.	Bland	New Orleans red bean dishes and Southwestern chili.
Split pea	Small, with one round side and one flat. Green, yellow varieties.	Earthy	Soups. Good alone or mixed with other beans.
Fava (Broad beans)	Large, flat ovals, with nutty brown color.	Rich, meaty	Purées.
Chickpea (Garbanzo)	Small, round, white.	Mild	Middle Eastern cuisine, bean salads.
Black (Turtle beans)	Pea shape, small, black.	Full, earthy	Caribbean and South American cuisine. Black bean soup. Adds color to salads.

Buckwheat

Posole

Basmati rice

Wild rice

Quinoa

GREAT GRAINS

Want to get out of the white rice rut? Nothing could be easier. Experiment with wild rice, quinoa, buckwheat, and posole, the top recommendations from Rebecca Wood, author of *The Splendid Grain* and *The Revised Whole Foods Encyclopedia*.

■ Wild rice is prized for its intense flavor, which Wood likes in pilafs and soup. She combines wild rice with wild mushrooms for a totally wild soup.

■ Quinoa, the sacred grain of the Incas, is versatile, quick-cooking, and, nutritionally, a whole protein. The trick: It must be well-rinsed before using or it will have a bitter flavor. Try it in place of rice in pilafs, salads, casseroles, or even pudding.

■ Buckwheat is the most "comforting" of these grains, says Wood. It's great served with milk, butter, and honey for a winter breakfast, and you also can form leftovers into croquettes and pan-fry or grill them.

■ Posole, also known as hominy, can be purchased dried, frozen, or canned. Dried posole is soaked before using, the way beans are. Wood likes the distinctive flavor and texture of posole when it is combined with beans, cooked in a soup with squash and chilies, or as a pasta replacement in minestrone soup. When posole is ground, it's known as hominy grits, a staple of Southern cooking in the United States.

BEAN AND GRAIN SALADS

Your possibilities are really limited only by your imagination when it comes to cold bean and grain salads. Joanne Weir, author of *Beans and Rice* in the Williams-Sonoma Kitchen Library, shares some of her favorites. All these salads can be served chilled or at room temperature, with a vinaigrette dressing. Bean salads soak up a lot of dressing, so taste before serving. You may want to fold in some additional vinaigrette.

Grains and shellfish make good salad partners. You might want to experiment with flavored rice, such as brown, basmati, or jasmine, combined with cooked scallops or shrimp. Or, for a slightly crunchier taste, substitute millet for the rice or add chopped raw vegetables.

Cooked black beans and cooked corn niblets mixed with diced raw green, red, and yellow peppers and chopped red onions produce a bean salad bursting with flavor and color.

A South-of-France salad is built around cooked chickpeas, diced red onions, pitted black olives, and lots of chopped fresh herbs—oregano, basil, chives, and rosemary, for instance.

A salad with a Mediterranean flair combines cooked lentils, chopped raw red peppers, chopped mint, and crumbled feta cheese.

Mix and Match

Dana Parkes, promotions coordinator for the Ontario Bean Producers' Marketing Board in London, Ontario, points out that Canada is one of the world's major bean producers, exporting its crop to more than 70 countries. Parkes says not to be too concerned about using the exact bean a recipe calls for because many beans are interchangeable. Either dried lima beans or Great Northern beans, for example, can be used in the same recipes. So can different varieties of small white beans, sometimes called navy beans or pea beans.

True Stories

At the House of Commons' parliamentary restaurant in Ottawa, Executive Chef Judson Simpson uses different beans to prepare Harvest Vegetable Phyllo Purses with Skillet Browned Leeks and Plum Tomatoes:

½ cup diced celery
½ cup diced yellow pepper
1 cup sliced mushrooms
1½ cups broccoli fleurettes
1½ cups cauliflower fleurettes
½ cup diced red onion

1 tsp extra virgin olive oil
1 cup cooked Adzuki beans
1 cup cooked red lentils
1½ cups cooked chick peas
2 tbsp fresh chopped basil
1 tbsp fresh chopped oregano
16 oz (1 package) phyllo pastry
Black pepper, to taste
No-stick spray

For the leeks and tomatoes:
1 tsp extra virgin olive oil
2 leeks, cut in half, sliced
8 medium plum tomatoes, cut in half, sliced

1. Sauté the vegetables together in **olive oil** until softened. Add the **beans**, **lentils**, **chick peas**, **basil**, **oregano**, and **black pepper**. Heat this bean and vegetable mixture thoroughly and put it in reserve.
2. Cut the **phyllo** into 8-inch circles and layer four sheets thick by spraying each layer lightly with no-stick before stacking.
3. Place 1 cup of the vegetable/bean mixture in the center of each phyllo round. Fold like a turnover. With the edges pointing up, gather the edges toward the middle to form a purse. Bake on a cookie sheet sprayed lightly with no-stick at 350°F for 10 to 15 minutes.
4. In a sauté pan, heat the remaining olive oil and shallow fry the **leeks** until light brown. Add the **tomatoes** and cook until softened. Season with salt and black pepper.
5. To serve, place some of the leeks and tomatoes in the center of the plate and top with the phyllo purse. Garnish with basil.

From Angel Hair to Ziti

Pasta, dressed in sauces from delicate to hearty, makes a perfect meal.

COOKING BASICS

Sticky pasta. Mushy pasta. Crunchy pasta. Oily pasta. Sauce on the plate, pasta on the fork. How can such a seemingly simple dish go so wrong? There are some basic guidelines that will help you produce perfect pasta every time. Jay Sparks, executive chef with D'Amico and Partners in Minneapolis/St. Paul, Minnesota, recommends trying the following:

■ If you can, use artisan (handmade but packaged) dry pastas rather than the commercial types you find in most supermarkets. The artisan brands, often available in gourmet food shops, have lots of indentations that hold the sauce better.

■ When cooking pasta, use a large pot with lots of water—about five to six quarts per pound of pasta. Crowding too much pasta into a small pot with not enough water makes the pasta sticky. Don't add oil to the water, but do add salt along with the pasta once the water has come to a full boil.

■ Never rinse your pasta after cooking. But do save some of the pasta water. If your sauce is too dry or too thin, a little pasta water can always come to the rescue.

■ When using fresh pasta, use butter or cream in the sauce, not olive oil. Fresh pasta absorbs fats, and olive oil gives it a peculiar texture. Olive oil is the fat of choice for dry pasta, though.

Sparks says the biggest problem for some pasta cooks is trying to be too interesting. A good antidote: When making sauces, stick to two or three ingredients. "They'll work a lot better than a dozen," he reassures. One of his new favorite sauces uses grapefruit juice with a sprig of rosemary, reduced until it's almost a glaze, with butter melted in. This, combined with seared sea scallops (slice them if they're too thick) and some chopped fresh chives, makes a light and different sauce for linguine or tagliorini.

LAST-MINUTE MEAL

The beauty of pasta is that, though it can be made in minutes, it's "happy, heart-warming food," says Biba Caggiano, owner of Biba, a restaurant in Sacramento, California, and author of six cookbooks. She points out that a pantry stocked with a few essentials—spaghetti, canned tomatoes, garlic, anchovies, sun-dried tomatoes, olives, capers, canned tuna, and olive paste—along with some fresh vegetables and pancetta or prosciutto, can yield a number of quick, family-pleasing main dishes.

Using these ingredients, Caggiano suggests you try any of the following sauces to toss with the pasta:

■ Sauté a chopped onion in oil and butter, then combine with a can of tuna, a few anchovy fillets, chopped garlic, white wine, red pepper flakes, and chopped parsley.

■ Vary the dish by adding canned Italian plum tomatoes, crushed, and a tablespoon of bottled black olive paste.

■ Mix olive paste, sun-dried tomatoes, chopped garlic, and some good extra-virgin olive oil.

■ Combine sun-dried and canned Italian plum tomatoes in a pan where chopped garlic has been sautéed briefly and then removed. Season with hot red pepper flakes. Add coarsely chopped fresh arugula and mix it in.

■ Cook pancetta briefly, then add a few anchovy fillets, chopped garlic, and hot red pepper flakes. Add a few tablespoons of bread crumbs and cook briefly until they are brown (about 10 seconds).

■ Make a quick marinara sauce using chopped fresh garlic, canned

Cook pasta in lots of boiling water —five to six quarts per pound of pasta.

GOT TEN MINUTES? MAKE YOUR OWN!

It's quick and easy to make your own pasta if you have flour, eggs, a rolling pin, and a flat surface. The pasta will cook in just a minute or two in a pot of rapidly boiling water, providing almost instant satisfaction.

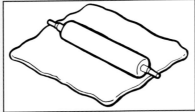

Beat three eggs in a large mixing bowl and sift in two cups unbleached all-purpose flour, stirring constantly until it forms a soft ball.

Put the dough on a lightly floured surface and knead until smooth and firm. Cut into six pieces, dust with flour, and roll into thin rec-

tangles. Using a sharp knife or pastry wheel, cut each sheet of dough into ribbons, hanging each batch on a drying rack as you go along.

Italian plum tomatoes, salt and pepper, and hot red pepper flakes. Simmer for 10 minutes, adding fresh or dried oregano and fresh basil leaves during the last few minutes of cooking.

PASTA ASIAN-STYLE

Asian noodles are an everyday staple with millions of people the world over. Now they are becoming as common in supermarkets as their Italian counterparts. These Asian "pastas" are made from rice, wheat, buckwheat, mung bean, pea, mountain yam, and even corn. You can buy them fresh or dried, raw or cooked, and in sheets like dumpling and egg roll wrappers and rice wraps.

Stephen Wong, food columnist for *The Vancouver Sun,* and Bill Jones, a chef-consultant, are co-authors of *New World Noodles,* which tells you how to turn this ingredient into one-pan dinners, tasty side dishes, healthy soups and salads. Wong recommends starting with the familiar:
- Choose a recipe similar to a noodle dish you may

already have enjoyed at a noodle house. For an authentic Asian flavor, stock up on soy and fish sauces, rice wine, rice vinegar, toasted sesame oil, chili pastes and red pepper flakes. Bottled sauces such as oyster sauce, blackbean sauce, curry sauce, and plum sauce help establish the key character of a dish. For best results, enliven prepared sauces with fresh herbs and aromatics like fresh ginger, garlic, and scallions.
- Try out different kinds of noodles. Generally, they cook faster than pasta, so watch them carefully to avoid overcooking. Soak most dried rice noodles briefly in hot water before adding them to stir fries or salads. To prevent noodles from sticking together, drizzle noodles with a dash of oil or rinse thoroughly in cold water.
- If your supermarket lacks a variety of noodles, go to an Asian market. Or, do what many Asian cooks do, and substitute pasta for noodles. After all, they are cut from the same cloth, as it were.

PASTA WITH A DIFFERENCE

What would happen if you threw away all your traditional notions of pasta? Let yourself think beyond spaghetti and marinara sauce? That's the challenge that was given to Mary Jane Wilan, and the result was *Pasta Exotica,* a collection of unusual pasta recipes that she created with Denice Skrepcinski. The basic approach, says Wilan, was "to let pasta itself be the star rather than having the sauces be the star." One of Wilan's favorites: bumble-bee lasagna, a black-and-yellow dish made by alternating pasta flavored

with squid ink and pasta flavored with saffron or dried Cheddar cheese.

Another result of Wilan's fun new look at pasta is pasta desserts. She deep-fries fresh raspberry-flavored pasta in little nests, using a long-handled basket usually used to create potato baskets. Then she fills the nests with fresh fruit or ice cream.

Wilan creates her pastas from scratch—a great family activity. Perhaps making pasta will lead a family to explore its ethnic culinary heritage, and create dishes like an East Indian sewain (sweet noodle dish) or a Jewish kugel (noodle pudding).

Tools of the Trade

Pasta pot with colander inside

Pasta serving utensil

Grilling to Perfection

How can you get great grilled flavor on your home barbecue?

THE BEST STEAKS

Steaks are often the centerpiece of a festive meal, so you want to be sure of exceptional results.

- Choose steaks that are at least 1 to 1½ inches thick, advises Dwayne Ennest, executive chef at the River Café on Prince Island in Calgary. This allows you to sear them on the outside while they stay juicy on the inside.
- Bypass lean cuts, such as round steak—they toughen on the grill. Instead, look for well-marbled steaks, which stay juicy and tender. Ennest's favorites are rib eye, tenderloin, strip loin, T-bone, and porterhouse.
- Before grilling, season steaks overnight. Ennest rubs in a special mix of herbs before letting the steaks marinate.
- Make sure the fire is white hot. If not, steaks steam rather than grill. Flip once—too much handling toughens the meat.
- Test for doneness using the hand test. If the center of the steak is soft, like the heel of your thumb, it's rare, says Ennest. If it is semi-firm, like the center of your palm, the steak is medium. If it's firm, like the tip of your finger, your steak is well done.

Quick Tricks

Charcoal Savers
Most folks use too much charcoal. Measure out just enough briquettes to extend one inch beyond the food. Mound the briquettes in the center and light. When coals are ready for cooking, spread them out, using tongs.

Is It Hot Yet?
To gauge hotness, place your hand over the grill. If you can only hold it there two seconds, the fire is hot; four seconds, medium; six seconds, low. Steaks, thin chops, and boneless chicken breasts should be grilled over a hot fire, and thick meats and chicken over medium heat.

Ready, Aim, Fire
Fire flare-ups can char meat. Douse flames quickly with a light spritz sprayed from a toy water pistol or a plant sprayer.

BARBECUED AND GRILLED TO PERFECTION

Before barbecuing beef ribs, Chef Stephan Dumas of Montreal's La Queue de Cheval Restaurant prepares a marinade of molasses, ketchup, tabasco sauce, brown sugar, brandy, Worcestershire sauce, crushed garlic, Dijon mustard, and pepper. After the ribs have marinated for 24 hours, Dumas places them over a fire, taking care not to overcook or burn, and serves them with a sauce made from the same ingredients, which has been freshly cooked.

For grilled pork chops, Dumas uses thick milk-fed chops from Quebec's Charlevoix region. His 24-hour marinade is made with olive oil, herbs, a little balsamic vinegar, and a dash of brandy. Dumas grills the chops over a medium fire, about five per side, and serves them with a reduction of balsamic vinegar, sugar, tomato, demiglace, spices, and brandy.

FLAVORING THE FIRE

For deep, smoky flavor, add hardwood or fruitwood chips to your fire. Soak them in water for two minutes and place on top of the briquettes just after lighting. For fresh, spicy taste add herbs, dried grapevines, corn cobs, fruit peels, or garlic. Soak them in water for two minutes, but wait until you're ready to cook before tossing them on coals. If using a gas grill, place flavor boosters on heavy-duty aluminum foil and set directly on coals.

Food	Hardwood and Fruitwood Chips (One handful)	Dried Corn Cobs and Grapevines (Use 4 dried cobs, 1 cup grapevines)	Herbs and Garlic (Use 2 tablespoons dried herbs, 1 cup fresh herbs, 4 to 6 cloves garlic)	Fruit Peels (1 to 2 cups)
Beef	Hickory, mesquite, oak	Corn cobs, grapevines	Basil, garlic, marjoram, rosemary, thyme	Lemon peels
Lamb	Oak, apple, cherry	Grapevines	Garlic, marjoram, mint, parsley, rosemary	Lemon & orange peels
Pork	Hickory, mesquite, oak, alder, apple, cherry	Corn cobs, grapevines	Cilantro, garlic, marjoram, rosemary, sage, thyme	Lemon & orange peels
Poultry	Hickory, mesquite, oak, alder, apple, cherry	Corn cobs	Garlic, marjoram, oregano, parsley, rosemary, sage, thyme, tarragon	Lemon peels

Tools of the Trade

Spring-loaded tongs. Restaurant-style tongs allow you to pick up food without piercing it and losing the juices. Plus, they spring back after every use, which is why they're the choice of the pros. Choose strong tongs that can handle heavy items without bending and that spring back automatically after each use.

WONDERFUL CHICKEN

To get deep, rich flavor, marinate chicken at least three hours and preferably overnight, says David Friedman, the man behind the succulent rotisserie chicken served at Boston Market. If a chicken marinates for less time, the flavor doesn't reach deep down into the meat.

"For rotisserie chicken, dry spice rubs and barbecue rubs work great," says Friedman, who is a graduate of the Culinary Institute of America. Delicate herbs are fine for smaller, individual pieces, but not enough to flavor a whole bird.

For golden brown color and crispy skin, Friedman suggests using fruit juice marinades. In addition to flavor, they add natural sugar for extra browning and tenderize the bird by breaking down the proteins in the meat.

If you're grilling with a rotisserie, you don't have to baste, because the bird bastes itself as it turns on the spit. But do truss the bird tightly, securing the legs and wings, so the whole bird turns evenly.

Grill whole chickens on a spit over a medium fire and direct heat so they don't burn. A 2½-pound bird needs about 70 minutes on the spit. Remove it from the grill and let it rest at least 10 minutes before carving and serving.

Myth: *Place food on the grill as soon as the flames have died down.* **Fact:** *That's too soon. Wait a little longer, until coals are white hot.*

WHAT WENT WRONG WITH MY BARBECUE?

If your meat doesn't taste grilled, your fire probably isn't hot enough, according to Chris Schlesinger and John Willoughby, authors of *Licensed to Grill*. That distinctive, old-fashioned flavor comes from the char created on the food's surface by a very hot fire.

If your fire doesn't get hot enough no matter how many briquettes you use, Schlesinger, who is also the proprietor of the famous East Coast Grill in Cambridge, Massachusetts, and Willoughby recommend hardwood charcoal. It's easier to start and burns hotter and longer than regular charcoal. Look for it in your local hardware store.

Steak may taste steamed and smoky if it is cooked in a covered grill. Despite what some manufacturers advise, Schlesinger and Willoughby recommend that you never cover the grill when cooking meat over direct heat. The fat can burn and smoke, trapping off-flavors.

If your problem is that your food is cooking too fast or burning, switch to indirect heat. Remove the food and grate. Using long-handled tongs, push the coals to one side of the grill. Place a foil drip pan on the other. Place the food on the grate over the pan, and continue cooking until done. If the fire gets cold before your food is fully cooked, you can transfer it to a 350°F oven to finish.

Seafood Sensations

**You can hook
some expert ideas
for serving fish.**

FRESH FISH

A good fish dish starts at the fish market. "Very fresh is more important than pink peppercorns or other exotic treatments," says Ann Chandonnet, food historian and author of *Alaska Heritage Seafood Cookbook*. She advises that finding a fish merchant you can trust is the key to overcoming the fear a lot of people have about cooking fish.

Look for whole fish that have glossy surfaces and clear eyes, says Chandonnet. Avoid fish that have bruises or a dull surface. A good market will have a thin barrier (usually a plastic wrap) between the ice and the fish so the top layer of the fish doesn't begin to freeze.

Chandonnet advises that you begin with a simple recipe that lets you appreciate the taste of the fresh fish. For example, rub the fish lightly with olive oil, drizzle a tablespoon of lemon juice over it, and bake it in an ovenproof dish in an oven preheated to 400-450°F. You can determine the cooking time by measuring the fish at its thickest point and baking for 10 minutes per inch. Then you can start to vary the recipe. "The slightest gradations of seasonings can change things," she points out. "If you start with a few excellent ingredients, then you don't need

to worry about the exotic."
- Add some chopped, fresh herbs.
- Substitute butter for half the olive oil in a recipe.
- Replace some of the lemon with balsamic vinegar.

One West Coast tribe perfected this approach and could prepare fish 200 different ways for a potlatch (festival). Each of their recipes involved just a slight adjustment so that, for instance, they might have a basic smoked salmon, a half-smoked salmon, a poached, half-smoked salmon broiled on sticks near the fire, and a salmon in seaweed broth.

PLANKED FISH

Cooking fish on a wooden plank over a fire is a delicious culinary tradition of West Coast native peoples. One way to do it: Go to a lumberyard and purchase a sanded, untreated cedar plank large enough to hold the fish you want to cook. Soak the plank in water four to six hours or overnight. Place the fish on it, and put the plank over a grill or fire, far enough away from the heat so the wood doesn't burn. An easier alternative: Buy a plank that can go into the oven.

Sharon Parker, co-founder of Chinook Planks, a company that designs and markets gourmet cookware,

Fish that is really fresh has clear eyes and a glossy surface.

wants to make plank cooking possible in the average kitchen. Her planks, cedar or alder wood, contain metal rods that stabilize the wood and keep it from splitting or warping when heated. Cedar imparts a subtle, smoky flavor to the fish and smells wonderful during cooking. Alder gives

a vanilla flavor and is not as fragrant.

You place the plank in the middle to upper section of the oven and roast fish at 350°F until done. A scooped-out section in the middle of the plank holds any juices that accumulate during cooking.

Smart Moves

When buying and preparing seafood, follow these procedures from Health Canada and the Canadian Food Inspection Agency:
- Buy seafood that has been kept properly chilled.
- Refrigerate seafood immediately, and keep at 40°F or less.
- Use fresh seafood within three days of purchase. Before use, examine it carefully and, if in doubt, discard it.
- Keep raw seafood separate from other foods during storage and preparation. Use separate cutting boards for fish and meat. After use, clean and sanitize boards, utensils, and containers.

True Stories

Ann Chandonnet's perusal of the journals of the men who accompanied Captain Cook on his explorations of Alaska in 1778 revealed that one man was served halibut with blueberry sauce when he visited a town at the tip of the Aleutians. It seems that mankind's search for interesting food combinations is as universal and long-standing as its search for new territories.

SOPHISTICATED FISH

The Oyster Bar Restaurant at Grand Central Terminal in New York City has been satisfying the appetites of the city's fish lovers for decades. As tastes change, so do the restaurant's recipes. One of the sell-out dishes today, says the Oyster Bar's executive chef and fish buyer, Sandy Ingber, is Pompadour of black sea bass—sea bass fillet surrounded by thinly sliced Idaho potatoes, pan-seared in butter, and served with a red wine beurre blanc on a bed of sautéed leeks garnished with chives. The small, delicate fish fillet gets steamed while the potatoes get brown and crispy.

Another, simpler Oyster Bar favorite is the lobster club sandwich. A 1½-pound steamed lobster is taken out of the shell, sliced, and placed on sourdough bread with a cayenne mayonnaise dressing. Keeping it company on the plate are sweet potato chips and jicama slaw. Similarly uncomplicated and popular is Caesar salad with jumbo lump blue crab meat and jumbo shrimp. Seasonal dishes like shad and shad roe, soft-shell crabs, and stone crabs fly out of the Oyster Bar kitchen, too.

When chef Ingber is cooking fish at home, he grills it. Firm fish can be placed right on the grill. For flaky fish, use a rack or place fish on aluminum foil that's been lightly oiled and punched with holes. Ingber's advice for the most satisfying results: Don't overcook fish, the most common mistake that home cooks make.

FARM-RAISED FISH

Aquaculture, or fish farming, is expanding in Canada. Fish farmers raise 50 different species of shellfish and finfish, says David Conley of Fisheries and Oceans Canada. Farmed products represent 22 percent of Canada's fish production. And that proportion is increasing. In British Columbia, the production of farmed salmon now exceeds the wild catch. Soon other farmed species, such as haddock, halibut, eels, and stripped bass will appear on the market.

Farmers grow seafood and fish in highly controlled conditions, says Sharon Pettipas, the planning and development officer of the Nova Scotia Department of Fisheries and Aquaculture. The provinces license fish farmers and lease freshwater and marine sites, except in the East where the federal government has jurisdiction. Once a farmer has obtained a lease, the site undergoes environmental assessment and must be checked by the Coast Guard to ensure that the farm will not interfere with commercial or recreational boating activity. During the farming operation, federal and provincial inspectors monitor water quality and do sediment testing. The Canada Food Inspection Agency checks the farm products to ensure they are safe.

With fast processing techniques, farmed products can be shipped to markets and restaurants within 24 to 48 hours. As Sharon Pettipas points out, year-round availability of farmed fish is a boon to consumers. Pettipas chooses red-fleshed steelhead trout. She bakes it in the oven and serves an accompanying dill sauce. She adds that this farm fish is just as delicious pan-fried or barbecued.

FATTY AND NON-FATTY FISH

Some fish, including cod, halibut, and red snapper, are lean, with less than 2 percent fat. Other types, including salmon, lake trout, and bluefish, have a fat content of 6 percent or more. Fatty fish are an excellent source of omega-3 long-chain fatty acids, which seem to help prevent blood clots, and lower cholesterol and triglycerides.

Cod   **Salmon**

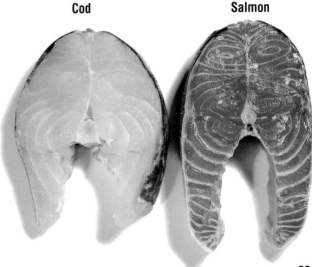

Prime Picks

Specialty produce invites special attention.

FRESH IS BEST

Whenever possible, North America's best chefs are serving organic produce. The Farm at South Mountain, an organic farm in Phoenix, Arizona, supplies fine local restaurants. Owner Wayne Smith says the chef's favorites include:

- Mesclun—a mixture of greens (usually 12) chosen for taste, color, aroma, and texture.
- Edible weeds, such as dandelion and lamb's quarter.
- Arugula and radicchio.
- Pea tendrils (the end of the pea plant that grasps the trellis).
- Edible flowers, such as Johnny-jump-up, nasturtium, and calendula.
- Baby vegetables.
- Artichoke leaves (similar to celery, says Smith).
- Tomatoes of all varieties—The Farm sells 37 varieties of tomatoes, including many varieties that have been around for 50 years or longer.

Smart Moves

- If you're buying heirloom or exotic fruit for the first time, buy a small quantity of anything unfamiliar until you discover which are your favorites.
- Store heirloom apples in the refrigerator, where they will stay firm and fresh longer.

OLD IS NEW

Heirloom fruits—those dating back to 1900—are making a comeback. Like heirloom quilts, each type is prized for its unique character, history, and name. Some heirloom fruits never go out of fashion. The McIntosh apple, discovered in an orchard in Dundas County, Ontario, about 200 years ago, remains one of North America's most popular eating apples. Emile Janssens of Campina Orchard in Parkhill, Ontario, grows about 500 different varieties of apples. He explains that when it comes to apples, many of the old varieties were chance seedlings, the results of settlers' planting seeds they brought from overseas or from nature's own seeding process. Apple trees grown from seeds tend to vary from the parent tree. A seedling from a McIntosh won't be a McIntosh. It'll be something different. Therefore, orchards use the techniques of grafting or budding to reproduce particular varieties and keep them available for new generations of fruit lovers.

Just the names of the heirloom apples are good enough to munch on:

- Ben Davis. A Janssens's favorite, this red apple was grown in England about 100 years ago. The widely grown Cortland is a cross of the Ben Davis

Delicate Korean melon is a delicious way to begin or end a meal.

and McIntosh varieties.
- Cox Orange Pippin. A favorite in England where it originated, this reddish-orange apple is good for eating.
- Lady Apis. Popular in France more than 200 years ago, Lady Apis was used as toiletry. Aristocratic ladies carried the apple in their drawstring purses because they loved its perfumed scent.
- Northern Spy. Thought by some to be the best pie apple ever grown, this apple was discovered in 1800 in New York State.
- Winter Banana. A yellow ornamental apple, it produces a banana aroma when it gets overripe.

Edible weeds: You can find delicious food in the great outdoors

Clover
Eat raw, or use dry for tea.

Chickweed
Eat raw or slightly cooked.

Dandelion
Eat greens raw and roots cooked.

Knotweed
Eat tuber and young shoots cooked.

Lamb's quarter
Eat leaves raw and seeds raw or cooked.

EXOTIC FRUITS

In the mood for some sweet sop ice? How about fruit salad with jack fruit? Then the island of Maui is the place to go. Chuck and Lilly Boerner run ONO Organic Farms, a tropical fruit and coffee family farm on this Hawaiian island, and supply health food stores and gourmet restaurants with the unusual fruits they grow. Chuck Boerner explains that papayas, bananas, avocados, and coffee are the farm's main products, but that interest in the exotic fruits is growing. Many of the fruits originated in Central America or Indonesia and are fairly new to Hawaii. These unusual products are also slowly making their way to the mainland, and may be available in specialty stores during certain times of the year. If the experience of the past holds true, they may soon be as familiar as the tropical fruits people have come to take for granted, such as pineapples and bananas.

Mangos are a tasty treat peeled and eaten whole, chunked into salads, or puréed and frozen as sorbet.

Fruit	Description	When Available
Star apple	Looks and tastes like a fig, but with the texture of a persimmon. When cut in half, the inside has a star shape.	February–May
Sweet sop	Red and white exterior. White flesh with black seeds. Tastes like and has the consistency of a sweet vanilla custard.	September
Rollenia deliciosa	Same family as the sweet sop. Bright yellow when ripe, with big knobs on the outside.	September
Sour sop	White flesh, dark seeds, green skin with small spines. Very tart, custard consistency.	May–July
Egg fruit	Bright yellow or yellow-orange exterior. Looks like the yolk of a hard-boiled egg.	September
Pumpkin cherry	Rose color, shaped like a miniature pumpkin. Single stone like a cherry.	August
White sapote	Green exterior. Taste and texture like a pear.	May–July
Jack fruit	Huge (12 to 15 pounds), oval, with golden, crunchy flesh.	Year-round

FRUIT, HOT OR COLD

Fresh fruit simply treated is pure ambrosia. Abby Mandel, author of *Celebrating the Midwestern Table*, suggests the following taste treats:

■ Make fruit sorbet for a low-calorie, refreshing, and delicious dessert. Take fruits in season—berries, sliced peaches, apricots, or bananas—and freeze in a single layer on a cookie sheet. Store in a double bag to prevent freezer odor and freeze until you want to use. Thaw the fruit for approximately 10 minutes, then process in the food processor with a little sugar and zest of a lemon or orange until it is the consistency of sorbet. (Add a little juice if you need liquid.)

■ Roast firm fruit, such as apples or pears, to enhance their flavor. Brush with honey or maple syrup and melted butter, or a mixture of orange juice, sugar, and melted butter. Roast in a 400°F oven until you can pierce the fruit with a fork.

Papaya is wonderful puréed in soups, sliced in salads, or mixed in a main dish. The black seeds make a beautiful, edible garnish.

Guavas can be a perfumy addition to a fruit salad or puréed as a sauce for chicken and pork.

Sweet Endings

Some favorite desserts are demystified.

THE FLAKIEST PIE CRUST

"Flaky is beautiful" when it comes to pie crust, and the queen of crusts is Shirley Corriher. Food writer and author of *CookWise*, Corriher adapted a technique she got from pastry chef Jim Dodge to achieve the flakiest crust.

1½ sticks butter

2½ cups of a low-protein pastry flour (such as White Lily) or a combination of 1¾ cups bleached all-purpose flour and ½ cup instant flour

½ teaspoon salt

2 tablespoons shortening

8 ounces sour cream

1 to 2 tablespoons whole milk, if needed

1. Cut the **butter** into four long logs, then cut the logs into thirds, so you have big chunks of butter.
2. Toss the butter with the **flour** and **salt**, put the mixture on a piece of wax paper, and place it in the freezer for 10 minutes.
3. Put the flour and butter mixture on the counter and roll it with a rolling pin. It will stick to the rolling pin. Just scrape it off, put it together, and roll over it again three times.
4. Put the mixture back in the freezer for another 10 minutes, then take it out and repeat the rolling and scraping procedure three additional times.
5. Cut the **shortening** into small pieces and add it to the pastry mixture.
6. Roll and scrape the mixture three more times. Return it to the freezer for 10 minutes, then take it out.
7. Add the **sour cream** and, if the dough is too crumbly, the **milk**. Chill in the refrigerator until you are ready to roll it out.

Another secret to Corriher's crusts: When prebaking the crust, instead of the old fill-it-with-beans method, she places waxed paper over the raw crust in the pie pan, places another pie pan on top, turns both pans upside down, and bakes the crust that way. Gravity pulls the sides of the crust down so they don't look shriveled.

Corriher takes the upper pie pan off to expose the bottom of the crust for the last few minutes of baking so it gets crisp, then replaces the pie pan before taking the crust out of the oven. Prebaking in a preheated 350°F oven takes about 15 minutes or until the crust is lightly browned. Then you can add your favorite filling, sweet or savory, and finish baking, following directions in the recipe.

CREAMY NO-CRACK CHEESECAKE

The biggest challenge in making cheesecake? Knowing when it's done, says Kraft Creative Kitchens manager Maureen Weiss. What to look for? Slightly puffed edges and a center area, about the size of a silver dollar, that appears soft and moist. Taking your cheesecake out of the oven at this point will yield a creamy result, promises Weiss, since the center area will firm up as the cake cools. Overbaking is the culprit behind dried-out cheesecake.

If your cheesecake has cracks on the top, another common complaint, it's because you peeked too soon. Opening the oven during baking lets cool air in and leads to those unattractive splits.

Cheesecake is a great choice when you want an impressive dessert for company but don't have time for last-minute baking. Cheesecake freezes and refrigerates well. You can store it for two months in the freezer, and up to three days in the refrigerator.

Tools of the Trade

Cake strips. Moistened and placed around the outside of the cake pan, these strips help to prevent the edges of a cake from browning and drying out before the center is done.

Pie tapes. Placed over the edges of the pie crust, pie tapes can prevent them from burning.

After baking and cooling, chill the cheesecake for three to four hours in the refrigerator, uncovered. Then, for refrigerator storage, simply place a sheet of plastic wrap or aluminum foil around it.

For freezer storage, first wrap the cake securely in plastic wrap, then foil. Place it in a plastic bag, seal it, and label it with the date. Before serving, thaw it in the refrigerator overnight.

Wait until shortly before serving to top your cheesecake, using whipped cream, strawberries, cherries or other fresh or canned fruit, chocolate curls, or whatever else strikes your fancy. You can have fun with your choice of toppings and correct any flaws in the cake's appearance at the same time. For a dessert that's truly eye-catching, you might try alternating wedges of a few varieties of fresh fruit or berries.

Myth: *Baking powder creates the air bubbles that make a cake rise.* **Fact:** *Baking powder enlarges the bubbles that are in the fat.*

CHOCOLATE AT ITS BEST

Chocolate is a bit fussy to work with. Improper storage or inept handling can mar chocolate creations. To help get the results you want, follow this helpful advice from Alice Medrich, author of *Cocolat: Extraordinary Chocolate Desserts* and *Chocolate and the Art of Low-Fat Desserts*:

■ Keep chocolate well wrapped, and store it in a cool, dry place away from foods with distinct odors. Over time, even wrapped chocolate will absorb odors from nearby herbs and spices.

■ Dark chocolate can be kept for at least a year. Milk chocolate and white chocolate, both of which contain milk, may develop rancid or cheesy flavors within months. For the freshest flavor and smoothest melt, try to use them within three months of purchase.

■ Use the type of chocolate called for in your recipe. Semi-sweet and bittersweet chocolate are generally interchangeable. Don't substitute milk or white chocolate for semi-sweet or bittersweet, and vice versa. Also, don't substitute chips or morsels for chunk chocolate.

■ To melt chocolate, first chop it into small pieces. The increased surface will allow it to melt quickly on low heat. (Chocolate burns at a much lower temperature than butter, so keep the temperature low.) Stir the chocolate frequently to hasten melting, and remove from the heat source as soon as (or even before) the last pieces of chocolate are completely melted. Continue to stir off the heat as necessary to complete melting. When the chocolate is completely melted, it should be warm, not hot, to the touch.

■ To melt chocolate in the microwave, use a medium setting for dark chocolate, low for white or milk chocolate. Use short time increments and stir after each one.

When you melt chocolate in a double boiler, simmer the water so no steam or water gets into the chocolate.

■ To melt chocolate in a double boiler, place it over, not in, gently simmering water. Or, place a heatproof bowl of chocolate directly into a water bath—a skillet of barely simmering water. When melting white or milk chocolate in a water bath, turn the burner off and wait about 60 seconds before placing the bowl of chocolate in it, and then stir constantly.

■ When using melted chocolate, keep it away from water. A wet bowl or a drip of water inadvertently added to melted chocolate may cause it to "seize" and turn into a dull, thick paste.

Unsweetened chocolate is chocolate liquor with cocoa butter, but no sugar.

Bittersweet chocolate is chocolate liquor with cocoa butter, sugar, and vanilla.

THE LIGHTEST BUTTER CAKE

If you envision a high, light butter cake, but get a dense, heavy one when you bake, try Rose Levy Beranbaum's approach. She's author of *The Cake Bible* and creator of a new way of creaming the butter and sugar to ensure aeration and prevent overbeating.

Combine all the dry ingredients and mix on low speed for 30 seconds. Add the butter and a small amount of liquid, mixing until the dry ingredients are moistened. Beat on a higher speed for a minute. Finish by adding the remaining liquid in batches, beating briefly after each addition.

■ Have all the ingredients at room temperature.

■ Choose your ingredients with care. Use cake flour, but not the self-rising kind. For a very fine texture, use superfine sugar. Use unsalted butter and fresh baking powder.

■ Follow the instructions. Measure or weigh ingredients carefully, use the correct pan size, and bake for the recommended baking time.

■ If you use a hand-held mixer, beat at high speed.

White chocolate has cocoa butter, sugar, milk solids, and flavorings, but no chocolate liquor.

Milk chocolate is chocolate liquor with cocoa butter, sugar, vanilla, and milk solids.

93

Cooking Light

Low-fat, delicious meals are the new standard.

SPA SECRETS

Spas are noted for their great low-fat food. If they can do it, why can't the home cook? Jean Jones, syndicated food columnist and author of *Canyon Ranch Cooking,* shares some of the tricks that help to make spa food so successful:

■ When sautéing, baking, or broiling, spray the food you're cooking very lightly with oil. For maximum flavor, fill a spray bottle with your favorite flavored oil. Try vegetables roasted this way— everything from asparagus to broccoli to sweet potatoes. Cook them in a 400°F oven until done.

Times will vary for each vegetable.

■ Reduce the fat in your salad dressings. In a vinaigrette, leave out the oil and replace three-quarters of the volume that's called for with water. Then add one tablespoon of an aromatic oil, such as walnut, hazelnut, or dark sesame. For a cheese dressing, use only one-quarter of the amount of cheese. Place all the ingredients in a blender and blend until smooth. Then pour the dressing into a bowl or jar and add about a quarter-cup of low-fat cottage cheese. The texture will be lumpy. Let the dressing marinate in the refrigerator overnight. The cottage cheese lumps will absorb the flavor of the original

cheese, giving the dressing the taste of the high-fat version.

■ Don't forgo your favorite dishes. Instead, find ways to make them more healthful. Prepare meatloaf with very lean meat, using three-quarters of the amount called for in the recipe. Make up the volume with a combination of whole-wheat bread crumbs and cottage cheese, and then add spices. (The rule of thumb is that any time

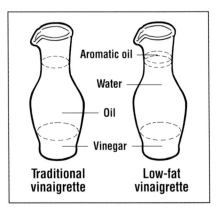

Aromatic oil
Water
Oil
Vinegar

Traditional vinaigrette　　**Low-fat vinaigrette**

you reduce volume in a dish, you need to replace it with an equivalent amount of something.)

■ Make a low-fat version of guacamole using cooked, puréed asparagus mixed with low-fat sour cream, tomatoes, and the usual guacamole seasonings.

■ When preparing fish, do not overcook it. Cook the fish fillets only until they change from translucent to opaque.

SPICED-UP RICE

Chef Arturo Boada's spicy rice dish has a startling ingredient—Coca-Cola. The combination of sweet and hot is a knockout.

1 tablespoon olive oil
1½ teaspoons Cajun Creole seasonings
1 tablespoon chopped garlic
1 cup rice
2 cups Coca-Cola

1. Preheat the oven to 375°F.
2. Heat the **olive oil** in an ovenproof pan and briefly sauté the **Cajun Creole seasonings** and the **garlic.**
3. Add the **rice** and sauté until it is translucent.
4. Add the **Coca-Cola** and bring to a boil.
5. Place the pan in the oven for about 12 minutes, or until all the liquid is absorbed.

You can add maximum flavor but minimal fat if you mist your vegetables with herb- or garlic-infused oil before roasting.

LAYER ON THE FLAVOR, TEXTURE, AND COLOR

Meatless meals provide a great opportunity to keep the fat down and the interest up. Carol Ritchie, cookbook consultant and recipe developer for the *American Heart Association Cookbook,* points out that meatless dishes provide a great way to create layers of flavor, texture, color, and aroma. For example, she starts with a large Portobello mushroom for each person, makes a few slits in the top, drizzles on some balsamic vinegar, and grills it for a few minutes on each side. She serves it over couscous or rice, topped with vivid greens like sautéed collard or kale, and some red bell pepper for contrast.

Another favorite is spinach and black bean enchiladas. In a bowl, mix blanched spinach with salsa, cumin, chili powder, black beans, and soy cheese. (Soy cheese tastes great, is healthy, and melts beautifully.) Roll in tortillas and bake for 15 minutes. Make a creamy topping using fat-free sour cream and lime juice. Serve with grated cheese, diced tomato, and chopped green onion.

ADD FLAVOR, NOT FAT

A lot of people equate low-fat food with bland food. Chef Arturo Boada, owner of Solero and Sabroso Grill in Houston, Texas, proves it's not necessarily so. Try the following methods he uses for infusing flavor into low-fat cooking:

- Zip up a main-dish salad. Poach chicken breasts, flavoring the poaching liquid with garlic, tarragon, lime juice, and a pinch of diced celery. Slice the chicken, toss it with a vinaigrette dressing, fresh herbs, and tomatoes or other vegetables you have on hand.
- Grill vegetables. Cut red onion, yellow squash, red potatoes, broccoli, and red peppers into different shapes, then toss with a little olive oil, garlic, fresh-cracked black pepper, a pinch of salt, and fresh herbs to taste. Place on a hot grill and char for about two minutes. Combine with grilled meat, chicken, or shrimp for a main course.
- Go South American. Make beans and rice, adding a cup of tomato paste to your rice-cooking water. This produces a flavorful, colorful dish. If you like, add a little sautéed chorizo, some grilled beef tenderloin, or cubes of cooked chicken breasts. It's the combination of flavors that makes a dish really interesting.

True Stories

When Carol Ritchie was 21 and learned that she had high cholesterol, she never realized that this "wake-up call" to her health would lead to her present career. Until then, Ritchie was unaware that high cholesterol could be a problem for women, especially young women. As a food lover, she was discouraged at first, thinking that she'd have to eat "boring, bland, flavorless food" for the rest of her life. Then she began to teach cooking classes at a local gourmet shop in order to supplement her work as a musician. That, combined with her passion for food and the need for a low-fat diet, inspired her to create delicious and heart-healthy dishes. Today, she's a cooking teacher, author, and television cook.

MARVELOUS MOUSSE

A fruit mousse makes a satisfying and elegant close to a meal. Laureen Gauthier, pastry chef and instructor at the New England Culinary Institute in Montpelier, Vermont, suggests this low-fat version.

Purée any frozen or cooked fruit (straining seeds as necessary) and adding sweetener to taste. Then fold in some whipped egg whites (instead of the traditional cream), pour into a parfait glass, and chill until serving time. If you like, garnish with mint leaves or fresh berries. For a tangier taste, whisk a little yogurt into the purée before adding the egg whites.

Just ¼ cup of egg whites...

Keep in mind that egg whites whip up to a greater volume than cream. To produce a cup of whipped whites, you'll only need about a quarter-cup of liquid whites. To ensure egg safety, pasteurize the whites by placing them in the top of a double boiler and holding them at 145°F for three minutes, whisking continuously. Use an instant-read thermometer.

Remember that when you're adding whipped egg whites, you'll get a lighter texture if you mix a quarter of the whites into the purée first. Then use a rubber spatula to gradually add the rest of the cup, turning the mixture over until the whites and purée are completely combined.

makes a full cup of whipped egg whites.

Smart Moves

- Get brown, crispy French fries without the usual fat. Peel baking potatoes and cut them lengthwise into eighths. Toss with a little olive oil and place on a jelly roll pan coated with nonstick spray. Bake at 475°F for 15 to 20 minutes. For added flavor, add spices after tossing with the olive oil—for example, a mixture of cumin, chili powder, paprika, and oregano, or other seasonings of your choice.
- When using nonstick cookware, spray the pan lightly with oil, then heat it until water dances on the surface. This will give you enough heat to seal the food. Too often, people use a pan that's not hot enough. As a result, the food steams rather than getting nicely browned.

Fast Food

Food can be quick and healthy at the same time.

DINNER UNDER WRAPS

Some of the easiest dishes can be created by wrapping meat, fish, vegetables, and spices in aluminum foil packets and steaming them quickly in the oven. Carol Owen, director, consumer services, at the Reynolds Metals Company, says that with this method, you can create dishes that use the whole gamut of flavors available today.

■ For a Caribbean-inspired meal, combine cooked rice, boneless chicken breast, sliced green onions, pineapple chunks, lime juice, brown sugar, and Caribbean jerk seasoning in individual foil packets. Wrap tightly and bake about 20 minutes.

■ For an Asian approach, combine sliced sirloin steak and snow peas, and top with a sauce made from teriyaki sauce, creamy peanut butter, and cornstarch. Bake about 15 minutes.

■ For a French flair, sprinkle white fish fillets like flounder or sole with thyme, marjoram, and lemon juice. Place the fish over frozen vegetables and top with sliced green onions, salt, and pepper. Or place the fillets on sliced onions and shredded carrots, top with grated fresh ginger, rice vinegar, sesame oil, salt, and pepper. Bake about 18 minutes.

The convenience of these individual packets is that they can be customized to each person's taste. If your kids don't like onions, just leave the onions out of their packets. If someone is going to be late for dinner, pre-wrap the meal and cook it when that person arrives home.

All recipes call for a pre-heated 450°F oven. If you put the packets over a hot grill instead, they will cook a bit more quickly, so be careful not to let them burn.

PIZZA IN NO TIME

Choose your toppings carefully and pizza can be not only delicious but also good for you. Evan Kleiman, chef/owner of Angeli Caffè

Carribean Wrap
Preparation time: 10 minutes
Cooking time: 20 minutes

Fritatta
Preparation time: 8 minutes
Cooking time: 10 minutes

be ready to roll out when you get home from work.

Stretch the dough, add good-for-you toppings, slide onto a pizza stone, and bake for about eight minutes in a very hot oven. If your family members are anything like the enthusiastic Angeli customers, they'll like the following types of pizza, all of which are quick and easy to prepare:

Pizza
Preparation time: 12 minutes
Cooking time: 8 minutes

in Los Angeles and author of *Angeli Caffè Pizza Pasta Panini*, suggests making pizza into a quick, healthy meal. Start by picking up fresh dough from your local pizza parlor. Or, if you freeze the dough, move it to the refrigerator in the morning of the day you want to use it, and it will

Tools of the Trade
Pizza stone to bake pizzas on

Pizza paddle for transferring stretched dough to the stone

VEGETABLES TAKE THE PLATE

Julee Rosso, co-author of *The Silver Palate* cookbooks and author of *Everyday Cooking*, says she's reversed the way she thinks about dinner. When she plans the meal she thinks of the vegetables first, rather than the protein. "It's the total opposite of the way I was brought up," she says.

When she envisions the dinner plate, she sees it half-filled with vegetables, one-quarter filled with starch, and one-quarter with protein.

Supper at the Rosso house often begins with salad. "With the array of washed greens available, there's no reason you can't whip a salad together," she says. The focus of the main course would be two vegetables—perhaps roasted, baked in a gratin, or steamed over a pot containing water infused with herbs, garlic, or ginger. To complement the vegetables, Rosso often turns to the local fish—whitefish, perch, and salmon. She broils the fish, or bakes it with fresh bay leaves on top and bottom and a little fish stock or citrus juice in the pan. To complete the main course, she'll add pasta, rice, or another grain. Supper frequently ends with fruit.

One way Rosso recommends cutting down on preparation time is by putting family and friends to work in the kitchen. It can be more fun, too.

THE PLEASURES OF POACHING

Most people associate poached food with flavorless food. But did you ever pull shreds of chicken off the bones you've used to make chicken stock? That wonderful chicken flavor is like the flavor you get with poaching, points out Shelly Young, chef and owner of the Chopping Block Cooking School in Chicago. Poaching means to cook below a simmer. When you poach, you should see no movement in the liquid. She recommends poaching when you don't want to spend a lot of time cooking but want a delicious meal that everyone in the family, including kids, will enjoy.

Great poached dishes start with homemade stock. When you have time, perhaps on a weekend, gather your stock ingredients—a chicken carcass or chicken bones, or fish bones if you're making fish stock, onions, carrots, celery, bay leaves, and peppercorns—put them in a pot and cover with water. Bring to a simmer and cook for an hour for fish stock, two hours for chicken stock. Cool the stock, skim the fat from chicken stock, and refrigerate or freeze until you're ready to use it.

Now for a poached meal: Heat up the stock, and drop in poultry (still on the bone) and some long-cooking root vegetables like carrots, potatoes, and turnips. Poach for 45 minutes while you check in with your kids, change clothes, and read the mail. Then add some quick-cooking vegetables, like fresh peas, kale, or fresh tomatoes, and fresh herbs. Cook for another 10 minutes. Serve in soup plates.

For a meal that takes less cooking time and is equally easy to prepare, poach fish (salmon will take about 20 minutes) and use only quicker-cooking vegetables. Add a salad and a tasty bread, and you're done.

- Puttanesca—tomato sauce, chopped garlic, sliced black olives, capers.
- Pesto—pesto sauce, sliced onions, pine nuts, Parmesan cheese.
- Rossi—mozzarella, sliced sweet red peppers, chopped garlic, capers, sliced olives, oregano.
- Tre Formaggi—ricotta, mozzarella, Parmesan, basil, prosciutto.

Another possibility for a quick meal, says Kleiman, is an open-faced sandwich made with bruschetta. Bruschetta is grilled bread, rubbed with garlic and drizzled with olive oil. (It's best when made with bread that has a firm crumb and hard crust.) The sandwich is great with arugula, chopped tomatoes, and mozzarella—or almost anything.

Kids in the Kitchen

Create food traditions with your kids.

HOME ALONE SNACKS

Be prepared for kids' snack attacks. Teenagers can prepare the following low-fat, nutritious snacks if you have the fixings on hand, says Mollie Katzen, author of *Pretend Soup and Other Real Recipes*. Don't hesitate to encourage younger kids to make these snacks, too. But just make sure you're around to supervise their culinary efforts.

Burrito: You'll need flour tortillas, a can of refried beans, grated Monterey Jack or other mild cheese, salsa, and/or chopped vegetables, such as tomatoes, onions, and peppers. Kids spread a tortilla with refried beans, heat it in a nonstick frying pan over medium heat, and sprinkle it with cheese, salsa, chopped vegetables, and, if desired, leftover cubed chicken or sautéed ground beef. Katzen points out that the flexibility and assured success of this snack will help teach your kids how to cook by feel, visuals, and their own preferences.

Vegetable dip: What could be easier? Some kids really go for cut-up vegetables dipped in a good brand of spaghetti sauce.

Pasta: If the kids are old enough to handle a pot of boiling water, keep ravioli and tortellini in the freezer so they can cook it for a snack. If they add tomato or pesto sauce and some freshly grated Parmesan cheese, the snack attack is solved.

It doesn't take kids long to decide cooking can be fun when they're part of the process.

YOUNG HANDS ARE WILLING HANDS

Young children ages three to eight love to join adults in the kitchen, but can feel underfoot unless you get into sync with what they enjoy and are capable of. "Children are much more interested in process than in product," says Margo Hammond, early childhood specialist at the Bank Street College of Education in New York City and author of *Let's Get Cooking*. "What you have to think about is not so much ending up with a perfect dish, but whether children will enjoy the time spent in the kitchen. You want them to learn something from the experience, and feel satisfied and connected to you."

When cooking with kids, keep the process very simple. Make sure there are as few steps as possible, and

KIDS' DO-IT-THEMSELVES FRUIT DIP

Fruit dip: All you need is a four-ounce package of cream cheese, a package of sweetened, frozen raspberries, plain yogurt, and cut-up fruit—apples, bananas, cantaloupe, strawberries, or whatever is in season. Kids can blend the cream cheese and raspberries in a food processor or blender until smooth, stir in some yogurt, and use this as a dip for the fruit.

Cream cheese, raspberries, and yogurt + Cut-up fruit + Food processor = Fun fruit dip

take one step at a time: "First, we have to scrub the potato... Now we're going to peel the potato... Now we're going to slice the potato."

Before they do something for the first time, demonstrate. Then offer support as necessary, but don't give in to the urge to help too much. Be content to let kids do as much as they can themselves—but don't expect perfect results.

What can kids do? Hammond advocates the use of "kid-powered tools" versus electric tools—egg beaters, sifters, whisks, mashers, hand-grinders, and juicers. She points out that using these tools not only helps kids develop small-motor coordination and strength, but also lets them feel powerful because they are making something work.

Dishes that kids love to eat and can learn to make include French toast, pancakes, fruit salad (especially if you have a melon-baller), muffins, stir-fry vegetables, mashed potatoes, guacamole, and salsa.

"The simpler the dish and the more able they are to feel in control of the process," says Hammond, "the more engaged they will be in the kitchen."

LEARNING THE BASICS

Connie McCalla, assistant director of The CookSchool at The Cookshop in Vancouver, teaches kids' classes during holidays. She also runs week-long cooking camps in the summer. Her aim is to ensure kids learn basic skills by building on their interest in food and their pleasure in eating.

Under McCalla's tutelage, kids learn to prepare their favorite foods: homemade chicken noodle soup, pasta, sushi, and wraps. At a class in Italian cooking, students prepare a dinner with minestrone soup, Caesar salad, lasagna, and ice cream. Another popular menu is Sunday dinner: soup, baked chicken, barbecued vegetables, rice or pasta, and a green salad with vinaigrette dressing. Salad preparation gives McCalla an opportunity to talk about different kinds of greens, nutrition, and shopping for quality.

McCalla chooses recipes that are appropriate to her students' age and abilities. Although the very young have short attention spans, McCalla points out that they can help with undemanding tasks. You can cut up some fruit and have them arrange it on a platter.

McCalla insists that her student dress like professional cooks. Her pupils wear aprons, close-toed shoes (never sandals), long pants, and short sleeves.

GIFTS FROM THE KITCHEN

Making gifts of food not only increases kids' kitchen savvy, it also helps to instill in them the notion that some of the most memorable gifts can be handmade. Try to think of something that can become your family's trademark gift, suggests Susan Costner, award-winning cookbook author.

Are you lucky enough to have a peach or plum tree or a strawberry patch in your backyard? Then jam might be the perfect gift. Use your favorite recipe and you've got something that your recipients will remember you by every time they spread it on toast.

A friend of Costner's buys giant jars of supermarket kosher pickles, adds garlic and red hot peppers, and marinates them for a month. The result is a delicious, inexpensive, and unusual gift.

Whatever your family's choice of homemade gift, make it extra-special with packaging. Put out all your art supplies and let the kids go to town with labels, ribbons, stickers, and other personalized decorations.

Smart Moves

Observe the following safety tips, says Connie McCalla, and you'll save yourself a lot of worry about kids hurting themselves in the kitchen:

- Be sure to have kids standing at a counter that's a comfortable height for them. If they are too short to stand and work, they may be a little too young to start cooking.
- Teach kids not to put their hands near something that's hot. Paper cut-outs of their hands can help. If you're using an electric skillet on a countertop, tape the cut-outs at a safe distance from the pan, and tell them to keep their hands on the cut-outs.
- When children are cutting, always have them use a cutting board or a thin, flexible plastic mat. Have them place the food on the board, not in their hand, and show them how to push down toward the board. Very young children can use regular dinner knives with serrated edges to cut soft foods like bananas and pears.
- Keep long hair tied back or clipped out of the child's face.
- Insist that kids always stay seated at the table while using kitchen utensils.
- Teach children to check the temperature of food before eating it.

A Sumptuous Spread

The buffet table is a gathering place for food, friends, and fun.

AN APPEALING BUFFET TABLE

For a different and inexpensive approach to arranging your buffet table, dare to be informal, using these suggestions from Bonnie Stern, director of her own cooking school in Toronto. Stern is also the author of eight cookbooks, including *Simply HeartSmart Cooking* and *More HeartSmart Cooking*, prepared with the Heart and Stroke Foundation of Canada.

■ Use upside-down milk crates and other containers to create different levels for displaying food on your buffet table. Cover these levels with cloths that complement the table cloth. Stern also likes to use rocks or large stones to vary the levels.

■ Use food as the decorative theme for the table: different-colored peppers, or a mass of fruit and vegetables all look beautiful.

■ If you do use flowers, try laying them on the table instead of putting them in vases.

■ Pile food high on the serving dish and crowd dishes together to make your buffet table look bountiful.

■ Serve cheeses in a way that guests won't hesitate to dig in. Arrange hard and semi-hard cheese in chunks, and place a knife or spoon with each soft cheese.

■ Always keep a second set of food platters in the kitchen, just in case those on your buffet table start to run low.

By creating a bountiful buffet with a casual air, you invite your guests to help themselves.

UNITED APPETITES

If you think your guest list is a challenge, imagine throwing a party for 250 people from all over the world. This is a regular occurrence for Louis Piuggi, executive chef at the United Nations in New York.

How do he and his team cope? "One thing that's not political about this place is the food," says Piuggi. "It cuts across all cultures and brings everybody together. We offer dishes in a variety of categories: fish, red meat, white meat, and vegetarian. We also have some international dishes, so we appeal to a wide range of tastes." A buffet menu might offer such varied items as a chicken tajine from Morocco, a whole roasted Chilean sea bass, and an Indian vegetarian curry.

Piuggi also organizes festivals featuring the food of one nation. For these, he includes some traditional dishes that may evoke childhood memories for the natives of that country. A recent example: An Icelandic festival featured Mama's Plokkfiskur, a dish made with haddock, codfish, and ocean perch, cooked with onions, garlic, potatoes, and cream, and covered with a sauce similar to Hollandaise.

What lessons from his job does Piuggi apply when entertaining at home? He plans his menus as far in advance as possible, and tries to get as much as he can done ahead of time so he's in the kitchen very little the day of a party. Perhaps most important, he's not afraid to use unexpected menu combinations to create a memorable meal.

The Right Way

- Cocktail parties shouldn't last longer than two hours. More than that, and you'll find guests will expect dinner.
- Don't cut corners on staffing. The service guests receive will be a critical part of their memory of the event.
- If you are planning to prepare some of the party food yourself, choose what you do best or what you can do most simply, and order the rest of the meal from the caterer.
- If you're planning a buffet meal to serve a large number of people, include two dishes of everything to ease the traffic flow around the buffet table.

WEDDING BUFFET

Having difficulty deciding between a sit-down meal and a buffet for an upcoming wedding? Carole Peck, author of *The Buffet Book* and owner of the Good News Café in Woodbury, Connecticut, explains why she likes buffets: People can mingle informally, which is a real plus if the two families don't know each other. You can offer more food choices so that everyone will find something they like and no one will have to pretend to eat a dish they hate. Equally important, the buffet table, especially a colorful one with lots of textures, is a beautiful focal point in a room that might otherwise be disappointingly nondescript.

Peck always includes a meat and a fish entree, and at least four side dishes, one of which is vegan (no animal products at all), in her buffets. She tries for a mixture of familiar and not-so-familiar dishes. Popular menus now might include duck, baked salmon with horseradish and leek topping, shrimp, wild rice-crusted goat cheese and leek tart, layered vegetable tarts, polenta with vegetables, or squash stuffed with grains. Peck likes the tarts and polenta because they can be cut in wedges for easy serving and eating. She emphasizes the importance of serving foods in season to get the tastiest results.

Smart Moves

The following tips from Carole Peck will help give your buffet maximum appeal and put your guests at maximum ease:

- Stay away from hard-to-eat dishes, like those containing long pasta, and dishes that don't wear well, like those with cream sauce. If serving shellfish, take it out of the shell.
- Steer clear of dishes that can go bad, such as those with hollandaise sauces and raw-egg dressings.
- Provide large-sized plates so that guests can take their fill without looking like gluttons.
- If using sit-down tables, preset the tables with salad and bread. That gives guests a chance to find their places, stow handbags, and stave off hunger before the main course. It also helps with traffic control when the buffet begins, since tables can be added to the line individually.
- If you're having a buffet where flatware is placed on the buffet table, put it at the end, after guests have gotten their food. That eliminates their having to hold it while serving themselves.

TEAMING UP WITH A CATERER

You've decided to give the party of your life, and to work with a caterer. What happens in your first few meetings is critical to the success of your party and your pocketbook, says Kenneth Wolfe, vice-president, Robbins Wolfe Eventeurs in New York City. So that everyone ends up happy, follow Wolfe's suggestions for a great partnership:

- Look for a caterer who has a reputation for top-notch organization, as well as for good food. It's critically important that the caterer show up on time and handle all the details efficiently.
- Have a clear idea of your budget, who your guests are (ages, dietary restrictions), the type of party you want (elegant, themed, casual), and the hours.

Before hiring a caterer, schedule a tasting to sample the foods that will be served.

- Reach an understanding with the caterer about a whole variety of details. This most obviously includes the menu, but also what you might need to rent (e.g., china, flatware, linens), the level of service you would like, when the catering staff will arrive and leave, how cleanup will take place, and what will be done with leftovers.
- Expect the caterer to do a complete breakdown of costs with you early on: food, staff, rentals, liquor and wine, gratuities, and flowers.
- Do a walk-through of the party site with the caterer, discussing the flow of the party.
- Once you've met and discussed all the issues, the caterer should give you a proposal that spells out everything, including costs. This should be signed by both you and the caterer to avoid any misunderstandings.

The Perfect Table

You can set a creative and beautiful table.

TABLETOP DESIGN: A MIXED BLESSING

On the traditional table, everything matches. On the contemporary table, things can be a bit more interesting. Peri Wolfman, author of *The Perfect Setting* and *Knives, Forks and Spoons,* doesn't like to use one set of dishes. She prefers to mix tableware, and creates a blended look through color. For instance, she might combine white, cream, and taupe—a taupe buffet plate topped by a cream dinner plate topped by a white salad plate. The color variations and layering of plates heighten the interest of the table and makes it look "less stuffy," says Wolfman. "It's not that it's informal or makes your table less proper. It's just a little more original."

Wolfman suggests that you can also add an element of surprise by bringing out a beautiful old piece, such as a Wedgwood serving plate, and by mixing pottery and fine china (a pottery buffet plate, for instance, with a fine china dessert plate). Glassware and silverware

don't all have to match each other, either.

When it comes to linens, Wolfman likes a big, old, damask tablecloth, "because it has that gentle, well-worn feeling." With it, she uses oversized linen napkins. (White is a great choice because you can bleach it and get all the spots off.) Wolfman doesn't

WINE GLASSES SIMPLIFIED

You know all those rules about wines and the glasses in which they must be served? "It's not really necessary to have a different glass for each wine," says Harriet Lembeck, author of *Grossman's Guide to Wines, Beers and Spirits,* Sixth and Seventh Editions, and wine director for The New School in New York City. She says a good all-purpose wine glass works for serving all kinds of wines, except for champagne or other sparkling wine. "Wines with bubbles require something narrower and elongated, with a point at the bottom to send the bubbles rising upward," she explains.

When shopping for an all-purpose glass, look for a round or tulip-shaped bowl. Both these shapes curve in at the top, trapping the

fold the napkins, but simply shakes them from the center and drapes them over the table to the left of the fork. This gives the table an inviting, easygoing look.

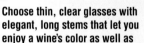

Choose thin, clear glasses with elegant, long stems that let you enjoy a wine's color as well as its aroma and taste.

bouquet. This allows you to enjoy the aroma of the wine, which gives you a clue as to what the wine will taste like.

As for size, Lembeck suggests 8 to 12 ounces. A smaller glass prevents you from swirling or smelling the wine, and a larger one tends to be unwieldy and makes it easy to serve too much wine at one time. When serving wine, fill the glass less than halfway, or to just under the widest point of the glass. That allows you to swirl and smell the wine without spilling it.

Lembeck also recommends a thin glass so you don't feel that there's a barrier between your mouth and the wine, and a clear (not colored) glass, which enables you to enjoy the color of the wine. You'll find lots of choices, in many price ranges.

Use plates of different colors at each place.

If you like the look of cut glass, consider a wine glass where the decorative work is on the stem or base, not the bowl, so it doesn't interfere with your ability to see the wine clearly.

If your budget allows, you might want to consider crystal wine glasses. They're thin and have a beautiful ring when clinked together at toasting time. Lembeck says there's no need to worry about lead poisoning since the wine does not stay in the glass long enough to be a health problem.

True Stories

Margaret Dickenson has accompanied her diplomat-husband, Lawrence, to his postings at Canadian embassies abroad. Her book *From the Ambassador's Table* is based on years of hosting parties around the world. She advises partygivers to develop a "do-able" style, relax, and have fun. Because lighting is so vital for creating that special mood at evening and holiday parties, she varies candle heights, or uses strings of lights and lanterns.

LOOKING AT FLATWARE

The four important factors that help determine the stainless steel flatware that's best for you are quality, design, function, and price, says Amira Taji, store manager of the Linen Chest in downtown Montreal.

■ The quality of flatware varies from low-end 13-chrome to higher-end 18/8 and 18/10. What distinguishes low- from high-end is the quality of the metals used. Better flatware will be less likely to break under stress, will last longer, and will develop a nice luster over time. The less-expensive 13-chrome might be a reasonable choice if you have young children, frequently drop flatware down the garbage disposal, or will be satisfied with something utilitarian. Choose 18/8 or 18/10 if you're buying for longer-term and like the feel of it when you're holding it in your hand. An easy way to tell low- from high-quality is to look between the tines of a fork. If the area is rough and hasn't been polished very well, this is a definite indication of a lower-quality item.

■ Design is a matter of personal choice. Always look for what you like and what will be compatible with the rest of your tableware.

■ Function is one of the most overlooked aspects in choosing flatware. You'll be happier with your choice if you consider how you're going to use your flatware, and how well it fits in your hands and your mouth.

■ Price is variable. You want to choose flatware that has character and elegantly represents you when you entertain, in a price range you are comfortable with.

Taji points out that "stainless" flatware means just that: it stains less than other kinds of cutlery. But stains can occur if you leave foods containing acids on flatware too long. To keep it shiny and bright, be sure to rinse off any food as quickly as possible, and place the flatware in the dishwasher. With proper care and the right detergent, your "stainless" flatware should give you years of good care.

PATTERNS FOR PLATEWARE

Choosing the pattern that suits you from among all the gorgeous tableware that's available today can be a difficult decision. But Charles Anderson, chef instructor and sommelier for the School of Culinary Arts at the Colorado Institute of Art, offers the following guidelines.

First, says Anderson, consider your dining style. Is it going to be formal or informal? Pottery is appropriate for all outdoor and most indoor dining, but if you have a very formal dining room and plan to entertain in that style, china is a more appropriate choice.

Another issue is the size of the dinner plate. "You can do more aggressive, elegant, dimensional presentations of food on a larger plate," says Anderson. Think half a rack of lamb with accompaniments. The same food on a smaller plate would look too crowded.

On the other hand, you might want to create an abundant effect, which you can do by putting a lot of food on a smaller plate. Big Italian or French pottery plates, for example, always look wonderful with informal, country foods such as paella, cassoulet, coq au vin, or pasta.

A third consideration when choosing plates is the design. Young couples frequently choose colorful, intricate designs and regret it later when they get tired of looking at them. Anderson advocates the approach taken by those in the restaurant business—show off the food on the plate rather than the plate itself, and choose something simple and elegant.

One solution is to have several sets of plateware—one for everyday dining, one for casual entertaining, and one for formal entertaining. Of course, that approach depends on your budget and the amount of storage space you have in your home.

Serve sparkling wine in long, narrow glasses designed to make the bubbles rise.

Mix old and new plates on the table.

Drape the table with an old damask cloth and oversized napkins.

Quick Tricks

Try something different:

■ Mix and match pieces of sterling silverware found at garage sales for an exotic, lavish look.

■ If you have a centerpiece, make it low enough so that everyone can see each other across the table.

■ Put candlesticks on decorative plates to protect your table from wax drips.

■ Keep large serving plates on a sideboard near the table to eliminate clutter and simplify serving.

Company's Coming

You can welcome friends and family and enjoy yourself.

PLEASING PEOPLE

Entertaining can be a high-stress experience because, as cooking and baking teacher Lauren Groveman points out, "People will carry with them the memory of that occasion and either remember it fondly or wish they hadn't come." Groveman, who wrote *Lauren Groveman's Kitchen: Nurturing Food for Family and Friends*, sees feeding others as a circular experience. By providing food, you make people happy. Their happiness makes you happy in turn. The pleasure derived from this exchange is a big motivation for many cooks, professional or home.

So design your entertaining in order to make yourself and others happy. How? Groveman suggests the following helpful hints and tips:

■ Entertain with food and in a style that fits your personality. Don't try to compete with your family members or friends.

■ Choose a menu that works for your guests. If you're feeding a lot of children, serve simple dishes. Children—and most adults—like good, comforting, wonderful-smelling food.

■ Check with your guests, especially those you're entertaining for the first time, to see if they have any food allergies or strong food dislikes. This lets them know you care and increases the chance that they will feel welcome and nurtured in your home.

■ Stay away from any dishes that you haven't prepared before. It can be a setup for failure.

■ Prepare as many dishes as you can a day ahead, but don't sacrifice flavor and texture. Many soups and stews improve with a day's rest, and you can also blanch and refrigerate vegetables, wash salad greens, and make bread dough. On the big day, prepare only those foods that must be done at the last minute, such as fresh-baked bread or a fruit tart.

■ Think about aroma. What will your guests smell as they enter your home? Certain smells say "welcome," or remind guests of their own beloved family traditions.

Be sure to make your table as beautiful and welcoming as your food—and as much a statement of your personal taste.

KITCHEN COORDINATION

To keep from getting overwhelmed by a big party, make lists, suggests Rick Rodgers, cooking teacher and author of cookbooks, including *The Perfect Party Series* and *Thanksgiving 101*.

■ A party preparation list of all the things you have to do in the month before the party, including foods you can make ahead and freeze, such as tomato sauce for lasagna or unfrosted cake layers.

■ A grocery list of nonperishables to buy a month before the party.

■ A beverage list, also for advance shopping.

■ A grocery list of items to buy one week ahead, such as onions, garlic, potatoes, and butter.

■ A grocery list of items to buy one or two days

Buy one month before paper goods and non-perishable groceries

Buy one week before onions, butter, garlic, potatoes

Buy 1-2 days before meat fish fresh vegetables

ahead, such as meat, fish, and fresh vegetables.

■ A utensils and serving dish list. Think big: 10- by 15-inch serving platters, a 10-quart stock pot, a 14-inch skillet. Indicate those items you will have to borrow and where you'll get them.

■ A tableware list. (You'll want to have enough so you don't have to resort to plastic and paper for some of your guests.)

THE LIGHTER SIDE OF ENTERTAINING

A successful dinner party doesn't mean guests leave your house feeling as if they've gained 10 pounds. Preserving the taste and enjoyment of food while cutting down on the fat is the approach used by Laurie Burrows Grad, broadcast journalist and author of *Entertaining Light & Easy.* Some lower-fat, company-pleasing dishes she serves regularly include:

- Osso buco made with veal shanks grilled (rather than sautéed in oil), then braised with broth and vegetables as usual.
- Veal and turkey loaf (instead of the usual ground beef and pork mixture) topped with a commercial sun-dried tomato pesto sauce.
- Stir-fried Szechuan shrimp and asparagus prepared in a nonstick pan with only a tablespoonful of oil.
- Oven-baked (versus fried) catfish, coated with mustard and chive-flavored bread crumbs.
- Fish, marinated and grilled, served with a roasted garlic sauce. Roast garlic until soft, and combine with yogurt, a tiny bit of mayonnaise, and fresh herbs.

Burrows Grad cautions never to skimp on flavor in order to cut down on fat. Rather than serve a mediocre low-fat baked dessert, for instance, she offers a beautiful fruit compote mixed with Amaretto and orange juice, and topped with yogurt.

COOKING IN THE WILDS

When home is the wilderness for five days or more, you can't just run out to a supermarket for a few items you forgot. That's why Black Feather Wilderness Expeditions, an Ottawa-based canoe-and-hiking outfitter, keeps all its basic menus on computer disks. When planning meals for a trip to an Arctic region or along one of Canada's remote rivers, guides check these menus to ensure there'll be the right amount of food for their hungry group.

Alison Galloway, Black Feather's administrative coordinator and a guide, says that, after a hard day on the river, canoeists appreciate hearty meals. But baked beans and oatmeal just won't do! A favorite Galloway menu includes a couscous salad, followed by curried chicken with pasta. Sometimes dinner consists of ingredients from the wild, such as freshly caught trout, with wild berries for dessert.

Dutch ovens are indispensable on these trips because they can be stacked on top of each other in such a way that several dishes can be cooked at once. They're great for baking biscuits, lasagna, corn bread and brownies, and can also be used as regular pots and pans over an open fire.

Guides are encouraged to be resourceful with leftovers, which can result in some unusual combinations. At the end of a 16-day trip to Baffin Island, a guide offered a "goulash" of rice and pasta.

Extra items list
(borrow if possible)
Large stock pot
Baking dishes
Serving platters
Punch bowl
Champagne glasses
Wine glasses
China
Coffee urn
Coffee cups
Flatware

Beverage list
(buy in advance)
Red wine
White wine
Champagne
Juice
Milk
Soda
Seltzer
Spring water

Smart Moves

- Let your seating arrangement dictate your menu. If you can accommodate everyone at a table, serve knife-and-fork food. If not, serve foods that can be eaten easily with just a fork.
- To save precious refrigerator space, store whatever refrigerated food you don't need for the party at a neighbor's. Put everything you can in plastic self-sealing bags rather than in space-wasting bowls or bulky containers.
- Test a new large-quantity recipe ahead of time by scaling it down and serving it to family or close friends.

Parties for Children

Try simple, fun entertaining for the younger set.

Nonpareils

Licorice

Chocolate bits

FOCUS ON THE BASICS

At Jeremy's Place in New York City, owner Jeremy Sage has been giving parties for four- to six-year-olds since 1981. He has learned (the hard way) that children this age will not spend more than eight minutes at the table, and so has devised a menu of least resistance for their parties: pizza and birthday cake. Here is his serving advice:

- Serve the pizza lukewarm. Piping hot burns.
- Cut pizza into sixteenths, not eighths. If you're serving three-year-olds, cut it into triangles.
- If a child doesn't want pizza, don't force it. Simply pass them by. Some kids just don't eat anything at all at parties.
- Offer one simple food. Food choices are too complicated.

- For beverages, serve juice or water.
- Ice cream cake is the cake to have, and it should be vanilla or chocolate. If you're going to have it decorated—with flowers, say—either get one flower just for the birthday child, or 27, one for every child at the party. Five flowers for 27 kids will only cause fighting and tears.
- To avoid the endless lighting-of-the-candles frustration, pre-light the candles, let them burn for 30 seconds, then blow them out. They'll light right away when it's time to serve the cake. (Never use trick candles with this age group.)

Other kid's-party experts agree with Sage's advice to offer one simple, easy-to-eat food. If pizza isn't your child's favorite, consider other things kids can eat with their fingers: chicken tenders, fish sticks, or sandwiches with familiar fillings cut into crustless triangles or cookie-cutter shapes.

CAKE'S THE THING

Whatever else you serve, the food kids look forward to the most is the cake, says Andrea Messina, lifestyle editor for *Parenting* magazine. Even so, she cautions, don't overthink the cake, because you won't get the payback in appreciation. Choose a simple flavor, and go to town on the decorating. One fun way is to get the kids involved. Make and ice a big sheet cake. Put out bowls of nonpareils, licorice, chocolate bits, gummy candy, miniature marshmallows, and whatever else strikes your fancy. The kids will love creating their own masterpiece, even if it looks like a disaster to you.

With a little imagination, you can turn standard cake shapes into great creations, says Messina. Make a caterpillar, for instance, by baking two bundt cakes, cutting them in half, and alternating the semi-circles so you have a wiggly-looking creature. Bake several mini-loaf cakes, decorate, and string together to form a train. Or use small round cake tins to create bright, edible "balloons".

A no-fail way to decorate a cake is to frost it, and then spread another color frosting on a plate. Press small cookie cutters into the contrasting frosting, then gently press the cutters on top of the cake to leave colored outlines of animals, flowers, or other shapes dancing on the cake.

COOKING UP A PARTY

For kids 10 and up, cooking can be the basis for a fun-filled party with a delectable finish. Leslie Bartosh, director of the Culinary Arts Academy at Galveston College in Galveston, Texas, ran two kids' cooking classes that could easily become parties:

- Make-Your-Own Pizza and Homemade Ice Cream. Pre-make the pizza dough, or buy prepared dough. Have kids help make ice cream, using an electric ice cream freezer. While the ice cream is freezing, have the kids roll out individual pizzas. Pour on

sauce, and dress them with toppings: mozzarella cheese, pepperoni, Italian sausage, onions, mushrooms, tri-color bell peppers, or black olives. When it's time for ice cream, let kids make their own sundaes. Provide cut-up fresh fruit, several sauces, nuts, and whipped cream.

- Homemade Pasta and Scoop Cookies. Use a pasta machine to make the pasta from scratch, or have kids roll it out and cut it (p.85). Cook and serve with a sauce of your choice. Afterwards, have kids mix cookie dough,

Smart Moves

- Kids of any age need to burn some energy rather than sit down with food when they first arrive at a party. Have some non-messy nibbles available just in case. Good choices are cereal party mix, pretzels, and celery sticks with cream cheese. For older kids, try fruit kebabs and vegetables with dip.
- A party at an ethnic restaurant can be a real birthday treat for kids old enough to appreciate it. Good choices are restaurants that are typically loud, and those with private rooms. Japanese restaurants, for instance, have tatami rooms where kids can take off their shoes and sit on the floor to eat. Chinese restaurants are usually popular with kids, as are Mexican. Another possibility is a restaurant with an open kitchen, where kids can watch the action. Be sure to call ahead for reservations and to pre-arrange the menu.

Miniature
marshmallows

Gummy candy

Tools of the Trade

A family collection of unusual cookie cutters can do double duty in creating sandwiches in inviting shapes. Try a peanut butter star or a tunafish hand.

such as chocolate chip or oatmeal raisin, then scoop onto baking trays. Bartosh advises that you plan the parties thoroughly ahead of time so kids will be engaged in some activity all the time. Downtime tests kids' limited patience.

COMING-OF-AGE PARTIES

At 13, kids are not much more ready to sit down to eat than they were at 6, says Stacy Gerber of Total Party Concepts in New York and Palm Beach. Nor are their

culinary tastes that much more developed. That's why Gerber recommends fairly straightforward party food that can be eaten while standing. He's had great success serving familiar foods like miniature hamburgers, mozzarella sticks, curly fries, chicken nuggets, and sliced steak. Baked potato bars and taco bars are big hits, too. For dessert,

says Gerber, serve ice cream bars. Kids never lose their love for ice cream, and these can be eaten on the run—a big plus.

At 16, food can get a little more serious. The typical Sweet Sixteen party, says Gerber, is a sit-down dinner that takes place at night. It might begin with a "mocktail" hour, which includes hors d'oeuvres and alcohol-

free drinks like piña coladas and strawberry daiquiris. Place the hors d'oeuvres on a buffet table so teens can help themselves. Having them passed butler-style can be too intimidating. Dinner menus can be as adventuresome as the teens' tastes, which vary a lot at this stage. Consult the best expert of all, the party girl or boy.

The Portable Feast

There are imaginative ideas for food on the go!

ENJOYING A PICNIC ON THE SEA

On their days off, graphic designer Sherry Streeter and her husband, Jon Wilson, founder of *Wooden Boat* magazine, head for their boat near their home in Maine, often with friends. Invariably, Streeter's food is one of the highlights of the day at sea. One of her picnic favorites is shortbread made without sugar that she serves as an easy appetizer or main course.

When creaming the butter to make the shortbread, she adds puréed smoked salmon or trout that's been seasoned with curry. Then she bakes it as usual and cuts it into small squares for serving. A larger square of the shortbread served with a green salad can also make a tasty main course for lunch or a light supper.

You can create your own versions of the recipe by adding cheese or artichoke hearts to the fish mixture, or by seasoning with chili powder, or cumin and turmeric. The results should be equally delicious.

Be prepared:

Don't get caught outdoors without picnic essentials. Have the following ready and waiting when you're ready to go.

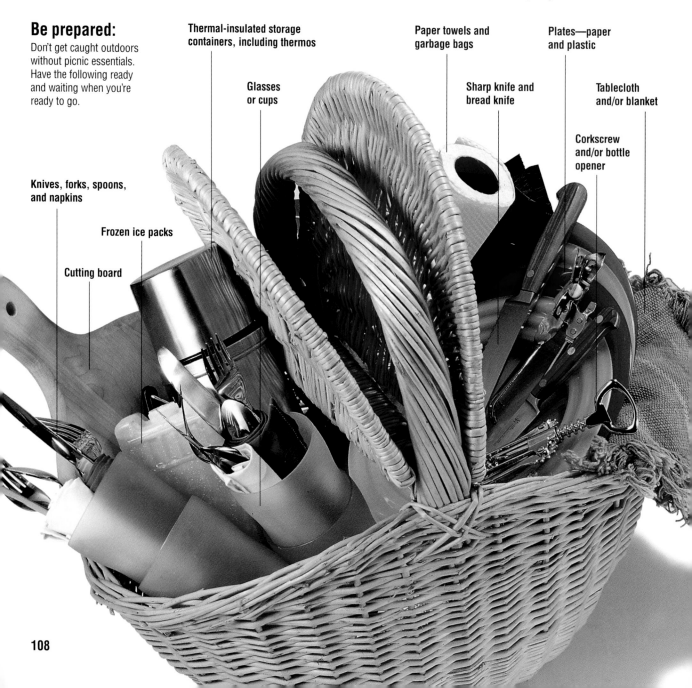

Thermal-insulated storage containers, including thermos

Glasses or cups

Paper towels and garbage bags

Sharp knife and bread knife

Plates—paper and plastic

Tablecloth and/or blanket

Corkscrew and/or bottle opener

Knives, forks, spoons, and napkins

Frozen ice packs

Cutting board

PICNIC IN THE WOODS

In the Pacific Northwest, a morning of hiking, waterfall hopping, or just watching someone else fish can build up an appetite. And guests staying at the Steamboat Inn on the North Umpqua River in Steamboat, Oregon, can always count on taking a substantial picnic with them when they venture out, thanks to co-owner Sharon Van Loan.

In a typical Van Loan basket, you might find:

- Spinach bread stuffed with ham or turkey and cheese, rolled in a spiral.
- Three different, complementary salads, such as marinated vegetable salad, pasta salad, and Italian bean salad.
- Fresh fruit.
- A rich but easy-to-handle dessert like a brownie or pound cake.

Van Loan's choices emphasize the essence of picnic foods. She stays with food that doesn't require anything fancy in the way of plates or flatware, so hikers won't have a lot of weight to carry. And she offers a great variety of tastes, textures, and aromas, so the guests are always deliciously satisfied. The whole meal can fit in an easy-to-carry backpack that does double duty—a handy way to take the tasty treats into the woods and the trash out.

PICNIC AT THE PLAY

Theater festivals are summer highlights throughout North America. So, too, are the picnics enjoyed by theatergoers. One special site for summer picnics are the spacious parks nearby Ontario's Stratford Theatre Festival. Ruth Klahsen, the festival chef, offers a choice of five menus for pre-show picnic lunches and dinners, from June through August.

A menu features a light three-course meal still substantial enough to sustain playgoers through five acts of Shakespeare. One of Klahsen's favorite picnics opens with chilled curried mango soup, followed by a main course of cold poached salmon, served with leeks vinaigrette and corn salad. For dessert, the playgoers can delight in oranges in red wine and homemade gingerbread. To enjoy these popular picnics, Klahsen advises festival visitors to book in advance.

A SAFETY REMINDER

Always choose picnic foods that will travel well. Pack your picnic basket with ice blocks, either the commercial ones or ones you have created yourself in empty one-quart juice containers. And try to eat within two hours of arriving at the picnic site so the food doesn't sit in the sun too long.

The Right Way

If a picnic opportunity presents itself and there's no time to prepare food, pick up dips and spreads, pickles, crackers, several interesting breads, cold cuts, and German potato salad at the market or deli. At the picnic site, set up a food bar and let the picnickers create their own meals.

Tools of the Trade

You'll enjoy your picnic a lot more if you aren't sharing your space with mosquitos and other bothersome flying insects. Look for citronella candles in creative shapes to suit your picnic's style. They can also double as a source of light. You can usually find a good supply early in the season, so stock up when you see them.

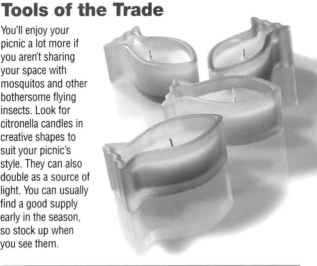

PICNIC AT THE BEACH

Heidi Cusick, editor of *Picnics* and author of over 500 articles, including many on picnics, used to live in Mendocino, California. She kept a picnic basket packed with utensils so when the fog rolled out, she could throw some food together and get to the beach. Since this could happen at breakfast, lunch, or dinner time, she developed favorite picnic dishes for all three meals.

- Cusick's breakfast special is a Spanish tortilla, which is served in tapas bars in Spain. Similar to a frittata, this dish consists of egg, potatoes, garlic, herbs, and onions cooked in a cast-iron skillet to a cakelike consistency so that it's easy to cut into wedges. She takes along muffins, scones, and a variety of fresh fruit.
- Lunch might consist of caponata (an Italian eggplant dish), smoked chicken or turkey, and a potato salad with a vinaigrette and mint dressing. Dessert? Something simple, like a pear with a piece of Gorgonzola cheese and a hard cookie

like biscotti. Cusick points out that the sweet-and-sour flavor of the caponata, the smokiness of the cold cuts, and the freshness of the mint are all enhanced when eaten outdoors in the fresh air.

- For dinner picnics, Cusick likes to start with pâté and cornichons, then follow with a whole roasted chicken covered in herbs, a salad, and fresh bread. Where cooking is permitted, she also likes to grill sausages and serve them on French rolls with mustard and a dressing made of sautéed red onions cooked with sugar, olive oil, and balsamic vinegar. Wine helps to make a picnic out-of-the-ordinary. With dinner she usually serves a Pinot Noir or spicy Zinfandel.

Some great picnics are completely spontaneous, Cusick explains, and can be a wonderful way to entertain. For an informal gathering, ask one friend to bring a wildflower centerpiece, another, a specialty dessert, and let the noncook pick up the bread.

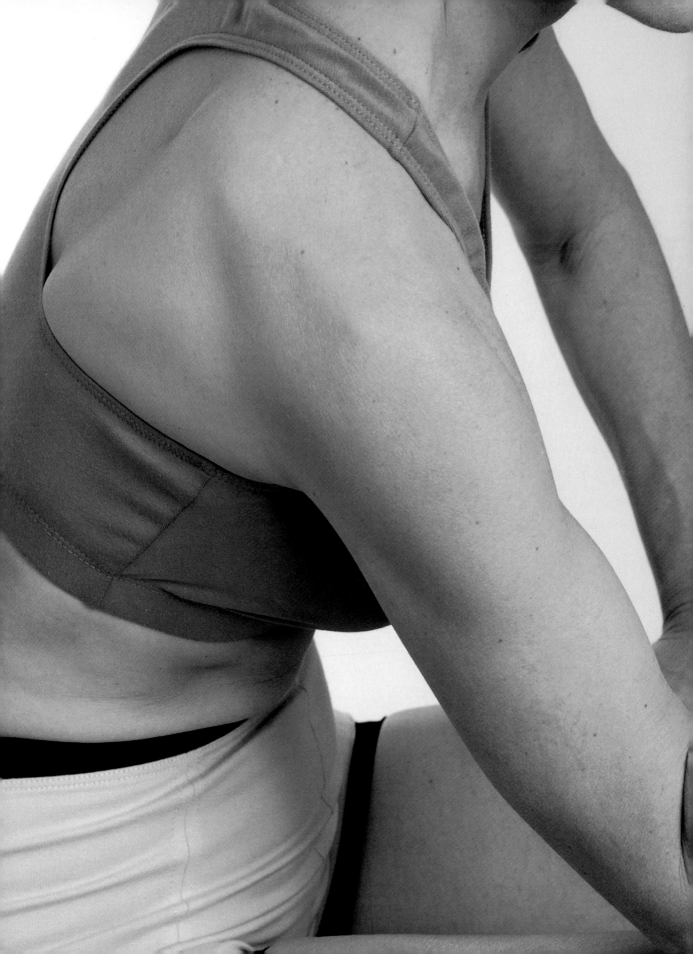

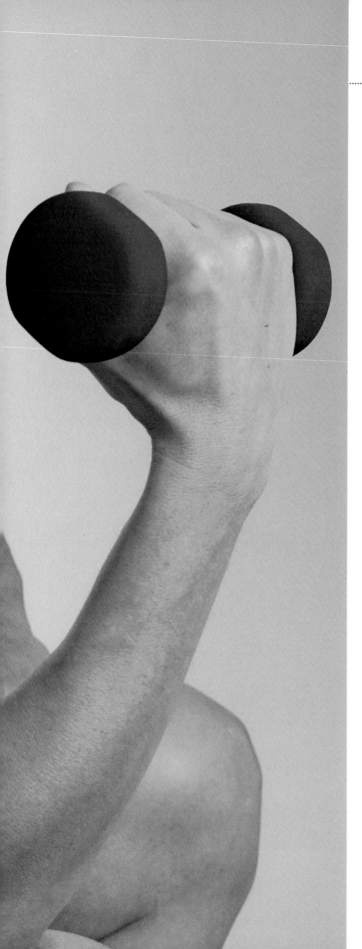

CHAPTER THREE

A Healthy Body

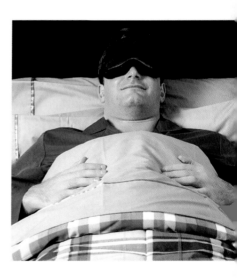

Tuning Up Your Body

Getting in shape can be fun, easy, and rewarding.

It's easy to find a few minutes to stretch every day, even in the busiest schedule.

TEN-MINUTE TUNE-UPS

If you can't find the time for a long workout in your hectic schedule, Rebecca Johnson and Bill Tulin have the answer. They co-authored *Travel Fitness*, designed to help busy business travelers keep fit while on the go. "New studies show that a regular, moderate amount of activity, spread throughout the course of a day, will keep you healthy. Even a 10-minute walk twice a day can get you on the road to feeling better," says Tulin.

The key to getting in shape when you're on a very tight schedule is flexibility. "Find hidden opportunities throughout your day to squeeze in a few exercises or stretches. Choose to be active whenever you can, and recognize that every bit of activity counts."

■ Walk whenever possible. Take the stairs instead of the elevator or escalator. Walk briskly to office meetings or when performing errands. Instead of parking your car right in front of your destination, park two or three blocks away and walk.

■ Try to accumulate 10 minutes or more of stretching per day. "Seize opportunities to stretch while watching TV, riding alone in an elevator, or waiting in line."

■ Think of your living room as your gym. You don't need expensive club memberships or fancy equipment to get a complete workout.

Quick Tricks

You can work at toning your muscles even while sitting at your office desk. Tulin and Johnson recommend these easy exercises for toning up while sitting down. Try to do these simple exercises once every hour or two when you are at your desk. Repeat each exercise five times when you do the routine.

Quadriceps extensions
Straighten your legs in front of you. Now tighten the muscles in the fronts of your thighs, and hold for two to three seconds before you release.

Abdomen tighteners
Press your lower back firmly against your seat, and pull in your abdominal muscles. Hold for two to three seconds, then release.

Fanny squeeze
Squeeze the buttocks muscles as tightly as you can for two to three seconds, and release.

WALKING FOR FUN AND FITNESS

Most fitness experts agree that walking is one of the safest and simplest ways to get in shape or stay that way. Janice McCaffrey of Calgary is an 11-time Canadian champion race walker. She is also a Commonwealth Games medal winner and has twice represented Canada at the Olympic Games. A former middle-distance runner, she took up race walking by chance in 1981.

An aerobic activity, race walking keeps McCaffrey's heart and lungs in top shape. An added bonus is that race walking helps to elevate mood and relieve stress. She calls the sport the ultimate in cross-training for a runner. In running, the calf and quadriceps muscles get a workout. In race walking, the shins and hamstrings do the work.

Walking can be enjoyed by almost anyone at any age or fitness level. Many people with osteoporosis, arthritis, and multiple sclerosis may reap the health benefits of walking.

Roger Burrows has been

True Stories

When Nona Black first set foot in an aerobics class five years ago, she never dreamed that she would end up teaching it. When her husband gave her a membership to the club where she now teaches, she weighed 220 pounds and was too intimidated by the fitness instructors to go very often. "Aerobics was just too hard, too choreographed, too much," she says.

Then she enlisted a friend to go with her, which helped her attendance. She also got a "new attitude." She decided that "just because the instructor was yelling 'push it!' didn't mean I had to." Black attended regularly and modified the moves that she found too difficult. "Lo and behold, I lost the weight," she says. After two years, one of the aerobics coordinators asked her if she would like to teach. Black was astonished. "I almost fell over in shock. Me? An instructor? One of those coordinated, energized, remember-everything people? I was flattered, scared, and excited."

Since becoming certified as an aerobics instructor, Black has been teaching step classes, high- and low-impact floor aerobics, aqua aerobics, cardiovascular conditioning classes, and abdominal classes. "I love the people," she says. "I especially love helping people who are heavy."

McCaffrey's coach for 24 years. Here are his tips for getting the most out of your walking workout:

- If you do not presently exercise, begin by walking normally—for longer periods. You should be able to stroll for 30 minutes before you move to the next stage.
- Start walking faster. The increased effort provides a good cardiovascular workout. By adding elements of a race walker's technique you can increase your speed. Bend your arms at the elbows so that your forearms are parallel to the ground, as if you were running. As you walk, use your shoulders to move your arms forward and back.
- Keep your strides short and quick—they are more efficient than long exaggerated strides. Alternate periods of your new "speedy" technique with normal walking. One minute of each.
- Wear clothes appropriate to the climate. Make sure you have well-fitting special fitness-walking shoes. Most competitors wear so-called "racing flats."

EVERYDAY EXERCISE

You don't have to be a marathon runner to stay in shape, says Darlene Sedlock, associate professor of kinesiology at Purdue University in Indiana. Even everyday activities such as gardening or mowing the lawn, if performed regularly, can help you keep your weight down, improve your cardiovascular condition, and boost self-confidence.

Sedlock calculated how many calories per hour an average 150-pound man would burn doing the following activities. If you weigh more or less than 150 pounds, you would burn more or fewer calories respectively. If you are trying to lose weight, Sedlock recommends trying to burn an extra 300 calories per day.

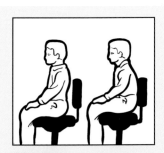

Pelvic tilts
Arch your back by pressing the small of your back forward. Then reverse the movement, pressing your lower back into the seat and pushing your hips forward.

Push-pull arm isometrics
If you have limited motion, clasp your hands in front of your chest and push them firmly together. Hold for a few seconds. Then clasp them tightly and pull out to either side.

Activity	Calories burned per hour
Standing still	115
Playing golf (without a cart)	265
Fishing, while walking and wading	270
Bicycling 5.5 mph	270
Walking 2 mph	315
Bicycling 9.4 mph	420
Playing tennis	460
Mowing the lawn	470
Digging in the garden	540
Running	615

It's a Stretch

Keep your body limber.

THE FUNDAMENTALS

Whether you're a weekend warrior or a seasoned athlete, stretching improves flexibility, helps prevent injury, reduces muscular soreness and tension, and helps you get in tune with your body. Michael J. Alter, a former gymnast, coach, and author of numerous

The Right Way

Michael J. Alter, physical education specialist, tells you how to make the most of your stretching routine.

Never stretch before a workout without warming up your muscles first. A short jog or three to five minutes on a stationary bicycle make good warm-ups. When it's cold out, take your time and make sure you're completely warmed up before exercising.

Lower leg stretch

Quadriceps stretch

Triceps stretch

Hamstring stretch

books on stretching, including *Sport Stretch*, recommends these safe, simple stretches, which engage many of your body's major muscle groups.

Lower leg stretch. Lean forward against a wall, with one leg bent forward and the other leg straight, with the rear foot planted firmly on the floor. Keeping both feet pointing straight forward and your forearms on the wall, exhale and flex your forward knee and shift your weight toward the wall. Keep your head, neck, spine, pelvis, rear leg, and ankle in a straight line.

Quadriceps stretch. Kneel with your knees, thighs, and heels together, and your toes pointing backward. Exhale and lean backward, resting on your extended arms, without letting your feet flare out to the sides. Do not arch your back or allow your knees to rise off the floor or spread apart.

Hamstring stretch. Sit on the floor with one leg straight and the other bent at the knee, the heel touching the inside of the opposite thigh (below). Keeping the outside

If you have trouble reaching your toes, try using a small towel to extend your reach.

of the thigh and calf of the bent leg on the floor, exhale and lower your upper torso toward the thigh of your extended leg.

Triceps stretch. Sit or stand with one arm flexed behind your head, the upper arm next to your ear and hand on your shoulder blade. Grasp your elbow. Exhale and gently pull your elbow behind your head.

Lower back stretch. Lie on your back with your knees bent. Grasping behind your thighs, exhale and pull your knees toward your chest and shoulders, elevating your hips off the floor. Re-extend slowly.

A DANCER'S PERSPECTIVE

Internationally renowned Canadian solo dancer Margie Gillis expresses her attitude toward life and dance this way: "If it's good for the soul, it's good for the muscles—and stretching the soul is good."

Gillis, who performs and tours actively, recently began working out in a gym to increase strength and endurance. During her daily hour-and-a-half workout, she warms up with a free-style hula dance, wiggling and moving different joints. In this way, she takes an inventory of her body's neuro-muscular system and works on each part. "Stretching comes in to lengthen a breathing muscle," she says. Lengthening muscles is important, as it gives her balance and a larger vocabulary of movement. It also helps maintain suppleness and range of motion. And as a dancer and artist, she is concerned with the quality of that motion.

Office stretches

Bob Anderson, one of North America's leading stretching experts, recommends these quick and easy stretches to prevent neck and back pain and repetitive strain injury. You can do them regularly at your desk.

Shoulder shrug

Head roll

Hand and wrist stretch

Lower back stretch

Full arm stretch

PREVENTING OFFICE INJURIES

"The human body was not designed for long periods of sitting," advises Bob Anderson, author of several books on stretching, including *Stretching at Your Computer or Desk*. Many sedentary people, especially those who spend long hours at computers, suffer from back pain, stiff muscles, tight joints, poor circulation, tension, and stress. More and more people are developing repetitive strain injuries, such as carpal tunnel syndrome, caused by repetitive movements—usually of the hands and wrists—that damage tendons, nerves, and muscles. "A word processor or programmer may perform as many as 20,000 key strokes with no breaks or variation," says Anderson. Here are his tips for avoiding office-related injuries and surviving a sedentary profession:

■ Take "micro-breaks" of about 30 seconds at least every 15 minutes or half-hour to stretch and move your muscles.

■ Make sure your desk and work space is set up for safety, comfort, and accessibility. Your monitor should be at least an arm's length from your eyes. Make sure your keyboard is at a height so that your forearms, wrists, and hands are aligned and parallel to the floor. Sit up straight—but not rigidly—in your chair, which should be both adjustable and comfortable.

■ Keep your arms and hands warm. Cold muscles and tendons are at greater risk of injury.

■ Don't pound the keys or grip the mouse tightly. Use a light, relaxed touch.

■ You want to stretch to a point of tension, never to a point of pain. Pain means you're pushing yourself too hard and are at risk of injury.

True Stories

Sharon Gannon fell down a flight of stairs 15 years ago, badly bruising the base of her spine. As a result, she lost the use of her right leg, was unable to stand up straight, and was told she might never regain her flexibility.

With the consent of her orthopedic surgeon, Gannon began to attend a yoga class. The deep breathing and gentle stretching immediately alleviated the chronic pain and muscle spasms, and she regained use of her leg. Now, after years of practicing yoga, she is much more supple and flexible than before the accident.

To find a yoga class, call the local "Y," a community center, or the continuing education department of your local school board.

Family Exercise

Stay healthy and have fun as a family.

MAKE IT FUN

People who've been exercising all their lives often have trouble adapting their routines to include their children, says Susan Kalish, author of *Your Child's Fitness*. That's because parents exercise to stay fit and look good. But kids exercise to have fun.

So, if you want to stay fit as a family, trying to include your kids in your existing exercise routine isn't going to work. Here are some ideas that will:

- Alter your routine to include your children's interests. You can jog with your children, but don't expect to run from start to finish. Plan to chat along the way and take time to stop at the pond and look for tadpoles, or to climb a favorite tree in the park.
- Find a way to include everyone. Kalish sometimes goes out running while her son rollerblades and her daughter cycles. Everyone can be together and no one worries about falling behind.
- Go at your children's pace. Let the slowest member lead the group so everyone can keep up. If you lead the way, your children will try to keep up with you and exhaust themselves, or they'll quit right away.
- Give positive feedback. Are your children learning to play baseball? Adults often don't realize how many different skills are involved in learning a new sport, or even just learning how to throw and catch a ball. Congratulate your children on each new accomplishment, such as holding the ball correctly or meeting the ball with the bat.

KEEP IT SIMPLE

Kids need to know they don't have to be talented athletes in order to stay fit, says Terry McGuinty of the Canadian Association for Health, Physical Education, Recreation and Dance (CAHPERD). Exercise is for everyone, not just kids who are privileged enough to do sports outside of school. That's why CAHPERD is trying to convince schools to offer quality daily physical education to all children.

Before television and video games, kids used to spend a lot more time being active. Today, many children go home and typically spend hours watching TV. Some children are so inactive that they're starting to show warning signs for stroke and heart disease.

CAHPERD has designed the Canadian Active Living Challenge, which teaches children and parents how to incorporate exercise into their day. Team sports can be fun, but kids can also get exercise by walking the dog or cycling after school. And children whose parents get involved see the best results. Set aside a couple of nights a week for a family walk after dinner, or go to the park and fly a kite.

The goal is to get children exercising while they're young. And kids who keep moving are likely to be healthier as they grow up.

Exercise built for two

Keep exercising fun by trying new experiences, such as sharing a ride on a tandem bicycle with your teenage son or daughter.

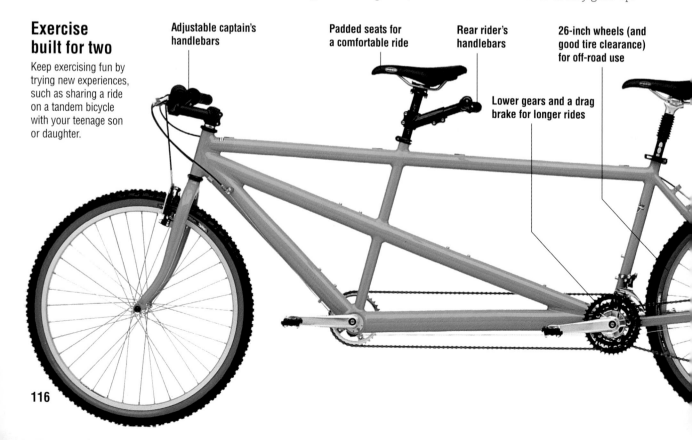

Adjustable captain's handlebars

Padded seats for a comfortable ride

Rear rider's handlebars

26-inch wheels (and good tire clearance) for off-road use

Lower gears and a drag brake for longer rides

Tools of the Trade

Get a stopwatch. Children like to time themselves, and love to break their old records. How long does it take to get to the top of the monkey bars? Run up the driveway backwards? Ride your bike around the park?

HOW FIT IS YOUR CHILD'S PHYS ED PROGRAM?

Every now and then parents get to see their child's report card and find out how the school rates their performance in physical education. But how does the school's phys ed program itself rate? Take the following quiz to find out:

1. Does the school provide your child with at least 30 minutes of instruction in physical education each day?

2. Does the program include opportunities for participation in school intramural activities and student leadership?

3. Is there a wide variety of physical activities offered?

4. Does the program include a cardiovascular component (activities such as running, skipping, aerobic dance or swimming)?

5. Does the program encourage children of all body types and abilities to participate?

6. Does the program emphasize fun, socialization, and active living rather than just competition and traditional team sports?

7. Are the teachers qualified?

8. Does the school provide a safe environment for physical activity?

9. Does the school make use of other facilities in addition to the gymnasium (such as the community skating rink or pool)?

10. Does your child look forward to physical education classes and intramural activities?

Quiz supplied by the Canadian Association for Health, Physical Education, Recreation and Dance.

If you answered yes to all 10 questions, your child has an excellent program. If you answered yes to between 6 and 8 questions, the program is good. If you answered yes to fewer than 6 questions, find out more about what the school offers and seek ways to persuade the administration to implement better programs. If you don't know the answers to some of the questions, the time to find out is now. A quality program should offer a wide range of activities. To find out how you can make a difference, call the Canadian Association for Health, Physical Education, Recreation and Dance at 1-800-663-8708 or visit their website at www.cahperd.ca.

FAMILY FIRST

Wallace Rolph, father of three and executive director of the Family Fitness Factory in Michigan puts family relationships first and fitness second. Rolph and his employees use exercise as a means of bringing families closer together.

■ When parents and children play competitive sports together, they begin to see each other in new ways—as teammates and equals on the field. Children see their parents make mistakes and keep on playing, learning that it's perfectly fine for them to make mistakes, too.

■ Taking martial arts classes can be a great way to spend time with your children. Everyone starts out on the same footing, and together the family can progress toward achieving higher belts and more skills. Often children learn certain skills even faster than their parents, putting them in a position to help mom and dad, which can be a great confidence-booster for any child.

■ Be enthusiastic about all your children's interests. If one child does ballet and the other plays soccer, spend an equal amount of time watching them and cheering them on.

■ Group activities that require team thinking and cooperative effort are great ways to get families talking. Look into family camps that offer this kind of activity.

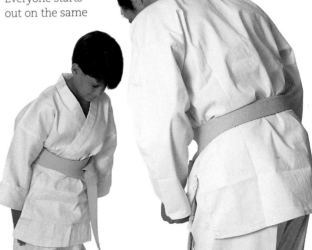

Smart Moves

■ Learn a little bit about the sports and activities your children participate in (whether it's modern dance, hockey, tennis, or gymnastics) to show you support them in what they're doing.

■ Focus on what your children are doing right, not what they're doing wrong. Otherwise they'll stop thinking of exercise as fun and start thinking of it as a chore.

■ Take the time to enjoy exercising with your children. Kids really do model their behavior after adults. If you have a good time, your children will as well.

Active at Any Age

As you get older, it's more important than ever to keep your body moving.

Myth: *People over 65 or 70 should avoid exercise because they're getting frail and will hurt themselves.*

Fact: *Regular exercise exposes most seniors to far more benefits than dangers, and can actually prevent the early onset of frailty.*

HELPING OLDER PARENTS

Dr. Robert Goode, professor of physical education and physiology at the University of Toronto, a member of the Institute of Aging, and author of *Fitness for the Fun of It*, explains that adult children of older parents can help them keep fit by encouraging them to join exercise classes. (If the person has been inactive and is older than 40, Goode recommends a checkup with a physician about the type and amount of exercise that are safe.)

- Let them go at their own pace. Whatever the type of exercise, they should be able to talk. If they cannot comfortably talk, they should slow down immediately.
- For health benefits, they should be able to work up to five or more minutes of exercise during which they can hear their own breathing. This means breathing is just audible and no louder, indicating that heart, lungs, and muscles are getting a good workout.
- Most healthy older people will prefer exercising to music of their era.
- Look for classes with gentle exercises that won't put them at risk of physical injury.

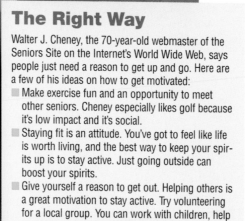

The Right Way

Walter J. Cheney, the 70-year-old webmaster of the Seniors Site on the Internet's World Wide Web, says people just need a reason to get up and go. Here are a few of his ideas on how to get motivated:

- Make exercise fun and an opportunity to meet other seniors. Cheney especially likes golf because it's low impact and it's social.
- Staying fit is an attitude. You've got to feel like life is worth living, and the best way to keep your spirits up is to stay active. Just going outside can boost your spirits.
- Give yourself a reason to get out. Helping others is a great motivation to stay active. Try volunteering for a local group. You can work with children, help out with animals, or pitch in at the park.
- Try something new. Many older people enjoy yoga classes, where they can do low-impact exercises in the company of others.
- Contact your local senior center for more ideas and information. Ask about exercise classes, walking groups, and day trips.

Smart Moves

Doing a variety of activities will keep you in good shape and keep your exercise program interesting. Here are some suggestions:

▪ Hockey is *the* Canadian sport at every age. The Canadian Adult Recreational Hockey Association (formerly known as Oldtimers Hockey) is an affiliation of leagues for men and women all over the country. To join a league, consult the association's website at www.carha.ca or call toll free 1-800-267-1854.

▪ The Canadian Senior Games Association sponsors competitions in chess and bridge, as well as active sports such as golf, swimming, and tennis. Every two years there are national events. Contact your provincial seniors organization for a referral or call (506) 847-3928.

▪ John Sellers of the Canadian Square and Round Dance Society says more than 26,000 Canadians belong to dance clubs. To find a club near you, consult the Web at www.csrds.ca.

Walking is one of the best exercises for older people because it's gentle and easy to do. Start out at a leisurely pace and slow down when you get tired. Gradually, you'll be able to walk faster and farther, perhaps even tackling a few hills. And because walking is gentle on the joints, you're less likely to injure yourself.

A NEW LEASE ON LIFE

Mollie Morris didn't start exercising on a regular basis until she retired to Florida, 19 years ago. Today, at 79, she regularly goes to her Jazzercize class four or five times a week. To Morris, exercise isn't just about keeping fit (although her doctor is full of kudos). It's about making friends and staying in touch with younger generations. Her Jazzercize class has introduced her to friends of all ages, and also keeps her up to date on the current pop music hits.

Here are some other ways to stay in shape suggested by Morris:

Take an exercise class. If the steps are too high-impact, you can easily tone them down to a level you're comfortable with. For example, Morris marches in place instead of bouncing. As an added plus, if Morris doesn't show up at her exercise class, several other members of the class wind up phoning her later to make sure she's okay.

Get a dog. Although Morris' housing community doesn't allow dogs, she takes over walking her children's dog when she goes to visit—which keeps her in shape while she's away from her Jazzercize class.

Walk every day. Walking is very popular in Morris' community, and she makes a point of parking a good distance from her destination so she can take a brisk walk to and from the car.

Quick Tricks

▪ Tap water weighs around 8.33 pounds per gallon. You can use this information to make your own hand weights. Simply consult the chart below to figure out how much water you need to use for the weights you want, and then pour that amount into an appropriately sized, leak-proof container.

▪ Or use pre-weighed grocery items instead. Food labels generally display the weight of the contents. And you can either use the original packaging (such as with soup cans) or put the product into a more manageable receptacle (such as sugar in a resealable plastic container).

WATER
1 gallon = 8 pounds
3 quarts = 6 pounds
2 quarts = 4 pounds
1 quart = 2 pounds
1 cup = ½ pound

Can of soup = 1 pound

USE IT OR LOSE IT

Age is no barrier to keeping active, says Sandra O'Brien Cousins, PhD, an exercise gerontologist at the University of Alberta in Edmonton. But neither is poor health, although many people use this as a reason not to exercise. Still, Cousins says, for some people, health problems, such as heart attack or arthritis, act as a trigger to get them moving. Lack of physical activity puts an older person at greater risk for disease and disability. Exercising will help you stay healthier and, therefore, more independent. Cousins puts the emphasis on "able" in the following types of exercises:

▪ EndurAble: endurance activities that improve heart health.

▪ LiftAble—strength exercises that help older people do things they need—and like—to do.

▪ StabAble—balance exercises that help prevent falls.

▪ FlexAble—stretching to keep the body limber.

Dress for Exercise Success

The right clothes and shoes can enhance your exercise routine.

Inline skaters need to wear a bicycle helmet as well as elbow and knee pads and wrist guards.

Football helmet
Impact-absorbing plastic and layers of foam dampen shock.

ON THE GO

When you are exercising outdoors—hiking, biking or running—you have to carry everything you bring with you. That's why it is essential to choose your apparel carefully, says Susan Bush, a musician who has ridden her bicycle more than 4,000 miles during the past three summers, as part of Tanqueray's American AIDS rides program, raising $24,000 for AIDS services.

To stay comfortable and dry no matter what the weather is doing, use layers, advises Bush. Here's her high-performance layering system:

Layer 1: A thin layer of synthetic fabric (often a combination of polyester, nylon, or spandex) next to the skin to wick away moisture and perspiration and keep you warm and dry.

Layer 2: A warm, breathable outer layer (often in synthetic fleece) that will keep you warm during chilly early mornings, but is lightweight enough to take off and carry with you when the temperature rises or you start to warm up.

Layer 3: A lightweight, breathable, waterproof top layer. Bush uses a simple plastic rain jacket with air vents on the side. However, she highly recommends the high-tech fabric Gore-Tex® if it's within your budget because of its comfort and durability.

Here are some of Bush's other suggestions for long-distance athletes:

Wear fitted, but not skintight, clothing. Baggy tops and bottoms weigh you down, flap, and billow in the wind, let in drafts, and won't keep you warm if they get wet.

Invest in a pair of arm warmers (polyester, nylon, and spandex) to get maximum warmth with a minimum amount of bulk.

Look for jerseys with pockets in the back where you can stow your top layer as the day heats up.

To keep your legs warm in winter, consider cycling pants that have warmer, wind-breaking material in the front and thinner, breathable fabric in the back to protect you from the cold while allowing your legs to move more easily.

Choose high tech synthetics over cotton, down, and wool. Natural fabrics are bulky, and don't dry out or wick away moisture as efficiently as synthetics. Plus, synthetics are usually comfortable against the skin and long-lasting.

The shoe for you

Different sports require different kinds of shoes. So when the salesperson tells you that one shoe is made for jogging and another for playing basketball, it's not just hype. Pete Gilmore, footwear product line manager for L.L.Bean, describes the differences among several popular sports shoes.

Batting helmet
Every player should have a helmet that fits perfectly.

Lacrosse helmet
Helmets should remain snug while players run.

Ice-Hockey helmet
Skaters need protection from collisions, falls, and flying pucks.

Smart Moves

Richard Cotton, an exercise physiologist and personal trainer from California, suggests the following tips for staying safe and comfortable while working out at the gym:

- Don't overdress in warm-ups and sweat pants to make yourself perspire more. Choose lightweight, breathable clothes that can be layered under a lightweight jacket until you're warmed up.
- Watch out for baggy clothing, or ties and zippers that can get caught in exercise machines. Play it safe by exercising in form-fitting athletic apparel.
- Wear form-fitting pants instead of shorts on the stationary bicycle to protect your legs from rubbing against the seat.
- Don't wear street clothes in the gym since they can inhibit movement.
- Wear shoes with good shock absorbency (not tennis shoes) for aerobics.
- Wear walking or running shoes to support your feet and legs if you spend a lot of time on the treadmill.
- Wear synthetic sports socks if you get blisters from wet cotton socks rubbing against your feet.
- Wear white sport socks to avoid dyes seeping into sweaty feet.

The Right Way

The most important thing to look for in any athletic shoe is a good fit. The problem, according to Pete Gilmore, sports outfitter at L.L. Bean, is that many people don't know what a good fit is. Here's what to look for when trying on new athletic shoes.

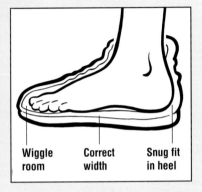

Wiggle room — Correct width — Snug fit in heel

PLAY IT SAFE

"Safety is the number one concern when it comes to kids playing sports," says Andy Escala, a physical education teacher who coaches varsity baseball and children's ice hockey. Make sure your child's coach is concerned with the safety of the team. If not, complain or find another coach.

The head is the most important part of the body to protect, emphasizes Escala. Make sure children always wear appropriate, high-quality head gear for every sport they play.

Sports helmets have become far more advanced in recent years. But even the most high-tech helmet won't work unless it's fitted properly. Helmets should be snug but comfortable, and shouldn't move around on children's heads.

Find out the safety standards for each sport. For example, batting helmets should cover the head and ears, and youth leagues are now using chin straps to keep them in place.

Make sure your children always take these safety precautions:

- Take off all jewelry before you play.
- Avoid shoes with replaceable cleats for baseball.
- Always wear a mouth guard during contact sports, which protects teeth and can prevent shock caused by a child's teeth banging together after an impact.

Walking shoes have to take less impact, so they offer lightweight cushioning, comfort, and breathability.

Running shoes feature a supportive upper and thick soles to absorb the impact of your foot striking the ground.

Basketball shoes feature extra cushioning and ankle support to keep your foot in place as you twist, turn, and jump around.

Outdoor cross-trainers are good all-around shoes, for active lifestyles, but not the best choice for any one sport or activity.

A Healthier Diet

**Enjoy the many benefits
of a healthy diet.**

FIVE TO TEN A DAY

Eating five to ten servings
of fruits and vegetables a
day as part of a healthy diet
may substantially lower
your chances of developing
cancer, heart disease, high
blood pressure, stroke, and
diabetes, says Allison Davis,
director of programs for the
Canadian Cancer Society's
5 to 10 a Day, a nationwide
nutrition campaign recently
launched with the Heart
and Stroke Foundation
of Canada. A diet rich in
fruits and vegetables may
also give you more energy,
aid your digestion, and
help you take off those
extra pounds.

- Choose fresh or frozen
  vegetables. Recent studies
  suggest that flash-frozen
  fruits and vegetables
  contain as many nutri-
  ents as fresh ones.
- Studies suggest that leafy
  green vegetables, such as
  spinach, and cruciferous
  vegetables, such as cabbage and broccoli, may
  protect against certain
  types of cancer.
- Orange and red vegeta-
  bles, such as carrots,
  winter squash, and red
  peppers, contain antioxidants which neutralize
  cancer-causing free-radi-
  cals and may decrease
  the risk of developing
  heart disease.
- The pectin—or soluble
  fiber—found in fruits
  such as apples may lower
  blood cholesterol levels.

ADDING HEALTHY INGREDIENTS

Adding these three tasty
and readily available foods
to your diet could provide
health benefits and significantly improve the quality
of your life, according to
Jean Barilla, MS, a biologist
and author of several natural health books, including
*Natural Health Secrets from
Around the World.*

Garlic. Fresh garlic is not
only delicious, but it contains lots of selenium, a
known foe of cancer and a
natural antibiotic. Garlic is
also a storehouse of antioxidants, and may decrease
the likelihood of developing
strokes, high blood pres-
sure, high cholesterol, blood
clots, and some cancers.
Garlic's antioxidant properties may also protect your
body from some of the
damaging effects of envi-
ronmental pollution.

Olive oil. Replace the saturated fats in your diet with
olive oil, and you may benefit from the lower heart disease and cancer rates
enjoyed by Mediterranean

peoples, who cook almost
exclusively with it.

"Olive oil is the best oil
you can eat," says Barilla.
It contains essential fatty
acids and antioxidants,
which protect the heart and
arteries, and act as an anti-
inflammatory. It also contains squalene, which can
help reduce cholesterol levels, lower your blood pressure, and protect against
abnormal blood clotting,
not to mention improve
your complexion. It is also
a source of oleic acid, which
keeps your cells youthful as
you age, says Barilla.

Yogurt. This ancient food is
an important source of aci-
dophilus, a "good" bacteria
that promotes a healthy
digestive tract. It is a natural antacid and aids the
absorption of nutrients in

the intestine. It helps the
body maintain a healthy
pH balance, killing germs
and preventing yeast from
growing in the blood
stream. Barilla especially
recommends it for sufferers
of yeast infections and for
people taking antibiotics,
which can strip the body of
important bacteria that aid
in the digestion of food.

Try these ways to add
them to your diet: If you
don't like garlic raw, finely
chop a clove or two, and
add to vegetables or main
dishes just before they've
finished cooking. Use olive
oil rather than butter or
other oils. Substitute plain
yogurt for sour cream or
mayonnaise in cold dips
and sauces, or combine
yogurt with fruit for a
delicious dessert.

Myth: *Artificial sweeteners are helping North Americans consume less sugar.* **Fact:** *Sugar consumption
in the US alone has increased by 20 percent in the last
15 years, despite the availability of artificial sweeteners.*

The Right Way

The current Health Canada voluntary guidelines for nutrition information labeling are in the process of being revised. The aim is to harmonize the Canadian and American food labeling systems. However, some manufacturers voluntarily list nutrition information that is useful in planning a balanced diet. Many experts recommend consuming less than 20 grams of saturated fat and less than 50 grams of total fat per day for optimum cardiovascular health. Saturated fats include all fats from animal sources, such as meat and dairy products, hydrogenated oils, such as whipped topping and non-dairy creamer, and tropical oils, such as coconut and palm oil. It's important too to track serving sizes and calories. Montreal-based nutritional expert Dr. Joe Schwarcz advises people to eat between 20 and 30 grams of fiber a day, and to avoid consuming more than 2,400 milligrams (one teaspoon) of sodium a day.

Nutrition Information

Per 30 g Serving Cereal (175 ml, ¾ cup)

Energy	Cal	100
	kJ	420
Protein		3.0 g
Fat		0.6 g
Carbohydrate		24.0 g
Sugars		4.4 g
Starch		16.6 g
Dietary fiber		3.0 g
Sodium		3.0 mg
Potassium		265 mg
Protein		168 g

SUGAR BLUES

Although Canadians' sugar intake has changed little in 70 years, it is still a matter for concern. Sugar triggers insulin release, and studies link fluctuating insulin levels with health problems. Young people can get up to 15 percent of their calories from refined sugars. Overindulgence pushes healthy foods out of the diet and contributes to tooth decay, obesity, and heart disease.

Soft drinks are a major source of sugar in the Canadian diet, says Tammy Cooper, a staff dietitian at the National Institute of Nutrition in Ottawa. They are replacing water, as well as more nutritious drinks, such as milk and juice. Try limiting soft-drink intake to once a day. Many packaged foods, such as some cereals, canned foods, and condiments are also loaded with sugar. When you look at the list of their ingredients, be aware that sugar comes in many forms. Anything that ends with the letters "ose" (as in fructose) is a sugar.

Instead of sugary foods, choose nutrient- and fiber-rich whole foods whenever possible to stay healthy.

Quick Tricks

Ask for air-popped popcorn when you go to the movie theater. Even without topping it with butter, movie theater popcorn that's been popped in tropical oil may have up to 20 or 25 grams of saturated fat—more than the recommended daily maximum. The same is true for french fries cooked in saturated fat.

EATING FOR A HEALTHY HEART

Cholesterol levels are expressed in millimoles per liter (mmol/l) or milligrams per deciliter (mg/dl). A value below 5.2 mmol/l (200 mg/dl) is considered safe. A figure of 6.2 mmol/l (240 mg/dl) or more is considered high. William Castelli, MD, director emeritus of the U.S. federal government's Framingham Heart Study, says people can substantially lower their risk of heart disease if they consume less saturated fat and fewer refined foods. According to Castelli:

■ People with cholesterol levels lower than 3.9 mmol/l (150 mg/dl) have the lowest incidence of heart disease, while people with levels above 5.8 mmol/l (225 mg/dl) have the highest. People with cholesterol levels above 7.8 mmol/l (300 mg/dl) have five times as many heart attacks as people with cholesterol levels of 3.9 mmol/l (150 mg/dl).

■ The fatty acids in fish oils lower cholesterol levels in the body and protect the arteries. If you don't like the taste of fish, add a daily fish oil nutritional supplement to your diet.

■ Soy proteins have also been linked to lower cholesterol levels. Try soy-based veggie burgers, tofu, roasted soy beans, soy drinks, and powdered soy supplements.

■ If you want to introduce your family to healthier eating habits, a gradual change works best. Begin by replacing some of the meat in your recipes with heart-friendly beans, grain, or soy products to reduce saturated fats.

The Great Diet Debate

Throw away the diet books and start losing weight permanently.

SHAPE UP NOW!

Obesity and weight-related conditions contribute to as many as half of the leading causes of preventable deaths in Canada, says Dr. Glen Berall, of the Nutritional and Eating Disorders Center. Maintaining a healthy weight can significantly reduce your chances of developing diabetes, heart disease, cancer, and other disabling illnesses.

Gradual weight loss, through a combination of sensible eating and moderate exercise, is the safest, healthiest—and easiest—way to reach your goals and feel good. But Dr. Berall says it's essential to identify and address factors that contribute to the weight-related condition.

Learn good food management. For instance, don't bring ice cream home if you can't keep it around for more than an hour without eating it. Instead, go out for a cone once in a while.

Exercise. This does not mean a grueling two hours at the gym. But it might mean a brisk daily walk. Try to be active for at least 30 minutes a day.

Don't turn dining into a duty. Eating is a pleasure, and it should remain so. If you completely deprive yourself of the foods you love, you could be setting yourself up for a binge.

Learn portion control. Educate your eye. A serving of meat should be no thicker than your hand and no bigger than your palm. A portion of mashed potatoes should be the size of your fist. Fill up your plate once, and don't go back for seconds.

Avoid surrounding yourself with saboteurs. Surround yourself with supportive family, friends, and colleagues. It may be beneficial to seek counselling from a qualified professional if you are an emotional eater.

Quick Tricks

- Spice up a low-fat tomato sauce with capers, olives, garlic, onion, fresh basil, anchovies, or hot peppers.
- Make a delicious, frothy fruit smoothie with low-fat milk and yogurt, frozen berries and bananas, and a touch of honey.
- Low-fat yogurt strained through a cheesecloth makes a tangy alternative to cream cheese, as a spread, or used in recipes.
- Try baked spaghetti squash instead of pasta as a base for your favorite sauces.

WHY WE OVEREAT

"People have hidden issues that sabotage their fervent wish to be slender," says Michelle Joy Levine, a certified psychotherapist and psychoanalyst and author of *I Wish I Were Thin...I wish I were fat.* "Unless they understand the underlying reasons that cause them to overeat in

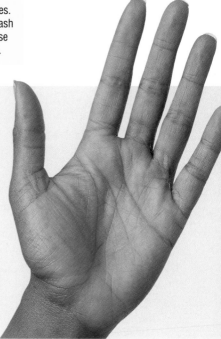

Learn portion control
A serving of meat should be no thicker than your hand and no bigger than your palm.

A piece of cheese should be no larger than your thumb.

True Stories

Cheryl Townsley went from being a high-powered sales executive with a six-figure income to 65 pounds overweight and too depressed and exhausted to hold a job. In her high-stress career, Townsley had completely neglected her health. She lived on junk food and rarely exercised. After five years, she finally sought help from a nutritionist, who got her on the road to feeling better with a healthy, natural diet and moderate exercise. Within six months, Townsley lost most of the weight and had her energy back.

Townsley recommends taking these steps toward good health and a sense of well-being:

- Counting calories doesn't work, says Townsley. Instead, enjoy whole foods, such as fruits and vegetables, and whole grains.
- Minimize chemicals, preservatives, food colorings, white flour, and hydrogenated fats, such as margarine and vegetable oil.
- If you're too depressed or tired to exercise vigorously, start simply with a little walking and light activity around the house. Eventually your energy level will improve and you're more likely to feel like exercising.
- Go one step at a time. If you expect miracles, you are setting yourself up for failure.

the first place, it is practically impossible for people to lose weight and keep it off. Many people who have problems with food are unconsciously expressing anger or fear or defiance, or the wish for control through overeating."

While the causes of overeating are individual and complex, there are some ways to help you get in touch with those reasons and your feelings about food. Here are some of the techniques Levine practices with her patients:

- Keep a food diary. On one side of the page list exactly what you ate and in what quantity. Next to

Psychotherapist Michelle Joy Levine recommends keeping a food diary.

that write down what you were feeling before you ate and afterwards. Be honest with yourself. Keep this record faithfully for at least one month.

- Set aside at least a few minutes at the end of

each day to think about the thoughts, feelings, and insights you've been recording in your food diary. The importance of this exercise is to help you identify and understand the causes of your

overeating and your feelings toward food.

- When you are about to eat something you know you will regret, wait for 10 minutes. After 10 minutes you may eat it if you still wish to, because you are in control of what you eat. Think about what feelings are evoking your desire to eat. Work on resolving that underlying issue, be it fear, anger, loneliness, or whatever is causing you to want to eat something you will regret. Addressing the underlying issues is the key to success in managing emotionally based eating problems.

A portion of mashed potatoes should be about the size of your fist.

Enjoy in abundance

Portion control is a big part of learning how to eat sensibly and recognizing the feeling of fullness. However, it's pretty difficult to become overweight by eating too many fruits and vegetables. Most raw, whole fruits and vegetables are low in calories and high in bulk—which means they will make you feel full and prevent you from overeating. They're also great sources of vitamins, minerals, and other essential nutrients—and they're surprisingly delicious.

LISTEN TO YOUR BODY

"Honor your hunger," says Evelyn Tribole, a registered dietitian and co-author of *Intuitive Eating: A Recovery Book for the Chronic Dieter*. Throw out the diet books and start listening to your body.

- Stop dieting now. Most overeating and binge eating is actually a result of dieting, says Tribole. It's a simple biological fact that if you undereat—in other words, diet—you set off mechanisms in your body and mind that cause you to binge and obsess about food. Dieting also lowers the metabolic rate, so even though you are starving yourself, the pounds will stubbornly remain.
- Give yourself permission to eat, says Tribole. If you tell yourself you can't eat a certain food, you'll end up feeling

deprived. That makes it likely you will experience cravings and possibly binges.

- Ask yourself these questions every time you eat: Am I truly hungry? If not, what am I feeling now? Is there anything I can give myself other than food that will make me feel better?
- Learn to trust your body to tell you when it is full. Listen for the signals in your body that you are no longer hungry. Do you feel satisfied? Are you still picking simply out of habit? Take time to enjoy your meals and the feeling of satisfaction they give you.
- Respect yourself. And your body. Stop comparing yourself to images of movie stars and models.
- Don't expect success overnight, warns Tribole. Intuitive eating is a long-term approach. But it works.

Supplementing Your Diet

There's no substitute for a healthy and varied diet.

NATURE'S MEDICINE CHEST

Our food supply is rich with nutrients that give us energy and protect our bodies from disease, says Rosie Schwartz, RD, a Toronto-based consulting dietitian and author of *The Enlightened Eater*. Medical experts are just beginning to understand the ways that nutrients in food interact together.

For example, the vitamins, minerals, and other disease-fighting chemicals in plant foods work together and in balance. Some nutrients and minerals cannot be absorbed without the presence of others, and many of these interactions are impossible to imitate in a pill at this time. In addition, the risk of supplements is that they may throw off nature's balance, creating overdoses of some nutrients and deficiencies in others. Schwartz's prescription? Eat plenty of plant foods and eat a variety. Sometimes moderate supplementation might be helpful for good health. Here's when:

■ Occasionally when people want to make sure they are getting enough of the various nutrients, a multivitamin and mineral supplement which contains no more than the recommended levels is suggested.

■ Everyone should get enough folic acid, which may help reduce the risk of heart disease and some cancers. Pregnant women in particular should get adequate folic acid, which lowers the risk of certain birth defects. To get the right amounts of nutrients, pregnant women should take a prenatal vitamin supplement, not a multivitamin, which may contain too much vitamin A.

■ If you are anemic, a vegetarian, or have food allergies that prevent you from eating certain foods, you may want to consider supplementation. For instance, if you can't eat dairy products, you may run the risk of a calcium deficiency.

FANTASTIC PHYTOCHEMICALS

Phytochemicals give you thousands of good reasons to eat a diet rich in plant-based foods. They give plant foods their distinctive colors and flavors and also may provide protection against cancer, heart disease, hypertension, and diseases associated with aging, according to Nancy Clark, MS, a registered dietitian and author of *Nancy Clark's Sports Nutrition Guidebook, Second Edition*. Among her clients are members of the Boston Red Sox and Celtics, as well as Olympic athletes.

Spinach is rich in vitamin A and potassium.

Greens are high in fiber and vitamins E and K.

Chili peppers contain vitamins A, C, E, P, and K+.

Onions contain dietary sulfur.

Pineapples are high in vitamin C.

Oranges are a great source of vitamin C, fiber, and potassium.

Peanuts offer protein, niacin, and pantothenic acid.

Strawberries are natural diuretics.

NANCY CLARK'S PHYTOCHEMICAL SHORTLIST

There are thousands of different phytochemicals, and scientists are discovering more all the time. Clark's list gives you an idea of some of their remarkable properties.

Food	Phytochemical	Action
Strawberries, pineapples	Chlorogenic acid	Helps block the production of carcinogens
Spinach, collard greens	Lutein	Helps reduce blindness in the elderly
Chili peppers	Capsaicin	Hinders the growth of cancer
Beans, peas, peanuts	Isoflavones	May reduce the risk of breast cancer
Citrus fruits	Terpenes	Help block tumor growth
Soy milk, tofu	Genistein	Helps protect against small tumors
Garlic, onions	Allylic sulfide	Slows tumor growth
All fruits and vegetables	Flavonoids	Help prevent carcinogenic hormones from attaching to cells

Lemons are rich in vitamin C.

Carrots provide vitamin A and fiber.

Garlic helps lower cholesterol.

A HEAD START

"Most kids are picky eaters," says Christine Williams, MD, MPH, director of the Child Health Center of the American Health Foundation. "And studies show that many kids aren't getting the vitamins and minerals they need in their diet." While Williams suggests that this is reason enough to add a daily children's multivitamin and mineral tablet to your child's breakfast menu, she emphasizes that supplements are no replacement for a wholesome, varied diet, especially for growing children.

Williams suggests trying to make these adjustments to your child's diet:

■ Children imitate parents' eating habits. Be a good role model for your kids and eat healthily.
■ If your child is picky about eating vegetables, grind them up and disguise them in soups, meat loaf, pasta sauce, meatballs, and chili.
■ Most children are not getting the dietary fiber they need. Fiber not only aids the digestion, but it may also reduce the risk of developing heart disease, cancer, diabetes, and stroke in adulthood. Children should eat an amount of fiber equal to their age plus 5 grams a day. For instance, an eight-year-old should eat at least 13 grams of fiber per day.
■ Forty percent of children have borderline high cholesterol. Try to restrict your child's intake of refined and fatty foods, such as french fries, hot dogs, ice cream, and processed meats.
■ Many children enjoy highly nutritious and low-fat soy foods, such as tofu, soy protein shakes, and veggie burgers.
■ Fish is a highly nutritious food. Try to serve it to your children at least twice a week.
■ If your child suddenly develops a dislike for a certain food, don't force him to eat it. There may be an underlying allergy.
■ Children who watch a lot of television instead of pursuing more active hobbies have a higher rate of obesity. Limit television to one hour a day.

Smart Moves

■ The body does not absorb minerals in supplement form very well. Incorporate high-mineral foods, such as wheat germ, seaweed, alfalfa sprouts, and nuts, into your diet.
■ Many women suffer from iron deficiency. Foods high in iron are organ meats, oats, raisins, peaches, beans, and leafy green vegetables.
■ Get the calcium without the saturated fat by eating low-fat dairy products.

CHOOSING A SUPPLEMENT

The vitamin industry is a $4 billion business, warns Nancy Clark. Although she advises "food first," she offers these guidelines for choosing a multivitamin and mineral supplement to add to your diet:

■ Ignore claims about natural vitamins. The body can't tell the difference between synthetic and natural vitamins. Besides, most "natural" vitamins are in fact blended with synthetic ones.
■ Don't pay premium prices for chelated supplements, which offer no special health benefits.
■ For best absorption, take your supplement with or after a meal.

The Right Way

"When it comes to supplements, more is not necessarily better," says Vivian Pincus, a registered dietitian who works with cardiovascular patients. Some vitamins, such as vitamins A and D, are toxic in large doses. Excess vitamin A causes calcium loss from the bones. Others cause unpleasant—even dangerous—side effects. To be sure that you don't exceed the upper tolerable limits of vitamins and minerals, consult with your physician or a registered dietitian about supplementation.

Look Younger, Feel Younger

Learn to look after your body and your mind.

PAMPER YOURSELF REGULARLY

"We can create some of the spa experience for ourselves," says Margaret Pierpont, co-author of *The Spa Life at Home*. As an executive editor at *Longevity Magazine*, Pierpont has had the good fortune to visit the best spas all over North America.

Here is a classic spa experience that anyone can do at home, says Pierpont. Set aside an hour every week to enjoy this easy and revitalizing ritual:

■ Create a pleasant environment for yourself. Turn off the phone. Let in the natural light. Or lower the lights and burn scented candles. Play soft, relaxing music.
■ Take an invigorating shower. Use a loofah, washcloth, or your favorite scrub to exfoliate the skin. Thoroughly scrub your skin and cleanse yourself.

■ Run a bath. Make the water warm enough to help you relax, but not so hot as to make you uncomfortable. Add inexpensive Epsom salts or other bath products or oils to help you relax and moisturize your skin. Give yourself at least 20 minutes to relax in your bath and daydream. "We all need time for reverie," says Pierpont.
■ When you're finished, take a quick, cool shower. Dry off with a clean, soft towel, and put on your robe and slippers.
■ Lie down for another 20 minutes. Pamper yourself by putting a scented eye bag or soft cloth over your eyes. To help relax your lower back, roll up a towel and place it under your knees. Let go of all your worries and allow yourself to rest.

THE MIND-BODY CONNECTION

"Stress is killing us," warns Lori Leyden-Rubenstein, PhD, a psychotherapist and author of *The Stress Management Handbook*. Approximately 100 million North Americans suffer from stress- and anxiety-related illnesses, and stress has been linked to heart disease, cancer, lung disease, accidents, and suicide.

Stress sets off powerful reactions in the body that depress the immune system and negatively affect your overall well-being, says Leyden-Rubenstein. Most of these reactions are avoidable if you learn how to respond to stressful feelings in a positive way. These easy exercises will get you on the path to emotional, physical, and spiritual healing:

Breathing. When you feel stressed or anxious, your breathing can become irregular and shallow, says Leyden-Rubenstein. Proper breathing can help you relax, get in tune with yourself, and feel more in control of your emotions. If you're feeling anxious, take a few moments to breathe deeply. Inhale slowly, and as fully as possible. Hold the breath for a few moments, then release. Now hold for a few moments again before inhaling. Repeat 10 times or until you begin to feel calmer and more confident.
Recognize distorted thinking and negative feelings about yourself. Are you constantly putting yourself down? Do you have negative feelings

Myth: *You can't control your health.* **Fact:** *Studies show that hope, trust, optimism, good relationships, a positive outlook, and a feeling of control can contribute to health and healing.*

Taking the time to relax and pamper yourself reduces stress and can help you stay healthy.

about your job, your relationships, or your life? Research suggests that the vast majority of the negative thoughts that people have about themselves and their lives are distorted and exaggerated, says Leyden-Rubenstein. When you sense you're being overly self-critical or you're feeling overwhelmed by worries at work or at home, take a moment to try to see your situation in a more positive and objective light.

Try to live in the moment. Most people spend much of their time feeling guilty about the past and worrying about the future rather than living in the present. Living in the present moment frees you from unnecessary worries about a past you can't change and a future you can't predict. And while you can't change what happened yesterday or predict what will happen tomorrow, you do have a certain amount of control over the here and now.

A STRONGER YOU

"Starting in the mid-thirties, every person loses approximately a third of a pound of muscle every year of their lives," says Miriam Nelson, PhD, an associate chief of the Human Physiology Laboratory at the Jean Mayer USDA Human Nutrition Research Center on Aging at Tufts University and the author of two best-selling books, including *Strong Women Stay Young*. Without exercising, most people will lose about five pounds of lean muscle a decade. This will be replaced with fat, making you more likely to develop heart disease, cancer, diabetes, and other chronic illnesses.

Women are especially at risk, since they live longer than men and naturally have less muscle and more fat. "If women want to be independent when they get older, they have to preserve their lean muscle mass," says Nelson.

Strength training is the only way to preserve or rebuild muscle. Lifting light weights, using weight machines, or doing strengthening exercises will all build muscle strength.

You only need to do it for 20 to 30 minutes twice a week to get the benefits. Nelson recommends a weekly regimen that includes both strength training and aerobics.

THE POWER OF THINKING POSITIVELY

Pessimistic thinking not only affects your outlook on life, it can also affect your emotional and physical health. Pessimistic people suffer from more depression, anxiety, and stress, and have poorer overall health than more optimistic people, according to a recent study by psychologist Susan Robinson-Whelen. While Robinson-Whelen doesn't recommend "going through life wearing rose-colored glasses," she does say that training yourself to think less negatively about the challenges in your life can pay off emotionally and physically.

Try to short-circuit pessimistic thoughts when they come up. Ask yourself if they are realistic, or if you could see your situation in a less negative light, suggests Robinson-Whelen.

Quick Tricks

Miriam Nelson recommends these strengthening exercises that require no equipment. Do them at least twice a week. If you have a history of back problems, check with your doctor before attempting abdominal and back exercises. Try to do eight repetitions of each exercise. Rest for a minute or two, and try to do another eight.

Chair Stand. This exercise will strengthen your thighs, abdominal muscles, and buttocks. Sit toward the front of the chair, with your feet flat on the floor, shoulder-width apart. Cross your arms and hold them against your chest. Leaning forward slightly but keeping your back straight, stand up slowly. Pause. Slowly lower yourself back into the chair. Don't fall into the chair. You should feel the effort in your buttocks and thighs.

Toe Stand. This exercise is a great calf toner. Stand about 12 inches away from a wall, your feet 12 inches apart. Place your fingertips on the wall to keep your balance. Slowly raise yourself as high as possible on the balls of your feet. Hold for three seconds, and slowly lower your heals to the ground.

Front Leg Raise. Sit on the floor, leaning back slightly, with your legs extended in front of you. Place your hands on the floor behind your buttocks. Place a rolled-up towel under your right knee. Bend your left knee, with your left foot on the floor next to your right calf. Lift your right leg as high as possible, with your toes pointing up. Pause. Slowly lower your leg to the floor. Repeat eight times. Switch legs and repeat again.

A Good Night's Sleep

Sleep is nature's way of restoring mind and body.

WAKE-UP CALL

One in four Canadians has some difficulty getting a good night's sleep. Approximately 4 million Canadians have a potentially diagnosable sleep disorder, says Bev Devens, executive director of Sleep/Wake Disorders Canada. Here are some common sleep disorders:

Insomnia. The most common sleep disorder, insomnia may be caused by stress, anxiety, poor sleep habits, and certain lifestyle habits, such as tobacco, alcohol, and caffeine. If you often have trouble falling asleep, or if you wake up before your alarm is set to go off and can't get back to sleep, you have insomnia.

Sleep apnea. If you are a loud snorer and you experience daytime fatigue and drowsiness, you may have sleep apnea. A breathing disturbance that causes repeated oxygen drops in the blood, apnea can cause irritability, depression, lack of concentration, high blood pressure, and cardiac irregularities. A person can suffer hundreds of apneas a night, in which the breathing stops and sleep is momentarily disturbed. For this reason, a person with apnea may be chronically sleep deprived without knowing it. Apnea is most common in people who are over 50, are obese, have allergies, large tonsils, or overbites. Apnea can usually be treated without surgery once diagnosed.

Restless leg syndrome (RLS). A common, sometimes inherited, disorder characterized by an annoying, tingling, but non-painful, sensation in the legs in the evening and at bedtime. Sufferers feel they must move their legs to get relief. The discomfort keeps people with RLS awake at night.

Narcolepsy. A rare but serious sleep disorder, narcolepsy is a disorder of the REM sleep mechanism. Sufferers are suddenly overcome with an attack of REM sleep, which can last several minutes or hours. Although there is no cure for narcolepsy, it can often be controlled with drugs.

Smart Moves

Carolyn Dean, MD, ND (naturopathic doctor), and author of *Dr. Carolyn Dean's Complementary Natural Remedies for Common Ailments*, recommends these naturally occurring substances for occasional sleeplessness. If you are pregnant or nursing, have a medical or psychiatric condition, or have frequent insomnia, talk to your doctor before taking supplements.

- One or two capsules of skullcap—a plant extract—at bedtime.
- A mild mood enhancer called 5HTP found in some foods, such as turkey and milk. A turkey sandwich will also provide the sleep-inducing combo of tryptophan and carbohydrates.
- St. John's Wort, a natural antidepressant.
- Valerian is a gentle, natural tranquilizer. You can take valerian as tea, capsules, or extract an hour before bedtime every night.
- Calcium supplements, taken at bedtime.
- A 100-200 mg B vitamin complex capsule daily.

The sleep cycle

Getting enough sleep helps keep the body and the immune system functioning at peak and may even help the mind process and order information. Gigi Kader, MD, medical director of the Unity Sleep Medicine and Research Center in St. Louis, explains the five stages you go through during a normal night's sleep.

Stage 1
This stage is the transitional phase between drowsiness and the first few moments of light sleep, as the muscles relax and the pulse becomes regular.

Stages 2 and 3
Sleep deepens as heart rate and body temperature drop.

If you're a light sleeper, invest in a comfortable blindfold and a pair of earplugs.

THIRTY WINKS

Good bedtime habits are the foundation for getting a good night's sleep, according to Martha Lentz, MD, a research associate professor at the University of Washington in Seattle.

- Try to go to bed and get up at the same time every day, even on weekends. It is especially important not to sleep in.
- Caffeine stays in the system for up to 12 hours. Avoid coffee, chocolate, and other caffeinated foods and beverages after midday.
- Try to avoid alcohol before bed. It can interfere with the quality of your sleep and cause you to have more difficulty sleeping in the long run.
- Do a little light exercise—such as taking a walk—in the late afternoon or early evening.
- Give yourself at least a half hour of quiet time before going to bed, when you leave behind all the worries of the day.
- Reserve your bedroom for sleep and lovemaking. Don't bring your check-

Quick Tricks

Relaxation techniques are safe and effective treatments for insomnia, says Dr. Virgil Wooten, director of the Sleep Disorders Center of Greater Cincinnati. Here are some of the procedures he teaches his patients and encourages them to use:

Progressive muscle relaxation. Gradually working up your entire body from toes to head, tense and relax every muscle. Spend 20 to 30 minutes doing this in bed every night.

Imagery. As you are lying in bed, imagine a place that you would like to be, or focus on a pleasant memory. Try to imagine the details, the colors, and the way things look and smell around you.

Thought-stopping technique. If you are having racing thoughts, firmly say "Stop!" to yourself each time a thought recurs.

Deep breathing. Take a deep breath and hold it for five seconds. When you breath out, imagine you are letting go of all the tension in your body. Repeat four times.

book or work from the office into bed with you.
- Make the most of bedtime rituals, such as brushing your teeth and preparing for the coming day.

ARE YOU SLEEP DEPRIVED?

Almost everybody needs eight hours of sleep a night or more, advises Thomas Roth, PhD, a representative of the National Sleep Foundation and chief of the Division of Sleep Disorders at Henry Ford Hospital in Detroit. "If you're only sleeping four or five hours a night, you're going to suffer for it in the long run." Sleep deprivation can affect mood, productivity, creativity, motor skills, and even your overall health. It can also put you in danger of having accidents on the job

or falling asleep behind the wheel, says Roth.

High-stress jobs and busy lifestyles are no reason to shortchange yourself on sleep, says Roth. "If you get rid of TV, cable, and the Internet, you can get the sleep you need."

FIBROMYALGIA ALERT

Fibromyalgia syndrome (FMS) is a common and chronic rheumatic condition, causing fatigue and muscle pain all over the body. It affects five times as many women as men, says

Gunnar Kraag, MD, chief of rheumatology at the Ottawa Hospital. Most FMS patients also suffer from an accompanying sleep disorder, which prevents them from getting deep, restorative stage-four sleep. If you suffer from chronic muscle pain, are tired all the time, and wake up feeling groggy and unrefreshed, you may have fibromyalgia and should see a doctor, says Kraag. Some of fibromyalgia's symptoms can be alleviated with good sleep habits, exercise, and medication.

Tools of the Trade

Machines that simulate natural sounds, such as a murmuring mountain creek, crickets and frogs on a summer night, or the tide coming in, block out noisy city streets and help you relax so that you can get the sleep you need.

Stage 4
This is the deepest stage of sleep, when the body repairs and regenerates itself. These restorative functions may be why people who are ill or under the weather crave lots of sleep.

Stage 5
Otherwise known as REM, or rapid-eye-movement sleep, this stage is the most active phase of each night's sleep cycle.

Once you have fallen asleep, stages 2,3,4, and 5 repeat in 90- to 120-minute cycles.

About REM
During REM, heart rate and blood pressure change rapidly, the muscles twitch, and the brain is very active. This is the stage of sleep in which we dream. Recent theories suggest that REM sleep is the body's way of ensuring the brain will wake up again, says Kader.

A Winning Smile

Good dental care begins at home.

Children can learn to brush for long enough by keeping it up for the duration of a music box tune.

YOUR CHILDREN'S TEETH

"Try to make brushing as much fun as possible for your child," says dentist and mother Kimberly Loos, DDS, who has an online dental column answering parents' questions about their children's teeth (www.smiledoc.com and www.parentsplace.com). To make sure your children brush long enough, says Loos, play or sing them a song and ask them to brush for the duration of it. Or buy them a timer so they can time themselves.

Children often don't listen as well to their parents as they do to other adults. So have a dentist, teacher, or other adult whom your children trust explain to them the importance of taking care of their teeth.

Use only a pea-sized amount of toothpaste on your children's toothbrushes so they don't ingest too much fluoride.

Brushing teeth can be a battle, especially at bedtime. So try to get your children to brush their teeth at other times of the day—perhaps right after dinner or at bathtime.

Nutrition plays a role in keeping teeth and supporting tissues healthy. Make sure your children are getting plenty of calcium in their diet. The sugars in starchy foods can also wreak havoc on oral health. Keep sugary sweets, soft drinks, and sticky foods, such as dried fruit, which adhere to teeth, to a minimum. Try to encourage children to rinse their mouths out with water if they've indulged in a treat.

HEALTHY GUMS

"Three out of four people will be affected with periodontal disease at some point in their lives," warns Hamilton, Ontario, periodontal specialist Dr. Marlene Mader. The good news is that it is almost always preventable, and can be reversed in its early stages.

Gum disease is caused by bacteria that invade gum tissue and can eat away at supporting bone. In early stages (gingivitis), there is inflammation of the gums; in advanced stages (periodontitis), the disease has begun to affect the bone.

"The leading cause of tooth loss in adults is gum disease," says Mader, "and recent studies have linked poorly controlled periodontitis to heart disease."

Gum disease can be difficult to detect in its early stages. Your dentist should use a *periodontal probe* to check for gum problems on a regular basis. This procedure is currently the only certain method of detecting gum disease.

Here are some of the warning signs that you may have gum disease:

■ Loose or separating teeth.
■ Bleeding while brushing or flossing.
■ Red, swollen, or tender gums.
■ Gums that pull away from the teeth.
■ Chronic bad breath.

PERIODONTAL ALERT

Certain health conditions make you susceptible to gum disease, says Mader. Also, certain habits can increase your chances of developing gum disease: **Smoking or tobacco use.** It is not fully understood how smoking is related to gum

Myth: Fluoride is good for you. **Fact:** While most dentists agree that topical fluoride strengthens the teeth, many express concern about the potentially dangerous effects of fluorosis, or fluoride toxicity. A tube of toothpaste contains a potentially lethal dose of fluoride. This can be especially dangerous for young children, who may be tempted to eat a good-tasting tube of fluoridated toothpaste.

disease. It may be that tobacco use decreases blood flow and lowers your resistance to infection.

Hormonal changes. Pregnancy, menopause, puberty, and oral contraceptives can make you more susceptible to gum disease.

Diabetes. Uncontrolled diabetes can make you a candidate for gum disease.

Poor nutrition. A balanced diet is important to your overall health, including teeth and gums.

Immune system disease. A compromised immune system can negatively affect periodontal health.

Medication. Tell your dentist if you're taking prescription medication; certain medicines can affect the health of your teeth and gums.

THUMB/PACIFIER SUCKING PROBLEMS

It is normal for babies to suck. It gets them food and also helps them to relax. "Thumb- or pacifier-sucking is only a problem after five or six years of age," says Kimberly Loos. Before then, it probably won't permanently affect a child's teeth. Here are tips for discouraging this common habit:

- Put a bandage over your child's thumb.
- Snip the top off the pacifier a little at a time so your child doesn't notice.
- Provide an incentive for your child to quit. Put a star on the calendar for every day your child refrains from thumb- or pacifier-sucking.

The Right Way

Flossing removes plaque, a major cause of tooth decay and gum disease, from between your teeth where a toothbrush can't reach.

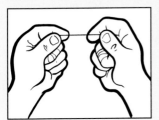

Wrap 15 to 20 inches of floss around your middle fingers. Start with most of it on one finger, and transfer it to the other as it's used up.

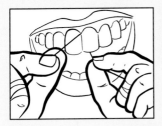

Use your forefingers to steer the floss gently in between every two teeth, and behind your back molars.

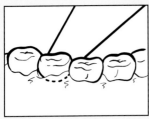

Concentrate on getting the floss into the gap between your teeth and gums, where plaque likes to hide.

Tools of the Trade

Old-fashioned manual toothbrushes have been on the market for over 200 years. But the last 20 years has brought many innovations to their design, including angled and textured handles, bi-level and textured bristles, color indicators that tell you when it's time to buy a new toothbrush, and different shapes and sizes.

Extra-long tip bristles

Bi-level bristles

Diamond-shaped head

NON-TOXIC DENTISTRY

Many oral health care providers are concerned about the mercury used in dentistry, say dentists David Kennedy, DDS, and Delbert Nichols, DDS, both preventive dentists. Although their views are still controversial and are not supported by the Canadian or American dental establishment, they are gaining wider currency.

Dental amalgam, or "silver," fillings are made of a compound that is 50 percent mercury, a substance that is "50 times more toxic than lead," according to Nichols. Toxic mercury vapors leech out of fillings when we eat, brush, chew gum, or grind our teeth.

Research has shown that the symptoms of low-grade mercury poisoning include anxiety, headaches, and depression. Mercury poisoning has also been linked to brain, kidney, and immune system damage. Recent findings have prompted countries such as Sweden, Germany, and England to restrict its use or phase it out completely. If you are concerned about amalgam, ask your dentist about non-toxic plastic composite fillings.

Smart Moves

- Brush your teeth twice a day for at least two minutes. Aim your brush at a 45° angle to your teeth, making sure the bristles penetrate gently into the gum line.
- Use a soft brush and brush gently. If your brush head is flattened out after a few weeks of use, you're brushing too hard.
- Floss your teeth daily.
- Have your teeth checked twice a year; a cleaning may be part of the checkup, depending on your needs.
- If you drink coffee or tea, swish some water around your mouth afterwards to prevent staining.
- If you have chronic canker sores, you may be sensitive to the fluoride in your toothpaste. Try brushing your teeth with baking soda.

The Eyes Have It

Don't wait until you have a problem. It may be too late.

PREVENTING BLINDNESS

Blindness in adults is often preventable, says Michael Henningsen, executive director of the Maryland-based Vision Care International Ministries. This medical-missions organization educates people all over the world about how to prevent blindness.

Fortunately most Canadians have access to the three most important contributors to eye health—nutrition, hygiene, and medical care. But some adults don't take even the most basic steps to protect their vision, even if they know they're at risk. Henningsen suggests these easy steps to help prevent vision loss:

- Get your eyes checked by an optometrist or ophthalmologist every two to three years. If you're over 64, you're at higher risk for certain eye diseases, and should see

an ophthalmologist or optometrist every three to four years.
- See your optometrist or ophthalmologist every year if you're in a high-risk group for eye disease. People with diabetes and high blood pressure are at high risk. People of African descent are five times more likely to develop eye disease than Caucasians.
- Always wear protective safety glasses when using power tools, playing fast-paced racquet sports, or doing other activities that could damage the eyes. People have even been blinded by nails that splinter during hammering. Lightweight safety glasses are now available.

TAKING CARE OF YOUR CHILD'S EYES

If there's one thing every parent should know, it's that there's more to good vision than 20/20, says Joel Zaba, an optometrist and visual consultant in Virginia. All 20/20 means is that you can see signs clearly at 20 feet. It doesn't mean you can see clearly at

Safety glasses protect your eyes from contact with foreign objects, whether you're in the science laboratory or in the wood shop.

Swimming goggles with a good seal can prevent infections, chlorine irritation, blurred vision, corneal breakdown, and loss of contact lenses.

Myth: *Contact lens wearers should wear only eye makeup labeled "hypoallergenic."* **Fact:** *Ilana Harkavi, creative director of Il-Makiage Cosmetics in New York City, explains that hypoallergenic doesn't necessarily mean it won't irritate your eyes. Instead, contact lens wearers should stick with using waterproof mascara and concealer, and creamy eyeshadows and pencils.*

16 inches, the distance from which most children read a textbook.

Over 80 percent of what we learn is through visual processing of information, according to Zaba. A child's undiagnosed vision problems can cause difficulties at school. But many children don't realize that they're having difficulty seeing, and they certainly don't know how to tell you what's wrong. Routine school vision screenings only check for a small number of problems. So it's important to take responsibility for your child's eye care, and take your child to an eye care professional as soon as you notice signs of a possible problem:

- Do they close one eye when they read, or squint? Do they get frustrated with close-up

work, and yet seem perfectly comfortable at the movies or watching television? They may be far-sighted. Do they bump into things more frequently than other children? They may be having trouble with their depth perception.
- "Notice whether your children's eyes work as a team," advises Zaba. Do they move together, or does one move more than the other or each in a different direction?
- Ask teachers to be very specific about problems your children have in school. Can they copy work from a textbook but have trouble copying from the blackboard? They may be having difficulty transferring the image from a vertical to a horizontal plane. Vision

Know Your Eye Care Team

Dr. Ralph Chou of the University of Waterloo's School of Optometry says it's important to know the differences among the three types of eye care professionals:

Ophthalmologists are MDs (physicians) who specialize in diagnosing and treating eye diseases.

Optometrists are professionals who diagnose vision problems and prescribe eyeglasses and contact lenses to correct them. Optometrists also treat minor eye diseases, but they are not physicians.

Opticians are trained to fit your eyeglasses and fill eyeglass and contact lens prescriptions.

Racquetball goggles protect your eyes while allowing you maximum vision to see the ball.

Ski goggles protect your eyes from sun, wind, and foreign objects, and allow better vision on the slopes.

Vision problems

Many vision problems are caused by one of these three conditions:

Myopia (Nearsightedness) is the result of wide eyeballs or very strong lenses. This causes eyes to focus visual images in front of the retina, making distant objects appear blurry.

Hyperopia (Farsightedness) is the result of narrow eyeballs or weak lenses. This causes eyes to focus visual images behind the retina, making nearby objects appear blurry.

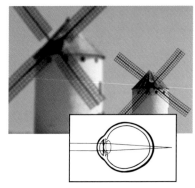

Astigmatism occurs when the eye's cornea is asymmetrically curved. This causes distorted vision, making it difficult to bring printed words and lines into focus.

problems can cause frustration that can lead to anti-social behavior or be mistaken for attention deficit disorder.

- Take hand-eye coordination seriously. Notice if your children think they can see a ball coming at them, but then grab for it in the wrong direction.
- Listen to what your children say. Do they describe seeing a green blob instead of individual leaves on a tree?
- Have your children's eyes checked by either an optometrist or ophthalmologist before they turn three and again before they enter school.

NEW SOLUTIONS

Laser vision correction has now become faster, easier, and more painless, according to Wendell P. Wong, MD, of the Natural Sight Laser Vision Center. Pioneered in Canada, the LASIK uses gentle, cool light to recontour the surface of your cornea (the outer window of your eye). The LASIK lets ophthalmologists use lasers to cure more serious vision problems than ever before. In fact, Wong himself has had his previously inoperable nearsightedness eliminated thanks to this new technology.

During surgery, the laser touches no nerve endings, which is why the procedure is so quick and painless. It can be performed in under 10 minutes and using only a topical anesthetic. And, since patients have 90-percent recovery in the first 24 hours, it's safe and practical to do both eyes in one session (unlike the practice with the PRK laser that causes more post-surgery pain and takes longer to heal).

The Right Way

Thirty million North Americans use contact lenses, according to Carol Norbeck, a Seattle-based optician in practice for almost 40 years. She is also a consultant for the U.S. eyewear industry and spokesperson for the Vision Care Institute. Most contact lens problems are preventable through proper use:

- Never switch or share contact lenses with anyone, warns Norbeck. For instance, high school students who use colored contact lenses sometimes trade lenses with schoolmates and friends. This practice is extremely dangerous and puts teenagers at risk for serious eye infections.
- Use disposable soft contact lenses as directed. These can be left in your eyes for up to one or two weeks and then discarded. To save

money or hassle, people often leave lenses in too long or try to clean them and wear them again. But it's very difficult to clean these fragile lenses sufficiently. Leaving them in too long puts you at risk for ulcerations (painful scar tissue on your lens that makes it impossible to continue using contact lenses) due to a reduced flow of oxygen to the eye. You're also impairing your vision as the lenses grow dirtier.

- Wear as little eye makeup as possible while you're wearing your lenses. Eye makeup can irritate your eyes and cause your lenses to get dirty more quickly. If you must wear makeup with contact lenses, makeup artists suggest choosing products that don't flake off easily. And check with your optometrist or ophthalmologist.

A Good Ear

Protect your hearing at all times.

IMPROVE YOUR HEARING NOW

Almost anyone with a hearing loss can improve his or her hearing with the high-technology equipment now available, says Ross J. Roeser, MD, of the Better Hearing Institute in Washington, D.C. Here are some of the possible options:

Hearing Aids. Until recently, hearing aids were simply miniature amplifiers, which would make sounds louder. Now computer technology has made hearing aids smaller and more powerful than ever. The new digital hearing aids not only amplify, but they also change the pitch and frequency of the sound according to each patient's individual needs. And these devices are so small you can't tell whether someone is wearing one. Some can even be inserted directly into the ear canal. Although people with slight to severe hearing loss may benefit from a digital hearing aid, "It's not like eyeglasses," warns Roeser. "It won't make your hearing perfect again. Background noise can still make it difficult to understand speech in crowded, noisy places."

Ear Implants. Surgically implanted hearing devices—called cochlear implants, because they are inserted into the cochlea, or internal ear—can substantially

This tiny hearing aid fits invisibly into the ear canal and produces a natural sound.

improve severe hearing loss. Cochlear implants convert sounds into electrical energy that is then interpreted as sound by the brain. Some patients with the implant may even be able to carry on a normal telephone conversation, says Roeser.

Assisting Devices. Assisting devices make life a little easier for someone who is hard of hearing. Alerting devices for the door bell and the telephone are common assisting devices, as well as vibrating alarm clocks that can be placed under your pillow. There are also special headphones that use infrared signals to increase the volume of the television for just one person, so that the rest of the family can keep the volume at the usual level. Similar devices are frequently supplied at the theater, opera, and symphony. Ask what's available before you buy your tickets.

RINGING IN THE EARS

If you have ever been to a rock concert or walked past a construction site, and then heard a ringing or buzzing in your ears for a few hours (or even days) afterward, you have experienced temporary **tinnitus**. People with chronic tinnitus perceive it all the time, says Pawel J. Jastreboff, PhD, ScD, of the Tinnitus and Hyperacusis Center in Baltimore. Not to be confused with **hyperacusis** or

EAR PLUGS

There are dozens of different types of ear plugs, many designed for use in specific situations, such as on construction sites or on stage at rock 'n' roll concerts. Here are a few of the most common:

These plugs alleviate discomfort on airplanes by helping ears adjust to cabin pressure.

Disposable foam earplugs help block out street noise and barking dogs for a peaceful night's sleep.

Swimmers with water-sensitive ears use malleable, water-repellent silicone plugs.

The Right Way

Parents need to recognize the symptoms of ear infections, advises Peggy Williams Goeschel of the Nebraska Commission for the Deaf and Hard of Hearing, who herself has a severe hearing loss due to chronic ear infections during her childhood. If you suspect an ear infection, see a doctor immediately, warns Goeschel. It may save your or a loved one's hearing. Here are some warning signs:
- Pulling on the ear or complaining of pain in the ear.
- High fever.
- Sudden hearing loss.

Smart Moves

- Keep the volume low when listening to portable headphones. If other people can hear what you're listening to, you are putting yourself at risk of ear damage.
- Cover your ears when an ambulance goes by.
- Use ear protection when running noisy equipment such as a chain saw or power drill.
- Wear earplugs to loud rock concerts.
- Never sit near the speakers at a concert.

hypersensitivity to real sound—tinnitus is a phantom auditory perception, or the real perception of a sound that does not exist. Jastreboff compares tinnitus to phantom limb or phantom pain syndrome.

About 17 percent of the population experiences tinnitus. Some of them suffer so badly that they would prefer to lose their hearing than listen to the constant jangling, ringing, buzzing, or hissing in their ears, according to Jastreboff. All of us experience what Jastreboff calls temporary "disco tinnitus" from time to time. But chronic tinnitus can cause anxiety, stress, depression, and sleeplessness.

"You can't enjoy life anymore," says Jastreboff, who has tinnitus himself and has taught himself to control it with the same techniques that he teaches to his patients. He has pioneered a highly successful treatment for tinnitus that trains the brain to block out the buzzing and ringing in the ears the same way people habitually tune out environmental noise, such as the hissing of a radiator or the humming of a refrigerator.

If you hear sounds that other people don't hear, which move with you and which you can't escape from, you may have tinni-

tus. And if you think you might, Jastreboff suggests these ways to keep it under control:

- Avoid silence. Everyone can get temporary tinnitus in a very quiet room. Try to have the radio or TV or a tape of nature sounds playing softly in the background.
- Avoid loud noise whenever possible. Musicians who play on amplified stages often develop tinnitus.

HOW LOUD IS TOO LOUD?

Most people don't realize which noises can have permanently debilitating effects on their hearing, says Lorraine Short, contributing editor to *Hearing Health* magazine (www.hearinghealthmag.com). Any prolonged exposure to sounds over 90 decibels can cause gradual hearing loss. And as the noise level increases above 100 decibels, you risk permanent hearing loss with even short-term regular exposure. Here are some examples of the decibel levels of several common noises that may require ear protection—and some that don't:

Noise	Decibels
Airplane takeoff	140
Rock concert	120
Snowmobiles	110
Power tools	100
Motorcycles	90
Traffic noise	80
Birds singing, normal conversation	60
Whispering	20

- Seek help. Tinnitus is much more common in people over 65. If you or someone you know is suffering from it, treatment is available.

RECOGNIZING THE SIGNS

"One in ten Canadians suffers from some level of hearing loss. About 300,000 Canadians are profoundly deaf. And some three out of four are late-deafened adults," explains Janice McNamara of the Canadian Hard of Hearing Association. Older people can be especially defensive about hearing loss, because it often comes upon them suddenly, fairly late in life, and they haven't had a whole lifetime to adjust. Here are some warning signs that a friend or family member might be having difficulty hearing:

- Your baby does not respond to your voice or other aural stimuli.
- Your child is having difficulties at school or is not picking up on what the teacher is saying.
- A friend doesn't turn toward you or seem to be listening when you talk to him or her.
- You have to repeat yourself frequently.
- Someone among your family or friends keeps making the volume on the television louder.

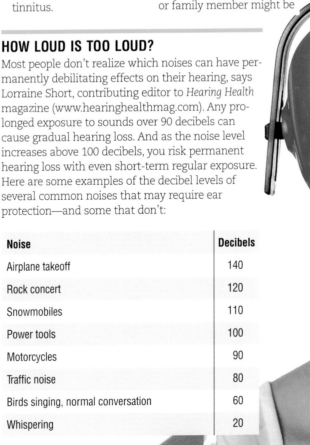

More Than Skin Deep

Have beautiful, healthy skin at any age.

A FRESH COMPLEXION

"Skin care is really a lifestyle," says Brian Gregory, MD, assistant professor of clinical dermatology at the University of British Columbia, and a practicing dermatologist. "It's not just about putting things on your skin."

What is good for the complexion's barrier of oil and protein? It is simple: prevent water loss, get enough sleep, reduce stress in your life, prevent sun damage, eat a well-balanced diet, and avoid alcohol and tobacco use.

■ Use a sunscreen of 15 SPF (sun protection factor) or greater, and put it on an hour before going out in the sun. Using a sunscreen doesn't mean you don't have to worry about sun exposure. You still have to take preventive measures, such as wearing a wide-brimmed hat and staying out of the sun during peak hours of 10 a.m. to 3 p.m.

■ Alpha hydroxy and glycolic acids—naturally occurring fruit and milk acids—will mildly exfoliate the skin by removing dead skin cells. Although the products with these acids claim to make skin look younger, they produce no lasting change.

■ Although there is no scientific evidence to back it, exercise may improve your skin's look, since it improves blood flow and circulation to the skin's surface. Wipe away excess sweat with a clean cloth during workouts.

■ Smoking causes wrinkling, and increases the likelihood of developing skin cancer.

THE SMART SHOPPER

About 1,700 anti-aging products are launched by over 600 cosmetic companies in North America every year, according to Paula Begoun, a cosmetic researcher and author of *The Beauty Bible: From Acne to Wrinkles and Everything in Between.* Health Canada sets guidelines for the cosmetics, toiletries, and fragrance industries. However, some consumer groups, like the Consumers' Association of Canada (CAC), are dissatisfied with the guidelines. "We want to see truthful, accurate claims, and access to more information. That means a company's toll-free number and website on the label," says Jennifer Hillard, vice president of the CAC. In the meantime, here are some of Begoun's tips on how to get the best-quality skin care products for your money:

■ Buy your moisturizers, including alpha hydroxy creams, at the drugstore. And don't spend more than $15.

■ Buy a day cream with an SPF of at least 15. "If your day cream doesn't contain a significant level of sunblock, it's a waste of money," says Begoun. "Dryness doesn't cause wrinkles. It is sun damage that does."

■ Avoid products that claim to reduce cellulite. There's no evidence that they have any effect at all.

■ Try to avoid using harsh cleansers including pure soap on your skin.

RUB-A-DUB-DUB

Use natural sea sponges, bristle brushes, loofahs, and other scrubbers gently and with caution. These tools can irritate your skin, causing redness, dryness, more blemishes, and increased sensitivity—especially on your face.

PROTECTING YOUR SKIN (AND YOUR HEALTH)

UV radiation doesn't just damage your skin. It damages your genes, says John DiGiovanna, MD, of the department of dermatology at Brown University School of Medicine. "UV damage is like money compounding in a retirement account," he says. "The earlier you sustain damage—from a bad sunburn in childhood, for instance—the longer the damage compounds as abnormal cells." And the more likely you are to develop skin cancer and wrinkles.

According to DiGiovanna, sun exposure is far more dangerous for children than adults. "There are changes in the skin as it ages that we don't really understand," he says.

Although people of all skin types should protect their skin from sun damage, certain groups are at particular risk. Be particularly careful if you:

■ Have a family history of skin cancer.

■ Burn, but don't tan.

■ Have had pre-cancerous cells removed.

■ Freckle easily.

Know Your Terms

SPF: Sun protection factor. A lotion with SPF 15, for example, provides 15 times the skin's natural protection.

UV: Ultraviolet rays have shorter wavelengths than visible light, and are the most damaging part of sunlight to the skin.

UVA: Most of the UV light that reaches the earth is in UVA rays, which penetrate deep into the skin and are associated with suppressing the immune system. Make sure your sunscreen also protects you against UVA rays.

UVB: A smaller portion of the UV light that reaches the earth is in UVB rays, which are more likely to burn the skin and are associated with damaging cell structure.

NO HEALTHY TAN

Experts are eager to dispel the myth of the healthy tan:

- Children and infants are at high risk for sun damage and heat stroke. They can even die. The Canadian Dermatology Association recommends no sun exposure for infants under six months. Put sunscreen on the exposed parts of your child's body every day. Keep your children out of the direct sunlight at midday. Protect them outdoors with sunblock, a hat, and protective clothing.
- Tanning and freckling are both signs that your skin is being damaged. Every time you tan, you increase your risk of damage and disease.
- Avoid tanning salons. There's no such thing as a healthy tan, despite their claims. Although they used to be thought less harmful, the UVA rays used by most tanning salons penetrate to deeper layers of skin and are associated with many sun-related diseases.
- The Canadian Dermatology Association recommends a broad-spectrum sunscreen that is effective against UVA and UVB rays, with an SPF of 15 or higher. Choose a lotion or cream and use it as your daily moisturizer.

COSMETIC SURGERY

People seriously concerned about the appearance of their skin sometimes look to surgical methods of improvement. Maritza I. Perez, MD, director of dermatologic surgery at St. Luke's Roosevelt Hospital in New York City, is working with some of the newest surgical skin treatments.

Here are some of the procedures she's using to temporarily or permanently rejuvenate the appearance of her client's skin.

Laser surgery. Whether you want to remove a tattoo, birth mark, acne scars, stretch marks, or want to improve the appearance of skin wrinkled from sun damage, some type of laser surgery might be the answer. "Laser surgery produces better results than plastic surgery, since it replaces skin rather than just lifting it," says Dr. Perez. The laser removes skin down to its deepest layer, and then the top is replaced with new, younger-looking skin.

Collagen or fat injection. Collagen or fat can be injected into laugh lines or small scars to minimize their appearance, says Perez. This process has to be repeated regularly.

Paralysis. You can stop deep wrinkles from developing on your forehead or from reappearing after laser surgery. An injection of botulin toxin paralyzes the muscles of the forehead, preventing lines caused by frowning or concentration, but the procedure must be repeated every six months.

Myth: It's not necessary to wear sunscreen on a cloudy day. **Fact:** Clouds don't block harmful UVA rays. Neither do windows. So you should wear sunscreen every day.

Quick Tricks

Ilana Harkavi, creative director of the cosmetics company Il-Makiage, explains that there are two basic kinds of red lipstick: warm (orange-based) shades, which look best on people with warm skin tones, and cool (blue-based) shades, which look best on people with cool skin tones. Determine your skin tone by looking at your eyes in a mirror. If you see any gold or yellow specks in the eye, that generally means you have a warm skin tone. If not, you have a cool skin tone.

Fragrance-free moisture cream for sensitive dry skin

Vitamin E, antioxidant intensive moisture cream

SPF 15 day moisture cream

Carrot moisture cream

Alpha hydroxy AHA sensitive skin cream

Jojoba moisture cream

Conditioning beauty bar with pH under 7

Healthy Hair

Home hair care is easy if you know how to do it.

A GOOD HAIR DAY

Every day can be a good hair day if you follow Jerome Lordet's advice. A top stylist at the Pierre Michel Salon in New York City, he numbers New York ladies who lunch and Hollywood stars among his regular clients.

■ If you have very fine hair, Lordet recommends washing it every day to give it movement and body. People with dry, thick, or curly hair need to wash less often. If you have curly hair, rinse it on the days you don't shampoo. This will bring natural oils from the roots down to the ends and keep it shiny and healthy-looking.

■ Apply conditioner just to the ends of your hair.

■ Rotate your shampoos from wash to wash, depending on the weather, humidity, and how your hair is "feeling." For instance, you may want to use a richer shampoo on sunny days.

■ Air dry your hair whenever possible. A good haircut should fall into place naturally and shouldn't need blow-dryer styling every morning.

■ Protect your hair from the sun with a hat or sunblock gel or shampoo.

■ Get your hair cut every five to seven weeks. Regular haircuts strengthen the hair and help it grow.

NATURALLY BEAUTIFUL HAIR

Almost everything you need to have rich, healthy hair you can find in your pantry, says beauty expert Janice Cox. Author of *Natural Beauty For All Seasons*, Cox recommends these gentle, inexpensive, and easy recipes for the hair.

Deep moisturizers	Coat damp hair with avocado, banana, or 2 tablespoons mayonnaise, honey, or coconut oil. Leave on at least 15 minutes. Shampoo.
Shampoos	Add the following to 1 cup of baby shampoo:
For dry hair	2 tablespoons olive or almond oil or 1 egg
For oily hair	2 tablespoons lemon juice or aloe vera gel
For normal hair	¼ cup beer or flat champagne

Styling gel	Soak 2 tablespoons flaxseeds in 1 cup boiled water until it thickens. The clear gel produced is ideal for setting the hair.
Cleansing rinse	Rinse hair with ¼ cup baking soda dissolved in 2 cups of warm water. Will remove build-up from hair spray and styling gels, as well as chlorine.
Dandruff treatment	Rinse with 2 tablespoons apple cider vinegar in 1 cup warm water.

Color rinses

For blonde hair
Chamomile tea warms the tones of blonde and light brown hair.

For red hair
Red hibiscus tea brightens red hair.

For brown hair
Sage and rosemary tea add warmth, while cinnamon produces red highlights.

Quick Tricks

If your hair is dried out from the sun, salt water, chlorine, or over-processing, Jerome Lordet recommends this conditioning treatment you can do at home:

■ Wash your hair and saturate it with your favorite deep conditioner.
■ Dampen a hand towel with fresh water. Microwave it for 30 to 60 seconds or until it is warm and steamy. If you don't have a microwave, you can put the towel in a sink or basin and cover it with very hot water.
■ Wait until the towel is cool enough to handle. If you used the second method, squeeze out the excess water. Now wrap the towel snugly around your hair.
■ Put a shower cap on over the towel. Leave on for as long as possible.
■ Rinse your hair thoroughly with warm water. If it still feels greasy, wash it gently with your favorite shampoo. Your hair will be silky and shiny after this salon-style treatment.

FEED YOUR HAIR

Good nutrition plays a vital role in keeping your hair healthy, says Ken Peters, a nutritional consultant and author of *Hair Loss Prevention*. If you are not eating well, your hair will be one of the first things to suffer.

■ Essential fatty acids help prevent hair loss and keep the hair shiny and thick. If you're having trouble getting enough in your diet, flaxseed, salmon, and evening primrose oil supplements are all excellent sources.
■ Eat plenty of whole—preferably organic—grains, such as brown rice and oats. They contain silica, a trace mineral that strengthens the hair and helps prevent breakage.
■ An adequate amount of fat in the diet—especially unhydrogenated fat, such as olive oil and other liquid fats—helps keep hair shiny and thick.
■ Vitamin C, the B vitamins, calcium, magnesium, and zinc are all essential to good hair health.
■ Hair loss is often caused by a hormonal imbalance. Soy foods, such as soy milk and tempeh, regulate the hormones and may help you save your hair. (If you are a woman experiencing significant hair loss, it could be an indication of serious illness or a vitamin deficiency. Consult your doctor.)

Some of the best deep moisturizers for your hair (honey, mayonnaise, banana, coconut oil) are already waiting in your kitchen.

The Right Way

Coloring doesn't have to be bad for your hair, says colorist Johanna Stella, owner of the Stella Salons in Miami and New York. Here are her tips for coloring at home:

■ Stella likes semipermanent color for at-home treatments. It's gentle to use, and is especially good at warming up hair that's grown dull or ashy-looking.
■ Stay close to your natural shade if you are coloring at home, advises Stella. It's least likely to damage the hair and easier to get right. If you're considering a radical, dramatic change, talk to a colorist at a reputable salon.
■ Semipermanent color will work if you have a sprinkling of gray to cover. Try a shade or two lighter than your natural color, recommends Stella. If you are a natural redhead and are trying to restore the color, add brown to a red tone, or your hair may take on a pinkish cast. If you are substantially gray, you'll have to use a permanent color.
■ If your ends are still light from a past process, put color on the roots but not on the ends. You can protect the ends during the coloring with a conditioner.
■ When using a highlighting kit at home, be conservative. Over-highlighting can leave you with ashy-looking hair. Leave the solution on for the minimum amount of time recommended in the instructions. You can always repeat the process a second time if you are not satisfied with the effect.
■ Condition your hair before and after coloring.
■ To keep color fresh and shiny, use shampoos and conditioners specially formulated for color-treated hair.
■ Always shampoo after swimming in chlorinated water. Water with a high mineral content can also have an unattractive effect on hair color.

Your Own Two Feet

Good health starts with your feet.

Give your feet and your lower back a break by lying on your back with your buttocks at the base of a wall and your legs extended upwards. Relax in this position for 15 minutes.

FIRST AID FOR YOUR FEET

The feet endure more wear and tear than any other part of the body. Orthopedic surgeon Michael Bowman, MD, tells you how you can care for your little aches and pains.

Ingrown toenails. Usually caused by narrow, tightly fitting shoes, ingrown toenails can be quite painful. Don't attempt to cut off or pull out the nail spur, or you may infect the area. Instead, trim the nail straight across, and round off the edges. Soak the feet for a few minutes to soften the skin. Now gently peel back the skin where the nail spur digs into the soft tissue on the side of the toe. Insert a small piece of cotton under the nail. Change the cotton daily, and wear comfortable shoes. The skin should heal within a few weeks. But if the area becomes swollen or hot to the touch, see a specialist.

Blisters. Usually due to poorly fitting shoes, blisters occur when the upper layer of skin becomes loosened by excessive friction and pressure. The fluid inside the blister is sterile, but can become infected. If the fluid beneath the skin is clear, just wash the area gently with soap and water and let the area breathe as much as possible. If the fluid looks cloudy or the area around the blister is red, lance it and sterilize the area with a topical antibiotic. Change the dressing daily, wear comfortable shoes, and it should heal within a week.

IF THE SHOE FITS

The world is divided into three kinds of people—those with **flexible** feet, those with **neutral** feet, and those with **rigid** feet. According to Paul Carrozza, footwear editor of *Runner's World* magazine and owner of RunTex, "the runner's store," in Austin, Texas.

The kind of feet you have determines what kind of athletic shoes you need. You can determine the flexibility of your feet by comparing the length of your feet when you're standing up to their length when you're sitting down.
■ If they're the same size, your feet are rigid, with high arches and tight Achilles tendons. Rigid feet do not absorb shock well. Look for soft, cushioned shoes, with a higher heel and plenty of room in the upper for your instep and arch.
■ If your feet are about half an inch—or half a size—longer when you are standing up, your feet are flexible, with high arches that flatten out under impact, and a low instep. Choose shoes with good arch support and a low heel for stability.
■ Neutral feet lengthen about a quarter inch from sitting to standing. Neutral feet are easiest to fit, because you can wear either a supportive or cushioned shoe.

The Right Way

Ill-fitting shoes are not only uncomfortable, but they can also cause costly and debilitating deformities and injury. Dr. Bruce Ramsden, podiatrist and president of the Ontario Podiatric Medical Association, suggests these guidelines for choosing safe and comfortable shoes:

- Shoe size varies from one brand or style to another. Judge shoes by the feel of the fit, not by the size.
- Have your feet measured regularly—especially when buying shoes. Feet tend to lengthen and spread as you get older. Ligaments and tendons loosen.
- Most people have one foot larger than the other. Fit shoes to the larger foot.
- Get shoes fitted at the end of the day when your feet are largest.
- Shoes should feel comfortable when you first try them on. Don't buy tight shoes expecting them to stretch out.
- Stand when you are being fitted. Make sure there is at least a finger-width of room at the end of each shoe for your longest toe.

SEAL OF APPROVAL

The Canadian Podiatric Medical Association evaluates shoes for comfort, healthfulness, and grants a Seal of Approval for products that meet their standards. "You don't have to be wealthy to be healthy," says Dr. Bruce Ramsden. He says that in general there are three zones in the pricing of shoes: the most expensive, the middle range, and the least expensive. He recommends buying shoes in the middle range. Look for good arch support and adequate width.

Quick Tricks

Marathon runners lubricate their feet before racing to cut down on chafing and keep their feet smooth and supple. For even better results, slather your feet with petroleum jelly at bedtime. Put on cotton socks to hold the moisture in. In the morning your feet will be smooth and soft.

GIVE YOUR FEET A TREAT

Dian Dincin Buchman, PhD, author of *The Complete Book of Water Therapy* and *The Complete Herbal Guide to Natural Health and Beauty*, recommends these natural remedies for common foot maladies. Herbal preparations are available at most health food stores.

For calluses and corns: Massage your feet with olive oil, castor oil, lanolin, or even face cream.

For itchy feet or athlete's foot: Apply lemon juice or apple cider vinegar directly to the feet.

For tired feet: Soak your feet in a bath of warm water with a few drops of lavender oil added. Or to revive your feet—and at the same time energize your body and stimulate your immune system—give yourself a brisk, cold-water foot bath every morning.

FEET FIRST

For massage therapist and reflexologist David Fairman, the foot is a window into the health of the entire body. Reflexologists believe that every part of the body corresponds to an area of the foot. By manipulating and massaging specific areas of the feet, you may find relief from illness and symptoms in the corresponding parts of the body. Here are two simple tips for pampering the most over-worked part of the body at home:

- Treat yourself—or even better, treat a friend—to a foot massage.
- Go barefoot. "Wearing shoes is like walking around in blindfolds," says Fairman. Going barefoot is a great way to give your feet a breather from constricting shoes, increase circulation and sensitivity, and wake up the feet.

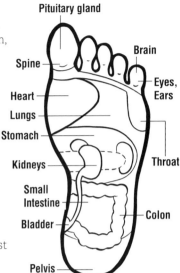

HEAL YOUR HEEL PAIN

If you are one of the 1.3 million North Americans who suffer from heel pain or plantar fasciitis, you may be able to find relief without spending hundreds of dollars on custom-made arch supports, says Dr. Glenn Pfeffer, an orthopedic surgeon in San Francisco. These stretching exercises combined with an inexpensive, off-the-shelf shoe insert are effective treatments for heel pain, according to a recent study. Repeat both exercises 20 times.

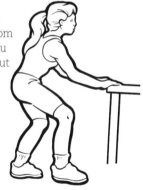

Lean forward, placing your palms on a table. Squat down slowly, trying to keep your heels on the ground. When you feel the stretch in the backs of your heels and your arches, hold the position for 10 seconds.

Lean forward against a wall, with one leg bent forward and the leg with the painful heel straight, further away from the wall. Try to keep your back heel on the ground.

What's in the Medicine Chest

**Learn to use
medications wisely.**

BE A SMARTER PATIENT

Prescription or over-the-counter medicines, including natural remedies such as herbal medicines, can be safe and effective, according to Barbara Jovaisas, an Ottawa-area pharmacist. But you have to use them sensibly.

■ Follow your doctor's prescription exactly. Be careful to take the correct amount of medicine at the specified times, and do not miss any doses. If you do forget to take your medicine, ask your doctor or pharmacist whether you should skip the dose altogether, take another dose immediately, or double up on your next dosage. But never double up without asking your doctor or pharmacist first.

■ Tell your doctor and pharmacist about other medications you are taking, either prescription, over-the-counter, or natural remedies, to avoid any potentially harmful interactions. And, of course, tell them if you are allergic to any medications, such as penicillin. People allergic to one medication may also be allergic to other similar ones.

■ Don't try to talk your doctor into giving you a medicine he or she is reluctant to prescribe for you. Doctors are occasionally pressured by patients to prescribe medications. If, however, your doctor prescribes a medicine you don't think you need, ask whether taking it is truly necessary, or if you might not be better off waiting a few days to see if you are getting better on your own.

■ If you experience any side effects from your medication, always discuss them with your doctor or pharmacist. Together you can decide if the benefits of medication outweigh the side effects, or if there is something you can do to minimize the side effects. Sometimes it takes a few days or weeks for the body to adjust to a new medication. After taking the medication for a short while, the side effects may disappear. Taking medicine with food or at a different time of day may reduce unpleasant side effects, but discuss this with your doctor or pharmacist first.

■ Don't be shy about asking questions. If your health-care providers do not have the time to answer your questions while you are in the office, be persistent and schedule a time to call and discuss your questions over the phone. It's your right to have the information you need to take your medicine properly.

AT THE PHARMACY

Just because certain medications are available without a prescription does not mean you don't have to be careful when you use them. Use common sense when taking any kind of drug, says pharmacist Barbara Jovaisas. And always follow the printed instructions for use of the medication.

■ Always go to the same pharmacy if possible. That way your pharmacist can keep track of your medications and warn you about any possible interactions. If you have to go to a different pharmacy to fill a prescription, make sure you tell them about any other medication you are taking.

■ When choosing over-the-counter medications, including herbal and other natural remedies, talk to your pharmacist. Be sure to mention any medications you are already taking. If you have asthma, high blood pressure, heart disease, diabetes, or if you are a pregnant or breast-feeding woman, talk to your doctor or pharmacist before using any nonprescription product.

■ Make sure to check the label to see if you should avoid certain foods, alcohol, or medicines when you take an over-the-counter medication.

■ Don't assume an over-the-counter medication is safe for children. Check the label or talk to your pharmacist.

Smart Moves

Help yourself and your family use nonprescription, over-the-counter medicine responsibly. Gerry Harrington of the Nonprescription Drug Manufacturers Association of Canada tells you how:

■ Always read the label of the medicine and follow the directions carefully. Don't take a higher dosage than the label indicates or continue taking it for longer than the label says.

■ Always ask your pharmacist or physician if you have any questions about the appropriateness of a drug or the correct dosage.

■ Don't use medicines after their expiration date. That date is clearly visible on the packaging. Though they probably won't harm you, they also may not be effective. It is advisable to take your medications back to your pharmacy for safe disposal.

■ Keep all medicines in their original containers to make sure that no one takes the wrong one by mistake, or the wrong dosage.

■ Be aware of common drug interactions that can produce unwanted results or reduce effectiveness. Follow the directions on the label to avoid drug interactions.

■ Store medicines in a cool, dark place (not in the bathroom) away from children.

■ Always take the recommended dosage, but not more than that. Don't confuse a teaspoon (tsp) with a tablespoon (tbsp).

■ Always check the package and the medicine itself for signs of tampering. Don't take the medicine if the seal is broken.

■ Don't take any medicine that looks discolored or different from usual.

The Right Way

Always keep these items on hand in your first-aid kit. Store the kit where it's easy to find—in a linen closet, perhaps. Don't keep it in the bathroom, where the moisture might make things damp.

- Ace bandage (3-inch width)
- Adhesive bandages in various sizes
- Adhesive tape (1-inch width)
- Antibiotic ointment
- Antiseptic washes
- Calamine lotion
- Cotton-tipped swabs, balls, or pads
- First-aid manual
- Flashlight and extra batteries
- Gauze bandages (2- and 4-inch widths)
- Hydrogen peroxide
- Large triangular bandages
- Painkillers, such as aspirin, acetaminophen, and ibuprofen
- Petroleum jelly
- Plain, nonscented soap
- Safety matches
- Safety pins
- Scissors
- Sterile gauze pads
- Thermometer
- Tissues
- Tweezers and sewing needles

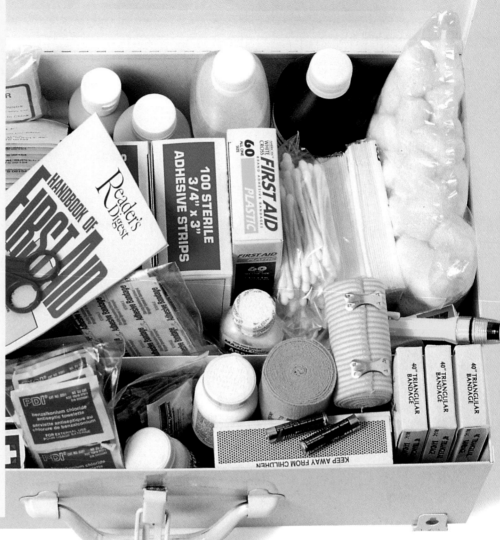

HELP FOR THE COMMON COLD

Too many over-the-counter medications take the shotgun approach to treating the common cold, says Michael Leff, editor of the *Consumer Reports On Health* monthly newsletter. Some cold formulas on the market even include ingredients that may counteract one another, such as combining an expectorant (which is meant to loosen phlegm and, therefore, make it eas-

ier to cough) with a cough suppressant.

Many experts who have studied the common cold suggest that you are much better off treating it without the use of drugs. If the cold symptoms become too difficult to live with, however, such as a dry cough that interrupts your sleep, you should look for individual medications that target each symptom separately. Otherwise, you are taking drugs—and possibly getting unpleasant side

effects—for cold symptoms that you don't even have.

Always look at the labels of the boxes and bottles for these ingredients that are meant to treat specific cold symptoms.

Dextromethorphan is the safest and most effective treatment if you have a dry, hacking cough. In general, don't treat a loose, productive cough with a cough suppressant.

Guaifenesin is an expectorant, and should help you to cough up phlegm.

Pseudoephedrine is an oral decongestant, which helps clear up a stuffy nose. This ingredient also tends to be a stimulant, which can make it difficult to use effectively if you are also trying to sleep.

Avoid **antihistamines** unless you are told otherwise by your doctor or pharmacist. These ingredients can dry out your mucus membranes—your body's natural healing system when you have a cold—and make you drowsy.

Fighting the Cold War

Follow these tips for beating the world's most common ailment.

Chicken soup helps prevent dehydration and eases congestion.

FACT OR FICTION

Joe Schwarcz, PhD, director of McGill University's Office for Chemistry and Society (MOCS) in Montreal, dispels some myths about colds and flu.

Myth: *Cold weather causes colds and flu.* **Fact:** *Although colds and flu are more common in the winter months, this has less to do with the weather than with confinement indoors. Viruses spread much more quickly in dry, heated, indoor areas where air doesn't circulate well, and direct contact with germs is far more likely. Plus, central heating systems dry out mucus membranes, which are the body's natural defense against viruses.*

Myth: *Kissing spreads colds and flu.* **Fact:** *According to Inlander, colds are much more likely to be spread by hand contact than by oral contact.*

Myth: *It's dangerous to exercise when you have the symptoms of a cold or flu.* **Fact:** *Provided you're not running a fever, some mild exercise—such as a brisk walk—will help your antibodies fight the virus.*

Myth: *Wet feet, wet hair, and exposure to cold weather and drafts can cause colds.* **Fact:** *Although getting chilled can lower your resistance if you're already run down, you can only catch a cold or flu if you come in contact with a cold or flu virus. In fact, a little fresh air can help clear your head if you are sick.*

Myth: *A low-grade fever should be treated with aspirin or acetaminophen.* **Fact:** *A mild fever is the body's way of fighting off viruses. Plus, a low-grade fever helps get antibodies circulating throughout your body.*

PREVENTING A COLD OR FLU

Catching a cold or the flu tells us our immune system is challenged or overburdened, says Bradley Bongiovanni, ND, a naturopathic doctor from Portland, Oregon. "Refined sugars, smoking, caffeine, sleep deprivation, alcohol, and stress all challenge the immune system," says Bongiovanni. If you want to optimize the function of your immune system and avoid getting sick, you need to accomplish two goals: The first is to decrease the overall burden placed on the body by making appropriate lifestyle changes. The second is to eat a varied, healthful diet emphasizing fresh whole foods, ensure adequate sleep, learn to manage your stress effectively, and engage in some sort of physical movement that stimulates the circulatory and lymphatic systems.

For an extra immune system boost during winter months, Bongiovanni suggests taking a high-potency antioxidant formula including vitamins A, C, E, and selenium as well as vitamin C itself up to a range of 1,000 to 3,000 mg a day. He also recommends flaxseeds or flaxseed oil, a "superfood" rich in essential fatty acids

Epsom salts help you get rid of toxins.

that act as a natural anti-inflammatory on irritated membranes. Flaxseed is also thought to be an aide in combatting heart disease, certain types of cancer, menstrual cramps, acne, and depression.

Flaxseeds or flaxseed oil act as a natural anti-inflammatory agent.

TRADITIONAL REMEDIES THAT WORK

Carolyn Dean, MD, ND (naturopathic doctor), combines the best of conventional medicine and alternative remedies to treat her patients. The author of *Dr. Carolyn Dean's Complementary Natural Remedies for Common Ailments*, she believes that preventive medicine "empowers individuals to take care of themselves." Here are some of her tried-and-true remedies:

Drink chicken broth. Not only does hot soup alleviate nasal congestion and help prevent dehydration, but studies show that chicken broth actually shortens the duration of colds, according to Dean's research.

Try taking a bath with Epsom salts. The magnesium sulfate in Epsom salts encourages sweating, which helps the body discharge harmful toxins.

Avoid dairy products and bread, which produce mucus and tend to worsen the congestion often associated with colds and flu.

HERBAL REMEDIES

Carolyn Dean, MD, also recommends these herbal remedies when you're under the weather. If you take medication, check with your doctor before taking herbs.

For a cough. Steep some sage in freshly boiled water for

Ginger tea helps tame nausea.

at least 20 minutes. Drink hot or cold.

For head congestion. Steep fenugreek in boiled water for five minutes. Drink this tea warm.

For nausea. Steep two tablespoons of freshly grated ginger in three cups of boiled water. Use it as a gargle or soak a hand towel in it, and hold towel to head.

To boost your immune system. Dean recommends a daily dose of echinacea during the winter months as a preventive measure. The herb should not be used by anyone with a severe illness or an autoimmune disorder such as multiple sclerosis, rheumatoid arthritis, or lupus.

For chest congestion. Steep the herbs mullein or lobelia in boiled water. Then saturate a hand towel with the warm liquid, place it on your chest, and relax.

YOUR CHILD'S COLD

"The single best measure you can take to prevent your children from catching a virus is encouraging them to wash their hands," says Jay Hoecker, MD, a specialist in pediatric infections at the Mayo Clinic in Rochester, Minnesota. Contrary to popular belief, children are no more susceptible to colds and flu than adults. But they tend to touch their faces and noses—and each other—more than adults and are less careful about hygiene. Encourage your children to wash their hands on a regular basis, especially before meals, after school, and before and after playtime to prevent the spread of viruses, suggests Hoecker.

Hoecker does not recommend over-the-counter remedies for children. Decongestants can agitate children, restrict blood flow, and stimulate heart rate, while aspirin can increase the likelihood of your child developing Reye's Syn-

Quick Tricks

Dian Dincin Buchman, PhD, author of *The Complete Book of Water Therapy*, suggests that you soak your feet in a relaxing footbath of warm water with two tablespoons of dried mustard powder added to relieve nasal and chest congestion.

Smart Moves

- Let a cold run its course. Over-the-counter medications can interfere with the body's natural healing process and can even depress your immune system. Use them sparingly.
- Don't treat a productive cough with a suppressant, since coughing is your body's way of ridding itself of accumulated phlegm.
- Disinfect your appliances such as telephones and remote controls to avoid infecting others and re-infecting yourself.
- Change the bed linens and bath towels frequently and use disposable towels in shared bathrooms and in the kitchen.
- Take zinc lozenges at the onset of a cold to lessen its duration and severity.
- Use a humidifier regularly during the winter months.

drome, a dangerous complication of viral infections that can cause liver or brain inflammation.

If your infant or child is stuffed up, try a homemade remedy first. Hoecker recommends salt-water nose drops made with half a teaspoon of salt to eight ounces of water. This homemade decongestant is safer, more effective, and less expensive than over-the-counter medicines.

Controlling Your Blood Pressure

Some simple lifestyle changes can keep your blood pressure under control.

DEFINING BLOOD PRESSURE

According to Norman Campbell, MD, FRCPC, faculty of medicine, University of Calgary, and president of the Coalition for Control of High Blood Pressure, your blood pressure is the force at which your heart pumps blood through your body.

The first (and higher) number refers to your **systolic** pressure, which occurs immediately after your heart contracts, and is the higher pressure. The

second (and lower) number refers to your **diastolic**, or lower pressure, the pressure which occurs when your heart is relaxed between contractions.

Physicians find your blood pressure by seeing how high the force of the blood pumping through your arm can push a column of mercury. If your blood pressure is 120/80—an optimal level—then your blood pushes the mercury up to a height of 120 mm when your heart is contracting, and 80 mm when it's at rest.

The higher your blood pressure, the harder your heart is working to pump

blood through your arteries. "It's similar to the air pressure in your tires," says Campbell. You need a certain amount of pressure to get rolling, but when it gets too high, the tires wear out quickly or can explode. That's what happens when someone has a heart attack or a stroke.

WHAT YOU CAN DO

A healthy lifestyle can be effective in preventing and treating high blood pressure (also known as hypertension), according to Thomas Pickering, MD, president of the Hypertension Network, a website that provides straightforward information about hypertension

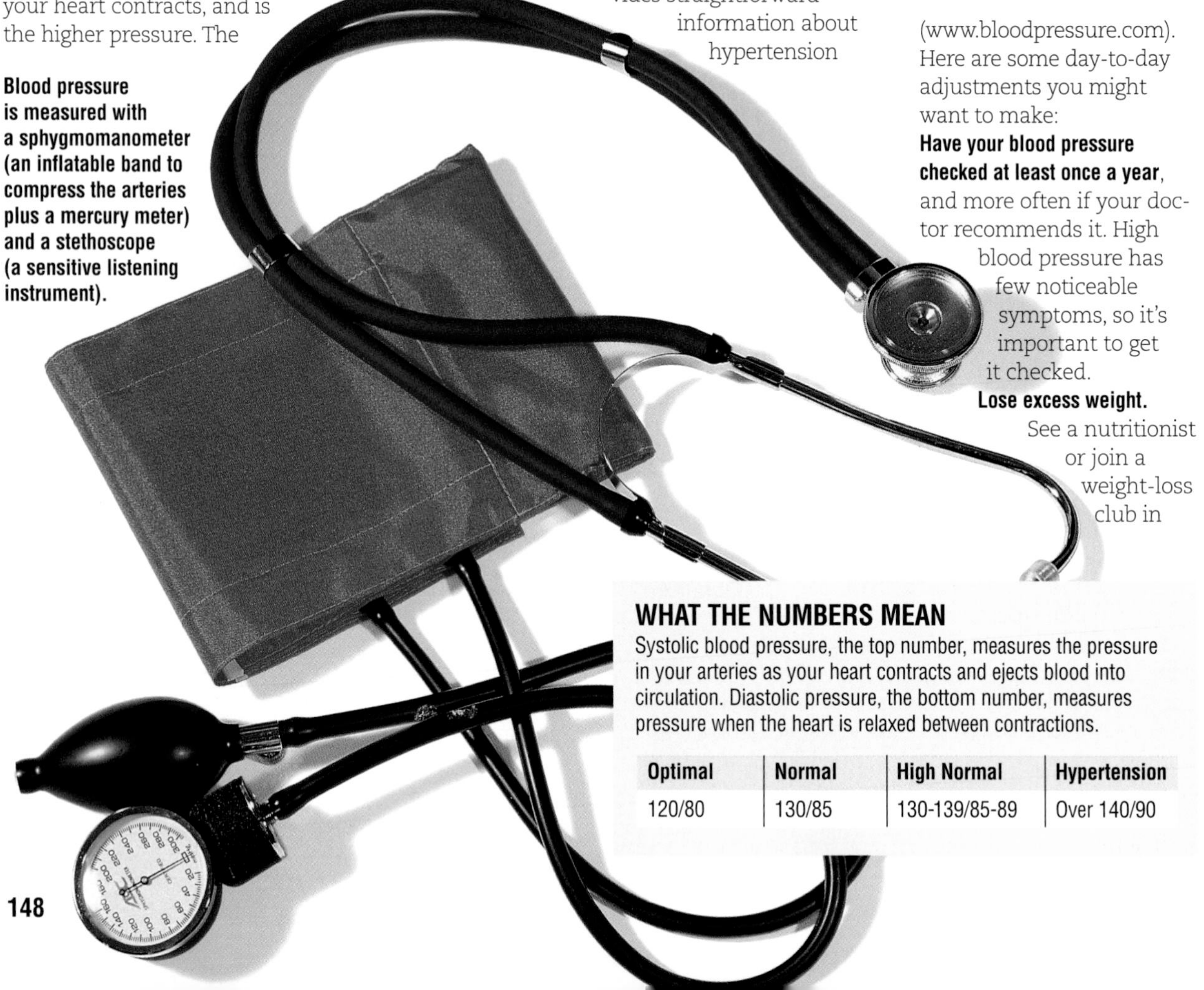

Blood pressure is measured with a sphygmomanometer (an inflatable band to compress the arteries plus a mercury meter) and a stethoscope (a sensitive listening instrument).

JAMES DUKE'S CELERY COCKTAIL
This beverage is a "very pleasant way to eat celery and garlic," says Dr. James Duke, a USDA phytochemist. These foods are thought to combat high blood pressure.

4 stalks celery
2 cloves garlic
1 carrot
Dash of fennel
Dash of parsley

Combine the ingredients and liquefy in a juicer. Drink once a day.

(www.bloodpressure.com). Here are some day-to-day adjustments you might want to make:
Have your blood pressure checked at least once a year, and more often if your doctor recommends it. High blood pressure has few noticeable symptoms, so it's important to get it checked.
Lose excess weight. See a nutritionist or join a weight-loss club in

WHAT THE NUMBERS MEAN

Systolic blood pressure, the top number, measures the pressure in your arteries as your heart contracts and ejects blood into circulation. Diastolic pressure, the bottom number, measures pressure when the heart is relaxed between contractions.

Optimal	Normal	High Normal	Hypertension
120/80	130/85	130-139/85-89	Over 140/90

The Right Way

The right reading. Caffeine, anxiety, or rushing to make an appointment on time can temporarily raise your blood pressure. To get an accurate reading, take a few moments to relax and breathe deeply before going in for your checkup. If you've had one or two high readings, have your blood pressure checked frequently for a few weeks or months. It may be a temporary increase, but if it isn't, you need to do something about it.

When can you stop? If your doctor prescribes blood pressure medication, it doesn't mean you have to take it forever. Once your blood pressure is under control, you may be able to keep it there by making some lifestyle changes. But, whatever you do, don't stop taking your medication without first consulting your doctor. Many people stop taking their pills once their blood pressure reaches a healthy level. More often than not, it skyrockets right back up after a period of time. If you are concerned about taking medication for the long term, ask your doctor about natural ways to control your blood pressure.

Do it yourself. Home heart rate monitors are inexpensive, easy to use, and accurate. If you have just been diagnosed with hypertension, take your blood pressure several times a week.

- Take the salt shaker off the dinner table.
- Make more foods from scratch. That way you're in control of the sodium content. Explore the recipes in the *HeartSmart* cookbook series produced by the Heart and Stroke Foundation of Canada.
- Choose fresh or fresh-frozen foods over canned and bottled goods.
- Reduce your intake of processed foods like smoke, cured, and deli meats, dry soup mixes, TV dinners, casserole mixes, pickles and snack foods.
- Avoid eating fast and convenience foods too often.
- Read food package labels and watch out when you see the following terms, since they indicate sodium: brine, baking soda, soda, baking powder, salt, monosodium glutamate, sodium chloride, NaCl, and any other sodium compound.

order to plan a weight management program.

Aerobic exercise is one of the most effective ways to lower your blood pressure. Many patients have been able to avoid medication with regular exercise. Dr. Pickering recommends biking, swimming, running, and brisk walking.

Quit smoking, which automatically doubles your risk of heart attack if you have high blood pressure.

EATING RIGHT

Foods that help lower blood pressure don't have to be bland, maintains Carole Dombrow, a registered dietitian. At the Heart and Stroke Foundation of Canada, where Dombrow is a nutrition consultant, she teaches people with hypertension how to cook tasty meals that won't raise their blood pressure. She says people with hypertension should be eating a variety of foods including vegetables, fruits, whole grains, leaner meats and meat alternatives, and low-fat dairy products, while cutting back on sodium intake.

"The one recommendation that is not easy for people to follow is cutting back on sodium," Dombrow says. The good news is we can teach our taste buds to desire less salt. She suggests some ways to do this:

NOT A MOMENT TOO SOON

According to the Canadian Heart Health Survey 1992, more than one in eight Canadians have high blood pressure. More men than women are affected: 16 percent of men and 13 percent of women registered diastolic blood pressure readings of 90 mm Hg or greater. Despite their doctor's warnings, many people have a hard time motivating themselves to take the necessary steps required to lower their blood pressure.

High blood pressure is called the silent killer. Many people with high blood pressure have no symptoms and lead normal lives, not realizing that if high blood pressure is not controlled, life-threatening problems can show up 10 to 20 years later. High blood pressure significantly increases the risk of developing heart disease, peripheral vascular disease, stroke, diabetes, kidney, and eye disease.

Increasing your life span and maintaining the quality of your life as you grow older are obvious, compelling reasons to lower your blood pressure. That is why medical education about blood pressure is so important. If people would go to their doctors and have their blood pressure checked regularly and treated when necessary, they could prevent the ravages of many of the diseases seen among older adults.

Quick Tricks

When preparing your food, consider replacing salt with these flavorful herbs and spices.

Herb/spice	Enhances
Basil	Tomato-based sauces and dishes
Bay leaf	Braised and stewed dishes
Chives	Salads, stews, and soups
Cinnamon	Desserts and beverages
Cloves	Meats and vegetables
Cumin	Marinades, chili, and tomato sauce
Curry	Meats, fish, poultry, and vegetables
Dill	Seafood, salads, light sauces, dips, and spreads
Ginger	Stir-fried poultry, lamb, or meat
Marjoram	Meats, fish, and vegetables
Mustard	Marinades and fish stews
Paprika	Potatoes, chicken, and fish
Parsley	Stocks and soups
Rosemary	Roasted or grilled lamb, chicken, or fish
Sage	Fish, lamb, pork, or poultry
Savory	Beans, stews, and lamb dishes

Getting Allergy Relief

Don't let your allergies run your life.

TREATING YOUR ALLERGIES

An allergic reaction occurs when your immune system interprets a harmless substance as a harmful invader. Allergic symptoms range from mild to life-threatening, and may include rash, runny nose, itchy eyes, worsening of asthma, drop in blood pressure, or swelling of the mouth and throat.

Frances A. Taylor, MA, co-author of *The Whole Way to Allergy Relief & Prevention: A Doctor's Complete Guide to Treatment & Self-Care*, recommends these natural ways to reduce your allergy symptoms:

- Use an air purifier to reduce hay fever allergens in your home, and avoid growing plants you're allergic to in your yard or garden.
- Keep your house pets clean and groomed, and don't let them roll around in the grass.
- Take vitamin C supplements, and pay attention to your nutrition. Vitamin C acts as a natural antihistamine.
- Avoid yardwork that worsens your symptoms, or wear a surgical mask while working in the garden.
- Avoid scented laundry products and cleaning supplies, which often trigger allergic reactions. Taylor says you can clean almost anything with common household items, such as lemon juice, baking soda and water.

BIG BAD BUGS

The stings and bites of honeybees, hornets, and wasps are extremely painful and, in some people, may cause serious allergic reactions. Jennifer Hay, author of *Allergies: Questions You Have... Answers You Need*, warns anyone who is allergic to insect bites to be wary of the yellowjacket. That's because yellowjackets are aggressive, tend to feed on garbage and fermenting fruit, and nest in the ground or walls near people's homes, where they may be easily disturbed.

There are two levels of allergic reaction. The first, and less dangerous, is merely an intensification of the normal reaction to an insect sting: localized pain, redness, and swelling that lasts for several days instead of several hours, sometimes combined with

Myth: *Children may outgrow their allergies as they reach adulthood.* **Fact:** *People can outgrow milk, egg, or soy allergies. However, peanut, tree nut, fish, and shellfish allergies usually last a lifetime. Strictly avoid the foods you are allergic to, and wear a Medic-Alert bracelet.*

The big eight

Over 90 percent of food allergic reactions are caused by these eight foods. Symptoms are often severe and may include hives, swelling of the mouth and throat, nausea, cramping, vomiting, and diarrhea.

fatigue and nausea. The second level of reaction is far more serious and leads to anaphylaxis, characterized by a drop in blood pressure, swelling (especially of the throat and tongue), breathing difficulties, dizziness, and nausea, possibly leading to shock or cardiac arrest. Fortunately, doctors can prescribe doses of epinephrine (a hormone that stimulates the nervous system) that can be self-injected in case of a reaction. It counteracts the anaphylactic reaction.

The best way to prevent a reaction is to avoid stings altogether, according to Hay. Here's how:

- Wear long sleeves whenever possible if you're going to be outside during the summer.
- Avoid scented cosmetics, perfumes, and hair sprays, which attract stinging insects.
- Wear blacks, greens, browns, and grays instead of bright colors which resemble the colorful flowers that also attract stinging insects.
- Try to avoid doing yardwork that could disturb a yellowjacket nest.
- Don't swat at anything that might sting you.
- Be especially careful when you are cooking or eating outdoors in the summertime.

Milk

Eggs

Peanuts

Fish

Shellfish

Wheat

Soy

Tree nuts

Tools of the Trade

Epinephrine can be injected into the thigh in the event of an allergic reaction. There are currently two kits available: The EpiPen, an autoinjector, contains one pre-measured dose; the AnaKit has two doses which must be measured and manually injected. Patients can administer the second dose if the first isn't working.

LIVING WITH FOOD ALLERGIES

People often confuse a food intolerance with a food allergy, says Antony Ham Pong, MD, an Ottawa-area pediatric allergies specialist. While a food intolerance can mimic the symptoms of a food allergy, it tends to be less severe. Real food allergies, on the other hand, may result in anaphylaxis and can be life threatening.

Between 1 and 3 percent of Canadians have true food allergies. The only way to prevent an allergic reaction is by strictly avoiding the foods you're allergic to. That means checking food labels carefully and asking about ingredients when not eating at home.

■ Most allergic reactions occur within two hours from the time the food

The Right Way

Anaphylactic reactions can be life-threatening. If you or someone else is having an anaphylactic reaction, call 911 immediately. Don't wait and hope it will get better or go away on its own. If the person is prescribed epinephrine, use it, but still get the patient to the hospital as quickly as possible. Even when the symptoms are relieved by epinephrine, the person could still have a second attack or a reaction to the medication.

was ingested. Often the reaction will take place within seconds. Symptoms can include hives, runny nose, itchy eyes, swelling and tingling of the mouth, cramping, nausea, vomiting, and diarrhea. One of the risks is dehydration which can have serious consequences if not treated.

■ Children may not have the words to describe the symptoms of a food allergy, and certainly won't know what's happening if it's the first time they are having a reaction. Parents should pay close attention to their children when first introducing them to one of the eight most common food allergens (facing page), and call for help at the first sign of swelling or difficulty breathing.

For more information about food allergies, Dr. Ham Pong suggests contacting Allergy and Asthma Information Association at (416) 783-8944, or Anaphylaxis Network of Canada at (416) 785-5666.

COOKING FOR A FOOD ALLERGY OR INTOLERANCE

Cooking for people with food allergies is all about making substitutions, says Marilyn Gioannini, author of *The Complete Food Allergy Cookbook: The Foods You've Always Loved Without the Ingredients You Can't Have.* To find the tastiest ones, you'll probably have to look beyond your local supermarket chain to health food stores and ethnic markets. Once you find the right substitute ingredients, however, you can find a new way to make your old favorites. Here are some of Gioannini's favorite substitutions:

■ Experiment with different grains if you have a wheat allergy.

Barley, rye, oats, rice, millet, and teff (a tiny grain 1/150 the size of wheat) are great, but may still be a problem for some people because they are related to wheat. Kamut and spelt are ancient varieties of wheat that may be tolerated by people who can't use modern wheat. People with severe wheat allergy or with celiac disease should not try these forms of wheat. Quinoa, amarynth, and buckwheat (related to rhubarb, despite its deceptive name) are safe even if you're allergic to all wheat-related grains.

■ Replace one type of flour with another. Substitute 1:1, and look at the texture. If it's too dry or too loose, add a little more flour or water.

■ Use arrow root powder or psyllium to replace eggs. Mixed with water, they will bind doughs together. You can also try adding more oil and baking powder to get the same effect.

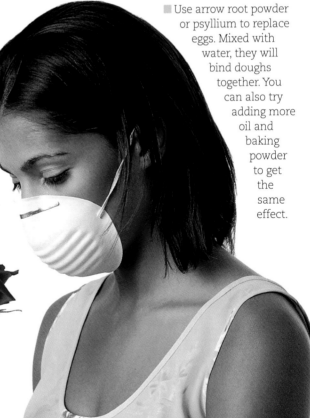

Conquering Depression

Get the help you need when you need it most.

DEPRESSION, OR JUST THE BLUES?

Depression is not just a state of mind. It's an illness that can have serious effects on your professional and personal life. Sometimes it's hard to tell the difference between normal mood swings and depression. It's natural to feel sad when something bad happens, such as the end of a romantic relationship or the death of a loved one. But while normal sadness tends to get better with the course of time, depression tends to get worse.

Aaron Beck, MD, professor of psychiatry at the University of Pennsylvania, identifies some signs to look for that can help you tell whether you're just feeling blue or might have a serious clinical depression and should find professional help.

Fatigue. Feeling tired or needing more sleep for several weeks or more with no physical explanation is the most common symptom of depression, and should be cause for concern. Some depressed people, however, experience sleeplessness instead of fatigue.

Sadness and self-hatred. Depression causes people to feel sad, often without knowing why. Depressed people often also experience intense feelings of guilt, helplessness, and worthlessness.

Gaining or losing a significant amount of weight without trying. Pay attention to any significant change in eating habits. Many people eat much less or much more than usual when they go into a depression.

Severe pessimism. When you're depressed, you believe the worst will happen. It's difficult to believe anything good will ever happen again.

Loss of pleasure and social withdrawal. Depression makes it practically impossible to enjoy anything, even activities you have always enjoyed.

Difficulty concentrating or remembering. Depression can cause thought processes to become confused and hazy, which can deepen the depression.

Clinical depression is a chronic progressive disease caused by biological dysfunction of the brain. People can inherit a biological predisposition to depression just as they might inherit a tendency to develop other chronic diseases, such as heart disease.

Two major differences set depression (and other emotional disorders) apart from other physical illnesses. First, since other people cannot see physical manifestations of depression, and there's no simple medical test to determine its presence, friends and family tend to blame depressed individuals for their disease, and say they should "snap out of it." That tends to magnify the depressed person's negative feelings.

Secondly, people suffering from depression have great difficulty understanding that their tremendous psychic pain is actually a disease process rather than a character weakness or personal failure.

Tools of the Trade

Mental health professionals use many tools to help alleviate the symptoms of depression.

- Cognitive psychotherapy teaches patients how to recognize and change negative thinking patterns, which feed their depression.
- Interpersonal psychotherapy involves learning how to handle personal relationships with other people in a more effective and positive manner.
- Antidepressant medications work to normalize the chemical balance in the brain to improve mood, sleep, appetite and energy levels, or decrease mania.
- Electroconvulsive therapy can be effective in cases of extremely severe depression when drugs aren't working and rapid improvement is necessary.

Light therapy has been used by some therapists to treat depressions they believe are induced by the darkness of the winter months.

WHEN DEPRESSION BECOMES LIFE THREATENING

Everybody should know the warning signs of suicide, says Dr. Paul Links, professor of psychiatry who holds the Arthur Sommer Rotenberg chair in suicide studies at the University of Toronto. If you see these signs in yourself or a friend or loved one, don't try to handle the situation yourself. Your best and only option is to get help from a qualified professional. Here are a few things you should know about suicide:

■ Depression itself is not life threatening, but it can become so quickly when accompanied by thoughts of suicide. The situation is even more dangerous when depression is accompanied by a second mental disorder (such as panic, borderline personality, or a thought disorder), or drug or alcohol abuse or both.

■ Take all threats of suicide seriously. Don't assume someone is just being melodramatic or trying to get more attention. Don't minimize their feelings or make moral statements like, "But you have so much to live for."

■ Pay attention to mentions of death and suicide in letters, poems, and everyday conversation. If you think something's wrong, ask. The most dangerous myth about suicide is that talking about it makes it happen. Talking about it is the first step toward getting help.

■ If someone confides their suicidal feelings to you, don't promise to keep it a secret. Offer to assist that person in finding help, or to go together to talk to a professional. No matter how bad and helpless someone feels, there are ways to get help.

■ Teach your children what to do if they hear their friends start talking about suicide. Explain that it's important to tell a trusted adult, even if their friend has told them not to. An often-repeated, but powerful, argument is "It's better to lose a friend than to lose a life."

■ Know where to go for help. You can contact your family physician, or a 24-hour crisis line, the number is on the first page of your local phone book. In an emergency, go to the nearest hospital emergency room or call 911. Call an organization like the Canadian Association for Suicide Prevention, (780) 482-0198, or visit websites like Suicide Information and Education Centre (www.siec.ca).

Myth: *Depressed people revel in their pain, and could just snap out of it if they really wanted to.* **Fact:** *Nobody enjoys being depressed. Depression is a serious disease that requires professional help.*

HELP YOURSELF

The essential difference between the blues and depression is that the blues come and go, while depression comes and stays.

It's not easy, but if you want to feel better, it's best to try to help yourself, says Diane Ryerson, MSW, LCSW, a Colorado-based expert on depression and suicide prevention programs for schools and communities. Ask your doctor or mental health professional what steps you can take, no matter how small, to help yourself get better.

Learn more about depression. Many people find it helpful to do some research about the causes and treatments for their disease.

Talk to other people. Ask a trusted friend or family member whether they've noticed any significant changes in your mood or behavior in the past few weeks. And let them know what they can do to help.

Do something. This sounds easy, but you probably don't feel like doing anything but sitting at home or sleeping. Instead, make yourself get up and do something, even if it's just cooking dinner or taking the dog for a walk.

Exercise. It's a fact that exercising makes you feel better, giving you a natural high. Choose something you used to enjoy, even if it doesn't sound enjoyable now, and just do it for a little while.

Give yourself a break. Many people blame themselves for their depression, making it even harder to feel better. Instead treat yourself like you would a loved one. Give yourself reassurance and encouragement. Talk back to any negative thoughts as you would if someone were harassing a loved one.

TWO KINDS OF DEPRESSION

Most people know about major depression, which can make it almost impossible to get through the day, perform usual activities like eating and working, or enjoy life. But there is also a second type of clinical depression, known as bipolar or manic depressive disorder, explains William P. Ashdown, president of the Mood Disorders Association of Canada. Both types require professional treatment.

People suffering from bipolar disorder experience severe mood swings, alternating between extreme depressive states and periods of excessive elation and euphoria called mania. Mania is also marked by irritability, a decreased need for sleep, racing thoughts, feelings of great self-importance, distraction, and increased talking, moving, and sexual activity. While major depression can show up at any age, people usually begin to show signs of bipolar disorder in their early twenties. This situation always requires medical intervention.

Living with Chronic Ailments

A positive attitude is the first step toward feeling better.

TAKING CHARGE

"Make sure your doctor is someone you trust—who listens to you, who works with you and for you," says James S. Gordon, MD, founder of the Georgetown University School of Mind-Body Medicine and author of *Manifesto for a New Medicine: Your Guide to Healing Partnerships and the Wise Use of Alternative Medicine*. Gordon explains how to take charge of your health—and of your life:

■ "Doctors tend to be very pessimistic," warns Gordon. They tend to present worst-case scenarios and statistical averages to their patients. "But you're not a statistic. Ask yourself, 'How do I become one of the people who beats the odds?'"

■ Become a partner with your physician. People who take an active role in their own health care do better physically.

■ Do what you can on your own to enhance your condition, whether it's improving your diet, exercising regularly, or practicing relaxation techniques or meditation. All of these life changes can play an important role in your well-being, and no one can do them for you.

■ Even small improvements and adjustments can have a positive effect on your progress. Start small. Start anywhere.

■ Don't get discouraged if one approach doesn't work. Everybody is different, and not every approach works for every person. There are dozens of other techniques to choose from.

BE A WINNER

"Winning is not always about being first," says Zoe Koplowitz, who was first diagnosed with multiple sclerosis over 25 years ago. "Sometimes it's about getting out of bed and putting your socks on." If you're living at your maximum physical capacity every day—whatever that may be—you're a winner.

■ If you are trying to stay active with a disability, learn the difference between "healthy tired and unhealthy tired." If you are feeling drained, woozy, and weak, you are

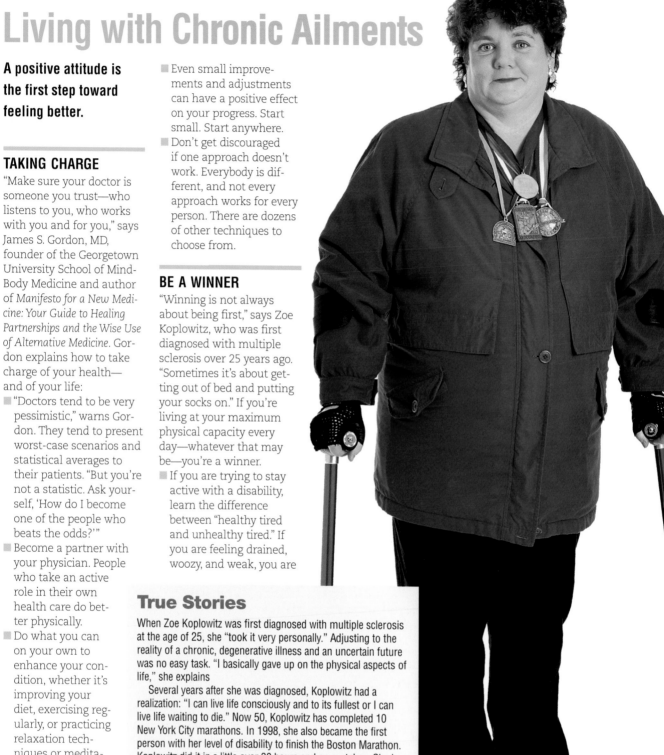

True Stories

When Zoe Koplowitz was first diagnosed with multiple sclerosis at the age of 25, she "took it very personally." Adjusting to the reality of a chronic, degenerative illness and an uncertain future was no easy task. "I basically gave up on the physical aspects of life," she explains

Several years after she was diagnosed, Koplowitz had a realization: "I can live life consciously and to its fullest or I can live life waiting to die." Now 50, Koplowitz has completed 10 New York City marathons. In 1998, she also became the first person with her level of disability to finish the Boston Marathon. Koplowitz did it in a little over 30 hours and on crutches. She is proud of the distinction she has earned as the "world's slowest marathon runner." Author of the best-selling *The Winning Spirit: Life Lessons Learned in Last Place*, Koplowitz attributes her success to discipline, self-acceptance, humor, and "a well-developed sense of the absurd."

- probably overdoing it. Know your limits.
- Practice visualization. Try to imagine yourself in vivid detail achieving your physical goals.
- Create morning rituals to remind yourself that every day is a new start.

COPING WITH OSTEOPOROSIS

According to the Osteoporosis Society of Canada, 1.4 million Canadians have osteoporosis. A painful, dangerous, and often disfiguring disease that causes thin and brittle bones, osteoporosis can be beaten with proper prevention and treatment.

Osteoporosis afflicts one in four women, and one in eight men over age 50. Two

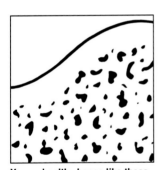

Young, healthy bones like these are strong and dense.

Bones with osteoporosis are porous and brittle by contrast.

million Canadians are at risk of developing the disease in their lifetime. "You may be at high risk if you are thin, smoke, have a history of breaking bones after age 45, are postmenopausal, or if your mother had a fracture from osteoporosis, warns Ethel Siris, MD, director of the osteoporosis program at the Columbia-Presbyterian Hospital. If you are in a high-risk group, ask your doctor about getting tested for bone density. The sooner

osteoporosis is diagnosed, the more effectively it can be treated and managed.

Adults reach peak bone density by the age of 20. Exercising (especially the weight-bearing variety) when you are growing up and in early adulthood is critical for building up as much bone mass as possible. Good nutrition—especially adequate calcium and vitamin D—is important for prevention and treatment. The recommended nutrient intake of calcium is at least 1,000 mg a day. Siris recommends getting your calcium from food sources.

Exercise is critical for preventing and treating osteoporosis. Weight-bearing exercise, such as walking, is wonderful for just about everyone. If you have osteo-

porosis, walking may be fine, but avoid carrying weights, which put too much stress on joints and can cause fractures. Low-impact aerobics may be a good option. Resistance exercise, such as swimming, yoga, and t'ai chi can help improve strength and balance. To prevent accidents that could cause fractures, fall-proof your house. Do away with throw rugs. Use a night light. Keep eyeglasses on hand. And avoid powerful sleep medication.

ASTHMA ALERT

According to Dr. Antony Ham Pong, an Ottawa-based pediatric allergies specialist, the number of Canadian children with asthma has jumped markedly, increasing from 1 in 40 children 20 years ago to 1 in 9 children in 1994-1995. Boys are more likely than girls to have asthma, as are children from low- or high-income households. "The rise in asthma cases may be partly due to increased exposure to indoor irritants such as smoke and fumes, including tobacco smoke and wood-burning stoves, and allergens such as dust mites and pet dander," says Ham Pong. Low-income families may have more asthma because parents are more likely to smoke. High-income families have more tightly sealed, energy-efficient homes, which also increases asthma risk.

Asthma is a serious disease that can cause decreased lung function and even death. "Children who have frequent bronchitis, pneumonia, or wheezy bronchitis several times each winter almost always have undiagnosed asthma as the reason for the recurrent chest problems," says Dr. Ham Pong. If you or someone in your family is wheezing, feels tight in the chest, or is coughing after vigorous exercise or when recuperating from a cold, see a physician. Dr. Ham Pong recommends the following tips for coping with this all-too-common illness:

- If you have been diagnosed with asthma, it does not necessarily mean you should stop exercising. Some world-class Canadian athletes, such as Olympic diver Sylvie Bernier and Olympic speed skater Susan Auch, have asthma. Children with asthma should be encouraged to participate in sports as long as they follow preventive and effective treatment. Sports which require prolonged periods of running or exercise, especially in hot, humid weather (track and field), or cold, dry weather (hockey), are most likely to provoke asthma. Swimming is one of the best tolerated sports. Ask your doctor for guidance.
- Keep your home well-ventilated and clean, especially the bedroom. Dust mites, roach droppings, animal dander, and other household pollutants can trigger an attack, and may even play a part in causing the illness. Tobacco smoke aggravates asthma. Avoid environmental tobacco smoke and certainly do not allow smoking in the home.
- It's important to maintain a positive attitude. Be diligent about following up on your treatment. Your attitude plays a significant role in feeling better and getting better, as it does with all chronic ailments.

How can you tell if your asthma is out of control?
- You need to use your bronchodilator three or more times per week (in addition to once per day before exercise).
- You wake up at night or in the morning with asthma symptoms once a week or more.
- You cannot do normal activities without such symptoms as shortness of breath, chest congestion, or coughing fits.
- You experience frequent prolonged or severe asthma flareups requiring hospitalization or emergency room visits.

Coping with Pain

Control your pain before it controls you.

A NATURAL REMEDY FOR BACK PAIN

Anne Holmes Waxman is a certified teacher of the Alexander Technique, which corrects posture to alleviate pain and reduce tension and stress in the body. Practitioners believe that body aches and tension are caused by the inefficient ways people use their bodies. Correcting your movements can soothe your pain. Waxman recommends this exercise, called an active state of rest, as a remedy for pain. Always check with your physician before trying an Alexander Technique.

Lie down on your back on a firm, supportive surface (not your bed).

Put a book under your head for support. If your throat feels constricted, try a thinner or fatter book.

Bend your knees while keeping your feet on the floor. Rest your hands on your belly, keeping your knees and feet aligned with your hips.

Imagine your spine elongating. Allow your whole torso to expand in width, depth, and length. Keep your neck loose.

Let go of the tension in your legs and arms, imagining your knees floating toward the ceiling and elbows out to either side.

Wall squats can help relieve back pain. Stand with feet shoulder-width apart, back flat against a wall. Slide down the wall until your thighs are parallel to the floor. Hold five seconds, then slide back up. Repeat five times.

NO TIME FOR PAIN

Mary Anne Lang, CRRN, is a nurse for the Pain Team, a pain rehabilitation program at a hospital in Allentown, Pennsylvania. The majority of Lang's patients have fibromyalgia, which is a difficult-to-diagnose rheumatic disorder characterized by multiple aches and pains throughout the body, and fatigue. Most patients have spent years trying to find relief from their pain, going from one doctor to another in search of a cure. By the time they arrive at Lang's program, many have given up hope and taken to their beds.

There are just no cures for some kinds of pain, says Lang. What the Pain Team does is teach their patients how to rule the pain instead of letting it rule them. Here's what Lang teaches her patients during the 24-week program:

■ Listen to your body. This is the most important thing the Pain Team teaches. When people learn how to change positions frequently throughout the day, or take a break when they need to, they can often return to their jobs or other tasks they haven't been able to do comfortably in years.

This is one of the hardest things for people to learn.

■ Keep moving. The worst thing you can do for chronic pain is take to your bed. The longer you lie still, the more muscle you lose. Physical therapists can teach you exercises to stretch or strengthen even the tiniest muscles in your body.

■ Learn to relax. People suffering from chronic pain can use a wide variety of yoga and meditation techniques to relax.

Quick Tricks

If you use a computer all day at work, try these methods to keep yourself comfortable and pain-free.

Keep your wrists loose. Extend your arms straight in front of you and flex your wrists up toward you as far as possible. Point them straight ahead, and then flex them down. Hold each position for several seconds.

Relieve neck strain. Sitting up straight, pull your chin in towards your neck, making a double chin. Hold. Then, link your hands behind your head and gently pull forward until you feel the stretch.

Rest your eyes. Look away from the computer screen and focus your eyes on objects at varying distances every 10 to 15 minutes.

Common causes of lower back pain

The way you move throughout your day could be the primary source of your back pain. Here are some of the common ways you could be hurting your back from day to day.

Poor working conditions

Improper sitting posture

Smart Moves

Try heat or cold. Most people think of heat as the most soothing thing for pain, but cold can work as well. Use a hot water bottle or cold pack where it hurts the most, but always give your body a 20-minute break after 20 minutes of applying heat or cold. Some people get the best results by alternating between hot and cold packs.

Try biofeedback. Biofeedback machines help you learn to control aspects of your own nervous system. It may help you learn how to relax your body and release some of your pain.

Stretch. Start gently and don't overdo it. Stretching keeps your muscles from tightening up and gets the blood moving through your veins.

Although you might not think so, cold sometimes brings more relief than heat.

DON'T FACE IT ALONE

Many people try to hide or ignore chronic pain until it becomes completely debilitating, says Ellen Schecter, a writer and filmmaker, who used her own struggles with lupus to create a video for patients, families, and medical professionals called *Voices of Lupus*. But there's no reason to suffer alone in silence. Here's what Schecter recommends to others living with chronic pain:

- Look into related foundations. They have groups of doctors, social workers, and people with the disease or condition working together and pooling their resources. Foundations usually provide general information, doctor referrals, support groups, and other services.
- Find a doctor who cares. Many doctors are afraid of pain because they're not properly trained to treat it. Don't put up with that. If you are not happy with the way your doctor responds to your pain, find a new doctor or seek out a clinic or specialist in pain management.

- Don't be afraid or feel ashamed to take medicine. Some patients and doctors avoid pain medications because they fear addiction. But sometimes medication is the best and only way to keep functioning on a daily basis. Learn to use your medicine as prescribed.
- Try a support group. Other people experiencing similar pain will understand what you're going through better than anyone else. Look for a group led by an experienced professional.
- Learn everything you can. Don't leave your treatment passively in your doctor's hands. Use books or newspapers, and search the Web for up-to-date information that could help you.
- Above all, don't let pain be the main focus of your life. Learn to push it aside by enjoying activities and people you love.

CONSIDERING THE ALTERNATIVES

When people with arthritis can't find the relief they need through over-the-counter painkillers and prescription medicines (or want to avoid the side effects of these treatments), they often turn to alternative medicine for new remedies. But Shanali Gayadeen of the Arthritis Society of Canada says that a new program teaches people with arthritis how to take a more active role in managing their arthritis pain.

The Arthritis Society trains people with arthritis to work as lay leaders and teach other people how to manage their arthritis. It's called the Arthritis Self-management Program. Here's how it works: Trained leaders teach basic information about arthritis, exercises, and relaxation techniques. Participants learn how keeping weight low helps to minimize pain. They learn about the side effects of arthritis medication and how to control them, as well as how to manage stress and depression, which often accompany the condition.

"It is crucial that people understand how a diagnosis of chronic pain can lead to a pain cycle," says Gayadeen. "When this happens, a person in pain goes through stages of denial, fatigue, and depression, which increase the pain."

Leaders in the program teach useful problem-solving techniques for everyday situations. For instance, people learn the least painful way to get on and off buses. For more information, call 1-800-321-1433.

Improper computer work habits

Improper standing

Improper lifting

Poor sleeping posture

Handling Emergencies

A few seconds can make all the difference.

DIAL 911

When you call 911, your goal should be to get help as soon as possible. Unfortunately, people faced with an emergency often panic and are unable to provide vital information quickly and accurately. It's important to know what the 911 operators may ask if you have to make such a call.

The first task of 911 operators in Ottawa is to determine the nature of the emergency, the type of service required, and the site of the emergency. Once the operators have this information, they transfer the call to the appropriate emergency service. "Our 911 operators stay on the line to make sure the call gets through," says Harold Murphy, manager of emergency services for the regional municipality of Ottawa-Carleton.

If you're in an emergency situation, here's what operators need to know to help:

Keep a list of emergency numbers next to every phone.

The location of the emergency. For routine calls, the operator asks for information including the phone number and location of the crime-in-progress or emergency. If you are using a cellular phone to report an emergency, take note of nearby landmarks.

Police emergencies. When a call is switched to the police, a screen provides an automatic phone number identification. The police dispatcher will ask a series of questions, such as: Is it a crime? Is it an accident?

SEPARATING MYTH FROM REALITY

Don't do more harm than good when trying to help the injured, says Brenda D'Amico, MD, an emergency room (ER) doctor in White Plains, New York. Here are things to avoid doing during an accident:

■ Don't use tourniquets on bleeding wounds. Apply constant, firm pressure to the injured tissue until you get to a doctor.

■ If a neck injury is a possibility after a serious accident, don't move the patient. Keep the injured person still and calm. Call for an ambulance at once.

■ If someone loses a tooth, don't throw it away. It can be put back in the socket if you act quickly. Wrap the tooth in gauze dipped in a saline solution (or, failing that, in water), put it in a jar, and take it to the emergency room as soon as possible.

■ Don't put butter, oil, or ice on a burn. Instead, lay clean gauze dipped in cool water on the wound to try to cool the burn.

■ Don't put calamine lotion all over a rash right before you want the doctor to look at it.

■ Don't use alcohol to cool off a child with a high fever. The skin may absorb too much of the alcohol. Instead, give the youngster a cool sponge bath and a child's dose of acetaminophen or ibuprofen. Never give aspirin to a child.

■ Do not rub frostbitten tissue or try to rewarm it. Get a doctor at once, and meanwhile, immerse the area in warm—not hot—water until the skin turns red or blue, and pat it dry.

True Stories

Samuel M. Katz, author of *Anytime Anywhere!: On Patrol With the NYPD's Emergency Services Unit*, spent weeks riding along the Manhattan North beat with the New York Police Department's Emergency Services. Katz saw rescue workers save people stuck in elevators, collapsed buildings, and crushed cars. He witnessed this unique team of police officers with emergency medical training (EMT) handling everything from pitbull attacks to rescuing people about to jump off high-rise buildings.

He has learned a great deal from his experience. For instance, many household accidents are cooking accidents with scalding water or electrical fires that could have been prevented.

In car accidents, people wearing seatbelts were inevitably better off than those who weren't. "No matter how bad you might be pinned into the car," Katz says, "they can get to you and cut you out. But people who are hurled from the car in an accident are in big trouble." Of the Emergency Services Units, Katz says, "These guys are real professionals, but when they see small children killed because they weren't wearing seatbelts, it really has a profound effect on them."

EMERGENCY NUMBERS

911

POLICE
FIRE
AMBULANCE

Dr. Jones (pediatrics) 555-1012
Dr. Smith (G.P.) 555-3210
555-4365

Apply constant, firm pressure to a bleeding wound.

If a neck injury is possible, stabilize the patient's head.

If a tooth falls out, put it in a jar to transport it.

MW0212
30mph FRONTAL
BARRIER IMPACT

EMERGENCIES WITH CHILDREN

Try to remain calm when handling a medical emergency involving a child, advises Lois Craumer, a New Jersey school nurse.

Children—especially those in primary school—can get very frightened when they are hurt. And when they pick up on adults' fears and anxiety, they can become hysterical, warns Craumer, a 25-year veteran. This can make it particularly difficult to assess the severity of a child's injury. If the adults react quickly and calmly, however, children feel more assured and tend to calm themselves down.

Since children spend a lot of their time running around and playing outdoors, chances are most of them will have a few accidents.

A services pamphlet from the Emergency Department of the Children's Hospital of Eastern Ontario (CHEO) has these following suggestions for coping with a situation of an urgent kind.

If you feel the condition is life-threatening, call 911 immediately. If you have the time, try to bring these items with you to the hospital emergency room:

- Your child's health card and hospital card, if your child has one.
- A record of your child's immunizations (shots).
- Containers of medications your child is taking.
- Containers of any toxic substances that your child has swallowed.
- Your child's favorite toy, blanket, or book.

Tools of the Trade

Never put ice directly on your skin, because the moisture can cause frostbite. Instead, keep freezer packs handy in case of an injury. Look for reusable ones you can keep in your freezer and single-use packs that can be stored at room temperature. Or use a bag of frozen peas or corn niblets instead. If the pack has frost on it, wrap it in a towel or cloth before putting it next to your skin.

Every child under the age of 16 should be accompanied by a parent or a legal guardian to provide written consent for treatment, if this is deemed necessary.

Smart Moves

There are some clear signs that you need to get to the emergency room in a hurry:
- Chest pain or tightness, particularly in people over 50.
- Trouble breathing.
- Sudden paralysis in parts of your body.
- Fever of 104°F or more (try to contact your physician first).

CHAPTER FOUR

The Green Thumb's Yard and Garden

Gardening Basics

Get your garden off to a good start.

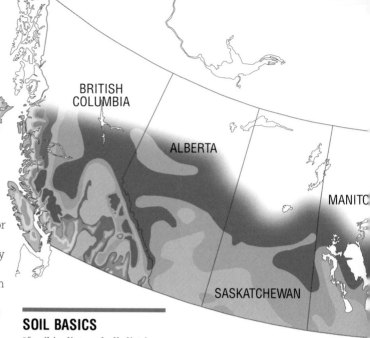

BRITISH COLUMBIA

ALBERTA

MANITO

SASKATCHEWAN

HARDINESS ZONES

Plants, like people, have different tolerances for heat and cold. They thrive or wilt based on how well suited they are to their climate. Unlike people, plants can't just escape to a climate-controlled environment when the outdoors gets uncomfortable. So choosing plants that like the weather in your region is a key to successful gardening.

Fortunately, there's help available. The Plant Hardiness Zone map, produced by Agriculture and Agri-Food Canada, divides the country into nine zones. This division was based in part on minimum temperatures and in part on the survival of indicator plants. Eight zones are further divided into "a" (colder) and "b" (warmer) regions. Over the years, most woody plants have been given a hardiness rating, indicating where they are likely to survive the winter. The survival of perennial plants is more dependent on the reliability

and persistence of snow cover, and their hardiness is harder to identify.

When you buy plants from a Canadian nursery or mail-order catalogue, the zone information will apply to you. If you buy plants from a mail-order source in the US, be aware that the hardiness map and ratings do not coincide with ours.

Also, remember the hardiness ratings are only a guide. Microclimates exist in every garden and a plant may die in one spot but live a few feet away. As David Tomlinson, a landscape architect in Aurora, Ontario, says, "I never consider a plant not hardy until it had died in three different locations in my garden."

In mountainous regions, elevation must be considered: a rise of 1,000 feet gives a drop of 1°F. Conversely, cold flows downhill and a spot on the valley floor may be a frost pocket and a zone colder than the surrounding region.

SOIL BASICS

If soil is dirt and all dirt is pretty much the same to you—think again. As Trevor Cole, former curator of the Dominion Arboretum in Ottawa, will tell you, soil consists of different-sized particles—clay, silt, sand, and organic matter, in ascending order of size.

In soil that's good for plants, these particles are combined so that there are holes for moisture and oxygen to get through. This is vital for root growth and plant nourishment. Imagine the relative sizes of the particles: clay is chickpea sized, silt is egg sized, sand is soccer-ball sized, and organic matter is beach-ball sized. You can see why clay soil doesn't allow for much movement of moisture or oxygen, while soil with lots of organic matter (i.e., dead plant or animal tissue) does. In ideal soil, called loam, a variety of particles are collected in groups. Loam is light and easy to stick your fingers into, and this is the texture you want to provide for your plants.

Soil pH—its level of acidity or alkalinity, expressed

on a scale of 0 to 14—is also important. The ideal level for most plants is about 6.5. If the pH is too low or too high, the plant can't take up nutrients as it should.

Plants also need soil that is rich in nitrogen, phosphorus, and potassium. Nitrogen aids in leaf and stem growth, phosphorus encourages root development, and potassium promotes growth and disease resistance.

If your plants are doing poorly, soil may be the culprit. To check the pH and mineral content, look in the Yellow Pages under "Soil Testing" to find private laboratories that will test your soil for a fee. Tell the lab what you're trying to grow, and it will advise what you need to add to your soil.

Home soil-testing kits are also available but you need to use caution. In parts of Atlantic Canada, for example, the red color of the soil can sometimes cause people to misread the results. The kits are useful for gauging the pH when you are altering the level.

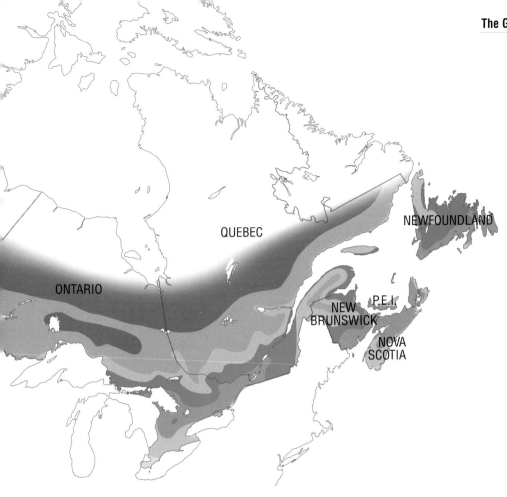

QUEBEC

NEWFOUNDLAND

ONTARIO

NEW
BRUNSWICK

P.E.I.

NOVA
SCOTIA

SEEDS OF YESTERYEAR

Do you yearn for the flavor of old-fashioned tomatoes? Dream about a flower garden like your grandmother had? If so, you're not alone. The desire to experience tastes and beauty from the past is one reason for a growing trend toward seed saving and exchanging, says Kent Whealy, director of the Seed Savers Exchange in the United States.

Seed saving is simply harvesting seeds from a plant so that you can grow it again. It's easiest to begin with seeds from self-pollinating plants, such as tomatoes, beans, peas, and snapdragons. Be aware, says Whealy, that you should not try to save seeds from hybrid varieties—those that result from the crossing of two different varieties. If you do, you'll get something different than the plant you started with. Only seeds from nonhybrid or open-pollinated plants result in plants that are true to type. That means they are genetically like their parents.

If you are new to the world of seeds, seed exchanging is a good way to get started. The Toronto-based Seeds of Diversity Canada is similar to Seed Savers Exchange. Bob Wildfong, president of Seeds of Diversity, says his organization has roughly 1,300 members, who collect and store seeds, and grow rare or endangered varieties of vegetables, fruits, and flowers. Seeds of Diversity also publishes an annual catalogue that lists names and addresses of members who have seeds they are making available, and the types of seeds they offer.

Hardiness Zones:
minimum temperatures

Zone 1

Zone 2

Zone 3

Zone 4

Zone 5

Zone 6

Zone 7

Zone 8

Zone 9

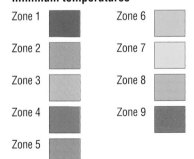

Know Your Terms

If you use commercial products to improve the structure of your soil and make it more fertile, you need to be able to decode the three-part formula—5-10-5, for example—that's printed on the box or bag. What it tells you are the percentages of the nitrogen (N), phosphorus (P), and potassium (K) in the preparation, always in the same order. A 100-pound bag of 5-10-5 fertilizer would provide 5 pounds of nitrogen, 10 pounds of phosphorus, and 5 pounds of potassium. The other 80 pounds is inert. Some formulas are created for general garden use, and others for meeting specific plant needs.

Choosing and Using

The right tools make gardening easier.

TOOLS YOU CAN'T LIVE WITHOUT

If you are just venturing into gardening, you'll need to stock up on some basic tools. Rob Lunan of Lee Valley Tools in Ottawa, suggests these essentials:

A long-handled round-point shovel for turning over soil, digging holes, and moving soil and other similar substances.

A waist-high digging fork with a D-handle or T-handle for dealing with tough situations, including breaking up big clumps of weeds and hard-packed soil.

A hand trowel or hand fork for digging small holes needed for planting. The hand fork can be used to sift soil and remove weeds.

A rake made of iron or steel for taking care of leaves, sticks, and other debris. A fan is useful for collecting material for grass clippings and small twigs.

A bypass spring-action hand pruner that has two moving blades, as scissors do, and is essential for pruning and cutting back unattractive new growth. It can be used on stems, twigs, and small branches.

A lopper for cutting thicker branches.

A sturdy cart or wheelbarrow for hauling loads of soil and garden waste, and to prevent back strain. Those with plastic trays are light and never rust. Large plywood carts are great for moving bulky stuff such as bales of peat or straw.

A high-quality, reinforced hose for watering. Lunan favors a multilayer vinyl hose.

A nozzle and a water wand are indispensable. Lunan says he uses the wand more than the nozzle.

A lightweight, two- to three-gallon watering can to water indoor plants, container plants, and seedlings. Lunan prefers plastic cans.

Buying a tool should be the beginning of a lifelong relationship, says Lunan. "It's always a wise idea to buy something of high quality, and then it will last for years."

COOKING UP COMPOST

Reaching temperatures upwards of 120°F, composters turn your everyday kitchen and garden waste into nutrient-rich compost for your garden. Before you buy a composter, however, you should take your own needs into consideration: Large composters hold more material, but process it more slowly. Active composters work faster, require mixing, and tend to cost more, but are sturdier than simple, passive models.

You may also want to consider a composter that stakes into the ground and has a locking cover (to deter curious wildlife and protect from high winds). Look for a composter that has air holes smaller than half an inch. Larger ones can be an invitation for mice. You can expect most heavy plastic composters to last between three and six years.

The ideal pruner should have:

Strong steel blades and solid construction

Bypass spring-action (both blades move)

Comfortable handle that fits your hand

PRUNERS

The most important thing to look for in pruners, says William Kennedy, president of Stillbrook Horticultural Supplies (www.stillbrook.com), in Connecticut, is the strength of the metal in the blade. Pruners that have strong steel blades won't bend if you find yourself twisting a branch during pruning. Thin blades are likely to bend, and once they do, they will never make a clean cut again.

Pruners that you will be comfortable using for years should have a good grip, with indentations for your fingers, and a nice heft in the hand. Some new models are ergonomically designed to reduce stress on the wrist, which is ideal if you are doing a lot of pruning or have problems with your wrists. Other features of high-quality pruners are "bypass action," where both blades move (as opposed to "anvil" pruners, where one blade comes down to meet a stationary base), and sharpness. Some companies provide blade replacements, which is convenient should you accidentally prune a stone or a wire fence and put a serious nick in your blade.

SHOVELS

What is the difference between a good tool and a bad tool? Materials, design, and construction, says Bob Denman, owner of Denman & Co., a gardening tool store in California. For example, a #2 shovel (the most common size) is designed to break ground, lift the soil, and toss it, as opposed to a spade, which is designed to push into the ground and turn.

Shovels range from about $10 to almost $100, and from a distance look the same. On closer inspection, though, you will see that the less-expensive models are made of stamped sheet metal, not forged metal. They have a "hollow back" design, which means the metal has been curved in back to form the socket, creating a hollow tube that allows moisture to get up into the wooden handle. The best shovels are made of forged metal, which is thicker and tougher than stamped sheet metal. Forged metal is also heavier, which is a plus in a shovel where you want gravity working with you when you push down into the earth.

The best wooden handles are made of American ash. There are several grades of American ash, so look for wood that is clear of knots and without any visible grain. The thicker the handle, the better. Be aware that wooden handles are designed to be thicker at the bottom and narrower at the top. Another, more-expensive, option is a hollow tube or solid core fiberglass handle. Both types of handles are stronger than wood. Denman feels they are not as pleasant to work with, though, because they are not shaped the way wood is.

POTS FOR OUTDOORS

Pots not only affect the health of your plants, they also contribute to the beauty of your outdoor setting. Jimi Meehan, a buyer for Sperling Nursery in Calabasas, California, recommends cement pots for

Cement pots hold moisture better than their terra cotta counterparts.

both reasons. Cement pots are healthier for plants because they do not dry out rapidly, a real plus in hot weather. They also age better than terra cotta, she thinks. Cement pots are available in acid-wash stains and with many different designs.

Terra cotta pots come in a huge range of sizes and

Smart Moves

- Set your outdoor pots on pot feet rather than in a saucer. Pot feet elevate the pot slightly, allowing air to circulate underneath. If the pot sits in a wet saucer, the bottom of the pot stays damp too long and algae and fungus begin to grow. Put three pot feet under each pot. Pot feet are available in whimsical shapes, such as frogs, hedgehogs, turtles, and lions.
- Sharpen your shovels, hoes, and any other tools designed to break ground with a whetstone or electric grindstone. Sharpening is the first thing you should do after buying a shovel, unless the supplier has already done it. After sharpening a tool, always maintain the edge.
- Maintain your pruners by cleaning after each use, especially if you have been working on a plant with sap. Gasoline, commercial bug and tar removers, or other solvents can be used. Oil and sharpen your pruners as necessary.
- Plan a space to store your tools to keep them easily accessible and protected from the elements. If you have a separate room, that's ideal. But you can be organized in a smaller space, too. A pegboard is handy for hanging hand tools, and nails or wall hooks work well for long-handled ones. Or store rakes, shovels, and hoes handle-down in a barrel or other deep container.

prices. Exciting newcomers are "terra chino" pots, which are lighter in color than terra cotta, and have a washed look. There has also been a surge in the popularity of Japanese water bowls, says Meehan. These pots are high-fired stoneware and come mostly in neutral tones, but also in teals, greens, and reds. Purchasers frequently use these pots, which do not have holes in the bottom, for container water gardens. Other popular sellers include Chinese cast-iron pots, urns, and ceramic pots with European designs.

"In Canada's cold climate, pots need special attention or they'll crack," says Marjorie Mason Hogue, owner of Mason Hogue Gardens near Uxbridge, Ontario. Her advice: Empty your small pots in fall and store them in a garage. If an empty pot is too big to move, fill it with pine boughs to create a winter bouquet. Lightweight plastic pots that resemble terra cotta are kinder on your back. Mason Hogue says newer frost-resistant pots are quite decorative. Some fiberglass pots, sprayed with an iron-oxide finish, look like cast iron.

Myth: *Rototillers are the best way to create a new garden bed.* **Fact:** *They don't turn over the soil deeply enough in a space that hasn't been cultivated before. Worse, they encourage the growth of perennial weeds and grasses by breaking up their roots. What they're better suited to is incorporating fertilizer and organic matter into the soil.*

Gardening with Native Plants

**There's added pleasure in an
ecologically sensitive garden.**

BACKYARD ECOSYSTEM

"When people think of extinction, they think of the rain forest," says Janet Marinelli, author of *Stalking the Wild Amaranth* as well as director of publishing at the Brooklyn Botanic Garden. "In fact, there's an extinction crisis going on in our own backyards."

She explains that as wilderness areas have shrunk and backyard areas have grown, native plants have been disappearing, only to be replaced by cultivated ones. This is a blow to the ecosystems in which we live, where plants, insects, birds, and mammals all work in harmony for continued survival.

The good news is, it's not too late. As Marinelli says, "I believe that home gardeners will be the true environmental heroes of the 21st century." How? First, learn what you can about the natural plant communities in your area, through books and horticultural organizations. Then, says Marinelli, "Try to recreate native plant communities, especially on the periphery of your property." She suggests edges of the property because she envisions a situation where many properties are linked together with native plants. This could make a big difference in helping to enlarge wilderness areas.

As it is now, with small pockets of wilderness, native plant seeds are trapped and can't disperse widely. If you're moving to a new home, especially one in a relatively unspoiled area on the "expanding urban fringe," don't rip out what's there, says Marinelli. Instead, work with the existing natural landscape. For instance, if it's a woodland, make a woodland garden, adding native plants for color and variety.

"In the forest, there are all kinds of vertical layers," says Marinelli, "canopy to understory to shrubs to wildflowers to mosses. It's an important way in which nature has packed a huge amount of diversity into the native landscape. The approach I advocate is to pack as much diversity into your property as possible," says Marinelli.

APPROPRIATE PLANTING

Putting the right plant in the right place is a familiar gardening mantra. Luckily, with native plant gardening, it's easy to determine where that "right place" is. "All you need to do is to look at where a native plant grows naturally—its habitat, in other words—and you're well on your way to understanding what the plant needs to thrive," says

Lorraine Johnson, author of *Grow Wild: Native Plant Gardening in Canada.* "Some native plants, for example, grow naturally in woodland habitats, underneath the shady canopy provided by trees. Obviously, these plants require shade in order to flourish."

Johnson points out that woodland habitats have nutrient-rich soil full of organic matter, and one way to ensure this rich soil in your own garden is to mulch with dead leaves in the fall; as the leaves decompose, they return their nutrients to the soil. Or replenish the soil annually with an application of well-rotted manure.

"Prairies and meadows are sunny habitats, and, in general, most prairie and meadow plants do best in full sun. They also tend to prefer soil that is not high in nutrients or organic matter, so regular applications of compost or rotted manure are not necessary and may cause excess foliage growth at the expense of flowering."

Many meadow and prairie plants are also drought tolerant, according to Johnson. After they are estab-

lished in the garden, they will thrive without any supplementary watering.

Plants that grow naturally in wetland habitats—whether wet meadows or ponds—require moist conditions in the garden. Wetlands tend to be nutrient-rich habitats, so wetland plants will benefit from regular additions of compost.

Once you're aware of these basic features of natural habitats, says Johnson, the job of matching native plants to the condition in your garden becomes easier. "For guidance, explore local natural areas where you'll discover many wonderful plant combinations that you can try out in your own native plant garden, whether woodland, prairie, meadow, or wetland."

DRYLAND GARDENING

Gardening in dry conditions can mean frustration and hard work, whether the drought is prolonged or only a matter of a week or two. Add wind, sun, high temperatures and rocky or sparse soil and many gar-

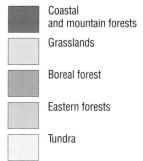

Legend:
- Coastal and mountain forests
- Grasslands
- Boreal forest
- Eastern forests
- Tundra
- Transition zones

sedums (*Sedum*), both upright and trailing. "There are dozens of these on the market, as gardeners are discovering their versatility in the garden," says Bennett. Perennials such as mullein (*Verbascum*), day-lilies (*Hemerocallis*), wormwood (*Artemisia*), and yarrow (*Achillea*) are also able to survive a few weeks without rain. Self-sowing annuals like rose moss (*Portulaca*), poppies (*Papaver*), pot marigold (*Calendula officinalis*), sage (*Salvia*), and bachelor's buttons (*Centaurea cyanus*) provide a burst of color all summer.

Most of these plants suffer if given too much water. Bennett says, "You should plant them in well-drained sandy soil and let them dry out between waterings. Terraced slopes suit them well, and so do raised beds and rock gardens."

A garden of drought-tolerant plants makes environmental sense too. Not only do these plants free you from most watering, but they are relatively disease and pest resistant and require little or no fertilizer. Adds Bennett, "I can go on vacation during the driest weeks of summer and know that my own dryland garden will still be alive and beautiful when I return."

spiny they should be kept well away from foot traffic. Venturing into naturalized or non-native plants increases the gardener's choices. Most hardy bulbs, including daffodils (*Narcissus*), crocus (*Crocus*), and tulip (*Tulipa*), thrive if given sunny, dry summers, their preferred conditions for dormancy. A range of colorful succulents, which are very good choices for containers and hanging baskets, as well as garden beds, include spurge (*Euphorbia*), yucca (*Yucca*), hens and chicks (*Sempervivum*), and

what it does not need or cannot tolerate."

Bennett points out that there are trees, shrubs, grasses, ground covers, annuals, and perennials for dryland gardens. "This type of garden need not look sparse, although it will probably look different, with more succulents and gray leaves than usual." Among drought-tolerant native plants of Canada are the white cedar (*Thuja occidentalis*), juniper (*Juniperus*), potentilla (*Potentilla*), blanket flower (*Gaillardia*), columbine (*Aquilegia*), sunflower (*Helianthus*), and Mexican hat (*Ratibida*), as well as a wide selection of penstemons (*Penstemon*). There are some cacti, too, especially prickly pears (*Opuntia*), which are hardy enough to survive in northern Alberta, but are so

den plants wilt or die. But Jennifer Bennett, author of *Dryland Gardening*, says, "Anyone who has noticed the greenery along a roadside in summer knows there are plants that can survive drought without watering. So, in the garden, it's just a matter of choosing what to grow, giving it what it needs, and avoiding

Smart Moves

To ensure that your dryland garden receives enough water to thrive but not more that it needs to survive, follow these guidelines:

■ If your soil has a high clay content, add coarse sand and organic matter such as compost to improve drainage.

■ Build raised beds if the ground is flat and water tends to puddle.

■ Allow lawns to go dormant and brown in summer, or replace lawns with patios or drought-tolerant shrubs or ground covers.

■ Water seedlings and new transplants including perennials, shrubs, and trees, regardless of their size, deeply and often the first year, or until they are established and growing on their own.

Gardening in Tough Spots

There are tricks to coping with less-than-desirable conditions.

1. Determine how severe the problem is. If grass is growing, that is a good indicator of what is going on below. Fairly healthy grass means soil compaction and toxicity are not too serious, whereas sick-looking grass is a tip-off that all is not well. You can find out how compacted the soil is by trying to drive a metal rod (about a half-inch in diameter) into it using your body weight. If you can not get it in about 5 inches, the soil is compacted. The cure is to till the soil. If you are going to plant only grass, till down 5 to 6 inches. If you want to plant shrubs and perennials, you will have to go much deeper—to 18 inches or so—to give their root systems space to take hold.

2. Assess soil drainage. Dig down six to eight inches, take a soil sample, look at it and smell it. If it has a rotting smell, or if the soil is gray, you have a problem. If the soil smells earthy and is brown, light yellow, or bright red, the drainage is probably okay. You have two options in dealing with a drainage problem. Either mound your planting areas with good soil from another source, or install an elaborate subsurface drainage system. Urban believes the mounding option is not only cheaper but more effective.

3. Assess soil quality. Look at both soil structure and nutrients, not only by observing the color and feel of the soil, but also by sending a sample of the soil for testing. Consult your Yellow Pages directory under "Soil Testing" to find a private soil-testing laboratory that will test your soil for a small fee. The laboratory will tell you how much and what kind of organic matter and minerals to add. "Once you've solved all these problems," says Urban, "You should be able to grow almost anything you want."

ABUSED SOIL

Whether it's an urban site that's been subjected to human feet, canine urine, and environmental pollution over the years, or a suburban one that's been visited by heavy machinery, construction debris, and topsoil stripping during a building project, the gardening challenge is soil.

"Soil is the most critical part of the equation," says James Urban, a Maryland-based landscape architect. Don't even think about planting in these problem areas, he advises, until you have done soil remediation. How? Urban suggests the following sequence:

MOUNTAIN GARDENING

Amy Hinman-Shade, owner of Shady Side Herb Farm in Montana, lives at an elevation of 3,100 feet. Winter temperatures get down to −44°F, wind is a constant visitor, and frost is not unusual in June and is back for good by late August. The soil is "rock with clay holding everything together."

When Hinman-Shade and her husband first bought the property, she optimistically set out to double dig a garden area, only to find that the shovel wouldn't go through the ground. Yet today Hinman-Shade manages to grow over 100 varieties of herbs and flowers as well as some vegetables. What's her secret? Two hundred and eighteen raised beds made from "gorgeous black soil" transported from 35 miles away.

Hinman-Shade uses the rocks that are so plentiful in her landscape to outline the beds and hold them together. The beds range in size from 2 feet square to 3 by 30 feet, and from 8 to 12 inches in depth. She constantly works in compost and manure to keep the soil healthy. "I wouldn't go back to tilling again, no matter what," says Hinman-Shade. "The beds warm up so much faster in the spring that I can be planting larkspur (*Consolida ambigua*) in April while my friends are still waiting. Beds are also easier to weed. And if production is down in one bed, I can let it go fallow, add organic fertilizers or whatever it needs, then cultivate it again later."

True Stories

In 1985, the citizens of Minneapolis spontaneously started to cultivate the six-foot-deep strip of land between their sidewalks and the street. This land is city property, but each resident is responsible for maintaining the portion of land in front of his or her house. The movement started out modestly, with a few dozen people just planting flowers, but quickly caught on and expanded. Now boulevard gardening, as it's known, has become a formal part of Minneapolis' City Beautiful program, functioning out of the city planning department.

John Parker, gardener and volunteer with the Neighborhood Environment Committee, explains that four levels of awards are given for the most beautiful gardens. Gardens vary from small raised beds around bases of trees to perennial beds that fill the median strip between the dual roadways of the broad boulevards. Not only has the city become more beautiful as a result, but the gardens also provide the occasion for neighbors to get to know one another.

It's a challenge to garden at high altitudes, but the results can be as spectacular as the natural scenery.

Topiary gardens enchant and amaze visitors, young and old.

© Disney Enterprises, Inc.

Hinman-Shade raises cold-sensitive vegetables, such as tomatoes, cucumbers, and peppers, in a greenhouse. To protect outdoor plants from occasional summer frosts, she covers the raised beds with a special fabric made for that purpose.

"Don't be afraid to try things," Hinman-Shade advises other gardeners living in challenging climates. There are many different microclimates in your yard, and a lot of times you'll find you can squeak something by that's not supposed to do well in your zone. You can try mulching it, planting it near your house, or changing its position."

GARDENING FOR THE PUBLIC

Any garden that has to handle visits from a large number of people is a tough spot. Add to that very high expectations of beauty, a hot, humid climate that bugs consider paradise, many different kinds of landscapes, and you have Walt Disney World in Orlando, Florida. Katy Moss Warner, director of Disney's Horticulture and Environmental Initiative, explains some of the gardening challenges at Disney World and how they are handled:

Climate. Florida has mild winters with the occasional killer frost and very hot, wet summers alien to standard bedding plants. Through extensive trial and error, Disney World gardeners learned that by adapting planting times to the Florida climate rather than following a northern schedule, they could successfully grow just about every one of the plants they wanted.

Landscaping style. Disney World's signature style relies on theme gardens that enable guests to feel that they have been transported to different parts of the world. Since many plants native to these environments won't do well in Florida, a solution has been to find look-alike plants that will thrive there.

Crowds. The number of visitors to Disney World effectively turns it into an urban landscape. Special care has been taken to make it more welcoming than the typical urban setting by including large shade trees, hanging baskets, and beautifully cared-for landscapes.

Fragile ecosystems. On Disney's highly developed resort property, it's a constant challenge to take care of the environment, but the organization is committed to it. It's been addressed by trying to preserve much of the native vegetation, using native plantings in the gardens wherever possible, conserving water and energy, and reducing the number of pesticides through the use of integrated pest management.

The Right Way

To cope with fungus—brown patch and powdery mildew, for instance—try compost tea. Mix compost with water, strain it, and spread it on lawns, roses, or other places where fungus can form. Compost resists fungus.

WELL-TRAVELED SPOTS

Two landscape areas that are notoriously hard to cultivate are alongside the driveway and around a children's play area. In both places, soil tends to become compacted from traffic—that of cars veering off the asphalt on the one hand and children's feet careening toward the swing set on the other. "Don't keep butting your head against the wall," advises Virginia L. Beatty, consultant, environmental education and horticulture.

Instead, she suggests using containers filled with flowering plants along the driveway, and giving kids free reign to have fun in the play space. You might, for instance, get a bunch of used tires and let the kids use them for building, bouncing, or even planting in. The point is, don't be bound by the convention that you have to have a perfectly manicured landscape, or you will only persist in something that's bound to result in failure.

Know Your Terms

Integrated pest management (commonly referred to as IPM) means controlling garden pests through a variety of approaches. These include the introduction of natural predators ("good bugs"), traps, hand picking of insects, and introducing sterilized male insects that will mate but the females produce no young. One goal of IPM is to avoid applying any toxic materials to the garden.

Decks, Patios, and Garden Walks

The places you gather help you make the most of outdoor living.

DESIGNING WITH PATHS

"The path is the place to start garden design," says Gordon Hayward, author of *Garden Paths* and a garden designer, writer, and lecturer. The first path to look at is the one leading from the street to the front door, which "should be broad and predictable, with a broad landing by the front door that welcomes guests in a generous, open way." He feels that the garden associated with that path should provide many experiences—potted plants, trees to walk under, and between them shrubs to create visual interest and a feeling of intimacy, and perennials for added color and fragrance.

Next, he tries to link the entrance path to other paths coming from the sides of the house, which then in turn link up to the paths from the back. "The result is to enclose the house in a garden and establish a clear itinerary around the house."

Once key paths around the house are determined, they can link up to less formal paths—to the garage, for example, vegetable garden, pool, or seating area. A guiding principle for design, says Hayward, is that "the closer to the house, the more the paths should echo the architectural lines of the house. That is, be straight and predictable. As you move away from the house, both the material and shape of the paths can become less formal."

Hayward suggests that the setting and direction of paths can help you determine places for plants. A curve in a path is a good place for a tree or shrub. A junction in a path lends itself to a tree, perhaps underplanted with shrubs and perennials, all timed to bloom together.

EVOKING A MOOD WITH PATHS

Secondary paths around and through your garden provide opportunities to set mood and tone. Kirk Himelick, visitor education landscape design specialist at Longwood Gardens in Kennett Square, Pennsylvania, points out that path size and shape, and the materials you select to create them,

all work together to produce a particular effect. A narrow, straight, concrete path from garage to garden shed says utilitarian, whereas a narrow, curving, cobblestone path is more charming and intimate. Curves also allow you to add a little mystery to the garden, making visitors wonder what's waiting around the bend.

When thinking about materials, says Himelick, consider the pace at which

Tools of the Trade

You can choose among a variety of paving materials.

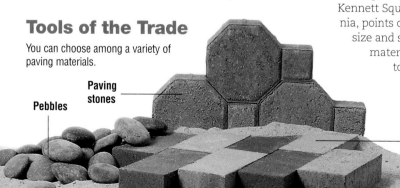

Pebbles

Paving stones

Bricks

you want people to walk. A smooth surface will allow them to move quickly. An uneven or rough-textured surface like gravel or cobblestone will slow them down and allow them to enjoy the space. Path materials can also be an inspiration for the kind of detail you add to the garden. If you use dyed concrete or colored stone, you might want to echo the color in the plants you position along the path.

Path materials can go beyond the usual stone, brick, gravel, or concrete. Himelick has seen paths covered with recycled materials, such as crushed brick or glass, or with a mulch that's different from the mulch used on the plants,

or with wooden boards. He especially likes the sound of walking on slightly elevated wooden boards, which creates the sensation that you are walking over water.

You can also use different materials on the same path to indicate a transition from one kind of garden space into another—from formal to informal, for instance. Varying the width of the path is another way to create this impression of transition.

DECKS WITH DISTINCTION

Decks are a handy answer to a number of outdoor design challenges. They allow you to create outdoor space if you live on a slope, have a house with lots of elevation changes, want to preserve trees near the house (you can build the deck around them), or want a more informal feeling than you might get with a patio. Suzanne Edney, a North Carolina-based landscape designer, gives some advice if you are considering building a deck:

- Think about when you will spend the most time on the deck and how much sun or shade you want. Then position the deck so it will receive that kind of light.
- Measure the size of an interior room in which you feel very comfortable. That is probably a good size for your deck.
- Keep the shape simple. The deck will be more useful, and you'll be more comfortable on it.
- Edge a small deck with built-in seats rather than railings to save space.
- Put trellises on the sides

of your deck that face neighbors and cover them with vines, such as clematis or honeysuckle, if privacy is an issue. You can buy ready-made trellises at garden centers.
- Think creatively about steps. Break up the steps to a tall deck into groups. For instance, divide 24 steps into groups of 8, with a landing between each group. Make steps broader than those in a typical staircase. Or consider a double staircase with steps going down in two directions, to each side of the garden.
- Consider the weight of big planters, a water garden, or a spa you would like to install.
- Stain the deck to coordinate with the color of the flooring in your house, extending the visual connection that links the inside to the outside.

A PEACEFUL PATIO

Barbara Blossom Ashmun, author of *Garden Retreats, 200 Tips for Growing Beautiful Perennials* and *200 Tips for Growing Beautiful Roses*, is an expert on garden design.
- The shape, style, and material of a patio should relate to those of the house, says Ashmun. For example, if the house is a rectangular brick Colo-

nial, the patio should be similarly conservative and at least lined in brick if not totally constructed of that material.
- Since there is often a fair amount of activity around a patio, don't plant anything too fragile or brittle there. Herbs are especially nice because they provide fragrance and texture without growing too tall and blocking the view.
- If your patio is a very high-activity area, Ashmun recommends putting plants in containers and having the lawn come right up to the patio. If you want a tree for shade, consider a smallish one, such as a flowering plum (*Prunus*) or cherry (*Prunus*). And because patios are usually close to the house, you don't want trees with messy fruit or large, heavy leaves that require a lot of clean-up.

Ashmun associates patios with quiet, peacefulness, and a beautiful view, and recommends using these criteria when you build. She feels that the view is too often the neglected element when planning patio design. For example, you should try to avoid looking out onto a fence or the neighbor's house, she advises.

The Right Way

Before building anything outdoors, follow these tips to get some sense of how it will look on completion.
- When planning garden paths, try laying them out with garden hoses or spray chalk.
- To get a feeling for where to place a deck, use a step ladder to see what the view would be from a number of different points.
- Simulate a patio by outlining it in string, or laying down cardboard in the shape you envision.

Garden Gates and Fences

There are lots of reasons for enclosing a garden.

Smart Moves

Know the difference between a mole and a vole? The creatures who eat your vegetation are mostly likely voles. Think of them as vegetarians. The ones who create tunnels in your lawn are moles. They're the carnivores and they're looking for grubs.

To discourage these visitors, you might try a sonic system. It consists of small units placed around your property that send out high-frequency sound waves designed to irritate the animals. It's one way to protect your young trees and flower bulbs from creatures that are almost impossible to fence out.

RUSTIC GATES

In a naturalistic garden with informal plantings, a rustic gate can make a nice focal point or a special transition between one part of the garden and another. David Robinson, owner of Natural Edge, creates and builds rustic, Adirondack-style gates and other garden structures, using branches and logs of trees such as locust, red cedar, and osage orange, a highly durable wood. This design concept dates back to 16th-century France and England, where it was used for furniture. He learned how to apply it while restoring the original garden structures in New York City's Central Park.

Because rustic gates use branches and logs, "they are just a bigger form of whatever is planted in the garden," says Robinson, who has built gates for a variety of settings—for a wooded garden, as a transition from a formal garden to a wooded area, and as an entrance to a swimming pool. While the feeling is rustic, the gates are constructed with state-of-the-art screws, fastening systems, and adhesives.

DEER FENCING

In the contest of wits between suburban home owners and deer, deer seem to be winning. The people at Benner's Gardens in New Hope, Pennsylvania, plan to change that with their deer fencing. Vice president and co-owner Al Benner explains that the fencing is black, polypropylene, high-strength mesh that is stretched between trees, fiberglass or metal posts, or wooden 4 x 4s. It can be used to enclose a small garden or a large property.

The fence is secured to the uprights with nails or special ties, and to the ground with steel stakes, so deer can't push their way through or under it. At eight feet, it's too high for deer to jump. White streamers are placed on the fence for the first few months after installation to warn the deer that a barrier is present and to keep them from running into the fence. The deer then re-route their trails to bypass the fenced property.

The key to success with this deer fencing, says Benner, is total enclosure. "If any space is left open, the deer will come right in and may get stuck inside." For enclosures that involve a

FENCE TIPS

Another approach to protecting vegetable gardens from deer is to subdivide the space into fenced squares 10 feet by 10 feet. Typically deer won't jump into enclosures that small.

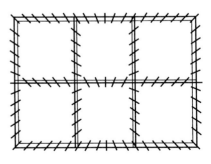

driveway, Benner suggests installing a deer guard—basically, a pit with bars on top. Similar to a cattle guard, it is placed in the driveway and connects to the fence on either side. Cars can drive over it, but deer can't cross it. Another alternative, of course, is a gate you open and close manually or by remote control.

COPPER GATES

Creator and builder David Burns, of Copper Gardens in California, has always had a fascination with entries, from the humble door of a potting shed to the grand entrance of a cathedral. "Entries give you a clue to what lies beyond—how important the next view will be," he says. So it's no surprise that he ended up, after a first career as a building contractor, making garden gates. His are copper, a material he chose because he likes the green of its verdigris (rust) and because of the ease with which it can be formed.

Burns' gates are designed after nature—a double driveway gate, for instance, in the shape of a mangrove tree, with the opening going up the tree trunk to the canopy, where it separates asymmetrically. A very pop-

Tools of the Trade

When you're ready to choose a fence, you may decide among the different types that are available based on the cost of the materials, the amount of work it takes to maintain them, and how difficult they are to install. The information in the chart below will give you an overview of that information for four basic fence types. Note that the cost per foot is based on a four-foot-high fence and does not include installation, which can vary dramatically.

Type/material	Cost per foot	Maintenance	Ease of installation
Picket	$15 to $20	Medium	Easy
PVC Plastic	$25 to $30	Low to none	Difficult
Split rail	$5 to $6	Medium	Easy
Steel mesh	$4 to $6	Low	Difficult

ular design involves vines and leaves, combined to make the gate look like a live bush. Other favorite shapes are willows and wisterias, but almost any organic theme can be adapted to fit into a particular setting or create a unique sense of place.

Burns' gates are not always on a grand scale. He has made some that serve as entries to tiny courtyards, or small openings from one garden space to another. No matter how modest, a gate makes a very personal statement.

WOODEN FENCES

Once upon a time, wooden fences were primarily picket fences. Now, says George Nash, author of *Wooden Fences* and *Renovating Old Houses*, there are so many styles of wooden fence, you can be sure to find one that complements your architecture. The strong lines of a vertical board fence or horizontal basket-weave fence, for instance, may go well with a house of a contemporary design, while a rail fence suits a ranch house,

and picket or more ornamental designs are the choice for older houses. In any case, a fence should be esthetically pleasing. If it is attractive, it's also likely to increase the property value of your house.

Nash says wooden fences are the ideal owner-builder project because they are relatively easy to put together. He suggests thinking through the following issues before you start:

Design. In addition to complementing your house's design, you have to consider terrain. If you have a slope or large trees, you'll have to accommodate them. Also, you want to consider the impact your fence will have on the shade pattern of your yard, and how wind will travel. Both will affect your current plantings.

Materials. The primary consideration is durability. Any wood that is in direct contact with the ground needs to be rot-resistant. Pressure-treated lumber, which fits the bill, is controversial from an environmental point of view. Woods that are naturally rot-resistant tend to be expensive or fall

into the category of endangered trees, so choices can be complicated. One place not to skimp is hardware. There is a lot of stress on a fence from extremes of temperature and weather. Your hardware needs to be able to handle that.

Gates. A gate can be an extension of the fence or something entirely different, and open automatically or manually.

Legal constraints. Fencing typically delineates boundary lines, and is therefore subject to local zoning regulations. It is advisable to check the local regulations about boundary issues, as well as any restrictions on fencing height, color, and design. Otherwise, you might find yourself caught up in a legal spat with a neighbor or your community.

Budget. What you can afford to pay will influence many of your other choices. Visit a local fencing company or lumber yard to get a sense of what the materials will cost. Then decide if you'll need professional help with the installation and get estimates for that part of the job.

Ready to build on your own? Read up on how to dig post holes and handle other construction details.

You can choose fencing that suits the style of your home and your neighborhood.

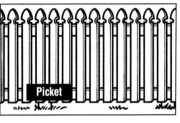

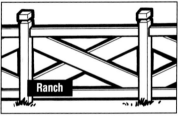

True Stories

Barbara Guy Long of Guelph, Ontario, has created a stir in Canada by reviving the age-old British wattle fence. To create her modern version, she uses cedar poles to support an interior grid framework. Then, she interlaces the framework with inch-thick willow branches to form a solid wattle. Wherever possible, she chooses curved or crooked willow branches whose shapes complement or emphasize the lines of the surrounding garden or landscape.

Gardens for All Seasons

You can plant your garden for year-round beauty.

DESIGNING A FOUR-SEASON GARDEN

"What I try to do is get a mix of plants in my garden, for spring, summer, and fall/winter interest," says garden writer and lecturer Stephanie Cohen, adjunct professor of horticulture at Temple University and education director at Waterloo Gardens in Pennsylvania. For spring, Cohen uses a combination of bulbs and the earliest-flowering perennials, such as hellebore (*Helleborus*), basket of gold (*Aurinia saxatilis*), and perennial candytuft (*Iberis sempervirens*). She tucks the bulbs in between perennials that are going to be fairly large later in the season so the yellow foliage of the bulbs won't be evident then.

The summer plants Cohen chooses tend to flower from summer into early fall. Where spring bloomers have finished and there are bare spots, especially in the front of the garden, she fills in with low-growing annuals like purple wave petunias and floss flower (*Ageratum houstonianum*). If you don't want to spend a lot of money on plants, you can also sprinkle fast-germinating seeds in places that you know will soon be bare—love-in-a-mist (*Nigella damascena*), for instance, or larkspur (*Consolida ambigua*).

For fall, Cohen tries to avoid what she calls "mumitis"—indiscriminate planting of chrysanthemums in reaction to a fading garden. Cohen tends to use more asters for late season because some will bloom into October and even November.

Her late fall and winter garden features ornamental grasses that are left standing and sedums allowed to dry on the stalk, as well as evergreen perennials.

A WINTER GARDEN

At Twombly Nursery (www.twomblynursery.com) in Connecticut, owner Ken Twombly and his staff have created a winter garden. Nursery sales manager Jay Nathans explains that "the basic philosophy that underpins the winter garden is combining five elements—color, texture, form, berries, and fruit—with flowers, so that there are many things to see."

The blues, yellows, and greens of a wide variety of conifers make an important contribution to the color palate. (There's hardly a conifer that doesn't have a color in its name). So do the brilliant reds of the Beni Kawa Japanese maple (*Acer palmatum* 'Beni Kawa'), the red twig dogwood (*Cornus sericea* 'Cardinal'), and bloodtwig dogwood (*Cornus sanguinea* 'Winter Beauty'). Lower to the ground, shrubs like heaths (*Erica*) and heathers (*Calluna vulgaris*) contribute to the garden's wonderful color array.

One of the great opportunities of a winter garden is the chance to notice the textures: textures of bark, such as the paperbark maple (*Acer griseum*) and lacebark pine (*Pinus bungeana*), and textures of foliage, such as ornamental grasses and evergreen perennials. The form of plants also becomes more apparent in winter, so the Twombly garden features a number of weeping trees as well as Harry Lauder's walking stick (*Corylus avellana* 'Contorta') with its fabulous contorted branches.

Plants with berries or fruits that persist through the winter include a number of winterberries (*Gaultheria*), as well as crabapples (*Malus*). Blooming plants are represented by, among others, privet honeysuckle (*Lonicera pileata*) and winterhazel (*Corylopsis*). "I can honestly say there's something

The combination of texture, form, and color is the key to a beautiful winter garden.

Garden ornaments can add focal points in winter, as flowers do in summer.

blooming all year," says Nathans. Visitors often wonder how they can re-create the garden on a smaller scale. "You can use just a few pieces and dwarf varieties, to create the same kind of effect," he advises.

A PERENNIAL BORDER FOR ALL SEASONS

The Northwest Perennial Alliance Mixed Herbaceous Perennial Border at the Bellevue Botanical Gardens in Seattle is the largest public perennial border in North America, according to Alliance secretary Bob Lilly. One of the creators and maintainers of the border, Lilly explains that the 22,000-square-foot area is divided into 10 different color sections, set off by

shrubs, including a "hot" (brightly colored) section, a pink section, a yellow, black, and blue section, and a "variegated and saturated" section (variegated foliage with deep purple and pink flowers).

The border has two great seasons: spring, when the bulbs and spring ephemerals, such as dicentra and cyclamen, are blooming, and summer, when the hot border is in full bloom. Still, the variety of plants in the border, and the attention the creators paid to combining many foliage textures and colors, ensures year-round interest.

In the summer, for instance, the yellow, black, and blue section features the yellow of coneflower (*Rudbeckia* 'Goldsturm') and assorted gold foliage plants contrasted with black mondo grass (*Ophiopogon planiscapus* 'Nigrescens') and other black foliage. In winter, the color theme is achieved through the blackish stems of *Cornus alba* 'Kesselringii' underplanted with golden feverfew (*Chrysanthemum parthenium*) and Bowles' golden grass (*Milium effusum* 'Aureum').

The fall color of deciduous shrubs, trees, and perennials, and the textures of ornamental grasses help carry the garden through to November, when the forms of trees, such as willow (*Salix*), begin to dominate the landscape.

A CHINESE GARDEN

Chinese gardens are enclosed spaces in which the overall design includes not just plants, but also—and equally important—water, rocks, and pavilions. Louis Rejean Deschenes, curator of the Chinese Garden and Penjing Collection at the Montreal Botanical Garden, explains that this type of garden dates back to the Ming Dynasty, when wealthy politicians would retire from public life and build a private garden in which to meditate, paint, write poetry, and gain inspiration.

Rocks and water are essential elements of a Chinese garden's four-season beauty.

Montreal's Chinese Garden includes plants that have staying power even through the area's very cold winters. The decorative flowers and berries of holly (*Ilex* × *meserveae*), Oregon grapeholly (*Mahonia aquifolium*), St. John's wort (*Hypericum calycinum*), wintergreen (*Gaultheria procumbens*), and cotoneaster (*Cotoneaster dammeri*), for instance, provide winter beauty and color, as do conifers, such as juniper (*Juniperus horizontalis*), Canada yew (*Taxus canadensis*), and mountain pine (*Pinus mugo*). But even without the existence of such plants, there is always something to look at and contemplate in this garden, also known as the Dream Lake Garden.

The major elements are the Dream Lake itself, Stone Mountain (an artificial mountain with sharp peaks), several distinctive buildings and pavilions, plus the cloistered entrance courtyard.

Deschenes says that part of the thrill of the Dream Lake Garden is the different views you can get, and the constant sense of discovery you have walking from one part of the garden to another. While most people can not re-create such a garden at home, you can incorporate elements of it, personalizing your garden with stones, water, statuary, and small structures that encourage quiet and contemplation.

The Right Way

The woody plants that characterize a winter garden should not be fertilized during the first year after planting. They need the time to get established and develop a strong root system, which encourages growth upwards. Flowering perennials, which have voracious appetites, should be fertilized right after planting.

Wildlife Habitats

**Gardens can attract
and nurture wildlife.**

Create a backyard habitat

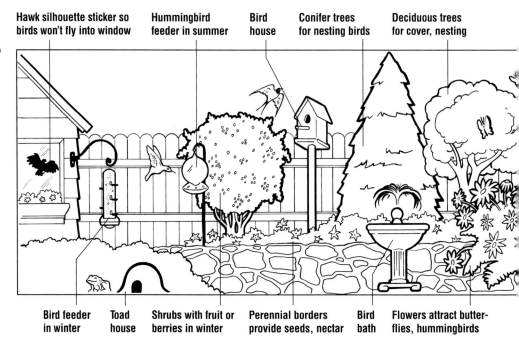

Hawk silhouette sticker so
birds won't fly into window

Hummingbird
feeder in summer

Bird
house

Conifer trees
for nesting birds

Deciduous trees
for cover, nesting

Bird feeder
in winter

Toad
house

Shrubs with fruit or
berries in winter

Perennial borders
provide seeds, nectar

Bird
bath

Flowers attract butter-
flies, hummingbirds

WHY CARE ABOUT WILDLIFE?

In the late 1800s, most of settled North America was farmland. There were wood lots, hedgerows, and weedy areas between fields where birds and other wildlife could find the food and cover they needed to survive, says Karen Williams, owner of Flora for Fauna, a nursery specializing in landscaping for wildlife in Woodbine, New Jersey. She also serves as a consultant to the Cape May Stopover Project, whose goal is to increase the habitat available for migrating birds.

As the land was divided up into small parcels, a lot of the cover and food sources were eliminated. As a result, wildlife populations declined. Does it matter? "A healthy environment enables many different animals and plants to survive and thrive," says Williams. "By encouraging wildlife, we are completing an ecosystem where everything works together."

If the mention of wildlife

calls up visions of skunks and raccoons, that's not what Williams is talking about. These animals are attracted by garbage, not by a backyard habitat. The wildlife she is talking about means birds, butterflies, and insects.

Landscaping for wildlife can include a lot of different elements. The trick is to choose plants not only for their beauty, but also for what they can provide. Take

into account their merits as bloom, fruit, and seed producers. For example, perennial borders and wildflower meadows contain flowering plants that are nectar and seed sources for wildlife. Trees underplanted with shrubs that produce fruit provide food and protection.

Won't encouraging a lot of insects lead to devastation in the garden? "Insect populations seldom get out of control because nature tends to create a balance," says Williams. One year, for instance, there was an outbreak of Japanese beetles in her garden. She waited out the invasion, and the next year had only a few beetles. "The predatory insects tend to eat the plant-eating insects. You have to have faith that nature is always shifting and that the pendulum will swing back."

Gardening for wildlife does mean your garden might not look like a garden catalog. "We've been lulled into the belief that gardens should look perfect," she says. In a diverse garden, "We have to learn to find what natural beauty is."

MEADOW GARDENING

"Forget the rule that says you need to supplement your soil with fertilizers. Also, the rules about regular watering and preparing your planting bed by digging in compost and manure." Is this horticultural heresy? No, it's meadow gardening, says Lorraine Johnson, author of *100 Easy-to-Grow Native Plants*.

For gardeners dealing with poor soil and drought, meadow

True Stories

At the Fletcher Wildlife Garden, part of the Central Experimental Farm in the heart of Ottawa, you'll find a model backyard wildlife garden. The half-acre site, developed by the Ottawa Field Naturalists with help from Agriculture Canada and Landscape Ontario (Ottawa chapter), provides the key ingredients wildlife needs to thrive: food, water, cover, and places to raise young. The garden's features include a pond teaming with aquatic life, nesting boxes, and bird feeders, and lots of indigenous plants and shrubs. The purpose of its creators is to encourage city dwellers to use their own backyards to restore a little bit of our lost natural world.

gardening saves the day. Meadow plants thrive in seemingly difficult conditions, but they also provide long-lasting color and exuberant blooms. And, once established, they require little maintenance.

How to start? According to Johnson, the most important work is right at the beginning. "You need to create a weed-free planting bed. Eliminating all weeds will save you an enormous amount of time down the road." Cultivate the soil repeatedly—perhaps over an entire summer—until you're sure that you've killed off all the weed seeds lurking in the soil.

"Once the bed is weed-free, broadcast seeds in spring or fall, or plant seedlings in spring. Remember, there's no need to dig in compost or manure—meadow plants don't need lots of nutrients in the soil." Seeds are cheaper and best for large areas, but seedlings will quickly have a more established look.

Water the new plantings regularly during the first summer. After that, they won't need supplementary watering. Be vigilant about weeding—especially in the first few years while plants are getting established.

Johnson suggests you buy your meadow seeds and plants from local nurseries. Ask for native plants adapted to local conditions. Also, think about adding native grasses, which will add structure and swaying beauty to the colorful meadow.

WHAT'S IN A BACKYARD HABITAT?

In 1973, the US National Wildlife Federation began its Backyard Wildlife Program as a way to acknowledge people who were making efforts to welcome wildlife into their backyards. Since then, the organization has certified over 20,000 Backyard Wildlife Habitat sites, says program manager Heather Carskaddan. All of them contain the following four elements, which are required for certification:

Food. Food sources include shrubs and trees that provide fruits and seeds throughout the year, and perennials and annuals that provide nectar for butterflies and hummingbirds. Planters and feeders can offer nuts, seeds, berries, and nectar.

Water. Possible water sources include bird baths, springs, water gardens, ponds (which also provide a habitat for dragonflies, fish, newts, frogs, and other aquatic life), and streams.

Cover. Places to shelter and hide might include deciduous shrubs, evergreen shrubs and trees, brush piles, log piles, rock walls, ground covers, meadow, or prairie patch.

Places to raise young. Evergreen and deciduous trees and shrubs provide nests for birds, as do nesting boxes and shelves. A variety of wildlife can nurture their young under the boughs of plants, in rock, log, or mulch piles, in dens, trees, or on the ground, and in meadow, prairie, or scrub patches. Aquatic and amphibious species deposit their eggs in ponds. Butterfly eggs and caterpillars are happy among herbs, flowers, shrubs, and trees.

WILDLIFE-FRIENDLY COMMUNITY

In 1998, the US National Wildlife Federation declared Alpine, California, the first Community Wildlife Habitat in the nation. This astonishing achievement began with one woman and her herb garden. Several years ago, Maureen Austin, a naturalist, and her husband realized that something they took for granted—the proliferation of wildlife in her herb garden—was unusual. Soon

Tools of the Trade

You can buy suet feeders constructed of durable, flexible, vinyl-covered wire with tops that open for easy refilling. Feeders designed to be used as hanging baskets suspended from a branch or pole may help deter squirrels—but don't bank on it.

she began giving monthly garden tours to educate people about gardening for wildlife. The next step was establishing CHIRP, a nonprofit organization devoted to instilling respect for and preserving garden wildlife. She is executive director.

"The selling point of my message is the beauty of the garden wildlife—hummingbirds, butterflies, songbirds—and of life itself," says Austin. "When people see my garden, they don't find it breathtaking as much as a place that makes them feel good because birds are singing, butterflies are drifting around, and a lizard is running over a rock. These things take you back to nature, to your roots."

Austin recognizes that the idea of creating a backyard habitat can seem intimidating if you've never done it, so she encourages people to start small, with a corner of a garden. It can make a difference.

Bluebird house

Bat house

Painted birdhouse

Toad house

Rustic birdhouse

Trees and Shrubs

Trees can create a garden legacy.

Plant both fast-growing and slow-growing trees.

Use shrubs to open some of the area to sunlight.

Create a winding path with interesting focal points.

Pick a ground cover that thrives in shade.

FAST-GROWING TREES

Many garden situations seem to cry out for quick results. If you have moved into a new housing development, just lost a much-needed shade tree, or want to block an eyesore being built next door, you will probably be tempted to choose a fast-growing tree.

But you have to realize, says Richard K. Sutton, PhD, a landscape architect in Nebraska, that "there's a correlation between how fast a plant grows and its susceptibility to breakage, as well as its life span." Sutton speaks from experience. In his backyard there's a fast-growing silver maple tree (*Acer saccharinum*) planted by previous residents. He has to clean up a yard full of its fallen branches after every wind storm.

Fast-growing trees fall into the "weed tree" category, says Sutton. "In the natural scheme of things, they are the colonizers. They don't stay around long because they are supplanted by sturdier, long-lived trees that grow in their shade and eventually take over." Weed trees have a life span of around 25 years, as opposed to 50 to 75 years for some classes of hardier trees.

If you want screening or shading quickly, consider mimicking nature—plant a fast-growing tree, and plant a slower-growing, longer-lived tree under it, recommends Sutton. Eventually, you will have to cut down the fast-grower in order to make way for the slow-grower. If you don't, you are likely to end up with the worst of both worlds, with the fast-grower dominating but falling apart under adverse weather conditions and the slow-grower stunted. An arborist or other specialist can help you choose trees that will work well in your growing zone, give advice on pruning, and recommend when to remove the fast-grower.

According to professionals, the trend in gardening is increasingly moving towards creating natural environments that can be sustained over the long term.

LANDSCAPE DIVERSITY

Tired of the same old view out your living room window? Think about enlivening it with some different shapes, colors, and textures in your garden, suggests Janet Meakin Poor, editor of *Plants That Merit Attention.* "It's a shame not to use more of the palate of plants available worldwide. It's like eating only hamburger or chicken every night for dinner," says Poor.

Exploring new cultivars is a great way to expand your plant repertory, vary your landscape, and in many cases, acquire plants specially adapted to your own climate. Poor cites examples such as the disease-resistant Kousa

Know Your Terms

A cultivar is a cross between two or more species, usually created to emphasize the best characteristics of each. For example, crossing a plant that has a vigorous root system with a plant that has a heavy bloom will result in a hardy, abundant variety.

True Stories

Gardener Cass Turnbull founded Plant Amnesty, a Seattle-based organization, to "stop the senseless torture and mutilation of trees and shrubs caused by bad pruning." Turnbull uses humor to get her points across: a "hall of shame," an ugly yard contest, and a mutilated tree protest, for example. But behind the humor, there's passion. "A lot of bad pruning is self-defeating," says Turnbull. "Cutting off tree tops, inappropriate shearing, and over-thinning all backfire because they create water sprouts that are ugly, weak, and rapid-growing. Good pruning improves the health and beauty of the plant instead of subverting it."

Turnbull objects to tree-topping, which she says is rarely justified. People tend to top trees because "the tree is too big for the person's idea of how big a tree should be." Turnbull's recommendation is to take the tree down and get something smaller. Before making any decisions, it is best to consult with an arborist certified by the International Society of Arboriculture (ISA). In Canada, you'll find ISA-certified arborists who follow its tree-pruning guidelines. In Ontario and Quebec, there are also certified arborists who follow provincially established guidelines.

dogwood (*Cornus kousa*), hardy new viburnums (*Viburnum*) with profuse berries and high winter tolerance, the Katsura tree (*Cercidiphyllum japonicum*) with a heart-shaped leaf and magnificent stature, and tree peonies (*Paeonia suffruticosa*), available in many different colors and hues.

Poor also recommends planting native shrubs and trees that have been neglected or fallen out of favor. The idea in landscaping, she says, is not to always settle for the usual.

From the enormous variety that's available, you should have no trouble finding trees and shrubs that will adapt well to your yard's environment. Start by visiting a local botanical garden, arboretum, or specialized nursery for ideas.

PRUNING KNOW-HOW

Doing the right kind of pruning when a tree is young can make the difference between a healthy, beautiful specimen in maturity and a misfit. Lee Reich, author of *The Pruning Book* and garden writer for the Associated Press, recommends the following prudent approach to pruning:

- For the quickest healing, prune just as growth is beginning.
- Prune anything that's dead, diseased, broken, or misplaced.
- Prune to develop a good structure. Keep your eye out for well-placed branches because those are the ones to preserve.
- Prune when a branch is small so the cut is small. Then leave the cut alone. If the cut is made correctly, it will heal best if left untreated.
- Ignore the old advice for pruning a just-planted tree by making a lot of little cuts. You may distort the tree's shape.

SHRUB SELECTION

Impulse buying might be all right for the odd perennial or two, but avoid it when you are shopping for shrubs. That's the advice of Fred Breglia, horticulturist at Landis Arboretum in Esperance, New York, who says that the key is picking the right plant for the right spot. When trying to decide what's best for the area you have in mind, consider the following:

Height and width. Choose a shrub you won't have to prune constantly in order to keep it from growing above the window line or across the back door.

Form. Decide if you want shrubs with a mound, pyramid, or vase shape.

Texture. Choose from coarse, medium, and fine bark and foliage textures.

Soil. Choose a plant that likes the kind of soil you have in your yard.

If you are planting more than one shrub, mix textures and forms for variety, and choose plants that will provide interest throughout the seasons.

Breglia also recommends that you see the shrubs as one part of the larger landscape. In the same way that you think about the ceiling, walls, and floor when decorating a room, you should think about the overstory (tall trees), understory (smaller trees), shrubbery (or back bone), and different ground covers when decorating outdoors.

Of course, you can't just move trees and bushes around if you want to try a new look, but annual and perennial flowers provide ideal—and almost infinitely variable—accents.

The Right Way

Many people plant shrubs too deep. If the root ball is lower than the soil around it, the plant can suffocate. Here are some guidelines to keep in mind:

Dig the hole two to three times as wide as the root ball and deep enough to work in fertilizer and peat moss.

Loosen and shake off the dirt that is tightly compacted around the roots so that they will be free to grow down into the soil.

Position the top of the root ball level with the surrounding soil so it is protected from winter frosts, but not suffocated.

Fill around the shrub with the soil you have removed and combined with peat moss. Water well, and mulch.

Caring for Lawns

Maintaining lawns doesn't have to be an exacting chore.

DRIP IRRIGATION

Drip irrigation systems deliver water to plant roots through emitters in hoses placed on the ground throughout the garden. Despite the fact that many people associate irrigation with drought areas, drip irrigation is appropriate anytime you have to water anything in the garden says Robert Kourik, author and publisher of *Drip Irrigation for Every Landscape and All Climates.*

As opposed to other forms of watering, drip irrigation gives you "more control with the same amount of water or less, and produces far better results and growth," says Kourik. The reason is that conventional watering methods, such as deep-soaking and sprinkling, put out so much water at a time that they tend to flood the pores in the soil, leaving no room for oxygen. Then, the soil has to drain so air can return to the pore structure. This places mild stress on plants, which can't absorb any nutrients or water until drainage has occurred.

Drip irrigation systems, on the other hand, emit water at the rate of one-half to one gallon per hour.

Longer is better for your lawn, especially in hot weather. Three inches is ideal.

Moisture slowly spreads outwards and down. About four to five inches below the surface, the entire root system of the garden is watered while leaving the soil aerobic. In addition, foliage stays dry (no mildew on the roses!) and less water is lost to runoff.

Looks can be deceptive with drip irrigation, advises Kourik. What you will see on the surface is a small wet area around each emitter, and some dry space until the next emitter. You might think the ground is not getting wet. In fact, if you dig down, you find that the wet area under the surface is much wider than what you see on top, because the water spreads out. As a result, you are "keeping the entire root zone happy," says Kourik.

Drip irrigation is appropriate for ground covers two to three inches high, and all plants higher than that. Hoses can be placed on top of the soil and covered with mulch or ground cover. They do not have to be buried. A new generation of drip irrigation hardware, called in-line drip tubing, has emitters built at regular intervals inside the hosing. Buy the hoses in rolls and cut off as much as you need to position emitters throughout the planting.

WHAT GRASS SHOULD I GROW?

"Choosing the right grass is critical in creating a great lawn," says Rob Witherspoon, director of the Guelph Turfgrass Institute in Guelph, Ontario. The institute evaluates new grasses, conducts turfgrass research, and provides consulting advice to professional turf managers across Canada. "There are three main types of grasses used for lawns in Canada," says Witherspoon, "Kentucky bluegrass, fine fescue, and perennial ryegrass." Each has specific uses, depending upon your needs.

Kentucky bluegrass is the most common grass, because it provides a high-quality lawn with a moderate amount of care. Fine fescues are great for dry, shaded locations but also grow well in full sun. They do not provide the plush carpet of a Kentucky bluegrass lawn, but are acceptable for lower maintenance lawns. Perennial ryegrass is a fast germinating grass used to repair damaged home lawns, but it is reliably hardy only in Canada's

You can liquefy moss in buttermilk or beer.

most southerly areas.

Lawn seed sold in Canada usually contains various amounts of Kentucky bluegrass, red fescue, and perennial ryegrass blended

Tools of the Trade

Use a broadcast or whirlybird fertilizer spreader rather than a drop spreader. Drop spreaders, useful in small areas, can leave green streaks on your lawn. Fill your spreader on the driveway, where spills can be easily swept up.

Although it usually takes a year or two to establish, a moss lawn can be an attractive, low-maintenance alternative to grass for moist, shady areas.

to provide the best characteristics of each grass. Quality lawn mixes are mostly Kentucky bluegrass. They also contain some red fescue, which grows better in any shaded areas, and perennial ryegrass, which germinates quickly and blends well with the bluegrass. Endophyte-enhanced grass seed can also be purchased to provide a lawn with more resistance to certain insect pests.

"Look for good-quality grass seed from a reputable supplier," says Witherspoon. For an instant lawn, consider using sod, which is more expensive but fast and easy. Watch out for miracle grasses with claims of rapid establishment, low maintenance and no need

for mowing. Some reasonable alternatives to the traditional lawn are grass and wildflower mixes. You can also let fescue grow long for that Scottish golf-course rough look. A good lawn is always a great ground cover that purifies the air, filters rainwater, prevents erosion, and provides oxygen.

Here are some more tips from the Guelph Turfgrass Institute:

- Soil preparation is key to a good lawn. Get rid of all weeds prior to seeding. The ideal seeding time is late summer and early fall.
- Keep the seeded areas uniformly moist until the grass plants are visible. Then, water deeper and less frequently.

- Mow your lawn as high as possible, especially in the heat of summer. Set your mower to cut grass three inches high. Always keep the blade sharp.
- To control weeds, keep the grass tall and thick. Remove individual weeds by hand or spot spray individual weeds.
- Fertilize in late fall after the grass has stopped growing. Follow up with an application in late May/early June and late August/early September. Add another application in midsummer if you irrigate or it is a wet summer.
- Use a slow-release fertilizer with an approximate ratio of 4-1-2 (20-5-10), and apply according to the maker's instructions.
- Try alternative ground covers or mulch for heavily shaded areas such as under trees and around buildings.

MOSS LAWNS

Looking for the ultimate low-maintenance lawn? Then consider a moss lawn, says David E. Benner, who created one on his property 30 years ago and has not looked back. Moss takes longer to establish itself than grass—1 to 2 years, versus a few months—so it requires

patience. But once it is nestled in, you can sit back, relax, and stare at your parked lawn mower.

Moss lawns are easiest to grow in shady conditions, though there are mosses that do well in the sun. Mosses grow best beneath beech, oak, and maple trees. They will not do well under evergreen trees because of the thick layer of needles covering the ground.

Here's what it takes to establish a moss lawn:

- Create a smooth, bare soil surface.
- Check soil acidification. Moss likes a pH of between 5 and 6. If your soil is not at this level naturally, you can lower the pH by adding aluminum sulfate, ferrous sulfate, or sulfur.
- Apply the moss to the soil. You can transplant moss when temperatures are cool and moisture is high. Scoop up clumps of moss with a spade, place them on the soil, and tamp down. Or try drying and crumbling moss plants into a powder and scattering them on the soil. In a third technique, you can mix moss with buttermilk or beer and pour the mixture over the ground. The moss has to be kept moist for several weeks until the plants begin to grow.

The only regular maintenance a moss lawn needs is a good raking in the fall.

Smart Moves

If you are going to use a drip irrigation system, you will need to have the following three things attached to the hose faucet:
A check valve or atmospheric vacuum breaker, devices designed to keep water from siphoning back into the house water system.
A filter, to keep sediment or rust from clogging the system. "Y" filters are the easiest to clean.
A pressure regulator, to keep water pressure at 25 pounds per square inch or lower.

Organic Gardening

Organic gardening is growing nature's way.

WHY GARDEN ORGANICALLY?

Life in a healthy garden is a strong tapestry of many diverse strands, woven together, interacting to keep any one organism from dominating and causing problems, says Jeff Cox, columnist for *Organic Gardening* magazine, host of the PBS television series *Your Organic Garden* and *Grow It!*, and author of 13 books on organic gardening and landscaping. Nature like good government, he says, is a delicate system of checks and balances.

Given this perspective, it becomes obvious why poisonous chemicals, whether fertilizers, fungicides, insecticides, or herbicides, wreak such havoc in a tightly knit system. These chemicals tear apart nature's carefully constructed and balanced web of life. Suddenly certain creatures are released from predation and their numbers begin to multiply unchecked. What was once merely a happy player in the garden becomes a major problem.

But organic gardening is not just about gardening

without chemicals. The organic approach is to maximize the diversity of life in the garden. The more kinds of creatures that inhabit any given system—whether garden, farm, or rain forest—the healthier it is. Each creature has an ecological role to play. Microorganisms decay fungus strands. Fungus helps disassemble the fallen leaves. Ladybugs eat aphids. Birds eat ladybugs. Mice eat birds' eggs. Foxes keep mice in check. And finally, when the foxes die, microorganisms break down their bodies.

IT'S ALL ABOUT SOIL

The main premise of organic gardening, says Charlie Nardozzi, senior horticulturist of the National Gardening Association (www.garden.org) in Vermont, is that building healthy soil will produce healthy plants. Healthy plants are better able to withstand diseases and are less vulnerable to pests, just as a well-nourished human body is better able to ward off illness. The healthier the

plant, the less need for intervention in the form of pest control, fertilizers, and disease treatment, which are the typical uses for chemicals in the garden.

Gardening organically starts with adding organic matter to the soil. Decaying organic matter breeds

Green manure

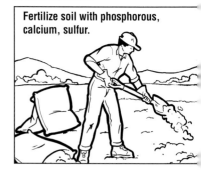

Fertilize soil with phosphorous, calcium, sulfur.

Smart Moves

One non-toxic method of pest control is companion planting—combining plants that naturally repel certain harmful insects with plants that attract the pests and are most susceptible to damage from them.

Basil

Basil repels flies and mosquitoes. Plant with tomatoes.

Borage deters tomato worms. Plant with tomatoes, strawberries, and all varieties of squash.

Coriander repels aphids and spider mites. Plant as desired throughout the garden.

Feverfew roots contain pyrethrin, which repels a variety of pests. Plant throughout the garden.

Garlic repels aphids. Plant near roses and raspberries.

Horseradish repels blister beetles. Plant with potatoes.

Hyssop deters cabbage moths, so plant near cabbage. Planted near grapes, it will typically increase their yield.

Nasturtium repels whiteflies and various cabbage pests. Plant with radishes and cabbage.

Peppermint drives away red ants from shrubs and flowers, and white cabbage butterflies from cabbage. Plant with cabbage, peonies, and tomatoes.

Pyrethrum (a daisy-like type of chrysanthemum) keeps a variety of pests away from nearby plants. Place strategically throughout the garden.

Rue deters Japanese beetles in roses and raspberries, so plant it near those bushes.

Sage deters cabbage moths, beetles, and carrot flies. Plant near cabbage and carrots.

Savory discourages cabbage moths. Plant near cabbage.

Nasturtium

Quick Tricks

There are over 100 varieties of edible flowers available to the North American gardener. They include:

Nasturtium	Calendula	Gardenia
Pansy	Chamomile	Primrose
Sweet violet	Chrysanthemum	Peony
Chive	Day lily	Gladiola

microorganisms. The microorganisms produce a mix of nutrients in the soil that create a well-balanced diet for plants, one which they are able to absorb in the right quantities and at the right times.

One form of organic matter is decaying plant matter, such as grass clippings, leaves, hay, straw, vegetable scraps, and so on. Another form is manure, which is now available from a wide variety of animals. Both types are usually applied to the garden after being composted to reduce the risk of any possible health issues.

If, after adding organic matter to the soil, soil tests reveal that it's still missing specific nutrients, you can add organic fertilizer. Organic fertilizer tends to be closely related to its original source, says Nardozzi.

You can use crushed rock phosphate, for instance, to supply phosphate, soy bean meal or alfalfa meal to provide nitrogen, and green sand (another mined material) to add potassium.

Most organic fertilizers act slowly in the soil, because they need to be digested by microorganisms before they can be absorbed by plants. If you need fast action, quick-release organic fertilizers are widely available. Fish emulsion is an example.

COVER CROPS

Many organic gardeners use cover crops, or green manures, as they are often called, to help build healthy soil. Annual, quick-growing cover crops are typically planted between growing periods to replenish the soil—in late fall and winter in cold climates, for instance, or during the summer in a hot climate.

The crops are allowed to grow until they are about a foot tall, and then they are tilled or dug into the earth. Perennial cover crops are used for longer periods of time—a year or so—to breathe new life into a worn-out area or one that won't be used during that growing period.

Cover crops, says Ann Clark, associate professor in the department of plant agriculture at the University of Guelph, provide substantial benefits to the soil, and they can:

- Increase the organic matter content, beneficial microorganisms, and nitrogen content of the soil in the garden.
- Stabilize the soil to prevent erosion.
- Improve water, air, and root penetration.
- Choke out weeds.
- Reduce pests.

Cover crops, which are planted from seed, include legumes, such as alfalfa, clover, vetch, peas, and beans, and non-legumes like ryegrass, buckwheat, and mustard. Clark says that a seed mix is a good way to start because it increases your chances of success. If one variety doesn't work well, something else will.

Cover crops do especially well if the soil is fertilized with phosphorous, calcium, and sulfur before you plant, says Clark. Seeds can be broadcast (tossed by hand) onto the loosened soil. Then water as necessary to promote growth.

COPING WITH PESTS AND DISEASES

Lynn Bycynski is a market gardener and author of *The Flower Farmer: An Organic Grower's Guide to Raising and Selling Cut Flowers*. For a professional grower, she has a casual attitude toward garden pests and diseases. "Keep in mind that not every insect pest is going to ruin a garden. The first thing to do is observe them to see if they're doing any real damage. If they are, there are usually a lot of simple things you can do to eliminate the problem. You can spray spider mites and aphids with a hose, for instance."

Bycynski's first line of defense in coping with these problems is to turn to an organic gardening book for advice rather than rushing out to the store for a chemical cure—especially a toxic one. "I want my garden to be a place that's safe for my children and nurturing for me. It wouldn't be worthwhile to have a garden if I had to spray it with pesticides or herbicides."

One of Bycynski's main strategies in avoiding pests and diseases has been to simply give up on the plants that have been most problematic in her garden. "A big challenge of gardening is finding out what works in your space. It involves trying lots of different things."

For a trouble-free annual cutting garden, Bycynski put together the following list of easy, prolific flowers that can be grown successfully virtually anywhere in North America. She urges you to look for these cultivars, or others that are identified as being 18 inches or taller. The flowers are listed in the order in which they bloom, from late spring until fall.

Consolida ambigua 'Giant Imperial'
Ammi majus
Antirrhinum majus 'Rocket'
Zinnia 'Blue Point' and 'Oklahoma'
Ageratum 'Blue Horizon'
Rudbeckia 'Indian Summer'
Celosia 'Pampas Plume'
Asclepias 'Silky Gold' and 'Red Butterfly'
Monarda 'Lambada'
Salvia farinacea 'Blue Bedder'
Celosia 'Flamingo Feather'

Bycynski also recommends some flowering perennials for your cutting garden, including *Salvia* 'May Night,' *Phlox paniculata* 'David,' and *Echinacea purpurea* 'Magnus.'

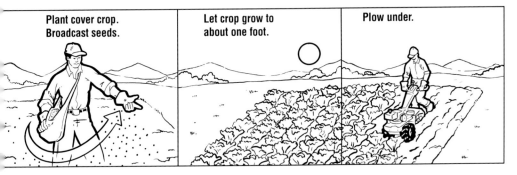

Plant cover crop. Broadcast seeds.

Let crop grow to about one foot.

Plow under.

Composting and Mulching

You can improve the quality of your soil to protect plants.

Kitchen composter bin

THE TRUTH ABOUT COMPOST AND MULCH

Are you confused about the difference between compost and mulch? Just remember, compost goes *in* the soil, mulch goes *on top*, says Charlie Mazza, senior extension associate at Cornell University for the Home and Grounds Community Horticulture Program for New York State. Compost is organic matter that is incorporated into the soil to improve soil conditions. Mulch, which can be organic or inorganic, is used to cut down on weeds and water evaporation during the growing season. During the winter, mulch is laid down to provide insulation for plant crowns, the point at which the root joins the stem.

Composting means taking organic materials such as yard waste and table scraps, heaping them in a pile, and allowing them to break down into a texture fine enough to be added to soil. "Compost serves the double purpose of adding organic matter to the soil and reducing the amount of waste we throw into our waste stream," says Mazza.

He explains that the breakdown process happens through the action of microorganisms feasting on the pile's contents. Like us, these microorganisms need a balanced diet, which you can supply by adding both "browns" for carbon—autumn leaves and twigs, farm animal manure, and straw, for example—and "greens" for nitrogen —grass clippings, plant cuttings, and fruit and vegetable parings. Stirring the pile helps to quicken decomposition. So does keeping it moist.

There are hundreds of varieties of mulch, which can be loosely divided into

Gravel

summer mulch for weed and evaporation control, and winter mulch for plant protection. Summer mulches include everything from inorganic materials, such as colored stone

Plastic sheeting

chips, black plastic, and the new geotextiles, to organic materials like bark chips, wood shavings, and cocoa

Cocoa hulls

bean hulls. Winter mulches tend to be lighter and looser—straw, pine needles, and dried leaves.

Mazza advises thinking about utility and price when you choose mulches.

The Right Way

If nothing is happening in your compost pile, and you have a mix of "browns" and "greens," chances are the pile is too dry. The microorganisms that work on the pile need air and water to survive. Rain may not wet the pile sufficiently if it only reaches the top layer. Everytime you turn the pile, hose it down thoroughly so everything gets a coating of moisture.

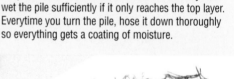

Cedar mulch

If you are mulching a high-visibility area, you will want something good-looking that may cost a little more. If you are mulching your vegetable garden, you can go with a more humble and less expensive material.

Wood shavings

CANADA'S "MASTER COMPOSTER" PROGRAM

If you're having problems getting your composter to work efficiently, there's lots of help at hand. Your city or municipality may have a recycling department that can tell you what's available in your area. They may also have pamphlets outlining composting basics.

Some Canadian cities have a "master composter" program in place. Trained volunteers man "composting hotlines" to help people with all their composting questions. If you have a problem, they may even send someone to your home to see what the problem may be.

Susan Antler of the Toronto-based Composting Council of Canada says that, all across the country, record numbers of people have taken on the task of composting in their own backyards. Antler's goal is to bring awareness to the general public that organic waste should no longer be thought of as merely "waste," but rather as a valuable resource that we can turn into a great product for our gardens. Her organization can tell you what resources you may have near you.

COMPOST CONNECTIONS

As a consultant for Woods End Research Labs in Maine, Jonathan Collinson does troubleshooting at compost sites that have problems. Here are some of his recommendations for successful composting:

- Choose a compost system that fits the time and energy you are willing to expend on it, as well as the size of your yard. Be aware that the only way to get quick results is by frequent and thorough mixing of the pile, whether with a rotary system or a pitchfork. It's fine to neglect your compost pile. Decomposition will take place anyway, but it will happen at a much slower rate.
- If your compost pile attracts flies, be sure to thoroughly mix in any new material you add, then cover it with a six-inch layer of leaves or straw. Keep a three-inch layer of leaves or hay over the sides of the pile. After covering it, water regularly so the contents degrade quickly.
- Compost piles attract rats only in areas where rats are already a problem. If you live in such an area, place a very strong hardware cloth—made of quarter- or half-inch galvanized mesh—on the bottom and top of your compost pile. Thoroughly mixing the pile will further discourage rats, who do not like having their food mixed with leaves and straw.
- If you want to compost newspaper, limit the amount you add to about five percent of the total volume. Newspaper has an extremely high carbon-to-nitrogen ratio—between 500 and 1,000 to 1. The ideal compost ratio is 30 to 1. To get it right, place a thin layer of newspaper between thick layers of "greens." You should not see any newsprint when composting is complete.
- Never use compost pure. Dig it into the soil. With a potted plant, remove the plant from the pot, mix the compost with the soil, then repot.

COMPOSTING WITH WORMS

You can use red wiggler worms to create your own compost. Placed in a bin in your backyard, they will eat all your kitchen scraps, and in a matter of months turn them into compost to nourish the soil. Here's how to start, from Jack Livingstone, owner of the Worm Factory in Perth, Ontario:

- Buy red wiggler worms. You will need about 1,000 (about a pound) to handle the food scraps from two to four people, in a container two feet by one foot by one foot deep.
- Use a wooden container, because it absorbs moisture. If you use a plastic container, it should have drain holes in the bottom to reduce excess moisture. Be sure both containers have loose-fitting lids.
- Place eight inches of damp yard waste (leaves and grass clippings) in the bottom of the container. Keep it moist at all times. Do not use potting soil unless you can be sure that it has no chemicals that could be harmful to the worms. The use of soil is not necessary for your worm bed.
- Place worms in the container and let them stay there for two days before placing any food in it.
- Begin to add food scraps—everything but meat, fish, bones, and acid fruits. If you grind the scraps before adding them to the container, the worms will eat them more quickly. Cover food scraps with a layer of dampened leaves, grass clippings, or newspaper to prevent odors or insects.
- To harvest the worm castings, dump the container's contents onto spread-out newspaper and remove the castings. Fill the box with fresh bedding and dump the worms and undigested matter back into the box.
- Keep your worms outside, if possible. During the frigid Canadian winter, put the worms in a well-insulated composter to protect them from freezing. Ensure that they get a large feeding once a week so they will produce enough heat. If you keep the worms indoors, you can prevent them from crawling out by placing them in an uncovered container under a low-watt light.

Smart Moves

The two most important things to do with compost:

Keep it aerated.

Keep it moist.

Biointensive Gardening

You can get a greater yield using fewer resources.

WHAT IS BIOINTENSIVE GARDENING?

Biointensive gardening is a method of growing food crops that can be traced back to ancient civilizations and, in more recent times, to European market farmers. This type of gardening was introduced in North America by English master horticulturist Alan Chadwick. It has been popularized by John Jeavons, author of *How to Grow More Vegetables, Fruits, Nuts, Berries, Grains and Other Crops Than You Ever Thought Possible on Less Land Than You Can Imagine*, and *Lazy Bed Gardening*. Jeavons practices biointensive farming on steep, tough terrain in California.

GREENHOUSE GARDENING

Steve Moore is director of the Center for Sustainable Living at Wilson College in Chambersburg, Pennsylvania. Using biointensive raised gardening beds, both outdoors and in a solar greenhouse, Moore and his students produce 34 types of vegetables, as well as herbs and flowers, for 34 weeks of the year.

During the cold winters in the area, the greenhouse beds are covered with plastic sheeting draped over arches. The plastic can be pulled back to expose the beds to light. When the plastic is draped again, it traps heat within the plastic tunnels. "This puts us several zones south," says Moore, who has managed to grow lettuce in the greenhouse when nighttime temperatures dipped to 17°F.

Moore says that choosing cold-tolerant varieties is also important for winter gardening. In addition, says Moore, the dense plant spacing "enhances the microclimate right around the plants, making them more stress-free, and more resistant to temperature and insect damage."

Moore acknowledges that the initial effort needed to create double-dug beds is substantial. But, he says, "people cannot conceive of how much food can come out of a small area. If you can grow that much food, the investment in double digging is rewarded many times over down the road. And, you don't have to weed and water a big garden."

Stringbeans

Squash

The Right Way

To do biointensive gardening, you have to double dig a bed by hand. Here are instructions on how to do it:

- Mark the area where you want the bed.
- Remove sod if necessary.
- Loosen the soil.
- Using a shovel, dig a trench one foot deep and one foot wide at one side of the bed. Put the soil in a bucket or wheelbarrow. Then, with a spading fork, loosen the underneath layer another foot down.
- Moving backwards, repeat this process, but put the top 12 inches of soil in the trench you dug just before.
- Work your way in this fashion to the end of the bed. Place the soil you removed from the first trench in the last trench.
- Work compost and organic fertilizer into the top six inches of soil.

A whole gardening method

Biointensive gardening is a system whose components must be used together to produce the best results. Leaving out one or more aspects of the method can have a detrimental effect on the soil, on crop yields and quality, and on beneficial insects that are important to the system.

1. Double-dug, raised beds
These are beds created by loosening the soil to a depth of 24 inches. The loose soil enables plant roots to penetrate vertically rather than horizontally. In addition, the soil is aerated, moisture retention and nutrient content are improved, and weeding is simplified.

2. Intensive planting
Seeds or seedlings are planted close together in three- to five-foot-wide beds in a hexagonal pattern. When they grow, their leaves touch, shielding the soil, protecting microorganisms, contributing to moisture retention, and retarding weed growth.

Corn

COMPANION PLANTING

Companion planting, explains biointensive mini-farmer and teacher Linda Sickles, combines plants that perform better when they are clustered together. There can be a variety of reasons why companion plants enhance their partners.

One may have an extensive root system and the other not, so they don't compete for space. One may be a heavy nitrogen feeder and the other a heavy nitrogen giver. One may attract an insect the other needs for pollination. One may repel an insect that may damage the other. "Sometimes we don't know quite why the companionship works," says Sickles, but it seems to. Since companion planting has been practiced successfully for many years in many cultures, anecdotal evidence is often the basis for companion choices.

Popular plant pairings you can try in your garden include celery and leeks, strawberries and green beans, dill and fennel, and the three sisters—corn, beans, and squash. Tall tomatoes can provide a nice mini-climate for lettuce planted underneath. Any of the aromatic herbs, such as mint, sage, or rosemary, are useful for repelling insects that like vegetables.

PLANTING MATTERS

At the Occidental Arts and Ecology Center (www.oaec.org) in California, Doug Gosling manages the 25-year-old organic biointensive garden. Gosling explains the hexagonal planting method used in biointensive gardening:

"Hexagonal planting saves space. If you plant in rows, you waste the space between the rows. In fact, half your surface is empty. Hexagonal planting maximizes the planting you can do in a given area."

Smart Moves

If you are willing to wait, you can let microorganisms and earthworms do the kind of soil cultivation you can achieve through double digging, says Doug Gosling. This technique is called "sheet mulching." To sheet mulch, add organic matter, such as plant debris or cut cover crops, to the surface of the soil, then mulch with straw. Microorganisms and earthworms will make their way to the surface to feed on this material, and in the process will cultivate the soil. It takes about four to six months for cultivation to occur.

To plant hexagonally, you can imagine a hexagon and plant on the points. It is probably easier to plant in rows 12 inches apart perpendicular to the length of the bed. Then plant between those rows, so that plants are between, not in line with, the existing plants.

Continuous planting all year long is another characteristic of biointensive gardening. One reason is that if you leave soil exposed to the elements, it can get damaged. Another is that continuous planting lets you plant cover crops that help to enrich the soil. Crops from the legume family, such as vetch and fava beans, take nitrogen out of the atmosphere and fix it on their roots. If you compost these cover crops, the nitrogen becomes available to other plants.

3. Composting
Healthy soil is maintained by the regular addition of composted organic matter—organic waste products, such as food scraps, manure, and vegetation. Chemical fertilizers and pesticides are not used.

4. Companion planting
Certain plants grow better in the company of certain other plants. Biointensive gardening uses these natural pairings to produce fine-quality vegetables and maintain a vigorous soil.

5. Open-pollinated seeds
These help to preserve genetic diversity and enable gardeners to develop their own cultivars, or crosses between two plants.

Perennial Gardens

Some planning creates long-term beauty.

PLANTS THAT GRACE THEIR SPACE

If you are looking for a never-fail perennial garden, seek out never-fail plants. That's the advice of garden writer, teacher, and lecturer Sydney Eddison, author of *The Self-Taught Gardener.* "Start by familiarizing yourself with really sturdy plants for your area. Among those that work well in many parts of North America are day lilies (*Hemerocallis*), peonies, globe thistles (*Echinops*), blue star (*Amsonia*), and boltonia."

Eddison looks at the perennial garden as a checkerboard, divided into one-foot squares. Each square should be a good investment of space—one that will pay off in visual appeal for the longest time possible. Bearded iris (*Iris × germanica*), for example, is a bad investment because it looks gorgeous for a week in the spring, then leaves unsightly foliage for the summer. Sedum autumn joy (*Sedum spectabile*), on the other hand, is a good investment because it's beautiful from the time it is a rosette in the spring until you cut down the stems in late fall. "Plants have to earn their keep," says Eddison, especially if you have only limited room. Long-blooming perennials and those with handsome foliage all year can be counted on to enhance the beauty of your garden.

Perennial gardening is so satisfying because the process of growth and change is so dynamic —not only week to week and season to season, but year to year.

"The most important place for your best performers is at the edge of the flower bed," says Eddison. "It directs your eye, tells you the shape of the bed, and describes the shape of whatever is adjacent to it. If the edge is neat and tidy, and the plants look healthy and happy, you won't notice any disasters that may be going on elsewhere in the flower bed."

Another key to a great-looking perennial garden is repetition. "Repetition," observes Eddison, "whether of plants or colors, ties it all together. So instead of a spotty, one-of-a-kind effect, repeat successful plants throughout the bed."

A PERENNIAL PALATE

Experienced gardeners sometimes compare what they do in a garden to making a painting. In both cases, the creator has a vision involving color and form. Less-experienced gardeners can find this a daunting challenge.

Renée Beaulieu, public relations coordinator and horticulturist at White Flower Farm (www .whiteflowerfarm.com) in Litchfield, Connecticut, suggests that it's best to pick a theme—either warm or cool—and start off with just a few colors. For a warm effect, go with yellow, orange, and red, being careful to choose orange-reds, not blue-reds. If you want to go cool, try blue and the softer pinks. Blue and purple are very hard to do well together, cautions Beaulieu, as are yellow and pink.

Your vantage point can help you determine which way to go with color. If you see the garden primarily from a distance, consider hot colors, which leap out at you. The cool colors, by contrast, won't be very noticeable. If your usual view is

Smart Moves

- Spring can be a quiet time in a perennial garden unless you plant bulbs. Bulbs can give you a whole season of bloom by themselves, says Sydney Eddison. Plant bulbs in the middle or back of the garden where their browning foliage won't be too noticeable once they are finished blooming. Be sure to mark where you have put them so you won't dig them up when planting other things.
- Conventional wisdom says to place white flowers between warring colors to separate them. That might work if the flower is light and cloudy like baby's breath (*Gypsophila*), says Renée Beaulieu, but some white flowers—phlox (*Phlox paniculata*), for instance—really call attention to themselves, effectively adding yet another discordant note to the palette.

Know Your Terms

Perennial: A plant that regrows from the same root year after year. Perennial life spans can vary anywhere from three years to a lifetime.

Annual: A plant that lives only one year.

Border: A flower bed placed against a backdrop, such as shrubs, a hedge, or a wall.

Parterre: An ornamental garden area where the beds and paths form a pattern.

Topiary: A plant trimmed into ornamental shapes.

Espalier: A plant trained to grow flat against a lattice or trellis, or the trellis on which the plant grows.

blood grass (*Imperata cylindrica* 'Rubra') and Bowles' golden grass (*Milium effusum* 'Aureum') make attractive edgings, while taller grasses like zebra grass (*Miscanthus sinensis* 'Zebrinus') provide interest farther back.

"Grasses are really at their best in fall," says Cole, "when the plumes of seeds, swaying in the gentlest breeze, add height and movement to the border."

Much of Canada has long winters, and any plants that can add interest to the garden at that time are welcome. The stately plumes of the many named forms of Japanese silver grass (*Miscanthus sinensis*) can withstand many winter storms.

gram for Macintosh computers, called Mum's the Word Plus, works. "It combines a drawing program with a plant database. The database lets you look up information on plants—zone, appearance, soil conditions, sun, height, color, and so on. You can also do searches through the database—for example, you can find all blue flowering perennials that bloom in your zone during June and July. The drawing program lets you do a layout of your property and garden bed to scale, and then drag plants from the plant database window to the drawing window. The program draws a symbol for the plant, and you can move it around and change its size."

Norin's program—and others like it on the market—also allow you to do bloom sequencing, letting you see in color on your screen what your garden will look like in a particular season. Once your garden is growing, the program provides a map of your plantings and a place to record notes about what worked and the changes you want to make.

up close, you can use cools, or a striking combination of hot and cool colors.

How many different plants does it take to make a beautiful perennial garden? There's no absolute number. Beaulieu's rule of thumb is that at least half of the plants should be chosen because of their interesting, long-lived, and sturdy foliage—hakonechloa, lady's mantle (*Alchemilla*), and Russian sage (*Perovskia*), to name a few. "They'll have presence all year whether they have flowers or not."

Beaulieu points out that in the traditional perennial border, plants typically appear in odd numbers—one (if the plant is fairly large), three, five, or seven. Curiously, using odd numbers helps achieve a natural, informal look. With even numbers of plants, the tendency to line them up symmetrically in neat rows can create a blocky and unnatural look.

WAVING IN THE WIND

For virtually every kind of garden, you'll always find suitable ornamental grass. Blue, green, golden, or striped, a 6-inch pygmy or a 10-foot giant, grasses fit in everywhere. "They have become the plant of choice for the discerning gardener," says Trevor Cole, former curator of the Dominion Arboretum in Ottawa and author of *The Ontario Gardener*. While a few are thugs, Cole says, most grasses are excellent plants that deserve a place in every garden.

From spring to fall, grasses are worth growing for their foliage alone, while the flowers and seed heads are a bonus. "The seeds on some small grasses are delightful," says Cole, "but you have to get down to their level to appreciate them."

In spring and summer, the colorful foliage of grasses adds contrast to a perennial border. Dwarf grasses, such as Japanese

PLANNING A PERENNIAL GARDEN

Most garden experts agree that sketching a plan for a perennial garden before starting to plant is a must. In the past, plans were done on paper. Now, more and more plans are being created on a computer.

Roberta Norin, president of Terrace Software in Massachusetts, explains how her company's pro-

The Right Way

If you find a plant is pot-bound—the roots wrapped tightly in a circle—when you remove it from its pot in preparation for planting, don't plant it that way. If you do, the roots will continue to grow in a circle rather than extending down into the soil, which helps anchor the plant. Instead, gently pull the roots apart with your fingers. If necessary, snip an X across the bottom of the roots to free them, and then pull them apart.

Growing Roses

Roses are one of the wonders of the plant world.

Plant a bare-root rose bush by creating a mound of soil at the center of the hole, spreading the bare roots over the mound, and packing soil around them.

ENSURING ROSE SURVIVAL

When most people get interested in gardening, one of the first plants they try are roses, especially the hybrid tea and floribunda types. Unfortunately, many gardeners become disillusioned by the failure of their roses to survive the winter and give up on these plants.

"This is a pity," says Trevor Cole, former curator of the Dominion Arboretum in Ottawa and consultant for Reader's Digest's *Easy Roses*. "The main mistake is not planting deep enough. To survive our cold winters, you have to bury the bud union down deep."

Cole explains that, for years, gardening books recommended planting with the bud union—where the branches grow out of the roots—about an inch below soil level. But the method of planting deeper has improved survival rates of roses. "We now tell people to plant the union 4 to 6 inches below the soil. So, even if the top is killed to soil level, enough of the bush survives to grow again."

Where winters are severe, deep planting is best. In milder parts of Ontario and British Columbia, shallow planting is acceptable. But it is still worthwhile to mound soil up around the crown of the plant in late fall. Even without protection, most roses in these areas will survive the win-

ter and grow away in spring.

"Climbers are different," says Cole. "Unless you grow Explorer roses such as 'John Cabot', 'William Baffin', or 'John Davis', climbing roses need extra protection to survive the cold." Deep planting will protect the crown. But climbers have long flower-producing canes, which must also be protected. In late fall, take climbers down off their trellis, lay them on the ground, and cover them with straw and boards. Add some bait to stop mice from stripping the bark from the canes.

NORTHERN ROSES

For decades, Canada's agricultural research stations have developed hardy roses for Canadian gardens. As early as 1922, the Ottawa station introduced 'Agnes', a creamy-white rugosa hybrid that is still available.

In recent years, the number of hardy rose introductions has increased greatly. Work at Ottawa and, later, L'Assomption, Quebec, produced the Explorer series, while the station at Morden, Manitoba, introduced the Parkland series.

Cole points out that these hardy roses can survive without additional protection down to Zone 3, while many are hardy to Zone 2. There may be some tip-kill, but the plant will survive.

Myth: *Roses are too time-consuming and expensive to try to maintain.* **Fact:** *Roses can be easy to grow if you plant those that do well in your area. And roses are just as happy with inexpensive fertilizers and mulches as they are with more expensive ones.*

Smart Moves

- When buying a rose in a nursery, look for the All-American Rose Selections symbol, which indicates that the rose has gone through at least two years of rigorous testing.
- Buy just a few bushes of a variety and see how they do for a year before committing to a large number.

Cole says, "It is vital to get these roses growing on their own roots. Grafted roses are only as hardy as their roots. Own-root plants grow from the base, even if the top is killed. Sadly, since grafting gives more plants from the same parent, many nurseries use this method."

While hardiness is a primary consideration in selecting these roses, disease resistance is also a factor. Most of these roses strongly resist mildew and black spot. Their colors range from pale pink to dark red. 'J. P. Connell' is creamy white with a yellow center. Parkland's 'Morden Blush' is palest pink in cool weather and ivory-white in hot.

"My favorite is 'Champlain'," says Cole. "It is a dwarf bush, about 3 feet high, with bright red double flowers from early summer until frost. It makes a good informal hedge, but it has only a slight fragrance."

Several of these roses have trailing stems that can be trained up a support as climbers. Unlike most climbing roses, they don't need to be taken down and protected when winters are harsh. Says Cole, "I particularly like 'John Davis'. The buds are like miniature hybrid tea blooms, just right for boutonnieres or small arrangements."

NEW BLOOMS

Tom Carruth is director of research for Weeks Roses (www.weeksroses.com), a 60-year-old wholesale rose business in California. He develops new roses by crossing two separate parents and germinating the offspring, doing about 800 cross-breedings a year. Typically, three new roses will result from that crop. What follows is a 10-year evaluation period involving test trials in 42 sites throughout the US. These trials look at a variety of factors: vigor, hardiness in different climates, fresh color at the onset of blooming, finish color as the flower ages, and whether the rose sheds its petals well, among others.

Two of Weeks' new varieties—Betty Boop and Fourth of July—recently won awards from All-American Rose Selections. One of the privileges of developing new varieties is the chance to name them. Betty Boop, for example, is a floribunda (multibloom) rose that's yellow with red edges—"Boopy colors," says Carruth.

CROWNING ROSE ROYALTY

Roses, with their showy blooms, lend themselves to competition, and rose growers are happy to participate. All entrants in rose exhibitions are amateurs who get no rewards but the thrill of competing and the potential for winning a prize, such as a silver plate or crystal bowl.

Lynn Hunt, an accredited judge of rose exhibitions for the American Rose Society (www.ars.org), explains that at every rose show selections are made of a queen and king rose, a princess and a prince, and members of the court. The only varieties of roses eligible for queen are hybrid tea roses and grandifloras, with one bloom per stem.

The rose qualities judges look for are form, color, and substance, with form being the most important. The rose should be one-half to three-quarters open, nicely presented with good foliage, and free of disease or damage. The stem should be in proportion to the bloom. In general, the bigger the bloom, the better the score, as long as stem and bloom are in proportion. Exhibitors are prohibited from using any artificial products on the roses.

To qualify as a judge, you must be a member of the American Rose Society, have been an exhibitor in the past, and have a broad knowledge of all types of roses. Potential judges attend a two-day course and take a two-part exam. There is no money in being a judge, but there's "lots of fun," says Hunt.

Hunt started growing roses 20 years ago after seeing a rose exhibition in a shopping mall. Her special interest is in David Austin roses, which look like old-variety roses but have been bred with modern roses to have repeat blooms. Many old-fashioned roses bloom only once a season.

PRUNING FOR GENERAL MAINTENANCE

Pruning serves three purposes. It promotes blooming, opens up the shape of the bush so that the flowers are more visible, and lets light and air into the center of the bush, which helps prevent disease and encourages growth.

You'll need:
- A sturdy pair of gloves to protect your hands.
- Bypass-style hand pruners to trim tight to the branch.
- A pruning knife to cut off dead twigs.

Prune out older canes.

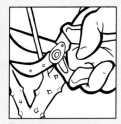
Remove stray growth.

Remove dead wood.

Trim at dormant leaf bud.

Herb Gardens

Some beautiful plants are also useful.

Dill

Thyme

Mint

THE MANY FACETS OF HERBS

Delve into herbs, and you will discover a "very big world, far beyond the traditional perception of garden plants," says Holly H. Shimizu, managing director of Lewis Ginter Botanical Gardens in Richmond, Virginia. She points out that many herbs date back to Biblical or medieval times and that one possible definition of herbs is "plants with stories." In our own times, herbs are used for cooking, healing, fragrance, and industry.

Shimizu loves to teach people about the complex role that herbs play in our lives because it helps them "see the connection between themselves and the natural world." In particular, she cites being able to show Madagascar peri-winkle (*Catharanthus roseus*) to people who have received it as an alternative medical therapy.

It is difficult to generalize about the care of such a large group of plants, but the most widely grown category of herbs, the culinary herbs, need about six hours of sunlight, good drainage, and a neutral pH—roughly 6.5—to thrive, says Shimizu. She points out that herbs do not have to be confined to a separate garden. They are great companions for vegetables, perennials, and roses. Moreover, they are esthetically pleasing in every type of garden.

Shimizu especially prizes herbs for their fragrance. "All kinds of things are associated with fragrance—emotions, hunger, sex drive. Herbs are a wonderful way to have more fragrance in our own spaces," she says.

DESIGNING AN HERB GARDEN

If you want a garden devoted just to herbs, you have a choice between two very different styles: the formal approach associated with medieval monasteries and French parterre, or the informal gardens found in many backyards. In either case, locate your culinary garden in a sunny spot as close to the kitchen as possible, advises Rosalind Creasy, landscape designer and author of *The Complete Book of Edible Landscaping*. Then you can clip and cook.

Creating and maintaining a formal herb garden is a major commitment, says Creasy, but it can be a fascinating experience. Formal herb gardens involve the use of symmetry, geometric shapes, and the repetition of elements—for example, you might have an even number of rectangular beds with the same border, type of structure, and focal point. Potted plants, topiaries, or espaliered fruit trees can be included.

Often, formal gardens are enclosed by a boxwood hedge or picket fence to accentuate their lines and formal nature. The look is refined, clipped, and tidy. A big challenge, says Creasy, is the continual tending and coping to keep it that way. Keep in mind, too, that the repetition required by the design means you can have fewer species in the garden.

An informal herb garden can work in a variety of settings: tucked into the corner of a flower or vegetable garden, lining the front walk of a house, or placed around a patio. As the name implies, there are no strict rules

Kitchen topiaries, like this rosemary, look beautiful, smell wonderful, and are a great source of fresh herbs.

CREATING A FORMAL HERB GARDEN

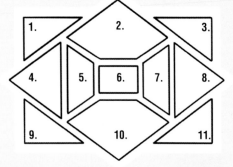

1. Tarragon
2. Oregano
3. Dill
4. Sage
5. Sweet basil
6. Thyme
7. Parsley
8. Chives
9. Coriander
10. Nasturtium
11. Rosemary

Cilantro

Lemon balm

Myth: *Herbs always grow better outdoors than in pots in your kitchen.* **Fact:** *They need light, so a sunny window beats a shady garden.*

for creating such a garden. Here are some key guidelines:

- Place short plants in the front and tall plants in the back.
- Put dark plants next to light ones, stiff next to frilly.
- Create interest by combining foliage colors and textures.
- Avoid arranging herbs by the color of their flowers because their bloom time is typically quite short.

Research how each herb grows in your region. In much of Canada, some herbs will survive the frigid winter. Tarragon, thyme, mint, oregano, and marjoram are all pretty tough, says Sharon Channer of The Herb Garden near Almonte, Ontario. You may have success over-wintering tender herbs indoors by placing them on a sunny south- or west-facing window. Bay laurel and rosemary usually do well indoors and grow large enough to make attractive houseplants. For a wide herb selection, she advises you to treat them as annuals, and buy new plants every year.

MEDICINAL HERBS

Interest in herbs as alternative medicines, combined with the deterioration of native habitats, has depleted native stands of certain plants in North America, says Nancy Scarzello of United Plant Savers, a Vermont-based nonprofit organization dedicated to the cultivation and conservation of medicinal plants. In the United States, ginseng (*Panax quinquefolium*), goldenseal (*Hydrastis canadensis*), and purple coneflower (*Echinacea angustifolia*) are endangered in some areas. In Canada, wild leek and wild garlic are threatened. The problem is acute because the plants are removed by their roots, from which herbal medicines are derived. This makes regeneration impossible. When only the leaves are removed and the root is left behind, as is the case with some medicinal herbs, the plant can grow again.

Taking plants or parts of plants from the wild is called "wildcrafting." An ethical approach to wildcrafting, where it is not prohibited by law, involves getting permission from the landowner to remove plants, taking only 5 to 10 percent of the plant population, and taking bark only from branches that have been removed from a tree. Seeds should be planted to replace plants that are removed. The problem is that a plant like ginseng takes six to seven years to mature.

United Plant Savers encourages people to plant their own medicine gardens, says Scarzello, and will provide seed and plant resource lists, as well as a growing guide. Many of the medicinal herbs, including ginseng, goldenseal, and bloodroot (*Sanguinaria canadensis*), are woodland plants that like shade. Others, like purple coneflower, grow well in a sunny border.

GROWING HERBS IN CONTAINERS

Culinary herbs do well in containers, whether indoors on a window sill or outside on a patio. For best results, observe these guidelines offered by Robin A. Siktberg, who is horticulturist for the Herb Society of America (www.herbsociety.org):

- Place containers where they will get full sun.
- Plant in a soilless mix. Siktberg buys a commercial one and combines it with perlite and compost in a 1:1:1 ratio. The perlite helps drainage, which is important for herbs. Coarse sand also helps drainage.
- Combine herbs with similar watering requirements—for example, tarragon and basil need more water than rosemary, thyme, and lavender. Mint, which spreads quickly, should always be in its own container.
- Let the top inch (for larger containers) or half-inch (for smaller containers) dry out before watering. But make sure you do not let the soil dry out completely.
- Use a 12-12-12 granular fertilizer in the soil when planting. Use no more than half the amount normally recommended for flowers and vegetables. For most herbs, one feeding a year is enough, but fast-growing, leafy herbs like tarragon and basil may benefit from additional fertilizing during the growing season.
- Pinch off flowers to keep plants from going to seed.

Smart Moves

- There is a great variation in the quality of herbs available for planting. Buy herbs in person so you can bruise the leaves and smell them, or buy from a catalog. There are a number of excellent sources, some of which you can order online as well as by phone or mail.
- Annual herbs like basil, parsley, and cilantro that are sold in two-inch pots from a garden center often have not been thinned out. Eight to 10 seeds were planted in the pot and all allowed to grow. Ideally, all but one of the plants should have been removed so its roots had room to spread out. After you take these herbs out of the pot, separate the plants, and plant each one separately. If you plant the whole clump, none of them will grow well.
- You can use any kind of container to plant herbs. Terra cotta provides good drainage and allows air to get to the roots. Plastic tends to hold moisture in, but usually not so much that it is a problem. Wood is also acceptable. Whatever container you use, make sure it has drainage holes in the bottom, which you can cover with shards of a broken pot or a flat rock, so that water can seep out but soil can't.
- Your container should be one-third as big as the overall above-ground area of the plant at maturity. Overly large pots prevent the plant from taking root in the soil.

Rock Gardens

Sometimes small things are the most beautiful.

THE NATURE OF ROCK GARDENING

"The whole point of rock gardening is to grow little plants," says Panayoti Kelaidis, curator of the rock, alpine, and environmental gardens and plant evaluation coordinator at the Denver Botanic Gardens. "Rock gardening is focused less on creating a scene or vista, although a good rock garden usually does that, than on revealing a subtle interplay of color and form."

Kelaidis, the world's leading expert in this field, suggests that for city dwellers with limited space, the miniature landscape of a rock garden is a good alternative to the conventional annual or perennial garden. Besides being on the right scale for a small setting, rock gardens are low maintenance and can provide more interest for a longer period. Kelaidis says, "The urban gardener can have a real diversity of plants, which makes the small garden feel big and dynamic."

In larger yards, rock gardens require an intimate spot to show off their small-scale beauty. Small hills and slopes are a logical choice, says Kelaidis. If you have a flat space, you need to create a spot for an inti-

The rocks you choose can be the most permanent garden decisions you make. You'll want to weigh the effect of size and texture on the effect you want to achieve.

mate garden. There are three reliable ways to achieve that:

- Build small mountains on your site, which is what Kelaidis' wife did on their property. "This is the most exciting but also the most challenging option," says Kelaidis, because you are effectively resculpting the site and have to know what you are doing.
- Create raised beds, a defining feature of most rock gardens.
- Garden in containers, which you can move around easily.

It takes imagination and creativity, but not a lot of material, to arrange rock gardens artistically, says Kelaidis. You can make something beautiful out of a boulder and a few conifers, or different-sized plants in a tiny crevice garden. The choice to include plants, rocks, and other elements is a highly individual enterprise, and the resulting garden is a true expression of its creator. It's also extremely satisfying.

Create an informal garden by growing creeping rock plants, such as several species of thyme, in the crevices between the stone slabs of the patio. Or make a moss-covered stump a focal point.

DEMYSTIFYING ROCK AND ALPINE GARDENING

The terms rock and alpine gardens tend to be used interchangeably by rock-gardening aficionados. This can be confusing for the beginner trying to sort out what's what. Brent Hine, curator of the E.H. Lohbrunner Alpine Garden at the University of British Columbia, explains that a rock garden is simply a small-scale version of a mountain environment, created to grow and display plants whose normal habitat is high above the tree line.

Strictly speaking, an alpine garden would include only rocks and alpine plants. In fact, though, because of the

Russian sage

Yellow aster

Fieldstone

River pebbles

looseness with which these terms are used, you may find gardens called alpine that have some non-alpine plants. Interestingly, the 2½-acre UBC garden mixes both kinds. According to Hine, it is believed to be the largest in North America, and its displays reach their peak in May and June.

Many alpine plants will do well at lower elevations, though they may not be as tight and compact as they would be in their natural habitat. Most like full sun and very well drained soil. Alpines are particularly susceptible to rot because they traditionally grow in dry, wind-swept areas. Most are early bloomers. Alpines that are fairly easy to find include creeping phlox (*Phlox stolonifera*), miniature dianthus (*Dianthus deltoides*), saxifrages, gentian (*Gentiana*), edelweiss (*Leontopodium*), dwarf penstemon (*Penstemon davidsonii*), and miniature columbines (*Aquilegia*).

FOR THE LOVE OF PLANTS

Rock garden plants are perennials, points out Harvey Buchite, avid rock gardener and co-owner of Rice Creek Gardens (www.ricecreekgardens.com) in Minnesota. This group

of plants includes not only flowering perennials (typically less than 12 inches high), but also dwarf conifers and other dwarf shrubs.

Buchite suggests that a few basic plants can provide a rock gardener with blooms for every month of the growing year: May—rockcress (*Arabis*) and Pasque flower (*Pulsatilla*), June—creeping phlox, July—miniature dianthus, August—bellflower (*Campanula carpatica*), September—asters. Since rock garden plants are prized as much for their fine detail in foliage as for their flowers, though, they are interesting in any season.

Before starting a rock garden, look at as many as possible to see what you like. A rock garden 10 feet long and 6 feet wide is about the minimum amount of space needed. As long as you choose plants carefully, you can have either a sun or shade rock garden.

Maintaining your rock

Smart Moves

One advantage of trough gardens is that you can replant them easily if you want a change of scene or if you want to experiment with things you haven't grown before. And if the plants get too big, you can move them to a rock garden or individual pots and start your trough garden again.

garden is fairly easy:
- Well-drained soil is the key to success.
- Alpine plants need fertilizing only once in early spring. Too much fertilizer encourages rapid growth, making plants more susceptible to winter injury.
- Clip plants occasionally to keep them from getting too leggy and to prevent them from going to seed.

TROUGH GARDENS

The original troughs were hand-hewn from freshly quarried limestone and used to feed and water horses, says Sydney McCrea, Washington State University master gardener coordinator. In England, they were rediscovered by Edwardian gardeners who planted annuals in them. Today's rock gardeners use them for creating miniature landscapes. You'll find troughs as part of a larger rock garden, or as *the* rock garden for terrace or rooftop gardeners. UBC's Brent Hine says some gardeners fill troughs with plants from one part of the world or from one mountain range!

Since there are a limited number of original troughs in circulation, many rock gardeners make their own with cement, vermiculite, and peat moss. Vermiculite helps to keep the container light, and peat moss gives it a brown, earthy color. The cement mixture is placed in a mold (a wooden box lined with plastic), where it dries before being removed. Some people like to grow moss on the outside of the trough for a weathered, natural look.

For her trough gardens, McCrea uses a planting soil made from potting soil, peat moss, and fine pea gravel. The pea gravel ensures the good drainage that rock garden plants need. Plant choices for a trough garden include all the rock and alpine plants, and are determined by size and the look the person is trying to achieve. McCrea suggests incorporating different textures, including small grasses.

Trough gardens have to be kept moist—they should not be allowed to dry out completely. Other than that, they do not need much tending.

One advantage of trough gardens is the ease with which they can be changed. If the gardener wants a change of scene or if the plants get too big, they can be removed and placed in the rock garden.

Slate — Granite — Ground cover thyme — Ground cover oregano

Water Gardens

**Water helps create a
tranquil garden space.**

BUILDING A POND

A pond can be the focal
point of a garden, and a
serene place from which to
contemplate the beauty of
nature. Ponds provide water
for birds and homes for
aquatic wildlife. For these
and other reasons, ponds
are a wonderful investment.
To make the most of your
pond, consider this advice
from Jim Lawrie, manager
of Waterford Gardens
(www.waterford-gardens
.com) in New Jersey:

■ Choose a reliably sunny
spot for your backyard
pond, since aquatic
plants need six to eight
hours of sunlight daily in
the summer. Place it in
proximity to well-used
living areas so it can be
enjoyed not only from
your patio or deck but
also through the win-
dows of your home.

■ Avoid putting the pond
under deciduous trees,
which will drop their
leaves into it in fall, or in
a low-lying area where
water accumulates. If the
pond is located in a low
spot, you risk that the
runoff after rainstorms
may wash lawn fertilizers
into the pond, causing
algal bloom.

Myth: *Japanese koi (a type of fish) are a welcome
addition to a water garden.* **Fact:** *Koi will eat your
aquatic plants. If you want to have these fish, build them
a separate pond they can call their own.*

The Right Way

Use natural algae control. Include one bunch of submerged
plants (such as anacharis or
myriophyllum) for every
square foot of pond surface.
Plant them in pots filled with
sandy soil and place them on
the bottom of the pond.

■ Put in the largest water
garden that your land-
scape can accommodate
and your budget can
stand, says Lawrie. People
who approach a first
pond timidly usually
regret it later, when they
have come to love their
pond and wish they had
a larger one. In addition,
larger ponds are easier to
control because they are
less subject to the rise
and fall of air tempera-
tures. Large ponds also
have more room for
plants and fish.

■ Plan on running an electrical line to the pond
area, as most ponds have
lights, a filter, a moving
water feature, and a de-
icer for the winter, all of
which are powered by
electricity. Outlets should
be equipped with ground
fault interrupter receptacles "because you're going
to be putting 110-volt
appliances in the water."

■ Locate a waterfall, if you
include one, in the back
of the pond, away from

Colorful flowering
plants of different
heights and leaf
shapes help create
an appealing setting
for your water garden.

Aquatic
plants shade
the water
and help
keep algae
in check.

water lilies, which don't
like moving water.

■ Familiarize yourself with
city bylaws and regula-
tions governing pond
depth and security fenc-
ing. To some extent, pond
depth is a matter of individual choice, but if you
want to have goldfish, the
pond must be at least
36 inches deep. If, how-
ever, you wish to con-
struct a water garden
that will feature Japanese
koi, it must be at least
42 inches deep.

POND PLANTS

There are four basic types
of plants used in ponds,
explains Alan Sperling,
publisher of *Pondscape* magazine. Each has its purpose
in the pond ecology:

Floating plants, as their name
suggests, float on the surface of the water. They help
to shade the water and

absorb nutrients that might
otherwise support the
growth of algae.

Submerged plants live underwater. They are typically
planted a couple of inches
deep in a shallow pan of
gravel that is sunk into the
pond. This keeps them
close to the surface so sunlight can strike their vegetation. Submerged plants
compete with algae for
nutrients, so they make a
valuable contribution to
keeping the pond algae-
free. In spring, their shallow
home heats up quickly,
encouraging plant growth.
They also provide a good
place for spawning fish.

Water lilies (*Nymphaea*) are
the esthetic stars of the
pond. In addition, they pro-

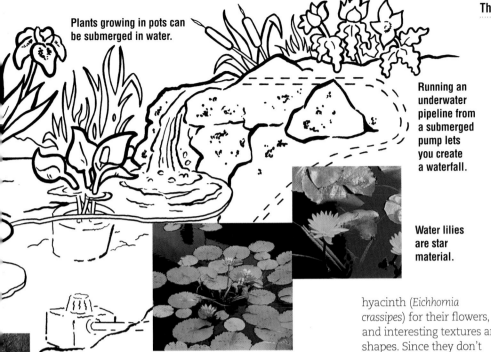

Plants growing in pots can be submerged in water.

Running an underwater pipeline from a submerged pump lets you create a waterfall.

Water lilies are star material.

Marginal plants at the water's edge provide a habitat for aquatic wildlife.

vide essential shade for fish and prevent the sunlight from heating up the water too much. Hardy lilies live outdoors year-round. Tropical lilies are hardy only in frost-free climates.

Marginal or bog plants live at the edge of the pond, some about five inches below the surface of the water and some in the soil beside the pond. Fish, frogs, and other pond life can find a comfortable home among the water plants in the marginal area of the pond. The plants growing in the soil help make a visual transition between the pond and the rest of the landscape.

Algae is almost always the number-one plant in any pond, warns Sperling. "Algae is Mother Nature's way of balancing the ecosystem." Pond lovers might want to quarrel with Mother Nature on this issue.

CONTAINER WATER GARDENS

If you love the idea of water and aquatic plants in your garden, but are not able or ready to commit to a pond, consider water gardening in containers. "Containers are a good way to start," says Joseph Tomocik, curator of the water gardens at the Denver Botanic Gardens. "If something doesn't work, it's no big deal. You just empty out the container and try again in another location or with different plants."

Anything that holds water is a potential water garden container. Tomocik started out with half-barrels lined with plastic, and says that both plastic and clay half-barrels are popular choices. But you can use any soup-bowl-shaped container as a replacement.

Tomocik chooses from a variety of aquatic plants to create interest in his water gardens. He prizes floating plants such as water lettuce (*Pistia stratiotes*) and water

hyacinth (*Eichhornia crassipes*) for their flowers, and interesting textures and shapes. Since they don't need soil, you can place them right in the water.

Water lilies need their roots in loam or claylike soil. It's easiest to plant them in a separate pot and lower the pot into the water. Tomocik recommends small-sized varieties for container gardens.

Tomocik calls on a large group of plants called marginals for the variety of sizes, forms, and colors they can add to water gardens. Marginals with upright foliage include cattails (*Typha*) and sweet flag (*Acorus*). In the broad-leaf category are arrowhead (*Sagittaria*) and taro (*Colocasia*). Trailing plants are nice for the edges of the container. Aquatic mint (*Mentha aquatica*), for example, is very fragrant, and parrot feather (*Myriophyllum verticillatum*) has wonderful delicate and lacy foliage.

Aquatic plants should last all summer with very little maintenance. In cold climates, you will need to dismantle your container gardens for the winter.

FOUNTAINS

The appeal of fountains, says Michael Zimber, owner of Stone Forest, a Santa Fe, New Mexico, supplier of hand-carved granite fountains and garden ornaments, is that "they distill the essence of something grand in nature—a creek, a waterfall, a pond." They work on the principle used in Japanese gardens that something miniaturized can give you the same feeling as its larger counterpart in nature.

The history of fountains goes back a long way, especially in dry desert environments, says Zimber. Today, you can have a fountain without feeling guilty, since most fountains recirculate water. "You will use less water than if you planted the same area with Kentucky bluegrass." A standard fountain uses about a gallon of water a day, equivalent to one toilet-bowl flush. Fountains usually have a reservoir that stores water. You can fill it up about once a week using a garden hose, tie it into your drip irrigation system, or have a dedicated water line for it.

Fountains can be a focal point for your garden, or can anchor a section of the garden, such as the corner of a courtyard. "Often, people choose a place where they hang out a lot so they can hear the running water," says Zimber.

Another popular water item is stone basins. In the days of Japanese tea ceremonies, stone basins were used for ritual cleansing. Today, the basins tend to be used for fountains, bird baths, or simply as a small body of water.

Gardening in Small Spaces

You can plant on rooftops, in containers, and in window boxes.

ROOFTOP GARDENING

In recent decades, gardening hasn't just been limited to ground level, says Art Drysdale, Toronto-based horticulturist, broadcaster, and author. In *Gardening Off the Ground*, Drysdale describes the ins and outs to growing plants in containers on rooftops and apartment balconies. Here he offers some tips:

- Summer's heat and sunlight can quickly dry out the soil and other planting medium in containers. To prevent this, use large, light-colored (white is best) or heat-resistant Styrofoam-lined containers. You can lengthen the time between waterings by adding a good-quality compost material to your planting medium. Work low-cost polymers into the soil. These tiny particles, which resemble coarse salt, swell with water and release it when the plants need it most.
- To protect your garden from the havoc that stiff winds can sometimes cause, put up cloth or wooden baffles at the ends of balconies or all around your rooftop garden. Also, it might be wise to use heavy planting mixes, rather than those with peat moss.
- If you're going to overwinter woody plants, choose trees, shrubs, and herbaceous perennials that are proven hardy to at least two zones colder than the zone in which you live. Just before the fall freeze-up, make sure to water all your trees and shrubs thoroughly.
- Use some of the many new annual vines, such as climbing nasturtium, to cover up any unsightly rooftop vents, smokestacks, or air conditioners that can mar the appearance of your roof garden.
- If you're planning to create a reasonably large garden, put in an electrical outlet and a source of running water. Also, consider installing an automatic irrigation system. These systems are available for all types of gardens and containers, even hanging baskets.

PLANTING IN CONTAINERS

Before choosing plants for outdoor containers, says June Hutson, supervisor of the Kemper Home Demonstration Garden at the Missouri Botanical Garden, think about where you will place them. This will determine whether you get sun or shade plants. Then, for each container, select plants with similar requirements for light, water, and feeding.

Some of Hutson's low-maintenance favorites for containers are zinnia *angustifolia*, vinca *rosea* (*Catharanthus roseus*), globe amaranth (*Gomphrena globosa*), and New Guinea impatiens. She likes the red ornamental fountain grass (*Pennisetum rubrum*) as a central specimen plant, and scented geraniums, with their many different leaf patterns and wonderful aroma, for textural change and filler material. *Coreopsis verticillata* 'Moonbeam' is a non-stop summer bloomer, and goes well with Eulalia grass (*Miscanthus zebrinus*) and two varieties of speedwell (*Veronica grandis holophylla* or *Veronica spicata*).

Marjorie Mason Hogue, owner of Mason Hogue Gardens, a nursery near Uxbridge, Ontario, uses the phrase "potscaping" for the process of arranging plants in containers. June Hutson says that it is helpful to think in terms of layers, with a tall, central plant surrounded by medium-height plants surrounded by shorter plants, with filler material trailing over the edge. Create interest by combining different textures. You will get a full, lush look if you pack plants a few inches from each other.

Don't limit yourself to traditional flowerpots and vases when it comes to arranging your own plants.

True Stories

Roger Miller designs, installs, and maintains rooftop gardens in New York City. Consequently, he's dealt with a few strange and difficult situations. One of the most memorable was a de-installation. A client's 25-year-old English-style roof garden had to be removed because the building's roof needed to be redone.

So Miller and his team cut up and carted away 25-foot herb trees, a wisteria with a four-inch trunk, and all the other large, beautiful plants that had been grown and tended over the decades. The soil, watering system, and planters were stored away for two years. The good news is that the owners started all over again and created a gorgeous Italianate garden.

WINDOW BOXES

According to Tovah Martin, author of *Window Boxes* for *Taylor's Weekend Gardening Guide*, the common mistake people make with window boxes is getting them too shallow. Window boxes should be about one foot deep, says Martin, to accommodate the roots of the many plants one tends to crowd in. She suggests that two to three feet is a good length, and likes a width of at least five inches. Deep window boxes are showing up more often at garden centers, so you should not need to have them custom-made.

Martin says window boxes are a great place to get creative, so don't be bound by convention. For example, she suggests trying to create theme window boxes:

- A fragrance selection, with plants such as heliotrope (*Heliotropium arborescens*), herbs, older varieties of fragrant verbena, and scented geraniums.
- A hummingbird attractor, using plants with red and orange tubular flowers.
- A color theme—for example, all white flowers such as petunias, artemisia, baby's breath (*Gypsophila*), and creeping lamium (*Lamium maculatum*).
- A fragrant and tasty herb selection, using the herbs from the song "Scarborough Fair": parsley, sage, trailing rosemary, and thyme.
- A vegetable garden, with cherry tomatoes, brussels sprouts, leeks, and flowering kale.

Other plants that Martin would choose for a window box include scaevola, nasturtiums (*Tropaeolum majus*), petunias, brachycomes, fuchsias, and coral bells (*Heuchera*).

SMALL-SPACE GARDENING

Linda Yang, author of *The City and Town Gardener*, believes that small spaces require plants that "give the biggest bang for the garden because they provide more than one season of interest." Too often, she says, urban gardeners focus only on the season in which they happen to be buying the plant. Yang suggests, for example, that a small weeping tree such as a weeping dogwood (*Cornus florida*) is a good choice because it has an interesting sculptural form in the winter, beautiful flowers in the spring, and attractive autumnal coloration.

Another way to get mileage out of a small space, says Yang, is by using woody species trained to grow flat on an espalier (a lattice or trellis). Junipers, cotoneaster, and winged euonymus (*Euonymus alatus*) work well. Whether a formal shape like a candelabra or an informal fan shape, espaliers are interesting to look at, take up minimal space, and can be underplanted with seasonal flowers.

Dwarf shrubs can also help you make the most of limited space. Depending on your light conditions, you can consider dwarf azaleas (*Rhododendron*) and rhododendrons, dwarf Alberta spruce (*Picea conica* or *Picea albertiana*), or compact Japanese holly (*Ilex crenata compacta*).

Vines are also useful in the small-space gardener's repertory. The only caveat is that vines tend to demand more than their share of soil space, so root competition can be a problem.

Gardening with Children

It's important to nurture a child's relationship with the earth.

PERSONALIZING A CHILD'S GARDEN

Ask a child to describe the perfect garden and you are likely to get a very different answer from the one you would give yourself. Would you include a place to hide? To play in the mud? That's why, if you have the room, it makes sense to give a child his or her own garden space.

Linda Mazar, gardener, teacher, and creator of two websites, Linda's Garden and Kid's Garden, provided one for her son and let him make the space very much his own. Here's how to do the same for your child:

- Locate the garden close to the swing set and sandbox.
- Put up a little white fence and let the child paint a sign that identifies the owner of the garden.
- Mix up some "quick crete"—instant concrete—and form it into stepping stones where your child can make hand and foot prints. Then place the stepping stones around the garden.
- Create a hiding space— a teepee formed out of scarlet runner beans tied to and growing up a trellis made out of branches. This is a perfect place to explore bugs and other critters.
- Create a scarecrow using the child's old clothes.
- Let your child put a pink flamingo in the garden or whatever else appeals to his or her imagination.

Quick Tricks

Kids can grow potatoes in a plastic garbage bag. Fill the bag halfway with a combination of compost and gardening soil. Make small holes in the bag for water drainage. In it, plant some seed potatoes that have sprouts, making sure they are covered by the soil. Water well, and continue to water as needed. As the sprouts appear above the soil line, add more soil. Harvest the new potatoes as they gradually mature.

You can grow a menagerie of plants and shrubs:
- Bearberry
- Butterfly bush
- Cardinal flower
- Catnip
- Dogtooth violet
- Foxglove
- Fawnlily
- Goatsbeard
- Ostrich fern
- Oxeye daisy
- Pussy willow
- Sheep laurel
- Tiger lily

Let your child choose and plant the kinds of seeds and plants that are interesting and are likely to be successful— sunflowers, pumpkins, popcorn, and morning glories, for instance.

FAMILY GARDENING

The key to gardening with kids, says Patti Kraemer-Doell, family garden coordinator at the New York Botanical Gardens, is "letting them experience it themselves. We have tried to guide them, but not tell them to put the sunflowers here and the tomatoes there. The emphasis is on developing their imagination and their appreciation for being out in the garden."

Guidance comes in the form of a string grid that is stretched across a planting bed, which divides it into one-foot squares. Kids get advice about how many seeds or seedlings to put in each square and how deep to plant them. Volunteers show kids pictures of how the full-grown plants will look, so they understand how much room each plant needs.

Theme gardens have been a big hit in the program, and are easy to do in a home garden. Try a barnyard garden, suggests Kraemer-Doell, using plants whose names have associations with barnyard animals—lambs ears (*Stachys byzantina*), hen and chicks (*Echeveria*), and cowslip (*Pulmonaria*), for example. Let kids grow a salsa garden, with all sorts of tomatoes, hot peppers, onions, and cilantro. A pizza garden can have basil, oregano, and tomatoes. In a Persian carpet garden, kids can focus on colored flowers. A seed garden can include plants that disperse their seeds in different ways, from milkweed (*Asclepias*) to sunflowers (*Helianthus*).

Kraemer-Doell also suggests trying a sunflower house. Let kids plant sunflower seeds in a square, leaving space for a door in front. As the sunflowers grow, put a hay fence around them for protection and stake if necessary. Plant morning glories or sweet peas around the base of each sunflower, and they will grow up the stems, eventually forming a roof over the top. By summer's end, kids will have a sunflower house to play in.

Some kids might just want to play in the garden, says Kraemer-Doell. At the family garden, there's a special place set aside just for digging and looking at insects and worms. It's a very popular spot.

GARDENING FOR CITY KIDS

If you are an urban parent worried that your child will never put hand to soil, check to see if there's a botanical garden near you. Many have programs that introduce kids to gardening. In Montreal, the Botanical Garden has had a program for kids since the 1930's. In the Youth Gardens (Jardins-jeunes), each kid has his or her own 6- by 14-foot plot. The kids meet twice a week, from planting time in spring until fall harvest, to learn all about the joys of gardening.

The Chicago Botanic Garden's program works with the schools to teach kids about gardening. The program begins with teacher training at the start of the school year, blossoms in the classroom during the winter, and comes to fruition in spring and summer when classes get to plant and maintain their own plots. In every plot, there are marigolds, sunflowers and snapdragons. Vegetables include basics like tomatoes, carrots, and lettuce, with more unusual choices, such as kohlrabi and jalapeno peppers. The kids make weekly trips to the Botanic Garden from May through August so they can cultivate the soil, plant, water, weed, and best of all, harvest the crop!

A lesson kids learn from gardening, says Sara Fretzin, the Chicago program's coordinator, is that it's okay to make mistakes. Along the way the kids may lose some plants, or decide they don't like others, but that is all part of the experience.

RESPONSIBILITY FOR THE EARTH

Andy Lipkis is president of Treepeople, an organization dedicated to inspiring the people of Los Angeles to take personal responsibility for the urban forest—educating, training, and supporting them as they plant and care for trees and improve their neighborhoods. In a certain sense, it all started with gardening.

As a young child, Lipkis tended vegetable gardens at his grandmother's house. When he was 14, at a summer camp in the mountains, he had the transformative experience that led to Treepeople. He and a group of other teens reclaimed a dead piece of forest, used by the camp as a baseball field and parking lot, as a picnic garden. They stripped off the tar, roto-tilled and cultivated the soil, and planted smog-resistant trees and a lawn. It was back-breaking physical work, "yet it was the greatest joy," says Lipkis, "because we saw the profound difference we could make with our caring and creativity. Everyone was turned on by what we could do with our hands."

Treepeople's extensive education program focuses on providing new generations of kids with the same realization. Kids learn how to analyze the environmental problems in their own ecosystems—their backyards and schoolyards—and think about how trees can provide solutions.

Smart Moves

To instill a love of gardening, make it fun for kids, not a chore. Here are some ways to make that happen:

- Give kids tasks appropriate to their age. Very little ones can sprinkle some water from a small can. Slightly older ones can plant some seeds—but maybe only 10 now and 10 later. Older kids can take on bigger projects that give them a sense of accomplishment and pride, and results they can show off.
- Keep your expectations realistic. Most kids just won't enjoy weeding for more than a few minutes.
- Grow surprising, out-of-proportion things, such as giant sunflowers and small pumpkins.
- Grow colorful things. Look for vivid reds, purples, and yellows when shopping for plants.
- Start growing seeds indoors under lights or on the window sill, so kids have seedlings by outdoor planting time.

Greenhouse Gardening

You can garden year-round in a temperature-controlled environment.

NEVER-ENDING GARDENING

Greenhouses are for "frustrated gardeners"—people in cold climates who want to garden year-round, those who want to grow vegetables in the winter, and those who want to grow plants with special culture requirements, says Janice L. Hale, editor of *Hobby Greenhouse* magazine. Greenhouses are the answer because you can manipulate the temperature, humidity, light, and soil.

What size and material should you use? A minimal size is 6 by 8 feet, but Hale recommends going as large as your budget will bear. She thinks 12 by 14 feet would work for most people. "It's amazing how quickly you can fill up a greenhouse with plants."

Aluminum is the most common framing material. Wood and steel are other possibilities, with redwood being the most attractive and durable. Greenhouses can be glazed with polyethylene film, rigid plastics, such as acrylic or polycar-

bonate, or glass. A polycarbonate glazing is a good choice because you can get double or triple wall panels that help to provide excellent insulation.

Temperature is controlled by heaters and fans, humidity with a humidifier and misters, and light through the use of shade cloths of various densities.

A greenhouse, whether it's a lush environment of exotic plants or a shelf for your old favorites, can provide enormous pleasure in all seasons.

TO ATTACH OR NOT ATTACH

Greenhouses can be either freestanding or attached to the house. Miranda Smith, author of *Greenhouse Gardening*, favors using attached solar greenhouses. This type of greenhouse has some mechanism for retaining the heat collected during the day—for instance, water in tanks, tile floors, or stones—that it releases at night. The greenhouse is built against the southern side of the house, covering doors and windows, which are left open. In winter, heat collected in the greenhouse heats the home. Or, if there's a heat deficiency in the greenhouse, heat in the house can be increased a lit-

tle to raise the greenhouse temperature. While this can add a bit to your home heating bill, overall it's much less expensive than heating a freestanding greenhouse. There is also an exchange of carbon dioxide and oxygen between the house and greenhouse, which is beneficial to both.

Freestanding greenhouses can be built from kits, but an attached greenhouse has to be custommade to fit your house. Smith recommends a wooden structure glazed with glass or rigid plastic.

Building a greenhouse involves a serious investment of energy and money.

Smart Moves

- Resist the impulse to stock your new greenhouse with every plant you have ever wanted. Instead, choose plants with similar requirements for light, temperature, and watering so you can keep things manageable at first. As you begin to understand the different microclimates in your greenhouse, you can add plants that will do well there.
- Install an automatic watering system, such as a drip system, if you're away for periods of time.

Maintaining the plants within is an ongoing commitment. Smith cautions, "If you can't spare the time to take care of the plants, you'll find yourself with a large useless room attached to your house. And you can't 'sort of' greenhouse garden or you'll find you're raising the biggest, most beautiful crop of aphids anyone ever saw."

Smith grows vegetables—leafy greens like kale, collard, bok choy, and arugula are favorites—in raised beds that are typically 2½ feet deep. She plants tomato seeds in January and harvests her first crop in May, when most people are just putting their seedlings outdoors. Because greenhouses are an ideal environment for growing pests as well as vegetables, Smith is vigilant in her use of natural predators, such as ladybugs, lacewings, and beneficial mites, to handle the plant-eaters.

GREENHOUSE MECHANICS

A greenhouse needs at least six hours of sunlight, says Rick Heinen of B.C. Greenhouse Builders Limited (www.bcgreenhouses.com) in Burnaby. Heinen adds you also have to have mechanisms to create the right kind of climate. The three main things to consider are air circulation, cooling, and heating.

For proper air circulation, you have to have a fan going at all times. It can range from a simple oscillating fan, to more elaborate varieties, such as the "heat-saver fan," which hangs from the ceiling of the greenhouse. To calculate the fan size you will need (expressed as "cfm" or cubic feet per minute), multiply the greenhouse area by 10. For example, an 8- by 12-foot greenhouse is 96 square feet and needs 960 cfm.

Cooling the greenhouse is crucial to the life of the plants. On hot sunny days, greenhouses must be covered on the outside by a shade cloth or screen. Ventilation is a key element of cooling, says Heinen. There are automatic ventilation systems that include fans and intake shutters. Also available are solar openers that are heat activated and open only when the sun shines. A misting system in the greenhouse adds humidity and helps cool the greenhouse by evaporation.

Greenhouses can be heated with electric, natural gas, or propane heaters, which need to be on a thermostat, or with kerosene heaters that need venting. Many people mistakenly think greenhouses will stay warm overnight, but unless there is some kind of solar collector, that is not true. Often the temperature inside a freestanding greenhouse is only one or two degrees above the outside temperature. Insulating the greenhouse or using polycarbonate, double-wall glazing helps you to keep your plants warm enough in cold temperatures.

CARNIVOROUS PLANTS

Greenhouses are great homes for all types of delicate, flowering plants. But how about carnivorous plants? James Pietropaolo, owner of Peter Pauls Nurseries (www.peterpauls.com) in New York, says the carnivores are good candidates for greenhouses because they like high humidity year-round. Air in the average house is too dry for them.

There are over 600 species of carnivorous plants, explains Pietropaolo, and they grow around the world. Some popular carnivorous plants (also known as insectivorous) include Venus flytrap (*Dionaea muscipula*), pitcher plant (*Sarracenia*), Australian pitcher plant (*Nepenthes*), cobra lily (*Darlingtonia*), sundew (*Drosera*), butterwort (*Pinquicula*), and bladderwort (*Utricularia*).

Carnivorous plants have different ways of attracting insects—by the colors they display, the nectar they produce, or the odor they emit. Some, like the Venus flytrap, have traps for catching insects, while others—the pitcher plant, for instance—catch them in funnel-like tubes.

You can observe the process firsthand by feeding a carnivorous plant. All you need is an insect, dead or alive. For a plant with a trap, simply touch the trigger hair that causes the trap to close. For a funnel plant, just drop the insect into the funnel.

"Some people expect to see the plant chewing the insect," says Pietropaolo, "but that doesn't happen. Basically what you see is the trap closing or the insect disappearing down the tube."

Running water is important. Having both hot and cold available facilitates clean-up and lets you give plants warm rather than ice-cold water.

Ventilation

Shade cloths

Misting system to add humidity

Self-contained kerosene heaters

Growing Orchids

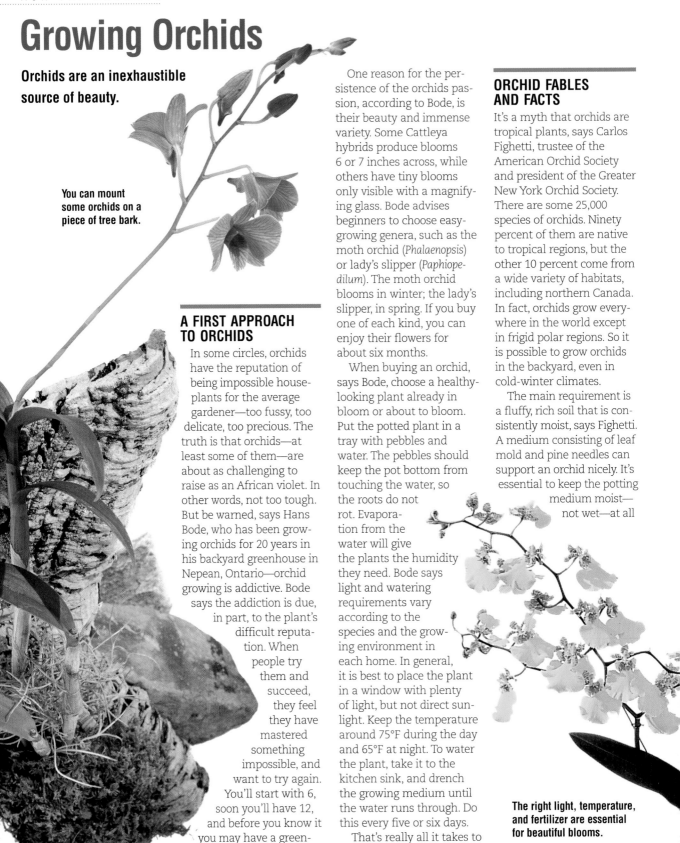

Orchids are an inexhaustible source of beauty.

You can mount some orchids on a piece of tree bark.

A FIRST APPROACH TO ORCHIDS

In some circles, orchids have the reputation of being impossible house-plants for the average gardener—too fussy, too delicate, too precious. The truth is that orchids—at least some of them—are about as challenging to raise as an African violet. In other words, not too tough. But be warned, says Hans Bode, who has been grow-ing orchids for 20 years in his backyard greenhouse in Nepean, Ontario—orchid growing is addictive. Bode says the addiction is due, in part, to the plant's difficult reputa-tion. When people try them and succeed, they feel they have mastered something impossible, and want to try again. You'll start with 6, soon you'll have 12, and before you know it you may have a green-house full of orchids.

One reason for the per-sistence of the orchids pas-sion, according to Bode, is their beauty and immense variety. Some Cattleya hybrids produce blooms 6 or 7 inches across, while others have tiny blooms only visible with a magnify-ing glass. Bode advises beginners to choose easy-growing genera, such as the moth orchid (*Phalaenopsis*) or lady's slipper (*Paphiope-dilum*). The moth orchid blooms in winter; the lady's slipper, in spring. If you buy one of each kind, you can enjoy their flowers for about six months.

When buying an orchid, says Bode, choose a healthy-looking plant already in bloom or about to bloom. Put the potted plant in a tray with pebbles and water. The pebbles should keep the pot bottom from touching the water, so the roots do not rot. Evapora-tion from the water will give the plants the humidity they need. Bode says light and watering requirements vary according to the species and the grow-ing environment in each home. In general, it is best to place the plant in a window with plenty of light, but not direct sun-light. Keep the temperature around 75°F during the day and 65°F at night. To water the plant, take it to the kitchen sink, and drench the growing medium until the water runs through. Do this every five or six days.

That's really all it takes to grow orchids!

ORCHID FABLES AND FACTS

It's a myth that orchids are tropical plants, says Carlos Fighetti, trustee of the American Orchid Society and president of the Greater New York Orchid Society. There are some 25,000 species of orchids. Ninety percent of them are native to tropical regions, but the other 10 percent come from a wide variety of habitats, including northern Canada. In fact, orchids grow every-where in the world except in frigid polar regions. So it is possible to grow orchids in the backyard, even in cold-winter climates.

The main requirement is a fluffy, rich soil that is con-sistently moist, says Fighetti. A medium consisting of leaf mold and pine needles can support an orchid nicely. It's essential to keep the potting medium moist— not wet—at all

The right light, temperature, and fertilizer are essential for beautiful blooms.

times, keeping in mind that outdoors most orchids grow in bog-like conditions. Although watering schedules will depend on the microclimate in your house, generally orchids need to be watered every three or four days.

Buy vials to hold your orchid cuttings.

Fighetti says it is fascinating to hybridize orchids—to breed different plants in order to produce a specimen with specific characteristics such as greater vigor, a certain color, a more beautiful flower, or the ability to grow faster. It takes three to four years to see progeny produce, and it can take five to six generations to get the results you want. But for some people, that's all part of the orchid obsession.

EASY GROWING

For good results and least fuss, Kenni Judd, co-owner of Juno Beach Orchids in Florida, recommends the thin-leaved Oncidium orchid (*Oncidium* 'Gower Ramsey'), commonly known as the dancing lady, or a Cattleya hybrid. You'll find more suggestions at Judd's website (www.jborchids.com). When in doubt about any aspect of orchid growing, Judd suggests joining an orchid society. In Canada, you can call the Canadian Orchid Congress, an organization consisting of more than 20 local societies, or visit its website (www.orchidmall.com) for more information.

In cold climates, Hans Bode thinks the basement is a good place to grow orchids. It's humid, and there's usually access to water. You can try using regular fluorescent lights, but Bode says high-pressure sodium lights provide greater intensity and are suitable for virtually every kind of orchid.

Orchids should be watered regularly and fertilized weekly, using half the recommended strength of regular fertilizer. Full-strength fertilizer can burn their roots.

ADVICE FROM THE ORCHID LADY

Utah-based Linda Fortner, who is also known as The Orchid Lady, runs a website (www.orchidlady.com) devoted to orchids. Many people turn to her for help when their orchids are not behaving according to expectations. One of the most frequently asked questions is "Why won't my orchids bloom?" She responds that three factors may be responsible—light, temperature, and fertilizer.

Light. The natural habitat of each orchid determines its light requirements. You need to know the type of orchid you have and what light levels it would normally receive in nature.

Temperature. Again, each genera and species of orchid has a preferred temperature range. In general, orchids grow best when there is a difference of temperature between night and day. Many orchids won't flower without a "cool-down" period where the night temperature is 10 to 15 degrees cooler than the daytime temperature.

Fertilizer. Orchids planted in bark should get a 30-10-10 fertilizer because bark robs the plant of nitrogen. Orchids grown in other media need a 20-20-20 or 23-19-17 mix.

Know Your Terms

Genera: A group of plants that are closely related.
Species: A smaller group within the genera.
Variety: A group within the species that differs in small ways from other plants of the species.

If you buy orchids at a discount chain, you will probably be told only the genera. If you purchase them from a florist or garden center, you are more likely to find out the species as well, which will make it easier for you to buy the same plant again and to provide the growing conditions it needs.

Spectacular Indoor Bloomers

You can grow beautiful blossoms indoors.

FORCING BLOOMS

Forcing bulbs means manipulating the environment of spring-blooming bulbs so that they will bloom earlier indoors than they would in nature. Walter Fisher Jr., who is a perennial winner at the Philadelphia Flower Show, where forced bulbs are a highlight, details the steps required for successful forcing:

Buying. For large, strong blooms, buy the largest-sized bulbs available. Like onions, bulbs should be solid to the feel and have no signs of mold. "This is a critical part of the process," says Fisher. "If you're going to go through 16 to 18 weeks of forcing, you want to start out with strong bulbs that have no defects."

Potting. Any kind of clean plastic or clay pot will do. (If the pot has been used before, sterilize it with a mixture of 1 part bleach to 10 parts water.) Fisher uses bulb pans or azalea pots, which are shorter than the standard pot, because he likes the way blooming plants look in them.

Keep in mind that the bigger the pot, the more bulbs you can get in it. Contrary to popular opinion, you can squeeze bulbs into the pot, allowing them to touch each other and the sides of the pot, as well as come up a little above the surface of the soil. Fisher suggests 15 average-sized bulbs in an eight-inch pot.

Prepared planting mixes are fine for bulbs, as long as they are able to retain moisture, provide good drainage, and have enough substance to anchor the plants, which get top heavy when they bloom. Remember, too, to water after potting.

Cold storage. This is the step that speeds up the normal blooming of the bulb. What you are trying to achieve is a steady temperature of about 40°F, which is refrigerator temperature.

Dark is essential. So is keeping the bulbs moist, by watering about once a week. The rule of thumb is 15 weeks of cold storage. After that, remove the pots from storage and water thoroughly. Leave them in a cool, dark place for a day or two to allow the bulbs to acclimatize to their new, warmer environment.

Heat and light. To encourage blooming, keep the plants in bright light at a temperature between 65°F and 70°F. If you are using lights, keep them on 16 hours a day, but be careful not to get the plants too close to the lights because the foliage can burn.

Amaryllis

Know Your Terms

Insecticidal soap is a commercially prepared soap used to treat a number of plant pests. It is safer to use than household soaps or detergents, which can burn plant leaves if not rinsed off with water within 5 to 10 minutes.

Pyrethrum is a natural organic poison made from ground-up chrysanthemum flowers and is used to kill a number of insects.

Hyacinth

The Right Way

You can experiment with different container shapes and try different planting media until you find the potting style that pleases you.

If you plant bulbs in potting soil, they'll absorb enough nutrients to grow and bloom again if they're transplanted to the garden.

You can force bulbs in containers filled with small rocks or pebbles, which provide excellent drainage.

You can force hyacinth and crocus bulbs in plain water. Look for special vases or forcing bowls in garden shops and through mail order.

REBLOOMING TIPS

How do we encourage houseplants to rebloom? Many radio listeners have asked Ed Lawrence, horticultural expert of CBC's *Ontario Today* weekly gardening program, and chief of the National Capital Commission's official residences, greenhouse and grounds services section. Lawrence says light is crucial. Gardenias and hibiscus are indoor-flowering plants that can easily be persuaded to rebloom.

Gardenias like to be kept in a south- or west-facing window, where their fragrant white blooms will respond best to a consistent temperature, between 60° and 65°F. If the temperature changes, the buds may drop off before opening. Mist them regularly during their budding period. After flowering has finished, cut the plants back. This gives them the maximum amount of time to produce new growth and new flower bud.

From the end of February until early October, feed gardenias once a month at half strength with a soluble fertilizer for flowering houseplants. Keeping them evenly moist but allowing them to dry out somewhat between waterings, as well as providing a well-drained soil (up to 30 percent sharp sand), will help avoid root rot. Mulch lightly with used tea leaves to maintain soil acidity. Gardenias are susceptible to spider mites, which can be treated with insecticidal soap.

Hibiscus bloom all summer and fall, helped by a monthly feeding of fertilizer for flowering houseplants. Apply at the same rate as gardenias. Cut them back by at least 50 percent after flowering. This will foster new growth, which will produce new flower buds. Hibiscus attract aphids and whitefly, so check for these pests regularly. If need be, treat with insecticidal soap or natural pyrethrum.

HOLIDAY BLOOMERS

What do you do with the amaryllis and poinsettia (*Euphorbia pulcherrima*) plants that looked so beautiful at Christmastime? You can probably make them bloom again says Ed Lawrence, who suggests these rigorous methods:

Amaryllis. After blooming, cut the flower stalk close to the bulb. Keep the leaves growing on in a bright sunny window. Water once the soil gets dry, applying a balanced soluble fertilizer once a month. Put the plant outside into a sunny location after all danger of frost has passed. For Christmas bloom, withhold water from early July on. Early in August cut the foliage off one to two inches above the neck of the bulb, and put the pot on its side on a cool (55°F), completely dark spot. Check the dormant bulb for an emerging flower bud about the end of October. Once the bud appears, bring the plant into a bright light, and water well. Allow the soil to dry between waterings. The flowers should appear in time for the holidays.

Poinsettia. As days grow longer, poinsettias stop blooming, but their foliage remains attractive. Water thoroughly when the soil dries out, and use a balanced soluble fertilizer every two weeks year-round. After the danger of frost has passed, put the plants outdoors into full sun. Prune by late July to ensure flower production. Bring plants indoors before frost. In late September, put them on a strict schedule: 14 hours of total darkness and 10 hours of bright daylight. Once the flowers have formed and the bracts begin to color up, bring the plants back to normal conditions.

Daffodil

Hibiscus

Tulip

Cyclamen

Easy-care Houseplants

Successful indoor gardening can be painless, too.

HARDY HOUSEPLANTS

When Dr. H. Marc Cathey, president emeritus of the American Horticultural Society, set out to identify three iron-clad houseplants, his criterion was that they had to be able to do well in the bathroom. The bathroom? It has the worst kind of growing environment conceivable—frequently little or no natural light, usually too hot, and sometimes too cold. In addition, he looked for plants that didn't need much water, didn't need to be fed, and weren't subject to insects or diseases. The winners were:

Philodendron scandens, the well-known heart-shaped philodendron.

Aglaonema, commonly known as silver queen or Chinese evergreen.

Dracaena, especially 'Janet Craig' dracaena.

All three plants are found naturally on the floor of rain forests, where they receive very little natural light, and where the soil is often low in nutrients. They can be acclimatized to survive on very little water—as little as one watering a month.

If the plants will get extremely low levels of light, water, and food, they probably won't grow very quickly, so buy them the size you want them to be, Cathey says. As to appearance: "They look like they're made out of Naugahyde."

For an easy blooming alternative, Cathey recommends bromeliads, a large and varied group of plants. They tolerate a variety of light conditions, don't need much water, and have spectacular blooms. Guzmania is a favorite.

A plant that flourishes in the bathroom will probably thrive anywhere in the house.

GO TROPICAL

You can grow a pineapple plant in your living room.
- Cut the top off a pineapple and let it dry out for four days.
- Stick toothpicks into the top and press it into soil in a six- to eight-inch pot.
- Water and feed as you would any other plant. In about six months, it should have new leaves.
- Put an apple and a couple of paper towels in a polyethylene bag and place it over the plant. Close it up and leave it for four days. The gases from the apple will cause a baby pineapple to germinate.
- Remove the bag, and in nine months you will see a new little pineapple growing on your plant.

Quick Tricks

- Cacti and succulents need the least attention.
- For low-maintenance gardening, try a terrarium.
- Match the plants to the available natural light.
- Deal with pests such as bugs, scales, or aphids with a mild soap spray.

The Right Way

- To keep from overfertilizing your plants, choose a balanced fertilizer, like 20-20-20, but use just a quarter of the recommended amount when you mix it with water.
- To help plants survive the drying effects of heat in the winter, place them close together so they can create small moisture zones. It helps to have them near a humidifier or sitting on pebbles in a tray of water.
- Or, when placing plants over a tray of water, suspend them on overturned plant saucers or on egg crate sheets purchased at the hardware store. This will keep their roots from rotting.
- If they are small enough, put your houseplants in the sink once a week and wash off their leaves. Larger plants can be sponged off or rinsed off in the shower.

PLANT CARE REALITIES

Five conditions to consider if you want to grow houseplants are light, temperature, feeding, water, and air circulation, says Judy Becker, owner of Lauray of Salisbury in Connecticut. The rule of thumb says that if you get three out of the five right, your plants will probably survive. Five out of five ensures that they will thrive.

In order to meet the requirements of your particular plants, Becker suggests that you "treat each one as an individual." Find out what each needs by reading up on it or asking for advice at your nursery or a local plant society. And be honest about the amount of time you want to spend nurturing them. Some plants are more demanding and temperamental than others.

African violets need humidity. You can provide it by putting the pots on small rocks in a water-filled pan.

Plants need the full spectrum of light.

SMART SELECTIONS

To understand why there aren't more easy-care flowering houseplants around, it helps to understand something about flowering plants in general. Maggie Stuckey, author of *The Houseplant Encyclopedia* and *Gardening from the Ground Up*, explains that "plants that flower depend on sunshine, which is why there are very few indoor plants that flower reliably and satisfactorily." Stuckey recommends the following as your best bets:

- Bromeliads have big, unusual flowers with lots of color. Since these plants are succulents, they don't require much watering or other care. The only problem is that, once they flower, they die, so you have to make repeat investments if you want to have these plants around.
- Kalanchoes, another group of succulents, can brighten up the house with clusters of long-lasting flowers— yellow, orange, peach, apricot—above the thick, fleshy leaves. Given the bright light they crave, kalanchoes will bloom over and over.
- Spathiphyllum, also known as white flag, has a flower that sits way above the beautiful foliage. It's the perfect choice for apartment dwellers or for interior rooms because it requires almost no light.
- Cyclamen, which come in many bright colors, will bloom for months. They like a slightly cool temperature.
- Streptocarpus is a flamboyant cousin of the African violet. It has the same violet-shaped heads, only bigger and flashier, and on longer stems.

AFRICAN VIOLETS

Contrary to popular opinion, African violets (*Saintpaulia*) do not require any more care than the average houseplant, says Paul Sorano, owner of Lyndon Lyon Greenhouses, Inc. (www.lyndonlyon.com), in New York. He should know. His grandfather, Lyndon Lyon, bred the first double-pink African violets and won many gardening awards. Today, Lyndon Lyon Greenhouses specializes in African violets, as well as other plants. In order to thrive, African violets need:

- A constant year-round temperature range of 65°F to 75°F.
- A location with early morning or late afternoon sun. "They're just like we are," says Sorano, "in the sense that they shouldn't be exposed to the bright noonday sun."
- Moderate humidity, which you can create by setting the pots on rocks in a tray of water. As the water gradually evaporates, it will provide the necessary moisture.
- Weekly fertilizing following the directions on any good commercial African violet fertilizer.

African violets also need to be watered thoroughly, then left until semidry. A good test is to stick your finger in the pot as far as your first knuckle. If the soil is still damp, wait longer to water. Violets benefit from some drying because it allows their root systems to get more oxygen.

Sorano advocates the use of plastic pots because they make it easier to tell when a plant is dry, simply by lifting it. A dry plant is much lighter than a wet one. "We do a lot of things by heft around here," says Sorano. "We just walk through the greenhouse and lift up the pots one by one. If they're light, we water them. Clay pots make it hard to judge the wetness of the plant."

CHAPTER FIVE

Car
Smarts

Getting a Great Deal on a New Car

A little research goes a long way.

KNOWLEDGEABLE CUSTOMERS PAY LOWER PRICES

Paige Amidon, director of the *Consumer Reports* New and Used Car Price Services, says that getting a good price on a new car begins with a better understanding of the dealer's final cost for the car. According to Amidon, people frequently believe the invoice price (the official price the dealer pays the manufacturer) is the same as the dealer's final cost—something that dealers would like you to believe. In reality, the dealer's final cost is almost always below the invoice price because of special incentives, promotions, and hold-backs offered by the manufacturer. In general, you should expect to pay a price somewhere be-

You can almost always get a better deal than the sticker price on a new car.

tween the manufacturer's suggested retail price (MSRP—the sticker price on the car window) and the dealer's final cost.

"It is difficult to get up-to-date information on invoice prices," says George Iny, president of the Automobile Protection Association (APA), a nonprofit auto industry watchdog group. The APA and the Automobile Consumer Coalition can help supply you with information on invoice prices. The dealer's actual cost is more difficult to determine because it can be affected by the manufacturer's promotions. However, it is not enough to know the dealer's cost. You still have to work to get the best price for a new car:

Shop around. Even if you can't go to more than one dealer for the same manufacturer, you can look at comparable cars. Let the dealer know that you're shopping for other comparable cars, and will go with the one you get the best deal on. Of course, you can't take advantage of this technique if you have your heart set on a certain vehicle. So keep your options open and shop for a certain class of car, rather than for a particular model. **Avoid dealers who quote you a price that's good only for that same day.** A reputable dealership should be able to hold the price for a week. Special promotions, however, do expire, so ask for documentation stating any expiration dates. **Let dealers know you've done your research.** Sometimes, if they see you've researched their cost and know what you want, they'll give you their best price. **Be a hard bargainer.** Don't believe dealers who tell you they're losing money on a deal. They're not, or they wouldn't sell. When dealers have to move inventory, they may sell below the invoice price—but they're still making money.

EXTRAS AND FEATURES

Sandra Kinsler, the editor of *Woman Motorist* (www.womanmotorist.com) and author of the online *New and Used Car Buying Handbooks*, explains what you should know about options and features:

Features are included by the manufacturer on every car in a given model.

Options are features that you can have added to your car for extra money. Cars on dealers' lots frequently already have several options added to them.

"Don't go for options you don't need," warns George Iny. For instance, if you can live without air-conditioning, you will save yourself a substantial amount of money. Some options, for example moon roofs, which may leak, can be an invitation to trouble and expense later on.

Some of the best deals around can be manufacturers' promotions.

MANUFACTURERS' PROMOTIONS

Auto manufacturers some-times help dealerships sell their cars with promotions or incentive programs for consumers, says Ron Pinelli, president of Autodata Corporation in New Jersey, which helps auto compa-nies stay competitive by analyzing prices. These promotions can feature rebates, discounts, free equipment, or special low-interest financing.

Some times of year are better than others for find-ing promotions, explains Pinelli. In Canada, look for deals in the months of August and September, or at the end of the month, because many dealerships get a bonus for selling a cer-tain number of cars within a specific time period.

Know where to look for the best promotions. Manu-facturers offer special pro-motions on cars for very specific reasons: The com-pany may be vying to have the top-selling car (such as the Chevrolet Cavalier or Honda Civic) in a certain category. Less-popular brand names, on the other hand, such as Nissan and Hyundai, make quality cars but have to lower their prices in order to compete with more-popular brands like Honda and Toyota, and are often eager to move excess inventory.

Deals often show up across the board when one manufacturer comes into the market with a rebate because the compe-tition is forced to match it to stay competitive—unless, of course, one brand is far more popu-lar than the others and can keep selling its cars at full price.

BUYING A CAR THAT WILL HOLD ITS VALUE

Charlie Vogulheim, editor of the *Kelley Blue Book* (www.carpoint.msn.com), the leading US used vehicle pricing information guide, suggests that you consider the resale value of your car before you even purchase it. If you plan on reselling your car or trading it in someday, you should look for one that will hold its value. In Canada, consult the *Cana-dian Red Book*. It provides the relative value of new and used cars, giving prices for many models and options. The *Canadian Black Book*, a trade publication used by car dealers, rates the dollar value of used cars. These sources for car data can be found at public libraries.

Broad market appeal. Current-ly, in Canada, the Chevrolet Cavalier, Pontiac Sunfire, and Ford Taurus are very popular cars, Hondas and Toyotas are also popular, and that's likely to continue for at least the next few years. Minivans are popular, and have good resale value. Manual transmis-sions do better in sports cars. Air-conditioning is the most important option in terms of a car's resale value. Power windows and locks are important in mid-size cars.

Popular colors. Although color has little or nothing to do with a car holding its value, George Iny says the most popular colors with car thieves tend to be dark greens and dark blues. In North America, basic black and white are consistently popular colors. The popularity of red cars goes up and down in erratic ways. Earth tones, silvers, and golds are currently doing well. Usually, classic colors are better choices than trendy colors.

Appropriate options. To have a good resale value, vehicles should have the options appropriate to their class. For example, inexpensive economy cars don't need too many options, but mid-to high-end vehicles should have power windows, power locks, power seats, and cruise control. Moon roofs and high-quality sound systems are also popular. Leather is popular in luxury vehicles, but make sure to take good care of it, or it could be a negative instead of a posi-tive. And don't expect to get a good return for your money on personalized features, such as expensive wheel treatments or special aerodynamic kits.

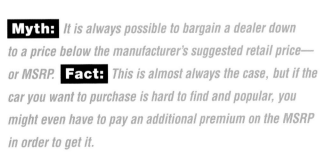

Myth: *It is always possible to bargain a dealer down to a price below the manufacturer's suggested retail price—or MSRP.* **Fact:** *This is almost always the case, but if the car you want to purchase is hard to find and popular, you might even have to pay an additional premium on the MSRP in order to get it.*

Buying a Used Car

Learn how to find what you're looking for.

THE USED-CAR MARKETPLACE

The essential advice for purchasing a used car has always been "Buyer beware." That advice still holds true, but over the past few years, the prices of new cars and light trucks have outpaced many consumers' incomes, sending demand for used cars up. While buying a used car is still filled with uncertainty, there are ways to increase your chances of making a satisfactory purchase.

Doug Mayhew, manager of public relations for the Canadian Automobile Association (CAA), suggests that would-be buyers consult the CAA's annual *Autopinion* magazine. Published each December, and based on members' appraisals of their own cars, it gives very useful general information and details about problems with specific models, the cost of repairs, and overall satisfaction. *Autopinion* also contains articles by automotive journalists on subjects ranging from car-buying trends, leasing, and the latest features.

INSPECTING A USED CAR

The scariest part of buying a used car is not being completely sure of what condition it's in. A car that's been in a major accident is always a bigger risk, but sellers often try to hide this information. Andrew Bleakley, evaluator-inspector, runs a mobile vehicle inspection service in Montreal. For about $80 he will perform a full, unbiased inspection on a used vehicle. In his 10 years as a professional inspector, Bleakley has seen a lot. He warns, "Watch out for dealer demonstration vehicles which are used, not new. They may have been in a collision." He adds that it is not uncommon in Ontario and Quebec especially for unscrupulous sellers to roll back the odometer or to even disengage it. Bleakley has special tools to check for this.

Bleakley always recommends hiring an independent technician to inspect the condition of a used car before you buy it. The problem is finding someone qualified to do the inspection, which he says generally doesn't mean just any mechanic. A thorough mechanical inspection includes checking the compression, all major systems, including the engine, electrical and charging systems, transmission and drive line, fluids, brakes, suspension, and steering. Essential, too, is an inspection of the car's body and finally a road test.

There are, however, a few things everyone can do before buying a used car:
- Do a visual check of the car. Look at the right rear door hinges. If they are

Myth: *When you buy a used car, you never know what you're getting.* **Fact:** *Some dealers offer used cars with enhanced warranty packages that cover repair costs for a specified period of time.*

very worn, or the door doesn't close well, the car may have been used as a taxi. Holes in the roof could mean the car was used for deliveries.
- Check for oil leaks on the pavement. Note that leaks are not necessarily a significant problem—it depends on the cause.
- Don't assume that new-looking brake and accelerator pedals mean the car hasn't been driven much. Resellers know people check these details and can buy new pads for around $6.
- Copy down the vehicle identification number (VIN), a 17-character combination of numbers and letters, from the vehicle's dashboard. In Ontario, ask the dealer or seller for the Used Vehicle Information Package. This gives details of previous owners, any outstanding liens on the car, and the fair market value of the vehicle.

The Right Way

It is not easy to determine how much you should pay for a used car. A vehicle's depreciation, or loss in its original value, depends on many variables, including how old the car is, its current popularity, and whether you are buying from a dealer or directly from the original owner.

In general, the value of a three-year-old car can range from half to two-thirds of its original purchase price, and some cars retain even more of their original purchase prices. For example, the popular Ford Explorer retains about 75 percent of its sticker price after three years, while the high-end Lincoln Continental retains only about half of its original cost after the same amount of time.

Unfortunately, increased demand has caused used-car prices to rise even faster than new-car prices over the past few years. You need to do your research to get a good deal.

DETERMINING THE BEST USED CARS

Bob Beattie, executive director of the Ontario Used Car Dealers Association (www.ucda.org), offers his advice for buying a used car:

- Once you have decided on a car, have it checked by your own mechanic. It will be money well spent.
- During negotiations, look closely at any guarantee offered by a dealership. Ask if an extended warranty is available. This could be for a period of three months or up to three years.
- Check the quality of the car, not the odometer. At the end of the day, a guarantee, warranty, and inspection, are more important than other factors such as the odometer reading, or whether a car has had just one owner. How well a car's been cared for is critical. For example, if one car has low mileage but was not well serviced and another car has higher mileage but was well cared for, the second car may be a better deal.
- If you are buying a used car privately, beware of "curbsiders." These individuals pass themselves off as private sellers of their own vehicles. In fact, a curbsider is in the business of selling cars. If you are looking for a used car in the classified section of a newspaper, cast your eye down the ads. Does one phone number appear alongside more than one ad? If so, it is probably a curbsider. Beattie says his organization has found that about 20 percent of so-called private sellers in Canada are actually curbsiders. In Ontario, go to the Ministry of Transport, License Office, and ask for a Used Vehicle Information Package (UVIP). This gives you vital information and history about a used car.
- Be suspicious of any car that has signs of being freshly painted. This may indicate serious damage from an accident.

FITTING A CAR TO YOUR NEEDS

People buy used cars because they want to save money, says Matthew Grabowsky, a car-buying consultant from Pennsylvania. So the first thing you should decide is what features matter the most to you. That means determining how much importance you want to give to utility versus image. "For example, the same $3,000 could probably get you an 8-year-old Honda Civic with reasonably low mileage or a 15-year-old BMW with moon roof and loads of miles. You have to know what you want before you start looking."

To help focus the search, Grabowsky has a list of questions he asks his clients to answer before giving them any advice. The answers to these questions can help you determine the kind of car you're looking for:

- How much do you want to spend on the vehicle? Factor in the costs of maintenance, repairs, and insurance.
- How important to you is a car's appearance versus its reliability?
- What's the maximum number of passengers you need to carry, and how frequently will you need to carry that many? If you only need to carry seven people once a year when your family comes to visit, you probably shouldn't waste money on the high premium of a minivan.
- How many kilometers do you drive on a weekly basis?
- What kind of driving do you do (commuting versus recreation, and highway versus local or off-road driving)?

Arranging a Car Loan

**Explore your financing options
before shopping for a car.**

**Bring everything
you need to fill
out the applica-
tion form and
to speed up the
review process.**

THE TRUE COST OF OWNERSHIP

"People are often attracted to a certain car dealer because of an ad hyping one aspect of the transaction—whether it's a low monthly payment, a rebate, or a sale price," says Steve Larkin, Customer Communications Manager for Ford Credit US, the world's largest firm devoted to auto financing. Instead, Larkin advises buyers to focus on the cost of purchase and subsequent ownership, including insurance and maintenance.

Larkin's advice applies equally to Canadians, says Don Whitehead, Assistant Regional Manager of Ford Credit Canada, the Canadian arm of the US firm. According to Whitehead, Ford Credit Canada handled about 200,000 finance/lease loans in 1999, and has 400,000 accounts outstanding. You can check out its website at www.fordcredit.ca.

Here are factors affecting the cost of a car loan:
Down payment. A higher down payment, no matter from whatever the source or sources, reduces your monthly payment and your total financing costs. If there is a rebate available, add it to any down payment you already have and reduce the amount you need to finance.
Loan term. A typical loan lasts for four or five years. Contracting for a longer

loan will reduce your monthly payment, but you'll pay more overall for credit—a trade-off you may be happy to make.
Prepayment penalty. Even with a longer loan, you always have the option of paying more any month you're able to. Although prepayment penalties are often assessed in the US, they are relatively rare in Canada, says Whitehead. Ford Credit does not assess prepayment penalties to their customers.

Most lenders use the simple interest formula for allocating your monthly payment between finance charges and principal finance charges for loans, says Whitehead. Ford Credit Canada switched to this method in 1995. Simply put, it means that the finance charge you pay is based on the principal balance outstanding for the actual number of days that it is outstanding.

Another formula, now rarely used, is the Rule of 78s. It works on the principle that, if you take the 12 months of the year and add them up, they would equal 78. If you pay out in the first month of the year instead

of paying 1/12 (.08333) of the year's interest, you would pay 12/78 (.15385) of the year's interest charge. If you pay out the loan in the second month, you would pay 12/78 + 11/78 (.029488) of the year's interest charge instead of 2/12 (.16667) as in straight-line calculation. Lenders who calculate loans by using this method make you pay more interest in the initial months of a loan. As a result, you get less of a break on the financing expense if you pay off the loan before maturity.

Don Whitehead recommends that you ask your lender what refund you would be entitled to if you repay your loan early. If the lender is using the Rule of 78s or another method that makes you pay most of the interest early in the loan repayment period, there may be no advantage to repaying early.
Loan rate. All auto manufacturers run loan specials at certain times of the year with terms that can't be beat. Call the dealers to ask when these happen, or check their websites. The offer is often for specific vehicles and loan terms.

Value of service. Steve Larkin adds that "there's usually a trade-off between price and convenience. Before choosing a lender, ask yourself what extent you're willing to compromise on conveniences, such as access to service, ability to check loan information over the Internet, payment options, and obtaining statements of account, to get a better overall price."

Smart Moves

The more detailed and accurate the information you provide, the quicker your loan will be processed. Be prepared to apply for a car loan by bringing the following information when you go to the dealership:

- Account numbers and addresses for all bank accounts, loans, and credit cards.
- Address and account information for mortgage lender, or address and phone number for landlord.
- Full name and address of employer.
- Phone numbers and addresses for three references.
- Sources of additional income, such as investments.

DEALERS' LOANS

If customers do not have their own loan from a bank or financial institution, car dealers will try to find one for them. Many dealerships are now using low interest rate financing as a marketing tool for car sales, and they have greatly streamlined the procedures for obtaining car loans. The dealerships employ business office managers whose primary expertise is the financing of vehicles and explaining warranties to customers.

Every dealership has its own computer system to facilitate loan applications. North American manufacturers have credit arms that provide financing for vehicle purchases. They may provide dealers with a small computer to assist with loan applications.

Dealers may also work with five or six lenders such as banks, finance companies, and trust companies. After you have selected your vehicle, you sit down with the business office manager who takes credit information from you. Then the business manager sends a loan application to the lending institution that the manager believes will provide financing. If the loan application is turned down, the business manager will try another lending institution:

- A bank will charge a higher interest rate if it considers you to be a high-risk credit customer. If you think you are being charged a rate that is too high, shop around. Loan institutions all have different ways of looking at an application.
- In general, banks pay a flat fee to a dealership for each can loan that they send to them. This doesn't add to the cost of the vehicle to the consumer. In this way, car dealers provide banks with an opportunity to market their loans. And for the customer, there is the convenience of one-stop shopping for vehicle and loan. In the past, dealers earned higher commissions by encouraging customers to borrow larger amounts and incur higher financing charges. This is no longer the situation. Now, dealers operate under a policy of full disclosure, which benefits the consumer.

- Paying cash is not an effective leverage point when negotiating a car's price with a dealer. Dealers make money by marking up loans—usually by about one percent.

HOME EQUITY LOANS

Another way of financing an automobile purchase is available to consumers who borrow on a line of credit at their banks or financial institutions. Using your home as equity, you can obtain a line of credit worth up to 75 percent of the appraised value of your house.

For the average consumer who is buying a car, a home equity loan may be an attractive way to borrow. This type of loan may be of most interest to consumers who have paid off their mortgage. A home equity loan, compared with other bank or financial institution lending rates, offers the advantage of a low interest rate. Another advantage is the convenience of a line of credit. After you have paid off your loan, you still have credit available should you need it.

There are drawbacks to home equity loans, however. A line of credit may take time to set up (unless you are already a loan customer with the bank), and there may be associated costs such as appraisal and legal fees. The interest rate on a line of credit fluctuates according to the prime interest rate, so there is no guaranteed rate of interest. If you take longer to repay the loan, the extra amount you spend in interest could eat up your savings. And, if you default on the loan, you risk losing your home.

CREDIT UNION LOANS

Sharon Leonard of the retail division of Credit Union Central of Canada says there are 2,130 credit unions and Caisses Populaires in Canada, with 10 million members. Every credit union has a defined membership criteria. Some serve specific communities; others, certain occupations, such as police, municipal workers, and firefighters. For details about credit unions in your area, call the Credit Union Central of Canada at 1-800-433-9122.

Credit unions offer car loans and, recently, they have started to offer a leasing service to members.

Information. At the very least, credit unions help you compare loans and let you know the blue book value of your trade-in. At the next level, you'll find fully equipped libraries, where you can read auto reviews, compare options, surf the Web for more information, or attend car-buying seminars. The peak level of service is available from some credit unions who coach you through the entire purchasing process.

Car-buying service. Members can get a preapproved car loan and select the type of car they would like to purchase. The buying service contacts dealers that the credit union has alliances with, and requests competitive quotes.

Members' only sales. At some credit unions, you can buy a new car or used car on-site. The seller sets low prices in expectation of doing volume sales, and the credit union usually reduces its already low loan rates for the event.

Is Leasing for You?

The answer depends on how you use your car.

LOOK BEFORE YOU LEASE

"Leasing has become highly popular and competitive in Canada," says Zvi Richman, owner of First Rate Auto Leasing in Toronto. "Many consumers find leasing an attractive alternative to purchasing a car because it is a good way to minimize the monthly cost of driving a vehicle."

Manufacturers and private leasing companies are all getting into the act. Leasing now accounts for a significant amount of manufacturers' business. In 1998, for instance, Ford of Canada, through Ford Credit, did roughly 45 percent of its retail business through leasing.

Many people are familiar with traditional car loans, but are less familiar with leasing. "Before you lease, you really have to read all the fine print and understand the lease agreement," advises Richman.

In Canada, some provinces have a mandatory full disclosure lease document, says Richman. That makes it easier to understand the full costs of leasing.

But it is up to the consumer to get the right information to ensure you know what you are getting into.

Make sure that the gross capitalization cost (also called the capital cost) of the vehicle is clearly noted. This is the value of the car that you and the dealer agree to. It's an amount you can negotiate just as you would the price of buying a new car.

Also, be sure that the leasing form the dealer gives you states the residual value of the car, or the amount it will be worth at the end of the term of the lease. The residual is also called the resale value of the vehicle. At the end of the lease, you may decide you want to purchase the car you have been leasing. If so, the residual is the amount you will have to pay. The residual is an estimated value. It is not negotiable. The rate of interest should be clearly stated. These numbers are the key to determining the amount of your monthly payment that covers depreciation of the vehicle.

Customers should be aware of distance limits when they lease, says Richman. The standard lease allows for about 20,000 to 24,000 kilometers a year. A distance of 18,000 to 20,000 kilometers per year is considered low. If you do not need the higher limit, you may be able to negotiate a lower monthly payment in exchange for a lower distance limit. But it is better to be realistic about your distance needs. It is much more expensive to pay for the extra distance at the end of your lease.

It makes good sense to get a reference to a leasing company, just as you would before you hire any professional, says Richman.

The majority of luxury vehicle drivers now lease their cars rather than buy. Leasing can be a good deal in this situation—but only if you're willing to do your homework to get the best deal available to drive your dream car.

WHO SHOULD LEASE?

Fred M. H. Gregory, contributing editor for *Car and Driver* magazine, advises drivers who are uncertain about whether to lease their next car to ask themselves about their driving habits and the kind of car they'd like to have.

Gregory maintains that leasing can make sense for a buyer who wants to:
- Change cars every two, three, or four years.
- Put down very little money up front.
- Make smaller monthly payments.
- Drive a more expensive car.

In contrast, Gregory says that leasing doesn't make sense for a driver who:
- Tends to drive the same car for a long time.
- Is a hard user and puts lots of miles on a car every year.
- Wants to pay the least possible amount for a car.

SHOP AROUND FOR THE BEST LEASE

According to Jeff Ostroff, creator of a consumer advocate car buying and leasing site on the Web (www .CarBuyingTips.com), the most important thing consumers need to know about a lease is that it's a contract. Frequently, people decide they want to get out of their lease after a year or two—and only then realize that they'll have to pay big fines to do it. You might, in fact, have to pay the entire amount you would have paid if you'd kept the car for the full term.

When you are shopping for a lease, find out what kind of down payment will be required. Also, find out what penalties will apply if you decide to get out of the lease. Some companies will charge a financial penalty. Others may charge all the remaining lease payments.

If you have to break a lease, do it in the cheapest way possible, says Zvi Richman. Call the manufacturer's financial arm, get your buyout and purchase the car. Then sell the car yourself, rather than return it to the dealer.

If you lease a vehicle, you will be responsible for paying for insurance, maintenance, and repairs. Some manufacturers offer special deals in which they pay for some maintenance. Discuss this option. Also, find out

what the lessor considers normal wear and tear.

When you lease a car, the dealer actually sells it to the leasing company or the financial arm of the manufacturer. You then rent the vehicle from these organizations. To make the most on the sale, dealers usually try to get you to focus on your monthly payment, not on the actual price of the car. But you shouldn't lose sight of the cost of the car. Getting a lower price for the car will benefit you in the end. If in doubt, contact the Automobile Protection Association for a recommendation to an independent leasing company.

Although banks are generally prohibited from leasing automobiles, some offer car loans called "buybacks," which are similar to leases. This type of loan sets a residual value for the vehicle and finances the balance of the cost. Terms may be as long as five years.

THREE STEPS TO A BETTER LEASE

"If you're not prepared, you will almost surely pay too much for your lease," says Al Hearn, author of "Automobile Leasing: The Art of the Deal" on the consumer website www.leaseguide.com. To get the best deal, you need to understand three basic elements of automotive leasing before you set foot in the dealer's showroom.

1. Know the fundamentals of leasing. Read up on how leasing works in books, magazines, or on the Internet. Make sure you understand how monthly payments are calculated and how specialized terminology is used in the lease

agreement. Then, get your dealer or leasing company to give you a blank contract to review. Ask about anything you don't understand.

2. Research the vehicle. If you let the dealer educate you, you'll only learn what the dealer wants you to know. Prepare as you would if you were going to buy the car: Know your models, options, and prices (including dealer invoice prices). Look for information in new-car

guides at automotive websites, or from the Automobile Protection Association.

3. Shop around for your lease. You may not know that you have a choice of which firm you can use to lease your car. The dealer will only offer you the manufacturer's leasing firm, but you may find better terms at an independent leasing company. Use the Yellow Pages or the Internet to shop around for the best deal.

LEASING LANGUAGE

Make sure you understand all the terms in a lease before you sign it. Here are some common phrases used in lease agreements. Ask the lessor to explain any you don't grasp.

Lease: a contract by which the owner of property allows another to use it for a specified period of time, usually in return for money.

Lease term: the length of time a lease is in effect.

Lessee: the person who leases a car or truck.

Lessor: the dealer or finance company that offers and administers the lease.

Closed-end lease: monthly payments can be slightly higher than with an open-end lease. There are two types: one sets the residual at fair market value near the end of the lease term; the other offers a fixed, or guaranteed, residual value.

Residual or **lease-end value:** the estimated market value of a vehicle at the end of its lease. The residual value is established before you sign the lease. Setting this value determines how much monthly payments will be.

Net capitalized cost: this is the total cost of the vehicle you wish to lease. It includes the base vehicle price, options, additions, delivery costs and predelivery inspection charges minus any down payment. Sometimes a trade-in value may be applied to a down payment.

Excess mileage: any mileage above the standard annual allowance (about 20,000 to 24,000 kilometers per year) set for the lease. At lease end, you are often obliged to pay a penalty for excess mileage.

The Right Way

You might want to consider buying GAP insurance. (GAP stands for Guaranteed Asset Protection.) It covers the difference between the vehicle's book value in a lease contract and the amount the insurance company will pay out in case the vehicle is stolen or damaged beyond repair. Sometimes it is included in the lease contract; sometimes you have to purchase it separately. Either way, it is recommended.

Tips on Tires

Learn what to drive on for the safest ride.

WHAT YOU NEED TO KNOW

Most people who shop for tires don't know anything about them, says John Penney, president of TireNet (www.tirenet.com). Here are a few key pieces of information to help you find the right tires:

■ First, find out the exact model of your car? That means not just knowing that you have a 1990 Honda Accord, but whether it's an LX or an SX. Only then can the dealer tell what size tires you need. You can also double-check the size by looking in your owner's manual, or on the yellow label on the doorjamb, the glovebox door, or the console bin.

■ How long you plan to keep the car? If you're going to be driving the car for years, consider buying high-quality tires that will give you the most kilometers for your dollar. It makes no sense, however, to buy top-of-the-line tires for a car you're planning to get rid of in a few months.

■ Keep in mind how many kilometers you have on your car. On the average, North American con-sumers turn in their cars after they reach 150,000 to 160,000 kilometers. And if your car has over 160,000 kilometers on it, how many more can you expect it to last before you have to get rid of it—along with the tires?

■ Finally, how much do you want to spend?

HOW TO READ YOUR TIRES

A tire's side-walls contain information that shows what size they are, and what type of wear and perfor-mance they'll

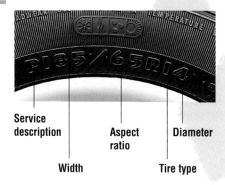

Service description

Width

Aspect ratio

Tire type

Diameter

deliver. Tom Torbjornsen, automotive tool and equipment dealer, and host of his own talk-radio show about cars in Buffalo, New York (www.carshowtomt.com), explains what the markings mean on a typical tire reading **P185/65R14**.

P: This **service description** means the tire was designed for a passenger car (LT means the tire is designed for a light truck).

185: This number is the **width** of the tire in millimeters.

65: This is the tire's **aspect ratio**, or relationship between its height and width. This tire is 65 percent as tall as it is wide.

R: This letter indicates the **tire type**. This is a radial tire.

14: This number is the diameter of the wheel in inches.

TIRE PRESSURE

"The tires may be the most mundane parts of a car, but they're the only contact between your car and the road," declares John Rastetter, the director of product information services for The Tire Rack (www.tirerack.com), North America's largest phone- and mail-order tire retailer. "A tire is actually a pneumatic device (which means it's mechanized by air) that supports a vehicle's load, acts as a spring, and translates acceleration, braking, and cornering inputs to the driving surface. As such, tires profoundly influence safety, performance, ride, comfort, and fuel economy."

It's not your tires that carry the load of your car—it's the air inside them that does. That's why it's vital to check the pressure weekly or, at least, once a month. It takes about a minute, and you'll be likely to notice any pressure loss caused by minor punctures before it causes a major problem. It's best to check the pressure in the morning, when the

TIME FOR NEW TIRES?

Many people continue driving on their old tires long after it's time for them to be replaced, which can cause significant safety hazards. Tom Torbjornsen suggests looking for these signs that it's time to replace your tires:

■ Tread is worn down to tread wear indicators.

■ Hydroplaning, or losing tire contact with the road, in wet weather.

■ Uneven wear patterns on your tires caused by poor alignment.

■ A low roar coming from the tires as you drive.

■ Visible sidewall damage from rubbing against curbs while parking.

All-season radial tire with sturdy steel belts, two-ply radial polyester cord, and water grooves.

Off-road tire with wide tread and deep grooves for better mileage and traction.

Tools of the Trade

Experts suggest investing in a high-quality tire pressure gauge, and using it to test the pressure in your tires on a weekly basis. Under- or over-inflating your tires could lead to tire failure, resulting in potentially deadly accidents.

tires are cold, since air expands when it's hot.

Set your tire pressure according to the range recommended by the vehicle's manufacturer. This information is listed on a label located on the doorjamb, engine compartment, or glovebox door. Also check your owner's manual about recommended pressure adjustments for driving a fully loaded vehicle or in extreme temperatures.

Inflating your tires at the maximum pressure may improve high-speed performance and fuel economy, since it reduces rolling resistance, but it can also produce a harsher ride and reduce the tires' resistance to damage from potholes, bumpy roads, and other hazards. Proper tire pressure levels make handling, steering, and braking safer and easier.

BALANCING

Mike Whitaker, Big O Tires store manager in Wyoming (www.idahotires.com), suggests getting your tires balanced every time you change winter tires to summer tires and vice versa.

Tire or wheel balance is important for both vehicle stability and your comfort.

As a tire wears, its mass becomes unevenly distributed. When balancing, mechanics put the tire on a machine that tests for heavy spots, caused by uneven wear. These spots can cause vibrations in your

Quick Tricks

A Canadian buying US tires should be aware of the US Department of Transportation's Uniform Tire Quality Grading System (UTQG) rating, designed to let consumers compare styles and brands of tires. Here are the three categories that make up a tire's rating:

Treadwear: This rating indicates how well a test tire wore in a controlled testing environment. A tire rated 200 delivers twice the wear as one rated 100.

Traction: This broad-based rating indicates how well the tire grips the pavement. The ratings, from best to worst, are A, B, and C.

Temperature: This rating tells how much friction the tires create, and thus how much heat affects them. As with traction, the ratings, from best to worst, are A, B, and C.

wheel, seat, or entire vehicle. They can also make your car wobbly and difficult to handle. For about $6 a tire, you can get your tires tested and rebalanced to help ensure a consistently smooth and safe ride.

EQUALIZE TIRE WEAR

Ideally, all four tires should wear at the same rate. However, the front tires of front-wheel-drive vehicles wear almost three times faster than the rear tires. And rear-wheel- and all-wheel-drive vehicles tend to wear their front tires' shoulders and rear tires' center portions more quickly. However, your individual driving style will also affect the way the tires on your car wear.

To equalize tire wear, rotate them periodically. If you have a full-size spare, you will want to include it in your rotation schedule. While many drivers rotate their tires at 8,000- to 12,000-kilometer intervals,

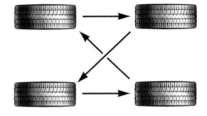

John Rastetter of The Tire Rack recommends a different schedule. The first rotation is the most important, he maintains, because it is done at the stage of a tire's life when the greatest wear occurs.

For the first 25,000 kilometers, rotate the tires every 5,000 kilometers. For the next 25,000 kilometers, rotate every 8,000 kilometers, and from that point on, rotate the tires every 12,000 kilometers.

STUDDED TIRES

Pierre Trudeau of Transport Canada says that for traction on ice, studded tires are your best choice. Many provinces permit studded tires during winter—the exact period varies from province to province. Check with your local department of transport to make sure they are permitted in your province. Today, the studs are made in such a way that they no longer damage asphalt highway as they once did.

Rain tire
with special channels to sweep away water for the best wet traction.

Wide high performance tire
with curved pitch boundaries for a smooth ride.

Fuel Efficiency

Getting better mileage takes less of a toll on your wallet—and the environment.

DRIVE SMARTER

Whatever kind of vehicle you have can be driven more efficiently if you exercise patience and work on learning some simple skills, maintains Tony Swan, a senior editor at *Car and Driver* magazine and noted amateur road racer. The single most important thing a driver can do to improve mileage is to drive smoothly. In addition, Swan recommends the following:

- Apply the throttle, or accelerator, progressively and consistently, and don't use more power than you need.
- Don't accelerate using the vehicle's maximum ability. Build up speed as gradually as the flow of traffic allows.
- Cruise at a steady speed. Your fuel efficiency significantly decreases if you're continually going back and forth from one speed to another.
- Try to anticipate the stop signals. Zooming away from one light, only to come to a screeching stop at the next one, uses up lots of fuel.
- Use the highest possible gear. With a standard transmission car, shift into the next gear as soon as you can, and cruise in the highest possible gear. This takes some practice, but once you get the hang of it, this style of driving becomes second nature. (If you're traveling to Europe—where gasoline is three to four dollars a gallon—and you take a taxicab, watch the driver: You'll be amazed at how quickly he gets from first to fourth gear.)
- Try fresh air. It takes a lot of fuel to run an air conditioner. An open window may be all the cooling you need.
- Lessen your load. Clean out the trunk and don't carry around any more stuff than you need to.

BUYING GREEN CARS

Buying a more fuel-efficient car can make a real difference in public health and the health of the planet. When you buy a new car, you probably consider what you'll spend on fuel and repairs. But there are environmental costs, too, such as the adverse health impacts of air pollution, oil spills and fouling of water supplies, damage to habitats, and the growing risks of climate disruption.

Buying green goes hand in hand with better mileage because the lower your fuel consumption, the fewer emissions. Here are tips for improved fuel economy from Pierre Trudeau:

- Don't idle. Start your car and go. Even at 0°F, most cars need only 15 to 30 seconds of idling before driving. Excessive idling increases fuel consumption. Ten seconds of idling consumes more fuel than restarting your engine. Of course, the "start and go—don't idle" advice doesn't apply to normal driving situations when you must come to a stop at stop signs, traffic lights, and to wait your turn to proceed in traffic.
- Properly inflated tires save fuel. Inflate your tires to the pressure recommended by the manufacturer.

DETERMINING YOUR FUEL CONSUMPTION

Pierre Trudeau of Transport Canada explains how to figure out your car's real fuel consumption:

- Fill the tank and jot down a first odometer reading.
- Next time you fill the tank, note the number of liters you just purchased and jot down a second odometer reading.
- Step 1: Multiply the fuel consumed in liters by 100.
- Step 2: Find the distance traveled.
- Step 3: Divide that result by the distance traveled to get the fuel consumption in liters per 100 kilometers (L/100).

31 LITERS — **18100** Second odometer reading.

x100 − **17700** Minus first odometer reading.

3100 ÷ **400** Distance traveled.

Driving with a lead foot can significantly lower your fuel efficiency, while following the speed limit will improve mileage.

FUEL EFFICIENCY OF THE FUTURE

It's not that we can't make a more fuel-efficient car, says Marc Ross, professor of physics at the University of Michigan. It's that consumers aren't very interested in buying one. Ross has been working on automotive, energy, and emissions issues for the last 10 years, and has come to the conclusion that there are a variety of innovations that could enable cars to get twice as much work out of the fuel they take in than they currently do. Here are some of the ideas he's considering:

■ Automate the manual transmission gear changes, except during the brief moments while shifting. Quite a bit of energy is lost here because the transmission keeps spinning in between gear changes. (The Mercedes-Benz line is planning to implement this change over the next 10 years.)

= 7.7 LITERS PER 100 KM

■ Improve the power of an engine for its given size. Smaller engines use less fuel. If we adopted engines that got higher (horse) power-per-unit displacement, we'd get better mileage. Some Japanese and a few of the newer American cars are experimenting with this innovation. Unfortunately, small engines are unpopular in North America.

■ Use lighter materials. If manufacturers used lighter materials, they could make larger cars that still had good fuel efficiency. Of course, for safety reasons, the materials would have to be as strong as those used in current production.

■ Use a lean-burn engine. During normal operation there's a lot more air in a lean-burn engine relative to fuel than there is in a normal engine, and having a higher air-to-fuel ratio is more efficient.

■ Develop alternative fuel vehicles that are competitive with traditional vehicles. In Europe, electric and hybrid buses are being used on some mass transit routes. In North America, the electric streetcar, or trolley, is coming back into use.

Underinflated tires increase fuel consumption substantially. Check tire pressure every time you tank up, or at least once a month. Watch for uneven tread wear. For every two pounds per square inch (14 kPa) of under-inflation, you increase fuel consumption by 1 percent.

■ Get a tune-up. A well-tuned car can save you between 15 and 50 percent in fuel. Have your car serviced in spring and fall and as the manufacturer recommends.

Smart Moves

Automotive engineers aren't the only people who can make a difference in a car's fuel efficiency. Marc Ross suggests trying these techniques for choosing a new car with low gas mileage and using less gasoline every time you drive:

■ Drive an aerodynamic car. The greater the surface on the front of your car for air to hit, the more fuel you need to use to push the car forward. That's why sports cars get much better mileage than boxy sedans.

■ Obey speed limits. Air resistance increases exponentially as your driving speed increases, which means that slowing down by even 15 km/h can make a big difference in how much gas you use.

■ Drive a car with a lower overall mass. Bulky SUVs and luxury sedans use more fuel than lighter cars.

■ Keep your tires properly inflated, and check their air pressure frequently. Soft tires use up a great deal of extra energy.

■ Choose a manual transmission, which is more fuel-efficient than an automatic.

■ Take advantage of the Drive Clean Program if you live in Ontario, and have emission levels checked if your car is more than three years old (www.driveclean.com).

The Right Way

Consider fuel efficiency when buying a car, urges the fuel efficiency division of Transport Canada.

■ Get only the options you really need. Optional equipment that adds weight to your car can increase your fuel consumption (especially heavy options, such as four-wheel drive).

■ Automatic transmissions generally degrade fuel economy. Larger engines and higher horsepower typically result in lower gas mileage. If you need the additional power and torque, be aware that your fuel efficiency will suffer.

■ Buy the most fuel-efficient model in the size category that meets your needs. Consult Natural Resources Canada's Fuel Consumption Guide and their Auto$mart Program (call 1-800-387-2000).

The Opel Calibra
Sold in Europe, the Opel Calibra leads the industry in aerodynamics, creating the least wind resistance and improving fuel efficiency.

Alternative Fuels

Consider the pros and cons before buying an alternative-fuel car.

OVERVIEW

"The demand for alternative vehicle fuels exists mostly because we need to reduce vehicles' pollution output and decrease our dependency on strictly fossil fuels," explains Bob Storck, electrical engineer and syndicated automotive and history of technology writer for newspapers, popular magazines, and the Internet. Storck explains that it's hard to replace gasoline because it's so simple to use. "It's very easy to carry a few liters of gasoline—all you need is a container. But it's much harder to carry around a unit of electricity or compressed gas." Alternative fuel proponents need to solve these distribution problems to offer a truly viable alternative.

According to Storck, there are three main types of alternative fuel vehicles currently in development:

Electric: These vehicles run on a battery, which must be plugged into a recharging station, either in your own garage or at a public station, when the battery runs low. It takes eight hours to fully charge an electric car, which has a limited range before needing to be recharged. Several companies, including Bombardier, are testing these cars in the US and Canada.

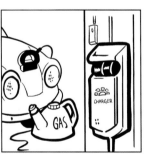

Hybrids: These cars use a combination of electricity and gasoline, and put out a minimal amount of pollution. Hybrid cars switch back and forth between electric and gas power, taking advantage of the best performance characteristics of each energy source.

True alternative fuels: These include ethanol, methanol, diesel, and gaseous fuels (compressed natural gas, propane, and hydrogen). Fuel cell vehicles break down raw fuel, such as gas or methanol, and run it through the engine's fuel cell to create energy.

The Right Way

The electric cars available today are most appropriate for people who have their own garages, use their cars mostly to commute on the highway from the suburbs into town, and can recharge the battery at home each night, advises Joanne Brickman. Don't even think about getting an electric car if you live in an apartment building in the city and don't have your own garage, she adds.

HYBRID POTENTIAL

Hybrid vehicles combine the best of both electric and gasoline vehicles, maintains Jeremy Barnes, a product safety and environment administrator at Toyota. The Toyota Prius, the world's first hybrid production vehicle (containing both a gas engine and electric motor), is currently available in Japan, and will be available in the US in mid- to late 2000. The Japanese version of the Prius gets up to twice the mileage of conventional cars. This is an attractive feature where gasoline is expensive.

The beauty of the Toyota Prius, says Barnes, is that you never have to plug it in. It has a clean, quiet operation, and you can refuel it quickly at the gas station. Hybrids bypass the drawback of battery electric vehicles (their limited kilometers per charge), while emitting far less pollution than gasoline-fueled vehicles.

Here's an example of how the Prius works:
- When you stop at a traffic light, the gas engine turns off.
- When the light turns green, you start moving on battery power, and then the gas engine turns on at around 12 to 15 kilometers per hour. The car continues to run on both power systems until you reach a cruising speed.
- When you reach a steady cruising speed (usually around 50 to 55 kilometers per hour), the electric

True Stories

Canadian businesses are leading the way in the development of alternative, nonpolluting technologies for vehicles. Here are two examples:

Bombardier has recently introduced the world's first Neighborhood Vehicle™—the Bombardier NV™. This is the first mass-produced neighborhood electric vehicle, and its manufacturer claims that the NV™ is as easy to charge as a cellular phone. It runs on six regular 12-volt, lead-acid batteries, plus one auxiliary battery for accessories. The battery takes about eight hours to recharge at a cost of $0.40 per charge.

The NV™ can accelerate from 0 to 32 kilometers per hour in six seconds and has a top speed of 40 kilometers per hour. Bombardier claims that the NV™ is the perfect vehicle for getting around "gated communities," university campuses, or industrial complexes, and on designated low-speed paths. With a range of 50 kilometers, the NV™ is said to be the ideal vehicle for daily short-distance errands. For further details, check out the Bombardier website at www.recreation.bombardier.com.

Ballard Power Systems of North Vancouver, British Columbia, is a pioneer in the fuel-cell technology, which can power public transit buses and, perhaps in the future, personal automobiles.

Fuel-cell technology may sound like science fiction. But the fuel cell creates power without combustion, without moving parts, and without any emissions. The fuel cell works by converting hydrogen and oxygen into electricity and water vapor. The hydrogen for the cells is stored in a tank or manufactured in the vehicle from other fuel, such as methanol.

Some of the benefits of fuel-cell technology are that it is emission-free, high energy efficient, operates quietly, gives more power at lower speed, and is low maintenance. Fuel-cell engines, in comparison with battery engines, are low in weight, quick and easy to refuel. Moreover, they give the vehicle a superior driving range of between 400 to 500 kilometers.

motor shuts down and you run on the gas engine alone.

- While the car is cruising, the system bleeds energy off of the gas engine and uses it to recharge the electric battery.
- If you step hard on the accelerator while running on the gas engine, the electric motor turns on to give you an extra boost of power. It shuts off again when you take your foot off the accelerator.
- When you brake, the system uses regenerative braking, taking advantage of the kinetic energy that would otherwise be lost to the wheels in order to help recharge the battery.

THE CATCH

"The search for alternate fuels and forms of powering cars and trucks is guided by the need for low-emission vehicles and preparation for any future fuel oil crunch. But many experts say it could be a decade before alternative-fuel vehicles are widespread," says Barry Winfield, US West Coast editor of *Car and Driver* magazine. Such factors as limited cruising range, long recharging cycles, and a relatively small number of charging stations will limit electric vehicles, while the scarce number of ethanol or methanol pumping stations could keep flexible-fuel rigs running mainly on gasoline, Winfield maintains.

Another of the obstacles to alternative-fuel vehicles is that there's no consensus among industry leaders as to what the ideal fuel would actually be, Winfield explains. Even if there were agreement, the widespread adoption of any alternative would require fundamental changes in the automotive infrastructure, including the creation of massive new distribution systems.

Consequently, many experts predict that gasoline and diesel cars and trucks will most likely continue to dominate the roads for decades to come. They're reliable, comfortable, and affordable.

Existing technologies are also continually improving, resulting in overall lower emissions and better fuel economy. The current automotive technologies are also sustained by an enormous economic infrastructure, including the factories, petroleum refineries, service stations, and all the people—from auto workers to garage mechanics—who come together to make the current system work.

Keep Your Car Looking Good

The products you use determine the results you'll get.

CLEANING YOUR CAR

The number one no-no in cleaning your car —using dishwashing detergent—is the one thing most people do, says Barry Meguiar, who is president and CEO of Meguiar's (www.meguiars.com), manufacturer of a wide variety of car care products since 1901. Detergent is the worst thing you can use because it's formulated to strip everything off surfaces, and therefore washes away the very wax coatings and polymers you put on to protect your car's finish against oxidation, dullness, and color loss. Car washing shampoos and conditioners, on the other hand, are specially formulated to clean your car gently.

Here are some of Meguiar's tips for keeping your car looking its best:

■ Start at the top and work down. Hose down the whole car first. Lather one section at a time and hose it off so that the soap doesn't dry onto the finish.
■ Use 100-percent-cotton deep-pile terry cloth toweling to dry your car. These plush towels prevent any little particulates left on the car's surface from skidding across the finish and leaving tiny scratches, something that frequently happens when you use smooth cloths.
■ Don't use any fabric softener when washing the towels you will use to dry your car after cleaning it.
■ Don't wash your car when it's warm after driving. Wait until the surface is cool, then wash it in a cool, shady spot to prevent water spots.
■ Keep your car waxed. You can tell if your car isn't waxed very well because washing it will be a slow, tiresome job. If your car is well waxed, however, the cloth should glide quickly and easily across the finish.
■ Be careful of car washes, especially if they haven't been updated recently. Some of the older brushes can scratch your car's finish.

The Right Way

Here's Barry Meguiar's method for testing the cleanliness of a car's surface: After you've washed and dried your car, rub the finish with the face of your hand. It should feel as smooth as glass. If it feels gritty, invisible contaminants have bonded to your finish, making it impossible to achieve a clear, high-gloss finish.

You can get rid of these contaminants with detailing clay. Rubbing this putty-like substance across your car's finish is the best way to remove bonded contaminants without scratching the finish. You can finish the whole car in around 20 minutes.

CLEANING YOUR PAINT

Cleaning your car is not the same as cleaning your car's paintwork, says Larry Reynolds, owner of Car Care Specialties, a one-stop online shopping center for all your car care needs (www.carcareonline.com). Washing your car is, however, the first step in cleaning your paint. Next, select a high-quality paint cleaner. There are two types of paint cleaners: chemical and friction. Friction cleaners smooth out the paint's surface, creating the glossiest finish. Harsher chemical cleaners strip the surface, and are best for removing sticky debris.

Friction cleaners usually come in different strengths. Compound, the most aggressive, should only be used if your paint finish is badly marred. Glaze, the finest cleaning agent, refreshes the paint, and will create a lustrous finish if your paint is in good condition. When in doubt, use the gentlest products that will do the job.

Cleaning your paint will:
■ Remove oxidation and add emollients back

Smart Moves

Here are Barry Meguiar's five steps for keeping your car's finish looking good:

1. Wash. Be sure to use a car wash product made especially for automotive finishes.

2. Prep the finish. Use detailing clay to get bonded contaminants off the paint's surface.

3. Polish to achieve a high gloss. This step is optional, and will achieve the most noticeable results on dark-colored (black, red, dark blue, dark green) vehicles.

4. Add protection. Barrier coats that will protect your car's paint finish from wear and tear include waxes, polymers, silicones, and resins.

5. Perform daily maintenance. Use quick detailer and a soft cloth to wipe off any dirt or contaminants before they have time to bond to the finish.

into the paint (without which the paint turns dull and lifeless).

■ Prepare and smooth the paint surface for car wax. Reynolds recommends working on one panel at a time so your car isn't left unprotected if you can't finish the job.

WAX IT WELL

The purpose of waxing and cleaning your car is to protect its paintwork from dirt, the elements, pollution, road debris, oxidization, and anything else that can mar the color and the finish. Yet many people don't realize that some waxes and most cleaners have abrasives that can damage some car surfaces, warns Don Prieto of the Prietive Group, a Los Angeles-based company that maintains fleets of press vehicles for several auto manufacturers.

Never use an abrasive cleaner on a paint surface unless it is so badly oxidized that waxing will not bring out a shine. And never use a wax that contains abrasives on a clearcoat finish. This kind of wax works very well on cars with solid color finishes, but not with clearcoated finishes because it scratches and dulls the transparent surface layer.

A wax or sealer that is applied by hand-rubbing will always give you better protection than a product that's sprayed on at a car wash. Car wash waxes give a nice temporary shine, but don't provide lasting protection. But the kind of wax you use won't make much difference if your car's finish is in poor condition.

Here is Prieto's step-by-step advice on how to wax your car for a beautiful protective finish:

■ Wash and dry your car to remove all dirt and dust. Park it out of the sun, and allow the paint to cool down. If you need to use a paint cleaner, follow the recommendations on the container carefully.

■ Apply the wax using a very soft, slightly damp, cheesecloth rag or the applicator that comes with the wax.

■ Pour a small quantity of liquid wax, or smear a small amount of paste wax, on the applicator. Apply the wax in a straight line or rotary motion to a small section of the body, a door, or fender. Let it dry to a dull haze, and then use a soft cheesecloth rag to hand-buff it off the paint.

■ A thorough waxing may take several applications. You can tell if there is enough wax by pouring water on the paint surface. If it beads up, there's enough wax. If it appears to soak into the paint, you need more wax. In high humidity, the wax may not dry thoroughly between applications. If you will be waxing in humid weather, allow your car to stand out in the sunlight for a day or two between coats, then buff the surface again to a high-gloss finish. The heat will activate and dry the wax more quickly.

Tools of the Trade

Carnauba wax comes from plants and offers better depth of shine than polymer wax, but lasts for a shorter period of time.

Polymer wax is a petroleum distillate that offers less depth of shine, but lasts longer than carnauba wax. German finishes don't react well to polymer wax, although it often works well on Japanese and American car finishes.

STUBBORN STAINS

Sometimes soap and water may not be enough. Professional detailers suggest the following specialized methods to get rid of hard-to-remove grime:

Tree sap, road tar, and other sticky residues: Use a solvent-, petroleum-, or citrus-based degreaser or tar remover. Citrus cleansers are the gentlest.

Bird droppings: Immediate action is the key, before the acidic mess can bake into your car's paint. Apply a wet towel to the stain and let it sit for a while before wiping the white stuff away. Then rinse to remove all residue.

Bugs: Soak thoroughly with water, then use a wash mitt and a plastic scrub brush (make sure it won't scratch your car) to get inside the grille and around lights and light covers. A paint brush can help you reach tight corners, and an old toothbrush can be even handier for getting into smaller crevices.

Preventive Maintenance

Pay a little bit for prevention now—or a lot for repairs later.

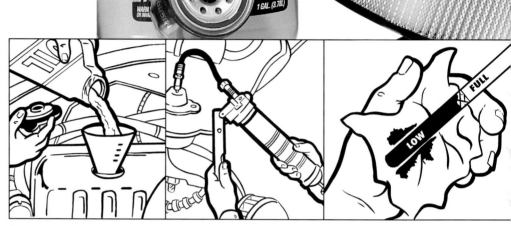

IMPORTANT MEASURES

Maintaining the condition of your car as it grows older lies squarely in your hands: You can choose to keep it in good shape or to run it into the ground.

There are a few simple procedures you can follow that will help your vehicle last longer and make driving it more enjoyable, maintains Deanna Sclar, author of *Auto Repair for Dummies*. Here are some basic steps she advocates for keeping your car running smoothly:

Change the oil on a regular basis: every 5,000 km, or two to three months—whichever comes first. In between oil changes, add oil periodically if necessary to keep the level constant.

Get a lube job. Cars over 15 years old should get one every 5,000 km. (Consult your owner's manual for newer cars.) During a lube job, mechanics apply grease and oil to some of the moving and rubber parts.

Check your fluids. Once a month, check the levels of your radiator coolant, automatic transmission fluid, brake fluid, windshield-washer fluid, and power-steering fluid, and add fluids as necessary.

TUNE-UPS HAVE CHANGED THEIR TUNE

Mike Allen knows what people really want to know about their cars because he makes it his business to find out. As associate automotive editor for *Popular Mechanics* magazine, Allen answers drivers' questions in the "Car Clinic" and "Saturday Mechanic" columns. Tune-ups are a frequent topic of discussion, he reports, often because drivers aren't sure what the term actually means.

"The best rule of thumb is to refer to your vehicle's owner's manual. It will specify how often your car really needs to be serviced," advises Allen. Most vehicles manufactured since the early 1980s require a tune-up only once every 50,000 kilometers.

Actually, there's really no such thing as an old-fashioned tune-up anymore. "Today, it's considered preventive maintenance, and involves changing the spark plugs, air and fuel filters, and PCV valve, and checking engine performance," Allen explains.

Another common misconception that many drivers have is that an oil change is part of a tune-up, but it's actually a separate maintenance service. Don't assume you don't need to get your oil changed because you've had a recent tune-up. Oil should be checked frequently, on a monthly (preferably weekly) basis, and changed every 5,000 kilometers.

HEALTH INSURANCE FOR YOUR CAR

Lisa Christensen is best known as the "lady mechanic" on her popular CJAD radio car show in Montreal. Christensen is a licensed automotive mechanic nationally certified with ASE, and a full-time diagnostic specialist with CarQuest Canada Ltd. Here are a few of her suggestions for keeping your vehicle in healthy driving condition:

■ Check your tire pressure regularly. The contact surface between your tires and the road is about the size of your palm. To help maintain proper handling of your vehicle, check your tire pressure once a month. Check the spare tire, too. It is usually forgotten unless it is needed, and by then it may be too late.

■ Clean your windows—inside and outside—at least once a week. The materials used in the interiors of cars give off fumes. These fumes collect on the windows and cut down on your vision.

■ Install a new set of windshield-wiper blades every six months to ensure good visibility.

■ Use a fuel of the octane level the manufacturer recommends for your vehicle. Cars that require a higher level of octane or diesel will say so. Using a higher level of octane than recommended is a waste of money.

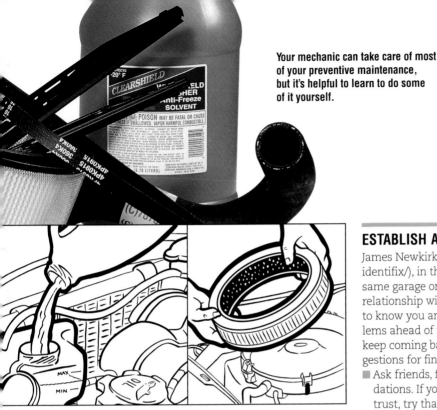

Your mechanic can take care of most of your preventive maintenance, but it's helpful to learn to do some of it yourself.

Smart Moves

Keeping an eye on your antifreeze can prevent an unpleasant surprise mid-winter. Some new vehicles come with antifreeze that lasts five years before it needs changing. Regardless, check the fluid level when you fill the gas tank, and have the solution analyzed before each winter.

Change your coolant at least once a year, or every 30,000 km, whichever comes first. Throughout the year, you can add coolant periodically to maintain a constant level.

Change your filters. Get a new air filter every 30,000 km (more often in very dusty areas), a new fuel filter every time you take your vehicle in for a tune-up, and a new oil filter every time you change the oil.

ESTABLISH A RELATIONSHIP WITH A GARAGE

James Newkirk and Jan Lee of Identifix (www.itan.net/identifix/), in the US, recommend taking your car to the same garage on a regular basis, and establishing a friendly relationship with the mechanics there. This way, they'll get to know you and your car (helping them pick up on problems ahead of time), and want to make you happy so you'll keep coming back. Here are some of Newkirk and Lee's suggestions for finding a good garage with reliable mechanics:

■ Ask friends, family, and coworkers for shop recommendations. If you find a shop that several people like and trust, try that one first.

■ Look for shops with mechanics certified by the National Institute for Automotive Service Excellence (ASE). Certification indicates that the mechanics have passed certain knowledge and performance tests, and were interested enough in their work to pursue certification.

■ Choose a shop that specializes in the areas your car needs the most help with. Find a place that focuses on tune-ups for regular maintenance, but consider specialty shops (like those for brakes or mufflers) when you're looking for expertise in a particular area.

■ Feel free to ask a shop for references. The manager should put you in touch with a couple of customers who can give you testimonials about the quality of service they have received.

■ Check your driver's manual before taking your car into a shop for the first time. If the manual says it's about time to change certain belts, and then the shop recommends changing those belts, you can get the sense that the mechanics know their stuff.

DOING IT YOURSELF

"Modern cars, with their complex systems and computer controls, have limited the extent of do-it-yourself repairs," says Dr. Fran Lockwood, vice president of technology at Valvoline, a consumer products company specializing in automotive products and services. But you can head off future problems with a few routine maintenance procedures:

■ When you flush your radiator or add coolant, use a 50/50 mixture of antifreeze and distilled water, which helps reduce the amount of mineral deposits that form in the engine and radiator.

■ Examine your belts, hoses, radiator cap, and thermostat. Look at the back side of belts for cracks and splits. Hoses are a different story: They rot from the inside out, and a hose that looks perfectly fine on the outside may be ready to burst. If you can reach the hoses, however, you can squeeze them all around to feel for soft spots.

■ Pay attention to smoke from your tailpipe: Some white vapor puffing out when you start the car is normal, but blue smoke while you're driving could mean you're burning oil, black smoke probably means you're using too much gas, and blue-white smoke could mean a blown head gasket.

The Right Way

The owner's manual is your most important tool for keeping your car running efficiently. By taking a careful look at the maintenance calendar, you can stay on top of when you need to take your car in for preventive maintenance procedures, and estimate your costs for each visit. Unfortunately, few people ever do.

If you don't have the car's original manual, request a replacement from the manufacturer or ask your mechanic to access the maintenance schedule for you (usually through a CD-ROM).

It's also smart to follow the "severe driving" maintenance schedule provided in the manual—rather than the normal service schedule—to ensure a long life for your engine.

Troubleshooting

Diagnose problems with your car by knowing what clues to look for.

SURE SIGNS OF TROUBLE

Doug Haviland, division manager of training at the Midas International Corp. (www.midasautosystems. com), suggests keeping an eye out for these warning signs that something could be wrong with your brakes, exhaust, or steering/suspension system:

Brakes: warning lamps on the dashboard, a change in the feel of the brake pedal action (such as the pedal going all the way to the floor when you step on it), and unusual noises, such as grinding, squeaking, or scratching, when you apply the brakes. A red warning lamp on the dashboard or a grinding sound when the brakes are applied warrant immediate attention by a trained technician.

Exhaust: an obvious loud noise, an odor like rotten eggs, any kind of smoke coming from underneath the car, reduced engine per-

formance (indicating a blockage), rattles and vibrations from under the car, or the muffler actually falling off or hanging down—two drastic conditions that need to be repaired as soon as possible.

Steering/Suspension: the car pulling to the left or right while you attempt to drive straight—which can be quite dangerous—any kind of abnormal tire wear, knocks or other noises when the vehicle goes over bumps, a shaking or vibrating steering wheel, and noticeable changes in the ride and handling.

SNIFF OUT THE PROBLEM

If your vehicle isn't running well, you can usually tell. But it's not so easy to determine just what the cause of the problem might be—and it's even harder to accurately explain what's wrong to your mechanic.

Daniel Garrison, an ASE-certified master technician representing ACDelco and GM Parts, says that identifying strange vehicle odors can help you figure out the cause of the problem. Here are some typical odors you may smell in your car, and the problems they commonly indicate. Identify the odors and explain to your technician specifically when they occur, where they come from, and what they smell like.

- A sweet odor, often accompanied by steam under the hood, may indicate a leak in the antifreeze or coolant system.
- A thick, heavy odor, possibly coinciding with smoke from under the hood or exhaust pipe, is a sign of burning oil.
- An acrid odor, like burnt toast, may mean that something in the electrical system has shorted out and fried a wire or other component.
- A continuous, heavy sulfurous odor, like rotten eggs, points to a problem in the emission control system, which might be a malfunctioning catalytic converter.
- A burning rubber odor may be caused by overheated brakes or a slipping clutch.

The Right Way

To diagnose a problem with your vehicle, you have to pay close attention to the details, maintains Eric Gartner, president of AutoTech Software (www.metacog.com), which manufactures AutoTech for Windows 98, 95, and 3.1, software that enables the average person (the non-mechanic) to easily diagnose a wide variety of automotive problems by answering simple yes or no questions.

If you can precisely identify the symptoms, you may be able to identify the problem with your vehicle through a layperson's diagnostic manual or software. "There's a lot you can figure out on your own from your car's smells, sounds, and driving history," says Gartner. Then you'll know what you're talking about when you take the car to a technician, and will have a good idea of how much it might cost to fix.

LIQUID EVIDENCE

Finding fluid on the pavement underneath where you park your car may indicate a problem. Robert Taylor, master certified technician and president of Taylor Automotive Tech-Line (www.4door.com), which offers technical support for auto repair professionals, tells you what different-looking fluids under your car might mean:

A clear, thin liquid leaking toward the front of the passenger side is caused by water condensing on the air conditioner system, which is perfectly normal.

Your radiator may be leaking coolant if you find a sweet-smelling green or orange liquid under the engine compartment or radiator.

Red fluid with a burnt odor may be a leak from your automatic transmission.

■ A hot metallic odor, usually accompanied by the sweet, cloying smell of antifreeze or coolant, is often an indicator that your engine is overheating. White smoke leaking from under the hood may also tip you off. (Check the temperature gauge on your dashboard.)

Smart Moves

If your car starts making strange clinks, clunks, or grinding noises, it's a cry for help. These sounds may indicate a problem:

Boom: A constant bass drum roll or thunder.
Click: Like a camera shutter or a retractable pen.
Clunk: Like a heavy door closing.
Grind: Like sharpening an ax on a grinding wheel.
Growl: Like an angry dog.

Knock: Like the tapping on a door.
Rattle: Like a baby's rattle or a stone in a can.
Roar: A whooshing, waterfall sound.
Rumble: Like a bowling ball rolling down the alley.
Spit: Sizzling like a drop of water on a hot skillet.
Squeak: Like tennis shoes on a wooden floor.
Squeal: Like the high-pitched squeal of a pig.
Whine: Like an electric drill motor.

TERMS OF THE TRADE

Few people actually pay close attention to what's happening with their car while they're driving. It's important, however, to be aware of how your car drives, so that you'll notice any subtle changes that could indicate trouble. That way you may be able to catch something just starting to occur that could otherwise turn into a serious problem.

Watch your dashboard warning lights, and don't ignore small changes in the way your vehicle operates. If your car does some strange things while you're driving, you may have a potentially serious problem. Identifying these symptoms and knowing how to describe them to a mechanic will make it easier to fix your car. If you notice any of the following symptoms, here are the words you can use to describe them. Say:

Brake fade if the stopping distance seems to increase, causing longer braking distance, similar to braking at high speeds. The brake pedal may also feel unresponsive.

Brake pedal pulse if the brake pedal feels like it's pulsing when you apply the brakes.

Detonation if you hear mild to severe pinging that's usually worse under acceleration, and is especially severe when you're going uphill.

Dieseling if the engine continues to run after the ignition switch is turned off, or if the engine runs unevenly and makes knocking noises.

Engine cuts out when there's a temporary, complete loss of power, or the engine quits at sharp, irregular intervals. This may occur regularly or intermittently, but it is usually worse under heavy acceleration.

Hesitation if there's a momentary lack of response when you depress the accelerator. This can occur at all speeds and is usually most severe when you are starting from a complete stop. The condition may also cause the engine to stall.

Pulls/grabs if the vehicle has a tendency to move right or left when you step on the brakes, or the brakes engage suddenly when you apply steady pressure to the brake pedal.

Rough idle if the engine runs unevenly while idling. The car may also shake.

Shimmy if you feel a rapid side-to-side motion from both front wheels in the steering wheel.

Sluggish if the engine delivers limited power under a heavy load or at high speeds, won't accelerate as briskly as it usually does, loses too much speed going up hills, or has less overall speed than normal.

Sounds like popcorn popping if the engine makes sharp, metallic knocks that change as you open the throttle.

Spongy if you experience less-than-anticipated response to increased throttle opening, or little or no increase in speed, when you step on the accelerator.

Surge if the vehicle speeds up and slows down although you aren't changing the pressure on the accelerator pedal. This can occur at any speed.

Sway/pitching if the ride is mushy or spongy, or the vehicle takes a long time to recover from bumps in the road.

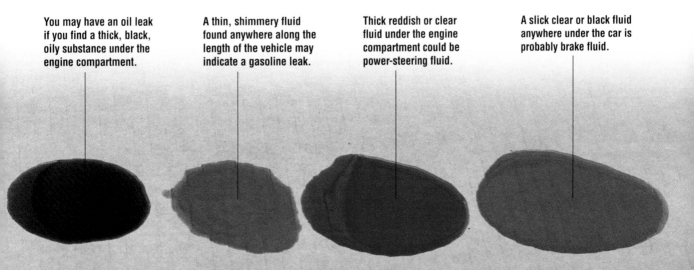

You may have an oil leak if you find a thick, black, oily substance under the engine compartment.

A thin, shimmery fluid found anywhere along the length of the vehicle may indicate a gasoline leak.

Thick reddish or clear fluid under the engine compartment could be power-steering fluid.

A slick clear or black fluid anywhere under the car is probably brake fluid.

At the Mechanic

You can find a trustworthy, capable repair shop.

Myth: *If you have a problem with your mechanic, change repair shops immediately.* **Fact:** *Experts caution that this is not the best way to correct a problem. "It's inadvisable to hop around from technician to technician, just as you wouldn't jump around from doctor to doctor. Instead, go back and politely tell the same technician that your vehicle needs more attention."*

FINDING A TECHNICIAN

Finding a capable technician is the biggest quest of every car owner. "Don't wait until an emergency arises to find a good repair shop," cautions auto repair shop owner Cathy Reichow. Instead, try a new shop whenever you need preventive maintenance. "Be a secret agent," she advises. "Get an oil change and hang around the shop while your car is in the bay." Here are some of Reichow's other tips for finding a reliable technician:

- Determine what's important to you. Do you want the lowest price? Are you willing to pay a bit more for a technician's immediate attention?
- Trust your first impression. How are you greeted? Are the shop and the parking lot clean and neat?
- Make sure you can communicate with the technicians. Are you comfortable with them? Do they treat you with respect and answer your questions?

Quick Tricks

Reichow knows that customers' biggest misgivings concern high labor costs and unwarranted work. While it pays to be picky, consumers should also be aware that proper diagnosis and repair takes time and technical sophistication. Keep the following in mind when rating a shop's performance:

Your old parts should be given back to you automatically. Even if 9 out of 10 people don't want them, technicians should be trained to put old parts in a bag and offer them to you.

Make sure that you get a computerized, itemized bill detailing the labor cost, what was done for each step in the repair process, and an item number for each new part installed.

You should sign a repair order that includes the bottom-line cost before having a technician begin work on your car. On routine repairs, this number can vary by no more than 10 percent.

- Listen to how they treat other customers on the phone. Is that how you want to be treated?
- Observe how they handle people who come back dissatisfied with the work done on their cars.
- Scope out the place. Do they have modern equipment? Are there cars like yours in the parking lot?

HELP AUTO TECHNICIANS HELP YOU

Bob Weber has worked on cars for over 30 years and has held a master technician certification since 1976. These days, he uses his knowledge to answer drivers' questions as a contributor at The Car Connection, www.thecarconnection.com, a consumer website for car buyers, and writes a twice-weekly automotive column called "MotorMouth" for the *Chicago Tribune*.

You can help your mechanic to do good, efficient work, Weber says:
- Be honest and expect honesty back.
- Tell them the whole story, and be specific.
- Be up front about work done by other mechanics.
- Keep records of repairs, especially if you don't always go to the same shop.
- A good mechanic will appreciate a customer who becomes involved in the repair process by asking questions, inspecting the work, and reviewing the itemized bill.

"Consumers need to pay attention to their automobiles, and use their senses to describe what's wrong," Weber advocates. "Make the sound for us. It helps! Mechanics will try to extract the information, and will take a test ride with you, but it is quicker if you take note of the sounds and smells of the problem for them ahead of time."

The Right Way

Cars, like people, sometimes complain about their problems. To help speed up the diagnosis, pay attention to the unhappy noises your car is making, and share them with your technician.
- What does the noise sound like? Does it click, clunk, squeak, grind, or groan?
- When do you hear it? Does it happen while you're starting the car, while the car is idling, only when it is hot or cold, while you're accelerating, or while you're braking?
- What part of the car is the noise coming from? Is it in the front, rear, right, or left?
- Is the noise accompanied by other symptoms? Is there jerking, smoke, burning smells, or vibrating sensations?

CONFIDENCE FOR WOMEN DRIVERS

Cathy Reichow is an Ohio-based automotive repair shop owner and certified parts specialist who's in tune with the challenges women face at the mechanic's. Reichow addresses these concerns as a member of the Woman's Board of the Car Care Council, a non-profit organization that educates consumers about vehicle maintenance. The Council's recent survey shows that 81 percent of women have full responsibility for their car repairs, yet most feel uncomfortable taking their car in for more than regular maintenance. It doesn't have to be that way, asserts Reichow. "The more educated you are, the less likely you'll be taken advantage of. Start by reading your owner's manual, which is full of basic information about the care and maintenance of your vehicle."

ASE CERTIFICATION

Experts agree that one of the basic signs of a good technician is ASE certification. This voluntary credential is administered by the National Institute for Automotive Service Excellence (ASE), an independent, non-profit organization dedicated to improving the quality of automobile repair and maintenance services. Nancy Guzik, director of consumer relations at the US Institute, says, "ASE is the only nationwide certification system for the automotive industry. Currently, about 4,300 working technicians in Canada are ASE-certified." Ask if your auto technician is certified in the specific area in which your vehicle needs work. There are 36 exams in seven specialties, from Engine Machinist to School Bus Technician.

Before automotive workers can take the ASE certification test, they must have had two years of experience. The test is rigorous, and one out of three people fail. In addition, those with ASE credentials must be retested every five years to maintain their certification. "The tests change to keep up with the changing technology," notes Guzik.

To achieve ASE Master Technician status, automobile technicians must pass at least eight comprehensive exams in engine repair, automatic transmission/transaxle, manual drive train and axles, suspension and steering, brakes, electrical/electronic systems, heat and air conditioning, and engine performance.

Look for the ASE Blue Seal of Excellence® in the window of your repair shop. Individual certificates are usually posted in the customer waiting room.

Better Body Work

You have more control than you might realize.

PARTS AND REPAIR SHOP CHOICES

"Body work is the process of restoring a vehicle to pre-accident condition," says Tony Molla, editorial director of *Motor Age* and *Automotive Body Repair News* magazines. "The average person has a collision once every 10 years. Most people let their insurance company handle the body work choices, but the reality is that people have rights they are unaware of."

If your car insurance policy says your vehicle will be restored to pre-loss condition, you need to take responsibility and be fully informed about the repairs involved. That means staying on top of who's making the repairs, what repairs they're making, and what parts they're using.

CHOOSE YOUR PARTS

For replacement parts, there is a choice:
Original Equipment Manufacturer (OEM) parts that have been made by the vehicle's manufacturer. These are the most expensive on the market.
Salvage parts that have come from another car. These less-expensive parts can be the best choice. Be aware that their quality may be suspect.
After-market parts that don't have the original vehicle manufacturer's name on them. The insurance company will usually recommend these to help control costs. But be warned that using after-market parts might decrease the value of your automobile. "If the car is five years old, and is out of warranty, the owner may find it acceptable to use after-market sheet metal. But in a new car, the use of after-market sheet metal may diminish its value," says Tony Molla.

Also, using after-market parts for a repair job on a new car may void some parts of the new-vehicle warranty. And repairing a leased car with parts that are not from the original manufacturer might also be a problem when it's time to turn it in.

CHOOSE YOUR BODY SHOP

When insurance firms give their customers a recommended list of body shops they have prenegotiated prices with, it is called a direct referral plan. Check with your insurance company to find out whether it has such a plan. Even if this is the case, you still have a right to take your car to a shop you know and trust, says Bob Dance, the owner of a body shop in Nepean, Ontario.

PAINTLESS DENT REMOVAL

Back in 1993, Todd Sudeck was working in his driveway trying to repair a dent in his Porsche Speedster. Common sense told him that he could rub the inside of the metal to push out the dent. So he wrapped duct tape around a bent screwdriver and tried out his theory. A neighbor saw what he was doing, and told him that there was a new process that used the same concept.

Sudeck went to a training class to learn the basics of paintless dent removal. Now he is president of The Ding King, headquartered in California. He and his team of technicians have massaged the dents out of more than 1 million cars!

The cost of traditional body work—sanding, filling,

Before

and painting—has never been higher due to environmental concerns, more expensive paint, and rising labor costs. Paintless dent removal costs under $100, and saves both insurance companies and consumers millions of dollars each month. And it requires only a set of tools in different lengths, diameters, and tip styles. Check the Yellow Pages for a paintless dent-removal specialist.

Myth: *Most people think that the amount of their deductible is set in stone.* **Fact:** *The fact is that insurance companies may waive a deductible when paying for a minor repair that will save them money in the long run. For instance, they may cover filling in a chip in a windshield because replacing the whole windshield later would cost over $1,000.*

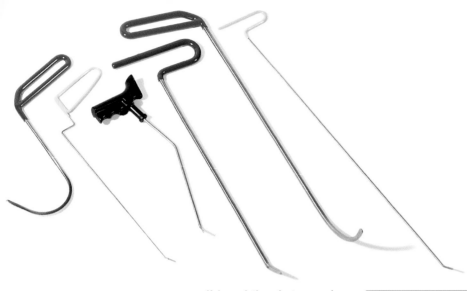

Quick Tricks

Here's how you can tell whether or not a dent is a good candidate for paintless dent removal:

- Dime- or quarter-size dents on the flat, hard body of the car are the best candidates for dent removal.
- Large dents in soft metals can be improved but may leave a bent, wavy pattern on the surface.
- Dents located on edges or corners cannot be removed.
- Large and deep dents can be improved, but not removed.

After

Using paintless dent-removal tools like these, technicians may be able to massage a dent out of your car for significantly less than it would cost to have it repaired in the traditional way.

TAKE RESPONSIBILITY FOR REPAIRS

Bob Dance of Maaco Auto Painting and Bodyworks in Nepean, Ontario, acknowledges that body work can be very expensive. "The average cost for repairing your basic fender bender can range from $1,000 to $1,500," says Dance.

Here are some simple steps to follow in case you should ever become involved in an accident:

- Always be aware of just exactly what your car insurance coverage entitles you to. For example, does your insurance policy entitle you to a replacement car when yours is being repaired?
- Find if there is a direct referral program through which your car insurance

company selects the body shop? If so, how many repair shops are on the list? Are any of these shops located in your immediate vicinity?
- Know what your deductible is.
- Before selecting a repair facility, it is advisable to contact your local Better Business Bureau to find out whether any complaints have been filed against the facility you are considering. If so, get details about the number and nature of those complaints.
- Tell the body shop all of the details of your accident (for example, how it happened, where the car was hit).
- Ask how the repairs will be done. What type of parts will be used? What type of paint? Does the sheet metal have a corrosion problem? Ask the repair shop to put everything that is being done in writing.

SPEAK TO A WORLD-CLASS TECHNICIAN

Toledo, Ohio-based Dan Pietras is the co-host and technical expert for the Consumer Automotive Repair (CAR) Show on radio. He is certified as a World-Class Technician by the National Institute for Automotive Service Excellence (ASE) for his expertise in 32 of 36 of their technical fields. Pietras' advice to people who have been in collisions is to rely on their adjuster. "Your adjuster is your mouthpiece," says Pietras. "Most claim adjusters have been in the repair industry a long time, and know what they're talking about."

One of the most common questions asked on the CAR Show is "Will my car be the same after it is repaired?" Pietras answers, "Yes, 99 percent of the time." Through sophisticated technology and skillful technicians, a vehicle can be repaired to within three millimeters of the original manufacturer's dimensions. However, there is a psychological devaluation because it has been in an accident, says Pietras. People consider it "not right."

BODY SHOP TERMS YOU SHOULD KNOW:

Bob Dance defines the following terms used in body shops around the country, and how they relate to your car:

Totaled. The condition of a car when the cost of repairing it exceeds the value of the car. When a car is referred to as totaled, it is generally beyond repair, or totally wrecked.

Rebuilt title. A "salvage" vehicle that has been repaired and certified as safe for the road. In Ontario, for example, this requires a Structural Inspection Certificate and a Safety Standards Certificate.

Section or clipping. The practice of using the salvageable parts of wrecked cars to repair other damaged cars.

Betterment. Repairing a vehicle to be in better condition than it was. For example, if an insurance company pays to replace a rusted fender with a new one, the owner may be charged a betterment fee.

LKQ—Like Kind and Quality. If you see this on your estimate, it indicates that salvaged parts may have been used, and that these parts were in roughly the same condition as the original parts before they were damaged.

Keeping Your Car Safe

The security you need depends on your vehicle and your location.

Audible alarm system

Tire lock

LAYERED PROTECTION

"Auto theft has become a major social problem which costs Canadians one billion dollars annually," says Terri MacLean, chief operating officer of the Insurance Crime Prevention Bureau (ICPB), a nonprofit organization that has worked to combat vehicle theft and insurance fraud since 1923.

Today's car thieves are not joyriders. They are well-organized criminals who steal cars for profit.

Core Protection: Immobilizing Tools

Prevent thieves from by-passing your ignition and hot-wiring your car by using one of the following:

Smart key: an ignition key that contains specially coded computer chips or radio frequencies. Without the exact key, the vehicle's engine cannot be started.

Kill switch or starter-, ignition-, or fuel-disabler: interrupts the flow of electricity from the battery or fuel to the engine, preventing the car from being started until a hidden switch or button has been activated by the driver.

Layer 1: Common Sense

Whether you are parked in your own garage or running in to pay the gas station attendant, always secure your vehicle. Remove your keys from the ignition, close your windows, and lock your doors. If you're parking on the street, choose well-lit, well-traveled areas.

Layer 2: Visible or Audible Deterrents

Alert thieves that your vehicle is protected. Popular second layer devices include:

Audible alarms: motion or impact sensors that trigger a 120-

decibel siren when tripped.

Steering column collars: devices that prevent thieves from attacking this part of your ignition system.

Steering wheel locks: metal bars designed to prevent someone from turning the steering wheel.

Theft deterrent decals: stickers that warn thieves your vehicle is protected by an alarm or other antitheft device—inexpensive ways to bluff a thief.

Tire locks: similar to the circular steel boots that are often used by city police departments. These prevent your car from being driven.

Window etching: service that etches the vehicle identification number (VIN) onto your car's windshield, making it more difficult for thieves to resell the vehicle or its parts.

Steering wheel lock

A STANDARD FOR THEFT DETERRENTS

The Vehicle Information Centre of Canada (VICC), in conjunction with other interested stakeholders, has formed a coalition that developed the Canadian Standard for Automobile Theft Deterrent Systems, which sets a minimum acceptable level of security for a vehicle.

"Until we developed this standard, consumers had no way of determining the effectiveness of antitheft systems on the market," says Henning Norup, president of VICC.

At the core of the standard is an electronic immobilizer that arms automatically when the vehicle is shut down and prevents it from being started. Extra security devices such as alarms can be layered on. So far, one security system, the Autowatch 329 Ti, has passed the rigorous testing and evaluation process, and received VICC's approval.

In addition, factory-installed theft-deterrent systems by the following vehicle manufacturers on most of the new models have been approved by VICC: Ford, Nissan, Daimler-Chrysler, and Honda.

When shopping for security systems, consumers should look for the VICC approval logo. If a system doesn't sport the logo, consumers should ask the manufacturer why. Approved security systems installed as standard equipment by the vehicle manufacturer will automatically receive a discount through the CLEAR vehicle rating.

APPROVED THEFT DETERRENT SYSTEM

Layer 3: Tracking System

A tracking system is the most effective device for recovering a stolen car. Users purchase a transceiver for an annual fee. Then, if they report their car stolen, the police can broadcast a signal from a radio tower that triggers the transceiver to send out a homing signal to police cars and helicopters. LoJack is the most widespread stolen vehicle recovery system, and the only one that is operated by the police department. "We have a 90-percent recovery rate," says Paul McMahon, the marketing manager for LoJack, "and we find most cars in less than 24 hours—often in less than 2."

Stolen vehicle tracking system

True Stories

Several years ago, Officer Paul Cohen was doing undercover surveillance on a street in New York City when he saw a well-dressed man walk up to a car and open the trunk. Immediately, the car's alarm began sounding. The man took a few bags out of the trunk and walked away, while the alarm continued. Disgusted with the noise pollution, Officer Cohen went up to the man and said, "Excuse me, sir, that's very obnoxious," showing his police identification. Taken by surprise, the man replied, "You got me!" It turned out that he was a thief, and had stolen the bags out of the car. "The moral of the story," says Officer Cohen, "is that no one pays attention to car alarms. If you want protection, get another type of security system, such as a tracking system, or fuel- or ignition-disabler."

DETERMINING YOUR CAR'S SECURITY RISK

Some cars need more protection than others.

Most frequently stolen vehicles manufactured in 1997 and 1998:	Major metropolitan areas with the highest motor vehicle theft rates (1998):
Acura Integra (2 door)	Montreal, QC
Hyundai Tiburon FX (2 door)	Vancouver, BC
Jeep TJ (4WD)	Toronto, ON
Chevrolet Cavalier Z24 (2 door)	Winnipeg, MB
Volkswagen Golf (2 door)	Calgary, AB
Toyota 4Runner (4WD)	Ottawa, ON
Mazda MPV (4WD)	Hamilton, ON
Hyundai Accent (2 door)	Edmonton, AB
Dodge Dakota (4WD)	Quebec City, QC
Honda Civic (2 door)	

DETER AUTO THEFT

Hands-on experience backs up John Galeotafiore's recommendations about auto security: He's been testing anti-theft devices for *Consumer Reports* for the past 10 years. During that time, he's found that many theft deterrents are surprisingly simple to get past, and that they often lead you to think your car is more protected than it actually is. These deterrents include The Club and The Shield, about which he says, "I've sawed completely through a steering wheel and its protective shield in under a minute."

Galeotafiore maintains that professional thieves can find a way to steal any car, no matter what you use to protect it. But there are a few ways to make it harder for professionals and far less attractive to the novice thief:

- Get a security system that has passive arming. Active arming is when you set the alarm with your remote control every time you leave the car. Passive arming is when the system arms itself. "Every time you leave the car, even if you are running into a store for a few minutes, you want your alarm to go on automatically," Galeotafiore explains.
- Have your alarm system installed by an industry professional. "The install-it-yourself options tend to malfunction or be more complicated to operate than the average driver expects," Galeotafiore explains.
- Get a system that disables the engine as well as setting off an alarm. If they can't start the car immediately, most thieves will move on to another vehicle.

WHAT'S IN A VIN?

Every vehicle has a unique 17-digit Vehicle Identification Number (VIN) that police can use to help determine whether it's been stolen. The VIN will appear on the owner's registration, on the dashboard, and in

other locations on the car. "The VIN is like a car's DNA," says Ron Giblin of the Insurance Crime Prevention Bureau. "It gives information about the car's model, when and where it was assembled, and links it to its registered owner."

Police can often tell if a car has been stolen if its VIN is missing, has been visibly tampered with, or doesn't conform to the numerical formula prescribed by the automobile manufacturer.

Police recommend you print your name, address, and VIN on the inside of your car manual, as well as on a business card, which you should slide behind the dashboard. If your car is stolen for its parts, tagged for resale, or recovered in a chop shop, these clues will help the police connect the car to you.

Driving with Children

Preparation leads to safety and sanity.

CAR SEATS SAVE LIVES

France Legault is an engineer with Motor Vehicle Safety and Road Regulation for Transport Canada. Along with her other work, Legault fields questions about car seats. The number-one question she is asked is which car seat is the safest. Legault tells people the safest seats are the ones you use all the time, according to the manufacturer's instructions, for the longest time. The seat doesn't have to be permanently installed in the car; however, it must be properly installed. All seats sold in Canada are required to meet federal government standards. Look for the label bearing the maple leaf icon and the letters CMVSS (Canada Motor Vehicle Safety Standards).

"Child safety seats, when properly installed, can reduce the risk of death by 90 percent for children of all ages and reduce the risk of injuries by 70 percent," cites Legault. The following guidelines can help you determine which device is the most appropriate for your child:

Infant seats (Stage 1) should be used until your child is one year old. Some guidelines suggest a weight of 22 pounds as the upper limit for infant seats. Unless your child is very large for her age, stick with the infant seat until age one. Infant seats should be used in the back seat of the car, buckled securely with the car seat belt. Never place a rear-facing car seat in the front seat of a vehicle, whether it has a passenger-side air bag or not.

Convertible seats (infant-child seats and child booster seats) are safe as long as they are installed properly and used according to manufacturers' instructions.

Forward-facing child seats (Stage 2) should be used until a child is 4½ years old. Some guidelines suggest 40

Infants under one year must ride in a rear-facing car seat that meets Canada Motor Vehicle Safety Standards. These seats have shoulder harnesses that you must adjust to fit the baby snugly, without gaps.

pounds as the upper weight limit, but Legault believes the child's age is a better guide. Also called "toddler seats," these front-facing seats should be secured firmly to the car by the car seat belt and the top tether strap. If your vehicle doesn't have a tether strap anchor (on the shelf behind the seat, on the floor, or on the seat frame), have an anchor installed. Proper installation and use are vital. Harness straps should be adjusted to fit snugly according to what a child is wearing.

Booster seats (Stage 3) ease the transition from Stage 2 child seats to adult seat belts. They are for children between the ages of 4½ and 8. Boosters are used with car lap and shoulder belts. Adjust the seat belt low and snugly over your child's hips, not across the abdomen. Never slip the shoulder belt behind the child or under the child's arm.

The Right Way

"Only a third of car seats are properly installed. Two out of three seats are misused in some way," says Legault. Not all car seats fit all vehicles well. Follow both the car seat instructions and your vehicle owner's manual to install your car seat correctly. Here are some common mistakes:

Not buckled in tightly enough. Cinch the seat belt so that the seat does not move more than one inch side-to-side or back to front.

Harness straps too loose around the child. Make sure you can get a good, snug fit. After buckling your child into the seat, you should be able to fit no more than one finger between the child and the harness strap. Adjust the straps according to what the child is wearing. This is a consideration when you are buying the seat. For more advice, contact Transport Canada's hotline at 1-800-333-0371.

Seat belts. All children over age 8 should use the car's lap and shoulder belts as intended. The lap belt should be fastened snugly over the hips. Never let a child slip out of the shoulder belt. Legault recommends that children ride properly restrained in the back seat of the car until they are 13.

SECONDHAND CAR SEATS

"A used car seat is certainly better than no car seat, but it's only a good deal if the seat is a recent model and has never been in a crash," says Dr. Jill Courtemanche, a pediatrician who also works with the Eastern Ontario Car Seat Coalition. She offers these suggestions for parents interested in buying a used car seat:

- Buy from the original owner or a reputable source who can vouch for the seat and can assure you it has never been in an accident. If it has been in a crash or has been damaged, or if you don't know, don't buy it.
- Buy from a consignment shop where the staff has been trained to inspect and install car seats. A shop that specializes in car seats may be able to give you a waiver that the seat has never been in a crash. They also have a list of car seats that have been recalled by the manufacturers.
- Contact your local public health office or children's hospital to find out if your region has a car seat coalition, consignment shop, or loan program.
- Once your child has out-

grown it, pass along your gently used car seat to a consignment shop or maternity hospital so that someone else can use it.
- Call the manufacturer for a copy of the instructions for your specific model.

AIR BAG SAFETY

"Automobile crashes are the leading cause of death among children," says Janet Dewey. As executive director of the Air Bag & Seat Belt Safety Campaign in the US, Dewey is charged with making sure the public knows how to keep children safe while traveling in motor vehicles, particularly those with air bags. "Air bags can save an adult's life, but can also pose serious risks to children," maintains Dewey. "It is critical that children 12 and under ride properly restrained in the back seat. Infants, in particular, should never, ever ride in the front seat of a car that has a passenger-side air bag."

Should you consider an on/off switch? Medical experts agree that most families are better off without a switch if everyone wears a seat belt and all children 12 and under are able to ride in the back seat. On/off switches are essential, however, if a child must ride in front—if you have an infant who must be in the front seat for constant medical monitoring, for example, or you must regularly transport more children than you can buckle up in the back seat.

The bottom line, whether your car has air bags or not, the back seat is always the safest place for kids to ride.

BEST PRODUCTS FOR CHILDREN IN CARS

Karen Scott is the president of the One Step Ahead catalog, headquartered in Illinois. Her product selection has earned the catalog the Parent's Choice award three years running. "We pick through literally thousands of products, and only feature the best ones," says Scott. Here are some of her favorite products for use in the car:

Hindsight safety mirror. Allows the driver to see baby's face in the rearview mirror while using a rear-facing infant seat. The mirror, decorated as the face of a happy bear, attaches to the car's back seat.

Inflat-o-potty. Lets children who are being toilet trained stop anytime to use it. You can keep it in the trunk, and it uses standard-sized kitchen garbage bags.

Buckle alert. Signals to the driver when a car seat's buckle has been undone by small hands.

PARENTS' ADVICE FOR CAR TRIPS

Ruth Natzel has logged over 1 million miles driving with children: first in the back seat with her five younger siblings, and now in the front seat driving her own three children to weekly sports practice. Here's some advice from Natzel and other parents to help make long car trips more enjoyable:

- Get together several children's atlases. Your children can learn map-reading skill as they follow the roads you are driving on. They can also

help plan the vacation as they gather information about each region, points of historical interest, and provincial capitals.
- Plan picnic stops to take advantage of scenic parks or rest areas along your route. Although it may be tempting to let your children eat or drink in the car, France Legault recommends against it: "There is too great a danger of small children choking."
- Bring along tapes and CDs of your children's favorite music for sing-alongs. It's a wonderful way to pass the time.

Quick Tricks

Try out one of these perennial car game favorites:

The license plate game. Look for a license plate from every province in the country. Also, look for as many US state license plates as you can find.

The alphabet game. Find the letters of the alphabet, in order, on signs and license plates.

Buckle, buckle. Kids try to find an imaginary coin hidden in the car, asking questions and getting hints from you (or another child) about whether they're hot or cold.

Car Insurance Assurance

Understand what you're paying for.

ANATOMY OF AN INSURANCE POLICY

According to Mark Yakabuvski, president of the Insurance Bureau of Canada, people need to change their outlook on car insurance. Drivers should think about what they're buying and why, Yakabuvski maintains. Car insurance is protection against financial destruction, either due to a lawsuit or serious damage to self. When you think of it as insuring the well-being of yourself, your home, and your family—and not your car—it's a little easier to swallow the annual payments (and to be glad to never have to collect).

Here's Yakabuvski's specific advice on how to get the best coverage:

- Take a collision and comprehensive deductible of no less than $500. This is the simplest way to protect yourself against paying too much in annual payments. Almost everyone should be able to come up with $500 in case of an accident. And those who budget and plan well might want to raise their deductible as high as $1,000.
- Shop around. What you're trying to do is find the companies that are competing for your business—and they're not the same for every driver. Companies try to find their niche among the competition in the insurance market, and you want to find those that cater to drivers like you. These could be major national brand names or small, local companies.
- Learn about discounts. Most people know that if you get your homeowner's and car insurance from the same company, you can usually get a discount. Also look into defensive driving courses, alarm systems, antilock brakes, dual air bags, and other safety features. Ask about what discounts you might qualify for because the agent may overlook a discount that could be to your advantage.
- When your car is six years old or older, consider dropping your collision insurance completely. But be sure you're in a position to take on the risk of repairing or replacing your vehicle. Discuss this with your insurance representative. Comprehensive coverage should be maintained however.
- Write down the coverage you want and start calling around. Speak with at least two representatives. Ask them, "What is the best you can do for me?"
- Contact the Insurance Bureau of Canada for their brochure *Automobile Insurance in Canada*, which describes the automobile insurance situation in each province and territory. Phone toll-free at 1-800-387-2880. or visit their website (www.ibc.ca).

RENTAL CAR INSURANCE

Most drivers are responsible when it comes to buying adequate insurance for their own cars, but some may be negligent about insurance for their rental car. "There are three ways to obtain insurance for your rental car," says Doug Mayhew, manager, public relations for the Canadian Automobile Association (CAA) in North and East Ontario. "You can purchase insurance from the car rental firm. This is the most expensive option. Your credit card may provide insurance for a rental car. Or you may have an endorsement under your own insurance policy that provides additional coverage for rental vehicles." To save money and to protect yourself, Mayhew advises: find out what coverage you may already have, for example with your credit card, but make 100 percent certain that you have the coverage you need.

PROTECT YOURSELF

Cheryl Randle, president of Montreal- and Kingston-based Randle Insurance Agencies Inc., explains that it's much easier to depend on your own insurance in case of personal injury than to risk the time and money it would take to sue someone. It's also important to make sure you're fully covered in the event that someone else sues you—especially if you have significant assets to protect. "The first step is to look on the declaration page of your automobile insurance policy to determine how much coverage you cur-

Call several insurance representatives. Ask them, "What is the best you can do for me?"

WHO PAYS MORE? WHO PAYS LESS?

Certain types of drivers are considered high-risk by insurance companies, and consequently pay higher-than-average premiums, says Mark Yakabuvski. For others, there are ways to cash in on discounts. Check out the information below to see if you fall into one of these groups:

■ Owners of cars that are popular with thieves or have expensive replacement parts generally have to pay higher premiums to cover losses.

■ People who live or commute in densely populated metropolitan areas tend to pay more for their auto insurance because they have a greater chance of being in an accident or having their car stolen than comparable drivers who live in rural areas.

■ Drivers with moving violations or several accidents on their record generally pay more for insurance because they statistically pose a greater risk of loss.

■ Males under 25 years pay more for their insurance policies because they are more at risk of being involved in serious accidents.

■ Some companies give discounts to anyone who takes a defensive driving course. Some provinces require these for teenagers, learners, and drivers 70 years and over. Talk to your representative.

■ If you have not been involved in a moving violation or a driving accident in the past two to five years you may qualify for a discount.

■ You may qualify for an age discount once you reach 40.

■ Insurance companies may give discounts if you insure several vehicles with them. You may also qualify for a discount if you consolidate all your insurance policies (for example, life, home, and automobile insurance) with one carrier.

■ Discounts may be available if you have your vehicle equipped with safety devices. These could be antilock brakes and antitheft systems.

rently have," Randle says.

To be fully covered, you may need more. In Canada, there is universal coverage for damages caused by an uninsured automobile driver, the coverage provides up to $200,000. This is protection in the event you or your family members are injured in a crash caused by someone with no insurance or minimal insurance.

You may wish to purchase additional coverage of this type on your own insurance policy. Some insurance representatives recommend a Family protection endorsement that matches your own liability limits. When you can't recover full damages for bodily injuries, this protection covers the difference between your claim and the noninsured driver's liability. The coverage only applies to you, your spouse, and any dependent relatives you have.

Basic compulsory coverages may not be adequate if you were held responsible for a collision which caused serious injuries to other people. The minimum coverages are $50,000 in Quebec for Civil Liability and $200,000 in other provinces and territories for Third Party Liability. Insurance representatives usually recommend more than the minimum coverage.

THE CLEAR SYSTEM

More and more, insurance companies are using the CLEAR system (Canadian Loss Experience Automobile Rating), rather than the manufacturer's suggested retail price, to calculate the cost of insurance, says Henning Norup, president and chief operating officer of the Vehicle Information Centre of Canada (www.vicc.com). The CLEAR system rates each vehicle model according to its road performance and claims history. As a result, car safety features, such as air bags, antilock brakes, and antitheft devices may translate into lower premiums for car owners because these devices help curb insurers' claim costs. Other rating factors, such as your driving record or where you live are not affected by CLEAR. The CLEAR system is also estab-

lishing separate vehicle ratings for collision, comprehensive and personal injury. This means that if a particular vehicle make and model is costly to repair following the collision, the rating for collision is affected but not the other parts of the policy.

Before CLEAR was introduced, insurers simply paid the collision repair costs and passed them on to every one in the policy holder's rate class, calculated based on the manufacturer's suggested retail price.

With the CLEAR system, motorists with safer vehicles that are less expensive to insure do not subsidize those with higher loss costs. "CLEAR rewards consumers for buying cars that are less likely to incur losses," says Norup. It also helps encourage automakers to build vehicles that are safer, less damage-prone, and more theft-resistant.

"How Cars Measure Up is a tool for consumers to use before they actually go out and buy a car," says Norup. With this pamphlet, you can check how one model's insurance claim record compares to another. For a copy, call 1-800-761-6703 or visit VICC's website.

Quick Tricks

Cheryl Randle says, "It's certainly worth doing a few extra minutes of research to find the best automobile insurance deal." Here are some tips:

As an insurance broker, Randle always looks at four or five insurance carriers for each customer. Then she gives quotes from the three best carriers.

You may benefit from a special group rate. Randle provides group rates to Chamber of Commerce or Automobile Protection Association members.

Reassess your insurance policy every year when it comes up for renewal. It's also a good idea to reassess your policy whenever you have a major lifestyle change, such as a marriage.

After a Collision

Know the steps to follow in case you are involved in an accident.

HELP IS ON ITS WAY

After a collision, the first officer on the scene is responsible for the site, unless there is a catastrophe such as a toxic chemical spill, where the appropriate environmental authorities take charge.

The first priority is to attend to the living, says Jim Plumb of the Ottawa-Carleton Regional Police, Traffic Unit. This involves clearing a path to get ambulances and other official vehicles to the scene. The officer in charge will assess the situation and order more assistance, such as helicopters to airlift victims to the hospital, if needed. The officer will direct traffic around the collision to reduce any chance that more vehicles will become involved.

Other members of the emergency team are paramedics and firefighters. Paramedics prepare any patients who have to be moved and, if needed, provide emergency treatment, such as administering drugs or applying defibrillators to treat cardiac arrest. Firefighters are brought in to prevent fires, and make certain vehicles are secure. They may also be called on to extricate victims from vehicles.

Once the emergency medical needs of the victims have been attended to, the officer in charge conducts interviews with victims and witnesses and writes up collision report.

Smart Moves

- Carry the following in your car in case of emergencies: flares, blanket, medical kit, and flashlight.
- If your car is on fire, get out and away. Don't try to put the fire out. And if the fire is under the hood, leave the hood closed.
- If you're involved in an collision, pull your vehicle over to the right-hand shoulder if possible.
- If you are injured in an collision, don't try to move. Don't assume you are not hurt even if you don't feel any pain right away.
- When you drive past an collision scene, don't stare. Help keep the traffic moving so you don't cause another accident.

STEPS TO FOLLOW AFTER AN ACCIDENT

The Canadian Automobile Association (CAA) has chapters across the country with more than 4 million members. They respond to over a million calls for emergency service a year. Based on those calls, Douglas Mayhew, manager of public relations, CAA North and East Ontario, offers this list of some basic things to do if you're in a collision:

- Stay calm and attend to anyone who may be injured.
- If anyone is injured or killed, notify the police immediately. Make sure an ambulance or rescue squad has been called to the scene.
- When it does not conflict with provincial law and is safe to do so, move your car off the road. Protect the collision scene with reflectors or flares, but be alert for leaking fuel. Protect yourself and others from oncoming traffic.
- Do not argue, admit liability, or disclose the limits of your insurance coverage.
- Record the license plate numbers of any other vehicles that are involved.
- Get the names and addresses of drivers and passengers in the other vehicle, and those of witnesses, too.
- Notify your insurance company as soon as possible following the accident to be sure you're covered.
- Remember that most provinces require that an accident be reported to the appropriate authorities on the proper form unless the accident is a minor one.
- When you call the police, ask if there is an alternative reporting method. Many cities have special offices where you and the other driver can go to report the collision.

CONSULTING A LAWYER

Howard Yegendorf is a trial lawyer with Yegendorf, Brazeau, Seller, Prehogan and Wyllie in Ottawa. He represents people who have been hurt in accidents and are suing for personal injury.

"Personal injury law is not well understood," says

Quick Tricks

If you're looking for a personal injury lawyer, ask your real estate or family lawyer for a recommendation. You can also:

■ Call the local bar association and ask for a referral to a personal injury lawyer.

■ Look in the telephone book to see who practices personal injury law. Then find out what you can about the lawyer you select. Talk to other lawyers. What are the strengths and weaknesses of the lawyer you're considering? Be certain that you are comfortable with your lawyer. If not, find a new lawyer.

Yegendorf. "In Canada, the insurance programs vary from province to province, so it's important to get legal advice. Yegendorf suggests that you contact a personal injury lawyer if:

■ The other driver's insurance company asks you to give a statement or sign any releases.

■ You experience pain and suffering as a result of a collision. Most injuries are painful soften tissue problems. Whiplash, for instance, only reveals itself days, weeks or even months after the collision, Yegendorf says.

■ Under Ontario's no-fault system, your own insurance company pays for medical benefits, rehabilitation, loss of income up to a maximum limit, and certain other expenses. In most cases, you cannot sue for damages from pain and suffering and loss of income above the limit. The exception is when you can prove you've suffered a"threshold injury," which the law defines as a "permanent and serious injury." This may be an obviously catastrophic injury, or an injury which has permanent and serious consequences for you. Consult a lawyer for advice. You have two years to begin legal action.

■ You can sue for pain and suffering in all other provinces except Saskatchewan and Manitoba.

■ In Quebec's no-fault system, accident benefits for bodily injury are covered by a public plan run by the Société de l'assurance automobile du Québec (SAAQ), which covers all Quebec residents, as well as nonresidents to the extent that they were not at fault. You may need to consult a personal injury lawyer in Quebec should you wish to contest the amount of the benefit awarded by the SAAQ.

THE POLICE REPORT

"Our role is to be there to take down the facts, to be investigators," says Constable Jim Plumb, about police officers present at the scene of an accident. Plumb says in his 29 years on the force he has seen everything, and many things he wishes he hadn't seen. His advice to all drivers: Avoid collisions.

Any time there is a collision that involves personal injury or property damage amounting to more than $1,000, the police must be contacted to see if a criminal or provincial law has been broken," Plumb says.

The police report about the collision is sent to the Ministry of Transportation. The report should provide an accurate picture of how the collision happened. The insurance company must request a copy of the report from the Ministry.

Constable Plumb cautions motorists involved in a collision: "Information is a useful tool. Be prepared for anything. Keep accurate records while your memory is still fresh." Plumb suggests that people involved take photo of their cars as soon after the accident as possible, before the vehicles have been fixed. It is also extremely useful to record or to take photos of anything they feel may have contributed to the collision, such as road barriers or bad weather conditions.

Tools of the Trade

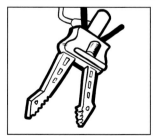

Jaws of Life
Hydraulic rescue tool used to pry metal apart, frequently used to remove a vehicle's doors to free a person inside.

Power ram
Works with a spreader rescue tool to separate and support, or hold apart, heavy pieces of a crushed vehicle.

Belt cutters
Strong tool used to cut through seat belts or other restraints preventing trapped victims from being safely removed.

Air bag
Strong inflatable bag, made out of bulletproof Kevlar, that fills instantly with compressed air to lift heavy objects.

Polish Your Driving Skills

Classes are the best way to become a better, safer driver.

SAFE DRIVERS KEEP CURRENT

Raynald Marchand, manager of Traffic Safety and Training, Canada Safety Council (CSC) in Ottawa, is committed to reducing the terrible cost of traffic injuries and fatalities. He feels one of the best ways to improve the situation is through the Defensive Driving Course (DDC), a six-hour program that teaches drivers how to stay collision-free. The Canada Safety Council sets the curriculum for the DDC and makes certain it reflects current traffic laws and conditions.

"We know that the problem is not that drivers are ignorant of the rules of the road," says Marchand. "Drivers have collisions because they are too aggressive behind the wheel, and they don't know how to drive defensively."

In 1997 alone, there were 2,927 fatalities as a result of collisions. In the same year, there were 217,614 injuries. But when you count all the fender benders and parking lot collisions, there were about 750,000 collisions. "The most dangerous thing you do in a day is get into your car and drive to work," says Marchand.

To save lives and lower the number of collisions, Marchand recommends drivers take a DDC every three to five years. It's the only forum for serious discussion about driving attitudes and behaviors, he says. Other facts worth noting about the Defensive Driving Course are:

- Insurance companies may give discounts to drivers who have followed a DDC.
- The Ministry of Transport of Alberta recognizes the DDC and rebates up to three demerit points to drivers who take the course.
- In Nova Scotia, new drivers, through the graduated license system, are required to take a DDC.
- Some companies, courier services for example, make DDCs mandatory for all their drivers.
- In some cases, companies also make a DDC available to their employees and families as a company benefit.

The CSC also writes curricula for motorcycle, all-terrain vehicle, and snowmobile drivers. In fact, the CSC figures that 85 percent of all licensed motorcycle drivers have taken their course. For more information about these courses and other issues affecting the safety of Canadians, visit www.safety-council.org.

Smart Moves

- Drive with your headlights on at all times to make it easier to see you.
- Use two-way left-turn lanes only when you are going to make a turn.
- If you doubt you can pass and make a right-hand turn in front of a bicycle, slow down and pull in behind the cyclist. Then complete your turn after he or she passes the corner.
- When merging onto a highway, use the entire length of the on-ramp to accelerate up to the speed of traffic.
- Stop to let pedestrians cross the street at all crosswalks and intersections.

SAFETY RULES FOR TEENAGE DRIVERS

When Peter Christianson, president of Young Drivers of Canada, was only three years old, his life changed. "We hit a patch of ice, lost control, and slammed into an oncoming bus. My father, a young surgeon, reached over and pushed me down onto the floor of the car. He was thrown out the door and died instantly."

At 16, Christianson, afraid of driving, practiced for over a year before attempting his test. As he gained confidence, he went on to race cars.

"While I was apparently risking my life on the racetrack, five of my friends were killed on the road. None of these crashes needed to happen," says Christianson.

Twenty-five years ago he began to develop a program, Young Drivers of Canada, to teach specific defensive driving techniques to help people avoid all types of collisions. "We are also committed to improving driver licensing and testing standards," says Christianson.

Here are some recommendations for young drivers and their codrivers:

- Enroll your teenager in a reputable driver training course. "The best advice for parents is to start your new driver as soon as they are eligible," says Christianson.
- "Parents need to know how to codrive with their children," he adds. For anyone planning to assist

THE THREE-SECOND RULE

It's important to be far enough away from the driver in front of you that you could stop safely in an emergency. If it's dark or you're having difficulty gauging the distance, try using the three-second rule: Select a stationary object in front of both you and the other driver. When the other driver passes the object, start counting slowly. You should be able to count to at least three by the time your own car passes the same object.

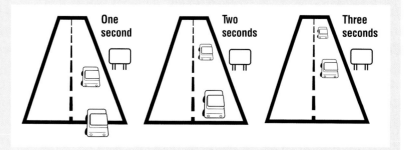

One second | Two seconds | Three seconds

a new driver, Young Drivers offers a free Co-Driver Program to help understand modern defensive driving techniques.

- Codrivers should gradually introduce new drivers to the risks of night driving, highway driving, and the peer pressure created by additional passengers. "Driving experience is a major key to reducing collisions," says Christianson. Supervised training practice with a codriver in cooperation with an approved driver training program will create proper driving habits in the new driver.
- Practice with your new driver for 2,000 kilometers before attempting the first test. Parents in British Columbia must sign that they and the driving school have provided at least 30 hours of supervised driving.

ADJUST YOUR ATTITUDE

As a driving safety instructor for 11 years, Randall Coleman has helped thousands of people change their bad driving habits. His unique focus is on attitude adjustment, and how it has an effect on your driving.

Coleman's number-one driving tip is to make sure that you take a few minutes to unwind before leaving work so you don't bring work-related stress into the car with you. "Once you are behind the wheel, you have the same attitude you had at work, but now you're operating a powerful, 9,000-kilogram machine."

People average about 200 driving violations before they are stopped by a police officer, says Coleman. Because of this, drivers tend to be complacent, which perpetuates bad habits. In an effort to reverse this dangerous inattention, Coleman teaches drivers to watch out for road conditions, weather, and the behavior of other drivers. And he teaches the following defensive-driving habits:

- Check for blind spots. You can't see these areas to the right and left of your vehicle in your rear-view mirror. Turn your head and take a quick look back. Remember that other drivers have blind spots, too.
- Watch for oncoming traffic by remembering your **four R's**: **Read** the road ahead. Stay to the **Right** when you drive. **Reduce** your speed, and **Ride** off the road if necessary to avoid any potentially dangerous situations.

TIPS AND TECHNIQUES FOR OLDER MOTORISTS

There are more than 4 million drivers aged 55 and over in Canada. The Canada Safety Council sponsors the 55-Alive Program for mature drivers who wish to refresh their skills. Although the course is voluntary, some provinces let mature drivers "redeem" driving demerit points after completing the course, and some insurance companies may give discounts.

As drivers age, their natural abilities to respond in a timely manner to traffic situations decrease due to dimmer vision, impaired hearing, and slower reflexes. Research has revealed some common problems for older drivers: failure to yield right of way, improper left turns, and entering and leaving expressways improperly.

Here are some basic tips and techniques that older drivers should observe to protect their own and other people's safety:

- Make sure you've had a recent vision examination. Keep a pair of sunglasses in the car all year long.
- Give your eyes time to adjust when driving at night.
- Do flexibility exercises so that you can turn and look over your shoulder, not just depend on your rear-view mirrors.
- Roll down windows to hear outside traffic noises, and turn down the radio.
- Scan for hazards, such as stalled cars. Keep looking about 500 meters ahead of your position. Drive cautiously.
- Avoid areas of high traffic when possible.
- Don't drive when tired or upset.

WHAT YOU CAN'T SEE CAN HURT YOU

A quick look can compensate for your mirrors' blind spots at the left and right of the back of your car.

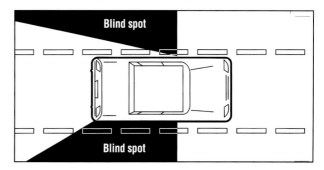

Blind spot

Blind spot

When the Driving Gets Tough

Learning new techniques can make you a better driver in tricky situations.

DEALING WITH AGGRESSIVE DRIVING

Paul Boase is a psychologist and chief, Roads Users, Motor Safety and Regulations at Transport Canada. Boase defines aggressive driving as a basic behavior that becomes habitual and endangers other traffic and other people. Some examples of aggressive driving include: speeding in excess of the posted limits, weaving in and out of traffic, or driving in a way that is inappropriate for the conditions, such as speeding during a blizzard or in heavy fog. Such behavior can lead to violent incidents, sometimes called road rage, and collisions. Aggressive driving consists of three stages:

1. The Zone of Impatience and Rushing includes behaviors such as driving over the speed limit, failing to signal, making illegal turns, running red lights, and swearing at other drivers.

2. The Zone of Hostility includes yelling, honking, making insulting gestures, tailgating, and blocking the passing lane. Between 30 and 50 percent of drivers admit to sometimes expressing anger in this way.

3. The Zone of Road Rage includes braking suddenly in front of a tailgater, cutting off drivers, chasing, fighting, using your car as a weapon, and even shooting.

Boase recommends the following strategies to control any aggressiveness you may feel while driving:

■ Do some advanced planning. Be sensitive to the traffic situation. If you are driving during rush hour, don't weave, speed, or tailgate.

■ Practice time management. If you have a 20-minute car journey, don't leave the house 15 minutes before you have to be somewhere and expect to make up the five minutes on the road.

■ Leave ample time to get to your destination. Be sensitive to the weather and traffic conditions. Know where you're going. Get clear instructions or use a map.

■ Never retaliate when others drive badly. Give a short, judicious blast on your horn if another car endangers you. Don't use your horn aggressively.

■ If you're being followed or tailgated, don't stop and get out of your car. Drive to the nearest police station or public place, such as a mall.

Myth: *You should keep a two-second cushion between you and the driver in front of you.* **Fact:** *"Anyone within three seconds of your vehicle is in your strike zone," says Ken Coffin. "This blows out the two-second rule."*

TAKING HEAVY TRAFFIC BY THE HORNS

"People pay no attention to driving, and yet there isn't any single thing you do each day more likely to affect your future," asserts Ken Coffin, co-owner of the Seattle-based Defensive Driving School, Inc. In Canada, the Canada Safety Council and other organizations offer defensive driving courses, which also teach measures that drivers can take to reduce the risk of collisions.

Coffin uses fine-tuned teaching techniques to help new drivers—as well as those with two to five more years experience under their belts—learn to make good decisions. Here are some of Coffin's methods for defending yourself in heavy traffic:

1. Secure space early. Your goal is to establish a comfort zone around your car, so that there is a good distance between you and the cars both in front of and behind you. It's harder to have an accident when there are no other cars around you.

2. Maintain a safe speed for current driving conditions. That means keeping up with the speed of traffic.

3. Pace pockets, not traffic. Coffin says 75 percent of drivers follow a herd mentality, merely following along with their eyes fixed on the bumper of the car ahead of them. Instead, try to get away from the herd, either by moving ahead or dropping back. When you've found a pocket, you should have a wave of intensity ahead of you, and a herd of cars behind.

> **You can maintain a comfortable pocket of space around your car and increase your safety by letting reckless drivers pass you by, and avoiding the herd mentality by staying aware of the other cars on the road.**

4. Pass me, you're bear bait. If the herd of cars behind you becomes restless, it's usually because of bear bait: speeding, reckless drivers who weave in and out among the rest of the cars. The best thing you can do with bear bait is to get them to pass you. Once they're gone, the herd should stabilize again. You can encourage bear bait to pass by speeding up 3 km/h, holding that speed for a few moments, and then dropping back 3 km/h. The bear bait should fly right past you.

5. Keep working the herd. Your goal is to maintain an expanding pocket around your vehicle. If you pay attention and maintain a good rapport with the herd behind you (keeping a smooth pace and reacting to obstacles ahead of time), they won't challenge you for your position.

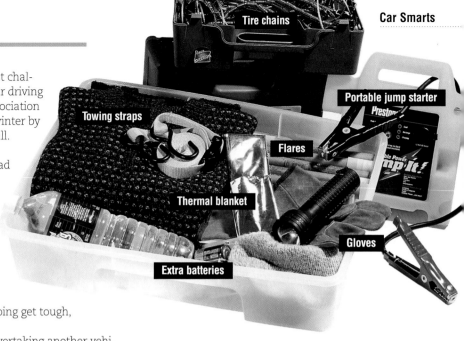

Tire chains

Portable jump starter

Towing straps

Flares

Thermal blanket

Gloves

Extra batteries

WINTER DRIVING TIPS

Winter weather presents the greatest challenge to your car, its engine, and your driving skills. The Canadian Automobile Association (CAA) advises that you prepare for winter by getting a complete checkup in the fall. Heed Environment Canada weather warnings. If you still must drive in bad weather, the CAA offers this advice:

■ Plan ahead and make sure you have enough fuel. Clear snow from the hood, roof, windows and lights. Clear windows of fog. If visibility becomes poor, find a place to safely pull off the road.

■ Let someone know your route and intended arrival time. If the going get tough, turn back or seek refuge.

■ Try to keep to main roads. Avoid overtaking another vehicle when roads are bad. Measure your speed.

■ Wear warm clothes that don't restrict movement.

■ Buckle up at all times. Properly secure small children in child restraints.

■ Tune your radio to a local station for weather advice.

Emergency Kit
You should keep emergency supplies in your car at all times, but especially in winter, when jumper cables, gloves, or an extra sweater can be a real lifesaver.

DRIVING AT NIGHT

Traffic death rates are higher at night than during the day, according to Transport Canada. Yet many of us are unaware of night driving's special hazards, or don't know effective ways to deal with them.

Why is night driving so dangerous? One obvious answer is darkness. Ninety percent of a driver's reaction depends on vision, and vision is severely limited at night. Depth perception, color recognition, and peripheral vision are all compromised after sundown. Night drivers are also more likely to be affected by fatigue and alcohol.

Here's how to prepare your car for night driving:

■ Clean your headlights, taillights, signal lights, mirrors, and windows once a week, and more often if necessary.

■ Aim your headlights properly. Misaimed headlights blind other drivers and reduce your ability to see the road.

■ If there is any doubt, turn your headlights on. Lights will not help you see better in early evening, but they make it easier for other drivers to see you. Being seen is as important as seeing.

■ Reduce your speed and increase your following distance. It is more difficult to judge speeds and distance at night.

■ Don't overdrive your headlights. You should be able to stop inside the illuminated area. If you can't, you are creating a dangerous blind crash area in front of your vehicle.

■ If an oncoming vehicle doesn't lower its beams from high to low, it can temporarily blind you. Avoid glare by watching the right edge of the road and using it as a guide.

Quick Tricks

Long-distance truck drivers often have a lot of experience with driving-related back pain. Steve Krott is a truck driver based in Pennsylvania who writes a monthly health column for www.layover .com, an online publication for the trucking industry. Here are Krott's tips for reducing back pain on long road trips:

■ Take frequent breaks. Don't try to drive straight through. Get out of the car and walk around at least once every two hours.

■ Adjust your seat, or use a lumbar pillow or other cushion to support your lower back while you drive.

■ Empty your pockets before you start driving. Sitting with a wallet in your back pocket can pinch your body, change your posture, and cause temporary numbness.

■ Stretch your hamstrings. Krott sees many truck drivers get out of their cabs and stretch out by bending over and reaching for their toes. The stretch you should really be doing, he says, is lying down on your back and gently pulling your knees to your chest, one at a time. Do this stretch every couple of hours when you get out of your car to take a break.

Automotive Gizmos: Computers in Your Car

New products can customize your car and make drive time more efficient.

MOBILE ELECTRONICS WORK FOR YOU

"You spend a lot of time in the car. People in our industry are working to make electronics work for you," says Lisa Fasold, a spokesperson for the Consumer Electronic Manufacturer's Association in the US. It's Fasold's job to go to all of the trade shows, know the manufacturers, understand the products, and be in touch with consumers.

"What is new and expensive now will become standard issue in just a few years," predicts Fasold. For those who want the latest automobile accessories, her advice is to purchase a car with no extras—not even a radio—and then install exactly what you want, from sound to security systems. "You pay double the price for electronics when they come with the car," Fasold explains, "and anything pre-installed in a new car is already at least three years old technologically."

"Safety is consistently the number-one concern in consumer surveys," says Fasold. To meet that need, mobile electronics companies are developing innovative products, such as:
Mobile Mayday, from Alpine. Customers are linked through their cellular phones to a 24-hour emergency response center. Using a special tracking device, the center can pinpoint the exact location of any customer's vehicle, and send out road-side assistance if needed.
ValetCarCom, from Directed Electronics Inc. You dial a special code on your phone to communicate with your car. For example, if you locked your keys in the car, you can open the door over the phone. You can also instruct the car to start warming up, turn off the headlights, and activate a security device—all remotely over the phone.
The Safety Warning System, available in new radar devices. This technology warns drivers of potential road hazards, such as approaching emergency vehicles, railroad crossings, accident scenes, and heavy fog.

NAVIGATION SYSTEMS SHOW AND TELL YOU THE WAY

The Alpine navigation system has been rated the most user-friendly in the industry. "We deliver voice instructions with a visual back-up using simplified graphics," explains Stephen Witt, Alpine's vice president of brand marketing and communication. The system adds significant value to any car. "Our Navigation and Information System gives the driver new utility: a highly productive, convenient, and safe vehicle."

Several companies already have electronic navigation systems on the market.

Users input their address and destination by placing a cursor on the map or using their preprogrammed address book. The Navigator gives them voice guidance plus a map that appears on a dash-mounted monitor. "Eventually, the system will include almost every road in the country," says Witt. Avis, Hertz, and National have all incorporated navigation systems into their rental fleets, and most customers agree that not having to ask strangers for directions is well worth the added fee. Here's what else the Navigator can do:

Your new car could have as many as 35 to 40 microprocessors to process more than 40 million instructions each second.

Tools of the Trade

The key to car navigation is a technology called GPS, or Global Positioning System. Since the 1970s, the Department of Defense has spent $13 billion dollars on this constellation of 24 satellites that help pinpoint military troop movements. Using at least 7 satellites, the GPS can locate a vehicle containing an onboard antenna to within a few yards of its exact longitude and latitude. This same technology that allowed Desert Storm troops to know where they were going in the dark can help lost drivers anywhere from New York to California find their destinations.

- Because it has huge information databases, the Navigator can organize your list of errands into the shortest route, locate the nearest ATM machine or gas station.
- If you run into a traffic jam, the Detour function can instantly set you a new route.
- The navigation system can provide you with real-time information about traffic and local weather conditions.

BEFORE YOU BUY

"I've been in this business for 30 years," says Derek Lee, certified technician and owner of Mobile Dynamics in Richmond Hill, Ontario. "I train people to fix faulty installations and incompatible systems that other people can't. Even a leased vehicle is not an obstacle to good sound—I've moved an expensive system through five of my own vehicles."

Before buying any automotive accessory, Lee suggests taking these steps:

- Ask yourself how long you plan to own your vehicle. "Even if you lease a car and change vehicles every two to three years, you can take your technology with you," says Lee. "You won't be disappointed if you stick to brand names. Most come out with new versions of their products every six months, but good quality will last."
- Increase your chances of good workmanship by choosing a technician who has three separate qualifications, says Lee.

First, see if the person has a certificate from Mobile Dynamics or a US school. In the last decade, Mobile Dynamics has trained about 2,000 technicians in Canada. Next, ask if the technician has training or certification from the manufacturer of the products that he is selling. Finally, look for a technician who has qualified as a Mobile Electronics Certified Professional (MECP).

- Educate yourself before purchasing. Read electronics magazines, such as *Car Audio and Electronics, Audio Sound and Security,* and *Car Stereo Review.* Get on the Internet and find out what the manufacturers have to say about their products.
- Visit an auto accessories shop. If it is selling only one product and that is not a recognized brand, investigate further to be sure you really want to do business there. "There's no such thing as a bad product in this business. Every two years, new,

improved products appear, and consumers can be confident," says Lee. If it's junk, you will find it at a flea market or one of the big sales advertising "warehouse brands."

THE CUTTING EDGE

"The new buzzword in mobile electronics is convergence," comments Dean Kanemitsu, director of marketing for advanced technology for Clarion, a leading American manufacturer of car audio and electronics products. "With our newest product, the Auto PC, we're bringing the automotive, computer, and wireless industries together. We're helping users be more efficient and entertained in their vehicles by customizing features they need and allowing drivers to control them from one voice-activated point." For example:

- If you are a parent chauffeuring a car full of kids, the audio system can play their favorite CD while you talk hands-free on your cell phone by accessing a phone book

- Lee points out that some components have longer lives than others. Tape decks and CD players last from 5 years to 12 years. And speakers typically last only about 5 years.

that listens to you and then places your call.
- If you are a road warrior who travels constantly from appointment to appointment, you can check your e-mail, create voice memo reminders, and access real-time traffic information to help you avoid the crunch.
- If you are a business person with a long commute, you can receive e-mail messages and listen to customized information about your stocks, knowing that your radio will interrupt if any traffic conditions occur that you should be aware of.

The Auto PC is the size of a standard car radio, and can be easily installed in the dashboard. And more Auto PC-enabled products are already in development.

Smart Moves

Automotive technology experts agree that these two products provide services that are well worth their price tags:
Hands-free cellular phones. This type of cell phone allows you to keep your hands on the steering wheel and your eyes on the road.
Mobile videos. Rear seat entertainment screens are installed in the back of the front-seat headrests, or flip down so passengers can watch videos and play games—great for keeping the kids quiet on long family road trips.

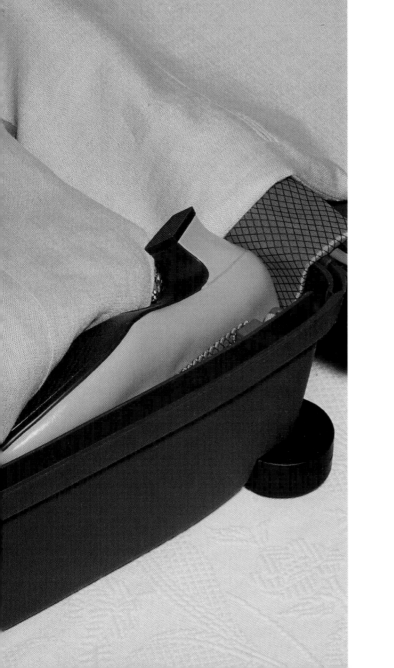

CHAPTER SIX

The Experienced Traveler

Using a Travel Agent

A good agent can help you enjoy your vacation.

THE BENEFITS OF USING A TRAVEL AGENT

Herbert Teison, editor and publisher of *Travel Smart* magazine, believes that most travelers are better off if they use a travel agent. Although it's becoming easier and easier for people to make their own travel plans, Teison maintains that travel agents continue to have far more training and experience than the average traveler. He suggests these additional reasons for taking advantage of a good travel agent:

- You get the personal touch. Your travel agent wants to keep your business and so has a real vested interest in keeping you happy.
- Travel agents have more clout. An agent has the potential to bring a good deal of business to a resort, hotel, or cruise line. Chances are, your agent will have a better

shot than you do at getting the exact seat, room, or flight you want.
- You can do it all in one phone call. Travel agents can save you the legwork of making all of your reservations yourself. It's not that expensive.
- Some people have the impression that making

your own travel plans saves you a lot of money. Travel agents, however, can often match the prices you find on your own, and any small additional cost is usually well worth the service.
- Travel agents understand the industry. They know what the going rate is for particular airplane routes or a week-long cruise in the Bahamas. Therefore, they know a good deal when they see one, while you may have no basis for comparison. They can also keep checking prices to get the best deal.

Ticket agents have quick access to the lowest ticket prices.

A good agent will give you a professionally prepared, glitch-free itinerary.

The Right Way

Some people use travel agents in ways the industry considers unethical. Sometimes, however, people don't realize that what they are doing is considered inappropriate. Here are a few simple guidelines to follow if you want to treat your travel agent with respect.

- Don't ask a travel agent to do in-depth research for you on a complicated vacation and then book the trip with someone else to save a few dollars. Agents provide information for free. Their earnings depend on the bookings.

- Don't expect your agent to spend hours finding you an airline ticket that will save you only a few extra dollars.
- Reward a travel agent's good work by becoming a loyal customer.
- Give your agent as much time as possible to book your trip and find you the best prices.
- Don't blame the agent when airlines or resorts are charging more than you want or are able to pay. In high season especially, agents have very little room to maneuver.

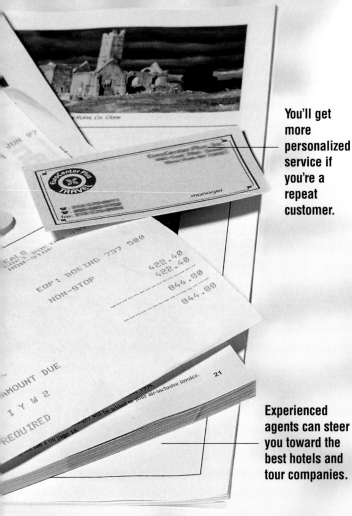

You'll get more personalized service if you're a repeat customer.

Experienced agents can steer you toward the best hotels and tour companies.

Quick Tricks

Asking these questions is a quick way to find out whether travel agents know what they're doing, according to Coralie Belman, executive director of the Canadian Institute of Travel Counsellors. If you don't like the answers, look for another agent. Comparison shopping at this stage can have big benefits.

■ Have you planned trips like mine before?
■ What kind of traveling have you done?
■ Have you ever been to the resorts you're describing?
■ What's your specialty?
■ Where do your clients typically travel?
■ What types of resources do you use to plan vacations?
■ Why do you prefer one tour operator over another?
■ Do you refer clients to other agents for cruises or other travel outside your specialty?
■ Are you reimbursed for booking with a particular airline or tour group rather than one with a better price?

WHEN TO USE YOUR TRAVEL AGENT

Robert Powell Sangster, author of *Traveler's Tool Kit: How to Travel Absolutely Anywhere*, describes the best times to use your travel agent—and the best times not to.

Use your travel agent when:

■ You are short of time.
■ You lack knowledge about technical issues like visas and permits.
■ You want to review tour brochures and get recommendations.
■ You are planning a complicated trip to several destinations.
■ You don't speak the language of a country you're planning to visit.
■ You're going somewhere you've never been before.

Don't use your travel agent when:

■ The agent is unfamiliar with your destination.
■ He refuses to use consolidator tickets (see p. 257).
■ You're sure you can find far less expensive tickets on your own.
■ The agent doesn't understand your areas of interest or dismisses them.
■ You need only one element of a trip, such as a car rental.
■ You're taking advantage of a special discount.

FINDING A GOOD TRAVEL AGENT

The best way to find a good travel agent is to get a friend's recommendation, says Dick Knodt of the American Society of Travel Agents. Ask your friend to introduce you. That way, the agent has the possibility not only of getting a new client, but also of losing an existing one if you're not happy with the service.

Here are some other ways to assess a prospective travel agent:

■ Check accreditations on the agent's stationery or business cards. Certified travel counselors (CTCs) and certified travel managers (CTMs) have met industry-based requirements for training, education, and work experience. "This in-depth knowledge about prices, services, accommodation, transportation, and tour destinations lets consumers make knowledgeable decisions," says Coralie Belman of the Canadian Institute of Travel Counsellors.
■ Find out how long the agent has been in business. Agents who have been around for a while and have an established reputation tend to be more reliable. And you can always check with your local Chamber of Commerce or Better Business Bureau to find out if there are any complaints against the agent.
■ Check references. Never make arrangements with an agent who calls you out of the blue. Speak to a few of the agent's other customers before charging a big trip to your credit card number.
■ Make sure the agent asks you about trips you have liked and disliked in the past, what kind of airline seats you prefer, and what frequent flier clubs you belong to. The agent should keep this personal data in the computer so you don't have to answer the same questions every time you book a new trip.
■ Book a trip. Then assess how important the agent's help was in making the experience a pleasant (or unpleasant) one.

Using the Internet for Travel

Get the information you need quickly and accurately.

GETTING STARTED

Neal Salkind, travel writer and host of Online Epicure, offers his suggestions for those who have never re-searched travel online:

- Start with the simplified search engine Yahoo! and go to the travel section. Yahoo! organizes infor-mation into categories. Follow the hierarchy down to the subject of your choice and visit the sites listed there.

- If you are comfortable with a particular guide-book series, travel mag-azine, or writer, do a search on that name. Most publishers have websites with informa-tion on their products and latest industry news.

- Likewise, most airlines, car rental companies, and major hotel chains have a site that offers special deals and general infor-mation. Start with the companies you are famil-iar with, but then visit their competitors' sites to compare quality and prices. You'll also save time by making your reservations online.

- Go to an online book-store—www.chapters.ca, www.indigo.ca, www .Barnesandnoble.com, or www.Amazon.com—and search for any type of trip or destination. You'll have access to more resources than you would at any one bookstore.

BEST DEALS ON THE WEB

Chelsea Mauldin, editor of Fodor's Travel Online, sug-gests some of the best ways for you to use online travel information:

Compare prices. Visit several airline or hotel reservation sites and compare their prices for similar products. You can do in a few min-utes on the Internet what used to require hours on the telephone.

Buy tickets. Save yourself time and money by buying airplane tickets online. Many airlines offer incen-tives to encourage you to buy tickets on their web-site, such as a reduction in regular prices or bonus frequent flier miles.

Choose a seat. Some airlines have websites that let you view the seat assignments and select which seat you want from those not already reserved. If you want a bulkhead seat or one away from the bath-rooms, here's an easy way to find it.

Get information on specific attractions. Once you know where you are going, check out websites on your desti-nation and decide what you want to see and do there. Websites can afford to carry far more detailed informa-tion than travel brochures— such as a virtual tour of the Renaissance paintings in the Louvre or a real-time image of New York's Empire State Building.

Get instant service. When you're using an online ser-vice, you're not left waiting on hold until a customer representative is available.

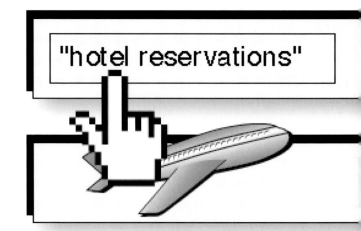

Smart Moves

One of the most useful ways to use the Internet is to take part in one of its many travel forums—discussion groups focused on a particular topic, such as discount travel or traveling alone. At forum sites, such as www.fodors.com/forums/ and www1.sympatico.ca/ Contents/Travel, people can discuss anything and everything by posting and answering questions, or just following along. Last year on the Fodor's travel forum, one of the best on the Web, people discussed over 20,000 different topics, known as threads.

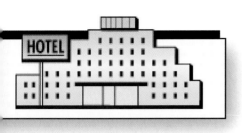

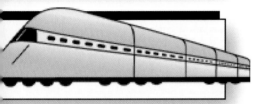

Surfing the World Wide Web is not an exact science. If you don't find the kind of websites you're looking for when you type one phrase into a search engine, try another. For example, *rental cars* could get you some different listings than *car rentals*. Also, try putting phrases in quotes or attaching them by hyphens, such as *"budget airfares"* or *budget-airfares*, to ensure that the search engine is looking for the phrase rather than the individual words.

Myth: *It's dangerous to make a credit card purchase online.* **Fact:** *If you have one of the major browsers, such as Netscape Navigator or Internet Explorer, and the site uses encryption to transfer your card number, it's at least as safe as making a purchase over the telephone.*

EVALUATING YOUR SOURCES

Lee Foster, writer for www.fostertravel.com, says that you have to be able to evaluate the reliability of different websites in order to find the information you seek. The trick, Foster says, is to figure out how each site is funded. Here's what to expect from the differently funded sites:

Subscriptions. It costs money to publish high-quality, objective travel writing. Sites that charge a fee for access can afford to pay respected travel writers to put their articles online. Subscription sites include major commercial sites like CompuServe and America Online.

Banner advertising. Free-access sites have to find another way to support themselves, and many do this by selling advertising space on their webpages. Like traditional magazines and newspapers, these sites use advertising revenue to support their content. While many of these sites contain valuable travel materials, be suspicious when they run a glowing review of one of their major advertisers.

Selling goods and services. A third way that sites finance their content is by selling something. Travel sites like Microsoft's Expedia use travel articles and tips to attract people to their site. They hope these people will then purchase airline tickets or hotel reservations through their service, generating a profit for the site. The better their free content is, the more traffic they'll get and the more chances they'll have to sell their merchandise, which is why these sites often feature top-notch information. As another source of income, these sites frequently carry banner advertising as well.

Outside funding. Some websites are funded by an outside source, such as a city's convention and visitors bureau. These sites often have detailed information on what's happening in their neighborhood, including year-round calendars of events and local entertainment listings. But remember that their primary goal is to sell you on their city, so judge their content accordingly.

AIRLINES ON THE WEB

According to Peter Frank, news editor of *Condé Nast Traveler*, making travel plans online is best for people who like to make their own decisions, research their destination, and investigate ways to get the best deals. Travelers who prefer to leave the legwork to someone else should work with a travel agent.

To make your own plans online, here's what Frank says you should know:

- If you are interested in last-minute ticket deals for weekend getaways, go to the site of every airline that flies out of your local airport and sign up for their weekly e-mail containing last-minute offers. Air Canada's site is www.aircanada.ca

- Try to coordinate your choice of airline with your rental car or hotel. Many sites offer low prices or bonus miles if you use an affiliated service.

- Don't overestimate your savings. In a recent study, *Condé Nast Traveler* found travel agents match or beat Internet fares about half the time, and come close the rest.

- Some sites will mail your airline tickets to you. Consider electronic or virtual tickets instead. By showing a confirmation number, and either the credit card you used or a photo ID, you get your tickets at the airport the day of your flight.

Hotel Hints

Are you looking for more than just an ordinary place to sleep?

FINDING THE PERFECT HIDEAWAY

The terms inn, bed and breakfast, and small hotel are often used interchangeably, explains Sandra W. Soule, host of the website www.inns.com. And they're applied to a wide variety of accommodations, both in the US and abroad. Bed and Breakfast Online Canada (www.bbcanada.com), started in the mid-90s by Doug White, now has more than 3,000 listings, photos included, with information on price, location, size, private or semi-private bathrooms, and policies on smoking and pets.

The places that are the most different from hotel or motel chains are those that are owner-operated. This means that the people at the front desk and those cooking and serving breakfast are often the owners themselves. It makes for a cozier and more personable atmosphere than a large hotel would have, so it's the first thing you should inquire about before making your reservations. Here are some other questions to ask before you book:

- Where is it located? Most small places are outside the center of town, away from the hustle and bustle. But some may be in relatively busy urban neighborhoods. In that case, ask about parking.
- What is the general atmosphere? Try to find pictures of the building and guest rooms, either in a brochure or on a website. Inns run the gamut from ruffles and lace to hunting decor.
- Does the place welcome families, or cater mostly to couples? If you're looking for privacy and romance, you'll probably want a different atmosphere than if you're taking your children along.
- What's for breakfast? Most small places serve a family-style breakfast (hence the term bed and breakfast). But while some places provide French toast, eggs, hash browns, and bacon, others offer only a choice of breads and coffee. Ask about afternoon tea or evening wine and cheese gatherings, when you get to chat with the owners and other guests.

Smart Moves

Here are a few questions you'll want to ask before you reserve your room:

- Will I have to pay a penalty if I cancel my reservation or check out a day early?
- What is the earliest time I can plan to arrive and get into my room?
- Will I be able to arrange to stay past the official check-out time?
- Does the rate I'll be paying include all tax and service charges?

Hotels
Hotels cater to business people more than do other accommodations. If you want access to a fax machine, health spa, conference hall, or cable TV, your best bet is a large hotel.

Inns
Luxury inns in the city or countryside typically provide more local flavor and variety than chain hotels.

Hostels
If you want to spend as little as possible, and don't require much in the way of amenities or privacy, hostels are the place to stay.

HOSTELS AREN'T JUST FOR STUDENTS

Hostels aren't just for young people anymore. According to Greg Brockmann of Ottawa-based Hostelling International—Canada (HI-Canada), more than seven percent of their members are 55 or older.

Hostels are inexpensive, dormitory-style accommodations. Found all over the world, the largest concentration is in Western Europe and North America. HI-Canada's more than 80 hostels are in settings ranging

Bed and Breakfast
Bed and breakfast lodgings let you feel more like a guest in someone's home than an anonymous customer.

from downtown Montreal and Toronto to Banff and Jasper in the Rockies.

Most hostels separate men and women into different areas. There are usually several beds or bunks to a room, but most hostels offer private, family, or couples' rooms as well. All hostel guests share the same bathrooms, kitchen, and other facilities.

Here's what else Brockmann thinks people should know about hostelling:

- Anyone can stay in a hostel. Becoming a member of an organization like HI-Canada gets you a discount at affiliated hostels and a directory of where to find them.
- In high season, call ahead and make a reservation, even if you are alone.
- Not all hostels are affiliated with a larger association, and there are plenty of great independent hostels. But association members are required to keep up certain health and safety standards, which is why some travelers are more comfortable with them.

- A night's stay in a Canadian hostel usually costs around $8 to $23, which is much less expensive than even a budget motel. Prices tend to be higher in cities, but you can spend the night in a hostel in downtown Vancouver for around $19 ($23 for non-members).
- Most hostels limit your stay to a week, but you may be able to arrange an extension during the off season. If you're staying for more than one night, you can leave your belongings with the manager during the day so you don't have to lug them around with you.
- Hostels are a great place to meet other travelers and share stories. People on their own can usually find someone to spend a day with or join a hostel-organized tour. Most hostels have a recreation area where travelers can relax together after each day's adventure.

YOUR CONCIERGE
A hotel's concierge can be a fabulous source of information, if you know what to ask. And if you're visiting for the first time, it's a good idea to get in touch with the concierge a couple of weeks before you arrive, according to Joy Connor, the head concierge at The Little Nell in Aspen, Colorado, one of the top-rated hotels in the US. Here are some of the subjects you may want to discuss with the concierge:

Restaurants. Ask about the one in the hotel and others nearby. If you like fish, ask which restaurants carry the freshest fish. If you want to meet people from the area,

ask where the employees go to eat. If you want to eat at the hottest new restaurant, call a month in advance and ask the concierge to make a reservation for you.

Nightlife. Be as specific as you can. Ask for the bar with the best selection of beers or the place with the best live band or country and western music.

Weather. Call ahead and ask what the weather should be like when you arrive so you know what clothes to bring.

Transportation. Find out whether the hotel offers an airport pickup service and arrange a pickup for your arrival. Ask about local buses and trains, and find out how much a taxi ride should cost.

HOTEL CONSOLIDATORS
Hotel consolidators—hotel brokers or discounters, such as Room Exchange—are a great place to call for a hotel room in a big city. Robert P. Tanzola, president of Accommodations Express, which handles reservations for hotels in 20 major US cities, explains some things you should know about consolidators:

- Unlike hotels themselves, consolidators offer the same rates for most of the year, usually saving you around 30 percent.
- They can usually find you a room in the most convenient hotel for you. Tell them if you want to be near the park or as close to the downtown business district as possible.
- Consolidators deal mostly with mid-level and luxury hotels, but can sometimes get you a room at a less-expensive hotel. If price is more important

to you than location, let the operator know.

- The best consolidators have operators who know the hotels personally. Ask whether the operator has actually stayed there.
- Consolidators sell to travel agents as well. So if you use a travel agency, ask your agent to check with a couple of consolidators before booking your room. Check the agent's price by getting a quote yourself.

Trading Homes

Get all the comforts of home on vacation, at no charge.

HOME EXCHANGE CLUBS

One way to visit another province or country is to find someone with a home in that area to swap accommodations with you. Many people swear by these home exchanges, saying they give you the most space and amenities for the lowest cost. Scheduling is usually flexible, too.

Most people interested in swapping homes join exchange clubs, which provide thick catalogs or internet listings of home exchanges worldwide. Suzanne Cassin, Canadian representative for Intervac International, one of the largest home exchange clubs, suggests you consider the following before joining a home exchange club:

■ Does the club have any special focus? Some cater especially to high school teachers, professors, or members of particular religious groups, which may or may not suit you.

■ How many people belong? The more members there are, the more chances you have to find the type of exchange you're looking for.

■ Does the club have a large number of members in the provinces or countries you're most interested in visiting?

■ How long has the club been in operation? Choose a club with an established reputation.

■ How much does it cost? Most clubs charge reasonably low fees. Find out what the initial fee covers, what it costs to repeat your listing during the current season, and if there are extra charges for photos.

■ How will you receive listings of available swaps? Some home-exchange clubs send out updated catalogs several times a year, while others do only one annual mass mailing; many post listings on the Internet with password protection. Seeing new listings every few months gives you an up-to-date view of what's available.

Tools of the Trade

Among popular home exchange clubs are:
HomeLink International (Canada)
(604-987-3262, www.ca.homelink.org)
Based in North Vancouver, British Columbia.
Intervac Canada
(1-800-665-0732, www.intervac.com) Based in Calgary, Alberta.
The Invented City
(415-522-1900) Based in San Francisco, California.
Trading Homes International
(800-877-8723) Based in Hermosa Beach, California.
Vacation Homes Unlimited
(800-VHU-SWAP or 805-298-0376) Based in Santa Clarita, California.
Worldwide Home Exchange Club
(202-588-5057) Based in Washington, DC.

Foreign swaps
Make sure you have names and telephone numbers of maintenance and repair people to contact in case of an emergency.

Urban swaps
Ensure that you'll be in a safe neighborhood, close to public transportation, museums, restaurants, and other sights.

FINDING THE BEST EXCHANGE

Once you find a possible exchange partner, it's important for both of you to be comfortable with one another before making a final agreement, according to Anne Pottinger, former president of the International Home Exchange Association. Here are some of the areas to make sure you cover:

Rural swaps
Find out what outdoor activities are available nearby, and make sure you will have access to a vehicle so you can get around.

- Find out if the other people have done a home exchange before, and ask for references. You'll be far more confident after you've spoken to someone they've exchanged with. If it's their first time, ask to speak to a couple of their friends or neighbors instead. Personal references are more useful than professional ones.
- Make a written agreement that covers both of your concerns. You may want to include a provision that they will repair or replace anything that is broken, stay out of a particular closet, or keep anyone under 25 years old from driving your car.
- Discuss whether you will exchange certain day-to-day responsibilities, such as taking care of the other family's pets.
- Make sure your house insurance policy and theirs will provide coverage while you are in the other's home. See that your car insurance permits another person to drive your vehicle, and covers you driving someone else's car.
- Explain how your appliances work. Kitchen gadgets vary in how they operate, so leave written instructions for the microwave, blender, coffee maker, even the washer and dryer. Find out whether they have fixtures that are important to you, such as a dishwasher or shower. Many European homes have bathtubs only.

MAKING YOUR HOME MORE APPEALING

Finding a home exchange in an area that appeals to you is only half the battle. You also have to find people interested in spending time in your home. Bill and Mary Barbour, co-authors of *Home Exchange Vacationing,* offer these tips for making your home even more appealing in your catalog listing:

- Don't worry if you don't have a mansion. Most people are far more interested in your location than the specifics of your home. Even the tiniest apartments in Manhattan attract a good deal of interest, while a magnificent home in rural Ohio finds fewer takers.
- In light of this, play up your neighborhood. Include every nearby attraction that might pique someone's interest. Mention ski areas, rivers for white-water rafting, beaches, big cities, national parks, shopping outlets, sports teams, or theme parks. You might be surprised by what draws people to your home, such as its proximity to a blue heron nesting area or their daughter's college.
- Mention what athletic activities are available nearby. Is there a golf course, bicycle path, volleyball court, hiking trail, tennis court, or good fishing in the neighborhood?
- Describe any special features of your home as well. Mention your vegetable garden, swing set, large back yard, Jacuzzi, pool, deck, beautiful view, or sun room.
- If you can include a picture, do it. And use one that captures your home's most charming or unusual feature.

True Story

By swapping homes with other families, Pat Greening of Oakville, Ontario, and husband Harry have had delightful holidays in Strasbourg, France, and in Britain's Yorkshire countryside. Walls of her 300-year-old exchange home there were so thick, the windowsills were deep enough to sit in. From the kitchen window, she could watch neighboring farmers train their sheepdogs.

Both Greening's swaps were through Intervac, an international home exchange program. Many ask if she locks up her silver and her crystal before leaving. Such a thought never occurred to her. By the time the exchange takes place, the parties are no longer strangers, having spent months working out details by fax, e-mail, or telephone. Besides, "Home exchangers are of the same ilk." It's common practice to leave a refrigerator stocked with the basics, including a bottle of wine. Sometimes, as occurred with the Greenings and one of the exchanges, the friendship continues when the holiday ends. "Just another benefit of trading homes."

Meeting your exchange partner is not necessary. However, on their first exchange, in 1994, the Greenings left their car at the Toronto airport for the incoming Strasbourg couple, whom they met on deplaning in France. On their second exchange, their Yorkshire partners were overnight guests of the Greenings before the Oakville couple left for Britain.

Greening points out that shopping where locals shop, meeting the neighbors, and eating at restaurants not usually frequented by tourists is a great way to really get to know a place. Both homes they visited were well equipped, but she suggests that anyone planning an exchange should ask about household appliances and local medical and dental care. Insurance coverage should also be clarified before leaving. And she suggests bringing a voltage converter, and leaving "stacks" of local tourist information for the incoming family.

Scotland, Ireland, or the west coast of France are all on the Greenings' short list for their next exchange. But all options are open and the possibilities are endless. "It's an adventure," says Greening.

Packing Smart

The art of travel begins with packing your bags.

WHAT'S YOUR BAG

G. Anderson Niccolls knows his bags. He was a baggage handler at Kennedy Airport. Now he's a salesman at a top-notch luggage store in New York City.

Niccolls recommends luggage that is streamlined, with handles and wheels that recess so they don't get caught in conveyor belts and luggage carousels.

Cloth bags are light and easy to handle. An 800- denier nylon polyester weave works well for people who travel occasionally. For durability, however, buy a 1200–1600 denier weave or—even stronger—a bag made from ballistic nylon, a military weave that's used to make bulletproof vests.

Most garment bags are made with men in mind. For women travelers, Niccolls suggests a 52-inch garment bag—the longest available, and a better choice for dresses.

For ultimate travel versatility, several manufacturers have introduced the convertible backpack/carry-on/shoulder bag-in-one. Some models even have wheels.

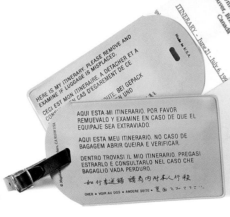

Retriever luggage tags can mean the difference between getting your lost luggage back later—or not at all.

DON'T LEAVE HOME WITHOUT THEM

Clever, compact travel accessories, from pocket-size currency converters to dual-voltage surge protectors, make it easier than ever to take the comforts and conveniences of home and office along—wherever your travels take you. "I always pack as if I'm heading to the wilderness," says John McManus, founder and president of Magellan's (www.magellans.com), supplier of travel equipment and supplies.

You'll wonder how you ever managed without these innovative accessories:

Pilots and flight attendants know that the least taxing way to carry your luggage is to pull it behind you.

- An international translator with 400 universally recognized drawings that can help you communicate basic ideas in any language.
- A compact telephone adapter that lets you check an e-mail—even send a fax—from virtually anywhere in the world.
- Retriever luggage tags that hold an extra copy of your itinerary. If your bags are temporarily lost, they can be forwarded to you at your hotel.
- A portable personal air purifier that weighs five ounces and can be hung around your neck if you're sensitive to smells.
- A special high-tech, compact, seven-ounce travel umbrella.
- A five-inch, five-ounce heating coil that will boil water for a quick cup of tea or coffee, or a freeze-dried soup.

Myth: *The longer your vacation will last, the more you need to bring along.*

Fact: *Smart travelers pack about the same amount of gear, whether they're traveling for one week or three months.*

PACKING STRATEGIES

For Judith Gilford, packing is a profession. She teaches classes on the subject and has written *The Packing Book*, proclaiming the virtues of packing light. The key to Gilford's packing system is her Bundle Method, which protects even tailored clothes and delicate fabrics from creasing and wrinkling, and allows easy access to daily items like underwear, socks, and accessories. The Bundle Method is ideal for soft-sided luggage. Here's how to do it:

- Assemble everything you will be taking along. Put aside what you will be wearing on the plane and what you will be needing the first day or two of your trip.
- Lay your open suitcase flat on the bed. Pretend the base of your suitcase is a clock face. Think of your clothes as the hands of the clock and layer them alternately in 12 o'clock, 3 o'clock, 6 o'clock, and 9 o'clock positions, draping each article over the edge of the bag. Start with the largest and heaviest items of your wardrobe, such as jackets and straight dresses. The lightest and most delicate items should be in the top layers.
- Once you have laid out all the main pieces of your wardrobe, place socks, lingerie, undergarments, and other soft accessories in the middle of your clothes. This is your core. It acts as a cushion, protecting each of the layers of clothes from wrinkling.
- Fold your garments back over the core, starting with the topmost layer. Wrap each layer tightly around the core, smoothing out wrinkles as you go.
- Tuck shoes, belts, and other accessories into the sides of the suitcase around your

Wrinkle-free packing

Drape your garments (from the heaviest to the most delicate) in a circle around the edges of your suitcase.

Put items that won't wrinkle, such as socks, pantyhose, underwear, and your toiletries kit, in the middle of the circle.

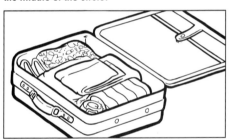

Fold the circle of garments neatly over the core items, and tuck shoes and accessories into any empty spaces.

bundle. Lay the clothes you set aside for the beginning of your trip on top for easy access.

The Right Way

To prevent that troublesome wobbling as you wheel your suitcase down the airport concourse, pack all your heaviest items at the bottom of the suitcase toward the wheels. Putting as much weight as you can on the wheels will keep your bag in better balance and make it easier to pull.

READY-TO-WEAR

New lightweight, high-tech, low-maintenance fabrics make it easier than ever to look and feel great when you're on the road. Whether you're trekking to Katmandu or doing business in Boston, you'll want to bring along clothes that are compact, wrinkle-resistant, and easy to care for, says Chuck Slaughter, founder and co-president of TravelSmith (www.TravelSmith.com), a mail-order travel outfitter. And that doesn't mean cotton. Slaughter describes some of the new miracle fabrics to look for when you are shopping for your travel wardrobe:

Coolmax™ looks and feels like cotton, but wicks moisture away from the skin and dries out in a jiffy. It's terrific for travel essentials, such as underwear, T-shirts, and polos.

For dressier travel, look for skirts, blazers, trousers, even trench coats, in durable yet lightweight microfiber, a nylon or polyester weave that is virtually impervious to wrinkles.

New Tencel™ Denim—made with wood pulp—is softer, comfier, and half as bulky as traditional denims.

Smart Moves

- Use a combination lock on your luggage rather than a lock with a key. They take a little longer for thieves to crack.
- Bring a change of clothes along in your carry-on bag in case your luggage gets lost. Most bags catch up with their owners within 24 hours of arrival.
- A fold-up nylon tote bag will do triple duty as a laundry bag, a beach tote, and an extra carry-on for your souvenirs on the way home.
- Many foreign hotel sinks don't have plugs. Bring along a flat rubber sink stopper on your

international travels so you can wash out your underwear.
- All-purpose travel soap, which can be used on hair, clothes, skin—even dishes and utensils—is a great space-saver.
- If you're going overseas for business, you may need to reset your modem software to recognize overseas dialtones. Call your Internet service provider before you go to find out how.
- Always pack several resealable plastic bags so you'll have someplace safe to keep wet clothes, food, or leaky bottles.

Travel Safety

Make your trip as safe as it is rewarding.

TRAVEL SCAMS TO WATCH OUT FOR

"Common sense is your main weapon against unscrupulous schemes to separate you from your travel dollars," says Steve Gillick, who is the executive director of the Canadian Institute of Travel Counsellors of Ontario (www.citontario.com).

Gillick, a travel industry veteran of 20 years and an inveterate globe-trotter to some 40 countries, has written two highly informative booklets on travel scams—*Scam Watch: Defining Travel Common Sense* and *Son of Scam.* The purpose of Gillick's booklets is to help travelers "anticipate, recognize, and avoid" the scams that they may possibly encounter on their journeys. With this greater awareness, Gillick says, you are "on your way to an enjoyable, safe, and healthy travel experience."

Here are some of the scams that Gillick says are commonly used to hoodwink unwary travelers:

Free trips. If you get a notice in the mail saying you'll receive a free trip provided you pay a sum of money up front—a so-called "confirmation fee"—it's more than likely a phony deal.

In some instances, scammers may call about a free trip and ask you to call a 900 or other long-distance number. If you make the call, you are charged by the minute, most likely to an overseas location, and the scammers make money on the call. Scammers often get your name from ballots that you've filled out for draws or contests at shows or fairs.

Phony tickets. There's a lively underground market in stolen tickets. To protect yourself, always buy tickets with a credit card from the airline, or from an agent you know, or one who has been recommended to you by a friend. Gillick also recommends you deal with a certified travel counselor (CTC), a designation that indicates a certain level of training, work experience in the travel industry, and professionalism.

Time-shares. Although there are legitimate offers, the time-share industry is full of scams, says Gillick.

Before committing yourself to a time-share, you should check with the Better Business Bureau, the Chamber of Commerce, or a visitors bureau in the area where the time-share is located. In any case, unsolicited offers for time-shares should always be regarded with skepticism.

Bait and switch. Although this is one of the most common scams in the US, it is relatively rare in Canada. Newspaper ads may lure you with the possibility of impossibly low airfares. When you call the number in the ad, however, the operator tells you that particular fare is all sold out, and then quotes you another, substantially more expensive fare.

WHAT *NOT* TO DO WHEN TRAVELING

- Carry your wallet and other valuables in a backpack, fanny pack, or other easily stolen carrying case.
- Take a ride with someone driving an unidentified vehicle but claiming to be a taxi.
- Ignore your instincts about a potentially dangerous situation.

HOTEL FIRE SAFETY

What to do in a hotel fire? Former New York City Fire Department Lieutenant Jim Powell ought to know. A firefighter for 22 years, Powell was twice decorated for bravery.

- The primary danger is that people are unfamiliar with their surroundings. Always check the fire exits and the fire safety instructions on the back of your hotel door. Count how many doors you'll have to go through to reach the emergency stairs.
- Plastics and other synthetics create toxic fumes when they burn, a concern in modern hotel rooms, where furniture and fixtures are often made of synthetic substances. Crawl on your hands and knees through smoke. Because heat and toxic gases rise, the coolest and most breathable air is close to floor level. Captain André Chamberlain of the Montreal Fire Department reiterates that you should crawl,

In Case of Fire

Touch the doorknob and door gently with the back of your hand. If it's hot, don't attempt to open it.

Put wet towels around the bottom of the door to deter the spread of smoke. If you must open a door, do so from a crouching position and be ready to close it immediately.

not slither along the floor, as there may also be toxic fumes at a very low level.

■ Try not to stay above the sixth floor in a hotel, which is as high as most aerial ladders can reach.

■ In an actual fire, try to wait for instructions. Call the hotel's front desk or the local fire department before doing anything.

BIG-CITY SAVVY

Big cities provide lots of excitement, entertainment, and opportunities for cultural enrichment. But they can also be hazardous—

Myth: *Throw the windows open wide during a fire to attract help and get fresh air.* **Fact:** *Fresh air attracts and feeds a fire. Hang a sheet out the window to alert rescuers. Then quickly shut the window.*

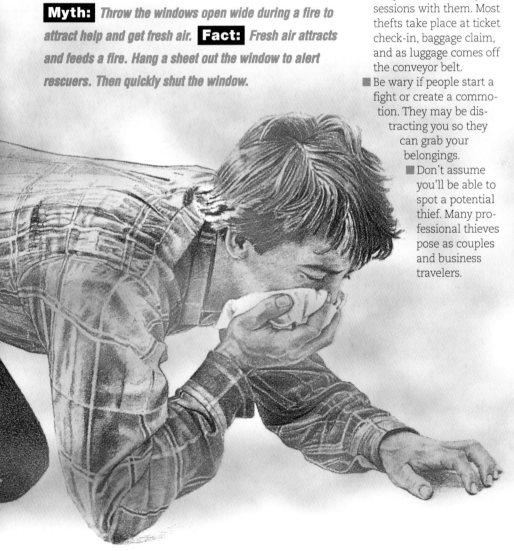

especially for jet-lagged travelers distracted by having to manage their luggage and children in unfamiliar and often crowded surroundings.

Detective/Sergeant Kevin Coffey has been with the Los Angeles Police Department for 17 years and has worked with the Airport Crimes Investigations Detail. He shares his years of experience in an audiobook called *Traveler Beware! An Undercover Cops Guide to Avoiding Pickpockets, Luggage Theft, and Travel Scams.* Here are some of Coffey's helpful hints for negotiating the

complexities of visiting a big city:

■ Many people like the ease and mobility of traveling with a fanny pack. Unfortunately, fanny packs are a magnet for thieves and pickpockets who don't hesitate to cut them off the waist of an unsuspecting tourist. It is better to keep your important documents and cash in a money belt or neck pouch worn underneath your outer clothing.

■ Keep a close eye on your carry-on luggage. Thieves know that most travelers carry their valuable possessions with them. Most thefts take place at ticket check-in, baggage claim, and as luggage comes off the conveyor belt.

■ Be wary if people start a fight or create a commotion. They may be distracting you so they can grab your belongings.

　■ Don't assume you'll be able to spot a potential thief. Many professional thieves pose as couples and business travelers.

A hotel door alarm that detects motion will alert you if someone opens the door.

A WOMAN'S PERSPECTIVE

Nanette C-Lee, editor and publisher of *Maiden Voyages*, a magazine and website (www.maiden-voyages.com) for "intrepid women travelers," never leaves home without the three A's: awareness, assessment, and appropriate response.

Awareness. Pay attention to your immediate environment. If you're driving to a nearby city, be certain of your highway exit. If you're traveling by airplane halfway around the world, be mindful of each country's cultural norms and behaviors. Ask yourself: Where am I? Who is following me? What is my next move if something goes wrong?

Assessment. Take stock of how you're feeling moment to moment. Are you prepared? Vulnerable? Tired? Managing kids? Watching luggage? Don't be afraid to make a scene if you think you are in danger. Remember, if you don't feel safe, you won't be safe.

Appropriate response. You can prepare yourself for almost any situation. Being prepared might include buying a hotel door alarm. It might mean taking self-defense classes. It might mean being sure that you have enough money for cab fare.

Budget Travel

You can have a really great vacation with a little bit of money.

BEST MONEY-SAVING TRAVEL TIPS

Ed Perkins, former editor of the *Consumer Reports Travel Letter*, shares his best advice on saving money when you travel:

- Get a good bargain guidebook. There are several series of high-quality bargain travel guides with names like *Let's Go, Berkeley,* or *Lonely Planet* available at libraries and bookstores. And for a step up from bare-bones travel, you can't beat *Frommer* guides.
- Join a half-price hotel program. Companies like Encore and Entertainment charge about $100 a year for a membership that will save you half off the published room rate—also known as the rack rate—in up to 4,000 participating hotels, whenever the hotel is less than 80 percent full.
- Join the Canadian Association of Retired Persons (CARP) as soon as you turn 50. Your membership gets you at least a small discount on most hotel rates, car rentals, and package deals.
- Use a discount travel agent to book a cruise. There are great deals on cruise vacations, but you won't get great prices by calling the cruise line. If you're flexible about when and where you sail, ask the agent to recommend the best deal.

IT PAYS TO BE FLEXIBLE

Make sure you have realistic expectations. "Budget travelers shouldn't expect to stay at five-star hotels," says Ann Klug of Travel CUTS/Voyages Campus, a Canada-wide travel agency geared to student, youth, and budget travelers. But, by following these tips, even a shoestring traveler can have an enjoyable vacation:

- Plan, plan, plan. Last-minute decisions on where you want to go and what you want to do might cost you. Plot your itinerary before your trip, and use guide books and local information to research the least expensive way to complete it. That way, you won't end up staying in an expensive hotel when there's a cheap hostel you didn't know about right around the corner.
- Consider traveling during the off season, when prices fall fairly dramatically. You might try traveling to Florida in the summer, and California in the winter.

- Always look around for the best deal. Even among inexpensive hostels, there are marked price differences.
- Call for the most recent prices at hotels and other accommodations. Their prices are constantly fluctuating.
- Make lunch your big meal instead of dinner. Lunch prices can be half as expensive as those for dinner, meaning you can eat twice as well for the same price by eating earlier in the day.
- If you are a student, get an International Student Identity Card available for $16 at Travel CUTS, most Via rail stations, and many student associations. It will save you money on airfare, trains, buses, accommodations, museums, and many other tourist services.

Don't leave home without it.

Camping is probably the cheapest way to spend the night, but don't forget these outdoor essentials:
- Bug spray—and lots of it.
- Easy-to-assemble tent with a rain fly and waterproof tarp for underneath.
- Bucket to carry your toiletries to and from the bathroom, and flip flops for the shower.
- Warm clothes for cold nights.
- Flashlight or lantern.

True Stories

Bargain travel doesn't have to mean spending your entire vacation counting your cash. On a recent vacation, Bruce Northam and his father decided to walk across England from coast to coast. They took their time, meandering in and out of little towns and spending time with local people most tourists never get to meet. They ate and drank in local pubs and slept in town inns.

When their trip was over, they came away with money in their pockets and an unforgettable portrait of the English countryside.

CHANGE YOUR TRAVEL PHILOSOPHY

One of the least painful ways to cut back on your travel expenditure is to change the way you think about traveling, says Bruce Northam, popular university lecturer and author of *Frugal Globetrotter, Your Guide to World Adventure Bargains*.

The secret is to have a mission for your next vacation. That way, you know what you want to do from the moment you arrive.

Choose a mission that relates to a favorite interest or hobby, such as listening to stringed instruments, bargain hunting, birdwatching, learning new massage techniques, viewing local artists, or attending religious services. Then decide to do and see as much related to your quest as you possibly can. Chances are, you'll have more adventures and meet more interesting people than if you spent your time wandering around the usual tourist attractions.

HOW LITTLE DO YOU WANT TO SPEND?

The word budget means different things to different people. Balance the cost and the level of amenities you're comfortable with.

Campground — $10 to $25 per site per night
This bare-bones option is usually the least expensive, but make sure you're really prepared to sleep in a tent and get up close and personal with nature.

Hostel — $8 to $23 per person per night
Hostels provide a roof over your head for very little money, but be willing to share your bathroom and bedroom with strangers.

Budget hotel — $50 to $100 per room per night
You should be able to find a good, clean hotel room with private bath for under $100 in major Canadian cities and for considerably less in smaller towns.

WHEN YOU HAVE MORE TIME THAN MONEY

In the travel industry, you pay a big premium for convenience, which is why business travelers with tight schedules often pay more than twice as much as tourists for the same airfare, car rental, or hotel room. A. J. Meier, a New York-based freelance writer and frequent traveler, maintains that her flexible schedule has enabled her to save a substantial amount of money on her travel expenses. Here are her suggestions on ways for people with flexible schedules to save:

- Fly at odd hours. Tell your ticket agent that you're willing to travel at less popular times if it will save you money. You can often get a better deal if you fly late at night, have a Saturday night stayover, or travel on holidays. Also, domestic flights frequently cost less on weekends, and international flights less on weekdays.
- Make plans at the last minute. Resorts like Club Med frequently offer wild card deals to fill up their empty rooms. For a reduced price, you get to pick a general time period during which they'll send you to one of a number of different resorts.
- Be adventurous. Every Tuesday or Wednesday, most of the major airlines post last-minute deals on the Internet. The prices are low, but the number of restrictions is high. You often have to depart on a Saturday and return on the following Monday or Tuesday, and destination cities are different each week. But if you just want to get away, you could find a great fare for a weekend jaunt to Chicago, London, or Amsterdam.
- Consider flying in and out of smaller airports, if they are closer to your destination, thus saving you money on ground travel. But be aware that smaller airports may be less competitive and so more expensive than larger ones.

Great Family Vacations

Make the most of your holiday time together.

INTERGENERATIONAL VACATIONS

It just takes a little planning and ingenuity to keep everyone from children to grandparents happy on an intergenerational vacation, says Pamela Lanier, author of *Family Travel: The Complete Guide* and host of the website www.travelguides.com. Above all, respect everyone's privacy and independence. Lanier suggests several approaches to picking the location:

- Accommodate everyone's budget and travel preferences by choosing an area that has an inn, an RV park, and a campsite near each other.
- Try a family resort with supervised activities that keep children busy and allow adults time to do things together.
- One cost-effective option for large gatherings is to rent a block of condos in a vacation community. If reserving rooms for a large group at a hotel, ask to speak directly to the sales or marketing departments. You might get a better deal.

FAMILY REUNIONS

Planning a big family reunion can be a lot of fun, but also a lot of work. Delegate responsibilities, advises Lanier. Put one person in charge of finding accommodations for out-of-town guests. Let another plan outings and activities. Have somebody else plan meals. Here are some other super tips for your next reunion:

- Plan a potluck night, when everyone brings their special signature dish. This is guaranteed to be a big hit.
- A fishing trip is fun for all generations, and you can reward yourselves with a fish fry.
- Have all your relatives contribute to a family cookbook. Put it together on your computer, and give everyone a copy.
- Arrange for a photographer to capture the event.

CHOOSING A FAMILY-FRIENDLY DESTINATION

Laura Sutherland wrote the book on family vacations. In fact, she wrote five

Make sure the camera fits the generation.

Teenagers can have fun with waterproof cameras that can be used in and out of the water.

Young children hate being left out, so get them their own inexpensive, single-use cameras.

books, including *The Best Bargain Family Vacations in the U.S.A.* Include all the members of your family in the planning process, she advises: "Let your kids help decide where to go and what to do once you've arrived." Having a say means they'll probably have a better time.

- When choosing accommodations, make sure your children will be welcome: An antique-filled B&B might be great for a couple, but a nightmare for a young family.
- Families with very small children might prefer a low-key vacation, perhaps

in a cottage by the beach. Location, convenience, and flexibility are key when traveling with toddlers: Too much scheduled activity will frustrate children and parents alike.

- Children between the ages of 5 and 12 will have a great time socializing with other kids at campgrounds and hotels that offer organized activities for kids.
- Older children and teens love active vacations, such as supervised rafting expeditions, watersport holidays, and dude ranch stays.

A True Story

For two decades, Jim and Anna McCrea of Queen's County, New Brunswick, have been renting out a three-bedroom house on their 5,000-acre farm. With dairy and beef herds, a fish hatchery, and lumbering operations that include a model wood lot, visitors can try their hands at milking cows, feeding calves, and haying in season. There are several kilometers of hiking trails and a convenient swimming hole. Weekly fees run $400 to $450. "It's a great place for families to learn about farming," said McCrae. "A lot of them that come to the farm don't know where milk comes from."

Myth: *You shouldn't try to travel anywhere with infants or young children.* **Fact:** *Many parents take even quite ambitious vacations with their little ones. Very small children are easily portable and might sleep quietly through grown-up activities, such as museum visits and sightseeing.*

Adults with a penchant for taking lots of photographs should buy film in bulk ahead of time, take their good camera, and remember to pack all of their lenses.

BUILDING FAMILY BONDS

"All family vacations are in part about bonding together," says Christine Loomis, author, mother of three, and travel editor of *Family Life* magazine. Outside daily routines and responsibilities, children and parents have an opportunity to connect in a special way.

Loomis thinks adventure vacations help strengthen family bonds, and that "travel changes the family dynamic." On supervised outings with an instructor, parents are learning with their children—taking a break from traditional roles and exploring on an equal footing with their kids. This can be an important bonding experience, especially between parents and young teenagers.

Traveling together can give parents an opportunity to learn from their children. "Adults are focused on the future. Children are focused on the here and now. Their curiosity reawakens our sense of awareness."

HOW TO STAY SANE WHEN TRAVELING WITH SMALL CHILDREN

"Children will pick up on parents' anxieties about traveling," says child psychologist Nancy Marks. If parents find traveling fun, more than likely their children will as well.

- It's important to try to maintain some of the regularity of home on the road. Children will feel more secure if you try to keep their eating and sleeping schedules as regular as possible.
- Long car rides can be a particular challenge. Schedule lots of stops, so children can snack and run around. Play word games and visual games. Sing together. Let your children take turns looking for landmarks or navigating with your road map. Try to make the trip as much fun as possible for everyone.
- To prepare for your child's first flight, take a trip to the airport ahead of time. Play airplane together. On the travel day, bring along a favorite toy from home for the trip.
- Electronic games, portable tape players, and compact travel toys are handy on long trips. If you have two children but only one tape or CD player, invest in an extra set of earphones.
- Involve your children in the adventure of travel. Encourage them to save up some of their allowance to purchase their own souvenirs. Buy them a disposable camera so they can take pictures to remind them of what they saw. Bring along a few art supplies so they can record their experiences.

- If you're traveling with teenagers, consider bringing one of their friends along. Teens are very peer-oriented and crave a little independence from their parents.
- Consider a family learning vacation. Learn how to dig for dinosaur bones at an archeological site or to play banjo or old-time fiddle at a folk heritage center. Many universities offer summer programs and classes for kids and parents to participate in together.
- Or try going to camp together. Many youth camps offer one- or two-week programs when they host entire families. "Family camps are a great buy and lots of fun," says Sutherland. Parents get the chance to be kids again and everyone gets to spend time with their families as well as other people their own age.

Pets on the Go

Keep your animals safe and happy on the road.

PET-FRIENDLY HOTELS

Frustration led Kathleen Devanna Fish to comb the country looking for pet-friendly accommodations and to write *Pets Welcome: A Guide to Hotels, Inns, and Resorts that Welcome You and Your Pet* (available by calling 1-800-524-6826). Here's what she recommends:

■ Call ahead to find out what special services the hotel offers, such as pet-walking and pet-sitting. Always call to make sure your pet is welcome if it's something other than a dog or cat.

■ Bring your pet's own food, litter, litter box, ID tags, leash, collar, favorite toys, bedding, and a bottle of water from home.

■ Bring vaccination and health records for all out-of-province as well as US visits.

■ Add a laminated card with the address and phone number of your hotel, and the dates you will be there, to the back of your pet's ID tag.

■ Don't leave your pet alone in an unfamiliar room. A nervous pet is liable to have an accident or tear up the furniture. And a lonely dog may bark the entire time you're away, making you thoroughly unpopular.

CAMPING FOR PETS AND PEOPLE

Gail Beebe, webmaster of the Delphi Pet Forum, has been taking her pets (including dogs, cats, and even birds) camping for over 10 years. You can benefit from what she has learned on these adventures:

■ Along with a first aid kit, bring pliers and wire cutters—dogs have an uncanny tendency to pick up fishhooks. Have tweezers on hand to remove ticks.

■ Never let your animal out of your car or camper without a leash or other restraint. Yes, you should put a harness on your cat. Practice at home first. Try distracting the cat with a catnip toy or treat as soon as you put the harness on. Soon, your cat will start getting used to it.

■ Call ahead to your destination to get a local veterinarian's phone number in case of an emergency. Park rangers don't always have this information.

Myth: *Getting to run around outdoors all day is the best part of a vacation for a dog.* **Fact:** *Dogs can overexert themselves, just like humans. Don't let your dogs exercise longer than they are used to. They don't know how to tell you they are tired, so they will do their best to keep up with you until they literally keel over.*

To tie up your pet outdoors, bring a curved screw-in restraint that goes into the ground and attaches to a lead line of ten feet or shorter. It's an ideal pairing of exercise and safety.

PETS ON JETS

There are strict rules concerning animals on airplanes, according to Air Canada spokesperson Michèle Meier. If you're planning on flying with your pets, make sure you get all the facts first. Ask for the airline's specifications in writing several weeks before you fly.

At Air Canada, very small dogs and cats, that can fit comfortably in a carrier with a maximum size of 23 by 40 by 55 centimeters, can be carried on board and kept under the seat in front of you. Larger animals must travel in a crate or carrier that is stored in a pressurized, temperature-controlled compartment separate from the main cabin. If you can't carry your pet on the plane with you, ask if someone will confirm that your pet is on board before takeoff.

Never expect to take your pet on board if you haven't made previous arrangements. Most airlines limit the number of animals per flight. There may also be

To keep ants out of pet food, use a metal pan and a heavy ceramic food bowl. Put the food bowl in the center of the metal pan and fill the pan with an inch or two of water. The ants will get stuck in the water and never make it to the food. Be sure the bowl is ceramic or it will float on top of the water.

other restrictions. Some airlines don't accept snakes or carry pets in their luggage sections during winter.

Fees for pets vary. Air Canada charges $65 for an animal to travel one way in North America.

Feed your pet four to six hours before departure, and water up until departure time. Leave an empty bowl in the carrier so somebody can give your pet water during a layover, or include a spill-proof bowl of ice with a sponge on top for your pet to lick.

Mark your pet's carrier with "Live Animal" on the top and at least one side, as well as with signs indicating "This End Up," plus your name, and a contact address and phone number for both your departure and destination cities. Put your pet's name on as well.

Familiarize your pet with the carrier ahead of time. Put a few favorite toys inside and leave it near your pet's sleeping area.

At home on the road

You want to make your pet's carrying case as cozy as possible, so line it with familiar-smelling towels or a blanket. Then, leave the carrier open near where your pet sleeps for a few days before you travel. Your pet will have the chance to get familiar with it ahead of time and maybe even try it out for a quick nap.

Proper labeling

Top lifts off so bottom can be a bed

End-opening door

LIVE ANIMAL

Wheels and handle for easy transport; wheels must be removable for aircraft luggage compartments

Good ventilation

Sturdy water tray

Locking device secure enough to prevent escape, but easily released in an emergency

---

KEEPING YOUR PET COMFORTABLE AND SAFE ON ROAD TRIPS

Dr. Brent Walker, a California veterinarian, offers these tips for keeping your pet safe and healthy on vacation:

Bring your pet's vaccination and other medical records in case you need them quickly. Make sure your pet has a collar tag with your home address and phone number (including area code). If you are a frequent traveler, consider one of the new microchip implants, which are put into place under the skin to identify your pet if its collar is lost.

Bring a photograph of your pet to identify it if it gets lost when you are away.

Have your pet examined before making a long trip, especially if it's older and more prone to heart disease and other maladies. Ask your veterinarian if there are any particular health concerns for your pet where you are going. For example, warm climates with high rainfalls are the worst for mosquito-transmitted heartworm and ticks. And certain areas of the southern US have a high incidence of airborne fungal diseases. Ask what symptoms you should watch for.

Keep your pet cool in the car. Pets are far more susceptible to heat than you are, and being locked in a hot car can kill them in minutes. Keep the cage out of the sun at all times, even in cool weather, by using window shades. If your car doesn't have air conditioning, leave the windows open slightly for a constant supply of fresh air.

Crate train your pet well before your road trip begins. Animals loose in the back seat of automobiles have been killed during sudden stops that hardly jolted the people in the front seat. Make sure the carrier is well padded and secure. If your pet is particularly high strung, ask your veterinarian whether using tranquilizers would be a good idea.

Your pets need to take frequent breaks during long drives, even if you don't. Take your dog for a walk to urinate and get some exercise every two to three hours. Allow enough time at the beginning and the end of the day for a long walk or real run. The exercise will be good for you as well as your dog.

Quick Tricks

Nerve calmer. Traveling makes some pets very nervous. To help them stay calm, line their crate with comfortable bedding. Include a familiar toy and one of your old T-shirts. Smells are very important to animals, and familiar ones help keep them relaxed under stress.

Fast food. Bring pet food that's easy to dispense. The semi-moist packets with single servings are easier to use than cans or large bags. They may not be the most nutritious choice, however, so take the length of your vacation into consideration as well.

Hotel finder. Before you leave, check out the website www.petswelcome.com. As well as travel tips and information on emergency clinics, it lists pet-friendly accommodations in Canada, the US, and France.

Better Business Travel

There are simple ways to ease the strain of business travel.

MAXIMIZING YOUR FREQUENT FLIER MILES

Christopher McGinnis, author of *The Unofficial Business Traveler's Pocket Guide*, says that many business travelers don't take full advantage of frequent flier miles. Here's his advice for accumulating as many as you can:

■ Concentrate your flying on one airline to make your frequent flier miles add up faster. With 25,000 miles on one airline, you'll be eligible for a free ticket, while 50,000 miles spread among several airlines might not add up to any reward at all.

■ Try to qualify for the elite level with the airline you use most often. You'll have to fly a specific number of miles each year, but elite frequent fliers have real perks. You can call a special number for reservations and information, get preference in upgrading your seats, and can check in at first-class desks even if you're flying economy. Some-

times you can even carry on more luggage than other passengers.

■ If you're really interested in using your frequent flier miles, make it a priority when you buy anything that offers a tie-in. For example, one phone company might offer five miles per calling minute on your choice of nine different airlines, while other carriers offer only bonus miles restricted to just one airline.

■ Boost your mileage by signing up for a credit card that offers frequent flier miles with the airline you use most frequently. Then use it to make large purchases, such as your new car, your child's college tuition, or family medical bills, to keep the miles adding up. Make sure,

though, to pay off the balance each month or you may end up paying more in interest than you're gaining in extra miles.

MAKING BUSINESS A PLEASURE

It's easy for frequent business travelers to become bogged down with the drudgery of their travel schedules. But that doesn't have to be the case, according to Chantal Beauchamp, media relations and communications coordinator with the Ottawa Tourism and Convention Authority. If you build a little flexibility into your schedule when you travel, Beauchamp says, you can make even a short stay in another city more enjoyable.

Here's what she advises

No matter how busy your business schedule, try to make some time for personal enjoyment.

to make business trips something you can look forward to:

■ If your schedule isn't too tight, call ahead and find out whether there are any special events scheduled in the area you're traveling to, such as a a special concert, festival, or rodeo. Then schedule your trip so that you'll have at least part of a day to attend the event.

■ If you're short on time, call the local convention and visitors bureau to find out what's going on the nights you'll be in town anyway. Then try and catch an Oilers' game if you're in Edmonton, or visit the Biosphere, say, or the Planetarium if you're in Montreal. Cities' websites are another great source of local information.

■ Sample some local flavor. Ask the concierge what the local food specialty is, and the most authentic place to get it. If you want to experience something a little different, don't always take the first, easiest piece of advice.

■ Business trips can be the kickoff for great, inexpensive family vacations, since your share is being paid for by your company. If you're going to Toronto, consider taking your children along for a visit to the Toronto Zoo. If you're going to Niagara Falls, leave the kids with your mom or a babysitter and plan a romantic weekend.

GETTING A BETTER PRICE

Business travel is rarely cheap, but there are a few things you can do to keep your costs down, says Nancy Barrows, executive vice president of Woodside Travel Trust, a consortium of corporate travel agencies.

■ Be flexible. If you're committed to one airline or departure time, you'll have to pay a premium.

■ Establish a relationship with a reliable travel agent. While you may be far too busy to look for the lowest fare, it's your agent's job to research all your possibilities.

■ Ask your agent to keep checking for lower fares up until the last minute. It may be worth a cancellation fee to get a much cheaper ticket.

■ Remember, though, that when it's essential that you get to a meeting on time, it might be worth the extra money to choose the most reliable flight instead of the least expensive one.

Smart Moves

You'll want to carry a plug and a converter, if necessary, so that you can use your computer on the road.

■ Pick up a copy of the local alternative weekly newspaper when you arrive in a new city. They're usually free, and provide detailed listings of what's going on in town. And unlike the daily paper, the weekly has listings that last all week so you can plan ahead.

■ Instead of asking the hotel concierge for a restaurant recommendation, ask the bellman where he and his friends eat, or what bar they frequent. That way you'll get a chance to mingle with the locals instead of other tourists.

■ Try to plan your trip so you can wear casual clothes on the plane, especially if you're traveling any distance. It's a lot easier to sleep, and your business clothes will arrive in better shape too.

■ Check with the hotel where you'll be staying to find out what kind of exercise facilities they have and whether the rooms have blow dryers. That way, you'll have what you need.

■ Ask whether there are connections in the room that you can use to send e-mail or whether there's a business center you can use.

■ Find out what long-distance phone service the hotel uses and what surcharges apply to calls from your room.

WHEN YOUR BUSINESS IS OVERSEAS

It takes a little planning to keep international business travel running smoothly, says Junius Peake, now the Monfort Distinguished Professor of Finance at the University of Northern Colorado, and formerly a securities industry executive and international consultant who traveled frequently to Europe, Asia, and South America. Here are his tips for staying comfortable and confident when doing business in another country:

■ Have some foreign currency in cash on hand when you arrive. Airport money exchangers offer the worst rates, and you'll want some cash for food, taxi rides, and unexpected emergencies.

■ If you've never been to the country before, read up on it. You'll want to find out local customs and business practices so you can make a good impression and avoid inadvertently being rude to both your clients and local people.

■ Find out about local transportation and whether most people take the bus or train to and from the airport. If you want to take a taxi, find out how much a ride should cost so you can avoid getting fleeced by a cabdriver.

■ Talk to people who've done business there before. Ask what they were surprised about or what they wish they'd known before they'd gone. Ask what you should look out for, whether it be gangs of youthful pickpockets or looking to the right instead of the left when you cross the road.

■ Pack only as much as you can carry on the plane with you. You don't want to waste precious time hunting down lost luggage or shopping for new clothes and shoes.

Solo Travel

Traveling is a great time to enjoy your own company.

ME, MYSELF, AND I

For many people, traveling alone isn't a necessity but a choice—and a passionate one. With no one else but yourself to rely on, you're likely to see more, do more, meet more people, and have more interesting experiences. In fact, many committed solo travelers make sure they find the time to travel alone even after they've settled down with their family.

Marybeth Bond has been an ardent solo traveler since she struck out on her own to travel the world at the age of 29. Her books, *Travelers' Tales: Gutsy Women, Travel Tips and Wisdom for the Road* and *A Woman's World*, document her two-year adventure and provide helpful hints for others:

■ Traveling alone gives you a rare opportunity to experience the world unfiltered by the opinions of other people, according to Bond. It's an ideal way to celebrate a life change, such as a new job or a big birthday—or to learn about yourself.

■ Traveling solo definitely has its rewards, but also its hardships. It can be a challenge at times to keep your solitude from sliding into loneliness. If you're feeling isolated, head out to a busy café and strike up conversations. Hostels are also great places to meet other travelers from

You'll never feel awkward eating alone if you bring reading and writing materials. And tuck a few family photos in your journal to share with new friends.

Smart Moves

When you travel by yourself, you may want to plan your itinerary in greater detail than you would if you were traveling with a companion. Having activities lined up at every stage of the trip is a good defense against being at loose ends. And you can indulge yourself with visits to places that travel companions might not be especially interested in.

■ If you are traveling with an organized tour group, sign up for the extra excursions that interest you, especially if you're a first-time visitor, and the tours will give you a richer sense of the region you're visiting.

■ If you've designed your own trip, get in touch with the tourist information offices in the regions where you'll be going. These offices stock the most current information about outdoor and indoor activities, from walking tours

to musical concerts, and they'll mail you information if you can't visit in person. Or, if you're traveling overseas, get in touch with the Canadian travel offices of the countries you'll be visiting. You can usually find the addresses in travel guides or by contacting their embassies or consulates here.

■ Do as much research before departure as you can make time for, and be sure to ask friends and colleagues who've made the trip about details that made their experience special. You don't want to learn about something that you would have enjoyed doing or an exceptional restaurant after you've left the area.

■ Don't do things that don't interest you. One of the great pleasures of solo travel is doing what you like, on your own schedule.

anywhere in the world, whether you're 17 or 70.

- In some cultures, it can feel a little awkward being by yourself, especially if you're a woman. Bringing a book or journal along to a busy restaurant can help you feel less conspicuous.
- And remember, the difference between being lonely and being alone is in your attitude.

SINGLES-FRIENDLY TOURS

If taking to the road on your own is a little more solitude than you bargained for, consider a singles-friendly tour or resort, suggests Betty Sobel, director of Solo Flights, a Connecticut-based firm catering to singles.

- Singles may be happier at one of the many all-inclusive resorts, such as Club Med and Breezes. Meal times and organized activities provide terrific opportunities to meet other solo travelers.
- Bus tours are an especially good option for singles, where small groups, close quarters, and shared experiences build bonds.
- Cruise lines will sometimes accommodate single travelers who are willing to share rooms with other singles. Ask ahead of time if you would like to be seated with other singles during meals. And get involved right away in activities that will introduce you to new people.
- The intimacy of small cruise ships, such as Windjammers, make them an ideal place to meet other vacationers traveling on their own.

PLAYING IT SAFE

Contrary to popular belief, solo travel doesn't have to be dangerous—even for a woman, says Sharon Wingler, a flight attendant for 26 years and author of *Travel Alone & Love It: A Flight Attendant's Guide to Solo Travel*. Although it is especially important to be prudent and take precautions when traveling alone, many women go solo—safely—all over the world.

- "Solo travel restored my faith in humanity," says Wingler. During her extensive travels, she has found people to be friendly and willing to go to extraordinary lengths to be helpful. If you ever need assistance or directions, don't hesitate to ask. A friendship or an invitation to a family dinner may even follow.
- Research your destination before you go. Once there, get to know your hotel staff. Not only will they be able to provide valuable information about what to see and do, but they will be able to tell you what kind of precautions to take in the area. If they get to know you, they will look out for your safety.
- "North Americans are the most casually dressed people on earth," says Wingler. If you're traveling abroad, dress more conservatively and more formally than you would at home. Women especially should observe the cultural norms of the country they're visiting. If you feel inappropriately dressed when you arrive, consider buying some clothes that will make you feel less conspicuous.

- Wingler recommends Canada, Australia, Greece, and Singapore as particularly hassle-free destinations for solo women.

TWO'S COMPANY

Perhaps you would like company on your next vacation, but your best friend can't make it or you'd like the opportunity to meet new people, whether for friendship or romance. A travel companion club might be the answer. Jens Jurgen, founder and president of Travel Companion Exchange in Farmingdale, New York, helps people with similar interests and itineraries meet one another.

Compatibility is very important when choosing a travel mate, advises Jurgen. The right companion to share your experiences with could greatly enhance your trip. The wrong companion could turn your vacation into a disaster. When you choose your partner, look not only for someone who has similar interests, but who's on a similar budget. If you are content picnicking in a park, for instance, you may feel stuck with a companion who wants to feast in four-star restaurants. People with very different lifestyles and financial means may find

they have to work much harder to get along.

Once you've chosen a partner, Jurgen recommends pooling shared expenses, such as hotels, and paying for personal items, such as souvenirs, separately. Don't haggle over small change—whoever ends up spending a little more will be rewarded by the convenience of sharing costs.

SOLO TRAVEL TIPS
Sharpen your mind and your social skills by bringing along a favorite game to teach new friends.

Take up an outdoor hobby that is inexpensive and can become a lifelong pursuit, wherever you travel.

Bringing along a sketch pad is a great way to exercise your creativity and document your trip—and will be a sure-fire conversation starter.

Senior Travel

Finally, you've got the time to take the trips you want.

THE BEST TRAVEL DEALS FOR SENIORS

Younger travelers have reason to be jealous of the travel discounts available for older adults. Gene and Adele Malott, owners, editors, and publishers of *The Mature Traveler*, a monthly newsletter highlighting "deals, discounts, and destinations for 49ers-plus," make it their business to tell you what these discounts are and how you can get them:

- Many hotel chains offer discounts to seniors, or membership in discount clubs. These deals are often good overseas as well as at home.
- You may also be able to get price cuts on flights, cruises, rail tickets, and ski vacations. The older you are, the more discounts you are eligible for. Always compare the standard senior rate to other discounts the company may be offering, though. Some vendors pretend to be doing you a favor when they're not.
- At age 60, travelers become eligible for substantial "pensioner" discounts and reduced rates on trains and tours and at hotels, museums, and other attractions in Western Europe.
- "Some bargains come and go very rapidly," says Malott, "such as a special rate marking the anniversary of a hotel, or other limited-time offers." The best approach is to turn your bargain-hunting into a game of discovery. For example, there may be a limited-time 50-percent-off deal you'll miss if you automatically accept the senior discount.
- Anyone 50 years and older who belongs to the Canadian Association of Retired Persons (CARP) can count on 10- to 30-percent discounts on travel and resort costs.

Smart Moves

Here are some tips on how to stay spry on the fly:

- Traveling in climate-controlled buses, trains, and airplanes can be dehydrating. Make sure you drink plenty of water.
- Changes of altitude can be a concern, especially if you have heart problems. If you are going to a higher altitude, don't overexert yourself for the first day or half-day.
- Many tour operators and cruise lines will accommodate special dietary needs if you ask ahead of time. Some even run special programs for people with special health concerns, such as dialysis or Parkinson's disease.
- Arrange for travel insurance for your trip. Then you can recover at least some of your money if a health emergency or other eventuality prevents you from traveling.

ADJUSTING FOR AGE

Getting older doesn't mean giving up your interests and your pastimes. But it may mean taking stock of how you're feeling from time to time and adjusting your goals accordingly. If you're nervous about traveling independently, an organized tour can provide extra security, says Linnea Jessup, managing editor of *Senior Travel Tips Magazine*.

- If you're traveling to an unfamiliar destination, it can be comforting to have an experienced person in charge who knows the area.
- If you feel a little shaky about your travel skills, bring along a younger friend or family member, perhaps a daughter or nephew. Intergenerational travel is more popular than ever, says Jessup.
- Sometimes the adjustments you'll want to make are subtle. Maybe it means insisting on the comforts of a three-star hotel, rather than settling for two stars. Maybe it means giving yourself more time to see fewer attractions. There are no hard and fast rules.

THE JOYS OF LIFELONG LEARNING

If you're like many older North Americans, your retirement years are a time to explore your personal interests and develop intellectual passions. Elderhostel, which offers a wide variety of travel and cultural programs across Canada, the United States, and in some 50 countries overseas, is dedicated to the philosophy of lifelong learning—what director Daniel Dowd calls "sightseeing for the mind."

He recommends Elderhostel for people age 55 and older with "inquiring minds, who want to share their years of experience and enjoy spending time with other people."

Whether your passion is philosophy, botany, archeology, art history, folk culture, or literature, there is a program for you. You can explore life in Nova Scotia's coastal communities, learn trapping techniques in the Northwest Territories, study the northern lights in Churchill, Manitoba, or almost anything that strikes your fancy. For possibilities, visit www.elderhostel.org.

The fee includes your chosen course, and meals, excursions to nearby sights, round-trip transportation, and accommodations.

Tools of the Trade

Using a convenient, day-by-day pillbox lets you leave bulky medicine bottles at home and see at a glance whether you've taken your required daily dosage.

Be a prepared traveler.

A hat to keep you out of the sun

Sunglasses or clip-ons

A bag you can carry comfortably, but large enough for a bottle of water, a snack, and your pill case, or other necessities

A walking stick that unfolds into a seat

Sturdy, comfortable walking shoes

Myth: *Senior travel discounts are available only to people over 65.* **Fact:** *Many resorts, hotels, and car rental agencies will give "senior" discounts—typically as much as 10 to 30 percent—to people as young as 50. A Canadian Association of Retired Persons (CARP) membership—which you can purchase for $15.95 when you turn 50—will get you discounts at many travel-related establishments. And you don't have to be retired to join, but you do have to ask about discounts you qualify for!*

NEVER SAY NEVER

Think you're too old or too inexperienced to go hiking in the Himalayas, trekking on the Silk Road, or visiting remote jungle tribes in New Guinea? Only if you think so, says Gary Murtagh, one of the founders of ElderTreks, a Toronto-based company that organizes adventures in exotic places for people 50 years and up. "It's an attitude thing," says Murtagh, who believes anyone in reasonable physical shape could handle ElderTreks tours. Convinced that many older Canadians want a vacation experience that goes beyond sightseeing bus tours, ElderTreks has made adventure and nature key components of their trips. Participants actively interact with the land, the people, and the culture. You might become part of an impromptu geography lesson at a faraway school or find yourself sharing a meal with a family in some remote village, says Murtagh.

Typical accommodations are tourist-class hotels and guesthouses, but if you choose the Adventure Option—and most Elder-Trekkers do—you might wind up sleeping on the floor of a tribal chief's hut or camping under the stars.

ElderTreks' core clientele are 65-year-olds. Half are married couples; the remainder, single. "There are so many older travelers looking for an active vacation," says Murtagh. "A lot are in better shape than people in their 30s and 40s."

The Right Way

Wherever you travel, always ask for the seniors' discount, advises Adele Malott. Many people working in the tourism industry are embarrassed to ask if you're a senior, so you may miss out on a 10- to 30-percent savings if you don't check.

Traveling with a Disability

The secret to a great vacation is in the little details.

THE WORLD BY WHEELCHAIR

Being in a wheelchair is no reason not to get out and see the world, says Carol Randall, co-founder of the Access-Able Travel Source website, which offers a wide range of resources for travelers with disabilities. People in wheelchairs can enjoy traveling to a wide variety of places worldwide if they research their destination ahead of time. Here are some of Randall's tips:

- Find out how wheelchair-accessible the city or country you will be visiting is. Countries around the world are improving accessibility, but no country has come as far as the US, although Canada, Scandinavia, and Australia are close behind. So prepare to run into a few obstacles along the way and consider them part of the adventure.
- How accessible is your hotel room? Ask about steps or narrow doorways. Is the bed the right height for you to transfer into? Is there a Hoyer lift if you need one?
- Consider taking a cruise on one of the larger cruise ships. Cruise lines have become very accessible, and allow you to visit multiple destinations without continually packing and unpacking.
- Be flexible and don't rush. You're sure to be disappointed if you expect your entire trip will go smoothly. Allow yourself more time than you think you will need whenever you go someplace new.
- Try not to travel alone. Having other people with you reduces some of the inevitable stresses of traveling and makes problems easier to solve.
- Keep an open mind. The more adventurous you want to be, the more you have to be willing to compromise. If you want to get to the top of Machu Picchu in Peru, you've got to let someone carry your chair up the last little way.

An increasing number of cruise ships can now accommodate guests with wheelchairs.

- Find a handicapped-friendly resort like the Mersey River Chalets in Nova Scotia, or a travel agent, such as Kéroul in Montreal, who specializes in travel for people with special needs. To explore other possibilities, check websites of organizations such as the Society for the Advancement of Travel for the Handicapped (SATH), Handicap Guide, Global Access, and Access-Able.

FAVORITE DESTINATIONS

Travel accessibility has improved dramatically during the past 15 years, according to Robert Samuels, a New York writer and travel editor for *New Mobility Magazine*. Samuels, a quadriplegic, has found some destinations far more wheelchair-accessible than others:

- Transportation is usually the biggest problem abroad. You can't ride the London buses or the Underground, although you can roll right into about half the taxis there. In Paris, there aren't even accessible taxis.
- The Americans with Disabilities Act of 1990 has made it much easier to get around in the US. In New York and some other cities, public buses are now wheelchair-accessi-

Tools of the Trade

Experienced travelers with disabilities recommend the same resources again and again. Here are some of the most popular newsletters, magazines, and books.

- *Open World*, newsletter for the Society for Advancement of Travel for the Handicapped.
- *Access to Travel*, a magazine about travel for people with disabilities that comes out six times a year.
- *Great American Vacations for Travelers with Disabilities*, published by Fodor's.

Quick Tricks

For help overseas. If you have a medical emergency in another country, you can always call the Canadian Embassy to find a local doctor who speaks English. Better still, know who to contact before you leave home: the Guelph, Ontario-based International Association of Medical Assistance to Travellers can advise you.
To find local transportation. In a North American city, call the local Center for Independent Living for information.
For accessibility information. Call the hotel directly (not the 800 number). If the operator can't answer your questions, ask to speak with a person in engineering or housekeeping, who may be more familiar with the actual rooms and equipment.

ble, as is the subway in Washington, DC.

■ Bed and breakfasts and other small hotels tend not to be accessible. So, especially in remote locations, you may have to stay in a larger (and often more expensive) hotel.

■ Beach areas often lack disabled facilities. If your friends or family have their heart set on a beach vacation, Miami's a great choice because there are a lot of things to see and do besides the beach.

■ In terms of public transportation, Vancouver is a model accessible city, according to Kathryn Underwood of *Abilities*, a Toronto quarterly publication for the disabled.

INSIDE INFORMATION

Both Canada and the US have come a long way in making airplanes and hotels accessible for people with disabilities. But if you

want to take a different kind of vacation, by traveling to rural areas, beach hotels, or family-friendly resorts, you can certainly find other ways to travel and other places to visit.

Some rental motor homes are equipped for people with disabilities, making available a wide range of previously inaccessible destinations. And people who need refrigerated medicine or bulky equipment can bring it along with them. Be sure to ask the dealer you're renting from about lifts, driver's hand controls, and accessible bathrooms.

In Puerto Rico, some resorts have beach chairs with large wheels that go right into the surf and lifts to get you in and out of their pools. A Nova Scotia resort, Mersey River Chalets, has specially designed docks to allow handicapped people access to swimming, canoes, and kayaks, which come with specially designed paddles for quadriplegics.

Many national parks in Canada and the US have accessible trails.

Disney World, and Disneyland are very accessible. The biggest hit at the Disney parks is a special entrance on most of the rides that lets you cut in front of the entire line. (Often you will also avoid crowds if you use the wheelchair entrance at some major museums.)

Many cruise lines, including Princess, Disney, and Norwegian American, are well equipped for people with a range of disabilities. There's even a company called Dialysis at Sea that plans tours for people who need this daily treatment.

IN CASE YOU GET SICK

Travelers with diabetes and other chronic diseases have to pay careful attention to prevent serious illness while they are traveling. Diabetic Maury Rosenbaum, a frequent traveler and editor of the newsletter *The Diabetic Traveler,* maintains that a few basic precautions can make the difference between a great vacation and a health crisis:

■ Address your fears and anxieties. Many people avoid traveling because they are afraid of leaving their hometown where they can always get the kind of food, medicine, or

medical assistance they need. If you are going to enjoy your vacation, you will need to address these concerns before you go to give yourself peace of mind.

■ If you are on a strict diet for health reasons, call your destination ahead of time to make sure that the ship or hotel kitchen offers food following your dietary restrictions. If not, determine whether you will be able to bring the necessary food items with you.

■ Always bring an extra supply of your medication, and ask your doctor for additional prescriptions in case you lose it. Keep your medicine with you at all times, but you may want to divide it among two or more bags in case one is lost or stolen. Do not check important medicine in your luggage.

■ Have the name, address, and phone number of a doctor near your destination who is familiar with your condition. Ask your own doctor for a recommendation or find out if there is a local organization that can arrange referrals quickly.

■ Ask your doctor ahead of time about adjusting your medication or eating schedule across time zones. Otherwise, you may upset your dosage. If you have a strict diet or need to eat at designated times, bring food with you onto the plane.

At Home in the Air

There are some simple secrets to flying right.

GET THE BEST DEAL ON AIRFARES

Want the best seats at the best prices? Louise Gross, president of the Smart Traveller, a Miami-based discount travel agency with clients all over the world, tells you how:

- Book early—at least three weeks in advance.
- If the price is right, but you're unsure about the safety record of the airline, keep in mind that all airlines flying in or out of Canada—whether domestic, international, or discount—have to meet the same Transport Canada airline safety standards, which are extremely high.
- Use a charter company. Charter flights, now highly regulated, are much more reliable than they used to be and offer big discounts.
- Consider taking an alternate route or flying into a nearby airport if you can't find the right price on your preferred route. Then rent a car or take ground transportation to your destination.

- Whenever possible, pay for your ticket or excursion with a credit card, advises Gross. That way, if your flight is canceled or your airline goes bankrupt, you can dispute the charge with your credit card company. Your credit card purchase may even be guaranteed.

CREATURE COMFORTS AT 35,000 FEET

Air travel can be an adventure, but it can take its toll on mind and body. Here are some helpful tips from Dr. Claude Thibeault, Air Canada's senior director of Occupational Health and Employee Assistance Services.

Nighttime flights can wreak havoc on your internal clock. If possible, fly during the day and sleep

A little bit of planning means the difference between a comfortable, relaxed flight and a cramped, miserable trip.

Quick Tricks

Flight attendant Caroline Fasoldt uses a rich night cream before and after a flight to protect her skin from the dehydrating effects of flying.

BE A SMART FREQUENT FLIER

"Now that almost everyone belongs to a frequent flier program, you must have a plan when trying to use an award to a popular destination," says Randy Petersen, editor and publisher of *Inside Flier* magazine. Some days offer better opportunities than others. The best days to redeem your miles are marked ✓. The worst days are marked ✗.

	MON	TUES	WED	THURS	FRI	SAT	SUN
US	✓	✓	✓		✗		✗
Florida	✓	✓	✓		✗		✗
Hawaii	✗	✓	✓	✓	✗	✗	✗
Asia		✓	✓	✓	✗	✗	✗
Caribbean	✗	✓	✓			✗	✗
Europe		✓	✓	✓	✗	✗	✗
Mexico		✓			✗	✗	✗
South America		✓	✓		✗	✗	✗

when you get to your hotel. Your internal clock will adjust to the new time zone much more quickly.

Airplane air is dry. Drink plenty of water and juice. Avoid caffeine and alcohol, which are dehydrating.

Limited space and inactivity may make you uncomfortable. A walk to the washroom, exercising your legs in your seat, or simply standing up helps, especially if you have vascular problems. Avoid tight, restrictive clothing. Wear comfortable layered clothing to help with temperature changes on board. Wear your seatbelt all the time.

ELBOW ROOM AND LEG ROOM

The seats in the middle of the center section are the last to fill up on wide-body planes, according to flight attendant Caroline Fasoldt. Book an aisle seat in the center section and you may end up with an empty row all to yourself!

Or, for extra leg room, try to reserve a seat in the emergency exit rows or in the bulkhead, the first row of seats in economy class.

These seats have twice, even three times, the leg room of regular seats.

BETTER FOOD ON BOARD

It's easier than ever to eat tasty and nutritious meals on board, says Siegfried Lang, managing director of food and beverage planning at Continental Airlines. Continental is one of many airlines that has revamped its onboard meal plan to make the food better.

Celebrity chefs, such as Don Pintabona of the Tribeca Grill in New York and Michael Cordua of Churrascos and Americas in Houston, collaborate with nutritionists and dietitians to ensure that Continental's meals are as good-tasting and nutritious as possible. United Airlines has the most comprehensive meals program, offering 26 different types of meals. Other airlines offer similar programs. Some tips on airline food:

- Most major airlines offer a range of special meal and snack options to economy, business, and first-class customers, at no extra charge. Many air carriers offer low-fat, low-sodium, diabetic, and high-fiber meal options, as well as special meals for members of the Hindu, Moslem, and Jewish faiths. Depending on your carrier, other choices may include Asian, vegetarian, Indian, salad plates, fruit plates, and special meals for infants and toddlers. Ask what's available next time you book your flight.

- Air travel can magnify the effects of alcohol. To arrive refreshed and alert, limit your alcohol consumption before your flight and on board to a glass of wine with dinner.

- Enjoy your onboard meal, but don't overeat. Even if you're not on a restricted diet, it might make sense to choose a vegetarian or low-fat meal to prevent in-flight indigestion.

- If you're concerned about nutrition, most carriers will supply a nutrition card on request, listing the nutritional content of your in-flight meal.

Tools of the Trade

Whether they're on duty or off, flight attendants prefer carry-on luggage with built-in wheels and retractable handles. You can roll right through customs and onto the plane. At your destination, while everyone else is still standing around waiting for their bags, you'll already be settling comfortably into your hotel room. Most airlines allow you to carry on a 9- by 22- by 14-inch case.

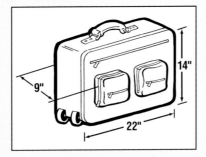

9" 14" 22"

Riding the Rails

Train travel is back in vogue—and for many good reasons.

THE NATION'S BACKYARD

Train travel lets you see the country from a whole new perspective, according to Cliff Black, director of public affairs for Amtrak. Traveling by train gives you a glimpse of "the nation's backyard," whether it's spectacular natural scenery, small-town life, or inner-city industrial areas

that the railways have historically served.

For the business person, train travel offers practical advantages. Modern technology, such as cellular phones and laptops, make it easier than ever to get your work done on the move. "Unlike a plane, you don't have to put away your laptop for take-off or landing. You can keep working from the moment you board until you pull into the station."

And when you travel by train, you're taking one trip instead of three—if you consider the typically long

drives to and from suburban airports, Black adds. "This gives you uninterrupted time to rest, think, or get something accomplished. And the seats are a whole lot bigger."

RAIL ADVENTURES AND CLASSIC TRAIN TRIPS

Think that rail travel is boring? Think again. Dixie Fowler, tour and operations manager with the Rail Travel Center in Brattleboro, Vermont, organizes about 30 rail tours a year around the world—from fall excursions to Churchill, Manitoba, to

see the polar bears and northern lights to luxury train trips along the South African coast. She and her husband, Carl Fowler, between them have clocked about 400,000 miles on the world's trains. Here are some of their favorite runs:

- One of the most popular and beautiful routes in the US is the *Coast Starlight*, which runs from Los Angeles to Seattle.
- The *Sierra Madre Express*, which runs from Tucson, Arizona, to the Copper Canyon in Mexico, is an eight-day round trip on a luxury private train.

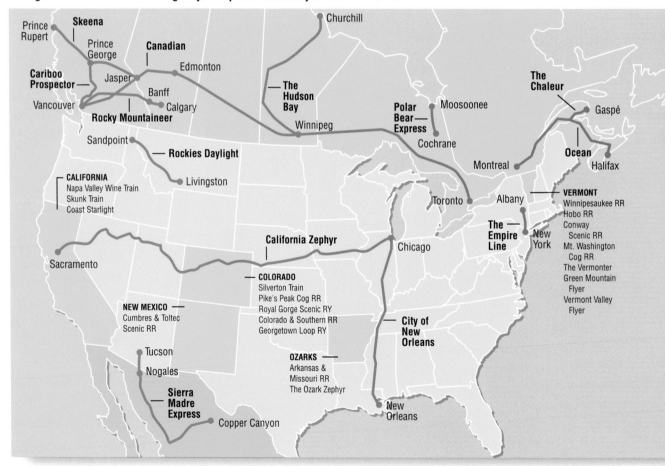

Taking the train is an exhilarating way to explore the beauty of North America.

- The *Adirondack Scenic Railroad* offers travel in vintage open-windowed coaches through the gorgeous scenery of the wilderness Adirondack Park in New York.
- Popular Canadian routes include Via Rail's transcontinental *Canadian* trip, between Toronto and Vancouver, and the *Skeena*, from Prince Rupert, British Columbia, to Jasper National Park in Alberta, and the Great Canadian Railtour Tour Company's *Rocky Mountaineer* route from Banff to Vancouver.
- Switzerland's *Glacier Express* passes through

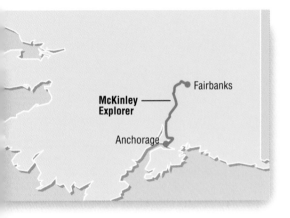

the tourist meccas of St. Moritz and Zermatt.
- The *Eastern Oriental Express* is a luxury train running from Bangkok to Singapore—not to be confused with the famous *Venice-Simplon Orient Express* running from Paris to Istanbul.
- Probably the most luxurious train in the world, the ultimate-luxury *Royal Scotsman* will take you on a six-day circle tour of the Highlands. Its restored dining car is over 100 years old, and its lounge observation car is the longest in the world.

TIPS FOR LONG-HAUL RAIL TRAVELERS

John Pitt, an English travel writer and author of *U.S.A. By Rail*, thinks that train travel is the best way to appreciate the breadth, natural beauty, and variety of North America.
- The best times to see the US and Canada by rail are spring and fall, when the trains are much less crowded, says Pitt. Fall foliage is a particular attraction in the North.
- Many schedules are arranged so you travel through the most scenic or historic parts of the trip during daylight. On some US routes, national park rangers and tour guides join the train to provide commentary and answer travelers' questions.
- One practical advantage of rail travel is that you can bring a lot of luggage with you at no charge. Via Rail will let you carry on two bags and check another three for free. Just remember to check

in at least a half-hour before the train departs.
- Pitt urges travelers to take advantage of conductors' or service managers' interests and expertise. They can be great sources of historic information about sites along the way.

TRAVELING IN EUROPE BY TRAIN

European trains are fast, efficient, and comfortable. If you plan to travel extensively in Europe, consider purchasing a Eurail pass, suggests Mary DiThomas of Rail Pass Express. Although Eurail passes may not be the most economical option for travelers—unless you will be covering a lot of ground in a short time—they offer the ultimate in flexibility and convenience.
- A standard Eurail pass offers unlimited first-class travel in 17 European countries. They can be purchased for 15-day to 90-day periods.
- If you will be traveling at a more leisurely pace, consider a Eurail Flexipass. Flexipasses offer a certain number of days of travel

Myth: *Trains are for budget travelers only.* **Fact:** *High-standard services such as private suites and full-service dining cars are now being reintroduced on passenger trains in the US, says conductor Rick Palmer.*

within a specified time period. For instance, they can be purchased for 10 or 15 days of travel within a two-month period.
- Several rail pass/car rental combinations are available in Great Britain and continental Europe. Your travel agent will be able to help you choose one that suits your plan.
- If you will be traveling in only one or two countries, regional passes, including BritRail and France Rail passes, are often a smart, economical choice.

TIME TO UNWIND

A train conductor for over 25 years, Rick Palmer now works on the *Empire Line* from New York City to Albany. Although Palmer knows plenty of business travelers who use their time on board to get their work done, he recommends taking advantage of uninterrupted time on the train for relaxation and contemplation. The peace and quiet afforded by train travel can significantly cut down on the stresses of modern-day living, says Palmer.

Smart Moves

- Weather and temporary track conditions can delay trains. Give yourself at least an hour or two of leeway to make connections.
- Choose a seat away from the doors, which can be noisy, congested, and distracting.
- Make sure when you choose a seat that the reclining mechanism and leg rests are in good working order.

- If you take a platform break, be sure to listen for announcements. It could be a long wait before another train is heading your way.
- Lunch in the dining car is usually a better value than dinner.
- You can take your own food if you prefer, but you can't count on being able to replenish your supply at train stations.

Traveling by Bus

You can leave the driving to them.

NEW HORIZONS

"You'll never get a better view of America than from the front seat of a bus," says author Irma Kurtz, who spent five months touring the US on her own by motorcoach. "And it's the best way to get to know the people of the land." In fact, she still keeps in touch with many of the friends she made during her cross-country adventure.

Best known for her column in *Cosmopolitan* magazine, Kurtz wrote a book documenting her journeys: *The Great American Bus Ride: An Intrepid Woman's Cross-Country Adventure*. And she has lots of insights for people who want to hit the road by bus:

■ Long-haul bus rides are a great way to beat the solitude of traveling solo, but you have to be a people person to enjoy bus travel. Fellow travelers will pour out their life stories to you.
■ About onboard politics: "Bad boys sit in the back, and show-offs in the front." If there's ever any trouble on board, it always comes from the "mean seats" in the last few rows.
■ If you're picky about what you eat, bring food along with you. Although all long-haul buses make meal stops, they're almost exclusively at fast-food restaurants.
■ Although the area around bus terminals can be unsavory, the bus stations themselves are safe and heavily policed. As a precaution, Kurtz recommends carrying as little luggage as possible and taking a cab to and from the station, especially if you're a woman who is traveling alone.
■ Best of all, Kurtz thinks that buses are one of the safest ways to travel: "You see a lot of elderly women traveling alone on the bus. There's a lot of camaraderie on board. People really do look out for each other."

RIDING THE HOUND

Bus travel might not only be the best way to see the country—it is also the cheapest. Greyhound serves some 2,100 destinations in Canada and offers numerous discounts to get to them. Many of these deals require advance purchase or have other restrictions, so Greyhound's Judy Murray recommends that you plan ahead.

■ The Canada Coach pass offers unlimited travel on all Greyhound Canada routes. You can buy a 7-, 15-, 30-, or 60-day pass. A 30-day Go Anywhere fare offers unlimited travel in Canada and the US.
■ Greyhound offers a 10-percent discount on all fares for people 60 years and older.
■ All children 15 years and younger can travel free with the purchaser of a regular adult or senior fare.
■ Another popular option is the "companion fare": the purchaser of a regular adult or senior fare can bring along a companion at half price.
■ A student with an International Student Identity Card (ISIC) receives a 25-percent discount: the discount for other recognized student cards is 10 percent.

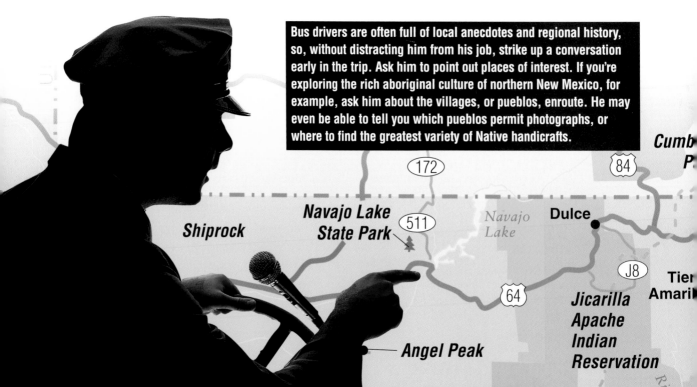

Bus drivers are often full of local anecdotes and regional history, so, without distracting him from his job, strike up a conversation early in the trip. Ask him to point out places of interest. If you're exploring the rich aboriginal culture of northern New Mexico, for example, ask him about the villages, or pueblos, enroute. He may even be able to tell you which pueblos permit photographs, or where to find the greatest variety of Native handicrafts.

LONG-HAUL SURVIVAL KIT

Water or juice to prevent dehydration

Your favorite healthy snacks

Pillow and blanket for comfortable naps

A portable CD or cassette player to pass the time

LEG ROOM

The notion of comfortable bus travel is "something of an oxymoron, at least for a 6-foot-4-inch basketball player." Jay Butler, head coach of Columbia University's women's basketball team, travels to and from 13 games every season by motorcoach with his team of 25 student athletes.

All buses were not created equal, according to Butler. When you have a choice, choose comfort. Deluxe coaches with plush, deeply reclining seats, onboard bathrooms, and video monitors to watch movies ease much of the discomfort of long-haul trips. But whatever the comfort level, Butler stocks plenty of juice and water on board to keep his athletes hydrated, something he suggests for all travelers. All 25 players bring blankets and pillows along to keep cozy on the long winter rides. And most of them travel with portable tape or CD players to help them pass the time.

His players' comfort is important to Butler. While many coaches require their athletes to wear suits or other formal clothes when arriving as the visiting team, he had smart-looking but comfortable travel suits designed for his athletes so they can relax on the road and still arrive looking sharp. You can choose a jogging suit in a durable, wrinkle-resistant fabric if you want the same combination of comfort and presentability.

HAPPY TRAILS

Thought about organizing a motorcoach tour with your bridge club, book club, or your church group? Barbara Koss and Sue Neuschel organize bus tours for their Illinois township that "people never forget." When you hear some of their ideas, you'll understand why:

■ Plan your trip around a theme, suggests Koss. On some of her tours, participants wear costumes or hats to help create a mood. Sometimes she and Neuschel plan a theme around a destination, such as a backroads tour, a lake tour, or a canal boat tour.

■ Try to switch seats between rest stops, advises Neuschel. It lets people mix and make new friends. And it gives people who have been sitting in the back a chance to come and sit up front.

■ The secret to keeping people from becoming cranky and uncomfortable on a long bus ride is to keep them entertained. Koss and Neuschel devise games and activities for people to play on the road.

■ Have a "happy hour" on board on your return trip. Koss and Neuschel sometimes dress up in maids' costumes or black tie and tails and serve cheese and crackers to participants.

■ Neuschel and Koss research their routes and plan their meal stops at rural family restaurants, rather than roadside fast-food joints. On one trip in rural Indiana, the group was invited to a Mennonite farm for a home-cooked Thanksgiving dinner made with fresh local ingredients.

■ Don't skimp on comfort when you arrange for a bus, says Koss. A little extra leg room and padding on the seats can make a big difference.

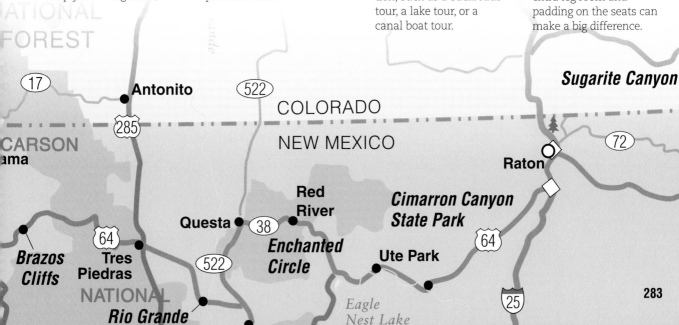

Cruising to Paradise

Choose a cruise where you'll be comfortable.

BEST CRUISE ON A BUDGET

These days, nobody should pay full price for a cruise. Almost every travel agent can get you a discount off the rack rate (the price in the brochure). John Lang, spokesperson for Toronto-based The Cruise People, Canada's oldest cruise agency, offers these suggestions:

■ Make your reservations as early as possible. Most cruise companies offer savings or discounts off retail prices for booking their cruises well in advance of embarkation.

■ If you can leave on a moment's notice, ask your travel agent about last-minute vacancies. Some ships regularly offer fabulous prices on last-minute bookings to fill their empty cabins.

■ Be flexible. If you are willing to cruise on any of a variety of ships and are open to different departure dates and destinations, your travel agent will have a much better chance of finding you a great deal.

■ Travelers 55 years of age and older at time of booking may receive preferred pricing from selected cruise lines.

■ Group bookings can yield big savings. Certain cruise lines offer one to four free cabins for group bookings, and a group can be as few as 10 persons. The group can be assembled by you from among your family and friends or put together by your travel agent to take advantage of a cruise's block-booking policies.

■ Passenger freighters can be a great way to see the world. Cabins are generally larger than on regular cruise ships and the cost is substantially less.

FINDING THE BEST CRUISE

How much you enjoy your vacation at sea depends on finding the cruise that best suits your interests, temperament, and budget. Jim Godsman, president of Cruise Lines International Association, the cruise industry's trade group, recommends these simple ways to help you choose the right ship:

Luxury hierarchy

There are four generally accepted levels of luxury in the cruise industry. When you find a cruise that fits your budget, compare it to others in its category before you book your cabin. (Adventure and expedition cruise lines are not included in these lists.)

■ Find a cruise specialist, an experienced travel agent who understands the cruise industry.

■ Ask yourself what you want to do on your vacation, and then tell your travel agent. If you enjoy partying all night with lots of people, you will want a very different cruise than someone looking for a week of peace and quiet. A little searching should turn up exactly what you want.

■ Look for cruises that cater to your lifestyle. Some ships have a formal ambiance and hold one or two black-tie affairs each week, while others have a more casual, relaxed atmosphere. Families usually want cruise ships with special programs for children.

■ Ask your agent for profiles on a variety of cruise lines so you find the one that best suits your interests, your budget, and the time you prefer to travel.

Ultra-deluxe
includes lines such as Crystal Cruises, Cunard, Radisson, Seaborn, and Silversea Cruises.

INTERPRETING CRUISE BROCHURES

Detailed reports of today's passenger ships and travelers' accounts of their shipboard experiences are regular features of *SeaFare,* an illustrated review of sea travel, published quarterly in Toronto for readers around the world. *SeaFare's* associate editor Philip Dawson offers these tips on getting the most useful information from a cruise brochure:

■ Pay particular attention to the photographs. They will give you a good idea of what amenities the ship has to offer.

■ Look at the people in the photographs to find out whether the ship caters to older or younger travelers, how formal the attire is, and whether there are children or mostly adults on board.

■ Note the square footage of the cabins. It is a more reliable way to compare

Smart Moves

■ Get a great deal on a cruise by traveling during the off season. Consider cruising to Alaska in the late spring or early autumn, or to the Caribbean during the summer. Not only will you pay less, but you will have a better chance of getting the ship you want.

■ To make sure your cruise doesn't wind up costing far more than you expected, determine an entertainment budget for yourself beforehand and stick to it. Cruise ships tend to charge high prices for drinks, in-room movies, and shore excursions in order to be able to offer low prices on cabins.

■ Before you send in the final payment for your cruise, ask your travel agent to look for any last-minute deals that might save you money.

Myth: *Cruises are for retirees, not young people and families with small children.* **Fact:** *There are cruise ships that cater to people of all ages. Within the past 10 years, the average age of cruise passengers has dropped from 56 to 44.*

Deluxe
includes lines such as Celebrity, Holland America, Orient, Renaissance, and Princess.

Moderate
includes lines such as Carnival, Costa, Norwegian, and Royal Caribbean.

Budget
includes lines such as Commodore, Premier, and Regal.

A PERFECT MATCH

Shirley Slater, author of Fielding's *Worldwide Cruises 1998*, recommends doing your own research on cruising, even if you're going to use a travel agent. Knowing the answers to these questions will help your travel agent find the best cruise for you:

What are you looking for in a cruise-ship vacation? Do you want to lie on the deck and watch the ocean, shop in local markets, or tour historic sites?

How long do you want to be away? You can choose to cruise for three days or three months.

Where do you want to go? The Caribbean or Alaska are the most frequently visited destinations, but there are also cruises sailing through the Mediterranean, in Asia, and throughout the rest of the world.

Do you plan to travel alone, as a couple, or with a group? If you'll be by yourself, you may want to look for a specialized cruise that's designed for singles. But if you're planning a family trip that will be fun for grandparents and children as well as parents, you may want a ship that offers many different kinds of activities.

Are you interested in a large, medium, or small ship? Large ships may hold up to 3,800 passengers, while small ships carry between 100 and 300. Generally the larger the ship, the more entertainment and activities there will be. But the advantage of a smaller one is a greater sense of being at sea.

What are you looking for in shipboard culture? Would you prefer to attend lectures on the places you will be visiting, spend most of your time in the casino, or do a little of both? Most cruise lines are clear about the lifestyle and activities on board, since they want happy passengers.

Do you want to combine cruising with shore visits? Some trips emphasize shopping, but some others schedule hikes or tours.

Learn the lingo

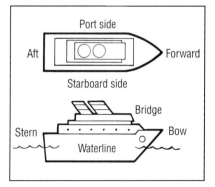

sizes than looking at brochure photographs.
■ Pay attention to the deck plan. You may want to avoid a cabin underneath the disco or next to the kitchen. People prone to seasickness often prefer cabins down low near the center of the ship, where there is the least movement.

Traveling Abroad

For many travelers, Europe's the place.

TOURS FOR THE FIRST-TIMER

Perhaps you've never been abroad before. Maybe you're nervous about negotiating a new language, culture, or city. Maybe you only want to see major sights like the Eiffel Tower or Picadilly Circus. Maybe you live alone, but don't want to travel alone. If any of these sound familiar, an organized tour might be the perfect answer.

On organized tours, your accommodations, meals, and transportation from city to city and site to site are all taken care of. Such tours are not the best choice, however, if you don't like getting up early during your vacation, prefer a less frenetic pace, or like to spend unscheduled time on your own. Also, organized tours tend to cater to North American tastes in food and accommodation. If you want a more authentic experience, consider traveling independently. Great Britain—or the Netherlands or Scandinavia, where many people speak English—are good destinations if you're nervous about being able to communicate.

Canadians traveling abroad can get excellent information on safety, security, health concerns, and visa requirements for some 215 destinations from the Department of Foreign Affairs and International Trade. Scores of booklets, such as *Bon Voyage But…*, *Her Own Way*, *Advice for the Woman Traveller,* and *Crossing the 49th* are chock-full of practical tips on everything from passports and health insurance to medical advice and how to contact consular services during emergencies. And they're all free.

You can get them by writing to Enquiries Service, Department of Foreign Affairs and International Trade, 125 Sussex Drive, Ottawa, ON K1A 0G2, by calling 1-800-267-8376, or by visiting the website www.dfait-maeci.gc.ca.

THE INDEPENDENT TRAVELER

Striking out on your own, fortified with a good map, a good guidebook, and a basket full of the local cheese, bread, and wine, is the only way to see Europe, according to medievalists Eileen Gardiner and Ron Musto of Italica Press, who travel there frequently for both work and pleasure. Here's how they travel:

Driving. Renting a car gives you the greatest flexibility and allows you to explore off the beaten path. It is usually cheapest if you make arrangements with a Canadian agent. You can find some very good deals, often through a travel agent, and airfare/car rental combinations can cut car rental costs by up to two-thirds. Small European cars are not only the most economical option but also the most practical for the tourist. Many of Europe's most interesting towns and hamlets—even neighborhoods in the major cities—have narrow, twisting streets and steep slopes. If you do manage to wedge a big car down one of these streets, you may never make it out again.

Accommodations. Unless you're very picky about where you stay, it's really only necessary to make reservations during the summer and in the big cities, say Gardiner and Musto. The tourist offices in most European towns provide listings of inns, B&Bs, and two- and three-star hotels, which usually offer perfectly adequate accommodation. Leaving yourself open to chance will also leave you open to new adventures.

Language. The further you travel from the major tourist centers, the more you'll have to improvise with your communication skills. Gardiner and Musto describe how their rusty classical Greek caused them to drive through a small, fast river. They had misunderstood the directions they were given by a Greek farmer.

MONEY MATTERS

"You'd be appalled if you knew how much money you'll lose over the course of your travels through bank fees," says Rick Steves, author of 13 European travel guidebooks and the host and writer of the PBS series "Travels in Europe." Although you can't avoid these losses, you can minimize them:

- ATMs are everywhere in Europe now. They give the best possible rates—better than travelers checks—but you'll be charged a modest fee by your bank for each use.
- All major brands of travelers checks are accepted in Europe. However, some

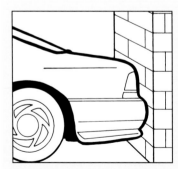

The Right Way

If you plan to travel in continental Europe with a car and will be stopping along the way to explore churches or ancient ruins, insist on a car with a trunk or concealed baggage compartment, say Gardiner and Musto, who make frequent research stops.

When parking, back the car up against a wall or railing so that it's impossible to open the trunk, even if it's jimmied. "We've heard too many woeful stories of people losing all their possessions within minutes of parking their car to explore a museum or stop for a caffè latte," they say.

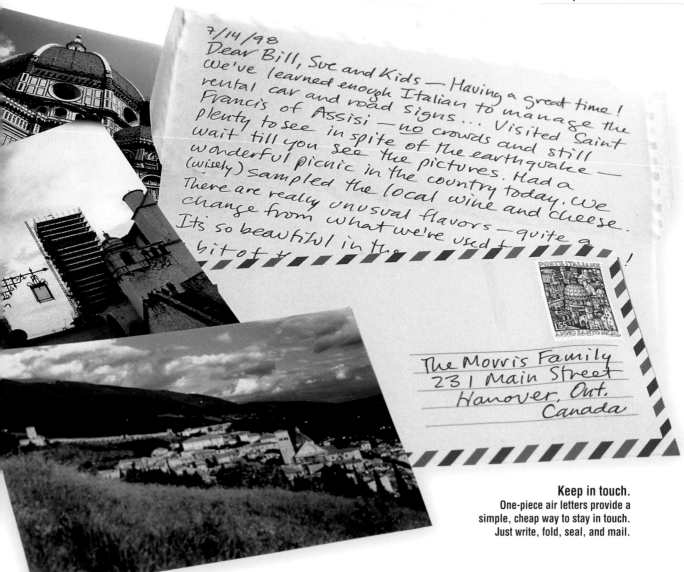

7/14/98
Dear Bill, Sue and Kids — Having a great time!
We've learned enough Italian to manage the
rental car and road signs... Visited Saint
Francis of Assisi — no crowds and still
plenty to see in spite of the earthquake —
wait till you see the pictures. Had a
wonderful picnic in the country today. We
(wisely) sampled the local wine and cheese.
There are really unusual flavors — quite a
change from what we're used t
It's so beautiful in the
bit of ☀

The Morris Family
231 Main Street
Hanover, Ont.
Canada

Keep in touch.
One-piece air letters provide a
simple, cheap way to stay in touch.
Just write, fold, seal, and mail.

Mail your vacation home.
Get your film developed while you're still away,
and send it home as personalized postcards.

merchants may ask you not to use them, and many banks charge a fee for cashing them, on top of the fee you may have paid to buy them.

■ Never offer to pay in dollars rather than local currency, says Steves. "It's simply bad style to think that your currency would be accepted in a foreign country." If someone does accept your cash, they will probably give you a poor exchange rate.

■ "Europe is a very safe place from a violent crime point of view but a dangerous place from a purse-snatching and pickpocketing point of view," says Steves. Keep your valuables in a money belt that you wear under your clothes.

A VILLA IN VERONA, A COTTAGE IN THE COTSWOLDS

If you want the excitement of a new culture, but the comforts of home, consider renting a house in your dream destination. "When you rent a home, you are a traveler, not a tourist. You'll come back feeling like you've *been* some place," says Suzanne B. Cohen, an Augusta, Maine-based rental agent who specializes in properties in Great Britain and Central Italy.

Rental properties are ideal for families, groups, or people who want to integrate with the culture or simply keep to their own schedule. There are homes available for virtually every taste or occasion, whether you want to be in a fortified farmhouse in Tuscany or a canalside townhouse in Venice, and whether you're going abroad for a week or a year. Start looking six months in advance, advises Cohen, and always ask for references from people who have stayed in the home.

287

Traveling Further Afield

The world is full of great travel destinations.

EXPANDING YOUR HORIZONS

For many people, a trip abroad means heading to the famous cities of Western Europe. Edward Hasbrouck, an Internet travel guru you can locate at www.practicalnomad.com, would like to change that. Hasbrouck dispels some common misconceptions:

■ One of the advantages of traveling away from the major tourist destinations is that you can afford a higher level of comfort for considerably less money. For instance, budget travelers visiting less-Westernized countries often hire a private guide or driver—a luxury that would be prohibitively expensive in Western Europe.

■ Although it is courteous to try and pick up a few words of the native language, the role of English as the "international language of tourism" makes it possible to travel

North Americans are often surprised at the generous hospitality of other cultures.

almost anywhere on the strength of English alone.

■ Far from being a gap on a résumé that needs to be explained away, time spent traveling can be a tremendous advantage in the job market now that all sectors of the economy express a demand for people with the ability to interact with a wide variety of peoples. According to Hasbrouck, it may even help you get a job.

Smart Moves

■ Don't try to do too much in too little time. For instance, it is routine for North Americans to try to "do" China in two or three weeks. But remember that China is almost as large as Canada.

■ If you take any prescription medications, take a double supply and get a note from your physician saying what they are for.

■ Check with someone who has visited an area recently to get information on safety concerns. Better still, contact the consular affairs bureau of the Department of Foreign Affairs and International Trade. It will provide you with up-to-date travel reports and information on changes in political and security situations worldwide (www.dfait-maeci.gc.ca).

TAKING THE CHILDREN

For many parents, planning a trip to a provincial park seems enough of a challenge, let alone a family vacation halfway around the world. But Chantal and David Watson took two of their three children trekking in Nepal last year.

Traveling with children is a great way to meet people, she says. In Nepal they were frequently invited to people's homes where they were "treated as family." Here are her tips:

■ Train your kids to travel, says Chantal, a freelance architectural designer. That means introducing them to a varied diet when they're young and getting them used to coping with makeshift bedtime arrangements. Camping trips and visits to friends and relatives can be good practice.

■ Pack light. You don't want to be weighed down or distracted by excess baggage. The Watsons took little more than a single change of clothes and their sleeping bags on their Nepal trip.

■ Adjust your schedule to your children's. An itinerary with lots of breaks works well with kids. And it's important to include time for them to talk about the things they're seeing and doing.

ATTITUDE ADJUSTMENT

For some people, traveling in remote areas or less well developed parts of the world can be an ordeal, whereas others may find the same experience exciting and adventuresome. Often the different reactions can be traced back to the traveler's mindset and

STAYING HEALTHY ABROAD

Protecting your health is a major concern if you're planning a trip to a tropical or less-Westernized area. Find out well ahead of departure time what inoculations you will need for admittance to the countries you propose to visit. The information sources below can be immensely helpful. In addition, Dr. Jay Keystone, staff physician at the Toronto General Hospital's Centre for Travel and Tropical Medicine, and the editor of *Don't Drink the Water*, a Canadian Public Health Association guide to staying healthy in warm climates, provides the following helpful guidelines:

- Map out a general itinerary and take it to a travel health specialist. Most cities have specialized travel clinics, many of them affiliated with universities, public health departments, or family practice units. Cross-Canada locations are listed on the Canadian Society for International Health website, www.csih.org.
- Vaccinations and preventive medications for diseases such as viral hepatitis (A and B), yellow fever, and malaria are required or recommended for many regions of the world. Since they can take four to

six weeks to reach full effect, you should seek advice at least two months before your departure. In addition, vaccination requirements not only vary from country to country, but from region to region within the same country. Make sure you are prepared.

- Day-biting insects can transmit serious diseases such as dengue fever; and night-biting insects, malaria. In high-risk areas, protect yourself by using an insect repellent on exposed skin, the insecticide permethrin on clothing, and sleeping under a permethrin-impregnated bed net. Avoid swimming, washing, or wading in slow-moving freshwater lakes or rivers in most tropical countries to avoid schistosomiasis (bilharzia) and infection with a water-borne parasite, which can penetrate unbroken skin.
- Avoid riding in overcrowded public vehicles or on motorcycles, and never travel by road in rural areas after dark.
- Make sure routine vaccinations for diseases such as tetanus, diphtheria, polio, and measles, mumps, and rubella are up to date. Other immunizations may also be recommended.

Hepatitis A	Typhoid	Yellow fever	Malaria
Vaccination recommended for travelers to developing countries and other areas with poor sanitation and water supplies.	In developing countries, vaccination recommended for long-term travelers and those traveling off main tourist routes in areas with poor sanitation and water supplies.	Vaccination recommended or required for parts of Africa and South America. A certification of vaccination is also required by immigration authorities in many countries for travelers from infected areas. In Canada, it is available only at Health Canada-designated travel clinics.	Anti-malarial medication, such as mefloquine or chloroquine, is recommended for many places in the developing world, but the type of medication depends on such factors as geographic regions, the traveler's activities, and season of travel. These medications need to be taken before and after travel. Also, since anti-malarial medications do not offer complete protection, travelers should take measures to protect themselves from exposure to night-biting mosquitoes in high-risk areas (see bulleted copy above). The International Association for Medical Assistance to Travellers (see below) offers its members a portable freestanding mosquito bed that also protects against spiders, ticks, beetles, flies, roaches, assassin bugs, bed bugs, and other insects.

Information sources

A 200-country immunization chart for diphtheria, viral hepatitis, measles, mumps, pertussis, plague, rabies, rubella, tetanus, typhus, typhoid fever, yellow fever, and other vaccine-preventable diseases such as encephalitis, as well as details on risk areas for schistosomiasis and the widespread fatal chagas' disease are available from the Guelph, Ontario-based International Association for Medical Assistance to Travellers (www.sentex.net/~iamat/mb.html). Health tips on preparing for travel and information on travel health clinics across Canada are available at www.csih.org, the website of the Canadian Society for International Health.

Check the Information for Travellers on Health Canada's website, hwcweb.hwc.ca. Up-to-the-minute travel information from the Travel Information Program of the Department of Foreign Affairs and International Trade is available toll free at 1-800-575-2500 or at www.dfait-maeci.gc.ca/travelreport/menu_e.htm.

preparedness, or lack of it.

Making the appropriate arrangements before you go and taking the right attitude along with you can make your travels considerably more rewarding, says Jeffrey Gettleman, a reporter for the *Los Angeles Times*. Gettleman became "smitten" with the peoples and cultures of eastern Africa when he went there as a college student. Here are his guidelines for planning a trip far afield:

Itinerary. Build some flexibility into your itinerary to accommodate spur-of-the-moment side trips and unexpected delays.

Wardrobe. Try to strike a balance between personal comfort and showing respect for the cultural norms of the host country. Gettleman prefers long pants and collared shirts—especially when visiting religious buildings or attending ceremonies. He recommends long skirts and sleeved shirts for women.

Money. Bring as much cash as you're comfortable carrying. You'll generally get a much better rate of exchange on cash than on travelers checks, which some stores may refuse. Don't rely on credit cards or ATM cards, although credit cards are welcome at some larger hotels and stores.

Recreational Vehicles

You can make an RV trip anything you want it to be.

RENTING AN RV

If you are considering a first-time vacation in an RV, you will probably want to rent, not buy. But renting an RV is not as simple as renting a car. You can't just pick up the keys and hit the road. Phil Ingrassia of Recreational Vehicle Rental Association suggests:

- Make reservations with the rental company ahead of time, especially if you want to travel during the peak season.
- When you pick up the RV, make sure the agent spends some time teaching you about it. Find out how to cut off the liquid propane (LP) gas, fill the fresh water tanks, empty the waste water tanks, and use the appliances.
- Check with your automobile insurance company to find out if it covers you

in a rental RV. Then find out if your homeowner's policy covers any belongings you take with you. You will want to buy additional coverage if you are not already insured.

- Decide whether you want to bring your own bedding and cutlery, or whether it would make more sense to rent a convenience kit from the rental company. If you decide to rent a kit, find out what is in it and bring anything else you will need.
- If you are not sure what kind of unit to rent, tell the agent how many people you'll be traveling with and where you'll be going. RVs range greatly in size, and you want to make sure you can fit everything (and everyone) comfortably inside, while not paying for extra weight and space.
- Take ease of driving into consideration as well. While driving a small motor home is almost like driving a van, a larger one can be trickier.

The Right Way

To help answer the question of whether to rent or to buy, consider that typical RV owners put 5,900 miles a year on their vehicle. If you drive more than that, consider buying. If not, you will be better off renting.

RV CLUBS

Other RV travelers can be a great source of information and camaraderie. Louise Morel of Go RVing Canada, an organization representing dealers, manufacturers, and RV campgrounds, explains that there are a wide variety of RV clubs to choose from.

If you are interested in finding other people who enjoy RV travel, Morel says, look for an RV club that caters to your particular interest. Although some clubs may welcome all RV travelers, most are more specialized. Many concentrate on a particular type of RV, such as the Safari owners' group, one of the largest motor home clubs.

The GMC motor home group focuses on these

classic vehicles from the 1970s, long since out of production. Members get together to share maintenance techniques and get leads on where to buy hard-to-find spare parts.

Most clubs have a geographic basis as well. There are usually multiple clubs or chapters based on location: many Canadians belong to US-based clubs. And some clubs focus on members' other interests, such as golfing, short-wave radio, or meeting other singles. There are even clubs for solo women RV travelers and those who travel despite physical disabilities.

Many RV clubs offer mail-forwarding and message services, great for staying in touch with friends and family when you're on the go. And most have a magazine

Motor coaches and trailers*

Class A motor home
- Range from $65,000 and up—to hundreds of thousands of dollars.
- Have the widest variety of luxury features.
- Usually between 23 and 40 feet long.

*Price ranges for all vehicles shown here are as in 1999

Class C motor home
- Range from $50,000 to $120,000.
- Built on van chassis.
- Have storage/sleeper compartment over driver's cab.
- Usually between 21 and 38 feet long.

Class B camper (camper-van conversion)
- Range from $55,000 to $80,000.
- Modified from standard vans.
- Extra compartment on top.

or newsletter to help keep you up to date. Find out more about RV clubs by asking for information from your RV dealer or from other RV travelers you meet on the road.

VARIETIES OF RVS

Harry Basch, co-author of *Freewheelin' USA*, says many people think that vacationing in an RV means buying into a particular type of lifestyle. But that's not the case. Instead, he says, taking a vacation in an RV means you can bring your own lifestyle with you. To do that, you need to choose the RV type that best suits you. That means answering these questions:

- Are you interested in spending as little as possible or willing to pay extra to get more space or luxury? Folding camping trailers are at the low end while a large Class A motor home is the most expensive.
- Do you want to drive the RV itself or pull it behind you in your own car? Class A and Class C motor homes propel themselves. Travel trailers, on

the other hand, always need to be towed behind other vehicles.

- How much space do you need for your family or guests and your belongings? You will need extra room to carry fishing gear or in-line skates for the whole family. You get the

most room for a large family in a Class A motor home, but a mini Class C motor home or a trailer is usually large enough for two people.

- Do you plan to travel the main roads, or do you want to be able to drive your RV on back roads,

through the woods, or near a lake? Truck campers, in which the RV unit is attached to the bed of the truck, are the easiest models to drive through rough and remote terrain. Other types of RVs are more likely to get stuck.

EATING ON THE GO

Preparing meals in your RV is all about finding simple ways to do things and cutting down on extra weight and waste, according to Janet Groene, author of *Cooking Aboard Your RV*. Here are her recommendations for preparing easy, delicious meals on the road:

- Carry as little water as possible. At eight pounds per gallon, water adds a lot of weight to your vehicle, getting you fewer miles per gallon of gasoline. Of course, you don't want to run out of water, either. So carry a little more than you think you will need while you're driving, and fill up again at your destination.
- To cut back on useless weight, buy dehydrated foods, concentrated juice, boned chicken, and dry mixes. Then add water when you stop at a trailer park.
- Eliminate as much packaging as possible. Combine dry casserole or soup mixes and baking ingredients ahead of time and store them in plastic bags. Mix spice blends in resealable plastic bags instead of bringing all the individual spice bottles. Choose plastic containers over glass whenever possible.
- Adjust your recipes to one pot and try to use as few dishes and utensils as possible to cut down on dishwashing.

A Great Meal in Minutes

Janet Groene's recipe for Barbecue Bombs is a big hit with hungry travelers. And family members can prepare their own serving just the way they like it. Start the coals about 30 minutes before you begin cooking.

4 lean, meaty, boneless pork chops
Dijon mustard
Large onion cut into four thick slices
4 medium potatoes, scrubbed and sliced
4 medium carrots, cut into rounds
Salt and pepper to taste

1. Spray four 12- by 12-inch squares of aluminum foil with nonstick pan spray and put a **pork chop** on each square.
2. Spread each chop with **mustard** and top with an **onion** slice.
3. Lift the foil edges and add the **potatoes** and **carrots**. Season with **salt and pepper**.
4. Bring the four corners of foil together over the ingredients and twist them.
5. Place each of the packets on the grill about three inches above the coals. Grill for 30 to 35 minutes. The pork chop on the bottom will brown gently and the vegetables will steam.

Travel trailer
- Range from $15,000 to $100,000.
- Able to be towed by wide variety of vehicles.
- Can measure anywhere from 13 to 36 feet long.

Fifth wheel trailer
- Range from $20,000 to $130,000.
- Able to be towed by pick-up trucks only—raised front section extends over truck bed.
- Usually between 20 and 40 feet long.

Folding camping trailer
- Range from $4,000 to $12,000.
- Fabric tops fold up to create sleeping compartments at campsite.
- Usually between 8 and 10 feet long when folded.

The Great Outdoors

When you're heading into the wilderness, be prepared.

PLANNING IS ESSENTIAL

Charlie Reade, a veteran instructor with *Outward Bound*, the wilderness adventure school that runs programs all over the world, believes that interacting with nature builds self-esteem, self-reliance, concern for others, and concern for the environment. Here are his guidelines for safe and responsible outdoor exploration:

- Proper planning is key to an enjoyable and safe trip. Get reliable, detailed maps of the area before setting out. Research the water quality. Find out what kinds of wildlife, poisonous plants, and insects you might be encountering and how to identify them.

- If you haven't done much camping, work up to a long outing gradually. Start with an overnight trip and, as your confidence builds, go out for longer expeditions.
- Always leave a copy of your itinerary with a friend or relative. Never go out alone—even for a short hike—without letting someone know where you're going.
- Good campsites are found, not made. Look for a raised, natural clearing. And leave no traces of your visit. Dig a six-inch-deep latrine, and then cover and disguise it before you leave.

STAYING SAFE IN THE WILDERNESS

Marsha Karle, who has worked at Wyoming's Yellowstone National Park for 15 years, offers these sometimes-surprising safety tips:

- Heart attacks caused by overexertion at high ele-

vation are one of the chief causes of death at Yellowstone, says Karle. Whatever your age, give your body a chance to adjust to the new elevation, and don't overexert yourself. (Heart attacks are not a chief cause of death at Banff National Park, according to park employees Mary Dalman and Julie Timmins.)
- Higher elevations can also mean sudden changes in weather conditions, so always be prepared for the worst. Nighttime especially can be quite cold—sometimes dipping as low as

freezing, even in the height of summer.
- Bears aren't the only animals to be wary of in the wilderness, Karle warns. Moose and elk may charge if they feel threatened—especially mothers with their young.
- Car accidents are the most frequent cause of injury at Yellowstone. So despite the distractions, it's important to keep your eyes on the road.
- Practice fire safety. Use a designated fire pit, and keep water on hand for emergencies. If you have long hair, keep it tied back near the fire.

Smart Moves

Weight is a consideration in backwoods camping. Trail mix and pasta are a lot lighter to lug in than canned goods.

Before using water from streams or lakes, boil for three to five minutes to prevent giardiasis, an infectious disease that causes diarrhea. Sometimes the natural water supply is contaminated by human or animal feces that carry the parasite giardia.

Wilderness checklist

Don't set out without these camping essentials.

Plenty of waterproof matches and lighters

A signaling device, such as a pocket mirror or flares

A map and a GPS receiver (plus a compass for back-up)

GREEN TIPS
WATERPROOF
SAFETY
MATCHES

GREAT GEAR

The high-quality, light-weight equipment and outdoor clothing now available make it easier than ever to plan trouble-free outings and enjoy the country's natural splendors. Kevin McKenna, a camping equipment specialist and outdoor photographer, tells you what to look for in your basic camping gear:

- A good backpack is essential. A poorly made pack that puts unnecessary pressure on your back and shoulders—or that falls apart on the road—could cause serious back pain and inconvenience. Buy your pack from a reputable dealer, who will help you find the fit that's best for your body type. Have the salesperson load it for you in the store, and walk around with it on your back. Try and imagine how it would feel after a 10-mile hike over rough terrain.

- Look for a pack made of rugged, water-resistant material, with a minimum of zippers and

Make sure your backpack has the proper weight transfer for your back.

openings that could split under a full load. The hip belt is the most important part of the pack. Look for one that transfers weight away from your shoulders and onto your hips, which should ideally support 80 percent of your load.

- Invest in a separate rain cover for your backpack, unless you don't mind sleeping in a soggy sleeping bag. Although most good packs are water-resistant, they are not truly waterproof.

- Look for a tent with good ventilation and a rain-fly made of Dacron, any polyester material or

Look for a tent that has good ventilation so your sleeping area doesn't turn into a sauna.

other fabric resistant to sun damage. And invest in a sturdy waterproof tarp to put under the tent in wet weather.

- For parents, a "kid carrier" is indispensable. Many models can hold up to a 40-pound child. Look for one with good padding and vertical seating with high sidewalls.

HASSLE-FREE FUN

Keep It Simple is the golden rule for Margaret Spicer and Margaret Gulino, camp directors and site inspectors for the Girl Scout Council of Greater New York. On a

A kid carrier allows you to keep hiking, even after your child's legs get tired.

camping trip, the greatest pleasures are often the simplest, whether it's contemplating a starry night sky or preparing a nutritious one-dish meal by the campfire. And keeping things simple—from what you pack to the outings and activities you plan—will not only cut down on potential hassles, but give you time to enjoy the natural environment with your family.

Research is the key. Call before you go to find out what facilities and activities a campsite or park offers. That way you won't take along too much gear or too little.

A first-aid kit

A large, insulating space blanket and 50 feet of heavy parachute cord to construct a makeshift shelter in an emergency

Extra batteries for flashlights and cellular phones

An emergency water filtration system or germicidal tablets

A cellphone. Even diehard wilderness adventurers are now carrying cellular phones in their backpacks. A cellular phone can be a lifesaver in an emergency situation. In fact, many companies offer special rates on cellular phones that you use strictly for emergencies.

Adventure Travel

What's your idea of a great adventure?

DEFINING ADVENTURE TRAVEL

People in the travel industry constantly disagree over the definition of adventure travel. One travel agent uses it to describe an afternoon tour through the rain forest in a minivan. Others claim it indicates a high level of risk, exposure to the elements, and the lowest level of creature comforts.

According to Brian Alexander, adventure travel writer and author of *Green Cathedrals: A Wayward Traveler in the Rain Forest*, this inconsistency means that you need to decide what level of adventure you are interested in before you call your travel agent or sign up for a tour. Determine your level of endurance to figure out whether you are interested in what the industry calls soft or hard adventure. "If you're planning a trip with an agent or outfitter," he says, "be very specific about what the trip's all about." That way you won't end up riding a yak through the Himalayas when you'd imagined biking through the rolling hills of Provence.

If you are relatively new to the idea of outdoor adventure, you want to make sure you don't get in over

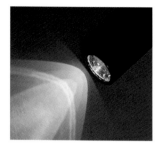

Tools of the Trade

Even minimalist packers will want to have a source of light with them at night in the wilderness. Tiny Mini Mag Lites are less than four inches long and well worth the little bit of extra weight. Head lamps allow you to see in the dark with both hands free, a great help when you have to set up camp after dark.

your head. But novices can still take part in plenty of exciting adventures. Consider a moderate river rafting trip, bicycling tour, or novice hiking excursion. It's always better to underestimate than overestimate your skill level and stamina.

PACKING FOR THE EXTREME

"Clothes may or may not make the man or woman, but they definitely can make or break a back-country trip," according to Philip Torrens, a product expert at Vancouver-based Mountain Equipment Co-op. Find out what the climate's going to be like, the possible precipitation, and the range of high and low temperatures, he advises. You'll find the desert can get awfully cold at night. Here are his tips on dressing for comfort in the outdoors:

- You'll want your clothes to perform a variety of functions. Nothing beats loose-fitting cotton in hot and dry conditions—it feels cool next to the skin, provides UV protection, and resists abrasion, especially in heavier canvas weaves—but cotton is clammy and dries slowly in damp and cool weather. So a better choice might be nylon and polyester fabrics, which have a near-cotton feel, dry quickly, and are virtually wrinkle-free. Or consider one of the synthetic/cotton blends that offer benefits of both.

Get the right shoe for the terrain.

Serious backpacking

- Flexible upper for rough terrain
- Insulated lining
- Steel-reinforced sole
- Metal grommets
- Waterproof upper
- Heavy-tread soles for a good grip

GORE-TEX®

Cold weather
Non-slip natural rubber soles, removable thermal innerboots, tight seal to keep the snow out.

- Mosquitoes and other pests can bite through fabric, so look for tight weaves—thread counts over 175 or 200—to keep them from your skin.
- To prevent blisters in hot weather, wear shoes that allow maximum ventilation. Less-ventilation shoes will help hold your body heat in cold weather.
- Choose shoes or boots specifically designed for hiking and try them on in the store with the socks you will wear on the trip. Reject any boot or shoe that pinches or chafes.

The Right Way

According to Philip Torrens of Mountain Equipment Co-op, layering gives maximum comfort for minimum weight and bulk.

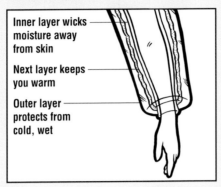

Inner layer wicks moisture away from skin

Next layer keeps you warm

Outer layer protects from cold, wet

Layer 1: Evaporative
Your first layer of clothing should be able to wick moisture away from your skin. Choose long underwear in polyester or spandex (not cotton).

Layer 2: Insulative
Your next layer should be lightweight and able to hold in heat. Consider pants, vests, and tops in good insulating fabric such as polyester fleece, which is durable, quick-drying, and nonallergenic.

Layer 3: Barrier
Your outer layer is responsible for protecting you from the elements. Choose a breathable rain jacket or shell, or an insulated jacket in very cold climates. Look for zipped vents that can be opened to increase breathability in insulated outerwear. Pockets in rain jackets should open vertically to prevent leakage.

HAVING AN EXCELLENT ADVENTURE

Kurt Miller, co-owner of Warren Miller Entertainment, which produces films aimed at outdoor sports enthusiasts, explains how you can increase your chances of having a great time on your adventure:

- Know what you're getting into. Do some research on the area before you go. Look at guidebooks to get an idea of the terrain. Talk to a friend who's been on a similar trip so you know what to expect.
- Be honest about your abilities. People who overestimate their abilities and find themselves overwhelmed and exhausted are more likely to get hurt.

- Listen to your guides. They know the area better than anyone else, and are the ones who can show you where to catch the most fish, ski the best terrain, or sail the best part of the island.
- Don't push your guides to do things that are unsafe. When something goes wrong on an adventure trip, it's usually because a guest ignores a guide's safety precautions. Instead, let your guides know if there's something you really want to do, such as ski some really steep terrain, if it's safe. Remember, you're paying your guides to keep you safe and to ensure that you have a good time.

THE FUN NEVER ENDS

Adventure travel is becoming more and more popular with the over-50 crowd, according to James Plouf, editor of *Marco Polo*, an adventure travel magazine for older adults. "These travelers are looking to get off the golf course and have some unique cultural experiences," he says. Here are Plouf's tips for older travelers looking for a genuine outdoor adventure:

- Use a tour group that has experience with older travelers. They are more likely to understand your health and safety concerns, as well as different areas of interest.
- Consult your doctor before you book your trip,

and again before you depart. Ask about vaccines, altitude sickness, regional diseases, and any precautions you should take. Also ask what medicines you should take with you, such as pain killers, antibiotics, or antidiarrheals.
- Consider an expedition cruise. You will travel on a smaller cruise ship that can make frequent stops in areas where larger ships are unable to go. And you will be able to get out and explore points of interest along the way.
- Look into walking trips. There are quite a few available on which you don't have to carry your pack and can keep an easy, gentle walking pace.

Hot weather
Breathable mesh and leather construction, quick-dry lining, lightweight build.

Wet weather
Waterproof leather uppers, latex-sealed seams, directly attached soles.

River rafting
Neoprene upper, no-slip non-marking soles, raised sidewells, secure fastener.

Mountain biking
Raised ankle cuff, stiff plastic toe box, deep-welled heel cup, snug fit.

Volunteer Vacations

Travel to new places, meet new people, help build a better world.

DECIDING TO VOLUNTEER

According to Bill McMillon, author of *Volunteer Vacations: Short-term Adventures that Will Benefit You and Others*, there are over 275 organizations around the world looking for people who want to spend their vacation time in volunteer activities. The vacations range from day trips to several-month excursions, and can be found halfway around the world or just a short drive away. To some people's surprise, they can be quite expensive, and you almost always have to pay for your own round-trip airfare or other transportation costs. But there are plenty of low-cost opportunities as well.

Here are some of McMillon's suggestions:

- If you want to take children, look for trips that welcome families, such as digs with the Texas Archaeological Society or working with the Heifer Project International.
- International work camps are great opportunities, especially for young adults ages 18 to 26.

There are a great number of projects in many different countries, so there is usually one to suit every taste, from rebuilding a community center in Haiti to painting a mural at an Italian summer camp for the young victims of Chernobyl.

- Seniors can enjoy volunteer vacations if they are in good physical condition. Elderhostel's volunteer division is particularly popular with the over-50 population.

Myth: *Volunteer vacations are just for college students and other young people.* **Fact:** *Some organizations cater to the college crowd, but other organizations have many older participants. On some of these trips, you could find half the volunteers to be over 40 or 50.*

HELPING TEENS HELP OTHERS

"Volunteering to build homes is especially eye-opening for young people who may never have thought about poverty or substandard housing—even in Canada," says David Beckerson, a spokesperson for Habitat for Humanity Canada. "It's a chance for Canadian youth to see a family move into their first safe, decent, affordable home."

Habitat, which welcomes volunteers of all ages and is currently building homes in 51 communities across Canada, has chapters geared to younger people at 14 universities, colleges, and high schools across the country. Here's some

Taking a hands-on role in creating new housing for people in need builds a real sense of community.

advice for parents and teen group leaders:

- Make sure teens know what they're getting into—that the real purpose of the work is to help others. Don't suggest it won't be any fun, but that the enjoyment will come from meeting people and working toward a common goal. And never force teens to go if they don't want to.
- Explain what they will actually be doing during the day, and the impact it will have.
- Encourage teenagers to interact at the work

site with people of all ages and different backgrounds.

■ Most importantly, take time at the end of each day to talk about anything these young volunteers want to discuss. They may feel overwhelmed by their first look at the inequalities of the world.

Volunteers on scientific expeditions help out with original research and have a great time, too.

ESPECIALLY FOR OUTDOOR TYPES

A one-week volunteer vacation offered from June through August by Alberta's Royal Tyrrell Museum of Palaeontology can be a dream come true for paleontologist wannabees. Open to adults 18 years and over, it is set in the world famous badlands of Dinosaur Provincial Park. You'll be part of a team that prospects for, collects, and prepares dinosaurs, turtles, crocodiles, and other fossils for museum display. Data

collected during field experience is used in published scientific studies. "The program is rigorous and the work can be difficult, but it is also the closest you can get to paleontology without being a paleontologist," says Marty Hickie of the museum's media relations department. "Best of all, there's no need for previous experience. We'll train you." The $800 participation fee includes accommodation, meals, and all work-related supplies.

Participants in the Parks Canada Research Adventure program also pay to participate in three to five days of hands-on wildlife research. Projects might involve monitoring bighorn sheep in Kootenay, or tracking grizzlies in Banff or Yoho national parks.

There are plenty of vacation opportunities if you want to volunteer outdoors.

Parks Canada has several other inexpensive opportunities for volunteers to spend a week or so camping and working in its parks. Volunteers might find themselves herding bison, building a cabin, maintaining trails, or observing birds. Program personnel suggest that anyone interested should:

■ Decide the level of work you're capable of, then check www.parkscanada.pch.gc.ca.

■ Know what you are getting into. Spend one or two days camping and hiking before you decide to go on a week-long trip.

■ Contact the park you would like to work in and discuss your abilities and interests with a staff member.

True Stories

At 64, Jerry Peterson of St. Cloud, Minnesota, has already taken part in more volunteer vacations than he can count. As both a group leader and regular volunteer, he has worked at such diverse places as a youth center in Mexico and a Quaker organic farm in Ireland.

His favorite part of every trip is getting to know people from all over the world, and the organizations he travels with, such as Volunteers for Peace, Global Network, and Citizens Network, include volunteers from more than one country in each project. During a recent trip to a center for children with disabilities in Manchester, England, Peterson remembers how it didn't matter what language you spoke. Everyone learned a bit of other people's languages, he says. At the end of the day everyone was laughing and joking in phrases from all over the world.

Ecotourism

Ecotourism is more than a vacation. It's an attitude.

DEFINING ECOTOURISM

If you're not sure what ecotourism is, John M. Snyder, PhD, chairman of Eco Tourism International, an interdisciplinary group that evaluates potential ecotourism projects, explains it: Ecotourism describes a vacation in a natural environment, where Native people are spokespersons for their country and share their nature, history, and culture with others.

Unlike most of today's tourist attractions, Snyder explains, the natural habitat of ecotourist destinations is not damaged by visitors, and the local culture not degraded. Instead of bringing in help from the outside, ecotourism companies hire and train local people, providing new jobs for the area. They also make every effort to keep industry profits in their native country. That's why many ecotourism advocates discourage cruising, which they say lets the tourists in but keeps their money on the boat.

HOW TO BE AN ECOTOURIST

According to Christopher P. Baker, author of the *Costa Rica Handbook*, Costa Rica is at the forefront of ecotourism, helping to protect the local environment by teaching visitors how to act responsibly. Here's how you can use ecotourism techniques that have been successful in Costa Rica to be an ecotourist wherever you might travel:

- Minimalize your impact on the land any way you can. Stay on trails instead of wandering off, harming local plants and native animals. Follow any instructions given by your guides.
- Be understanding if you can't get access to a particular area at the exact time and day you want. Many ecotourist destinations are very fragile, and can be destroyed by too many visitors. In recent years, popular locations like the Galapagos Islands have been endangered because they have been overwhelmed with people.
- Follow the well-known, well-respected edict, "Take only photographs, leave only footprints."

Bring along—don't expect to buy—basics like pens and pencils.

Handy items, such as handkerchiefs or bandanas, double as gifts, so bring extras.

WHAT TO EXPECT

In order to get the most out of your first trip as an ecotourist, you need to know what to expect. Carolyn Hill, manager of EcoSource (an ecotourism information organization and website), suggests you read up on local geography, weather, culture, plants, and animals ahead of time. Ask questions, she urges.

Here are some of Hill's tips on how to prepare for the adventure:

- Ecotourism destinations are in the great outdoors, so you should get ready to spend a lot of your time outside.
- Don't expect the creature comforts available at most vacation spots. Prepare to spend a few nights or more without

The Right Way

As ecotourism grows in popularity, many tour groups are jumping on the bandwagon. But there can be big differences in the quality of your trip, and in the extent to which an organization follows the principles of preserving the environment and the culture. Before you make your plans, contact the Vermont-based Ecotourism Society at 703-549-8979 for a list of recommended programs or tour operators for the area you want to visit.

Anything from socks to important papers can be kept dry in resealable plastic bags.

running water, electricity, and air conditioning.
- Get ready for bugs. If you're traveling to a warm climate, find out what kind of bugs to expect and make sure to bring any recommended long-sleeve shirts or bug repellent. You'll also want to find out if you need to get any special vaccinations or take any specific medications before visiting these areas.

- Respect and follow local customs. If women are expected to wear dresses, wear a dress. If you want to gain the respect of the local people, make the effort to learn a little of their language and culture. Chances are, if you make an effort to learn about and understand them, they'll be much more likely to do the same for you.
- Budget extra time at the end of your trip. Most ecotourist sites are in remote areas. If you miss your flight because of a flood, you may have to spend an extra day—or week.

PRESENTS FOR YOUR HOST

There's no easier way to make new friends (especially with children) than to give them a gift. And it's a personal way to express your appreciation for what your hosts are sharing with you. Consider some of Carolyn Hill's favorite gifts to squeeze into your suitcase:
- Balls for children.
- Bandanas for women's heads.
- Needles and thread.
- Pens, pencils, and paper.
- Solar calculators.
- Sunglasses.
- Swiss army knives.
- T-shirts.

ECO-PACKING

If you're going to be an ecotourist, bring only what you need. Watching a tour guide trying to get your gigantic luggage into a canoe or atop an elephant can be embarrassing. Of course, some things may be impossible to get at your destination.

Shoes. If you're a woman with a size 10 foot, you'll be hard-pressed to find a pair of hiking boots in all of Asia.

Clothes. North Americans tend to be larger than people in many countries. Finding big or long-enough clothing might be difficult.

Sealable plastic bags. If you're hiking or traveling in open vehicles, things can get wet. Pack with sealable plastic bags, which can do double duty to carry garbage out of the wilderness.

Essentials. You may not be able to find basics like feminine hygiene products, medicine, toothpaste and shampoo, batteries, and antibiotic cream.

MORE THAN TOURISTS

For a homegrown sample of ecotourism, the Conservation Nature Tours in Ontario's Bruce Peninsula are hard to beat. Run jointly by the Saugeen Valley and Grey Sauble conservation authorities, the one- to three-day tours adhere to ecotourism principles of small groups and local tour guides, says coordinator Chris Hughes. Outings include a canoe birding trip along the Rankin River system, kayaking along the Bruce Peninsula shoreline, and a Saugeen River adventure during which you sleep in teepees and learn traditional techniques such as leathercraft and foraging for food. The program pays for itself; any profit goes back to the conservation authority. For more information check the www.svca.on.ca website.

If you want to travel further afield, and you're interested in serious scientific field study, contact the US-based Earthwatch Institute (www.earthwatch.org), a non-profit group that sponsors and funds field-based scientific research in some 50 countries. It puts about 4,000 laypeople in the field every year. Participants range from age 16 to 80 plus. With Earthwatch:
- You get to work in a place or scientific field that appeals to you.
- The organization trusts you to get the basics down and to work hard. You get a brief orientation and then you're out in the thick of things—with supervision.
- Your fees, which average US$1,600, support the research.

The Business of Living

Making a Financial Plan

Take control of your financial future.

GOING SOLO

"The financial world has changed enormously in the last couple of decades," says Jonathan Clements, a columnist for *The Wall Street Journal* and author of *25 Myths You've Got to Avoid—If You Want to Manage Your Money Right: The New Rules for Financial Success*. "Brokerage fees used to be fixed," explains Bruce Cohen, former *Financial Post* columnist and author of *The Money Adviser*. "There were very few mutual funds, and it was quite difficult to get information about them." In short, you couldn't save money by investigating on your own. Now, with plentiful opportunities to save money with discount brokers, low- and no-load funds, and online trading and other web-based financial services, it can make good sense to do it yourself.

Even so, there may be circumstances when you can benefit from professional advice. These may include:

- If you're very busy and are willing to pay for the convenience of having a professional help you.
- If you panic over short-term market performance. Emotions play a major part in the financial decisions we make, notes Clements.
- If you're planning for something big, such as retirement, it might be helpful to get a "financial checkup."
- If you come into an inheritance or have some other type of financial windfall.

Don't use a professional just because you think financial planning is complicated. "It's not rocket science," says Jonathan Clements. And whatever path you choose, you can't avoid educating yourself and being involved in the process: "You have to supervise your investment advisor."

GOAL SETTING

If you want to win the Olympics, you need a coach. The same is true if you want to reach your financial goals, says Eileen Michaels, a financial planner in New York City who plays financial coach to her clients. She is the author of *When Are You Entitled to New Underwear and Other Major Financial Decisions*.

There are three major factors Michaels takes into consideration when developing a financial "blueprint" with her clients:

- Where are you now financially?
- Where would you like to see yourself?
- How much time do you have to reach your goals?

Time, she says, is the operative factor. It's not only a question of whether you'll be able to reach your goals, but when you'll be able to reach them. A timeline can help you put your goals in perspective:

Short-term goals are where you'd like to see yourself in a few years. For instance, perhaps you want to buy a home.

Intermediate goals might include sending children who are young now to college in the future.

Long-range goals are your plans for retirement and your estate.

Financial well-being starts with a solid foundation: Make sure you and your family are properly insured. Also, "level the playing field" by paying off high-interest debt, such as credit cards.

Tools of the Trade

Bruce Cohen points out that, in Canada, anyone seeking advice from financial planners should be aware of these points:

- Financial advisors use more than two dozen designations, but the most common one is Certified Financial Planner (CFP).
- The major professional bodies in Canada's financial planning world are the Canadian Association of Financial Planners and the Canadian Association of Insurance and Financial Advisors.
- Quebec is currently the only province that regulates financial planners, although others are considering regulation. Advisors must, however, be licensed with the provincial securities commission if they sell investments, and with the provincial insurance commission if they sell insurance products. Licensing is not required for financial institution staff who take deposits, which include Guaranteed Investment Certificates (GICs).

REALITY CHECK

Making a financial plan is full of tough choices, says Judith Martindale, a financial planner who works with middle-income clients. People who don't have a lot of disposable income have to prioritize. They can't necessarily have everything they aspire to, whether that means the house of their dreams, a new car every three years, or a higher education for their children. Sometimes, people have to be willing to make trade-offs.

Less-affluent people also tend be more conservative investors. It's important, Martindale says, to strike a balance between growing your money for the future and getting the sleep you need now. She favors index funds—funds that track an index of a particular market—for people on a tight budget because they provide lots of diversification and are more cost-efficient than those funds that are actively managed, which often have higher fees and generate lots of capital gains.

The Right Way

In Canada, some commissioned financial planners charge a fee for developing a financial plan. Once you've decided on your financial plan, you can have the advisor implement it or you can go elsewhere to get it done. If, however, your financial advisor implements the recommended plan, his or her fee should be reduced in whole or in part.

Myth: *You don't have enough personal income to start saving for the future.* **Fact:** *P.Y.F.—pay yourself first, say the experts, and invest it immediately in a rainy-day fund or tax-deferred plan. If you take money for savings off the top, you'll never miss that extra 5 or 10 percent of your gross monthly income.*

Here are some other tips from Martindale to get you and your family started on the right financial path:

- If you can't afford a financial planner with whom you feel comfortable, find a money buddy—a good friend or relative who has similar financial goals and with whom you can learn about financial planning and investing.
- Track your expenses, advises Martindale. She recommends any one of the many excellent software programs, such as Quicken, that can help you organize and consolidate your finances and financial records.
- Aim to save at least 10 percent of your take-home pay and increase that slowly to 10 percent of your gross pay. If that seems too ambitious, start with 2 percent and gradually increase.
- Whether you go solo or seek professional help, involve other members of your family whose financial lives are in any way intertwined with yours.

A HOLISTIC APPROACH

"Financial planning is a process," says fee-only planner Evelyne Yang in Potomac, Maryland, who takes a holistic, comprehensive approach. In her opinion, a person can only be in peak financial health if they are doing well on all financial levels. Here are some of the factors she takes into consideration with her clients:

- Are you financially well organized?
- Are you maximizing tax shelters, write-offs, and deductions?
- Do you have clearly defined financial goals?
- Are your goals realistic, and are you making financial provisions to meet them?
- Is your lifestyle appropriate to your income and your mid- and long-term financial goals?
- Are you maximizing returns on your investments while minimizing your risk?
- Are you properly insured at the minimum cost?

When Yang has reviewed a client's financial situation, she invites them in for a goal-setting session. This, she says, is the most important part of the process. "Success means different things to different people," says Yang. For some, it might mean owning their own home or early retirement. For others, it means having the time and financial independence to enjoy intellectual pursuits, volunteer work, hobbies, or travel. Knowing what's most important to you will help you structure a plan to meet your goals—and needs.

Smart Moves

Bruce Cohen offers seven tips for evaluating a prospective financial planner:

- What is the advisor's level of experience and education? Does he or she belong to any professional associations with a code of ethics and professional insurance?
- Does the financial advisor offer the kinds of products and services that meet your particular needs?
- Is the advisor used to dealing with clients at your stage of life and financial level? Does he or she prefer aggressive or conservative clients?
- How often does the advisor intend to communicate with you? In what ways? What does he or she do to educate clients?
- When does the financial advisor feel you will be able to fairly evaluate his or her service? How will you go about making this evaluation?
- Do you understand what the advisor is talking about? Does he or she appear to understand you?
- Do you understand how the financial advisor is compensated?

Keeping Good Records

Everything's easier if you're organized.

THE PAPER CHASE

"Running a house is a lot like running a business," says Stephanie Denton, a professional organizer based in Cincinnati, Ohio, who specializes in both residential and commercial paperwork and recordkeeping. To get a successful grip on organizing documents, bills, and other materials, Denton suggests the following tips:

■ Create a space in which you can always do your paperwork. This is perhaps the most important element of a successful system. If you can't devote an entire desk to the task, at least invest in a rolling file cart to store active paperwork and a two-drawer file cabinet

for family records. Store the rolling file cart wherever it is most convenient and comfortable to do your work, whether that is the kitchen, office, or family room.

■ When in doubt, throw it out. The first step to implementing a workable filing system is to eliminate paper you don't use, don't need, or that you could easily access again elsewhere. Throw out duplicate statements, old catalogs, and all of the coupons, mailings, or offerings you'll never have an opportunity to use or even read.

■ Set aside two days a month to pay bills. If a monthly due date doesn't

fit into your cycle, call up the creditor and suggest a more convenient date. Keep two manila folders at the front of your system for current bills—one to correspond with each bill-paying day—and file all incoming bills. Keep a list in the front of each folder of what needs to be paid in case the invoice never arrives or gets misplaced.

■ Think of your filing system not as a rigid tool, but as a living, breathing system that can accommodate your changing needs. A good filing system is both mentally and physically flexible. Everyone's needs are different, says Denton, but when devising a filing system, ask yourself: "Where would I look for this?" Create main headings for your filing system, such as *Investments, Taxes, Children*, and so forth, and file individual folders under the main headings. Never overstuff your files.

TAX RECORDS

Revenue Canada can audit your tax return for four years after you filed, and without time limit if they think you've committed tax evasion or fraud. Here's what Revenue Canada says you can do to protect yourself if you're audited:

Tax returns and supporting documents. Although it is important to hang on to your tax returns, it is even more important to hang on to supporting documents, such as all tax information slips (T3, T4, T5), canceled

checks, receipts for medical and professional expenses, and all other paperwork relating to your return. Revenue Canada advises all taxpayers to keep these records for four years. If you operate a business, you should keep your records for six years. You might also consider seeking permission from Revenue Canada to destroy these documents.

Housing records. Keep all records relating to home improvements, additions, repairs, and expenses incurred when buying or selling a home for as long as you own the home plus six years.

Investment records. Keep all purchase and reinvestment records for six years after the sale of the investment.

RRSP contributions. Records of nondeductible RRSP contributions should be kept indefinitely. When you make withdrawals in later years, you will be able to prove the tax has been paid on the money.

Smart Moves

Here are some simple but practical solutions to household chaos and disorganization:

■ Open mail over the wastebasket and throw out envelopes. Immediately route all opened mail.

■ File all your papers flat, not folded, to save space and make them easier to access.

■ Keep plenty of stamps and address labels on hand for easy and efficient bill paying.

■ Arrange automatic bill payment whenever possible to avoid extra paperwork and possible late charges.

■ For every new piece of paper you put in your files, take something out. For instance, if you are filing a recently paid bill, throw out the oldest one in the sequence—provided you don't need to save it to support your tax return. If you use this system, you never have to clean out your files.

■ Use staples instead of paper clips to keep all your paperwork together.

■ If you remove a file temporarily, use a place marker, such as a large index card or ruler, so that you put the file back in the right place and don't misfile it.

■ Consider using vertical files, which keep paperwork upright and visible, for your filing system.

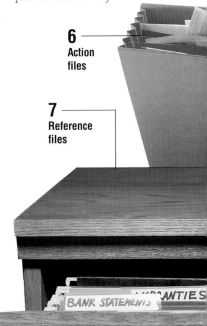

6 Action files

7 Reference files

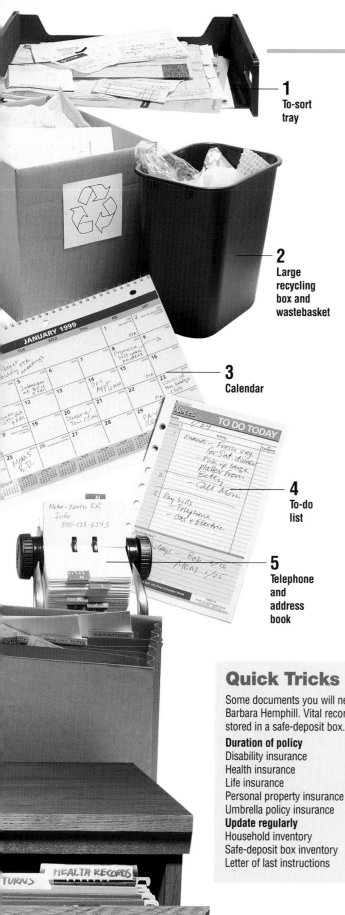

1 To-sort tray

2 Large recycling box and wastebasket

3 Calendar

4 To-do list

5 Telephone and address book

LUCKY NUMBER SEVEN

"In my experience, every piece of paper in your life can be managed effectively by putting the piece of paper, or the information on it, into one of seven places," says Barbara Hemphill, author of *Taming the Paper Tiger at Home,* creator of The Paper Tiger file index software, and a professional organizing consultant in North Carolina.

1. To-sort tray. This should be a temporary place to keep all incoming paperwork you haven't yet had a chance to look at, such as the day's mail, or papers brought home from work. For this approach to work, you must empty the tray regularly and use it consistently.

2. Large recycling box and wastebasket. "These are some of the most important tools in your work area," says Hemphill.

3. Calendar. Whether paper or electronic, a master calendar can help you eliminate a lot of clutter from your desktop. Get into the habit of entering important information, such as business and social engagements, deadlines, family outings, telephone appointments, and other commitments, as soon as possible, and dispose of the notice immediately.

4. To-do list. Create master to-do lists under headings, such as *Birthdays, Books, Errands, Goals, Letters,* and *Projects.* Enter commitments requiring attention in the near future on your master calendar.

5. Telephone and address book. A rotary card file or electronic card file on your computer that can be easily updated works best.

6. Action files. These are for papers that need your attention immediately or in the near future. Categories for action files depend on your personal needs and style, but might include *Pay* for bills, orders you need to place, and donations you wish to make, *File* for items to be filed in reference files you can't reach from your chair, and *Computer Entry* for information that needs to be filed on the computer and can then be thrown out or stored in your reference files.

7. Reference files. These are for papers you might need in the future, such as health and insurance records, bank statements, tax returns, and warranties. However you decide to organize your permanent files, always keep an up-to-date index in hard copy at the front of your filing system. Make changes in pencil and update the index as necessary.

Quick Tricks

Some documents you will need to keep easily accessible for many years, even permanently, says Barbara Hemphill. Vital records, such as birth and marriage certificates, should be permanently stored in a safe-deposit box. Here's Hemphill's schedule:

Duration of policy	Statute of limitations	Permanently
Disability insurance	Automobile insurance	Illness records
Health insurance	Homeowner's insurance	Vaccination records
Life insurance	Liability insurance	Academic diplomas
Personal property insurance	**As long as you own**	Birth and adoption certificates
Umbrella policy insurance	Automobile registrations	Citizenship papers
Update regularly	Major purchases	Divorce decrees
Household inventory	Automobile titles	Marriage certificates
Safe-deposit box inventory	Warrantees	Powers of attorney
Letter of last instructions	Instructions	Social Security records

Credit and Debt

Enjoy the convenience and flexibility of credit while avoiding the risks.

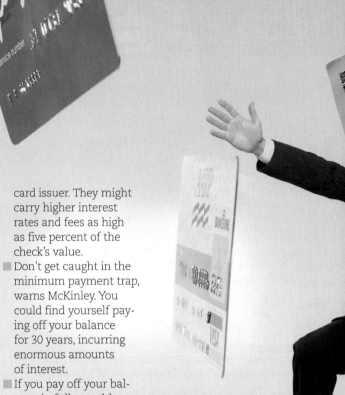

PLASTIC FANTASTIC

"It's never been more of a buyer's market for credit cards," says Gerri Detweiler, who is the author of *The Ultimate Credit Handbook* and co-author of *Invest in Yourself: Six Secrets to a Rich Life.* Nonetheless, she says, some consumers may find themselves confused and frustrated when trying to pick the right card from the variety of offers that are now currently available. Here are some tips to help you get started:

Low fixed annual percentage rate. A no-frills credit card with a low annual percentage rate (APR) is probably your best bet if you routinely carry a balance from month to month. "You have to be honest with yourself about your spending habits," says Detweiler.

Rebate offers. Some credit cards offer enticing rebates on airfares and vacation packages charged to the card, or they may award travel points for every dollar charged to the card; the points are redeemable in airfare reductions when you travel. However, because of their high annual fees, high interest rates, and nominal award levels, you'll have to charge enormous amounts—perhaps as much as $10,000 a year—and pay off your balance monthly to get any substantial benefit from the rebate.

No annual fee. These credit cards often carry high APRs, but might be a good choice for people who pay their balance in full monthly. For most consumers, Gerri Detweiler suggests that is probably to keep only two major credit cards—one low-APR card in case you will be carrying over a balance, and one "convenience" card that you pay off in full each month.

BEWARE OF CARD SHARKS

Despite the good deals that are now available, card issuers "are laying lots of land mines for consumers," says Robert McKinley, who is the president of the Cardweb website (www .cardweb.com), which tracks the payment card industry and provides information for consumers on thousands of current credit card offers.

Watch out for these charges on your monthly credit card statement:

- Late fees and overlimit fees have increased to 29 dollars or more in the majority of cases.
- If the APR seems too good to be true, check the disclosure box on the card offer. Often, low APRs apply only to transferred balances from other cards, or cash advances.
- Familiarize yourself with the terms of convenience checks offered by the card issuer. They might carry higher interest rates and fees as high as five percent of the check's value.
- Don't get caught in the minimum payment trap, warns McKinley. You could find yourself paying off your balance for 30 years, incurring enormous amounts of interest.
- If you pay off your balance in full monthly, you may have difficulty getting the best rate on your credit card. Many card issuers are trying to sift out convenience users, who take advantage of card perks while avoiding high interest charges.

SMART SHOPPING

"Comparison shop," advises Bill Anderson, president and CEO of Bank Rate Monitor (www.bankrate.com), an independent US consumers' source for banking and credit information. "There is tremendous variation in the prices of most banking products."

Whether you're shopping for a CD, auto loan, mortgage, home equity loan, or checking account, Anderson's practical advice is just as applicable to Canadians as Americans.

- The Internet, tables of rates in the newspaper, and the Yellow Pages are all excellent tools to help you with your search for a loan. If you don't find the product you're seeking being advertised, but the bank otherwise offers favorable rates, contact the bank and ask what it can offer you on what you're looking for.
- Check out the rates at smaller banks and credit unions. "The larger, well-advertised institutions are not always the cheapest," advises Anderson.
- If you have a lot of credit card debt, Anderson recommends consolidating it with a home equity loan or line of

credit, provided you have equity built up in your home. Generally, the interest rates are much lower than credit cards. Of course, if you default on the loan, you risk losing your home.

■ Fixed-term home equity loans or lines of credit are good if you are doing major renovations on your home. "They put discipline into the borrowing process and prevent overspending," says Anderson.

■ Car dealers will often negotiate on the price of a vehicle, but dig their heels in when it comes to financing. Before shopping for a car, get pre-approved for a car loan at your bank. Negotiate and fix your price without telling the dealer that you have other sources of credit.

■ Stay clear of finance companies, as they charge more than 30 percent on loans.

■ Beware of payday loan companies, which charge very high interest rates for short-term loans.

DEBIT CARDS

Debit cards are a great tool for people who have difficulty managing their credit card spending, says Laurie Campbell, program director of the Credit Counselling Service of Toronto. Debit cards—ATM cards that carry a credit card logo—provide most of the shopping conveniences of a traditional credit card without the risk of interest charges or running up a lot of debt, since money is withdrawn directly from your bank account.

TRADE SECRETS

Studies indicate that credit card use has slowed slightly whereas debit card use has soared. Some observers say the punitive interest rates and other aggressive fees charged by some credit card issuers is a factor. Financial experts advise consumers not to settle for punitive credit card terms. If you are being hit with hidden charges on your credit card, find another issuer.

Interest backdating. Interest on a purchase usually begins accruing the day the purchase amount is posted to your account. Some companies, however, charge interest beginning on the date of purchase—before they've even paid the store.

Teaser rates. If you sign up for a card with a low introductory rate, when the rate expires your existing balance will usually be subject to the higher interest rate.

Grace periods. Many issuers are eliminating grace periods altogether, which means you are charged interest on everything you buy from the day you buy it, even if you pay off your balance monthly.

Cash advances. Beware of hefty transaction fees, high interest rates, and stiff finance charges on cash advances from your card. Use only in an emergency.

Smart Moves

Credit reports enable lenders to offer a risk-based price when they give credit, says Norman Magnuson, vice president of public affairs of Associated Credit Bureaus, the trade association for the credit reporting industry. In other words, if you're a good risk, you'll be offered a competitive interest rate. If you're a poor risk, you'll be charged more in the form of higher interest rates. Here are some ways to ensure that your credit report is the best possible reflection of your financial situation:

■ It is important to pay your bills on time to protect your credit rating. Most lenders will report a delinquency to the credit bureaus if a payment is 30 to 60 days late.

■ Open lines of credit—whether you carry a balance or not—can negatively affect your credit rating. Cancel all open lines of credit, such as credit cards, if you're not using them.

■ Every time you apply for credit, it is reported to the major credit bureaus. Even if you make timely monthly payments to lenders, applying for credit too often can hurt your credit rating.

■ Mistakes can happen on your credit report. Check your report regularly for accuracy and address any discrepancies with the credit bureau. This is especially important if you will be applying for credit, a loan, mortgage, or apartment in the near future.

Credit Counseling

Many people may have financial difficulties from time to time.

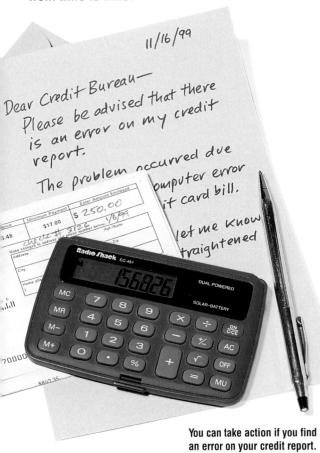

You can take action if you find an error on your credit report.

THE HELP YOU NEED

"We teach individuals and families how to be financially self-sufficient," says Laurie Campbell, program director of the Credit Counselling Service (CCS) of Toronto. This nonprofit, charitable organization, a member of the Ontario Association of Credit Counselling Services, has counseled clients in all financial circumstances, from people living on social assistance to those with six-figure incomes. Frequently people run into financial difficul-

ties after a divorce, when they allow their expenses to exceed their incomes, or after losing a job.

Among CCS services are professional counseling, educational programs, and debt management planning. In the last, counselors help clients design a stringent budget allowing only for necessities while working with creditors to reduce finance charges, cease collection actions, and agree to a payment plan manageable for the creditor. "We act as the liaison between the consumer and the cred-

itor," says Campbell. The plans are designed to last no more than three or four years, which is manageable for most people. "Clients understand they won't have to live on such a strict budget forever—that it's a temporary measure."

If you're using credit cards out of necessity to buy groceries or to pay your mortgage or utility bills, or if you can't keep track of your credit card purchases, it's time to re-evaluate your lifestyle, says Campbell.

Visit the CCS website (www.creditcanada.com) or call 1-800-267-2272.

DOWN WITH DEBT

When you put yourself in debt, you are selling a part of your future, says Steve Rhode, president of Debt Counselors of America, an Internet-based debt counseling agency. These five steps will help you get out of debt:

Stop going into debt. "If you immediately stop doing the things that got you into debt in the first place, you won't go any further into debt," says Rhode.

Track your spending. Carry a pad and pen with you wherever you go and track every penny you spend. "By simply writing down your expenses and reviewing the list, you will immediately cut some of your unnecessary spending." At the end of the month, subtract the amount you spent from the amount you earned. If you spent more than you earned, you will either have to adjust your lifestyle or increase your income.

Plan for the future. "Write down your plan for becoming debt-free and review it often. Set goals that are within your reach, such as spending less than you earn each month, making regular deposits into a savings account, or brown-bagging your lunch.

Don't expect instant miracles. "You didn't get into debt overnight, and you're not going to get out overnight," says Rhode. Most people slip into debt slowly over time. Getting out of debt means changing old habits, being patient, and staying on course.

Seek help. Professional counselors can help you meet your financial goals and develop realistic repayment plans. Visit one of the country's some 30 CCS offices, or get credit counseling by phone anywhere in Canada by calling the 1-800 number listed at left.

Make sure you understand your credit report, and check it regularly for accuracy.

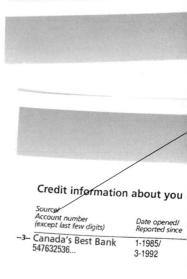

WHEN TIMES GET TOUGH

If your debts have got out of hand, there are solutions. Some of these are outlined in an Industry Canada publication, *Dealing With Debt: A Consumer's Guide.*

- If you cannot keep up to date with your bill payments, credit counseling may be the answer, especially if you have difficulty making a budget and sticking to it.
- Contact your creditors directly to renegotiate lower payments over a longer period. Speak to the credit manager, or whoever can approve a repayment plan.
- Another possibility is a debt-consolidation loan by which your bank pays off all your debts, leaving you with one manageable monthly payment.
- Residents of Alberta, British Columbia, Nova Scotia, Prince Edward Island, and Saskatchewan may seek a consolidation order. This sets out the amount and times when payments are due to the court, which distributes your payments to your creditors. A consolidation order lets you pay off your debts over three years, and frees you from creditor harassment and wage garnishment. Unlike bankruptcy, you do not lose your assets.
- Quebec's Lacombe Law, or Voluntary Deposit scheme, available at most courthouses, is similar to a consolidation order. Monthly payments based on income and number of dependents are paid to the court.
- One of your last resorts is a consumer proposal to your creditors to reduce the amount of your debts or to extend the time you have to pay them off. If this fails, you may have to file for bankruptcy.

IS BANKRUPTCY THE ANSWER?

Most people don't like to go bankrupt, according to Bob Sanderson of the Canadian Insolvency Practitioners Association. Yet thousands of Canadians regularly find themselves in this predicament. In Edmonton, for example, 15 to 20 people file for bankruptcy every day of the year.

People such as Darrell Shalley, who works in one of Industry Canada's bankruptcy offices in Alberta, say there is no one reason for the rise in consumer bankruptcies. Credit overextension, marital breakdown, student loans, loss of jobs, and, increasingly, gambling are all to blame.

Whatever the source of the problem, you can go bankrupt in two ways. You can declare bankruptcy if you owe $1,000 or more and cannot make regular payments or haven't property to cover your debts. Or you can be forced into bankruptcy by someone to whom you owe at least $1,000.

Either way, you must assign your assets, with certain exemptions, to a trustee in bankruptcy who will divide them among your creditors. Exempt property varies from province to province, but generally includes basic furniture and household goods, necessary clothing, tools of your trade, and any vehicle used for business. Some jurisdictions permit you to keep livestock, family portraits, medals, and other decorations, and items related to religious worship.

Although bankruptcy legislation is designed to help you get rid of debts and make a fresh start, it can still have ruinous consequences. Weigh these carefully before filing for bankruptcy. Even though you cannot be fired from your job if you do so, having a bankruptcy in your credit history can have other devastating effects.

Because the information can stay on your credit record for up to 10 years, you might have trouble renting an apartment, or getting a job where you have to be bonded. Most likely, you will have difficulty getting a bank loan, a mortgage, or a credit card.

A bankruptcy doesn't erase all debts. You will still be responsible for any court-specified damages for assault, for all spousal and child support payments, and for any debts related to fraud, court fines, and student loans.

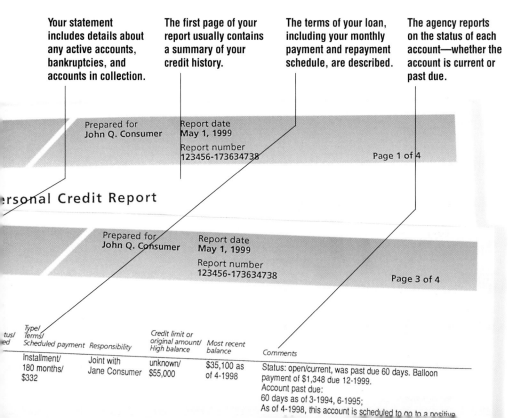

Your statement includes details about any active accounts, bankruptcies, and accounts in collection.

The first page of your report usually contains a summary of your credit history.

The terms of your loan, including your monthly payment and repayment schedule, are described.

The agency reports on the status of each account—whether the account is current or past due.

Prepared for
John Q. Consumer

Report date
May 1, 1999

Report number
123456-173634738

Page 1 of 4

ersonal Credit Report

Prepared for
John Q. Consumer

Report date
May 1, 1999

Report number
123456-173634738

Page 3 of 4

tus/ed	Type/ Terms/ Scheduled payment	Responsibility	Credit limit or original amount/ High balance	Most recent balance	Comments
	Installment/ 180 months/ $332	Joint with Jane Consumer	unknown/ $55,000	$35,100 as of 4-1998	Status: open/current, was past due 60 days. Balloon payment of $1,348 due 12-1999. Account past due: 60 days as of 3-1994, 6-1995; As of 4-1998, this account is scheduled to go to a positive

Buying a Home

**Make the right choice
the right way.**

TO BUY OR TO RENT?

According to Canada Mortgage and Housing Corporation (CMHC), 37 percent of Canadian renters could afford to buy a home. But when it comes to buying or renting, age, lifestyle, whether or not you're a parent, even where you live, all play a role. This was among findings of a late 1990s study by the CMHC, which wanted to know why, in Quebec, so many 25- to 34-year-olds—the so-called Generation X—were tenants rather than homeowners. At the time, 56 percent of this age group outside Quebec owned their homes, a figure that dropped to 34 percent in Montreal. CMHC's Kim-Anh Lam explained: "When we asked about their priorities, Gen Xers placed housing fifth—after recreational activities, retirement planning, consolidating their jobs, and repaying their debt." However, home ownership became a priority once a couple became serious, or the first child arrived.

Most experts agree that renting makes sense if you're highly mobile and don't want to be burdened with the slow pace of the buying and selling process, or if you can't or don't want to take on the long-term financial commitments of a mortgage and home maintenance. Renting may be necessary in order to save for the 10- to 20-percent down payment needed to buy a home.

Whether you buy or rent your home, you should use no more than 35 percent of your income on housing, including rent or mortgage, utilities, insurance, and repair. Most banks recommend that no more than 30 percent of your income should support a mortgage, and no more than 40 percent should go to a mortgage and other debt.

Look online.

Know Your Terms

Agent: An individual who represents either the buyer or seller in a real estate transaction.
Broker: An individual, sometimes an owner of an agency, who has met real estate licensing standards and is authorized to conduct real estate transactions.
Multiple Listing Service (MLS): Under this marketing system, agents from real estate companies other than the listing office will also show your house to prospective clients.
Realtor: A broker or agent who belongs to the Canadian Real Estate Association.

Drive around.

OFFER TO PURCHASE

Home buyers sometimes get stung because they or their representatives fail to include important conditions in the Offer to Purchase, or, as it is sometimes called, the Agreement of Purchase and Sale. Your offer can be conditional—it is good only on condition that you obtain mortgage financing, or the house passes a home inspection or a termite check. In *Homebuying Step by Step: a consumer guide and workbook,* the CMHC recommends your offer also include:

■ Basic details such as your legal name, the name of the vendor, and the legal and civic address of the property.
■ The purchase price and all financial details. Included in this should be the amount of the deposit and any interest to be paid on it. You may also want to spell out the specific amount of penalty should you wish to back out of the deal.
■ The chattel or items in the home that are included in the purchase price. This may include window coverings, appliances, a satellite dish,

carpeting, bookcases, or a backyard swing. Enumerate all of them, and stipulate that everything in the house—all appliances and systems—be in working order at the time of closing of title.
■ Date of closing and taking possession—usually 30 to 60 days from the date of the agreement, but it can be longer.
■ Request for a current land survey of the property.
■ Date and time at which the offer becomes null and void. A 48-hour limit on the seller's response time to your offer is reasonable.

FOR BUYERS ONLY

A typical real estate transaction often begins when prospective buyers drive by a house that looks appealing, take down the name of the real estate agent listed on the sign in the yard, and call that person for an appointment. The only problem? That agent—usually the listing agent—works for a commission paid by the seller, and the agent's legal responsibility is to get the best price possible for the current homeowners, not the prospective buyers.

Common sense calls for buyers to be honest about their priorities, preferences, and price range. But since the agent's commission comes from the vendor, and since this money is a percentage of the sale price, it is entirely possible that any information the buyers reveal to the agent—their finances, the top price they'll pay, their reactions to the house—could be used to sweeten the pot for the sellers.

Keep in mind, too, that the agent-vendor relationship doesn't change just because you ask an agent to help you find your dream house. The agent's services will be free to you since his or her fees will be paid by the vendor whose property you eventually buy. Commissions are divided between the listing agent and the agent who brings about the sale.

What can buyers do in these situations? They can be aware that agents will be motivated to get the highest price and the best terms from the seller's point of view. Also, the higher the price, the bigger the agent's commission. Accordingly, buyers should not expect any agent to volunteer information on a house's

Talk to a local realtor.

Check the listings.

defects. If an agent says it's a "fixer-upper," find out exactly what needs fixing up. Buyers should ask specific questions and expect factual answers. But, unless you ask, don't expect the agent to tell you the roof is 25 years old or the fireplaces don't work.

Smart Moves

Ask the following kinds of questions before choosing an agent. The answers will help you determine how buyer-focused he or she is:

■ How long have you represented buyers as a buyer's agent?

■ Do you or your company take real estate listings? Do you prefer exclusive or Multiple Listing Service listings?

■ What percentage of your personal business and your company's business comes from representing buyers? What percentage from representing sellers?

■ Will you try to sell me one of your listed properties before showing me listings from other sources?

■ Do you have information about For Sale by Owner properties?

■ Can I have the names and phone numbers of three to six of your most recent buyer clients?

■ What training have you had in being a buyer's agent?

■ How will you protect my interests as a buyer?

Check out the classified ads in your local newspaper.

Country Properties – Sales 2355

Passive Solar Contemporary, 14 Acres 7 rm, 2 Bths, greenhouse, garage, deck, South view, brook, mature trees. photos & site map. $139,000.

Country P

2 BR conte recreation r pvt courtyar acre lands

BUYING A NEW HOME

When buying a home that's been around for a while, you're getting a known quantity that's proven how it reacts to winter, summer, rain, wind, and other circumstances. When buying a newly built home, you're getting something that "hasn't been road-tested," says Alan Fields, co-author of *Your New Home: The Alert Consumer's Guide to Buying and Building a Quality Home.* So it's important to be careful.

He points out the three biggest mistakes people make when buying a new house:

■ Forgetting to get the "window sticker" for the house—the written list, similar to that on a new car, of specifications and materials used by the builder. "Deal with a builder who's willing to give you specifics about the construction process," advises Fields.

■ Failing to check out the neighborhood. "People fall in love with how pretty the new home is, and don't ask enough questions about what's going on around them with respect to schools, parks, zoning, traffic flow, and other details."

■ Not hiring an independent inspector or engineer to help evaluate the construction. "People think because it's new it's not necessary to inspect the home," says Fields, "or that the city or county housing inspector will check to ensure quality. Those inspectors are checking to ensure that the home meets the minimum standards—not the highest standards—for health and safety codes in the area. Just because a home passes a city inspection doesn't mean you got what you paid for, or what your family deserves."

Home Inspections

Uncover a home's good and bad points.

CHOOSING AN INSPECTOR

Buying a home is the largest investment most people make in their lifetime. A home inspection is a key step in determining whether that investment is a smart one because it identifies not only a home's strengths, but also its weaknesses—problems that can cost you a lot now or in the future, says Harry Janssen, 1998-99 President of the Canadian Association of Home Inspectors. The CAHI is a voluntary, nonprofit professional society dedicated to promoting excellence in the field of home inspection. How to be confident that you're getting a quality home inspection? Janssen suggests that you use recommendations of friends, work colleagues, and real estate agents to assemble a list of at least three inspectors. Interview each one, asking whether he or she has or can provide each of the following:

Credentials, such as membership in CAHI or other nationally recognized organizations and certification number. You should also inquire about the inspector's years of experience and time on location. This kind of information is vital, because there is as yet no nationwide licensing system for inspectors. Plus, there is no single type of professional experience or training that prepares someone for the field. There are courses in many aspects of home inspection. CAHI members must complete written exams and have conducted 250 inspections according to professional standards and ethical practices.

Professional insurance, in case the inspector makes a costly or dangerous mistake.

A written contract spelling out what the inspector will do for you, so you understand the process and are realistic about what it will provide.

Permission to attend the inspection. Your presence at the inspection will lengthen it, but it's important to hear and see firsthand what the inspector finds and to ask questions on the spot about the property.

A written report specifying the inspector's findings. The CAHI code of ethics stipulates that an inspector can represent only one client on a property and can send the inspection report only to those authorized by the client. The inspector is not allowed to repair anything on the property.

The Right Way

The home inspector's job is to identify problems in a home, not solve them. If your inspection report indicates a problem with a particular component or system in your home—the roof or foundations, for instance—call in specialists for advice on how to handle it.

THE INSPECTION REPORT

There are three different types of inspection reports, says Brian Crewe, owner of Bransen Enterprises, a Montreal home inspection company. One is the checklist report, completed during the inspection, where the inspector gives satisfactory or unsatisfactory status to all items he or she inspects. The second type is a narrative report, created after the inspection, which includes the inspector's commentary on what was seen.

The third type is the combination report, which verifies all points and includes narrative comments. As an inspector, Crewe prefers this report because it is completed on site when everyone involved in the project asks questions and clears up any ambiguities or concerns. This type of report is available in professionally prepared packages. Also available are computer programs for on-site report production.

Evaluating the report can be a challenge. That's one reason why it's important to be on-site during the home inspection, says Crewe. "As you're walking around with the inspector, you should get enough information to understand what's a big issue and needs attention, or what's typical of houses of that age and area."

It is vital to have a report on hand to back up any discussions that may arise after inspection has been concluded. Crewe advises going over the report with your real estate agent to get his or her point of view on what's worth taking back to the negotiating table.

THE HOME PRESENTATION

When a new home is completed, the builder or builder's representative takes the buyer on a home presentation, or final walk-through of the house. Tom Hrin, senior construction manager for US Home in California, and author of *Daily Field Guide: A Logbook for Home Builders,* points out that it's not uncommon for over 160 individuals to work on the construction of one house, so mistakes can be made. Hrin recommends you look for the following:

- Find out where all the gas and water shut-off valves and electrical breakers are, and know which switches operate what. You should know where the main shut-off valves are, and where the sewer is located.
- Make sure all the appliances and systems, such as the water heater, air conditioning, and heat, are working. Construction debris can get trapped in toilets, garbage disposals, and other receptacles, so be sure to turn them all on.
- Check all finished surfaces (wood, vinyl, granite, tile, plaster, sheetrock) for chips and scratches.
- Make sure all windows, cabinets, and drawers work properly.
- Double-check the fireplace flue to make sure it's working, and look up into the fireplace to ensure there are no obstructions or pipes out of place.
- Go over the terms of the warranty and understand everything that's covered and for how long.

Smart Moves

The following inspections are among those required by the Canadian Association of Home Inspectors:

Structural components: such as foundations, floors, walls, columns, ceilings, and roofs.

Exterior: including doors, windows, garage door operators, decks, balconies, stoops, steps, porches, eaves, soffits and fascias, drainage, driveways, patios, and retaining walls, as they affect the condition of the building.

Roofing: including roof coverings, drainage systems, flashings, skylights, and chimneys.

Plumbing: including interior water supply, drain, waste and vent systems, hot water system, and sump pump.

Electrical: including conductor, service and grounding equipment, main overcurrent device, main and distribution panel, amperage and voltage ratings, branch circuit conductors, their overcurrent devices and the compatibility of their ampacities and voltages, the polarity and grounding of all receptacles within six feet of interior plumbing fixtures, and the operation of ground fault circuit interrupters.

Heating: equipment, automatic safety controls, chimneys, flues and vents, solid fuel heating devices, and distribution systems.

Central air conditioning: including equipment, controls, and distribution system.

Interiors: walls, ceilings, floors, steps, stairways, balconies and railings, counters, cabinets, doors, and windows.

Insulation and ventilation: insulation and vapor retarders in unfinished spaces, ventilation of attics and foundation areas, kitchen, bathroom, and laundry venting systems.

Do the bricks need repointing?

Are the door frames warped?

Are floorboards sunken or uneven?

BE WISE ABOUT WARRANTIES

"A home warranty is only as good as the contractor who built it," says Brian Crewe. "That's why you don't buy a home just because it has new home warranty." Many warranties of this type are available in Canada. But, as Crewe points out, some are administered by contractors themselves, creating conflict-of-interest situations that lead to frustration and litigation. Given this drawback, the federal and provincial governments are introducing legislation covering home inspections and warranty programs. In some areas, legislation will cover old as well as new dwellings.

Inspection by a qualified professional is the best way to check out the condition of your home. Your sales contract should include provisions for satisfactory inspections and specific renegotiation conditions. If you're building a new home, have it inspected regularly, particularly just prior to drywall installation. Once this stage of construction has been completed, a contractor can easily hide any problems. As the house belongs to your contractor until the final payment, always get his agreement to any inspections.

Financing Your Home

Develop your financial savvy to get the best possible mortgage.

GET READY, GET SET...

If there's one time you want to be a smart consumer, it's going into the home loan process, recommends Peter G. Miller, author of *The Common-Sense Mortgage*. "Get as much information as you can so you can be an equal in the marketplace, not a dependent. That's how you get the best deals."

His recommendations include:

- Months before you're ready to apply for a mortgage, start educating yourself. Read and save articles and books, visit Internet sites, talk to new home buyers. Start making a list of the questions you want to ask when you speak with brokers and lenders. Approach this project as you might a college class or a new job. "It's very important to realize there are hundreds of loan programs out there," says Miller. "Some will work really well for you and some won't. You'll be way ahead if you're informed." Banks, trust companies, credit unions, pension funds, and insurance companies, all lend money for mortgages.
- About three months before you plan to enter the loan marketplace, check your credit rating with Equifax Canada and Transunion Canada. You may find items that are factually incorrect or out of date, and you'll want to remove them before applying for a loan.
- At the same time, start speaking to lenders. Learn about how much financing you qualify for, and what loan programs seem to make the most sense for you.
- Get your paperwork together before applying, and get prequalified. Both will significantly speed up the loan process.

HIGH-RATIO LOANS

There are lots of options that let you customize your mortgage to your financial goals and needs, according to the Canada Mortgage and Housing Corporation (CMHC). One is a federally sponsored, CMHC-administered insurance program that enables you to purchase a home with as little a down payment as 5 percent of the house's appraised value or purchase price.

Ordinarily, mortgage loans do not exceed 75 percent of the house value. When they do, most lending institutions require that such high-ratio loans be insured. Then, if the borrower defaults, the lender is paid back by the insurer.

As many as 2.7 million Canadians currently own homes with insured mortgages. Getting the insurance begins with a $235 application fee, followed by a one-time insurance premium of 0.5 to 3.75 percent of the loan amount, and possibly other charges. The premium can be added to your regular mortgage payments or paid in full at the outset. Your lender can obtain the insurance from CMHC or a private insurer. Both new and resale homes are eligible.

Criteria specify that:

- The home must be in Canada and must be your principal residence.
- Housing payments, including principal, interest, taxes, heating, and 50 percent of applicable condominium fees, can't be more than 32 percent of your gross household income.
- Your debt load can't be more than 40 percent of your gross household income.

The Right Way

There are many sites on the Internet that can help you unravel the mysteries of home loans and begin shopping around for a loan program that fits your housing needs. One of these websites, www.mortgagecanada.com, is run by Mortgage Depot, which has offices in Victoria and Colwood, British Columbia. John Zieman, one of the original partners in Mortgage Depot, outlines some of the things you can find at this site:

- A list of lenders, including banks, trust and insurance companies. Mortgage Depot will help you pick the lender that offers rates and options best suited to your needs.
- A 1-800 access number to Mortgage Specialists who use the latest computer technology to review your circumstances, check your credit,

consider all the alternatives offered by different lenders, and calculate the price you can afford.

- Up-to-date information on mortgage rates, based on data from lenders across Canada. Background information on mortgages generally, with easy-to-understand explanations of standard mortgage forms.
- Calculators that do the math for you on a variety of mortgage variables.

John Zieman says that people often think that they can only shop for a mortgage at a local financial institution. In reality, borrowers will often secure better rates and terms by shopping through the Internet. This opens the door to a much wider variety of lenders and forces banks with local branches to be more competitive.

CLOSING COSTS

Closing marks the point at which all the legal and financial obligations of your offer to purchase have been met and the seller transfers the deed to the property to you in return for the balance of the purchase price not covered in the deposit. In some provinces, a mortgage lender must provide the buyer with an itemized estimate of settlement costs. You would be wise to check also with your lawyer, so that you know well ahead of time what your closing costs will be.

Typically these costs include property survey and pest inspection fees; the lender's home appraisal fees; lawyer/notary fees; charges for title search; both owner's and lender's title insurance; government recording and transfer fees payable to the municipality for recording property documents at the local courthouse; and prepayment of fire and property insurance.

You may also have to make adjustment payments to the buyer if he or she has prepaid property taxes or maintenance bills such as oil or hydro.

Know Your Terms

Type of Mortgage	Pros	Cons
Open You can repay the loan at any time in part or in full without penalty.	A good choice if you plan to sell soon. Most lenders will allow you to convert to a closed mortgage at any time.	Interest rates are usually higher than on closed mortgages.
Closed A closed mortgage is for a set term and with fixed conditions. Prepayment may net a penalty.	Usually offers the lowest interest rates.	Closed mortgages are not flexible, and there are often penalties for prepayments or lump-sum payments.
Fixed-rate Same interest rate for the entire term of the loan.	Predictable expense makes budgeting easier. Good choice if you will own the home for many years.	Usually higher interest rates than VRMs. Harder to qualify for than VRMs.
Variable-rate (VRM) Variable rates over term of loan. Conditions vary with lenders. Some offer a protected or capped rate.	Discounted introductory rates. Often assumable by another buyer.	Your payment goes up if interest rates rise. Unpredictable payments make long-term budgeting difficult.
Amortization period*		
25-year Pay off over 25 years of monthly payments.	Lower monthly payments. Easier to qualify for.	Higher total amount of interest than shorter loan.
15-year Pay off over 15 years of monthly payments.	Lower total amount of interest. Build equity faster than longer loan.	May be harder to qualify. Higher monthly payments than longer loan.
How You Pay		
Amortized Payments go toward principal and interest. Loan paid back fully over term.	Gradually build equity in your home. No debt at end of term.	Higher monthly payment than on interest-only loans. Tax deduction decreases as interest payment decreases.

*Loans are generally for terms of 1 to 5 years but amortized over 15, 20, or 25 years.

TAKING CARE OF BUSINESS

As well as authorization for a credit check, most lenders require the following documentation for a mortgage application:

- Information on age, marital status, and dependents.
- All income and employment details backed by a letter from your employer, T-4 slips, and income tax returns.
- If self-employed, signed financial statements, statements of income and expenses, and federal tax returns for the past two years.
- Current banking information with verification, such as account numbers, addresses, balances, and statements for all bank and investment accounts.
- A list of assets including property and vehicles.
- Total liabilities including account numbers, addresses, current balances, and payment amounts on all debts, such as credit cards and car loans.
- Copies of the property listing and, on a resale home, of the Offer to Purchase.
- Plans and the cost estimates on a new home.
- Copies of the financial statements of the condominium or cooperative association if you are buying a condo or a co-op.
- A certificate for well and septic, if applicable.

Homeowner's Insurance

You can protect your most important investment.

CHOOSING AN INSURER

Before you purchase a policy, it is advisable to consult any source that will help you evaluate insurers. For information about service, check out consumer magazines, which sometimes do articles on homeowner's insurance, including customer satisfaction ratings. Your provincial insurance department may be able to provide information. Ask friends about their experiences with their insurers.

If you're concerned about the financial health of an insurer, turn to reports published by ratings agencies, such as TRAC Insurance Services, Dominion Bond Rating Service, Canadian Bond Rating Service, A.M. Best, Moody's, and others. Check out several ratings to find the high-ranking insurers. These reports are usually found in the business section of your library. Your agent or the company should also be able to provide ratings information.

Talk to your provincial insurance department or the Insurance Bureau of Canada (www.ibc.ca) about protection against insurance company failure.

POLICY QUESTIONS

It's important to know what questions to ask when interviewing an agent about a homeowner's policy. Here are some suggestions from the Insurance Bureau of Canada:

Property insurance

- What basic coverages are included in the policy? Damage from fire, lightning, wind, hail, and smoke are typically included in a basic policy.
- What is not covered or specifically excluded? Disasters, such as earthquakes and floods, are typically not covered. If you live in an area where your home is subject to any of these perils, ask if special coverage can be provided.
- What is the appropriate amount of insurance for your dwelling and personal property? How is the amount of coverage calculated? Is it enough to rebuild your home if it is entirely destroyed?
- Is replacement cost on the dwelling automatic or do you have to request it? If your home is unique in any way or older, will the insurance policy pay to replace it using materials similar to the existing ones?
- In addition to your home, is there enough coverage included in the policy for other property, such as outbuildings, fences, additions, pools, or decks? Is any of the coverage limited and if yes, how?
- Are there limitations in the policy? Typical limitations include trees and shrubs, money and securities, and theft of jewelry. Evaluate your personal needs to ensure that they are met in your coverage. Additional coverage can be purchased for most, but not all, situations.
- Does the policy provide for additional living expenses? If your home is rendered uninhabitable, is there coverage to pay your living expenses until it is repaired?
- How is a claim settled? Whom will you be dealing with?

Personal property insurance

- What is covered? Most homeowner's policies provide "named peril" coverage for personal property, as opposed to dwelling coverage, which generally provides "all peril" coverage. You must be aware of what the named perils are, since there is only coverage for damage due to them. Fire, smoke, vandalism, and theft are examples of the perils covered. Theft to jewelry is usually limited in the basic policy, and additional coverage must be purchased.
- If your personal property is damaged, will the policy pay for new property, or will the coverage amount be depreciated?

Liability insurance

- Are there any exclusions in your policy you need to be aware of?
- If you do business in your home, will the homeowner's policy cover those activities? If not, can you purchase the

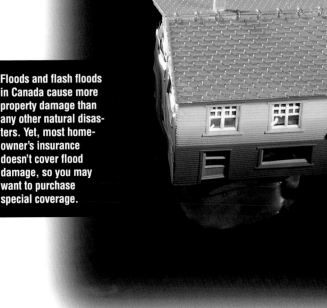

Floods and flash floods in Canada cause more property damage than any other natural disasters. Yet, most homeowner's insurance doesn't cover flood damage, so you may want to purchase special coverage.

Keep your insurance policies and other vital records in a fire-safe security chest.

DEALING WITH FLOODS

The average home policy in Canada doesn't cover flood damage. If you're in a high-risk area such as Manitoba's Red River Valley, make sure that this coverage is included in your policy.

In the event of a flood, the Insurance Bureau of Canada offers these suggestions that may assist you in getting the financial help you need in a timely manner:

■ Keep a record of your belongings. Some people keep track of their possessions on videotape. Others write a list, or take photographs, or make an audio list of collection such as books, stamps, and so. In all cases, be sure to record models, serial numbers, or other identifying marks. It is useful to know where you bought a lost or damaged item so the insurer can replace it with one of "like kind and quality."

■ If you have to evacuate, take your insurance policy with you if possible.

■ After the flood, contact your agent as quickly as possible. Save any remnants of damage for the adjuster.

■ Protect your property from further damage, keeping all related receipts. Don't make permanent repairs until the insurance company has inspected the property, and you've reached an agreement regarding reimbursement.

Fire extinguishers, smoke alarms, and chimney flares, designed to put out chimney fires, can help to improve your safety.

SIMPLIFYING SOME INSURANCE ISSUES

The Insurance Bureau of Canada can answer many of your questions about insurance. Here are its answers to some of the most common areas of confusion relating to homeowner's insurance:

The real estate value of a home versus the insurable amount. Most people think that if they buy a house for $300,000, they need that much in homeowner's insurance. But in the vast majority of cases that's not true because the amount you pay for a property includes the land as well as the structure. You need to be insured only for the cost of rebuilding the structure. Of course, if what you bought was a fabulous old home, the cost of rebuilding may be substantially higher. Consult with an insurance representative to get a sense of what it would cost to rebuild. That's the coverage you'll need.

Water damage. Water damage falls into three categories:

1. Damage caused by a flood, which is only covered through flood insurance.

2. Damage caused by serious weather and aging conditions, such as ice dams in the gutters or burst pipes. This is covered by homeowner's insurance.

3. Damage caused by neglect of small maintenance items, such as a drip under your sink. This is not covered. Your insurance agent and your policy should spell out exactly what is and is not covered. Read your insurance policy thoroughly.

"Replacement cost" versus "actual cost value" of personal property. A replacement cost policy pays you to buy something similar to what you had for what it would cost to buy it new. For example, if your 10-year-old living room couch was destroyed, it would pay you to purchase a new couch of the same quality. This is preferable to, but more expensive than, a cash value policy, which would only reimburse you for the current value of your 10-year-old couch.

amount of additional coverage you need?

■ Does your liability coverage extend to protect you at other locations?

Your premium

■ What is the premium for all the coverages you need? Is there any way you can reduce it?

■ Are there discounts if you install fire or burglar alarms, or other loss prevention equipment?

■ Are there discounts for good claim history or purchasing multiple lines of insurance with the same company?

■ What deductible options are available, and how could they affect your insurance premium?

■ What types of payment options are available (monthly, quarterly, direct bill)?

■ Does a claim affect your insurance policy or your premium?

The Right Way

Many people choose to go with a low deductible on their homeowner's insurance, worrying that they won't have the money to pay more when a crisis comes. It may, however, be best to take a higher deductible and to get a significantly lower premium as a result. Statistically, people have a claim only every 8 to 10 years. So you can save a lot by raising your deductible, and benefit by putting the savings aside toward better insurance (such as a replacement cost policy).

Selling Your Home

Learn to handle one of life's biggest financial challenges with ease and confidence.

Use a sign to attract potential buyers driving by your home.

The view from the deck — mountains and sky ...

Knotty pine kitchen — gas range and big fridge

Make your own brochure using snapshots of your home at its best.

SELLING YOUR HOME YOURSELF

Thinking about handling your own sale? "For sale by owner"—FSBO in the industry—with no agent's commission attached might move your house faster and net you some extra cash. But is it worth it? Even with professional help, selling the house you live in can be daunting and emotionally draining. Doing it yourself is a time-consuming task requiring much effort, patience, and flexibility. N'ann Harp, president of Virginia-based Smart Consumer Services (www.sconsumer.com) advises taking a good hard look at your strengths and weaknesses as well as the realities of your life before deciding to go FSBO. If you've got the time, temperament, and skills, you can do well. If not, selling your home can be a difficult experience, and might not be worth the effort.

Harp has created a to-do list for sellers going it on their own. Here are some of the key items:

■ Determine a proper asking price by educating yourself about "comparables"—the recent selling prices of similar homes in your area.

■ Create a one-page fact sheet—with a color picture and all the salient facts about the house, taxes, utilities, and the neighborhood. Use local real estate agency fact sheets as a guide. "Don't be afraid to get poetic," says Harp. If there's something that's really a "wow" about your home, let people know about it.

■ Advertise with a professional-looking lawn sign as well as in newspapers. Include day and evening telephone numbers in your newspaper ads. Keep the atmosphere quiet when showing the house. If necessary, send your kids and pets off when prospective clients are visiting.

■ Find out if potential buyers are already prequalified for a mortgage. If not, ask them to go through the process.

■ Be smart about legal issues. Find out what you have to disclose and do so, using the proper forms. Get a standard contract from a stationery store, real estate agency, or library, but before finalizing anything, have a qualified real estate lawyer review your agreements.

FINDING THE RIGHT AGENT

The agent with whom you list your house can make the difference between a selling process that's long, painful, and confusing, or one that's short and sweet. Marty Rodriguez, one of the most successful real estate agents associated with Century 21, advises you to:

■ See who's moving property in your area by checking lawn signs, newspaper ads, and word of mouth. "A hard-working agent will have a lot of exposure and will have created an identity."

■ Expect an agent to be enthusiastic. "It's not

The dining nook — all knotty pine, wounded woods!

enough to know the market," says Rodriguez. "You've got to have the enthusiasm to sell. I can sell nice and not-so-nice properties because I can help my clients see that the price is right and the value is there."

- Finding out what and how much agents have advertised and sold will help you determine how well they're operating.
- Expect an agent to be professional—to return phone calls promptly, to be organized and well-groomed, and to abide by a code of ethics, especially when it comes to honesty. Excellent communication skills are also important because open and clear communication is at the heart of any real estate transaction.

Adding to Rodriguez's list, Jennifer Braaksma of the Canadian Real Estate Association says:

- Find someone who specializes in selling properties like yours in the area.
- Find someone compatible with you and your goals. Interview several real estate agents to learn about their experience, track records, style, and market knowledge. Ideally, the person you choose should impress you with his or her competence, integrity, and way of doing business.

The Right Way

Want to know about recent sales, prices, and addresses of houses in your area? Check with your municipal clerk's office, which keeps a public record of these facts.

PREPARING YOUR HOME FOR DISPLAY

When your home is up for sale, it's like having your boss and your relatives and your worst enemy over for dinner, all at the same time. The scrutiny is intense. Martha Webb, author of *Dress Your House for Success*, recommends going out and looking at sale homes yourself to get an understanding of "how critical a buyer gets when looking. Begin to get a sense of what it's like when a house is completely clean and there isn't any work to be done." Then bring that objectivity back to your own home.

Webb suggests a five-step approach to bringing your house up to snuff. The first three basics are cleaning, uncluttering, and repairing. Don't stint on anything that will make the house look better.

The final two steps, which Webb calls neutralizing and dynamizing, help to create a feeling of home—something buyers will remember "long after they've been in the house."

Neutralizing involves creating an environment that will appeal to a broad range of people. This can mean anything from using neutral colors when repainting to removing highly personal items such as religious artifacts to eliminating pet or cooking odors.

Dynamizing involves looking at every room in your house and thinking about how to convey a special message about that space. In a den, for instance, you might drape an afghan over an easy chair and arrange a reading lamp next to it.

Tools of the Trade

Creating your own real estate ad? Here are some abbreviations you may find useful:

town	townhouse	fp or fpl	fireplace
mn flr	main floor	scsys	security system
br or bdrm	bedroom	c/air	central air-conditioning
mst bdrm	master bedroom		
fam rm	family room	f/air heat	forced-air heat
bth	bath	hrdwd	hardwood
fml	formal	brk	brick
bsmt	basement	w/o	walk out
fin lwr level	finished lower level	yd	yard
		txs	taxes
dble gar	double garage	mtg	mortgage

DISCLOSING DEFECTS

Admitting that your house isn't perfect can be one of the most anxiety-producing aspects of selling it. When it comes to serious flaws, however, telling all is not only the best policy; in many provinces it's the law: you must tell the buyer the truth about all physical defects of the house. Indeed most provinces also require sellers to sign either disclosure forms listing any known defects, or disclaimers affirming their lack of knowledge of any defects in the condition of the house.

In recent years, more and more buyers have sued sellers for not disclosing certain problems, or being outright deceitful about defects, before the sale. In these situations, the courts have increasingly sided with the buyers. Because agents have been sued with the sellers in some instances, some agents will no longer show a home unless the seller has completed a disclosure form.

Most provinces require sellers to tell buyers if there is any lead-based paint in or around the property and to report the presence of such environmental concerns as radon or asbestos. But, like most real estate laws, whether and how you're required to disclose the truth about other defects or structural problems, such as a wet basement, patched roof, or cracked foundation, may vary somewhat from province to province. So whether you're selling your home yourself or through a real estate agent, it's critical that you understand and abide by whatever disclosure laws apply in your case. Local consumer affairs offices can give you information on the specifics of your province's requirements, and the necessary forms are usually available in any real estate office.

As a seller, be aware that the frequency of home inspections in real estate transactions offers protection to buyers above and beyond provincial disclosure laws. A professional home inspection is likely to reveal the deepest, darkest secrets of your home. One possible strategy is to hire the inspector yourself and to repair any structural or systems' problems found before putting your house on the market.

Wills and Living Wills

Give yourself and your family peace of mind.

LAST WILL AND TESTAMENT

"Unless you're unmarried, childless, and without property, writing a will is one of the most important things you can do to protect your loved ones," says Mona Brown of Carman, Manitoba, a lawyer and executive member of the National Wills, Estates and Trusts Section of the Canadian Bar Association.

If you die without a will, your estate is turned over to the state, which divides your assets according to the succession laws of your province. This may mean costly and lengthy legal battles for your survivors, and even worse, your loved ones may not be provided for as you wished.

Some people make wills with the help of software programs or preprinted forms, but lawyers warn that some of these aids are "simply not right." American-produced packages, for example, may not take account of Canadian legislation, much less make allowances for distinctions in provincial probate laws.

If you do draw up your own will, have it checked by a lawyer. Better still, pay a lawyer to draw up a proper will in the first place, says Brown. Self-made wills are often challenged in the courts "because the deceased's intentions are unclear, or the deceased failed to anticipate certain events or deal with certain assets."

HARD FACTS ABOUT WILLS

Lawyer Stephen R. Elias, whose company publishes legal tools for nonlawyers, concedes that the more complex your estate, the more serious your need for legal help with your will. Similar advice is included with a Last Will and Testament package from Vancouver's Self-Counsel Press, one of Canada's leading publishers of legal books and packages for the layman.

In drawing up a will, remember that there may be restrictions on how you bequeath your assets. If you don't abide by certain laws on family relief—if you disinherit a spouse or dependent children, for example—your will can be overridden by the courts.

The law also prevents you from passing on certain kinds of property—life insurance proceeds, for example. These are paid to the beneficiary named in the policy. Also, assets held in a trust must be distributed according to the terms of the trust. In most provinces, the matrimonial home may not be given to a third party; the surviving spouse may have rights to the property. Here are other tips that apply whether you write your own will or seek professional help.

- Update your will after any major life change, such as marriage, divorce, the birth or adoption of children, the death of a spouse, or a move to another province. Otherwise, many income tax savings may be lost to your estate.
- Make sure your executor knows where your original will is located and can access it. When you

Writing a will is one of the most important ways you can protect your property and loved ones.

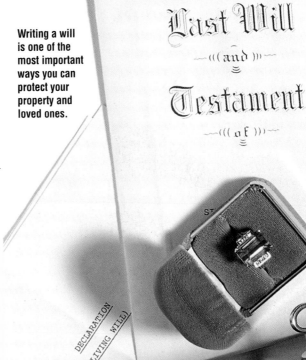

The Right Way

A valid will may be on scrap paper, provided it meets certain standards. These vary from province to province, but usually require:
- That the testator, or person making the will, is of "sound mind" (not senile or mentally incompetent), and not acting under the influence of another person.
- That the testator be a legal adult—at least 18 years of age in most provinces, but 19 in some.
- That the will is dated, and signed at the end by the testator and at least two witnesses who are not beneficiaries, or spouses of a beneficiary, and who are both present when the testator signs. (Wills handwritten by the testator do not require witnesses.)

update your will, destroy the earlier version.

- To be valid, a will must comply with the wills' act of your province. In most provinces, provided your will is executed properly and notarized on execution, your witnesses will not have to appear in court when your will is probated.
- Your will is the worst place to specify funeral arrangements, since often it is only examined after your burial. Instead, leave written instructions with friends or family.
- Some provinces recognize holograph or handwritten wills—ones that are set out, signed, and dated in the testator's handwriting. Holograph wills are not witnessed: they become invalid if anyone else writes on them. However, proof of the testator's signature and competence will be required for probate.

LIVING WILLS

"Everyone should have a living will," advises Cynthia St. John, executive director of Dying With Dignity, a national, nonprofit organization dedicated to fostering communication about end-of-life decisions and improving the way people die. A Canadian pioneer of living wills, Dying With Dignity has helped countless people ensure that their final wishes are carried out.

Everybody should have both a living will and a durable power of attorney for health care, says St. John. She considers the latter especially crucial for people with serious medical conditions.

A **living will** contains your written instructions about medical treatment in the event you are unable to communicate at the end of your life. You can, for instance, instruct doctors and family members as to the steps you do or don't want taken to preserve your life, and address issues such as whether you want to be an organ donor.

A **durable power of attorney for medical care** allows you to appoint someone to make medical-care decisions on your behalf if you are unable to do so yourself. You can appoint just about anyone to act as your agent—although not your doctor. St. John recommends choosing someone whom you trust and who will be a strong advocate on behalf of your wishes.

Legal recognition of living wills and durable powers of attorney for health care varies from province to province. Provinces that recognize living wills require health care workers to respect an individual's wishes. Talk to your family about your decisions, and ask them to support the person who will have durable power of attorney for your health care.

Discuss your wishes with your family physician while you are still in good health, and ask your doctors to place copies of your living will and durable power of attorney for health care in your medical files.

Inform your clergy and lawyers of your directives and give them, too, copies of the documents.

Kits on living wills and power of attorney for health care are available at nominal cost from Dying With Dignity. For more information, check its website (www.web.net/dwd/).

FINAL ARRANGEMENTS

It's very important for families to talk ahead of time about funeral arrangements, says Lisa Carlson, author of *Caring for the Dead: Your Final Act of Love.*

Openness about funeral preparations not only ensures that a loved one's wishes are carried out at death, but also protects families from deceptive business practices or overpaying for funeral services when they are at their most vulnerable. "Consumers need to be informed funeral shoppers," says Carlson.

- Be wary of prepaid funeral packages that are not transferable if you move, or ones, payable in installments, in which the prearranged price is not

locked in should you die before paying in full.

- You can save thousands of dollars if you plan ahead and shop around for a funeral home.
- Many people don't know that embalming, one of the costliest items on a funeral bill, is not always required. Provincial law sets rules for cremated remains; urns may not be required, or you may not have to have a casket.
- Ignore false claims that some caskets or vaults will preserve the body better than others.
- Memorial societies, which charge a nominal membership fee, provide information and resources to help people arrange affordable, dignified, prearranged funerals. For information on memorial societies, contact the Etobicoke, Ontario-based Federation of Ontario Memorial Societies.

Myth: *A living will could limit your access to health care in an accident.* **Fact:** *Living wills only go into effect when you're dying. In an emergency, medical technicians are charged with stabilizing you and getting you to a hospital.*

Power of Attorney

Sometimes it's necessary to appoint someone to act on your behalf.

AN OVERVIEW OF POWERS OF ATTORNEY

Power of attorney is a notarized document in which one person (the principal) authorizes another (the agent or attorney in fact) to handle certain affairs on his or her behalf. Provincial laws vary on who may serve as an agent, but it should be someone the principal trusts completely. Powers of attorney can include everything you do, including financial transactions, as well as some health care issues, such as making medical decisions on your behalf if you are incapacitated, or granting a babysitter authority to consent to medical care for your child in an emergency. The document can be general, limited, or a combina-

tion of general and specific powers. Typically, people grant a power of attorney in situations when they'll be unable to handle their affairs—they'll be out of the country, for instance.

A **regular** power of attorney gives the agent authority to sign legal documents and make almost any type of decision. The principal can cancel it at any time, and it ends if the principal becomes mentally incompetent or dies.

An **enduring** or **durable** power of attorney is not invalidated by incapacitation, and as a result is a good choice for people who are giving away powers in anticipation of physical or mental disabilities. It ends only when the principal revokes it or dies. Keep in mind that many provinces require very specific language for a durable power of attorney for health care decisions.

A durable power of attorney may give the agent

All powers of attorney must be notarized, but other procedures, such as those involving witnesses, vary from province to province.

immediate power, or it can "spring" into effect at a specified event, such as medical corroboration that the principal is mentally incompetent to handle his or her affairs. Accordingly, it is known as a **springing** power of attorney. It should be noted that all provinces do not recognize a springing power of attorney.

Because power of attorney forms and their uses vary from province to province, you should execute separate powers of attorney for each province where you live or have any assets.

The Right Way

Revocation of a power of attorney is an important, and often overlooked, consideration. Asking your agent to rip up the agreement may be enough—provided he or she destroys the document when you request it. A wiser policy would consist of sending a letter to the agent revoking the powers in addition to your verbal request. Be sure to keep a copy of the letter in your files. It is also advisable to notify anybody with whom the agent might have used or still could use the power of attorney.

CHOOSING AN AGENT

Absolute trust is the key when giving power of attorney to someone. "That trust needs to be based on some knowledge of you and your family," says lawyer Mona Brown of Carman, Manitoba. "It should be someone you go back a long way with, and there should be permanence to the relationship. You have to rely on the person's judgment and be confident that he or she will reflect your wishes." This is especially important if you're anticipating a long-term power of attorney, rather than a short-term one to cover a brief period of time when you will be unavailable.

Age and maturity are other qualities to consider, as are the willingness and ability to "deal with the essential triviality of the tasks, such as handling bookkeeping and signing cheques," says Brown. People sometimes assign two agents, such as two of their adult children, in hopes of making the work and decision making less onerous. The problem is, the two may not always agree, so you may want to consider how well they get on before choosing them. You should also name an alternate in case one person is unable or unwilling to act. Make sure those you name are willing to act as your agent. No matter whom you designate, review the decision from time to time. The relationship might have changed, making it important to assign someone different.

TIMING A POWER OF ATTORNEY

"The time to execute a power of attorney is before you need it," says Mona Brown. "I try to never do a will for anybody of any age without also doing a power of attorney. In doing a will, you recognize you could die. In doing a power of attorney, you recognize that something could happen that would make you unable to manage your affairs. When you're younger, such things are unexpected, but they're no less welcome when you're older. Either way, the document should be in place."

Brown advises people to designate an agent and a successor to that agent in case of an emergency, or the inability of the first agent to act. "Some people may not have another chance to do a power of attorney. So there should be a backup in case something happens to the first agent."

If you don't execute a power of attorney and you become unable to manage your affairs, your nearest and dearest may have to ask the courts to declare you incompetent and to grant someone guardianship over you and your assets. Once granted, the courts consider themselves a "watchdog" of your affairs. Inventories and financial accountings have to be filed with the courts regularly. Doctors, relatives, friends, and business associates may have to testify. Since you have the right to challenge all allegations, this court-intensive, expensive process can be emotionally difficult for all concerned.

Power of attorney is the better alternative in most cases. Not only can you select the person you want to handle your affairs, but you can also designate the precise amount of authority you wish to convey, and the circumstances under which the power should be revoked. Keep in mind that, once in effect, the agent's right to act on your behalf is virtually absolute and you are legally bound by his or her actions.

Smart Moves

There are several ways of protecting yourself and your best interests if you are at all hesitant about giving an agent unrestricted power of attorney:

- Write a separate letter to your lawyer, advising him or her that although the power of attorney is unrestricted, it's not to be used unless you are clearly not in a fit state to manage your own affairs.
- Name two attorneys who must act jointly, thereby reducing the risk that the power of attorney will be used improperly.
- Lodge the power of attorney with a third party, with clear written instructions stating the kinds of situations when it is to be released (for example, only if the named attorney provides the third party with a written statement from a qualified doctor attesting to the fact that you are no longer able to manage your financial affairs).

THE POWERS OF STEPPARENTS

Stepparents may wonder if they need a power of attorney to act on behalf of their stepchildren. It's not much of an issue as long as the parents are around. But if the parents get divorced and have joint legal custody, they're both still able to act on behalf of the child. If one of the parents remarries, he or she can't execute a power of attorney giving the stepparent power to override the wishes of the other parent. If one parent has sole custody, then the power of attorney is unnecessary for day-to-day transactions, except if the parent is going out of town or will be otherwise unavailable. Then the stepparent needs to be able to act in a medical or school emergency, and a power of attorney would be useful.

When choosing an agent to handle your financial affairs, make sure it's someone you trust to act in your best interests.

Acting as Executor

Understand what's involved in settling an estate.

TO BE OR NOT TO BE AN EXECUTOR

You're asked to be an executor. Should you accept? "I always tell people it's a two-sided coin," says Carman, Manitoba-based lawyer Mona Brown. "On one side, you have executive authority. On the other, you're answerable to the beneficiaries, so you're signing on for a position in which you are subject to scrutiny, and in which you're accountable. You are also personally liable for filing income tax and/or GST returns and for ensuring all income and GST taxes are paid prior to distributing any of the estate to beneficiaries. Therefore, you have to be prepared to justify your actions, and, if necessary, convince a probate (or surrogate) court judge that you acted prudently. It's not a job for someone who would be upset by that." Before deciding, consider the other aspects of the job:

- The need to keep meticulous records, detailing all receipts and disbursements.
- The responsibility to make decisions, such as choosing a real estate agent to sell the deceased's house.
- The reality of having to deal with conflict—for example, if the beneficiaries don't like some of your decisions.
- The time-consuming nature of the job, which can be overwhelming, even though you'll be compensated.
- Whether there will be a coexecutor. If so, you need to determine whether you can get along with that person.
- The nature of the deceased's estate—for example, how simple or complex the deceased's financial affairs are.
- The orderliness of the deceased's life. If the person is leaving behind a house crammed with years' worth of papers and junk, you may not want to get involved.

LIVING TRUSTS

Although most provinces have informal, inexpensive procedures for probating wills, probating involves mandatory reporting requirements. If the will is complicated, the process can also be time-consuming, and costly. Accordingly, people who own large estates and want to minimize probate costs and delays, as well as people who do not want details of their bequests to become public knowledge, often use an alternative legal device, a living trust, for handling their estates. People set up this trust while they are alive, often naming themselves as the initial trustees, and a successor trustee to take over when they die. At that time, assets from the trust can go directly to the beneficiaries, bypassing probate and executor's fees, or the suc-cessor trustee can take over managing the assets according to the terms of the trust.

Trust departments of banks are sometimes asked to take on a trustee or cotrustee role in these situations. Banks typically get involved in the process in the following situations:

- When assets need to be managed not only with the surviving spouse in mind, but also for the benefit of children, aging parents, or other beneficiaries.
- The person setting up

THE EXECUTOR'S ROLE

An executor is appointed in a will to ensure the will maker's wishes are carried out. Fees for the job are set by the province, and are usually a percentage of the estate's value. The role is for a finite period, from the date of death until all the assets are distributed (and longer, if certain tax issues arise), says Mona Brown, a lawyer specializing in trusts and estates. Brown lists the following typical executor responsibilities:

Presenting the will to probate (sometimes called surrogate) court. Having assets valued—getting the house appraised, for example.

Opening a chequing account in the name of the estate. Paying the deceased's debts, such as credit card balances, rent, and utilities.

Arranging probate in all provinces where the deceased held real estate. Claiming any life insurance, employee, or death benefits

The Right Way

If you've been named as executor of a will, your role doesn't become official until the first step in the process has taken place, the granting of probate or letters testamentary. This is an official certificate issued by the surrogate court or register of wills declaring that the will has been accepted as a valid last will and that the named person—in this case, you—has been certified as the executor.

the trust may desire a neutral party as trustee. For instance, a parent may not want his or her children managing the money when a choice would have to be made among them as to which child to designate trustee, or if a family business is involved.

- If "discretionary judgment" needs to be exercised. For instance, if the trustee has to approve purchases, it's a lot easier for a bank to say no to a Ferrari than for a kindly uncle to do so.

Setting up a living trust is quite complicated and can be quite expensive. Provincial laws on trusts vary, and you should get legal advice. Banks and financial planners charge annual fees for the cotrustee role.

MINIMIZING EMOTIONAL ENTANGLEMENTS

When a parent dies and his or her estate is being settled, "every single dysfunctional family dynamic is liable to leap into play," says Robert Gaines, PhD, a New York City psychologist. "Death being such a pivotal event, and money being so emotionally laden, all kinds of issues that seemed to have gone away can spring back. Sibling rivalries never die. After the death of a parent, these rivalries can become focused on their possessions and money."

And the executor, especially if it's one of the children, can get caught in the middle. Gaines continues, "The one chosen as executor shouldn't be surprised at the sentiments and anger coming from the other, less-enfranchised siblings or relatives."

How can this kind of strife be minimized, if not avoided entirely? Gaines suggests the following:

- Choose someone outside the family—someone you can trust to carry out your wishes—to be the executor of your will.
- Discuss the provisions of the will with family members in advance so there are no last-minute surprises. Explain how you understand your instructions and the reasons for your actions.
- If you are a relative of someone from whose will you have certain expectations, keep in mind that that person has the right to do whatever he or she wants with the estate. "At the end of their lives, people make decisions that are meaningful to them," reminds Gaines.

To avoid family conflicts, you may want to appoint a bank officer as executor of your will.

PAYING THE DUES

As an executor, one of your most important tasks will be paying the deceased's taxes and debts. However, you may hire lawyers and accountants to help you. As well as preparing the deceased's final income tax returns, and GST returns if applicable, you must pay all taxes due out of assets of the estate. Some personal liability can result if you don't follow correct procedures. You must also pay the estate's debts and contest any unjustified claims. Before getting a discharge from your duties, you will have to present the probate, or surrogate, court judge with an accounting of your actions as executor. (If the beneficiaries are adults, they may give a release and it won't be necessary to get a release from the court.)

Itemizing all real estate and personal property in the estate. Overseeing and keeping safe the deceased's personal property.

Informing banks, brokerages, and creditors about the death. Managing assets, such as stocks. Dealing with all personal financial business.

Filing income tax, GST, and estate tax returns, and paying taxes. Preparing an account of activities for the court. Distributing assets.

Smart Moves

Heirs are the last in line when an estate is being settled. Here are some of the disbursements your executor of an estate must see to first:

- Court fees
- Funeral expenses
- Estate settlement costs, including lawyer, accountant, and executor fees
- Taxes
- Debts, including any rent and wages owed by the deceased.

Resource Guide

The following pages list addresses, phone and fax numbers, e-mail addresses, and websites of some 300 Canadian organizations and firms, which may supply further information about subjects discussed in *Ask the Experts*. The names of the organizations are alphabetically arranged under the relevant chapter headings. Canadian federal government agencies are listed at the end of the guide.

Useful Internet Sources

Information on Canada
Internet: http://www.canadainfo.ca

Bell Canada Information
Internet: http://www.bell.ca

Directory of Over 1,000 Associations in Canada
Internet: http://www.sources.com

Information for Those 50+
Internet: http://www.seniorssearch.com

Seniors Guide to Federal Programs and Services
Internet: http://www.mbnet.mb.ca/crm/other/gencdn/sgfp/sgfp00.html

Bed and Breakfast Directory
Internet: http://www.bandbinfo.com

Directory B&Bs, Country Inns, Heritage Hotels, Historic Inns
Internet: http://www.bbselect.com/bbcan.htm

Chapter 1
Your Home, Inside and Out

Association of Registered Interior Designs of Ontario
717 Church Street
Toronto, ON M4W 2M5
Phone: (416) 921-2127, ext. 24
Toll free: 1-800-334-1108
Fax: (416) 921-3660
Internet: http://www.arido.on.ca
Governs the conduct of its 2,000 members; provides educational programs, advisory services, and information resources.

Canadian Alarm and Security Association (CANASA)
610 Alden Road, Suite 201
Markham, ON L3R 9Z1
Phone: (905) 513-0622
Toll free: 1-800-538-9919
Fax: (905) 513-0624
E-mail: staff@canasa.org
Internet: http://www.canasa.org
Represents the Canadian electronic security industry; provides lobbying, publications, research, and consumer information.

Canadian Antique Dealers Association
190 Davenport Road
Toronto, ON M5R 1J2
Phone: (416) 925-4720

Canadian Association of Professional Heritage Consultants
Box 1023
Toronto, ON M4Y 2T7
Represents and furthers the interests of heritage consultants; establishes and maintains standards; fosters awareness of heritage resources.

Canadian Association of Recycling Industries
50 Gervais Drive, Suite 502
Don Mills, ON M3C 1Z3
Phone: (416) 510-1244
Fax: (416) 510-1248
Promotes the commercial recycling industry.

Canadian Brush, Broom and Mop Manufacturers' Association
670 Bloor Street West, Suite 200
Toronto, ON M6G 1L2
Phone: (416) 533-7800
Fax: (416) 533-4795
Promotes the interests of the brush and allied manufacturing industries; develops educational seminars.

Canadian Carpet Institute
605-130 Slater Street
Ottawa, ON K1P 6E2
Phone: (613) 232-7183
Fax: (613) 232-3072
E-mail: carpet@magi.com
Members are institutional; publishes a carpet manual and newsletter.

Canadian Clay and Glass Gallery
25 Caroline Street North
Waterloo, ON N2L 2Y5
Phone: (519) 746-1882
Fax: (519) 746-6396
Focuses on public education and enjoyment of works of clay, glass, stained glass, and enamel artists.

Canadian Decorating Products Association
7895 Tranmere Drive, Unit 5
Mississauga, ON L5S 1V9
Phone: (905) 678-0331
Fax: (905) 678-0335
Provides information on products and services to retailers of paint and wallpaper.

Canadian Fire Alarm Association (CFAA)
Box 262
Markham, ON L3P 2J7
Toll free: 1-800-529-0552
Fax: (905) 479-3639
Internet: http://www.senecac.on.ca/~fire/cfaa/index.html
Volunteer, non-profit association; educates persons related to the fire alarm industry; provides an educational package to promote fire safety.

Canadian Fire Safety Association
2175 Sheppard Avenue East, Suite 110
Willowdale, ON M2J 1W8
Phone: (416) 492-9417
Fax: (416) 491-1670
Promotes fire safety through seminars, safety training courses, and scholarships.

Canadian Institute of Plumbing and Heating
295 The West Mall, Suite 330
Etobicoke, ON M9C 4Z4
Phone: (416) 695-0447
Fax: (416) 695-0450
Internet: http://www.ciph.com
Promotes the plumbing and hydronic industry; publishes a membership directory.

Canadian Interiors

E-mail: sheri@canadian
    interiors.com
Internet: http://www
    .canadianinteriors.com
*Website provides articles on the
interior design business.*

Canadian Kitchen Cabinet Association

27 Goulburn Avenue
Ottawa, ON K1N 8C7
Phone: (613) 233-6205
Fax: (613) 233-1929
*Promotes the interests of the
manufacturers, suppliers, and
dealers of kitchen cabinets and
bathroom vanities.*

Canada Mortgage and Housing Corporation (CMHC)

700 Montreal Road
Ottawa, ON K1A 0P7
Phone: (613) 748-2000
Fax: (613) 748-2098
Internet: http://www
    .cmhc-schl.gc.ca
*Develops new ways to finance
home purchases; encourages
innovation in housing design
and technology.*

Canadian Paint and Coatings Association

9900 Cavendish Boulevard,
    Suite 103
Saint-Laurent, QC H4M 2V2
Phone: (514) 745-2611
Fax: (514) 745-2031
*Represents 132 institutional
members.*

Canadian Retail Hardware Association

6800 Campobello Road
Mississauga, ON L5N 2L8
Phone: (905) 821-3470
Toll free: 1-800-268-3965
Fax: (905) 821-8946
E-mail: crha@crha.com
Internet: http://www
    .crha.com
*Advances the common interests
of its 1,600-plus members of the
hardware, houseware, and home
improvement stores.*

Canadian Roofing and Contractors' Association

155 Queen Street, Suite 1300
Ottawa, ON K1P 6L1
Phone: (613) 232-6724
Fax: (613) 232-2893
*Represents some 380 institu-
tional members.*

Consumer Protection

Canada Safety Council (CSC)

1020 Thomas Spratt Place
Ottawa, ON K1G 5L5
Phone: (613) 739-1535
Fax: (613) 739-1566
E-mail: csc@safety
    council.org
*Non-profit, public service orga-
nization dedicated to preventing
accidents and health hazards in
the home, workplace, traffic and
recreational environments.*

Canadian Council of Better Business Bureaus

115 Apple Creek Boulevard,
    Suite 209
Markham, ON L3R 6C9
Phone: (905) 415-1750
Fax: (905) 415-1752
*Promotes ethical business
practices; provides consumer
information and complaint reso-
lution services; comprised of
16 bureaus across Canada.*

Canadian Standards Association (CSA International)

178 Rexdale Boulevard
Etobicoke, ON M9W 1R3
Phone: (416) 747-2620
Fax: (416) 747-4292
*Independent, non-profit organi-
zation; provides services for
standards development, inspection, product certification and
testing, and management
registration.*

Consumer Association of Canada (CAC)

267 O'Connor Street,
    Suite 307
Ottawa, ON K2P 1V3
Phone: (613) 238-2533
Fax: (613) 563-2254

• CAC Alberta

10136-100th Street, Suite 304
Edmonton, AB T5J 0P1
Phone: (780) 426-3270
Fax: (780) 425-9578

• CAC Board Rep for Yukon Division

c/o 4823 Rue Sherbrooke
    Ouest, Bureau 225
Montreal, QC H3Z 1G7

• CAC British Columbia

306, 198 West Hastings
    Street
Vancouver, BC V6B 1H2
Phone: (604) 682-3535
Fax: (604) 682-6331

• CAC Manitoba

222 Osborne Street, Suite 21
Winnipeg, MB R3L 1Z3
Phone: (204) 452-2572
Fax: (204) 284-1876

• CAC Newfoundland

92 Old Topsoil Road
St. John's, NF A1E 2A8
Phone: (709) 737-4514
Fax: (709) 737-7680

• CAC Northwest Territories

5007-50th Street, Box 995
Yellowknife, NT X1A 2N7
Phone: (867) 920-2259
Fax: (867) 873-4058

• CAC Nova Scotia

5522 North Street
Halifax, NS B3H 1M8
Phone: (902) 452-0915

• CAC Québec

4823 Rue Sherbrooke Ouest,
    Bureau 225
Montreal, QC H3Z 1G7
Phone: (514) 931-8556
Fax: (514) 938-1311

• CAC Saskatchewan

116-103rd Street East
Saskatoon, SK S7N 1Y7
Phone: (306) 242-4909
Fax: (306) 373-5810
*Represents and informs con-
sumers; advocates action on the
behalf of consumers.*

Underwriters' Laboratories of Canada

7 Crouse Road
Scarborough, ON M1R 3A9
Phone: (416) 757-3611
Fax: (416) 757-8915
*Supplies authoritative informa-
tion on products and services to
inspection authorities.*

Canadian Textiles Institute

66 Slater Street, Suite 1720
Ottawa, ON K1P 5H1
Phone: (613) 232-7195
Fax: (613) 232-8722
E-mail: cti@textiles.ca
*Association comprised of mem-
bers of the Canadian textiles
manufacturing industry.*

Canadian Window and Door Manufacturers Association

27 Goulburn Avenue
Ottawa, ON K1N 8C7
Phone: (613) 233-9804
Fax: (613) 233-1929
*Promotes the manufacture, sale,
and distribution of doors, win-
dows, and other related products.*

Canadian Wood Council

1400 Blair Place, Suite 210
Ottawa, ON K1J 9B8
Phone: (613) 747-5544
Toll free: 1-800-463-5091
Fax: (613) 747-6254
Internet: http://www.cwc.ca
*National association representing
the wood products industry in
the areas of codes and standards,
education, and communications.*

Flowers Canada

7856 Fifth Line South, RR4
Milton, ON L9T 2X8
Phone: (905) 875-0707
Toll free: 1-800-447-5147
Fax: (905) 875-3494
*Promotes the Canadian floricul-
ture industry through education,
marketing, and representation.*

Interior Designers of Canada

260 King Street East,
    Suite 414
Toronto, ON M5A 1K3
Phone: (416) 594-9310
Fax: (416) 594-9313
*Represents 1,700 individual
members.*

International Institute for Conservation of Historic and Artistic Works—Canadian Group

Box 9195
Ottawa, ON K1G 3T9
*Disseminates knowledge con-
cerning the conservation of
works of art, museum objects,
archival material and monu-
ment.*

National Floor Covering Association
605-130 Slater Street
Ottawa, ON K1P 6E2
Phone: (613) 232-7845
Fax: (613) 232-3072

National Spa and Pool Institute of Canada
7370 Bramalea Road, Unit 5
Mississauga, ON L5S 1N6
Phone: (905) 676-1591
Fax: (905) 676-1598
E-mail: office@nspi.ca
Represents builders, retailers, service companies, manufacturers, and distributors in the swimming pool and spa/hot tub industry; nine regional chapters.

Royal Architectural Institute of Canada (RAIC)
55 Murray Street
Ottawa, ON K1N 5M3
Phone: (613) 241-3600
Fax: (613) 241-5750
Internet: http://www.raic.org
A voluntary national association that fosters public awareness and appreciation of architecture and lobbies government on architectural issues.

Waddington's Auctioneers
111 Bathurst Street
Toronto, ON M5V 2R1
Phone: (416) 504-9100
Fax: (416) 504-0033
E-mail: info@waddingtons auctions.com
Internet: http://www.wad dingtonsauctions.com
Canada's oldest and largest auction house; offers appraisal and sale of fine art, antiques, collectibles, and household furnishings.

Chapter 2
In the Kitchen

Beef Information Centre
2233 Argentia Road, Suite 100
Mississauga, ON L5N 2X7
Phone: (905) 821-4900
Fax: (905) 821-4915

Canadian Appliance Manufacturers Association
10 Carlson Court, Suite 210
Rexdale, ON M9W 6L2
Phone: (416) 674-7410
Fax: (416) 674-7412
Represents manufacturers and marketers of major consumer goods.

Canadian Federation of Chefs and Cooks
738A Bank Street, Suite 202
Ottawa, ON K1S 3V4
Phone: (613) 563-2433
Fax: (613) 563-2317
E-mail: essence@ ottawa.net
• **Edmonton Branch**
Phone: (780) 452-4891
• **Halifax Branch**
Phone: (902) 454-8178
• **Manitoba Branch**
Phone: (204) 783-1700
• **Moncton Branch**
Phone: (509) 865-2172
• **Montreal Branch**
Phone: (514) 631-5252
• **Ottawa-Hull Branch**
Phone: (613) 257-4938
Fax: (613) 257-4938
• **Prince Edward Island Branch**
Phone: (902) 831-2352
• **Regina Branch**
Phone: (306) 545-7913
• **St. John's Branch**
Phone: (709) 745-5323
• **Toronto Branch**
Phone: (905) 825-0205
• **Vancouver Branch**
Phone: (604) 737-1997
• **Victoria Branch**
Phone: (250) 386-6368
• **Yukon Branch**
Phone: (306) 633-3755
Develops the professions of cook and chef in Canada; publishes a chefs directory.

Canadian Health Food Association
550 Alden Road, Suite 205
Markham, ON L3R 6A8
Phone: (905) 479-6939
Fax: (905) 479-1516
Promotes the natural food and health products industry; conducts public relations programs.

Canadian Health Reform Products Ltd.
Box 80055
Burnaby, BC V5H 3X1
Phone: (604) 419-5008
Toll free: 1-800-663-6580
Provides information on health food and health products.

Canadian Pork Council
75 Albert Street, Suite 1101
Ottawa, ON K1P 5E7
Phone: (613) 236-9239
Fax: (613) 236-6658

Canadian Sugar Institute
10 Bay Street, Suite 620
Toronto, ON M5J 2R8
Phone: (416) 368-8091
Fax: (416) 368-6426
E-mail: info@sugar.ca
Sponsors public-health and information programs.

Dieticians of Canada
480 University Avenue, Suite 604
Toronto, ON M5G 1V2
Phone: (416) 596-0857
Fax: (416) 596-0603
E-mail: centralinfo@ dieticians.ca
Internet: http://www .dieticians.ca
Comprised of national and provincial associations promoting the nutritional well-being of the public.

Food Biotechnology Communications Network
1 Stone Road West
Guelph, ON N1G 4Y2
Phone: (519) 826-3440
Fax: (519) 826-3441
Internet: http://www .foodbiotech.org
A leading source of information and science-based facts about food biotechnology and its impact on our food system.

National Institute of Nutrition
265 Carling Avenue, Suite 302
Ottawa, ON K1S 2E1
Phone: (613) 235-3355
Fax: (613) 235-7032
E-mail: nin@nin.ca
Internet: http://www.nin.ca
Private, non-profit organization promoting the nutritional well-being of Canadians through research and education.

Ontario Aquaculture Association
Box 324
Elmira, ON N3B 2Z6
Phone: (519) 669-3400
Fax: (519) 669-2864
Represents the hatchery and fish farm industry; provides information to the public and its members.

Ontario White Bean Producers
4206 Raney Crescent
London, ON N6L 1C3
Phone: (519) 652-3566
Fax: (519) 652-9607
Internet: http://www.wwdc .com/whitepeabeans
Offers information on nutrition and recipes.

Paderno & Chaudier
Padinox Inc.
10 McCarville Street
West Royalty Industrial Park
Charlottetown, PE C1E 2A6
Phone: (902) 629-1500
Fax: (902) 629-1502
Toll-free sales:
1-800-565-0261
Toll-free customer service:
1-800-263-9768
E-mail: paderno@padinox.ca
Internet: http://www .paderno.com
Fine quality cookware, available by mail order.

Toronto Vegetarian Association
2300 Yonge Street, Suite 1101
Box 2307
Toronto, ON M4P 1E4
Phone: (416) 544-9800
Fax: (416) 544-9094
E-mail: tva@veg.on.ca
Internet: http://www .veg.on.ca
Canada's largest vegetarian organization; resource center provides information.

Chapter 3
A Healthy Body

Allergy/Asthma Information Association
130 Bridgeland Avenue,
Suite 424
Toronto, ON M6A 1Z4
Phone: (416) 783-8944, ext. 28
Toll free: 1-800-611-7011
Fax: (416) 783-7538
Non-profit association of allergic, asthmatic, and anaphylactic individuals, medical professionals and corporate citizens; provides information, referrals, and advocacy.

Allergy Foundation of Canada
Box 1904
Saskatoon, SK S7K 3S5
Phone: (306) 652-1608
Offers information and support for allergy sufferers.

Alzheimer Society of Canada
20 Eglinton Avenue West
Toronto, ON M4R 1K8
Phone: (416) 488-8772
Fax: (416) 488-3778
E-mail: info@alzheimer.ca
Internet: http://www
.alzheimer.ca
National voluntary organization providing support to those affected by the disease; ten provincial organizations.

The Arthritis Society
393 University Avenue,
Suite 1700
Toronto, ON M5G 1E6
Phone: (416) 979-7228
Toll free: 1-800-321-1433
Fax: (416) 979-8366
E-mail: info@arthritis.ca
Internet: http://www
.arthritis.ca
Non-profit organization; funds and promotes arthritis research, patient care, and education.

Asthma Society of Canada
130 Bridgeland Avenue,
Suite 425
Toronto, ON M6A 1Z4
Phone: (416) 787-4050
Toll free: 1-800-787-3880
Fax: (416) 787-5807
E-mail: asthma@myna.com
Internet: http://www
.asthmasociety.com
Programs include public education, support group assistance, and research.

Canadian AIDS Society
900-130 Albert Street
Ottawa, ON K1P 5G4
Phone: (613) 230-3580,
ext. 125
Fax: (613) 563-4998
Internet: http://www.cdn
aids.ca
Develops programs, services, and resources for its members.

The Canadian Association for Health, Physical Education, Recreation, and Dance (CAHPERD)
1600 James Naismith Drive
Gloucester, ON K1B 5N4
Phone: (613) 748-5622
Toll free: 1-800-663-8708
Fax: (613) 748-5737
E-mail: info@cahperd.ca
Internet: http://www
.cahperd.ca
A national volunteer organization promoting healthy active lifestyles.

Canadian Association for Suicide Prevention
c/o 201-1615 10th Avenue,
Southwest
Calgary, AB T3C 0J7
Phone: (403) 245-3900
Fax: (403) 245-0299
Internet: http://web.idirect
.com/~casp
Raises awareness and works toward the reduction of suicidal behavior.

The Canadian Association of Herbal Practitioners
1228 Kensington Road NW,
Suite 400
Calgary, AB T2N 4P9
Phone: (403) 270-0936
Fax: (403) 283-0799
Internet: http://www
.wrc.net

Canadian Centre for Occupational Health and Safety
250 Main Street East
Hamilton, ON L8N 1H6
Phone: (613) 957-2991
Toll free: 1-800-263-8466
Fax: (905) 572-4500
Internet: http://www.ccohs.ca
Provides information on noise and hearing protection, and other workplace issues, as well as ways to prevent disease and injury.

Sports Sources

Sport Canada
15 Eddy Street, 8th Floor
Hull, QC K1A 0M5
Internet: http://www.pch
.gc.ca/sportcanada

Sport BC (Vancouver)
1367 West Broadway,
Suite 509
Vancouver, BC V6H 4A9
Phone: (604) 737-3005
Fax: (604) 737-3097
Internet: http://www.sport
.bc.ca/SportBC/
Provides leadership and support to member organizations; promotes amateur sport.

Sport Manitoba
200 Main Street
Winnipeg, MN R3C 4M2
Phone: (204) 925-5605
Fax: (204) 925-5916
Develops amateur sport programs in Manitoba.

Sport New Brunswick Inc.
565 Priestman Street,
Suite 103
Fredericton, NB E3B 5X8
Phone: (506) 451-1320
Fax: (506) 451-1325
Promotes the benefits of sport and assists sport organizations throughout New Brunswick.

Sport Newfoundland and Labrador
Box 8700
St. John's, NF A1B 4J6
Phone: (709) 576-4932
Fax: (709) 576-7493
Promotes amateur sport throughout Newfoundland and Labrador.

Sport North Federation
Box 336
Yellowknife, NT X1A 2N3
Phone: (867) 873-3032
Toll free: 1-800-661-0797
Fax: (867) 920-4047
Promotes amateur sport in the Northwest Territories.

Sport Nova Scotia
Box 3010 S
Halifax, NS B3J 3G6
Phone: (902) 425-5450
Fax: (902) 425-5606

Sport Ontario
1185 Eglinton Avenue East
North York, ON M3C 3C6
Phone: (416) 426-7310
Fax: (416) 426-7326
Acts as the voice of amateur sport in Ontario.

Sport PEI Inc.
3 Queen Street
Box 302
Charlottetown, PE C1A 7K7
Phone: (902) 368-4110
Fax: (902) 368-4548
Comprised of 60 institutional members; publishes a sport directory.

Sport Yukon
4061 4th Avenue
Whitehorse, YT Y1A 1H1
Phone: (867) 668-4236
Fax: (867) 667-4237
Formerly: Yukon Sports Federation; comprised of 3,000 individual members.

Canadian Association of Retired Persons (CARP)
27 Queen Street East,
Suite 1304
Toronto, ON M5C 2M6
Phone: (416) 363-8748
Fax: (416) 363-8747
E-mail: publicrelations
@fifty-plus.net
Internet: http://www
.fifty-plus.net
Fosters the concerns of those over the age of 50; provides information on 50-plus lifestyle choices and political and economic issues; ten regional chapters.

Canadian Cancer Society
10 Alcorn Avenue, Suite 200
Toronto, ON M4V 3B1
Phone: (416) 961-7223,
ext. 318
Fax: (416) 961-4189
Internet: http://www
.cancer.ca
Cancer-related, fund-raising charity; donations help fund education, patient services, and research; ten regional offices.

Canadian Centre for Stress and Well-Being
1 Yonge Street, Suite 1801
Toronto, ON M5E 1W7
Phone: (416) 363-6204
Fax: (416) 369-0515

Canadian Cycling Association

1600 James Naismith,
    Suite 810
Gloucester, ON K1B 5N4
Phone: (613) 748-5692
Fax: (613) 748-5692
*Organizes and promotes both
recreational and competitive
cycling in Canada.*

Canadian Dental Association

1815 Alta Vista
Ottawa, ON K1G 3Y6
Phone: (613) 523-1770
Fax: (613) 523-7736
Internet: http://www
    .cdaadc.ca
*The authoritative national voice
for the dentistry profession; pro-
motes oral health for Canadians.*

Canadian Dermatology
Association

521-774 Promenade
    Echo Drive
Ottawa, ON K1S 5N8
Dr. David Gratton, President
Phone: (514) 931-3617
Fax: (514) 933-8798
Dr. Lynn From,
    President-Elect
Phone: (416) 323-6137
Fax: (416) 323-6306
Internet: http://www.derm
    .ubc.ca/jms
*Non-profit medical specialty
organization comprised of
560 dermatologists; administers
a sunscreen product evaluation
program.*

Canadian Diabetes Association

15 Toronto, Street,
    Suite 800
Toronto, ON M5C 2E3
Phone: (416) 363-3373
Toll free: 1-800-226-8464
Fax: (416) 363-3393
Internet: http://www
    .diabetes.ca
*Provides information on
diabetes.*

Canadian Fitness and Lifestyle
Research Institute

201-185 Somerset Street
    West
Ottawa, ON K2P 0J2
Phone: (613) 233-5528
Fax: (613) 233-5536
E-mail: info@cflri.ca
Internet: http://www
    .cflri.ca
*Conducts research on physically
active lifestyles, provides
research summaries and statisti-
cal information about physical
activity.*

Canadian Hard of Hearing
Association

2435 Holly Lane, Suite 205
Ottawa, ON K1V 7P2
Phone: (613) 526-1584
Toll free: 1-800-263-8068
Fax: (613) 526-4718
E-mail: chhanational
    @cyberus.ca
*Comprised of 46 regional
branches.*

Canadian Health Coalition

2841 Riverside Drive
Ottawa, ON K1V 8X7
Phone: (613) 521-3400,
    ext. 311
Fax: (613) 521-4655
*Mandate is to preserve and
improve medicare and Canada's
health care system; 39 affiliated
national organizations.*

Canadian Health Food Association

550 Alden Road, Suite 205
Markham, ON L3R 6A8
Phone: (905) 479-6939
Fax: (905) 479-1516
E-mail: admin@chfa.ca
*Resource for information on new
products and government legis-
lation related to herbs, home-
opathies, vitamins, organics,
cosmetics, and natural foods.*

Canadian Hearing Society

271 Spadina Road
Toronto, ON M5R 2V3
Phone: (416) 964-9595 (voice)
Toll free: 1-800-465-4327
    (technical devices only)
Fax: (416) 928-2506
TDD: (416) 964-0023
E-mail: info@chs.ca
Internet: http://www.chs.ca
*Provides services to the deaf,
deafened, and hard of hearing;
encourages the prevention of
hearing loss; 23 regional offices.*

Canadian Home Care Association

17 York Street, Suite 401
Ottawa, ON K1N 9J6
Phone: (613) 569-1585
Fax: (613) 569-1604
E-mail: chca@cdn
    homecare.on.ca
Internet: http://www.cdn
    homecare.on.ca
*Promotes the accessibility, qual-
ity, and development of home
care and community support ser-
vices, allowing people to stay at
home with safety and dignity.*

Canadian Hypertension Society

Department of Pharmacology
Room A329, Chown Building
University of Manitoba
753 McDermot Avenue
Winnipeg, MB R3E 0T6
Phone: (204) 789-3356
Fax: (204) 783-6915
*Promotes the prevention and
control of hypertension through
research.*

Canadian Institute
for Health Information

377 Dalhousie Street,
    Suite 200
Ottawa, ON K1N 9J6
Phone: (613) 241-7860
Fax: (613) 241-8120
Internet: http://www.cihi.ca
*Co-ordinates and maintains
Canada's health information sys-
tem; provides health information.*

Canadian Institute of Child Health

885 Meadowlands Drive
    East, Suite 512
Ottawa, ON K2C 3N2
Phone: (613) 224-4144
Fax: (613) 224-4145
E-mail: cich@igs.net
Internet: http://www.cich.ca
*Promotes the health and well-
being of children (from birth to
19 years of age); provides advo-
cacy, consultation, research, and
resources.*

Canadian Institute of Stress

Box 665, Station U
Toronto, ON M8Z 5Y9
Phone: (416) 236-4218
Fax: (416) 237-9894
Internet: http://www
    .stresscanada.org
*Offers training, counselling, and
seminars.*

Canadian Medical
Association (CMA)

Box 8650
Ottawa, ON K1G 0G8
Phone: (613) 731-9331
Toll free: 1-800-267-9703
Fax: (613) 731-9013
Internet: http://www.cma.ca
*Serves and informs members;
promotes ethics and standards
of medical practices; provides
a wide range of services; com-
prised of 12 divisions.*

Canadian Mental Health
Association

2160 Yonge Street, 3rd Floor
Toronto, ON M4S 2Z3
Phone: (416) 484-7750
Fax: (416) 484-4617
*Provides programs and services
for people with mental disorders,
their families, and support per-
sons; 12 regional divisions.*

Canadian Mothercraft Society

32 Heath Street West
Toronto, ON M4V 1T3
Phone: (416) 920-3515
Fax: (416) 920-5983
*Provides childcare and family
support services; provides train-
ing programs.*

Seniors Sources

Association of Mature Canadians
111 Queen Street East,
Suite 216
Toronto, ON M5C 1S2
Phone: (416) 601-0429
Toll free: 1-800-667-0429
Fax: (416) 601-0308
Provides information on a number of programs including travel insurance for frequent travelers or long-term vacationers worldwide, home and auto insurance, and health and dental programs.

Canadian Association of Retired Persons (CARP)
27 Queen Street East,
Suite 1304
Toronto, ON M5C 2M6
Phone: (416) 363-8748
Fax: (416) 363-8747
E-mail: publicrelations@fifty-plus.net
Internet: http://www.fifty-plus.net
Fosters the concerns of those over the age of 50; provides information on 50-plus lifestyle choices and political and economic issues.

Elderhostel Canada
4 Cataraqui Street
Kingston, ON K7K 1Z7
Phone: (613) 530-2222
Fax: (613) 530-2096
E-mail: ecpgmdpt@elderhostel.org
Internet: http://www.elderhostel.org
Provides educational opportunities for adults in their retirement years.

The Canadian National Institute for the Blind (CNIB)
1929 Bayview Avenue
Toronto, ON M4G 3E8
Phone: (416) 480-7644
Internet: http://www.cnib.ca
Provides rehabilitation services at no cost for people who are blind, visually impaired, and deaf-blind.

Eldertreks
597 Markham Street
Toronto, ON M6G 2L7
Phone: (416) 588-5000
Toll free: 1-800-741-7956
Fax: (416) 588-9839
Internet: http://www.eldertreks.com
Expressly for travelers 50 and older who love adventure and desire an active, participatory itinerary when visiting another country.

One Voice—The Canadian Seniors Network
1005-350 Sparks Street
Ottawa, ON K1R 7S8
Phone: (613) 238-7624
Fax: (613) 235-4497
E-mail: onevoice.lavoix@sympatico.ca
Non-profit organization addressing issues of concern to Canada's aging population.

Ontario Association of Non-Profit Homes and Services for Seniors
7050 Weston Road,
Suite 700
Woodbridge, ON L4L 8G7
Phone: (905) 851-8821, ext. 230
Fax: (905) 851-0744
Internet: http://www.oanhss.org
Represents 300 member organizations providing services, care, and housing for seniors.

Senior Tours Canada Inc.
225 Eglinton Avenue West
Toronto, ON M4R 1A9
Phone: (416) 322-1500
Toll free: 1-800-268-3492
Fax: (416) 322-1166
Internet: http://www.seniortravel.com
Operates worldwide escorted group tours for the 50-plus age group.

Canadian Natural Health Association
439 Wellington Street East,
Suite 5
Toronto, ON M5V 1E7
Phone: (416) 977-2642
Fax: (416) 977-1536
Promotes holistic health lifestyles; resource center.

Canadian Naturopathic Association
4174 Dundas Street West,
Suite 304
Etobicoke, ON M8X 1X3
Phone: (416) 233-1043
Fax: (416) 233-2924
For alternative approaches to medicine and health; comprised of 200 individual members.

Canadian Osteopathic Association
575 Waterloo Street
London, ON N6B 2R2
Phone: (519) 439-5521
Maintains high professional standards in osteopathic medicine.

Canadian Paediatric Society
100-2204 Walkley Road
Ottawa, ON K1G 4G8
Phone: (613) 526-9397
Fax: (613) 526-3332
E-mail: info@cps.ca
Internet: http://www.cps.ca
National advocacy association committed to the health and well-being of children and youth; offers publications, programs, and advocacy.

Canadian Pain Society
c/o 2136 West Mall
Department of Psychology
University of British Columbia
Vancouver, BC V6T 1Z4
Phone: (604) 822-3948
Fax: (604) 822-6923
Comprised of institutions, health care professionals, and research workers interested in pain.

Canadian Paralympic Committee
1600 James Naismith Drive
Gloucester, ON K1B 5N4
Phone: (613) 748-5630
Fax: (613) 748-5731
Promotes the Paralympic movement.

Canadian Paraplegic Association
1101 Prince of Wales Drive,
Suite 230
Ottawa, ON K2C 3W7
Phone: (613) 723-1033
Toll free: 1-800-720-4933
Fax: (613) 723-1060
E-mail: cpanational@canparaplegic.org
Internet: http://www.canparaplegic.org
Assists people with spinal cord injuries and other severe mobility impairments through counseling, information and advocacy services; nine regional branches.

Canadian Psoriasis Foundation
100A-824 Meath Street
Ottawa, ON K1Z 6E8
Phone: (613) 728-4000
Toll free: 1-800-265-0926
Fax: (613) 728-8913
E-mail: cpf-fcp@psoriasis.ca
Internet: http://www.psoriasis.ca
Non-profit organization serving the needs of those affected by psoriasis; provides information and support.

Canadian Rheumatology Association
1560 Rue Sherbrooke Est
Montreal, QC H2L 4K8
Phone: (514) 876-7131
Fax: (514) 876-6630
Fosters research, education, and care.

Canadian Sleep Society
3080 Yonge Street
Toronto, ON M4N 3N1
Joseph De Koninck, Ph.D.,
President
University of Ottawa
School of Graduate Studies
115 Seraphin Marion St. (205)
Box 450, Station A
Ottawa, ON K1N 6N5
Phone: (613) 562-5800, ext. 1234
Fax: (613) 562-5730
E-mail: jdekonin@css.to
Internet: http://www.css.to
Professional association of scientists, clinicians, and technologists in the areas of sleep research.

Canadian Society of Teachers for the F.M. Alexander Technique
465 Wilson Avenue
Toronto, ON M3H 1T9
Phone: 1-877-598-8879
Fax: (416) 631-0094
E-mail: canstat@istar.ca
Internet: http://www.canstat.ca

Canadian Sporting Goods Association
455 Rue St-Antoine Ouest,
Bureau 510
Montreal, QC H2Z 1J1
Phone: (514) 393-1132
Fax: (514) 393-9513
E-mail: sporting@csga.ca
Internet: http://www.globalsports.com/csga
Conducts trade shows and initiates programs designed to stimulate sports activity and participation.

Canadian Square and Round Dance Society

115 Holly Drive
Oakbank, MB R0E 1J2
Phone: (204) 444-3115
Fax: (204) 444-5768
E-mail: lkozera@mb
.sympatico.ca
Internet: http://www.csrds.ca
In co-operation with provincial, and territorial federations/associations, promotes the fun and enjoyment of square and round dancing.

Centre for Studies of Aging

222 College Street, Suite 106
Toronto, ON M5T 3J1
Phone: (416) 978-4771
Internet: http://www
.utoronto.ca/lifecourse
Conducts research on aging; supports educational initiatives.

Depressive and Manic Depressive Association of Ontario

214 Merton Street, Suite 101
Toronto, ON M4S 1A6
Phone: (416) 481-5413
Fax: (416) 481-5545
Support network of self-help groups for those experiencing depression or manic-depression and their families and friends; provides assistance and information.

Dieticians of Canada

480 University Avenue,
Suite 604
Toronto, ON M5G 1V2
Phone: (416) 596-0857
Fax: (416) 596-0603
E-mail: centralinfo@
dieticians.ca
Internet: http://www
.dieticians.ca
National and provincial associations promoting the nutritional well-being of the public.

Heart and Stroke Foundation of Canada

222 Queen Street, Suite 1402
Ottawa, ON K1P 5V9
Phone: (613) 569-4361
Toll free: 1-888-476-4636
Fax: (613) 569-3278
Internet: http://www.hsf.ca
National volunteer-led organization with 10 independent provincial foundations; promotes research, education, and prevention of heart disease and stroke.

Migraine Association of Canada

365 Bloor Street, Suite 1912
Toronto, ON M4W 3L4
Phone: (416) 920-4916
Fax: (416) 920-3677
Internet: http://www
.migraine.ca
Provides up-to-date information and education to the general public.

Multiple Sclerosis Society of Canada

250 Bloor Street East,
Suite 1000
Toronto, ON M4W 3P9
Phone: (416) 922-6065
Fax: (416) 922-7538
E-mail: info@mssoc.ca
Internet: http://www
.mssoc.ca
Supports MS research and provides services for people with MS and their families; more than 130 chapters.

National Cancer Institute of Canada

10 Alcorn Avenue, Suite 200
Toronto, ON M4V 3B1
Phone: (416) 961-7223
Fax: (416) 961-4189
Undertakes and supports cancer research and related programs; provides information related to cancer research and control.

The National Eating Disorder Information Centre (NEDIC)

CW 1-211
200 Elizabeth Street
Toronto, ON M5G 2C4
Phone: (416) 340-4156
Fax: (416) 340-4736
E-mail: nedic@uhn.on.ca
Internet: http://www.nedic
.on.ca
Non-profit organization that provides information and resources on eating disorders and weight preoccupation.

National Institute of Nutrition

265 Carling Avenue,
Suite 302
Ottawa, ON K1S 2E1
Phone: (613) 235-3355
Fax: (613) 235-7032
E-mail: nin@nin.ca
Internet: http://www.nin.ca
Private, non-profit organization promoting the nutritional well-being of Canadians through research and education.

National Network for Mental Health

490 York Road, Building A,
Unit 212
Guelph, ON N1E 6V1
Phone: (519) 766-1032
Fax: (519) 822-3732

North American Chronic Pain Association of Canada

150 Central Park Drive,
Unit 105
Brampton, ON L6T 2T9
Phone: (905) 846-0958
Fax: (905) 793-8781
Internet: http://www3
.sympatico.ca/nacpac
Non-profit, registered charity; assists people with chronic pain through education, research, and self-help groups.

Nutritional Consultants Organization of Canada

1201 Division Street
Kingston, ON K7K 6X4
Phone: (613) 382-8161
Toll free: 1-800-406-2703
Fax: (613) 382-8593
E-mail: noc@kings.igs.net
Internet: http://www
.canlink.com/ncoc

Ontario Podiatric Medical Association

900-45 Sheppard Avenue, East
Toronto, ON M2N 5W9
Phone: (416) 927-9111
Toll free: 1-888-220-3338
Fax: (416) 733-2491
E-mail: osc@osteoporosis.ca
Internet: http://www
.opma.ca
National, non-profit association of podiatrists; educates the public.

Osteoporosis Society of Canada

33 Laird Drive
Toronto, ON M4G 3S9
Phone: (416) 696-2663
Toll free: 1-800-463-6842
E-mail: osc@osteoporosis.ca
Internet: http://www
.osteoporosis.ca
Educates and supports individuals and communities in preventing, treating, and managing osteoporosis.

Overeaters Anonymous Canada

Box 11126
Edmonton, AB T5J 3K4
Phone: (780) 423-2546
Offers a Twelve Step program for individuals with a compulsive eating problem.

Sleep/Wake Disorders Canada

3080 Yonge Street, Suite 5055
Toronto, ON M4N 3N1
Phone: (416) 483-9654
Toll free: 1-800-387-9253
E-mail: swdc@global
serve.net
Internet: http://www.geo
cities.com/~sleepwake
National charity providing support and information to people affected by sleep/wake disorders.

Suicide Information and Education Centre

201-1615 10th Avenue
Southwest
Calgary, AB T3C 0J7
Phone: (403) 245-3900
Fax: (403) 245-0299
E-mail: siec@siec.ca
Internet: http://www.siec.ca
Collects and distributes information; provides training on suicide prevention, intervention, awareness, and bereavement.

Chapter 4

The Green Thumb's Yard and Garden

African Violet Society of Canada

Box 107
119 Maple Avenue
Hudson Heights, QC J0P 1J0
Phone: (514) 458-5398
Comprised of some 738 individual members.

Agricultural Groups Concerned About Resources and the Environment (AGCare)

40 Eglinton Avenue East,
5th Floor
Toronto, ON M4P 3B1
Phone: (519) 837-1326
Fax: (519) 837-3209
Internet: http://www
.agcare.org
Represents over 45,000 Ontario growers of field and horticultural crops on agricultural pesticide use, crop biotechnology developments, and other related environmental issues.

Agricultural Institute of Canada
141 Laurier Avenue West,
   Suite 1112
Ottawa, ON K1P 5J3
Phone: (613) 232-9459,
   ext. 303
Fax: (613) 594-5190
E-mail: news@aic.ca
Federation of provincial institutes of agrologists and scientific and agriculture-related organizations; provides information on Canadian agriculture.

Canadian Environmental Network
300-945 Wellington
   Street
Ottawa, ON K1Y 2X5
Phone: (613) 728-9810
Fax: (613) 728-2963
E-mail: cen@cen.web.net
Internet: http://www.cen
   .web.net
Non-profit umbrella organization for 1,500 Canadian environmental groups; publishes a guide.

Canadian Iris Society
c/o RR9
924 Bains Road
Dunnville, ON N1A 2W8
Phone: (905) 774-8360
E-mail: cris@netcom.ca
Internet: http://tor-pw1
   .netcom.ca/~cris/CIS.html
Promotes and provides information on the genus iris.

Canadian Nursery Trades Association
7856 Fifth Line South, RR 4
Milton, ON L9T 2X4
Phone: (905) 875-1399
Fax: (905) 875-1840
Promotes the horticultural industry through membership and public education.

Canadian Organic Growers, Inc.
Box 6408, Station J
Ottawa, ON K2A 3Y6
Phone: (705) 444-0923
Fax: (705) 444-0380
Provides information on the methods and techniques of organic growing, and associated benefits; nine regional chapters.

Canadian Ornamental Plant Foundation
Box 21083
North Bay, ON P1B 7N8
Phone: (705) 495-2563
Toll free: 1-800-265-1629
Fax: (705) 495-1449
E-mail: copf@efni.com
Encourages new plant development in the horticultural industry.

© Disney Enterprises, Inc.

Canadian Pest Management Society
Box 1000
Agassiz, BC V0M 1A0
Phone: (604) 796-2221,
   ext. 228
Fax: (604) 796-0359
Provides information on pest management.

Canadian Rose Society
10 Fairfax Crescent
Scarborough, ON M1L 1Z8
Phone: (416) 757-8809
Fax: (416) 757-4796
E-mail: crs@mirror.org
Internet: http://www
   .mirror.org/groups/cts/
Provides information on roses.

Canadian Seed Growers Association
Box 8455
Ottawa, ON K1G 3T1
Phone: (613) 236-0497
Fax: (613) 563-7855
Pedigreeing agency for all field crops in Canada (except potatoes).

Canadian Seed Trade Association
302-39 Robertson Road
Nepean, ON K2H 8R2
Phone: (613) 829-9527
Fax: (613) 829-3530
E-mail: csta@hookup.net
Comprised of 225 institutional members.

Canadian Society of Landscape Architects
Box 870, Station B
Ottawa, ON K1P 5P9
Phone: (613) 232-6342
Fax: (403) 938-2476
E-mail: csla@telusplanet.net
Represents 1,100 institutional and 1,035 individual members.

Canadian Wildlife Federation (CWF)
2740 Queensview Drive
Ottawa, ON K2B 1A2
Phone: (613) 721-2286
Fax: (613) 721-2902
Internet: http://www
   .cwf-fcf.org
Promotes living in harmony with the land; maintains programs in research and recovery; provides educational materials.

The Composting Council of Canada
16 Northumberland Street
Toronto, ON M6H 1P7
Phone: (416) 535-0240
Fax: (416) 536-9892
E-mail: ccc@compost.org
Internet: http://www
   .compost.org
Non-profit organization serving to advance and advocate the use of composting to government, industry, and the public.

Cruickshanks, The Garden Guild
Office/Warehouse
780 Birchmount Road
Scarborough, ON M1K 5H4
Phone: (416) 750-9249
Toll free: 1-800-665-5605
Internet: http://www
   .cruickshanks.com
This 70-year-old business is dedicated to flower bulbs. Their three times yearly catalogue, available upon request, also features perennials, shrubs, and garden accessories.

Dominion Herbal College
7527 Kingsway
Burnaby, BC V3N 3C1
Phone: (604) 521-5822
Fax: (604) 526-1561
E-mail: herbal@uniserve.com
Internet: http://www
   .dominionherbal.com
For information on herbal medicine and gardening.

Earthsave Canada
Box 34277, Station D
Vancouver, BC V6J 4N8
Phone: (604) 731-5885
Fax: (604) 731-5805
Internet: http://www
   .earthsave.bc.ca
Educational, non-profit society; promotes awareness of the health, ethical, and environmental consequences of food choices.

EcoSource Mississauga
161 Lakeshore Road West
Mississauga, ON L5H 1G3
Phone: (905) 274-6222
Fax: (905) 274-4387
E-mail: ecosource.missis
   sauga@sympatico.ca
Internet: http://www3
   .sympatico.ca/ecosource
   .mississauga
Provides information on reducing, reusing, composting, and recycling.

Garden Clubs of Ontario
4 Deer Park Court
Grimsby, ON L3M 2R2
Phone: (905) 945-2433
Coordinates activities of 14 garden clubs in Ontario.

GardenImport
Box 760
Thornhill, ON L3T 4A5
Phone: (905) 731-1950
Toll free: 1-800-339-8314
Internet: http://www
   .gardenimport.com
Mail-order source of hard-to-find, highly desirable selections of top quality perennials, flowering shrubs, climbers, seeds, and bulbs from around the world. Catalogue available upon request.

International Society of Arboriculture Ontario
Box 995, Station B
Willowdale, ON M2K 2T6
Phone: (416) 224-0182
Fax: (416) 224-9218
Affiliated with the International Society of Arboriculture; comprised of 250 individual members.

Landscape Alberta Nursery Trades Association
10215-176th Street
Edmonton, AB T5S 1M1
Phone: (780) 444-2152
E-mail: lanta@planet.eon.net
Comprised of 220 institutional and 18 individual members.

Landscape Manitoba
808 Muriel Street
Winnipeg, MB R2Y 0Y3
Phone: (204) 889-5981
Fax: (204) 888-0944
Promotes development of the industry; supports research and education.

Landscape New Brunswick Horticultural Trades Association
c/o RR 6
Fredericton, NB E3B 4X7
Phone: (506) 472-3357
Fax: (506) 457-1497
Promotes ornamental horticulture through educating and informing the public and membership.

Landscape Nova Scotia
Box 52
Shubenacadie, NS B0N 2H0
Phone: (902) 758-3512
Summertime only.

Landscape Ontario Horticultural Trades Association
7856 Fifth Line South, RR 4
Milton, ON L9T 2X8
Phone: (905) 875-1805
Toll free: 1-800-265-5656
Fax: (905) 875-3942
E-mail: lo@hort-trades.com
Internet: http://www
.hort-trades.com
Represents the Landscape/Garden Centre/Lawn Care sectors of the horticultural industry in Ontario; involved in education, communication, professional development, and advocacy.

National Community Tree Foundation
1550-220 Laurier
Avenue West
Ottawa, ON K1P 5Z9
Phone: (613) 567-5545
Fax: (613) 567-5270

Netherlands Flowerbulb Information Centre
78 Kingston Road
Toronto, ON M4L 1S6
Phone: (416) 690-3213
Fax: (416) 690-4427
Provides information on spring-, summer-, and fall-flowering flower bulbs.

Nova Scotia Coalition for Alternatives to Pesticides
Box 643
Baddeck, NS B0E 1B0
Phone: (902) 295-3053
Fax: (902) 295-1070
Comprised of over 200 individual members.

Nova Scotia Greenhouse Growers Association
RR 7
Amherst, NS B4N 3Y5
Phone: (902) 667-5940
Fax: (902) 667-0677
Comprised of 57 individual members.

Olds College
4500 50th Street
Olds, AB T4H 1R6
Phone: (403) 556-4703
Toll free: 1-800-661-6537
Fax: (403) 556-4704
E-mail: acryderman@admin
.oldscollege.ab.ca
Internet: http://www.olds
college.ab.ca
College specializes in agriculture, horticulture, environment, land management, and agri-business; provides facts and expertise.

Ontario Fruit and Vegetable Growers Association
355 Elmira Road North,
Unit 103
Guelph, ON N1K 1S5
Phone: (519) 763-6160
Fax: (519) 763-6604
Comprised of 12,000 individual fruit and vegetable producers in Ontario.

Ontario Shade Tree Council
75 The Donway West,
Suite 302
North York, ON M3C 2E9
Phone: (905) 884-8013,
ext. 905
Fax: (905) 851-9610
Provides information relating to planting, propagating, and preserving shade trees in Ontario.

Prince Edward Island Rose Society
c/o 55 Charlotte Drive
Charlottetown, PE C1A 2N6
Phone: (902) 672-2746
Comprised of 100 individual members.

Richters Herb Specialists
357 Highway 47
Goodwood, ON L0C 1A0
Phone: (905) 640-6677
E-mail: orderdesk@
richters.com
Internet: http://www
.richters.com
Mail-order source of unusual herbs from around the world. Fresh plants and organic seeds can be shipped anywhere in the world. Informative website. Catalogue available upon request.

Seeds of Diversity Canada
Box 36
Toronto, ON M4T 2L7
Phone: (905) 623-0353
Formerly: Heritage Seed Program; seeks out and preserves heirloom and endangered varieties of food crops.

Stokes Seeds Limited
PO Box 10
St. Catharines, ON L2R 6R6
Phone: (905) 688-4300
Internet: http://www
.stokeseeds.com
Mail-order distributor of quality flower, vegetables, herb, and perennial seeds. Free 122-page catalogue is filled with information on over 2,500 varieties of seeds.

Vancouver Botanical Gardens Association
5251 Oak Street
Vancouver, BC V6M 4H1
Phone: (604) 878-9274
Fax: (604) 266-4236
Comprised of over 8,000 individual members.

Wildlife Habitat Canada (WHC)
7 Hinton Avenue North,
Suite 200
Ottawa, ON K1Y 4P1
Phone: (613) 722-2090
Fax: (613) 722-3318
Works with citizens, governments, and industry to protect, enhance, and restore wildlife habitats.

Chapter 5
Car Smarts

Automobile Protection Association (APA)
292 Boulevard St-Joseph
Ouest
Montreal, QC H2V 2N7
Phone: (514) 272-5555
Fax: (514) 273-0797

• Toronto Branch
160 Pears Avenue, Suite 322
Toronto, ON M5R 3P8
Phone: (416) 964-6774
Mandate is to protect the automobile owner from manufacturing defects and dishonest repair and sales practices.

Auto Wise Educational Systems Inc.
First Canadian Place
Box 375
Toronto, ON M5X 1E2
Phone: (416) 264-4788
Fax: (416) 264-5088
E-mail: autowise@home.com
Internet: http://www.getthe
realdeal.com
Protects the consumer through education and information on improper automotive selling tactics and detection of substandard automobiles from abuse or accident.

B.C. Deer Guards
277-11444-119 Street
Edmonton, AB T5G 2X6
Phone: (780) 413-7258
Toll free: 1-888-863-2220
Fax: (780) 463-2281
Retailers of 'Deer Guards' for front-end protection to vehicles from collisions with wildlife.

Canadian Alarm and Security Association (CANASA)
610 Alden Road, Suite 201
Markham, ON L3R 9Z1
Phone: (905) 513-0622
Toll free: 1-800-538-9919
Fax: (905) 513-0624
E-mail: staff@canasa.org
Internet: http://www
.canasa.org
Represents the Canadian electronic security industry; provides lobbying, publications, research, and consumer information.

Ontario Safety League
5045 Orbitor Drive
Building 11, Suite 100
Mississauga, ON L4W 4Y4
Phone: (905) 625-0556
Fax: (905) 625-0677
E-mail: info@osl.org
Internet: http://www.osl.org
Non-profit organization dedicated to reducing preventable human suffering and injury; particularly through traffic safety education.

Recreation Vehicle Dealers Association of Canada
209-20353 64th Avenue
Langley, BC V2Y 1N5
Phone: (604) 533-4010
Fax: (604) 533-0795
Represents the recreation vehicle industry; concerns include education, use, safety, and shows.

Rein*Car* nate Vehicle Recycling Program
Recycling Council of Ontario
489 College Street,
    Suite 504
Toronto, ON M6G 1A5
Phone: (416) 960-1025, ext. 23
Hotline: 1-888-CAR-DIED
Fax: (416) 960-8053
Internet: http://www.rco
    .on.ca/reincarnate.html
Gives donated cars a second life by using all its parts, its metal, and fluids. Included are a free towing and a charitable tax receipt.

Transport 2000 Canada
117 Sparks Street, Suite 102
Box 858, Station B
Ottawa, ON K1P 5P9
Phone: (613) 594-3290
Fax: (613) 594-3271
Internet: http://www
    .transport2000.ca

• **British Columbia**
Phone: (604) 681-3192

• **Saskatchewan**
Phone: (306) 692-1742

• **Ontario**
Phone: (613) 721-6142
Fax: (613) 721-1804

• **Atlantic**
Phone: (902) 469-3474
Fax: (902) 469-3637
Non-profit federation of consumer groups and individuals promoting improved transportation; disseminates information, supports research, and advocacy.

Canadian Automobile Association (CAA)
1145 Hunt Club Road,
    Suite 200
Ottawa, ON K1V 0Y3
Phone: (613) 247-0117
Fax: (613) 247-0118
Internet: http://www.caa.ca

• **Victoria – CAA British Columbia**
Phone: (250) 380-1217

• **Edmonton – AMA**
Phone: (780) 430-5693

• **Regina – CAA Saskatchewan**
Phone: (306) 791-4327

• **Winnipeg – CAA Manitoba**
Phone: (204) 987-6037

• **Kitchener – CAA Mid-Western Ontario**
Phone: (519) 894-4959

• **St. Catharines – CAA Niagara**
Phone: (905) 984-8585

• **Toronto – CAA Central Ontario**
Phone: (905) 771-3434

• **Ottawa – CAA North and East Ontario**
Phone: (613) 721-3229

• **Hamilton – CAA South Central Ontario**
Phone: (905) 525-1520

• **Quebec City – CAA Québec**
Phone: (418) 624-2424

• **Saint John – CAA Maritimes**
Phone: (506) 653-9202
Provides emergency road service, automatic technical advice and services, travel and touring information, and various insurance plans.

Canadian Automotive Repair and Service Council
230-440 Laurier Avenue West
Ottawa, ON K1R 7X6
Phone: (613) 782-2402

Canadian Natural Gas Vehicle Alliance
243 Consumers Road,
    Suite 1200
North York, ON M2J 5E3
Phone: (416) 498-1994
Fax: (416) 498-4969
Promotes the development of natural gas for vehicles.

Central Ontario Four Wheel Drive Club
Box 7128, Station A
Toronto, ON M5W 1X8
Phone: (905) 858-9222
Comprised of 60 individual members.

DaimlerChrysler Canada
2450 Chrysler Centre
Windsor, ON N8W 3X7
Phone: (519) 973-2000
Internet: http://www
    .daimlerchrysler.ca
The third-largest manufacturer of passengers cars, trucks and automotive components in Canada.

Driving School Association of Ontario
557 Dixon Road, Unit 110
Etobicoke, ON M9W 6K1
Phone: (416) 247-2278
Fax: (416) 247-4883

Electric Vehicle Association of Canada
11-21 Concourse Gate
Nepean, ON K2E 7S4
Phone: (613) 723-3127
Fax: (613) 723-8275
E-mail: evac@evac.ca
Internet: http://www.evac.ca
Promotes the development of infrastructure and use of EVs in Canada.

Ford Motor Company Limited
The Canadian Road
Oakville, ON L6J 5E4
Phone: (905) 845-2511
Fax: (905) 844-1198
Canada's longest-established automotive company; central office in Oakville, ON, with parts distribution offices across Canada.

General Motors of Canada Limited
1908 Colonel Sam Drive
Oshawa, ON L1H 8P7
Phone: (905) 644-2848
Fax: (905) 644-3873
Internet: http://www
    .gmcanada.com
Manufactures and distributes passenger cars, trucks, locomotives, military vehicles, automotive components, parts, and accessories.

Infant & Toddler Safety Association
385 Fairway Road South,
    Suite 4A-230
Kitchener, ON N2C 2N9
Phone: (519) 570-0181
Fax: (519) 894-0739
Provides information and resource materials to increase safety awareness and knowledge.

Motor Vehicle Safety Association
13820 Dixie Road
RR 1
Inglewood, ON L0N 1K0
Phone: (905) 838-2918
Fax: (905) 838-4080
Promotes road safety on the roads and highways of Ontario; promotes driver training and fleet safety.

National Auto League
248 Pall Mall Street
London, ON N6A 4T4
Phone: (519) 432-8333
Fax: (519) 434-5220
Formerly: Canadian Motor Club.

Young Drivers® of Canada
21 King Street W
Box 38
Hamilton, ON L8P 4W7
Phone: (905) 640-6677
Internet: http://www
.youngdrivers.com
*Young Drivers® teaches specific
defensive driving techniques to
help avoid all types of collisions.
There are more than 150 centers
across Canada, in BC, AB, ON,
QC, NB, NS, NF, PE. They also
offer Collisionfree!™ for adult
drivers who want to learn the
skills of collision-free driving,
and a free co-driver session
for parents.*

Chapter 6
The Experienced Traveler

Alberta Country Vacations Association
Box 396
Sangudo, AB T0E 2A0
Phone: (403) 785-3700
*Develops and promotes charac-
teristic farm/ranch vacations
within Alberta.*

Alliance of Canadian Travel Associations
1729 Bank Street, Suite 201
Ottawa, ON K1V 7Z5
Phone: (613) 521-0474
Fax: (613) 521-0805
E-mail: acta.ntl@sympatico.ca
Internet: http://www.acta.net
*Represents the interests of its
members, primarily its retail and
wholesale members.*

Alpine Club of Canada
Box 8040
Canmore, AB T1W 2T8
Phone: (403) 678-3200
Fax: (403) 678-3224
Internet: http://www
.culturenet.ca/acc
*Promotes the study, exploration,
and appreciation of the Cana-
dian alpine and glacial regions.*

Canada World Youth
2330 Notre-Dame Ouest,
3e Etage
Montreal, QC H3J 1N4
Phone: (514) 931-3526
Toll free: 1-800-605-3526
Fax: (514) 939-2621
E-mail: cwy-jcm@
cwy-jcm.org
Internet: http://www
.cwy-jcm.org
*Non-profit organization which
provides young people with an
opportunity to participate in
international educational
programs.*

Canadian Business Travel Association
CBTA Secretariat
100-951-16th Street
West Vancouver, BC V7V 3S4
Phone: (604) 922-8654
Toll free: 1-800-757-3177
Fax: (604) 926-4115
*Promotes and facilitates the
exchange of information between
buyers and suppliers of corpo-
rate travel services; six regional
offices.*

Canadian Camping Association
1810 Avenue Road, Suite 303
Toronto, ON M5M 3Z2
Phone: (416) 781-4717
Fax: (416) 781-7875
Internet: http://www.kids
camps.com/canadian
camping
*National federation promoting
organized camping.*

Canadian Crossroads International
31 Madison Avenue
Toronto, ON M5R 2S2
Phone: (416) 967-1611
Fax: (416) 967-9078
E-mail: cci@crossroads-
carrefour.ca
Internet: http://www
.crossroads-carrefour.ca
*International exchange
program with developing
nations; sponsors community
education programs.*

Canadian Parks/Recreation Association
1600 James Naismith Drive,
Suite 306
Gloucester, ON K1B 5N4
Phone: (613) 748-5651
Fax: (613) 748-5854
E-mail: ghebert@rtm
.activeliving.ca
Internet: http://www.active
living.ca/activeliving/
cpra.html
*National, voluntary organization
encouraging healthy, active living and environmental awareness; provides education and
information.*

Canadian Recreational Canoeing Association
Box 398
446 Main Street West
Merrickville, ON K0G 1N0
Phone: (613) 269-2910
Fax: (613) 269-2908
E-mail: staff@crca.ca
Internet: http://www.crca.ca
*Provides information, programs,
and services for those interested
in canoeing, kayaking, and sea
kayaking in Canada.*

Canadian Recreational Vehicle Association of Canada
670 Bloor Street West,
Suite 200
Toronto, ON M6G 1L2
Phone: (416) 533-7800
Fax: (416) 533-4795
*Trade association of manufac-
turers of motor homes and
travel trailers.*

Canadian Tourism Commission
235 Queen Street, 8 West
Ottawa, ON K1A 0H6
Phone: (613) 946-1000
Fax: (613) 276-2841
Internet: http://www.canada
tourism.com
*National tourism marketing
organization.*

Earthroots Coalition
251-401 Richmond Street
West
Toronto, ON M5V 3A8
Phone: (416) 599-0152
Fax: (416) 340-2429
*Protects wilderness, wildlife, and
watersheds; funds research on
endangered species and ecosys-
tems.*

Earthsave Canada
Box 34277, Station D
Vancouver, BC V6J 4N8
Phone: (604) 731-5885
Fax: (604) 731-5805
Internet: http://www
.earthsave.bc.ca
*Educational, non-profit society;
promotes awareness of the
health, ethical, and environmen-
tal consequences of food choices.*

Hostelling International—Canada
205 Catherine Street,
Suite 400
Ottawa, ON K2P 1C3
Phone: (613) 237-7884
Fax: (613) 237-7868

• **British Columbia**
134 Abbott Street, Suite 402
Vancouver, BC V6B 2K4
Phone: (604) 684-7101
Fax: (604) 684-7181

• **Manitoba**
194A Sherbrooke Street
Winnipeg, MB R3C 2B6
Phone: (204) 784-1131
Fax: (204) 784-1133

• **New Brunswick**
150 Leeds Drive
Fredericton, NB E3B 4S8
Phone: (506) 454-9950

• **Northern Alberta**
10926-88th Avenue
Edmonton, AB T6G 0Z1
Phone: (780) 432-7798

• **Nova Scotia**
5516 Spring Garden Road
Box 3010 S
Halifax, NS B3J 3G8
Phone: (902) 425-5450
Fax: (902) 425-5606

• **Ontario East**
75 Nicholas Street
Ottawa, ON K1N 7B9
Phone: (613) 235-2595
Fax: (613) 569-2131

• **Prince Edward Island**
c/o 205 Catherine Street,
  Suite 400
Ottawa, ON K2P 1C3
Phone: (613) 237-7884

• **Quebec**
4545 Pierre-de-Coubertin
Montreal, QC H1V 3R2
Phone: (514) 252-3317
Fax: (514) 252-3119

• **Saskatchewan**
2014-14th Avenue
Regina, SK S4P 0X5
Phone: (306) 791-8160
Fax: (306) 721-2667

• **Southern Alberta**
1414 Kensington Road
  Northwest, Suite 203
Calgary, AB T9N 3P9
Phone: (403) 283-5551
Fax: (403) 283-6503

• **Toronto**
90 Gerrard Street West
Toronto, ON M5G 1J6
Phone: (416) 971-4050
Fax: (416) 971-4088
*Provides hostels for travelers,
especially young people.*

International Association for Medical Assistance to Travellers
597 Markham Street
Toronto, ON M6G 2L7
Phone: (519) 836-0102
Fax: (519) 836-3412
E-mail: kanat@syntex.net
Internet: http://www
  .syntex.net/~lamat
*Provides information on world
immunization requirements.
Also provides names of English-
speaking doctors worldwide.*

New Brunswick Farm Vacations Association
RR1
Centreville, NB E0J 1H0
Phone: (506) 276-4787
*Promotes improved relations
between rural and urban
families.*

Nova Scotia Association of Unique Country Inns
Box 102
Kentville, NS B4N 3V9

Nova Scotia Farm & Country Bed-Breakfast Association
2018 New Cheverie Road
Cheverie, NS B0N 1G0
Phone: (902) 633-2837
*Comprised of 76 individual
members; mandate is to provide
good, old-fashioned hospitality.*

Outward Bound Western Canada
1367 West Broadway,
  Suite 109
Vancouver, BC V6H 4H9
Phone: (604) 737-3093
Toll free: 1-800-254-6244
Fax: (604) 737-3109
E-mail: ob@uniserve.com
Internet: http://www.infinity
  .ca/outwardbound/
*Non-profit educational organiza-
tion teaching mountaineering
with a focus on personal growth.*

Outward Bound Wilderness School
150 Laird Drive, Suite 302
Toronto, ON M4G 3V7
Phone: (416) 421-8111
Toll free: 1-888-688-9273
Fax: (416) 421-9062
*Encourages self-reliance, respect
to others, responsibility to one's
community, and concern for the
environment.*

Saskatchewan Country Vacations Association
Box 428
Gull Lake, SK S0N 1A0
Phone: (306) 652-4350
Fax: (306) 665-0654
*Comprised of 48 individuals
providing a unique holiday and
accommodation.*

Skyline Hikers of the Canadian Rockies
Box 75055, Cambrian PO
Calgary, AB T2K 6J8
Phone: (403) 240-4016
*Promotes hiking in the Canadian
Rockies and the preservation
of the national parks in their
natural state.*

VIA Rail
Box 8116
Centre-Ville Station
Montreal, QC H3C 3N3
Phone: (514) 871-6604
Internet: http://www
  .viarail.ca
*Provides intercity and long-
distance passenger rail service
across Canada.*

Wilderness Canoe Association
1888 Yonge Street
Box 48022
Toronto, ON M4S 3C6
*Offers extensive and varied out-
ing programs; informs members
of developments in equipment
and techniques.*

Chapter 7
The Business of Living

Associated Credit Bureaus of British Columbia
400 Robson Street
Vancouver, BC V6B 2B4
Phone: (604) 691-2116
Fax: (604) 688-7329
*Formerly: Association of Credit
Bureaus of British Columbia.*

Canadian Association of Financial Planners
1710-439 University Avenue
Toronto, ON M5G 1Y8
Phone: (416) 593-6592
Toll free: 1-800-346-2237
Fax: (416) 593-8459
E-mail: planners@cafp.org
*Comprised of 1,500 individual
members.*

Canadian Association of Gift Planners
Box 4084
Edmonton, AB T6E 4S8
Phone: (780) 438-4837
Toll free: 1-888-438-4837
*Supports philanthropy, working
with both donors and charities.*

Canadian Association of Home Inspectors
Box 507
Brighton, ON K0K 1H0
Phone: (613) 475-5699
Fax: (613) 475-1595
E-mail: parkway@reach.net
Internet: http://www.telus
  planet.net/public/
  moemad/cahi2.html
*Comprised of seven provin-
cial/regional organiza-
tions; services include
educational and exam
requirements, and
directing the public
to qualified home
inspectors.*

Canadian Association of Insurance and Financial Advisors
41 Lesmill Road
North York, ON M3B 2T3
Phone: (416) 444-5251
Toll free: 1-800-563-5822
Fax: (416) 444-4356
Internet: http://www
  .caifa.com
*With 18,000 members, this is
Canada's largest association for
insurance and financial advisors.*

Canadian Bankers Association
Box 348
Commerce Court West
Toronto, ON M5L 1G2
Phone: (416) 362-6093
Toll free: 1-800-263-0231
Fax: (416) 362-5658
E-mail: cba@minacs.com
Internet: http://www.cba.ca
*Professional industry association
providing information, research,
and other support services pri-
marily to its members, the char-
tered banks of Canada.*

Canadian Bar Association (CBA)
50 O'Connor Street, Suite 902
Ottawa, ON K1P 6L2
Phone: (613) 237-2925
Toll free: 1-800-267-8860
Fax: (613) 237-0185
Internet: http://www.cba
  .org/abc
*Represents 35,000 lawyers
across Canada; provides a free
CBA directory.*

Canadian Coalition Against Insurance Fraud
151 Yonge Street, Suite 1800
Toronto, ON M5C 2W7
Phone: (416) 362-4550
Fax: (416) 362-4572
Internet: http://www
.fraudcoalition.org
Coalition of the property and casualty insurance industry and concerned groups improving industry practices, investigating practices, and raising public awareness.

Canadian Home Builders' Association (CHBA)
150 Laurier Avenue West,
Suite 200
Ottawa, ON K1P 5J4
Phone: (613) 230-3060
Fax: (613) 232-8214
Internet: http://www.chba.ca
Represents Canada's residential construction industry; publishes a magazine and newsletter.

Canadian Institute of Professional Home Inspectors
720, 999 West Broadway
Vancouver, BC V5Z 1K5
Phone: (604) 327-0262
Advises potential home buyers about problems associated with the home or condominium, before purchases are made.

Canadian Mortgage and Housing Corporation (CMHC)
700 Montreal Road
Ottawa, ON K1A 0P7
Phone: (613) 748-2494
Internet: http://www
.cmhc-schl.gc.ca
National housing agency; services include mortgage loan insurance, information on housing research and assisted housing.

Canadian Real Estate Association (CREA)
344 Slater Street, Suite 1600
Ottawa, ON K1R 7Y3
Phone: (613) 237-7111
Fax: (613) 234-2567
E-mail: info@crea.ca
Internet: http://www.mls
.ca/crea
CREA, representing some 68,000 realtors, is the national voice of organized real estate.

Canadian Shareowners Association
2 Carlton Street, Suite 1317
Toronto, ON M5B 1J3
Phone: (416) 595-9600
Fax: (416) 595-0400
Internet: http://www
.shareowner.ca
Non-profit educational organization comprised of 15,000-plus private investors and investment clubs.

Credit Association of Canada
Credit Bureau of Saskatoon
304A-4th Avenue North
Saskatoon, SK S7K 1K7
Phone: (306) 343-3200
Fax: (306) 343-3210
Formerly: Credit Granters Association of Canada.

Credit Counselling Service of Toronto
45 Sheppard Avenue East,
Suite 810
Toronto, ON M2N 5W9
Phone: (416) 228-3328
Toll free: 1-800-267-2272
Fax: (416) 228-1164
E-mail: ccstmt@credit
canada.com
Internet: http://www.credit
canada.com

Credit Institute of Canada
5090 Explorer Drive, Suite 501
Mississauga, ON L4W 3T9
Phone: (905) 629-9805
Fax: (905) 629-9809
Internet: http://www
.creditedu.org
Comprised of 2,300 individual professionals; 14 regional chapters.

Credit Union Central of Canada
300 The East Mall, Suite 500
Toronto, ON M9B 6B7
Phone: (416) 232-1262
Fax: (416) 232-9196
The national, financial, intermediary, and trade association for credit unions in Canada.

Dying with Dignity
55 Eglinton Avenue East,
Suite 705
Toronto, ON M4P 1G8
Phone: (416) 486-3998
Toll free: 1-800-495-6156
Fax: (416) 489-9010
E-mail: dwdca@web.net
Internet: http://www.web
.net/dwd
National society which informs, educates, and counsels persons on the issues of death and dying.

Equifax Credit Services
Toll free: 1-800-937-4093
Internet: http://www.equifax
.com
Canada's largest credit bureau, Equifax has offices in every region and major city in the country.

Federation of Ontario Memorial Societies
55 St. Phillips Road
Etobicoke, ON M9P 2N8
Phone: (905) 684-9180
Fax: (905) 684-7075
E-mail: preplan@npiec.on.ca
Internet: http://www.npiec
.on.ca/~preplan
Federation of non-profit memorial societies.

Funeral Advisory and Memorial Society
55 St. Phillips Road
Etobicoke, ON M9P 2N8
Phone: (416) 241-6274
Consultation service concerning funeral arrangements and costs, donating bodies for medical research and other matters of a similar nature.

Insurance Council of Canada
151 Yonge Street, Suite 1800
Toronto, ON M5C 2W7
Phone: (416) 362-2031
Fax: (416) 361-5952
Internet: http://www.ibc.ca

• Pacific Region
409 Granville Street, Suite 550
Vancouver, BC V6C 1W9
Phone: (604) 684-3635
Fax: (604) 684-6235

• Prairie Region
10080 Jasper Avenue,
Suite 801
Edmonton, AB T5J 1V9
Phone: (780) 423-2212
Fax: (780) 423-4796

• Ontario
151 Yonge Street, Suite 1800
Toronto, ON M5C 2W7
Phone: (416) 362-2031
Fax: (416) 362-6202

• Quebec
500 Rue Sherbrooke Ouest,
Bureau 600
Montreal, QC H3A 3C6
Phone: (514) 288-1563
Fax: (514) 288-0753

• Atlantic Region
1969 Upper Water Street,
Suite 1706
Halifax, NS B3J 3R7
Phone: (902) 429-2730
Fax: (902) 420-0157
Umbrella association of private-sector property and casualty insurance industry associations.

Investment Dealers Association of Canada
121 King Street West,
Suite 1600
Toronto, ON M5H 3T9
Phone: (416) 943-5870
Fax: (416) 364-0753
National trade association and self-regulatory organization of the Canadian securities industry, polices the activities of its 175 member firms.

Ontario Association of Home Inspectors
Box 38108
Castlewood R.P.O.
Toronto, ON M5N 3A8
Phone: (416) 256-0960
Fax: (613) 475-1595
Internet: http://www
.oahi.com
Granting body for registered home inspectors in Ontario; provides a membership directory.

Trust Companies Association of Canada
335 Bay Street, Suite 205
Toronto, ON M5H 3R3
Phone: (416) 866-8842
Fax: (416) 364-1993
Comprised of 20 institutional members.

Government Agencies

Government of Canada
Internet: http://canada.gc.ca
Links to over 450 government of Canada sites.

Agriculture and Agri-Food Canada
Communications Branch
Sir John Carling Branch,
Room E-122
930 Carling Avenue
Ottawa, ON K1A 0C7
Phone: (613) 759-1761
Fax: (613) 759-1019
E-mail: commbr@em.agr.ca
Internet: http://www.agr.ca
Develops policies and programs for the agriculture and agri-food sector.

Canada Customs and Revenue Agency
Formerly: Revenue Canada; promotes compliance with Canada's tax, trade, and border legislation and regulation. (Myriad regional tax service offices and centers.)
Phone: 1-800-959-8281 (for general inquiries)
Internet: http://www.ccradrc
.gc.ca/menu-e.html

Canadian Heritage Information Network
15 Eddy Street, 4th Floor
Hull, QC K1A 0M5
Phone: (819) 994-1200
Toll free: 1-800-520-2446
Fax: (819) 994-9555
E-mail: service@chin.gc.ca
Internet: http://www
.chin.gc.ca
Provides education and training concerning Canadian museums and Canadian heritage.

Emergency Preparedness Canada
Communications
Directorate
122 Bank Street, 2nd Floor
Ottawa, ON K1A 0W6
Phone: (613) 991-7077
Fax: (613) 998-9589
E-mail: communications
@epc-pcc.gc.ca
Internet: http://www
.epc-pcc.gc.ca
Provides for the safety and security of Canadians during national emergencies.

Environment Canada
Inquiry Centre
351 St-Joseph Boulevard
Hull, QC K1A 0H3
Phone: (819) 997-2800
Toll free: 1-800-668-6767
E-mail: enviroinfo@ec.gc.ca
Internet: http://www.ec
.gc.ca
Committed toward environmentally sustainable development; provides specialist and expert information and knowledge.

Canada Pension Plan
Consultation and
Communications Branch
Finance Canada
140 O'Connor Street
Ottawa, ON K1A 0G5
Phone: (613) 992-1573
E-mail: consltcom@fin.gc.ca
Internet: http://www.cpprpc
.gc.ca/homepage.htm
National pension system; provides numerous publications.

Fisheries and Oceans Canada
Communications Branch
200 Kent Street, 13th Floor,
Station 13228
Ottawa, ON K1A 0E6
Phone: (613) 993-1516
Fax: (613) 990-1866
E-mail: info@dfo-mpo.gc.ca
Internet: http://www
.dfo-mpo.gc.ca
Responsible for policies and programs relating to Canada's oceans and freshwater fish habitat.

Health Canada
A. L. 0913A
Ottawa, ON K1A 0K9
Phone: (613) 957-2991
Fax: (613) 941-5366
Internet: http://www
.hc-sc.gc.ca/english/
Develops health policy; enforces health regulations; promotes disease prevention and healthy living; provides numerous information services.

Health Canada
Canadian Food Inspection Agency (CFIA)
59 Camelot Drive
Nepean, ON K1A 0Y9
Phone: (613) 228-6682
Fax: (613) 228-6651
E-mail: cfiamaster@
em.agr.ca
Internet: http://www
.cfia-acia.agr.ca
Responsible for all federally mandated inspection services related to food safety, economic fraud, and animal and plant health programs.

Health Canada
Division of Aging and Seniors
Population Health
Directorate
Health Canada
A. L. 1908A1
Ottawa, ON K1A 1B4
Phone: (613) 952-7606
Fax: (613) 957-7627
E-mail: seniors@hc-sc.gc.ca
Internet: http://info.hc-sc
.gc.ca/seniors-aines/
seniors/english/new.htm
Focal point for information and center of expertise in areas pertaining to aging and seniors.

Heritage Canada
412 MacLaren Street
Ottawa, ON K2P 0M8
Phone: (613) 237-1066
Fax: (613) 237-5987
E-mail: hercanot@
sympatico.ca
Promotes the identification, protection, and enhancement of natural, cultural, and built environment and heritage.

Industry Canada
235 Queen Street
Ottawa, ON K1A 0H5
Publication inquiries:
(613) 947-7466
General information:
(613) 941-0222
Fax: (613) 952-9620
Internet: http://www.info
.ic.gc.ca
Industry Canada's three lines of business include: Marketplace Rules and Services, Industry Sector Development, and Microeconomic Policy.

National Archives of Canada
395 Wellington Street
Ottawa, ON K1A 0N3
Phone: (613) 996-2334
Fax: (613) 995-0919
E-mail: bcarey@archives.ca
Internet: http://www
.archives.ca
Preserves Canada's archival heritage, including photographs, paintings, and prints; provides reference and research services.

Parks Canada
25 Eddy Street
Hull, QC K1A 0M5
Toll free: 1-888-773-8888
E-mail: parkswebmaster
@pch.gc.ca
Internet: http://parkscanada
.pch.gc.ca
Provides information on National Parks and National Historic Sites administered by Parks Canada.

Transport Canada
330 Sparks Street
Ottawa, ON K1A 0N5
Phone: (613) 990-2309
E-mail: general@tc.gc.ca
Internet: http://www.tc
.gc.ca/en/menu.htm
Programs and services include: environmental affairs, research and development, statistics, air bag deactivation, and road safety.

Index

Acknowledgments

SPECIAL THANKS

Agriculture and Agri-Food Canada (Plant Hardiness Zone map, 162-163)
All-American Rose Selections (rose label, 191)
Asolo (wet weather boots, 295)
Dianne Athey (photo on mantel, 29)
Baer & McIntosh Real Estate (sign, 320)
Canadian Red Book, Inc. (booklet, 215)
Cannondale (bicycle, 116)
Coleman (tent, 264)
The Ding King Inc. (paintless dent removal tools, 234)
Kara W. Hatch (photo on mantel, 28)
Kaufman Footwear (cold weather boots, 294)
Jessica Krause (pedestal, 30)
Lax World Inc. (lacrosse helmet, 121)
Lightbulb Press, Inc. (book, 302)
LOOK, distributed in the USA solely by Veltec Sports, Inc. (mountain biking shoes, 295)
Maxiguard of America (alarm system, 236)
Karen Meldrom (photo on mantel, 29)
Simon Metz (photo on mantel, 29)
Kenneth M. and Virginia B. Morris (photos on mantel, 28-29; mounted photo, 28; beach photos, 266, 267)
O'Brien Pictures (photo on mantel, 28)
Pitbull Tire Lock Corporation (tire lock, 237)
Prestone Products (portable jump starter, 247)
Primex of California (river rafting shoes, 295)
Reebok International, Ltd. (shoes, 121)
Riddell Sports (football helmet, 120)
Jane and Leonard Schwartz (greenhouse, 202; orchids, 205)
Security Chain Company (tire chains, 247)
Stenciling by Michele (floor cloth, 20)
Urban Archeology (steam gauge clock, 30)
Vasque (hot weather boots, 295)
Vehicle Information Centre of Canada (logo, 236)
Ghislaine Viñas (mosaic flower pot, 30)
Widex (Senso 100% Digital Hearing Aid, 136)
Wisteria Design Studios (flower arrangement, 26)

PHOTO CREDITS

Airstream (travel trailer, 291)
Benner's Gardens, Inc. (moss garden, 181)
Bradbury and Bradbury (decorated room photographed by Douglas Kiester, 16)
California Closets (closets, 32, 33)
Carnival Cruises (moderate cruise line, 285)
Chinese Garden of Montreal Botanical Garden (Chinese garden, 175)
Chinook RV (camper-van conversion, 290)
Collinite Wax Products (car wax, 210)
Country Curtains (curtain, 22)
Cunard Line Limited (ultra-deluxe cruise line, 284)
The Ding King Inc. (before and after dent repair, 234)
Disney Enterprises, Inc. (topiaries, 169, 333)
frontera.com (cedar bench, 11, 38)
Garmin International (GPS receiver, 248)
Jeffrey Gettleman (African vacation, 288)
Grand Hotel (porches, 39)
Habitat for Humanity (construction group photographed by Don Dennis, 296)
Gordon Hayward (garden path, 170)
Heifer Project International (goat and child, 297)
Hostelling International (hostel, 256)
Jayco Inc. (class C motor home, 290; folding tent trailer, 291)
Jill Avery Murals & Artistic Finishes (child's room photographed by Rod Rolle, 35)
KARCO Engineering (crash test photographed by Jonathan Williams, 159)
King of the Road (fifth wheel trailer, 291)
Kolbe & Kolbe Millwork Co. Inc. (window box, 202)
Kraftmaid Cabinetry (kitchen cabinets, 36-37)
Alice Levien (garden photographed by Dianne Athey, 170, 178, 196)
LoJack Corporation (LoJack police scanner, 237)
Monaco Coach Corporation (class A motor home, 290)
Tom Monaco (home interior, 328)
Kenneth M. Morris (coneflower, New England aster, 167)

COVER CREDITS

Converting to metric measurements

TO CHANGE:	INTO:	MULTIPLY BY:
inches	centimeters	2.54
inches	millimeters	25.4
feet	meters	0.305
yards	meters	0.914
miles	kilometers	1.609
ounces	grams	31.103
pounds	kilograms	0.373
fluid ounces	milliliters	29.5
pints	liters	0.473
quarts	liters	0.946
gallons	liters	3.785

SPOONS AND CUPS

1 teaspoon	=	5 milliliters
1 tablespoon	=	15 milliliters
2 tablespoons	=	30 milliliters
1 cup	=	250 milliliters
2 cups	=	500 milliliters
3 cups	=	750 milliliters
4 cups	=	1 liter

TEMPERATURES

To change from degrees Fahrenheit to degrees Celsius, subtract 32, then multiply by 32.